D0404502

THE
BRITISH
MUSEUM

DICTIONARY OF
ANCIENT EGYPT

THE BRITISH MUSEUM

DICTIONARY OF ANCIENT EGYPT

IAN SHAW AND PAUL NICHOLSON

THE BRITISH MUSEUM PRESS

© 1995 The Trustees of The British Museum
Published by The British Museum Press

A division of
The British Museum Company Ltd
46 Bloomsbury Street
London WC1B 3QQ

First published 1995
First published in paperback 1997
This pocket edition first published 2002
Reprinted 2003

British Library Cataloguing in Publication Data

A catalogue record for this book is available
from the British Library

ISBN 0-7141-1953-9
Designed by Harry Green

Printed and bound in Spain by Grafos S.A.,
Barcelona

FRONTISPIECE *Detail of* wedjat-*eyes above a false door
with decoration imitating textiles. From the wooden
inner coffin of the commander Sepy. Middle Kingdom,
c. 2000 BC, from Deir el-Bersha, L. 2.13 m. (EA55315)*

PAGES 4–5 *Two male guests at the funeral feast of the
vizier Ramose in his tomb at Thebes. 18th Dynasty,
c. 1390–1336 BC. (GRAHAM HARRISON)*

CONTENTS

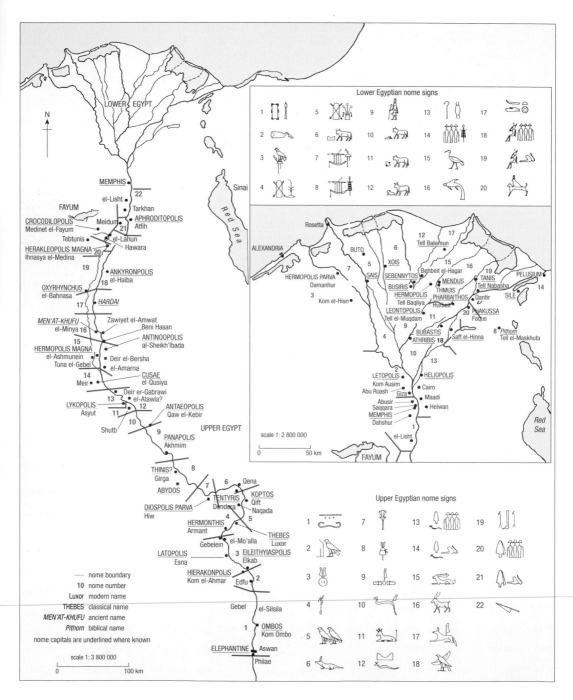

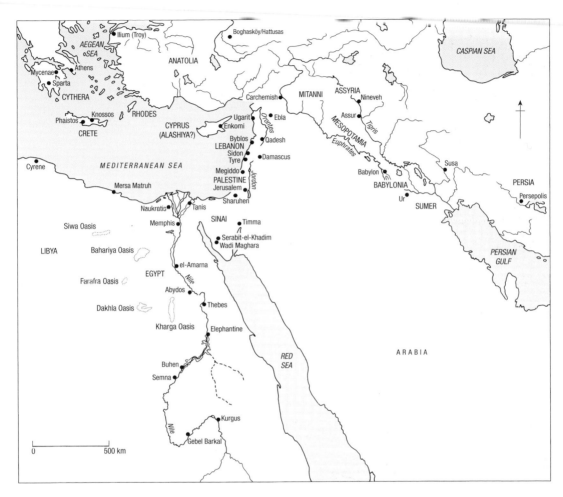

FACING PAGE Map of Egypt, showing the main sites mentioned in the text. The Egyptians themselves made a clear geographical distinction between Upper Egypt, consisting of the Nile Valley from Memphis to Aswan, and Lower Egypt (or the Delta), where the Nile fans out into several tributaries in its final descent to the Mediterranean. The twenty-two nomes (provinces) of Upper Egypt and the twenty nomes of Lower Egypt are also indicated, and the nome capitals, where known, are underlined. Each nome had its own symbol or standard, often incorporating animals, birds or fetishes sacred to the local deities.

ABOVE Map of the Ancient Near East, showing Egypt's neighbours in western Asia and the Mediterranean region. For most of the Pharaonic period Egypt was well protected by its natural geographical surroundings, consisting of the Sinai peninsula and the Red Sea to the east, the Sahara Desert to the west, and the Mediterranean Sea to the north. In the New Kingdom the Egyptians' 'empire' extended well beyond these traditional borders, as they vied with Mitanni and the Hittites for hegemony over the city-states of Syria-Palestine. It was only in the Late Period (c. 747–332 BC) that Egypt itself finally succumbed to the invading armies of Nubia, Assyria and Persia.

PREFACE

When this book was first produced, no reliable general dictionary of ancient Egypt was available in English, and the task of deciding what to include here and what to leave out was not easy. Many of the headings in this dictionary are derived from discussions with students and colleagues, but responsibility for the final list is ours. The book largely results from the need to find concise and accurate definitions of key terms in Egyptology, some of which have become obscure and archaic over the years. The principal aim has been to provide a reference work accessible to anyone with an interest in ancient Egypt, as well as to the academic community. The short bibliographies which accompany most entries are given in chronological, rather than alphabetical, order so that the list moves from early sources to more recent studies.

The spelling of ancient Egyptian personal names is a continual source of difficulty. Thus the kings cited here as 'Amenhotep' may be found elsewhere as 'Amenhotpe', or in the Greek form 'Amenophis'. We have chosen spellings that are as far as possible consistent with the transliteration of the original Egyptian, which has the added benefit of being consistent with those used by Stephen Quirke and Jeffrey Spencer in the *British Museum book of ancient Egypt* (London, 1992) and other BMP publications. In the headings of entries describing ancient sites, on the other hand, we have opted for the most commonly used name. Alternative forms of names are given in the text and index. We have endeavoured to make the index as comprehensive as possible in the hope that readers will find it helpful in researching topics or individuals not covered by specific headings in the text.

The chronological table provided here is that preferred by the Department of Ancient Egypt and Sudan in the British Museum. Because of the difficulties in establishing a single absolute chronology for ancient Egypt, both dates and lists of individual rulers tend to differ from one book to another, but most current chronological schemes will be found to be broadly similar to the one used here. Since Egyptologists tend to refer to 'dynasties' and 'kingdoms' in a way which can be confusing to the non-specialist, we have tried to give absolute dates BC and AD wherever possible.

The entries are supplemented by two appendices. The first of these lists the names and dates of Egyptologists mentioned in the text (some of whom have individual entrics and bibliographies in the main text). The second appendix lists the recognized numbers of Theban Tombs (designated TT) and those in the Valley of the Kings (designated KV), along with their occupants and dynasties. Throughout the dictionary there are frequent references to these tomb-numbers, as well as occasional mention of tomb-numbers at other sites, such as el-Amarna (EA), Beni Hasan (BH), Elkab (EK), Giza (G) and Saqqara.

Should readers require further detail on certain topics they are advised to consult both the bibliographies at the end of each entry and the following more specialized reference works: M. Lurker, *The gods and symbols of ancient Egypt* (London, 1974); W. Helck, E. Otto and W. Westendorf (eds), *Lexikon der Ägyptologie*, 7 vols (Wiesbaden, 1975–1988); G. Hart, *A dictionary of Egyptian gods and goddesses* (London, 1986); R. and A. David, *A biographical dictionary of ancient Egypt* (London,

1992); J. Baines and J. Malek, *Atlas of ancient Egypt* (Phaidon, 1984); and W. R. Dawson, E. P. Uphill and M. L. Bierbrier, *Who was who in Egyptology*, 3rd ed. (London, 1995). G. Posener's *A dictionary of Egyptian civilization* (London, 1962), although now somewhat in need of updating and out of print in English, provides a good range of information on many general Egyptological topics.

ACKNOWLEDGEMENTS

We would like to thank a number of individuals and institutions for their help during the course of this project. Firstly we would like to thank the staff of the Department of Ancient Egypt and Sudan at the British Museum, who have not stinted in sharing their scholarship with us. We are also grateful to many friends and colleagues with whom we have discussed subjects relevant to this book, including Dr W. Z. Wendrich, who wrote part of the entry on basketry and cordage, Joann Fletcher, who provided valuable information for the entry on hair and wigs, Dr Delwen Samuel, who supplied information on ancient brewing techniques, and Margaret Serpico, who kindly provided information on oils and incense. We would also like to thank Janine Bourriau, Sarah Buckingham, Barry Kemp, Professor Harry Smith and the staff of the various expeditions to Egypt with which we are involved. We should emphasize, however, that the final responsibility for the opinions expressed remains our own. In addition, we would like to acknowledge the support we have received from University College London and Cardiff University.

For assistance with various aspects of the production of the typescript and photographs we would like to thank Geoff Boden, Dr Caitlin Buck and John Morgan of Cardiff University and Dr Nick Fieller of the University of Sheffield.

Joanna Champness, Celia Clear, Emma Way and Julie Young of British Museum Press gave much useful help and advice concerning the production of the original book, and Carolyn Jones and Christine King on the present edition.

For illustrations we are grateful to the staff of the British Museum Photographic Service; to Graham Harrison; the Egyptian Museum Cairo (in particular Dr Mohammed Saleh); the Griffith Institute, Ashmolean Museum, Oxford; the Metropolitan Museum of Art, New York (in particular Dr Dorothea Arnold) and the Musée du Louvre. Unless otherwise stated the line drawings are by William Schenck, to whom we are also indebted.

Finally, we would like to thank Kate Trott, Ann Jones and Nia Shaw, who have helped in numerous ways.

IAN SHAW
PAUL NICHOLSON

A

Abu Gurab (Abu Ghurob)

Site on the west bank of the Nile between Giza and Saqqara, originally known to travellers as the 'Pyramid of Righa', although actually dominated by the remains of a sun temple erected by the 5th-Dynasty King Nyuserra (2445–2421 BC) whose pyramid stands a short distance to the south at ABUSIR. It became customary in the 5th Dynasty for the rulers to express their devotion to the Heliopolitan sun-god RA by building sun temples in addition to their own pyramid complexes. Abu Gurab is the best preserved of the two surviving examples (the other being that of Userkaf at Abusir), although at least six are known to have been built.

The central feature of the temple was a large, squat monument, the proportions of which were midway between a BENBEN STONE and a true OBELISK. Both the 'obelisk' and the tapering platform on which it stood were masonry constructions rather than monolithic. In front of the monument (of which only the core of the plinth remains) is a large open court, and in the centre of this open area is a massive travertine ALTAR comprising a disc

Plan of Abu Gurab.

BELOW *General view of the sun temple of the 5th-Dynasty King Nyuserra at Abu Gurab. The mound to the left is the base of the large squat obelisk; the travertine altar to its right is obscured by the enclosure wall. The Giza pyramids are visible on the skyline in the far distance.* (P. T. NICHOLSON)

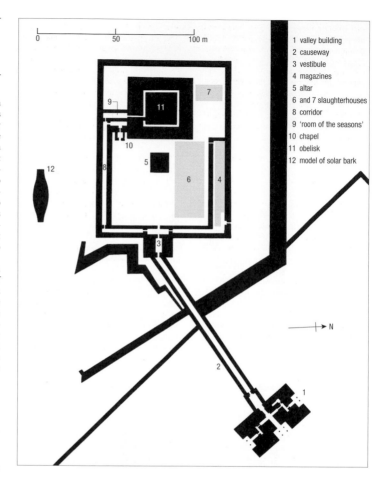

```
0        50              100 m
```

1 valley building
2 causeway
3 vestibule
4 magazines
5 altar
6 and 7 slaughterhouses
8 corridor
9 'room of the seasons'
10 chapel
11 obelisk
12 model of solar bark

N

an cannot on each side by four carved examples of the hieroglyphic sign *hetep* ('offering'), giving the whole an unusual cruciform shape. The altar is flanked on the north by a slaughter area and by temple magazines. The entrance to the temple is linked with a 'valley building' by a covered causeway, like those connecting pyramids with their valley temples. On reaching the temple proper, the causeway becomes a corridor running down the east side of the courtyard and along the south side. This corridor, which contained reliefs of the SED FESTIVAL (royal jubilee), led to the 'room of the seasons' (containing painted reliefs depicting the seasons of the Egyptian year) and ended in a chapel decorated with scenes of the dedication of the temple. Although these are evidently important scenes, they were carved on poor stone enhanced with a coating of lime plaster – such economies perhaps illustrate the strain on the finances of the Egyptian élite because of the need to build both pyramids and temples. To the south of the temple was a brick-built imitation of the BARK of the sun-god.

The site was excavated at the turn of the century by the German scholars Ludwig Borchardt, Heinrich Schäfer and Friedrich von Bissing, who sent many of the reliefs to museums in Germany, where a number of them were destroyed during the Second World War.

E. WINTER, 'Zur Deutung der Sonnenheiligtümer der 5. Dynastic', *WZKM* 54 (1957), 222–33.

E. EDEL and S. WENIG, *Die Jahreszeitenreliefs aus dem Sonnenheiligtum des Königs Ne-user-re*, Mitteilungen aus der ägyptischen Sammlung 8 (Berlin, 1974).

W. STEVENSON SMITH, *The art and architecture of ancient Egypt*, 2nd ed. (Harmondsworth, 1981), 128–32, figs 124–5.

D. WILDUNG, *Ni-User-Rê: Sonnenkönig-Sonnengott* (Munich, 1985).

Abu Roash (Abu Rawash)

Site of the unfinished funerary complex of the 4th-Dynasty ruler Djedefra (2566–2558 BC), the ancient name for which was 'Djedefra is a *sehedu* star'. The pyramid, situated to the north of GIZA on the west bank of the Nile, was evidently in better condition in 1839, when it was first examined by Richard Howard Vyse and John Perring. Since then, the site has suffered heavily, having been used as a quarry in the 1880s, but enough stone blocks remain to show that it was intended to be partly encased in red granite.

The mortuary temple on the east side of the pyramid and a large boat pit to the south were look excavated by Émile Chassinat in 1901. The boat pit contained many fragments of red quartzite statuary, including three painted heads from statues of Djedefra, one of which was probably from the earliest known royal SPHINX (Louvre E12626), as well as the lower section of a statue of the king accompanied by Queen Khentetka. Because of the nature of the local topography, the causeway (linking the mortuary temple with the valley temple) approaches from the northeast rather than the east.

To the north of the pyramid is Wadi Qarun, site of the still unexcavated valley temple, as well as a number of remains of a much later date, including part of a statue of Queen Arsinoe II, sister and wife of PTOLEMY II Philadelphus (285–246 BC). Objects bearing the names of the 1st-Dynasty pharaohs AHA (*c.*3100 BC) and DEN (*c.*2950 BC) have also been found at Abu Roash, indicating a strong Early Dynastic presence at the site.

To the east of the pyramid complex is an Old Kingdom cemetery, which was also excavated by Chassinat. About two kilometres to the south are the remains of a brick-built pyramid, comprising a knoll of rock and a burial chamber. This pyramid, the date of which is unknown, was still relatively well preserved when it was recorded in the early nineteenth century by the German scholar Karl Richard Lepsius.

F. BISSON DE LA ROQUE, *Rapport sur les fouilles d'Abu Roasch*, 3 vols (Cairo, 1924–5).

C. DESROCHES-NOBLECOURT (ed.), *Un siècle de fouilles françaises en Egypte, 1880–1980* (Paris, 1981), 44–53.

M. VALLOGIA, 'Le complex funeraire de Radjedef à Abu Roash', *BSFE* 130 (1994), 5–17.

Abu Simbel

Site of two rock-cut temples of RAMESES II (1279–1213 BC), located about 250 km southeast of Aswan. The temples were discovered by the traveller Jean-Louis Burckhardt in 1813 and cleared by Giovanni BELZONI four years later. The largest temple is dedicated to Amun-Ra, Ra-Horakhty, Ptah and the deified Rameses II. The façade is dominated by four colossal seated figures of Rameses II wearing the double crown and *nemes* headcloth. Between the two pairs of figures is the

The façade of the 'great temple' of Rameses II at Abu Simbel. The four seated colossi of the king are each 20 m high; the damaged figure was left unrestored when the temple was moved to higher ground as part of the UNESCO operation to preserve it from the waters of Lake Nasser. (P. T. NICHOLSON)

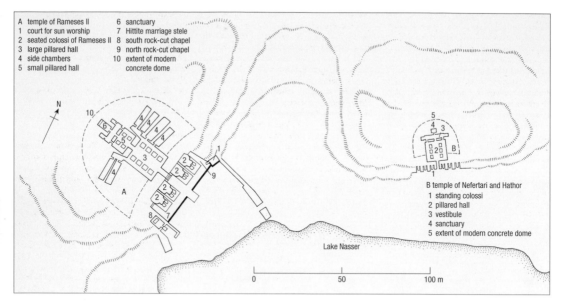

A	temple of Rameses II
1	court for sun worship
2	seated colossi of Rameses II
3	large pillared hall
4	side chambers
5	small pillared hall
6	sanctuary
7	Hittite marriage stele
8	south rock-cut chapel
9	north rock-cut chapel
10	extent of modern concrete dome

B temple of Nefertari and Hathor
1 standing colossi
2 pillared hall
3 vestibule
4 sanctuary
5 extent of modern concrete dome

Lake Nasser

0   50   100 m

The temples of (A) Rameses II and (B) his queen, Nefertari, and the goddess Hathor at Abu Simbel.

entrance to the cavernous interior of the monument, and flanking it, beneath the feet and throne of the king, are the NINE BOWS, the traditional enemies of Egypt. The monument thus symbolized Rameses II's domination of NUBIA, as well as his piety to the gods.

The 'great temple' is precisely aligned so that twice a year (during February and October) the rising sun illuminates the sanctuary and seated statues of the gods at the rearmost point of the temple. The temple is conventional in its overall layout, with a large pillared hall immediately beyond the entrance leading to a smaller pillared hall, followed by a vestibule and sanctuary. The standard of workmanship on the wall carvings is not high, though they are vigorous and retain their painted colour. The temple was decorated in the 34th year of Rameses' reign, and there is a discernible decline in artistic standard compared with the decoration of the earlier temples at ABYDOS. At the southern end of the external terrace a stele records the marriage of Rameses to a daughter of the HITTITE king Hattusilis III, valuable evidence of diplomatic relations at the time.

A little to the north of the great temple lies a smaller rock-cut temple dedicated to Queen NEFERTARI and the goddess HATHOR of Abshek. This façade features two standing figures of

the king, flanking those of his queen, on each side of the entrance. A passage leads to a six-pillared hall with SISTRUM-capital columns, followed by a vestibule, and finally the sanctuary, where a statue of the goddess Hathor protects Rameses II.

In the 1960s these temples were threatened by the rising waters of Lake Nasser resulting from the construction of the Aswan High Dam and were dismantled, moved and reassembled on higher ground, through the co-operation of archaeologists and engineers working under a UNESCO initiative.

W. MACQUITTY, *Abu Simbel* (London, 1965).
C. DESROCHES-NOBLECOURT and C. KUENTZ, *Le petit temple d'Abou Simbel*, 2 vols (Cairo, 1968).
T. SÄVE-SÖDERBERGH (ed.), *Temples and tombs of ancient Nubia* (London, 1987).

Abusir

Part of the necropolis of ancient MEMPHIS, consisting of several pyramids of the 5th Dynasty (2494–2345 BC), a sun temple (see ABU GURAB), and a number of MASTABA tombs and Late Period (747–332 BC) shaft tombs. Userkaf, founder of the 5th Dynasty, built his pyramid at Saqqara and a sun temple at Abusir, a short distance to the north. At least four of his successors (Sahura, Neferirkara, Raneferef and Nyuserra) therefore chose Abusir as the location for their funerary monuments, the ancient names of which were 'The ba of Sahura gleams', 'Neferirkara has become

a ba', 'The bas of Raneferef are divine' and 'The places of Nyuserra are enduring'. The finest of the mastaba tombs at Abusir is that of the 5th-Dynasty vizier Ptahshepses, a relative of Nyuserra, which incorporates two boat-shaped rooms presumably meant to hold full-sized boats, an unusual feature of a private tomb.

The funerary monument of Sahura (2487–2475 BC), the most complete of the four royal burials at Abusir, is the quintessential 5th-Dynasty pyramid complex, consisting of valley temple, causeway, mortuary temple and pyramid. The imposing portico of the mortuary temple gave access to a large courtyard with a well-preserved basalt-paved floor and a colonnade consisting of sixteen red granite palm columns (the latter now largely destroyed). The remains of the original limestone walls, with their fine painted decoration, have been transferred to the Egyptian Museum in Cairo and the Bodemuseum in Berlin. Beyond the colonnade were a series of store rooms surrounding the 'statue chamber', where the king's statues stood in niches, and immediately adjacent to the pyramid was the sanctuary with its alabaster altar. In the southeastern corner of the complex stood a small subsidiary pyramid.

When Ludwig Borchardt excavated Sahura's complex in 1902–8, he discovered the earliest temple relief of the king smiting his enemies, as well as reliefs depicting the cat-goddess BASTET in a corridor surrounding the palm-columned court. In the New Kingdom this corridor seems to have been re-roofed and used as a sanctuary for a local form of the lioness-goddess SEKHMET.

The complexes of Neferirkara (2475–2455 BC) and Nyuserra (2445–2421 BC) are both unfinished and poorly preserved. The complex of Neferirkara, although clearly intended to be larger than that of Sahura, is now best known for the large quantity of papyri from the mortuary temple, providing valuable evidence on the organization of royal funerary cults in the Old Kingdom. The papyri date from the reign of Isesi to that of PEPY II, and mainly consist of rotas for temple personnel, inventories of cult objects, and letters. Neferirkara's causeway

was evidently usurped by Nyuserra, who diverted it to his own mortuary temple. The poor quality of the rubble core used in these pyramids has left them in poor condition, especially since the fine blocks of outer casing have been plundered. To the northwest of the pyramid of Sahura are the remains of another unfinished pyramid complex, which probably belonged to Shepseskara (2455–2448 BC), the ephemeral successor of Neferirkara.

Since the 1970s the work of a team of Czech archaeologists, under the direction of Miroslav Verner, has revealed the mud-brick

mortuary temple of Raneferef (2448–2445 BC) whose unfinished pyramid was actually transformed into a MASTABA tomb. Their finds have included a second papyrus archive, a group of seals, a collection of cult objects, and the most important surviving group of 5th-Dynasty royal sculpture, including an unusual painted limestone statue of Raneferef himself with a Horus-falcon embracing the back of his head, as well as wooden statuettes of bound captives.

The Czech archaeologists have also uncovered the original pyramid complex and temples of Queen Khentkawes (mother of Sahura and Neferirkara), which was probably a cenotaph, since she also had a mastaba tomb between the causeways of Khufu and Khafra at GIZA. In 1988–9 they excavated the shaft-

tomb of the Persian-period 'chief physician', Udjahorresnet, who served as chancellor to Cambyses and Darius I (see PERSIA).

L. BORCHARDT, *Das Grabdenkmal des Königs Ne-user-Re* (Leipzig, 1907).

—, *Das Grabdenkmal des Königs Nefer-ir-ka-Re* (Leipzig, 1909).

—, *Das Grabdenkmal des Königs Sahu-Re* (Leipzig, 1910–13).

P. POSENER-KRIÉGER and J.-L. DE CENIVAL, *Hieratic papyri in the British Museum: the Abusir papyri* (London, 1968).

H. RICKE, *Das Sonnenheiligtum des Königs Userkaf*, 2 vols (Cairo, 1965; Wiesbaden, 1969).

P. KAPLONY, 'Das Papyrus Archiv von Abusir', *Orientalia* 41 (1972), 180–244.

P. POSENER-KRIÉGER, *Les archives du temple funéraire de Neferirkare (Les papyrus d'Abousir)*, 2 vols (Cairo, 1976).

M. VERNER, 'Excavations at Abusir, season 1978–9, preliminary excavation report: the pyramid of Queen Khentkawes ("A")', *ZÄS* 107 (1980), 158–64.

—, 'Remarques préliminaires sur les nouveaux papyrus d'Abousir', *Ägypten: Dauer und Wandel* (Mainz, 1986), 35–43.

Abydos (anc. Abdjw)

Sacred site located on the west bank of the Nile, 50 km south of modern Sohag. The site of Abydos, centre of the cult of the god OSIRIS, flourished from the Predynastic period until Christian times (c.4000 BC–AD 641). The earliest significant remains are the tombs of named rulers of the Protodynastic and Early Dynastic periods (c.3100–2686 BC). The earliest temple at the site is that of the canine god Osiris-Khentimentiu (Kom el-Sultan). An extensive settlement of the Pharaonic period and numerous graves and cenotaphs of humans and animals have also been excavated.

The site is still dominated by the temples of Sety I (1294–1279 BC) and his son Rameses II (1279–1213 BC), although an earlier chapel, constructed in the reign of Rameses I (1295–1294 BC), has survived in the form of a number of blocks of relief. The cult temple of Sety I is an L-shaped limestone building, and the iconography of its exquisite painted reliefs has been used to interpret the procedures of the religious rituals that were enacted there. In one scene Rameses II is shown reading out the names of previous kings from a papyrus roll in the presence of his father. The contents of the document are carved on the adjacent wall; this KING LIST (along with a similar list from the temple of Rameses II) has made an important contribution to studies of Egyptian chronology.

Behind the temple of Sety I is the Osireion, a building constructed of huge granite blocks which has been interpreted as a kind of cenotaph of the god Osiris. The structure is entered via a long descending gallery and decorated with excerpts from the *Book of Gates* and the Book of the Dead, as well as cosmological and dramatic texts. It was once thought to be an Old Kingdom building, because of the grandiose scale of the masonry, but it has now been dated to the reigns of Sety I and Merenptah and the style is generally presumed to have been an attempt at archaizing by New Kingdom architects.

The Abydos cemeteries, including the Early Dynastic necropolis now known as Umm el-Qa'ab, were excavated in the late nineteenth and

Plan of the 5th-Dynasty pyramid complexes at Abusir.

Map labels:
sun temple of Nyuserra
ABU GURAB
sun temple of Userkaf
N
ABUSIR
0 100 200 300 400 500   1000 m

1 pyramid complex of Sahura
2 mastaba of Ptahshepses
3 pyramid of Nyuserra
4 pyramid complex of Neferirkara Kakai
5 pyramid of Raneferef

early twentieth centuries by the French archaeologists Auguste Mariette and Emile Amélineau, and the British archaeologists Flinders Petrie and Eric Peet. In the 1960s Barry Kemp reanalysed the results of the excavations conducted by Petrie and Peet, and suggested that the Early Dynastic royal tombs were complemented by a row of 'funerary enclosures' to the east, which may well have been the prototypes of the mortuary temples in Old Kingdom PYRAMID complexes (see also GIZA and SAQQARA). In 1991 the excavations of David O'Connor revealed further support for this theory in the form of a number of Early Dynastic wooden BOAT GRAVES near the Shunet el-Zebib, the best preserved of the 'funerary enclosures'.

A team of German excavators, who have

BELOW *Two dolomite vases with gold covers, from the tomb of King Khasekhemwy at Abydos. 2nd Dynasty, c.2690 BC, H. of taller vase 5.7 cm. (EA33567–8)*

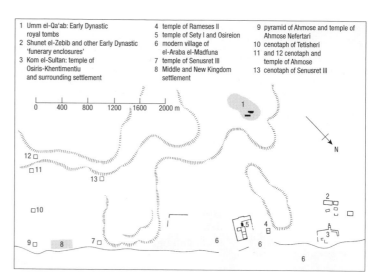

1 Umm el-Qa'ab: Early Dynastic royal tombs	4 temple of Rameses II	9 pyramid of Ahmose and temple of Ahmose Nefertari
2 Shunet el-Zebib and other Early Dynastic 'funerary enclosures'	5 temple of Sety I and Osireion	10 cenotaph of Tetisheri
3 Kom el-Sultan: temple of Osiris-Khentimentiu and surrounding settlement	6 modern village of el-Araba el-Madfuna	11 and 12 cenotaph and temple of Ahmose
	7 temple of Senusret III	13 cenotaph of Senusret III
	8 Middle and New Kingdom settlement	

ABOVE *Plan of Abydos.*

been working in the vicinity of the Early Dynastic royal cemetery since 1973, have obtained evidence to suggest that there are strong cultural links between Petrie's royal graves at Umm el-Qa'ab (traditionally dated to Dynasty I, the very beginning of the Early Dynastic phase at Abydos) and the adjacent late Predynastic Cemetery U. They therefore argue that the line of powerful historical rulers buried at Abydos may now be pushed further back into what was previously considered to be 'prehistory'.

The tomb of the 1st-Dynasty ruler Djer at Umm el-Qa'ab became identified with the tomb of Osiris from at least the late Middle Kingdom onwards, and during the 12th Dynasty (1985–1795 BC) it became common for individuals from elsewhere in Egypt to be buried at Abydos. It also appears to have become increasingly common for private individuals to make 'pilgrimages' to Abydos so that they could participate posthumously in the festivals of Osiris; large numbers of tombs

and cenotaphs (or 'offering chapels') were therefore constructed at the northern end of the site, in the vicinity of Kom el-Sultan. About two thousand stelae and numerous offering tables and statues have been plundered and excavated from these funerary monuments. The stelae have provided a great deal of information concerning the cult of Osiris, the literary structure of funerary autobiographies, and a wealth of details concerning the middle-ranking officials of the Middle Kingdom and their families.

The southern end of the site incorporates both Middle and New Kingdom archaeological remains; a pyramid temple, cenotaph and terraced temple of AHMOSE I (1550–1525 BC) and AHMOSE NEFERTARI were excavated by Charles Currelly in 1901. In 1993 Stephen Harvey undertook new excavations in this area, revealing fragments of painted reliefs of Ahmose I,

RIGHT *Plan of the temple of Sety I and the Osireion at Abydos.*

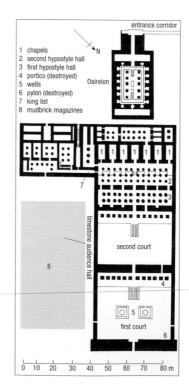

1 chapels
2 second hypostyle hall
3 first hypostyle hall
4 portico (destroyed)
5 wells
6 pylon (destroyed)
7 king list
8 mudbrick magazines

entrance corridor

Osireion

limestone audience hall

second court

first court

which perhaps depict his campaigns against the
HYKSOS at the beginning of the 18th Dynasty.

A. MARIETTE, *Abydos: description des fouilles exécutées sur l'emplacement de cette ville*, 2 vols (Paris, 1869–80).

W. M. F. PETRIE, *The royal tombs of the earliest dynasties*, 2 vols (London, 1900–1).

A. M. CALVERLEY and M. F. BROOME, *The temple of king Sethos I at Abydos*, 4 vols (London and Chicago, 1933–58).

H. FRANKFORT, *The cenotaph of Seti I at Abydos* (London, 1933).

B. J. KEMP, 'The Egyptian 1st Dynasty royal cemetery', *Antiquity* 41 (1967), 22–32.

W. K. SIMPSON, *Terrace of the Great God at Abydos: the offering chapels of Dynasties 12 and 13* (New Haven and Philadelphia, 1974).

A. R. DAVID, *A guide to religious ritual at Abydos* (Warminster, 1981).

D. O'CONNOR, 'The cenotaphs of the Middle Kingdom at Abydos', *Mélanges Gamal eddin Mokhtar* II (Cairo, 1985), 161–77.

—, 'Boat graves and pyramid origins: new discoveries at Abydos, Egypt', *Expedition* 33/3 (1991), 5–17.

G. DREYER, 'Umm el-Qa'ab. Nachuntersuchungen im frühzeitlichen Königsfriedhof 5./6. Vorbericht', *MDAIK* 49 (1993), 23–62 [preliminary reports on earlier seasons published in *MDAIK* 35, 38 and 46].

S. HARVEY, 'Monuments of Ahmose at Abydos', *Egyptian Archaeology* 4 (1994), 3–5.

administration

The process of social and economic control of the population was an area of life in which the Egyptians excelled. Many of the surviving artefacts and documents of the EARLY DYNAS-TIC PERIOD (*c*.3100–2686 BC), such as ivory labels and wine-jar sealings, were clearly elements of an emerging administrative infrastructure. The evidence for Egyptian administration consists of two basic elements: prosopography (i.e. textual records of the names, titles and professions of individuals) and the archaeological remains relating to supply and demand of commodities such as grain, beer and wine. The granaries surrounding the mortuary temple of Rameses II (the RAMESSEUM), for instance, are tangible remains of the increasingly elaborate system of storage and distribution that sustained those employed by the temple and state in Egypt.

The key factor in the administration of Early Dynastic Egypt, as in the early city-states of Mesopotamia, appears to have been the use of writing as a means of political control. The SCRIBE was therefore the most important element of the administration, a fact which is recognized both in 'pro-scribal' liter-

ary works such as the 12th Dynasty *Satire on the Trades* and in the popularity of statuary representing high officials in the scribal pose. It was the scribal profession that was responsible for assessing individuals' agricultural produce and collecting taxes on behalf of the king, provincial governor or temple official.

Fragment of a wall-painting from the tomb of Nebamun at Thebes, showing geese being counted for a tax assessment of agricultural produce. 18th Dynasty, c.1400 BC, H. 71 cm. (EA37978)

In the Old Kingdom (2686–2181 BC) there were two principal state offices apart from that of KING: the VIZIER (*tjayty sab tjaty*) and the overseer of royal works (*imy-r kat nesw*). The title vizier is first attested on inscribed stone vessels beneath the Step Pyramid at Saqqara, suggesting that the office was introduced at least as early as the 2nd Dynasty. After the unification of the country in the late fourth millennium BC, the various regions retained a degree of independence in their role as provinces (or NOMES) ruled by local governors (nomarchs). Whenever the central administration was weakened, whether through invasion or economic decline, power tended to devolve back to the nomes, as in the first and second so-called 'intermediate periods' (see CHRONOLOGY).

By the New Kingdom (1550–1069 BC) the Egyptian administration had considerably diversified; because it was no longer possible for the king to control all aspects of government, the role of the vizier had grown more important. The authority of both the king and his vizier had also been strengthened since the 12th Dynasty, apparently as a result of a policy of reduction in the power of the nomarchs. In the 18th Dynasty there were two viziers, northern and southern, but most of the surviving evidence concerns the southern vizier,

since fewer administrative documents have survived for this period in Lower Egypt. The walls of the Theban tomb of Rekhmira, who was southern vizier in the reigns of Thutmose III (1479–1425 BC) and Amenhotep II (1427–1400 BC), are decorated with his funerary biography as well as an inscription known as 'the duties of the vizier', which outlines the responsibilities of the post.

The New Kingdom national administration was divided into three sections: the dynasty, the internal administration and external affairs. The 'dynasty' consisted of royal relatives, most of whom held little political or economic power, perhaps because it was they who might have posed the greatest threat to the king. The internal administration comprised four sections: the 'royal domain', the army and navy, the religious hierarchy and the secular (or civil) officials.

The royal domain included such posts as chancellor, chamberlain and chief steward, while the army and navy were led by a commander-in-chief with chief deputies of north and south below him. The religious administration was controlled by an 'overseer of prophets of all the gods of Upper and Lower Egypt', a post which was actually held at various times by the vizier or the chief priest of AMUN. The secular part of the internal administration was headed by the northern and southern viziers, with overseers of the treasuries and granaries below them; it was these officials who controlled the national bureaucracy, judiciary and police. At a local level there were also 'town mayors' (*haty-'*) and councils (*kenbet*) in charge of the judiciary.

The New Kingdom external administration was divided into two sectors: (1) the governors of the three northern lands (i.e. the provinces of Syria-Palestine) and (2) the governor of the southern lands, who was also known as the VICEROY OF KUSH (or King's Son of Kush). Below the governors of the northern lands were local princes and garrison commanders, and below the Viceroy of Kush were the deputies of Wawat and Kush (the two regions of Egyptian-dominated Nubia), the mayors of Egyptian colonies and the local chiefs of the Nubians.

N. KANAWATI, *The Egyptian administration in the Old Kingdom: evidence of its economic decline* (Warminster, 1977).

T. G. H. JAMES, *Pharaoh's people: scenes from life in imperial Egypt* (London, 1984), 51–72, 154–80.

N. STRUDWICK, *The administration of Egypt in the Old Kingdom* (London, 1985).

B. J. KEMP, 'Large Middle Kingdom granary buildings (and the archaeology of administration)', *ZÄS* 113 (1986), 120–36.

S. QUIRKE, *The administration of Egypt in the Late Middle Kingdom* (New Malden, 1990).

aegis

Greek word for 'shield', used by Egyptologists to describe a representation of a broad necklace surmounted with the head of a deity. Depictions of sacred BARKS show that they had an aegis attached to the prow.

H. BONNET, *Reallexikon der Ägyptischen Religionsgeschichte* (Berlin, 1952), 8–9.

ABOVE *Jasper aegis incorporating a ram's head wearing sun-disc and cobra, H. 3.5 cm. (EA3360)*

RIGHT *Silver aegis with lion's head, H. 4.8 cm. (EA57903)*

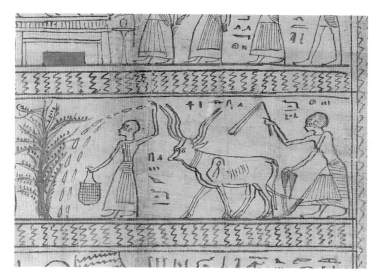

Aegyptiaca

Term usually applied to Egyptian objects found outside the borders of Egypt itself, particularly in the Eastern Mediterranean.

afterlife *see* FUNERARY BELIEFS

agriculture

The fundamental importance of agriculture in Egypt is attested from early times, with the development of land surveying as a means of re-determining land boundaries after the annual INUNDATION had deposited its load of silt on the fields, and also the measuring of areas of land for TAXATION purposes. Scenes of government surveyors measuring agricultural land are known from the decoration of many tomb chapels such as that of Menna, an

Detail of the Book of the Dead papyrus of Kerquny, showing the deceased ploughing and sowing. Ptolemaic period, c.250–150 BC. (EA9911, SHEET 2)

18th-Dynasty Theban official (TT69).

The development of the CALENDAR itself was linked to careful observation of the agricultural year, the seasons being named in accordance with stages of the annual Nile cycle. Flooding began in mid-June, the time of the New Year, and maximum depth was usually reached by mid-August, although the exact timing varied from north to south. The reach of the Nile was extended by the digging of irrigation canals which could also be used for moving water at times of low flood. Canals are first attested in the Early Dynastic period and it is likely that the reliefs on the macehead of King SCORPION show the use of irrigation in the late PREDYNASTIC PERIOD. As soon as the inundation began to subside the farmers blocked canals in order to retain the water, which was not released for a further month and a half. In October or November the seed was broadcast by hand and then trampled in by sheep and goats (as well as pigs, according to Herodotus).

The principal crop was grain, including barley (*Hordeum*; particularly the six-rowed variety) and three types of wheat: emmer (*Triticum dicoccum*), einkorn (*Triticum monococcum*) and spelt (*Triticum spelta*). These were used to make bread and beer, the two great staples of Egyptian life. The rich soil could support at least two crops a year, but if a second was desired, during the summer, then it had to be irrigated manually. In the Old and Middle Kingdoms, a simple yoke and vessels were used to move the water, but the introduction of the SHADUF in the New Kingdom and the *sakkia* (an animal-powered water wheel) in the Ptolemaic period not only made irrigation easier but also extended the area of cultivable land. Usually pulses rather than cereals were grown as a second crop, and although these 'fix' nitrogen and so enrich the soil, the environmental effect was probably relatively trivial compared with that of the Nile flood.

Numerous tomb-paintings depict grain being harvested with sickles, threshed using oxen, then winnowed and stored, while the quantities were carefully measured and recorded by scribes. Vegetables (including onions, garlic, peas, lentils, beans, radishes, cabbage, cucumbers and a type of lettuce) were usually grown in small square plots, attested both in tomb-paintings and in the archaeological record, as in the case of the vegetable plots outside the 'workmen's village' at EL-AMARNA.

OILS were extracted from sesame, castor and flax (*Linum usitatissimum*), the latter also supplying the principal fibre for the making of linen textiles. Grapes were grown for wine, particularly in the Delta region and oases, and there are numerous scenes showing wine presses in use. Many OSTRACA have also survived from wine-jars, usually recording the contents, date and origins of wine-jars. Wine and beer (see ALCOHOLIC BEVERAGES) were often flavoured with dates, and the fibres of the date palm were used in the making of cordage and BASKETRY.

Most of the agricultural land belonged to the king and the temples, and both kept copious records of its productivity. Officials often inflicted severe punishments on those who failed to meet grain quotas, and in many tombs, such as that of MERERUKA in the Old Kingdom, there are scenes of peasants being beaten for this reason.

L. KEIMER, 'Agriculture in ancient Egypt', *American Journal of Semitic Languages and Literature* 42 (1926), 283–8.

K. BAER, 'An eleventh dynasty farmer's letters to his family', *JAOS* 83 (1963), 1–19.

J. VANDIER, *Manuel d'archéologie égyptienne VI: Scènes de la vie agricole à l'ancien et au moyen empire* (Paris, 1978).

T. G. H. JAMES, *Pharaoh's people: scenes from life in imperial Egypt* (Oxford, 1984), 100–31.

H. WILSON, *Egyptian food and drink* (Princes Risborough, 1988).

E. STROUHAL, *Life in ancient Egypt* (Cambridge, 1992), 91–107.

W. WETTERSTROM, 'Foraging and farming in
Egypt: the transition from hunting and gathering to horticulture in the Nile valley', *The archaeology of Africa*, ed. T. Shaw et al. (London, 1993), 165–226.

A Group (A Horizon)

Term first used by the American archaeologist George Reisner to refer to a semi-nomadic Nubian Neolithic culture of the mid-fourth to early third millennium BC. More recently, W. Y. Adams has suggested that the A Group and their successors the C GROUP should be referred to as the A and C 'horizons', since the use of the term 'group' can give the misleading impression that they were two separate

Selection of objects from an A-Group grave, including two Egyptian imports (the tall jar and painted pot), c.3500–3000 BC, H. of tall jar 45 cm. (EA51193, 51187, 51188, 51191, 51192)

ethnic groups rather than simply two phases in the material culture of the Nubians.

Traces of the A Group, which probably evolved gradually out of the preceding Abkan culture, have survived throughout Lower Nubia. The archaeological remains at sites such as Afyeh (near Aswan) suggest that they lived mainly in temporary reed-built encampments or rock shelters, usually in the immediate area of the Nile, surviving through a diverse combination of hunting, gathering, fishing, the cultivation of wheat and barley, and the herding of sheep, goats and cattle.

Extensive A-Group cemeteries, typically including black-polished and 'eggshell' hand-made pottery, have been excavated at such sites as Sayala and Qustul (see BALLANA AND QUS-TUL). The grave goods sometimes include stone vessels, amulets and copper artefacts imported from Egypt, which not only help to date these graves but also demonstrate that the A Group were engaged in regular trade with the Egyptians of the Predynastic and Early Dynastic periods. The wealth and quantity of imported items appears to increase in later A-Group graves, suggesting a steady growth in contact between the two cultures. The A Group was eventually replaced by the C GROUP at some time during the OLD KINGDOM. See also B GROUP.

H. Å. NORDSTRÖM, *Neolithic and A-group sites* (Stockholm, 1972), 17–32.

W. Y. ADAMS, *Nubia: corridor to Africa*, 2nd ed. (London and Princeton, 1984), 118–32.

H. S. SMITH, 'The development of the A-Group "culture" in northern Lower Nubia', *Egypt and Africa*, ed. W. V. Davies (London, 1991), 92–111.

J. H. TAYLOR, *Egypt and Nubia* (London, 1991), 9–13.

Aha (c.3100 BC)

One of the earliest 1st-Dynasty rulers of a unified Egypt, whose name means 'the fighter'. His reign is attested primarily by funerary remains at ABYDOS, SAQQARA and NAQADA. When Flinders Petrie excavated at Umm el-Qa'ab (the Early Dynastic cemetery at Abydos) in 1899–1900, he discovered Tomb B19/15, which contained objects bearing the name of Aha. However, the earliest of the 1st- and 2nd-Dynasty élite tombs at north SAQQARA (no. 3357), excavated in the 1930s, was also dated by jar-sealings to the reign of Aha. Although it was once thought that the Saqqara tomb was the burial-place of Aha (and the Abydos tomb only a cenotaph), scholarly opinion has shifted since the material from the two sites was re-examined in the 1960s, leading to the suggestion that Aha was buried in Tomb B19/15 at Abydos and that the Saqqara tomb belonged to a Memphite high official. New research conducted in the Umm el-Qa'ab cemetery during the 1980s and 1990s (including the re-excavation of Tomb B19/15) also suggests that Aha was preceded by a relatively long sequence of earlier rulers of a united Egypt.

There is still considerable debate surrounding the possible links between Aha, NARMER and MENES (the semi-mythical founder of MEMPHIS), although two discoveries are particularly relevant to this problem. First, an ivory label, found in the tomb of Neithhotep (probably Aha's wife) in the late Predynastic cemetery at NAQADA, appears to give one of Aha's names as 'Men', which has led some scholars to suggest that he and Menes were the same person, or at least closely related. With regard to the place of Narmer in the chronological sequence, a seal impression discovered at Umm el-Qa'ab in 1985 appears to put him securely at the beginning of the 1st Dynasty, since it lists the first six rulers in the following order: Narmer, Aha, DJER, DJET, DEN and Merneith (the latter being a female ruler who may have been a regent). On the basis of these two pieces of evidence it is therefore possible that Narmer and Aha were father and son and that one of the two was also called Menes.

A. H. GARDINER, *Egypt of the Pharaohs* (Oxford, 1961), 405–14.

B. J. KEMP, 'The Egyptian 1st Dynasty royal cemetery', *Antiquity* 41 (1967), 22–32.

Ahhotep I (*c.*1590–1530 BC)

New Kingdom QUEEN whose lifetime spanned the crucial transition from the Second Intermediate Period to the New Kingdom, when the HYKSOS rulers were expelled from Lower Egypt, ushering in a new era of stability and indigenous Egyptian rule. As the daughter of the 17th-Dynasty ruler Senakhtenra Taa I, the wife of SEQENENRA TAA II and mother of AHMOSE I (and arguably also of KAMOSE), she appears to have played an important part in these wars of liberation. A stele erected by Ahmose I (1550–1525 BC) in the temple of Amun-Ra at KARNAK praises his mother's heroism: 'she is one who has accomplished the rites and cared for Egypt; she has looked after Egypt's troops and she has guarded them; she has brought back the fugitives and collected together the deserters; she has pacified Upper Egypt and expelled her rebels'. It has been suggested that this unusually active military role played by a royal wife (see QUEEN) might actually have been necessitated by the comparatively young age at which Ahmose I came to the throne – Ahhotep I might thus have served as regent for a few years until he reached maturity. An inscription on a doorway at the Nubian fortress of BUHEN links the names of Ahmose I and his mother in such a way as to imply a CORECENCY.

It has also been suggested that Ahhotep may have looked after the internal rule of Upper Egypt while her son was engaged in military campaigns. Certainly the titles given to Ahhotep in the Karnak stele include *nebet ta* ('mistress of the land'), showing that she probably wielded some power over a geographical area. The coffin of Ahhotep I was found in the royal cache at DEIR EL-BAHRI.

The intact burial of another Ahhotep (who was perhaps the wife of KAMOSE) was discov-

ered at Dra Abu el-Naga in western THEBES in 1859 by agents working for Auguste Mariette. Inside the tomb the excavators found a gilded wooden *rishi*-COFFIN containing the queen's mummy. There were also numerous items of funerary equipment, including several elaborate ceremonial weapons of Ahmose I, a necklace consisting of large golden FLIES, which was traditionally awarded for valour in battle, two model gold and silver BARKS (one placed on a bronze and wooden cart), and various items of jewellery.

F. W. VON BISSING, *Ein Thebanischer Grabfund aus dem Anfang des Neuen Reichs* (Berlin, 1900).

A. MACY ROTH, 'Ahhotep I and Ahhotep II', *Serapis* 4 (1977–8), 31–40.

C. VANDERSLEYEN, 'Les deux Ahhoteps', *SAK* 8 (1980), 233–42.

M. SALEH and H. SOUROUZIAN, *The Egyptian Museum, Cairo: official catalogue* (Mainz, 1987), cat. nos 120–6.

N. GRIMAL, *A history of ancient Egypt* (Oxford, 1992), 199–201.

Ahmose I (Amosis) (1550–1525 BC)

First ruler of the 18th Dynasty, who was the son of the Theban 17th-Dynasty ruler SEQENENRA TAA II. He came to the throne of a reunited Egypt after he and his predecessor KAMOSE had expelled the HYKSOS rulers from the Delta region. Recently excavated reliefs from ABYDOS apparently depict Ahmose's campaigns against the HYKSOS, which dominated his reign. The tombs of the soldiers Ahmose son of Ibana and Ahmose Pennekhbet at ELKAB are decorated with autobiographical inscriptions describing the role that they played in the campaigns of Ahmose I and his immediate successors. In western Asia he extended Egyptian influence deep into Syria–Palestine, and by the twenty-second year of his reign he may even have reached as far north as the Euphrates. He also undertook at least two campaigns into Nubia, establishing a new settlement at BUHEN as his administrative centre, under the command of a man called Turi who was to become the first known VICEROY OF KUSH in the reign of AMENHOTEP I (1525–1504 BC).

In his reorganization of the national and local government, which had probably remained relatively unchanged since the Middle Kingdom (see ADMINISTRATION), Ahmose I appears to have rewarded those local princes who had supported the Theban cause during the Second Intermediate Period (1650–1550 BC). Although he is known to have reopened the Tura limestone quarries, little has survived of the construction of religious buildings during his reign, apart from a few

Earliest known royal shabti *and one of the few sculptures of Ahmose I to be securely identified as such by its inscription. The king is portrayed wearing a* nemes *headcloth and a uraeus. 18th Dynasty, c.1550 BC, limestone, H. 30 cm. (EA32191)*

additions to the temples of Amun and Montu at KARNAK and mud-brick cenotaphs for TETISHERI and himself at ABYDOS.

The examination of his mummified body, which was among those transferred into the DEIR EL-BAHRI cache in the 21st Dynasty, suggests that he was about thirty-five when he died. The location of his tomb is still not definitely known, but he was probably buried at

Dra Abu el-Naga in western THEBES, where the pyramidal tombs of his 17th-Dynasty predecessors were located.

C. VANDERSLEYEN, *Les guerres d'Amosis, fondateur de la XVIII*e *dynastie* (Brussels, 1971).
C. DESROCHES-NOBLECOURT, 'Le "bestiaire" symbolique du libérateur Ahmosis', *Festschrift W. Westendorf* (Göttingen, 1984), 883–92.
A. M. DODSON, 'The tombs of the kings of the early Eighteenth Dynasty at Thebes', *ZÄS*, 115 (1988), 110–23.
N. GRIMAL, *A history of ancient Egypt* (Oxford, 1992), 193–202.

Ahmose II (Amasis, Amosis II) (570–526 BC)

Pharaoh of the late 26th Dynasty, who was originally a general in Nubia during the reign of PSAMTEK II (595–589 BC). He came to the throne following his defeat of APRIES (589–570 BC) at the 'Battle of Momemphis', which – according to a badly damaged stele – may actually have taken place near Terana on the Canopic branch of the Nile.

Ahmose II was proclaimed pharaoh by popular demand when Apries was blamed for the defeat of his troops at the hands of Dorian GREEK settlers. According to the Greek historian HERODOTUS, Ahmose II captured Apries and initially held him at the palace in SAIS; he is later said to have allowed him to be strangled, although eventually he appears to have accorded him a full royal burial.

Although Ahmose II found it necessary to continue to employ Greek mercenaries, he was

Green schist head from a statue of a Late Period king, possibly Ahmose II. 26th Dynasty, c.550 BC, H. 38 cm. (EA497)

more politically shrewd than his predecessor, presenting himself as nationalistic by limiting the activities of Greek merchants to the city of NAUKRATIS in the Delta, where they were granted special economic and commercial privileges (see TRADE). Later legend also has it that he married the daughter of Apries to the PERSIAN king in order to forestall Persian designs on Egypt, although this seems unlikely. By conquering parts of Cyprus he gained control of the Cypriot fleet, which he used to assist his allies in their struggles against the Persians. His friendly policy toward Greece included the financing of the rebuilding of the temple of Apollo at Delphi after its destruction in 548 BC, an act that earned him the epithet 'Philhellene'.

He is described by Herodotus as a popular ruler of humble origins, who is said to have had such a strong inclination for drink that he delayed affairs of state in order to indulge in a drinking bout. At the end of his long and prosperous reign he was succeeded by his son PSAMTEK III (526–525 BC), whose rule was to be abruptly ended some six months later by the invasion of the new Persian ruler, Cambyses.

Only a small number of sculptures representing Ahmose II have survived, and his name was apparently removed from many of his monuments by Cambyses. The buildings he constructed at SAIS, BUTO, MEMPHIS and ABYDOS have also been poorly preserved; although his tomb, located within the temple precincts at Sais, was ransacked in ancient times, a number of SHABTIS have been preserved.

HERODOTUS, *The histories*, trans. A. de Selincourt (Harmondsworth, 1972), II, 169–74.
A. B. LLOYD, 'The Late Period', *Ancient Egypt: a social history*, B. G. Trigger et al. (Cambridge, 1985), 285–6, 294.
N. GRIMAL, *A history of ancient Egypt* (Oxford, 1992), 363–4.

Ahmose Nefertari (c.1570–1505 BC)

Perhaps the most influential of the New Kingdom royal women, whose political and religious titles, like those of her grandmother TETISHERI and mother AHHOTEP I, have helped to illuminate the various new political roles adopted by women in the early 18th Dynasty (see QUEENS). Born in the early sixteenth century BC, she was described as *mwt nesw* ('king's mother') in relation to her son AMENHOTEP I and *hemet nesw weret* ('king's principal wife') in relation to her brother and husband AHMOSE I. She was also the first royal woman to have the title *hemet netjer* (see GOD'S WIFE OF AMUN) bestowed upon her, an act which was described in Ahmose I's Stele of Donations in

the temple of Amun at Karnak. This title was the one most frequently used by Ahmose Nefertari, and it was later passed on to several of her female descendants, including her own daughter Meritamun and Queen HATSHEPSUT (1473–1458 BC). It was once interpreted as an 'heiress' epithet, marking out the woman whom the king must marry to legitimize his claim to the throne, but it is now considered to have been simply a priestly office relating to the cult of Amun (carrying with it entitlement to an agricultural estate and personnel), which was to acquire greater political importance during the Late Period.

There is considerable textual evidence for Ahmose Nefertari's involvement in the cult of Amun as well as her participation in the quarrying and building projects undertaken by her husband. One stele even documents the fact that Ahmose I sought her approval before erecting a cenotaph for TETISHERI at Abydos. She seems to have outlived him by a considerable period, apparently serving as regent during the early years of Amenhotep I's reign. An inscription of the first year of the reign of his successor, THUTMOSE I, suggests that she was probably still alive even after the death of her son. She became the object of a posthumous religious cult, sometimes linked with that of Amenhotep I, particularly in connection with the workmen's village at DEIR EL-MEDINA, which they were considered to have jointly founded. More than fifty of the Theban tombs of private individuals include inscriptions mentioning her name.

M. GITTON, *L'épouse du dieu Ahmès Néfertary*, 2nd ed. (Paris, 1981).
—, *Les divines épouses de la 18*e *dynastie* (Paris, 1984).
G. ROBINS, *Women in ancient Egypt* (London, 1993), 43–5.

A Horizon see A GROUP

Aker

Earth-god whose cult can be traced back to the Early Dynastic period. He was most often represented as a form of 'double-sphinx', consisting of two lions seated back to back, but he was also occasionally portrayed simply as a tract of land with lions' heads or human heads at either side. The symbolism of Aker was closely associated with the junction of the eastern and western horizons in the underworld. Because the lions faced towards both sunrise and sunset, the god was closely associated with the journey of the sun through the underworld each night. The socket which holds the mast of the SOLAR BARK was therefore usually identified with Aker.

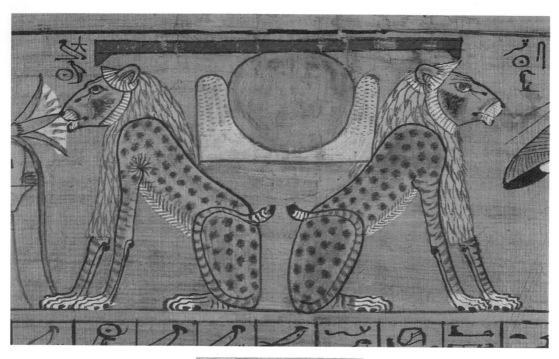

ABOVE *Detail from the Book of the Dead of Ani, showing lions representing the god Aker. 19th Dynasty, c.1250 BC, painted papyrus. (EA10470)*

M. F. BISSON DE LA ROQUE, 'Notes sur Aker', *BIFAO* 30 (1930), 575–80.
C. DE WIT, *Le role et le sens du lion* (Leiden, 1951).
E. HORNUNG, 'Aker', *Lexikon der Ägyptologie* I, ed. W. Helck, E. Otto and W. Westendorf (Wiesbaden, 1975), 114–15.
J. R. OGDEN, 'Some notes on the name and the iconography of the god '*kr*', *VA* 2 (1986), 127–35.

akh

One of the five principal elements which the Egyptians considered necessary to make up a complete personality, the other four being the KA, BA, NAME and SHADOW. The *akh* was believed to be the form in which the blessed dead inhabited the underworld, and also the result of the successful reunion of the *ba* with its *ka*. Once the *akh* had been created by this reunion, it was regarded as enduring and unchanging for eternity. Although the physical form of the *akh* was usually portrayed as a SHABTI-like mummiform figure, the word *akh* was written with the sign of the so-called crested IBIS (*Geronticus eremita*).

Detail of the coffin of Seni, showing a hieroglyph representing the crested akh-*bird. Middle Kingdom, c.2000 BC, painted wood, H. 15 cm. (EA30841)*

G. ENGLUND, *Akh – une notion religieuse dans l'Egypte pharaonique* (Uppsala, 1978).
J. P. ALLEN, 'Funerary texts and their meaning', *Mummies and magic*, ed. P. Lacovara, S. D'Auria, and C. H. Roehrig (Boston, 1988), 38–49.

Akhenaten (Amenhotep IV) (1352–1336 BC)

The infamous 'heretic' pharaoh, during whose reign the art and religion of Egypt were marked by rapid change. Born in the early fourteenth century BC, he was the son of AMENHOTEP III (1390–1352 BC) and Queen TIY. When he initially succeeded to the throne, probably some years before the death of his father (although there is still considerable debate as to whether there was any COREGENCY between the two), he was known as Amenhotep IV. However, in the first year of his reign, he set the tone for a new era by establishing a temple at KARNAK dedicated not to AMUN but to the god ATEN, the literal meaning of which was 'the (sun) disc'.

In his fifth regnal year Amenhotep IV made two crucial and iconoclastic decisions: he changed his name from Amenhotep ('Amun is content') to Akhenaten ('glory of the sun-disc') and he began to construct a new capital city called Akhetaten ('horizon of the Aten') at the site now known as EL-AMARNA in Middle Egypt. This newly founded settlement was evidently intended to replace both THEBES and MEMPHIS as the religious and secular focus of the country. The ensuing phase in Egyptian history, consisting of Akhenaten's reign and that of his ephemeral successor Smenkhkara, is therefore described as the Amarna period.

The major religious innovation of Akhenaten's reign was the vigorous promotion of the worship of the ATEN to the exclusion of

ABOVE *Colossal statue of Akhenaten from Karnak. 18th Dynasty, c.1350 BC, sandstone, H. 3.96 m. (CAIRO JE55938)*

the rest of the Egyptian gods, including even the state god AMUN. The reliefs and stelae in the temples and tombs of Akhenaten's reign repeatedly show the royal family (Akhenaten, his wife NEFERTITI and the royal princesses) worshipping and making offerings to the Aten, which was depicted as a disc with arms out-stretched downwards, often proferring WAS SCEPTRES and ANKH signs, symbolizing power and life respectively. The names of other deities – especially that of Amun – were excised from temple walls in an apparent attempt to establish the Aten as a single supreme deity, which has led many scholars to attribute the introduction of monotheism to Akhenaten mistakenly.

It has also been asserted, primarily on the basis of the evidence of the AMARNA LETTERS (diplomatic correspondence between the Amarna pharaohs and their vassals in SYRIA–PALESTINE), that Akhenaten neglected foreign policy and allowed the Egyptian 'empire' in western Asia to be severely eroded. There is, however, a certain amount of evidence for Asiatic campaigning during his reign, and it is also possible that the iconography of the period was deliberately underplaying the view of the king as warrior. It should also be borne in mind that the view of foreign policy in other reigns during the New Kingdom tends to be automatically distorted in that it derives principally from Egyptian temple reliefs and papyri rather than from genuine diplomatic documents such as the Amarna Letters.

After a sole reign of only about eighteen years, Akhenaten was succeeded first by an ephemeral figure called Smenkhkara (which may even have been a pseudonym for Nefertiti) and soon afterwards by Tutankhaten, who may have been a younger son of Amenhotep III or a son of Akhenaten. Within a few years the city at el-Amarna had been abandoned in favour of the traditional administrative centre at Memphis, and the new king had changed his name to Tutankhamun, effectively signalling the end of the supremacy of the Aten.

The final mystery of the 'Amarna period' is the disappearance of the bodies of Akhenaten and his immediate family. The royal tomb which Akhenaten had begun to build for himself in a secluded wadi to the east of el-Amarna appears never to have been completed and there is little evidence to suggest that anyone other than Meketaten (one of Akhenaten's daughters) was actually buried there. In 1907 Theodore Davis discovered the body of a young male member of the royal family in Tomb 55 in the VALLEY OF THE KINGS, apparently reinterred with a set of funerary equipment mainly belonging to Queen Tiy. This mummy was once identified as that of Akhenaten (a view still accepted by some Egyptologists) but most scholars now hypothesize that it may have been Smenkhkara.

G. T. MARTIN, *The royal tomb at el-Amarna*, 2 vols (London, 1974–89).

D. B. REDFORD, *Akhenaten the heretic king* (Princeton, 1984).

J. D. RAY, 'Review of Redford, D. B., *Akhenaten the heretic king*', *GM* 86 (1985), 81–3.

C. ALDRED, *Akhenaten: king of Egypt* (London, 1988).

Akhetaten *see* (TELL) EL-AMARNA

Akhmim (anc. Ipu, Khent-Mim)
Town-site on the east bank of the Nile opposite modern Sohag, which was the capital of the ninth NOME of Upper Egypt during the Pharaonic period (c.3100–332 BC). The earliest surviving remains are Old and Middle Kingdom rock-tombs, which were severely plundered during the 1880s, much of the

Coffin of the woman Tamin wearing daily dress, from the Roman-period cemetery at Akhmim. 2nd century AD, gilded and painted cartonnage and stucco, H. 1.5 m. (EA29586)

funerary equipment subsequently being dispersed among various collections. At around this time a large number of Late Period burials were unearthed. The tombs were first excavated by Percy Newberry in 1912 and more recently re-examined by Naguib Kanawati. The city originally included a number of temples dedicated to MIN, the god of fertility, but few stone buildings have survived from the Dynastic period, owing to the widespread plundering of the site in the fourteenth century AD. Recent excavations by Egyptian archaeologists, however, have uncovered colossal statues of RAMESES II (1279–1213 BC) and Meritamun. The cemeteries of the Christian period (AD 395–641), which were excavated in the late nineteenth century, have yielded many examples of wool, linen and silk fabrics which have formed part of the basis for a chronological framework for the study of textiles between the Hellenistic and Islamic periods (*c.*300 BC–AD 700).

P. E. NEWBERRY, 'The inscribed tombs of Ekhmim', *LAAA* 4 (1912), 101–20.

K. P. KUHLMANN, 'Der Felstempel des Eje bei Akhmim', *MDAIK* 35 (1979), 165–88.

N. KANAWATI, *Rock tombs of el-Hawawish: the cemetery of Akhmim*, 6 vols (Sydney, 1980–).

S. MCNALLY, 'Survival of a city: excavations at Akhmim', *NARCE* 116 (1981–2), 26–30.

K. P. KUHLMANN, *Materialen zur Archäologie und Geschichte des Raumes von Achmim* (Mainz, 1983).

E. J. BROVARSKI, 'Akhmim in the Old Kingdom and First Intermediate Period', *Mélanges Gamal Eddin Mokhtar*, I (Cairo, 1985).

Akkadian

Term used to denote a group of Semitic languages that first appeared in northern MESOPOTAMIA, in the third millennium BC, when the south of the country was still dominated by non-Semitic Sumerian speakers. By extension, the term is also used to refer to the material culture of northern Mesopotamia, particularly that of the dynasty founded by Sargon the Great (Sharrukin; 2334–2279 BC). The Akkadians adopted the Sumerians' CUNEIFORM writing system in order to write down their own language. They began gradually to infiltrate SUMER during its Early Dynastic period (*c.*3100–2686 BC). Such infiltration can be seen from the Semitic names of scribes at the southern site of Abu Salabikh who wrote in Sumerian; it is likely that many people were bilingual even before the unification of Sumer with Akkad. Akkadian is divided into Old Akkadian used in the third millennium and Assyrian and Babylonian in the second and first millennia and is related to Arabic

and Hebrew. The Sumerian language, on the other hand, has no close relatives.

Akkadian quickly became established as the lingua franca of the ancient Near East, and remained so over a long period, so that for example most of the AMARNA LETTERS (diplomatic correspondence between Egypt and the Levant in the mid-fourteenth century BC) are written in the Babylonian language, which is a late form of Akkadian.

J. OATES, *Babylon*, 2nd ed. (London, 1986), 22–59.

G. ROUX, *Ancient Iraq*, 3rd ed. (Harmondsworth, 1992), 146–60.

alabaster, Egyptian alabaster

The terms 'alabaster' or 'Egyptian alabaster' have often been used by Egyptologists to refer

Stone vessel from the tomb of Tutankhamun, inscribed with the cartouche of Thutmose III and details of its capacity (14.5 hin or 6.67 litres), c.1450 BC, travertine, H. 41.5 cm. (CAIRO, NO. 410, REPRODUCED COURTESY OF THE GRIFFITH INSTITUTE)

to a type of white or translucent stone used in Egyptian statuary and architecture, which is a form of limestone (calcium carbonate) more accurately described as travertine. From the Early Dynastic period onwards travertine was increasingly used for the production of funerary vessels, as well as statuary and altars; it occurs principally in the area of Middle Egypt, the main Pharaonic source being HATNUB, about 18 km southeast of the New Kingdom city at el-Amarna.

The use of the term alabaster is further complicated by the fact that the material often described by Egyptologists as 'gypsum', a

form of calcium sulphate quarried principally at Umm el-Sawwan in the Fayum region, may be legitimately described as 'alabaster'.

J. A. HARRELL, 'Misuse of the term "alabaster" in Egyptology', *GM* 119 (1990), 37–42.

D. and R. KLEMM, 'Calcit-Alabaster oder Travertin? Bemerkungen zu Sinn und Unsinn petrographischen Bezeichnungen in der Ägyptologie', *GM* 122 (1991), 57–70.

alcoholic beverages

Beer (*henket*), the most common of the alcoholic beverages, formed an important part of the Egyptian diet. This would be prepared in the household, or by brewers if it was for use in rations of state employees. The Egyptian process for making beer began with the preparation of partially baked cakes of barley bread. They were placed on a screen over a vat or jar, and water was poured over them until they dissolved and drained into the vat, whereupon the resulting mixture was left in a warm place to ferment. It has been suggested that stale bread may have been used as a substitute. Research by Delwen Samuel has challenged this traditional view by suggesting that bread was not used. However barley, emmer, or a mixture of both, are evident in beer residues. Often a variety of flavourings were added to the brew, including dates, honey and spices. The sugar from dates or honeyed bread would also have speeded up the fermentation. The brew was not necessarily very alcoholic, but had a high nutritional value, and was therefore an important part of the Egyptian diet (see FOOD). In the first century BC Diodorus Siculus praised the quality of Egyptian beer, describing it as barely inferior to wine.

Both red and white wine (*irep*) were regularly drunk and there are many tomb-paintings showing grapes being harvested and pressed, notably those in the tomb of Nakht at Thebes (TT52). The juice was collected in vats for fermentation, and when part-fermented was decanted into amphorae and left to mature, sometimes for several years. It then might be filtered again and have spices or honey added before finally being transported in amphorae. These vessels are frequently inscribed on the shoulder or have stamps impressed on the mud sealings. Often the inscription lists the king's regnal year, the variety of wine, its vineyard, its owner and the person responsible for production. In effect this served the same purpose as modern wine labels and as a result the locations of certain vineyards are known. The Delta, the western part of the coast, the Oases of KHARGA and DAKHLA and the Kynopolis area of Middle

ABOVE *Copy of a wine-making scene in the Theban tomb of Khaemwaset (TT261). New Kingdom.*

Ritual vase for 'Wine of Lower Egypt for the deceased lady Nodjmet'. 18th Dynasty, H. 79 cm. (EA59774)

Egypt seem to have been especially favoured. Wines might also be imported from SYRIA–PALESTINE and, later, GREECE, and there were a number of fruit wines made from dates, figs and pomegranates.

Alcohol was often taken in excess, and a number of private tombs, such as that of Djeserkaraseneb (TT38), are decorated with scenes showing guests exhibiting signs of nausea during banquets. In the depiction of a banquet in the tomb of Paheri at ELKAB, a female guest says, 'Give me eighteen cups of wine, for I wish to drink until drunkenness, my inside is like straw'. Such drunkenness was regarded as indicative of the abundance of the feast and therefore to be encouraged.

The best-known mythical instance of drunkenness was the intoxication of SEKHMET the lioness-goddess in *The Destruction of Mankind*, while the Greek historian Herodotus recorded that the festival of BASTET the cat-goddess was renowned for its drunkenness.

H. WILSON, *Egyptian food and drink* (Aylesbury, 1988).

J. GELLER, 'From prehistory to history: beer in Egypt', *The followers of Horus*, ed. F. Friedman and B. Adams (Oxford, 1992), 19–26.

E. STROUHAL, *Life in ancient Egypt* (Cambridge, 1992), 104–5, 127–8, 225.

Alexander the Great (352–323 BC)

In 332 BC the second Persian occupation of Egypt ended with the arrival of the armies of Alexander the Great. Born in Macedonia in 352 BC, Alexander had already conquered much of western Asia and the Levant before his arrival in Egypt, which appears to have been closer to a triumphal procession than an invasion. It was in keeping with this sense of

renewal rather than invasion that Alexander immediately made sacrifices to the gods at Memphis and visited SIWA OASIS in the Libyan Desert, where the oracle of AMUN-RA officially recognized him as the god's son, thus appar-

Silver coin bearing the head of Alexander the Great, c.330 BC, D. 2.7 cm. (CM3971E)

ently restoring the true pharaonic line. In a later attempt to bolster his claims to the royal succession, it was suggested, somewhat implausibly, in the *Alexander Romance*, that he was not the son of Philip II of Macedonia but the result of a liaison between his mother Olympias and NECTANEBO II (360–343 BC), the last native Egyptian pharaoh.

In 331 BC, having founded the city of ALEXANDRIA, Alexander left Egypt to continue his conquest of the Achaemenid empire (see PERSIA), leaving the country in the control of two Greek officials: Kleomenes of Naukratis, who was empowered to collect taxes from the newly appointed local governors, and PTOLEMY, son of Lagos, one of his generals, commander of the Egyptian army. Although certain monuments, such as the inner chapel of the temple of Amun at LUXOR, bear depictions of Alexander firmly establishing him as pharaoh, he must have had little opportunity to make any personal impact on the Egyptian political and economic structure, and it appears that, for a decade or so after his departure, the country suffered from a lack of strong leadership. In 323 BC, however, he died of a fever and although attempts were made on behalf of his half-brother Philip Arrhidaeus (323–317 BC) and his son Alexander IV (317–310 BC) to hold the newly acquired empire together, it eventually dissolved into a number of separate kingdoms ruled by his generals and their descendants. In Egypt Ptolemy at first functioned as a general alongside the viceroy Kleomenes, but eventually he became the first Ptolemaic ruler of Egypt after the death of Alexander IV, in 305 BC. It was Ptolemy I (305–285 BC) who was said to have placed the body of Alexander the Great in a golden coffin at Alexandria. His tomb was probably in the Soma (royal mausoleum), traditionally located under the Mosque of Nebi Daniel in central Alexandria, but so far it has not been found.

W. W. TARN, *Alexander the Great*, 2 vols (Cambridge, 1948).
A. BURN, *Alexander the Great and the Middle East*, 2nd ed. (Harmondsworth, 1973).
N. G. L. HAMMOND, *Alexander the Great: King, Commander and Statesman*, 3rd ed. (Bristol, 1989).

Alexandria (anc. Raqote)

Greco-Roman city situated on a narrow peninsula at the western end of the Mediterranean coast of Egypt. It was founded by Alexander the Great on the site of an earlier Egyptian settlement called Raqote, archaeological traces of which have so far been found only in the form of the pre-Ptolemaic seawalls to the north and west of the island of Pharos. Alexander is said to have entrusted the design of the city to the architect Deinokrates and the official Kleomenes, but the principal buildings were not completed until the reign of Ptolemy II Philadelphus (285–246 BC).

During the Ptolemaic and Roman periods (c.332 BC–AD 395) Alexandria was a thriving cosmopolitan city; by 320 BC it had replaced Memphis as the capital of Egypt and by the mid-first century BC it had a population of about half a million, including substantial numbers of Greeks and Jews. With its gridded street plan, it was essentially a Greek rather than an Egyptian city, and its identity was so strong that it was known as *Alexandrea ad Aegyptum*: Alexandria 'beside' Egypt rather than within it, as if it were a separate country in its own right. In the late first century AD the Roman orator Dio of Prusa even went so far as to describe Egypt as a mere appendage to Alexandria.

ABOVE *View of the underground chambers of Kom el-Shugafa, Alexandria. 1st–2nd centuries AD. (GRAHAM HARRISON)*

LEFT *Schist head from a statue of a young man, showing a combination of Greek and Egyptian sculptural traits, from Alexandria, c.1st century BC, H. 24.5 cm. (EA55253)*

The most famous ancient buildings at Alexandria were the Library and Museum, which are supposed to have been burned down, along with an irreplaceable collection of papyri, in the third century AD. The major monuments of the Ptolemaic and Roman periods were the SERAPEUM (a temple dedicated to the god SERAPIS, which may have housed part of the library collection), the Caesarium, a Roman stadium and Kom el-Shugafa (a labyrinth of rock-cut tombs dating to the first two centuries AD). The Alexandrian 'pharos', constructed in the early Ptolemaic period on the islet of Pharos about 1.5 km off the coast, was probably the earliest known lighthouse, but unfortunately virtually nothing has survived. Excavations at Kom el-Dikka, near the Mosque of Nebi Daniel, have revealed the remains of the central city during the Roman period, including a small theatre, baths, a gymnasium complex and a possible schoolroom. Apart from the fortress of Qait Bey on the Pharos peninsula, which may incorporate a few stray blocks from the ancient lighthouse, there are few surviving Islamic monuments at Alexandria.

The archaeological exploration of the city has

been complicated by the fact that antiquities from all over Egypt were gathered together in Alexandria either to adorn new temples or in preparation for their transportation to other parts of the Roman and Byzantine empires. Both Cleopatra's Needle (now on the Embankment in London) and the Central Park obelisk in New York once stood in the Caesarium, having been brought there from THUTMOSE III's temple to Ra-Atum at HELIOPOLIS.

Little excavation has taken place in the ancient town itself, which lies directly below the modern city centre, but parts of the road leading from the river port to the sea-harbour were examined in 1874. One of the most striking surviving monuments is Pompey's Pillar, a granite column which was actually erected by the Roman emperor Diocletian in c.AD 297, close to the site of the Serapeum.

E. BRECCIA, *Alexandrea ad Aegyptum*, Eng. trans. (Bergamo, 1922).

E. M. FORSTER, *Alexandria: a history and guide* (London, 1922).

P. M. FRASER, *Ptolemaic Alexandria*, 3 vols (Oxford, 1972).

H. KOLOTAJ, 'Recherches architectoniques dans les thermes et le théatre de Kom el-Dikka à Alexandrie', *Das römisch-byzantinische Agypten*, ed. G. Grimm et al. (Trier, 1983), 187–94.

A. K. BOWMAN, *Egypt after the pharaohs* (London, 1986), 204–33.

L. CANFORA, *The vanished library*, trans. M. Ryle (London, 1989).

altar

In the temples of ancient Egypt, the altar (*khat*) was used to carry offerings intended to propitiate deities or the deceased. The travertine ('Egyptian alabaster') altar in the sun temple of Nyuserra (2445–2421 BC) at Abu Gurab is one of the most impressive surviving examples. It consists of a huge monolithic circular slab surrounded by four other pieces of travertine, each carved in the form of a *hetep* ('offering') sign. In the temple of AMUN at KARNAK a pink granite altar in the form of a *hetep* sign (now in the Egyptian Museum, Cairo) was erected by Thutmose III (1479–1425 BC) in the 'Middle Kingdom court'. Relief scenes carved on the front of this altar show two kneeling figures of the king presenting offerings to Amun-Ra.

In the New Kingdom (1550–1069 BC) many large-scale stone temple altars were provided with ramps or sets of steps. A massive limestone altar dedicated to Ra-Horakhty, still *in situ* on the upper terrace of the temple of Hatshepsut at Deir el-Bahri, was furnished with a flight of ten steps on its western side. The Great Temple of the Aten at el-Amarna is

known to have included a large central altar approached by a ramp, as well as courtyards full of hundreds of stone offering tables.

From the Late Period (747–332 BC) onwards, Egypt began to be more influenced by Hellenistic and Syrian forms of worship

The great travertine altar at the sun temple of King Nyuserra at Abu Gurab. Around the circular central part of the altar are arranged four hetep *(offering) signs. (P. T. NICHOLSON)*

and the 'horned altar', consisting of a stone or brick-built block with raised corners, was introduced from Syria–Palestine. Such an altar was erected in front of the early Ptolemaic tomb of PETOSIRIS, a chief priest of Thoth, at Tuna el-Gebel. See also OFFERING TABLE.

G. JÉQUIER, 'Autel', *BIFAO* 19 (1922), 236–49.

I. SHAW, 'Balustrades, stairs and altars in the cult of the Aten at el-Amarna', *JEA* 80 (1994), 109–27.

Amara

The remains of two Nubian towns (Amara West and East) are located about 180 km south of Wadi Halfa on either side of the Nile. The walled settlement of Amara West, occupying an area of about 60,000 sq. m, was a colonial establishment founded by the Egyptians in the Ramesside period (c.1295–1069 BC), when most of Nubia was effectively regarded as part of Egypt. At Amara East there was once a town and temple dating to the Meroitic (see MEROE) period (c.300 BC–AD 350), but only the depleted remains of the enclosure wall are still visible at the site.

Amara West, perhaps initially set up as a base for gold-mining and trading expeditions further to the south, appears to have taken over from the town of SOLEB as the seat of the Deputy of Kush (Upper Nubia). The site included a stone-built temple of the time of

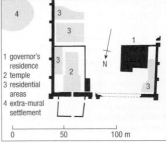

1 governor's residence
2 temple
3 residential areas
4 extra-mural settlement

0   50   100 m

Plan of the site of Amara West.

Rameses II, as well as cemeteries, some contemporary with the town and others dating to the BALLANA period (c.AD 400–543).

L. KIRWAN, 'Notes and news', *JEA* 22 (1936), 101–2.

H. W. FAIRMAN, 'Preliminary excavation reports on Amara West', *JEA* 24, 25, 34 (1938, 1939, 1948).

B. J. KEMP, 'Fortified towns in Nubia', *Man, settlement and urbanism*, ed. P. Ucko et al. (London, 1972), 651–6.

P. A. SPENCER, *Amara West* (London, 1997).

Amarna, (Tell) el- (anc. Akhetaten)

Site of a city, located about 280 km south of Cairo, founded by the pharaoh Akhenaten (1352–1336 BC). Abruptly abandoned following Akhenaten's death, after an occupation of only about twenty-five to thirty years, el-Amarna is the best-preserved example of an Egyptian settlement of the New Kingdom, including temples, palaces and large areas of mud-brick private housing. There are also two groups of rock-tombs (largely unfinished) at the northern and southern ends of the semi-circular bay of cliffs to the east of the city; these were built for the high officials of the city, such as the priest Panehsy and chief of police Mahu. The plundered and vandalized remains of the royal tombs of Akhenaten and his family, several kilometres to the east of the cliffs, were rediscovered in the late 1880s.

Unfortunately, because of the peculiarities of the site's historical background, the city of Akhetaten is unlikely to have been typical of Egyptian cities; nevertheless it presents an invaluable opportunity to study the patterning of urban life in Egypt during the fourteenth century BC. It was founded in about 1350 BC and abandoned about twenty years later; the dearth of subsequent settlement has ensured remarkable preservation of the city plan. The site as a whole is contained within a semi-circular bay of cliffs approximately 10 km long and a maximum of 5 km wide; the city itself stretches for about 7 km along the eastern bank of the Nile. The total population of the main city at el-Amarna has been estimated at between twenty thousand and fifty thousand.

Much of the western side of the city, including houses, harbours and the main palace of the king, has now vanished under the modern cultivation. However, a large number of structures have been preserved in the desert to the east, along with the wells, grain-silos, bakeries and refuse dumps that comprise the basic framework of production and consumption throughout the community. The nucleus of the city, the main components of which are described in contemporary inscriptions at the site, was a set of official buildings – principally temples, palaces and magazines – called the 'Island of Aten Distinguished in Jubilees'.

The three main residential zones of the city (the so-called north suburb, south suburb and north city) are characterized by a much more haphazard layout than the carefully planned central city; the manner in which they developed, with the spaces between the earliest large houses gradually being filled up with smaller clusters of houses, is usually described as 'organic'. There are also three small areas of planned settlement at el-Amarna: a block of

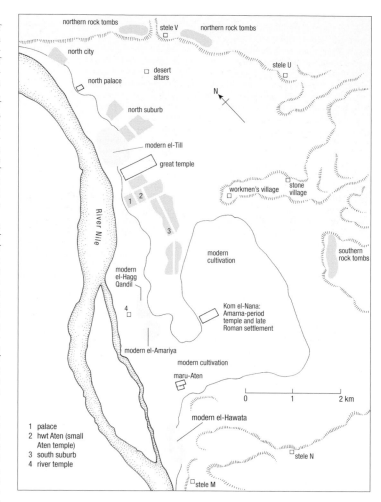

Plan of the city of Akhetaten at el-Amarna.

terraced buildings in the centre of the city (known as the 'clerks' houses'), a rectangular walled settlement located in relative isolation, more than a kilometre to the east of the main city (the 'workmen's village') and an area of drystone temporary accommodation situated about halfway between the latter and the cliffs (the 'stone village').

Over the last hundred years the site has been examined by a succession of excavators, including Flinders Petrie, Howard Carter and Leonard Woolsey. Since the late 1970s an expedition from the Egypt Exploration Society has produced the first detailed survey plan of the entire site, as well as excavating and re-examining a number of parts of the city, including the workmen's village, the small Aten temple and the newly identified Amarna-period temple of Kom el-Nana.

W. M. F. PETRIE, *Tell el-Amarna* (London, 1894).

N. DE G. DAVIES, *The rock tombs of El Amarna*, 6 vols (London, 1903–8).

T. E. PEET et al., *The city of Akhenaten*, 3 vols (London, 1923–51).

G. T. MARTIN, *The royal tomb at el-Amarna*, 2 vols (London, 1974–89).

L. BORCHARDT and H. RICKE, *Die Wöhnhäuser in Tell el-Amarna* (Berlin, 1980).

Fragment of painted pavement from a building called the Maru-Aten at el-Amarna, showing ducks flying out of a papyrus thicket. 18th Dynasty, c.1350 BC, painted plaster, H. 93 cm. (EA55617)

B. J. KEMP (ed.), *Amarna reports* I–VI (London, 1984–95).

B. J. KEMP, *Ancient Egypt: anatomy of a civilization* (London, 1989), 261–317.

Amarna Letters

Important cache of documents from EL-AMARNA, discovered in 1887 by a village woman digging ancient mud-brick for use as fertilizer (Arabic *sebakh*). This discovery led to further illicit diggings and the appearance of a number of clay CUNEIFORM tablets on the antiquities market. Their importance was not immediately recognized, and many passed into private hands, but Wallis Budge of the British Museum believed the tablets to be genuine and purchased a number of them; his view was confirmed by A. H. Sayce. The tablets are held by the British Museum, the Bodemuseum

in Berlin, the Louvre, and the Egyptian Museum in Cairo.

There are 382 known tablets, most of which derive from the 'Place of the Letters of Pharaoh', a building identified as the official 'records office' in the central city at el-Amarna. Their exact chronology is still debated, but they span a fifteen-to-thirty-year period (depending upon interpretations of co-regencies at this time), beginning around year thirty of AMENHOTEP III (1390–1352 BC) and extending no later than the first year of TUTANKHAMUN's reign (1336–1327 BC), with the majority dating to the time of AKHENATEN (1352–1336 BC). Most are written in a dialect of the AKKADIAN language, which was the lingua franca of the time, although the languages of the ASSYRIANS, HITTITES and Hurrians (MITANNI) are also represented.

All but thirty-two of the documents in the archive are items of diplomatic correspondence between Egypt and either the great powers in western Asia, such as Babylonia and Assyria, or the vassal states of SYRIA and PALESTINE. They provide a fascinating picture

of the relationship between Egypt and these states, although there are very few letters from the Egyptian ruler. The state of the empire under Akhenaten is poignantly documented in the increasingly desperate pleas for assistance from Syro-Palestinian cities under siege. As well as giving insights into the political conditions of the time, the letters also shed light on TRADE relations, diplomatic MARRIAGE and the values of particular com-

Tablet from el-Amarna, inscribed with a cuneiform letter from Tushratta of Mitanni to Amenhotep III. 18th Dynasty, c.1354 BC, clay, H. 9 cm. (WA29793)

modities such as GLASS, GOLD and the newly introduced IRON, while the various forms of address employed in the letters indicate the standing of the writers *vis-à-vis* the Egyptian court.

C. ALDRED, *Akhenaten, King of Egypt* (London, 1988), 183–94.

E. F. CAMPBELL, *The chronology of the Amarna Letters* (Baltimore, 1964).

B. J. KEMP, *Ancient Egypt: anatomy of a civilization* (London, 1989), 223–5.

W. L. MORAN, *The Amarna Letters* (London, 1992).

Amasis *see* AHMOSE II

Amenemhat (Ammenemes)
Four of the 12th-Dynasty pharaohs held the 'birth name' Amenemhat ('Amun is at the head'), while the rest, apart from Queen SOBEKNEFERU, took the name of SENUSRET.

Amenemhat I Sehetepibra (1985–1955 BC) was the son of a priest called Senusret and a woman called Nofret. He was the first ruler of the 12th Dynasty, but he is probably already attested at the end of the 11th Dynasty, when, as the vizier of MENTUHOTEP IV (1992–1985 BC), he led an expedition along the Wadi Hammamat to the Red Sea.

His Horus name, Wehem-mesut ('he who repeats births'), was no doubt chosen to celebrate the inauguration of the new dynasty. It is possible that the literary work known as *The Discourse of Neferty*, in which the emergence of a ruler called Ameny is supposed to have been foretold by a prophet in the Old Kingdom, was composed partly in order to legitimize his accession. He moved the royal residence to the newly established town of Amenemhatitjtawy, in the vicinity of EL-LISHT, thus shifting the focus of the country northwards. He also reorganized the ADMINISTRATION, ensuring that provincial power was in the hands of his supporters, appointing new governors at Asyut, Cusae and Elephantine and reintroducing conscription into the army. He founded a new fortress at Semna in the region of the second Nile cataract, thus creating the first of a string of 12th-Dynasty fortresses which probably gave the Egyptians a stranglehold over economic contacts with Upper Nubia and the countries further south in Africa.

He may also have introduced the practice of COREGENCY by allowing his successor to rule alongside him for the last few years of his reign, thus helping to ensure a smooth transition from one ruler to the next. Since he himself appears to have been assassinated as a result of a HARIM conspiracy, this precaution proved to be fully justified, and he was succeeded by his son Senusret I (1965–1920 BC), who had already been effectively in charge of foreign policy. The political and social repercussions of this traumatic end to his reign were reflected in two new literary works: *The Tale of Sinuhe* and *The Instruction of Amenemhat I* (the latter being the source of the assassination story). Amenemhat's funerary complex at EL-LISHT reintroduced the Old Kingdom pyramid-style royal tomb.

Amenemhat II Nubkaura (1922–1878 BC) succeeded to the throne after a two-year coregency with his father Senusret I, who had already consolidated Egyptian control over Nubia with the establishment of several further fortresses. Amenemhat II's reign was therefore relatively peaceful, and it is to his reign that the TOD 'treasure' dates: the variety of trade items or 'tribute' represented in this hoard suggests that contacts with western Asia and the Mediterranean world were flourishing. The discovery of statuary of Amenemhat's daughters and officials at a number of sites in Syria–Palestine also indicates that Egyptian influence in the Levant

was continuing to grow. The pyramid complex of Amenemhat II at DAHSHUR included a mortuary temple and causeway, excavated by de Morgan in 1894–5, but the valley temple has not yet been discovered.

Amenemhat III Nimaatra (1855–1808 BC) was the son of Senusret III and the sixth ruler of the 12th Dynasty. His reign evidently represented the most prosperous phase of the dynasty, with the military achievements of his predecessors allowing him to exploit the eco-

Granite head of Amenemhat III, bearing a usurping inscription of the 22nd Dynasty. Late 12th Dynasty, c.1820 BC, from Bubastis, H. 79 cm. (EA1063)

nomic resources of Nubia and Syria–Palestine as well as the mineral deposits of the Sinai and Eastern Desert. He is particularly associated with the economic and political rise of the Fayum region, where he completed a large-scale irrigation project inaugurated by his father. His surviving monuments in the area include two colossal granite statues of himself at Biahmu, temples to SOBEK and RENENUTET at Kiman Fares (Medinet el-Fayum) and MEDINET MAADI respectively, and two pyramid complexes. Like his father and grandfather, he was buried in a pyramid complex at Dahshur, where the mud-brick pyramid has been stripped of its limestone outer casing, but the black granite pyramidion, inscribed with his name, has survived. His second complex, at HAWARA, included the multi-roomed mortuary temple known to Classical authors as the 'Labyrinth'.

Amenemhat IV Maakherura (1808–1799 BC) was the son of Amenemhat III and the last male ruler of the 12th Dynasty. He completed his father's temples at Medinet Maadi and probably also built the unusual temple at Qasr el-Sagha in the northeastern Fayum, but his reign was otherwise short and comparatively

uneventful, perhaps representing the beginning of the decline of the Middle Kingdom. His pyramid complex was possibly the southern monument at Mazghuna, about 5 km to the south of those at Dahshur.

G. POSENER, *Littérature et politique dans l'Egypte de la XIIᵉ dynastie* (Paris, 1969).

N. GRIMAL, *A history of ancient Egypt* (Oxford, 1992), 158–81.

Amenhotep (Amenophis)

'Birth name' (or nomen), meaning 'Amun is content', which was included in the ROYAL TITULARY of four 18th-Dynasty rulers.

Amenhotep I Djeserkara (1525–1504 BC) was the son of AHMOSE I and AHMOSE NEFERTARI, and the second pharaoh of the 18th Dynasty. He appears to have pacified Nubia, established a temple at the Nubian town of Saï and appointed Turi as VICEROY OF KUSH. He was probably still very young when he came to the throne, so it is likely that his mother served as regent for the first part of his reign. They are jointly credited with the foundation of the royal tomb-workers' village at DEIR EL-MEDINA, where they consequently enjoyed personal religious cults until the late Ramesside period. His burial-place remains unidentified, although his tomb is mentioned in an official inspection list of the sixteenth year of Rameses IX's reign (c.1111 BC). He is known to have been the first pharaoh to build a separate mortuary temple (or 'mansion of millions of years') at DEIR EL-BAHRI, some distance away from the tomb itself. However, his mortuary chapel was later obliterated by the temple of HATSHEPSUT, and it is not clear whether he was buried at Dra Abu el-Naga (see THEBES), alongside his 17th-Dynasty ancestors, or in an unrecognized tomb in the VALLEY OF THE KINGS (perhaps the uninscribed Tomb KV39, although work in the 1990s suggests otherwise). His body, on the other hand, has survived, having been reburied in a cache at DEIR EL-BAHRI. It still has an excellent CARTONNAGE face-mask and had been rewrapped by the priests who moved it in the 21st Dynasty; it is the only royal mummy that has not been unwrapped in modern times.

Amenhotep II Aakheperura (1427–1400 BC) was the seventh ruler of the 18th Dynasty and coregent and successor to his father, THUTMOSE III (1479–1425 BC). He was born at MEMPHIS, his mother being Queen Meritra-Hatshepsut. The surviving reliefs and texts give the impression that he prided himself on his physical prowess, although it is equally possible that a new heroic image of the KINGSHIP was simply being adopted. Emulating the military successes of his father, he undertook three campaigns into Syria, but no military activity seems to have been considered necessary in Nubia, where he appointed Usersatet as VICEROY OF KUSH and ordered various projects of temple construction and decoration at Amada and KALABSHA. He built a number of shrines and temples in the region of THEBES, including structures at KARNAK, MEDAMUD and TOD. Little has survived of his mortuary temple at Thebes, but he was buried in Tomb KV35

Stele from a household shrine at el-Amarna, showing Amenhotep III with his principal wife Tiy beside a table of offerings under the rays of the Aten. 18th Dynasty, c.1350 BC, H. 30.5 cm. (EA53799)

in the Valley of the Kings. The decoration of this tomb, although unfinished, included a complete version of the book of *Amduat* (see FUNERARY TEXTS). When it was excavated by Victor Loret in 1898 it was found to contain not only Amenhotep II's mummy (still in his sarcophagus) but the bodies of eight other pharaohs (Thutmose IV, Amenhotep III, MERENPTAH, SETY II, Saptah, RAMESES IV, V and VI), three women (one of whom may be Queen TIY) and a young boy. These mummies were all brought to Amenhotep II's tomb, on the orders of Pinudjem (one of the chief priests of Amun at Thebes in the 21st Dynasty), in order to preserve them from the depredations of tomb-robbers.

Amenhotep III Nebmaatra (1390–1352 BC) was the son and successor of Thutmose IV (1400–1390 BC), his mother being Mutemwiya. He seems to have taken little interest in military affairs and, apart from quelling an uprising in Nubia in his fifth regnal year, he was content to maintain the order established by his predecessors. This policy was not altogether successful and during his long reign it is possible that some of the vassal states of Syria–Palestine began to break away from Egypt, paving the way for the HITTITES' expansion into the Levant during the last reigns of the 18th Dynasty. Some of his foreign correspondence has survived in the form of the AMARNA LETTERS.

The time of Amenhotep III is marked by the apparent opulence of the royal court and the high standard of artistic and architectural achievements, earning him the modern epithet 'the magnificent'. The high artistic skill of the time is exhibited in the tombs of such high officials as RAMOSE (TT55) and Khaemhet (TT57). His principal architect, AMENHOTEP SON OF HAPU, was responsible for the construction of the processional colonnade at LUXOR temple, the third pylon at KARNAK, the mortuary temple (the site of which is marked by the COLOSSI OF MEMNON) and his palace at MALKATA on the Theban west bank.

Some of the art of his reign shows the naturalistic, informal attitudes characteristic of the Amarna period, and it seems likely that he chose the ATEN as his personal god, whilst still honouring the other gods, thus anticipating (and presumably cultivating) the eventual religious revolution of his son, Amenhotep IV (AKHENATEN; 1352–1336 BC), whom he may have appointed as coregent towards the end of his reign, although this remains controversial. His eldest son, and the original heir to the throne, was Thutmose, who died young. It has been suggested that Amenhotep III may also have been the father of Smenkhkara, TUTANKHAMUN and Princess Baketaten, but the evidence for these links is tenuous. It has been suggested that his body may have been one of those reburied among a cache of royal mummies in the tomb of Amenhotep II (see above), although this identification has been disputed by some authorities. The body in question is that of a man who suffered from ill health and obesity towards the end of his life. Amenophis III's tomb (KV22) was located in the valley to the west of the main Valley of the Kings. It was decorated with scenes from the book of *Amduat* and when excavated by Howard Carter it still contained about fifty small fragments of the lid of the red granite sarcophagus in the burial chamber.

Amenhotep IV see AKHENATEN.

H. E. WINLOCK, 'A restoration of the reliefs from the mortuary temple of Amenhotep I', *JEA* 4 (1917), 11–15.

A. LANSING: 'Excavations at the palace of Amenhotep III at Thebes', *BMMA* 13 (March 1926), 8–14.

J. ČERNY, 'Le culte d'Amenophis Ier chez les ouvriers de la nécropole thebaine', *BIFAO* 27 (1927), 159–203.

B. VAN DE WALLE, 'Les rois sportifs de l'ancienne Egypte', *CdE* 13 (1938), 234–57.

W. C. HAYES, 'Egypt: internal affairs from Tuthmosis I to the death of Amenophis III', *Cambridge Ancient History*, ed. I. E. S. Edwards et al., 3rd ed. (Cambridge, 1973), 313–416.

A. KOZLOFF and B. BRYAN, *Egypt's dazzling sun: Amenhotep III and his world*, exh. cat. (Bloomington and Cleveland, 1992).

Amenhotep son of Hapu (*c.*1430–1350 BC) Born in the Delta town of Athribis (TELL ATRIB), about 40 km north of Cairo, in *c.*1430 BC, Amenhotep son of Hapu – also known as Huy – rose to a position of influence during the reign of AMENHOTEP III (1390–1352 BC). In about 1390 BC he moved from Athribis to the royal court at Thebes, where he is one of the guests portrayed in a banquet scene in the relief decoration of the tomb of his contemporary, the vizier RAMOSE (TT55). He was subsequently promoted to the offices of 'scribe of recruits' and 'director of all the king's works', which might be loosely translated as 'chief royal architect'. In this capacity he would have been in charge of the entire process of temple construction, from the extraction of the stone to the sculpting of reliefs, as well as the commissioning of such royal statues as the COLOSSI OF MEMNON.

Grey granite scribe statue of Amenhotep son of Hapu as a young man, from the Tenth Pylon of Karnak temple. 18th Dynasty, c.1365 BC, H. 1.28 m. (CAIRO JE44861)

He is known to have supervised the construction of the huge temple at SOLEB in Lower Nubia, where he is depicted alongside the king in several of the reliefs showing the ritual consecration of the temple. He also built two tombs for himself, and in the thirty-first year of Amenhotep III's reign he began to build his own cult temple on the west bank at Thebes. Amenhotep's importance during his own lifetime is indicated not only by the unusual size of his cult temple but by the fact that it was the only private monument situated among the royal mortuary temples on the west bank at Thebes (see MEDINET HABU).

In the precincts of the temple of Amun at Karnak he was permitted to set up several statues of himself. His career has been largely reconstructed from the texts carved on these statues – one limestone block statue bears inscriptions on all four sides. Although one text expresses his desire to reach the age of a hundred and ten, it is likely that he died in his eighties. He was buried in a rock-tomb at the southern end of the Qurnet Murai, on the Theban west bank, and a surviving 21st-Dynasty copy of a royal decree relating to his mortuary temple suggests that his cult continued to be celebrated at least three centuries after his death. Eventually, like the 3rd-Dynasty architect IMHOTEP (c.2650 BC), Amenhotep was deified posthumously in recognition of his wisdom and, from the LATE PERIOD, for his healing powers. In the Ptolemaic temple of Hathor at Deir el-Medina and the temple of Hatshepsut at Deir el-Bahri, chapels were dedicated to the worship of both Imhotep and Amenhotep son of Hapu.

C. ROBICHON and A. VARILLE, *Le temple du scribe royal Amenhotep fils de Hapou* (Cairo, 1936).

A. VARILLE, *Inscriptions concernant l'architecte Amenhotep fils de Hapou* (Cairo, 1968)

D. WILDUNG, *Egyptian saints: deification in pharaonic Egypt* (New York, 1977).

A. P. KOZLOFF and B. M. BRYAN, *Egypt's dazzling sun: Amenhotep III and his world* (Bloomington and Cleveland, 1992), 45–8.

Ammut

Creature in the netherworld, usually depicted with the head of a crocodile, the foreparts of a lion (or panther) and the rear of a hippopotamus, whose principal epithets were 'devourer of the dead' and 'great of death'. She is portrayed in vignettes illustrating Chapter 125 of the Book of the Dead (see FUNERARY TEXTS). The scenes show her waiting beside the scales in the Hall of the Two Truths, where the hearts of the dead were weighed against the feather of MAAT. It was Ammut who consumed the hearts

Detail from the Book of the Dead of Hunefer, consisting of the vignette associated with Chapter 125. Ammut is shown beside the scales on which the heart of the deceased is weighed. 19th Dynasty, c.1280 BC, painted papyrus. (EA9901, SHEET 3)

of those whose evil deeds made them unfit to proceed into the afterlife.

C. SEEBER, *Untersuchungen zur Darstellung des Totengerichts im Alten Ägypten* (Munich, 1976).

R. O. FAULKNER, *The ancient Egyptian Book of the Dead*, ed. C. Andrews (London, 1985), 29–34.

Amratian *see* PREDYNASTIC PERIOD

amulet

Term used to describe the small prophylactic charms favoured by the Egyptians and other ancient peoples. The Egyptians called these items *meket, nehet* or SA (all words deriving from verbs meaning 'to protect'), although the term *wedja* ('well-being') was also used. As well as affording protection, they may have been intended to imbue the wearer with particular qualities; thus, for instance, the bull and the lion may have been intended to provide strength and ferocity respectively. During the First Intermediate Period (2181–2055 BC), parts of the human body were used as amulet shapes, perhaps serving as replacements for actual lost or damaged anatomical elements. However, only the heart amulet became essen-

tial. Amulets frequently depicted sacred objects and animals, and, from the New Kingdom (1550–1069 BC) onwards, they portrayed gods and goddesses, not just state and powerful local deities but also 'household' deities such as BES and TAWERET. The range of funerary amulets increased greatly from the Saite period (664–525 BC) onwards.

Amulets could be made from stone, metal, glass or, more commonly, FAIENCE, and the materials were selected for their supposed magical properties. Specific combinations of material, colour and shape were prescribed for particular amulets in FUNERARY TEXTS from as early as the 5th Dynasty (see PYRAMID TEXTS), although recognizable types of amulets were being made from the Badarian period (c.5500–4000 BC) onwards. The names ascribed to different shapes of amulet are known from a number of textual sources, notably the Papyrus MacGregor.

A broad distinction can be made between those amulets that were worn in daily life, in order to protect the bearer magically from the dangers and crises that might threaten him or her, and those made expressly to adorn the mummified body of the deceased. The second category can include funerary deities such as ANUBIS, SERKET, SONS OF HORUS, but rarely (strangely enough) figures of OSIRIS, the god of the underworld. The BOOK OF THE DEAD includes several formulae with illustrative

Many amulets represented abstract concepts in the form of hieroglyphs, as in the case of the ANKH ('life') and the DJED PILLAR ('stability'). Among amuletic forms were the TYET ('knot of Isis'), the WAS SCEPTRE, the *akhet* ('HORIZON') and the *wedjat*-eye (see HORUS). See also SCARAB and COWROID.

G. A. REISNER, *Amulets*, 2 vols (Cairo, 1907–58).

W. M. F. PETRIE, *Amulets* (London, 1914).

C. ANDREWS, *Amulets of ancient Egypt* (London, 1994).

Amun, Amun-Ra

One of the most important gods in the Egyptian pantheon, whose temple at KARNAK is the best surviving religious complex of the New Kingdom. He is first mentioned (along with his wife Amaunet) in the 5th-Dynasty PYRAMID TEXTS, but the earliest temples dedicated solely to Amun appear to have been in the Theban region, where he was worshipped as a local deity at least as early as the 11th Dynasty. Amun's rise to pre-eminence was a direct result of the ascendancy of the Theban pharaohs from Mentuhotep II (2055–2004 BC) onwards, since politics and religion were very closely connected in ancient Egypt. In the jubilee chapel of Senusret I (1965–1920 BC) at Karnak he is described as 'the king of the gods', and by the time of the Ptolemies he was regarded as the Egyptian equivalent of Zeus.

His name probably means 'the hidden one' (although it may also be connected with the

Selection of amulets: faience hand, L. 3.1 cm, haematite headrest, W. 3 cm, faience papyrus, L. 5.6 cm, carnelian snake's head, L. 4.4 cm, haematite plummet, W. at base 1.8 cm, haematite carpenter's square, H. 1.5 cm, faience staircase, L. 1.9 cm, carnelian leg, H. 2.1 cm, glass heart, H. 5.3 cm, obsidian pair of fingers, H. 8.5 cm, red jasper tyet or 'knot of Isis', H. 6.5 cm. Old Kingdom to Ptolemaic period, c.2300–100 BC. (EA22991, 8309, 7435, 8327, 8332, 3123, 23123, 14622, 8088, 59500, 20639)

vignettes that endow prescribed amulets with magical powers; particular amulets were placed at specific points within the wrappings of a mummy, and Late Period funerary papyri sometimes end with representations of the appropriate position of each amulet on the body.

Grey granite statue of Amun in the form of a ram protecting King Taharqo, whose figure is carved between the paws. 25th Dynasty, c.690–664 BC, from the temple of Taharqo at Kawa, H. 1.06 m. (EA1779)

ancient Libyan word for water, *aman*) and he was usually represented as a human figure wearing a double-plumed crown, sometimes with a ram's head. It is implied, through such epithets as 'mysterious of form', that Amun's true identity and appearance could never be revealed. As well as being part of a divine triad at Thebes (with MUT and KHONS), he was also Amun Kematef, a member of the OGDOAD, a group of eight primeval deities who were worshipped in the region of Hermopolis Magna. Amun Kematef (meaning 'he who has completed his moment') was a creator-god able to resurrect himself by taking the form of a snake shedding his skin. Another aspect of Amun was an ITHYPHALLIC form, closely related to the fertility god MIN and described as Amun Kamutef (literally 'bull of his mother').

Part of the success of Amun's influence on Egyptian religion for most of the Dynastic period lay in his combination with other powerful deities, such as RA, the sun-god, who had been the dominant figure in the Old Kingdom pantheon. It was Amun-Ra, the Theban manifestation of the sun-god, who presided over the expanding Egyptian empire in Africa and the Levant. Eventually the Theban priesthood of Amun-Ra used the prestige of the cult of Amun in order to legitimize their rivalry with the pharaohs at the end of the New Kingdom (see HERIHOR).

The rise of the Kushite pharaohs of the 25th Dynasty led to a renaissance in the worship of Amun, since the Nubians believed that the true home of Amun was the sacred site of Gebel Barkal in northern Sudan (see NAPATA). Kushite kings such as PIY, SHABAQO and TAHARQO therefore associated themselves with the cult of Amun and thus sought to renew and reinvigorate his centres of worship.

K. SETHE, *Amun und die acht Urgötter* (Leipzig, 1929).

J. ZANDEE, *De Hymnen aan Amon van Papyrus Leiden 1350* (Leiden, 1948).

P. BARGUET, *Le temple d'Amon-re à Karnak: essai d'exegèse* (Cairo, 1962).

E. OTTO, *Egyptian art and the cults of Osiris and Amun* (London, 1968).

—, 'Amun', *Lexikon der Ägyptologie* I, ed. W. Helck, E. Otto and W. Westendorf (Wiesbaden, 1975), 237–48.

J. ASSMANN, *Egyptian solar religion in the New Kingdom: Ra, Amun and the crisis of polytheism*, trans. A. Alcock (London, 1995).

Anat

One of a number of deities introduced into Egypt from Syria–Palestine. The cult of Anat is first attested in Egypt in the late Middle Kingdom (*c*.1800 BC) and one of the HYKSOS

Stele of the chief royal craftsman Qeh. In the lower register Qeh and his family are shown worshipping the goddess Anat. In the upper register (from left to right) the deities Min, Qedeshet and Reshef are depicted; the inclusion of Min among a group of Western Asiatic deities is presumably explained by his association with the Eastern Desert. 19th Dynasty, c.1250 BC, limestone, from Deir el-Medina, H. 72 cm. (EA191)

kings of the 16th Dynasty (*c*.1560 BC) included the name Anat-her in his titulary. In the Third Intermediate Period her cult was celebrated in the temple of Mut at TANIS.

Although she held the beneficent epithets 'mother of all the gods' and 'mistress of the sky', she was primarily a goddess of war and was often depicted with shield, axe and lance. The myths surrounding Anat were concerned primarily with her savage exploits, and the Egyptians regarded her as protectress of the king in battle, a role sometimes shared with ASTARTE. Although Egyptian texts often used the names of the goddesses Anat and Astarte virtually interchangeably, their cults were in practice distinct.

The Syrian gods RESHEF and Baal were both regarded at various times as Anat's consorts, and she was said to have given birth to a wild bull by Baal. At times she is also portrayed as the wife of SETH (another god with Asiatic links), while private monuments sometimes depicted her alongside MIN, when the strong sexual aspect of her cult was being stressed. As with many other goddesses, her cult was sometimes syncretized with that of HATHOR.

J. B. PRITCHARD, *Palestinian figurines in relation to certain goddesses known through literature* (New Haven, 1943), 76–80.

R. STADELMANN, *Syrisch-palästinische Gottheiten in Ägypten* (Leiden, 1967), 91–6.

A. S. KAPELRUD, *The violent goddess Anat in the Ras Shamra texts* (Oslo, 1969).

ancestor busts

Term used to refer to small painted anthropoid busts serving as a focus for ancestor worship in the New Kingdom. Most were of limestone or sandstone, but a few smaller examples were made of wood and clay. They were rarely inscribed (the bust of Mutemonet, shown below, being one of the few exceptions), but the predominance of red paint (the typical male skin-colour in Egyptian art) suggests that most of them represent men. There are about 150 surviving examples, about half of which derive from the houses and funerary chapels of the tombworkers at the village of DEIR EL-MEDINA. The cult of the ancestors, each of which was known as *akh iker en Ra*, 'excellent spirit of Ra', was an important aspect of popular religion among the villagers. These 'excellent spirits' were also represented on about fifty-five surviving painted stelae, which, like the busts, could evidently be petitioned by relatives seeking divine aid.

Limestone ancestor bust of Mutemonet. 19th Dynasty, c.1250 BC. H. 49 cm. (EA1198)

J. KEITH-BENNETT, 'Anthropoid busts II: not from Deir el Medina alone', *BES* 3 (1981), 43–71.

R. J. DEMARÉE, *The "'h ikr n R'' stelae: on ancestor worship in ancient Egypt* (Leiden, 1983).

F. D. FRIEDMAN, 'Aspects of domestic life and religion', *Pharaoh's workers: the villagers of Deir el Medina*, ed. L. H. Lesko (Ithaca, 1994), 95–117.

Anedjib (Adjib, Andjyeb, Enezib) (*c*.2925 BC)
Ruler of the late 1st Dynasty who is thought to have been buried in Tomb X at ABYDOS, the smallest of the Early Dynastic royal tombs in the cemetery of Umm el-Qa'ab. Part of the wooden flooring was preserved in the burial chamber. Tomb 3038 at SAQQARA has also been dated to his reign by means of seal impressions which also mention the name of an official called Nebitka who was presumably buried there. This tomb contained a mud-brick stepped structure inside the MASTABA-like superstructure which is considered to be a possible precursor of step pyramids, and similar 'internal tumuli' have been identified in the recent re-excavations of the 1st-Dynasty royal tombs at Abydos.

Anedjib was the first to have the *nebty* ('Two Ladies') title and the *nesw-bit* ('He of the sedge and bee') name in his ROYAL TITU-LARY, although the *nesw-bit* title (without a name) had already been introduced in the reign of his predecessor DEN. A number of stone vessels carved with references to his SED FESTIVAL (royal jubilee) were excavated at Abydos. On most of these vases his name had been erased and replaced with that of his successor SEMERKHET, leading to suggestions that there may have been some kind of dynastic feud.

W. M. F. PETRIE, *The royal tombs of the first dynasty* I (London, 1900).

W. B. EMERY, *Great tombs of the first dynasty* I (Cairo, 1949).

—, *Archaic Egypt* (London, 1961), 80–4.

Anhur see ONURIS

Aniba (anc. Miam)
Site of a settlement and cemetery in Lower Nubia, founded as an Egyptian fortress in the Middle Kingdom (2055–1650 BC). During the 18th Dynasty (1550–1295 BC) Aniba became the administrative centre of Wawat, the area between the first and second Nile cataracts. The reception of tribute from the Nubian Prince of Miam is portrayed in the Theban tomb of Tutankhamun's viceroy, Huy (TT40). The site was partially excavated during the 1930s, but after the completion of the Aswan

Copy of a wall-painting in the tomb of Huy, showing Heqanefer, Prince of Miam (Aniba) and other chiefs, bowing before Tutankhamun. 18th Dynasty, c.1330 BC. (COPY BY NINA DE GARIS DAVIES)

High Dam in 1971 it was submerged by Lake Nasser.

G. STEINDORFF, *Aniba*, 2 vols (Glückstadt, 1935–7).

animal husbandry

The keeping and breeding of animals is attested as early as the Predynastic period at Lower Egyptian sites such as MERIMDA BENI SALAMA (*c*.4900–4300 BC). Even in the Old Kingdom, there was still an element of experimentation in the process of domestication of more unusual breeds, judging from such evidence as scenes of the force-feeding of cranes in the 5th-Dynasty tomb of Sopduhotep at Saqqara, and the depiction of the force-feeding of hyenas in the 6th-Dynasty tomb of MERERUKA at the same site. For most of the Dynastic period the most common domesticated animals were cattle, sheep, pigs, goats, asses and poultry. Ducks, geese and pigeons were the principal domesticated fowl; hens deriving from the African Jungle Fowl may have been introduced in the New Kingdom, but the earliest published skeletal evidence dates to the late fifth or early sixth century AD.

Cattle were important for their meat and milk but were also kept as draught animals. From the Predynastic period to the Old Kingdom, cattle were mainly of the long-horned type, but thinner short-horned varieties were gradually introduced from the Old Kingdom onwards, eventually becoming the norm. In the 18th Dynasty humped Zebu cattle were introduced as draught animals, but they never seem to have become common.

Cattle were tended by herdsmen who, as in parts of Africa today, stayed with the herd and moved them to new pastures as necessary. In the winter the herds grazed in the Nile valley, although many were moved to the Delta during the summer months. Identification of herds was facilitated by marking them, and a number of branding tools have survived.

It was the meat of oxen which was the most prized for offerings at temples and tombs, and which frequently figures in reliefs there. Wealthy landowners boast of enormous herds of cattle, and other animals, in their tomb inscriptions, and as a sign of wealth they were also a source of taxable revenue.

The HORSE, introduced around the time of the HYKSOS occupation in the Second Intermediate Period, did not become common until the New Kingdom, and was then used primarily for military purposes. Donkeys were extensively used as pack animals and, like cattle, for threshing. The CAMEL was not used until late in the Pharaonic period, and although there is some possible pictorial evidence from the late New Kingdom, the use of domesticated camels is not attested until the ninth century BC.

Sheep and goats were kept for meat, wool, hide and probably milk, although wool was never as important as linen in terms of textile manufacture. The Egyptians described both sheep and goats as 'small cattle', thus implying that all three animals were of being of roughly the same type. Goats, however, were more common than sheep, and better suited to grazing on poor land.

Pigs were regarded as animals of SETH, the god of chaos, and for this reason enjoyed somewhat ambiguous status. According to the Greek historian Herodotus, those who kept them formed a kind of underclass who could only marry the daughters of other swineherds. However, it is not clear whether this was the case in more ancient times, and a scene from the 6th-Dynasty tomb of Kagemni at Saqqara shows a swineherd giving milk to a piglet from his own tongue, perhaps implying that the herders of pigs were not held in any particularly low esteem relative to other farmers. Excavations during the 1980s at the site of the EL-AMARNA workmen's village have revealed surprisingly extensive evidence of pig rearing, and similar evidence has emerged from excavations at Memphis, Elephantine and Tell el-Dab'a, indicating that pork must have formed an important part of the diet of at least some classes of society. Although pork was never used in temple offerings, pigs are nevertheless included in lists of temple assets. Amenhotep, chief steward of Amenhotep III (1390–1352 BC), states that he donated a thousand pigs to a statue of his master at Memphis.

R. JANSSEN and J. J. JANSSEN, *Egyptian household animals* (Aylesbury, 1989).

E. STROUHAL, *Life in ancient Egypt* (Cambridge, 1992), 109–18.

K. C. MACDONALD and D. N. EDWARDS, 'Chickens in Africa: the importance of Qasr Ibrim', *Antiquity* 67/256 (1993), 584–90.

D. J. BREWER, D. B. REDFORD and S. REDFORD, *Domestic plants and animals: the Egyptian origins* (Warminster, 1994).

ankh

Hieroglyphic sign denoting 'life', which takes the form of a T-shape surmounted by a loop. The pictogram has been variously interpreted as a sandal strap (the loop at the top forming

Ankh, djed *and* was-sceptre *amulet. Late Period, c.700–500 BC, faience, H. 23.1 cm. (EA54412)*

the ankle strap) and a penis sheath. Temple reliefs frequently included scenes in which the king was offered the *ankh* sign by the gods, thus symbolizing the divine conferral of eternal life. In the Amarna period it was depicted being offered to Akhenaten and Nefertiti by the hands at the end of the rays descending from the sun disc (see ATEN). The *ankh* sign seems to have been one of the few hieroglyphs that was comprehensible even to the illiterate; therefore it is commonly found as a maker's mark on pottery vessels. The sign was eventually adopted by the COPTIC church as their unique form of cross, known as the *crux ansata*.

J. R. BAINES, 'Ankh sign, belt and penis sheath', *SAK* 3 (1975), 1–24.

C. ANDREWS, *Amulets of ancient Egypt* (London, 1994), 86.

antelope

Desert-dwelling horned bovid, which served as the symbol of the 16th Upper Egyptian nome (province). Three species of antelope are known from ancient Egypt (*Alcephalus buselaphus*, *Oryx gazella* and *Addax nasomaculato*). The goddess SATET of Elephantine was originally worshipped in the form of an antelope, and her headdress during the Pharaonic period consisted of a combination of antelope horns and the Upper Egyptian CROWN. Satet was responsible for the water of the first Nile cataract at Aswan, and a connection seems to have been made by the ancient Egyptians between water and antelopes, so that the goddess ANUKET could also be represented by another type of antelope, the gazelle, although she was more commonly depicted as a woman. The gazelle may also have symbolized grace and elegance, and paintings in the 18th-Dynasty tomb of MENNA (TT69) at Thebes show that it was sometimes used in place of a *uraeus* (see WADJYT) for minor queens and princesses.

The desert links of the antelope and gazelle also led to their association with the god SETH, and, correspondingly, the antelope was occasionally shown as the prey of the god HORUS in later times. One of the earliest forms of amulet took the form of a gazelle head, possibly in order to ward off the evil that such desert animals represented.

G. J. BOESSNECK, *Die Haustiere in Altägypten* (Munich, 1953).

L. STAEHELIN, 'Antilope', *Lexikon der Ägyptologie* I, ed. W. Helck, E. Otto and W. Westendorf (Wiesbaden, 1975), 319–23.

E. BRUNNER-TRAUT, 'Gazelle', *Lexikon der Ägyptologie* II, ed. W. Helck, E. Otto and W. Westendorf (Wiesbaden, 1977), 426–7.

Anubis (Inpw)

Canine god of the dead, closely associated with embalming and mummification. He is usually represented in the form of a seated black dog or a man with a dog's head, but it is not clear whether the dog in question – often identified by the Egyptian word *sab* – was a jackal. The connection between jackals and the god of mummification probably derived

Limestone statuette of Anubis. Ptolemaic period, c.300–100 BC, H. 51 cm. (EA47991)

from the desire to ward off the possibility of corpses being dismembered and consumed by such dogs. The black colouring of Anubis, however, is not characteristic of jackals; it relates instead to the colour of putrefying corpses and the fertile black soil of the Nile valley (which was closely associated with the concept of rebirth). The seated Anubis dog usually wore a ceremonial tie or collar around his neck and held a flail or *sekhem* sceptre like those held by OSIRIS, the other principal god of the dead. The cult of Anubis himself was eventually assimilated with that of Osiris. According to myth, the jackal-god was said to have wrapped the body of the deceased Osiris, thus establishing his particular association with the mummification process. Anubis was also linked with the IMIUT fetish, apparently consisting of a decapitated animal skin hanging at the top of a pole, images of which were included among royal funerary equipment in the New Kingdom. Both Anubis and the *imiut* fetish were known as 'sons of the *hesat*-cow'.

Anubis' role as the guardian of the necropolis is reflected in two of his most common epithets: *neb-ta-djeser* ('lord of the sacred land') and *khenty-seh-netjer* ('foremost of the divine booth'), the former showing his control over the cemetery itself and the latter indicating his association with the embalming tent or the burial chamber. An image of Anubis also figured prominently in the seal with which the entrances to the tombs in the VALLEY OF THE KINGS were stamped. This consisted of an image of a jackal above a set of nine bound CAPTIVES, showing that Anubis would protect the tomb against evildoers.

Perhaps the most vivid of Anubis' titles was *tepy dju ef* ('he who is upon his mountain'), which presents the visual image of a god continually keeping a watch on the necropolis from his vantage point in the high desert. In a similar vein, both he and Osiris are regularly described as *khentimentiu* ('foremost of the westerners'), which indicated their dominance over the necropolis, usually situated in the west. Khentimentiu was originally the name of an earlier canine deity at ABYDOS whom Anubis superseded.

H. KEES, 'Anubis "Herr von Sepa" und der 18. oberägyptische Gau', *ZÄS* 58 (1923), 79–101.

—, 'Kulttopographische und mythologische Beiträge', *ZÄS* 71 (1935), 150–5.

—, 'Der Gau von Kynopolis und seine Gotteit', *MIO* 6 (1958), 157–75.

Anuket (Anquet, Anukis)

Goddess of the first Nile cataract region around ASWAN, who is generally represented as a woman holding a papyrus sceptre and wearing a tall plumed crown. Her cult is recorded as early as the Old Kingdom, when, like many goddesses, she was regarded as a daughter of the sun-god RA, but in the New Kingdom she became part of the triad of Elephantine along with KHNUM and SATET. A temple was dedicated to her on the island of Sehel, a short distance to the south of Aswan, and she was also worshipped in Nubia.

E. OTTO, 'Anuket', *Lexikon der Ägyptologie* I, ed. W. Helck, E. Otto and W. Westendorf (Wiesbaden, 1975), 333–4.

Apedemak

Meroitic leonine and anthropomorphic lion-headed god, whose principal cult-centres were at the sites of Musawwarat el-Sufra and Naqa, both located in the desert to the east of the sixth Nile cataract in Sudan, although there

were also 'lion temples' at MEROE and probably Basa. Many aspects of religion and ritual in the Meroitic period (*c*.300 BC–AD 300) derived from Egyptian practices, AMUN in particular being as pre-eminent in Meroe as he had been in Pharaonic Egypt. But there were also a few important Nubian deities, such as the anthropomorphic ARENSNUPHIS and the creator-god Sebiumeker, foremost among whom was the war-god Apedemak.

In the lion temple at Musawwarat el-Sufra there were long inscriptions consisting of prayers to the god, inexplicably written in Egyptian HIEROGLYPHS rather than the Meroitic script, describing him as 'splendid god at the head of Nubia, lion of the south, strong of arm', possibly indicating that he was the tutelary god of the southern half of the Meroitic kingdom, where lions were still relatively common until the nineteenth century AD (few references to the god have survived in Lower Nubia). The lion temple at Naqa, founded by Natakamani and his queen Amanitere, consists of a PYLON followed by a pillared court (narrower than the front façade). The walls are decorated with reliefs in which Apedemak is depicted alongside Egyptian deities such as HATHOR and Amun, even forming a divine triad with ISIS and HORUS as his consort and child.

J. W. CROWFOOT and F. W. GRIFFITH, *The island of Meroe; Meroitic inscriptions* (London, 1911), 54–61 [temple of Apedemak at Naqa].

F. HINTZE et al., *Musawwarat es Sufra* 1/2 (Berlin, 1971).

L. V. ZABKAR, *Apedemak: lion god of Meroe* (Warminster, 1975).

W. Y. ADAMS, *Nubia: corridor to Africa*, 2nd ed. (London and Princeton, 1984), 325–7.

Apepi (Apophis)

The name Apepi (or Apophis), which occurs in MANETHO, was adopted by at least one of the HYKSOS pharaohs who ruled a substantial area of Egypt in the Second Intermediate Period (1650–1550 BC). Inscriptions in the temple at Bubastis (TELL BASTA) preserve the name of Aqenenra Apepi. A quasi-historical literary work known as the *Quarrel of Apophis and Seqenenra* describes the war between a Hyksos king called Apepi and his Theban rival, SEQENENRA TAA II, beginning with a letter sent by Apepi complaining that he is being kept awake by the sound of hippopotami in Upper Egypt. A more reliable version of the Theban military campaign against Aauserra Apepi is provided by two fragmentary stelae dating to the reign of the Theban king KAMOSE, and a later HIERATIC copy of the same text (known as the Carnarvon Tablet).

T. SÄVE-SÖDERBERGH, 'The Hyksos rule in Egypt', *JEA* 37 (1951), 53–71.

R. STADELMANN, 'Ein Beitrag zum Brief des Hyksos Apophis', *MDAIK* 36 (1965), 62–9.

J. VAN SETERS, *The Hyksos: a new investigation* (New Haven, 1966), 153–8.

Apis

Sacred bull who served as the BA (physical manifestation) or 'herald' of the god PTAH. His principal sanctuary was therefore located near the temple of Ptah at MEMPHIS, in the vicinity of which the 'embalming house' of the Apis

Bronze votive group statuette of an unnamed ruler kneeling before an Apis bull, his hands held out in offering. It was dedicated by Peftjawemawyhor, who is named on the bull's pedestal. 26th Dynasty, c.600 BC, H. of bull 12.5 cm. (EA22920)

bulls has been unearthed. Unlike many other sacred animals the Apis bull was always a single individual animal, selected for his particular markings. According to the Greek historian Herodotus, the Apis bull, conceived from a bolt of lightning, was black with a white diamond on the forehead, the image of a vulture on its back, double hairs on its tail, and a scarab-shaped mark under its tongue.

The cult of the Apis probably dates back to the beginning of Egyptian history, although Manetho, the Ptolemaic historian, claims that it originated in the 2nd Dynasty. The bull was closely linked with the pharaoh, both being divine manifestations of a god who were crowned at the time of their installation. Like the king, the Apis bull had his own 'window of appearances' (see PALACES) and, at least from the Late Period, he was thought to provide ORACLES. From the 22nd Dynasty onwards, the bull was represented on private coffins, as if accompanying the deceased westwards to the tomb or eastwards (presumably towards a new life) and serving as a protector of the dead.

At the death of each of the Apis bulls, there was national mourning, and the embalmed corpse was taken along the sacred way from Memphis to Saqqara, for burial in a granite sarcophagus in the underground catacombs known as the SERAPEUM, which were in use from at least as early as the New Kingdom. According to Herodotus, the Persian ruler Cambyses (525–522 BC) mocked the cult and caused the death of the Apis bull of the time, although it has been suggested that this story may simply have been an attempt to discredit the Persians, since it appears to be contradicted by a textual record of an Apis burial actually conducted by Cambyses.

Because of the divine nature of his birth, the mothers of the Apis bulls were venerated as manifestations of the goddess ISIS; they were accorded similar burials to their offspring, in the 'Iseum' (or 'mothers of Apis' catacomb), a set of galleries further to the north in Saqqara which were excavated in 1970 by Bryan Emery. The 'calves of the Apis' were also buried ceremonially, but their catacombs, like the early Pharaonic Apis galleries, remain undiscovered.

After his death, the Apis bull became identified with OSIRIS, being described as the syncretic deity Osiris-Apis or Osorapis. In the early Ptolemaic period the cult of SERAPIS was introduced, combining the traits of the Greek gods Zeus, Helios, Hades, Dionysos and Asklepios with those of Osorapis.

A. MARIETTE, *Le Sérapéum de Memphis* (Paris, 1882).

Detail from the Book of the Dead of Hunefer, showing the sun-god in the form of a cat symbolically decapitating Apophis. 19th Dynasty, c.1280 BC. (EA9901, SHEET 8)

E. BRUGSCH, 'Der Apis-Kreis aus den Zeiten der Ptolemäer nach den hieroglyphischen und demotischen Weihinschriften des Serapeums von Memphis', *ZÄS* 22 (1884), 110–36.

J. VERCOUTTER, 'Une epitaphe royale inédite du Sérapéum', *MDAIK* 16 (1958), 333–45.

M. MALININE, G. POSENER, J. VERCOUTTER, *Les stèles du Sérapéum de Memphis au Musée du Louvre* (Paris, 1969).

W. B. EMERY, 'Preliminary report on the excavations at North Saqqâra 1969–70', *JEA* 57 (1971), 3–13.

Apophis (HYKSOS rulers) *see* APEPI

Apophis

Snake-god of the underworld, who symbolized the forces of chaos and evil. Apophis is usually represented on New Kingdom funerary papyri and on the walls of the royal tombs in the VALLEY OF THE KINGS as the eternal adversary of the sun-god RA. It was the serpent Apophis who posed the principal threat to the bark of the sun-god as it passed through the underworld. Although in some circumstances Apophis was equated with the god SETH (and both had Asiatic connections), there are also vignettes showing Seth contributing to the defeat of Apophis. The evil 'eye of Apophis' was an important mythological and ritualistic motif, which could be thwarted only by Seth or by the eye of the sun-god. There are about twenty surviving temple reliefs showing the king striking a ball before a goddess (at Deir

el-Bahri, Luxor, Edfu, Dendera and Philae), apparently in simulation of the removal of Apophis' eye.

The so-called *Book of Apophis* was a collection of spells and rites intended to thwart the snake-god, the best surviving text being Papyrus Bremner-Rhind, which dates to the late fourth century BC. Other fragmentary examples of the *Book of Apophis* date at least as early as the reign of Rameses III (1184–1153 BC), and the text was probably originally composed during the New Kingdom, somewhere in the vicinity of Heliopolis. Like the EXECRATION TEXTS, the various spells were connected with elaborate cursing rituals.

H. BONNET, *Reallexikon der ägyptischen Religionsgeschichte* (Berlin, 1952), 51–3.

B. STRICKER, *De grote zeeslang* (Leiden, 1953).

J. F. BORGHOUTS, 'The evil eye of Apopis', *JEA* 59 (1973), 114–49.

G. HART, *Egyptian myths* (London, 1990), 58–61.

Apries (Haaibra/Wahibra) (589–570 BC)
Fourth king of the SAITE 26th Dynasty and son of PSAMTEK II (595–589 BC), he was the Biblical Hophra. Although HERODOTUS claims that the wife of Apries was called Nitetis, there are no contemporary references naming her. He was

an active builder, constructing additions to the temples at Athribis (Tuu mma), and the OASIS, MEMPHIS and SAIS. In the fourth year of his reign he had Ankhnesneferibra adopted as Nitiqret's successor as GOD'S WIFE OF AMUN. His foreign policy concentrated primarily on the defence of the northeastern frontier, with campaigns against Cyprus, Palestine and PHOENICIA. It was shortly after a defeat by Nebuchadnezzar II of BABYLON that he was deposed by the former general Ahmose II in 570 BC. He fled the country and probably died in battle in 567 BC, when he attempted to regain his throne by force with the help of a BABYLONIAN army (although Herodotus suggests that he was captured and later strangled). His body is said to have been carried to Sais and buried there with full royal honours by Ahmose II. Only one surviving statue has been identified as Apries by his name and titles (although several others have been assigned to him on stylistic grounds), and only a few figures of private individuals bear his cartouches.

W. M. F. PETRIE and J. H. WALKER, *The palace of Apries (Memphis II)* (London, 1999).

B. GUNN, 'The stela of Apries at Mitrahina', *ASAE* 27 (1927), 211–37.

H. DE MEULENAERE, *Herodotus over de 26ste Dynastie* (Louvain, 1951).

B. V. BOTHMER, *Egyptian sculpture of the Late Period, 700 BC–100 AD* (Brooklyn, 1969), 58–9.

Apuleius, Lucius (*c.*AD 123–after 161)
Classical writer, born at Madaura in Africa and educated in Carthage, who travelled widely, visiting Rome and Athens. He was the author of several literary works, including *Metamorphoses* or *The Golden Ass*, the only Latin novel to have survived in its entirety. It describes the exploits of a man called Lucius, who is said to have been redeemed by the 'mysteries' of the goddess ISIS. Apuleius' writings have thus provided insights into the cults of Isis and OSIRIS in the Roman period.

R. GRAVES, *The golden ass* (Harmondsworth, 1950).

archaeology *see* BELZONI, EGYPTOLOGY;
LEPSIUS; MARIETTE; MASPERO; PETRIE; REISNER; ROSELLINI and WILKINSON.

Archaic period *see* EARLY DYNASTIC PERIOD

Arensnuphis (Arsnuphis, Harensnuphis)
Meroitic god, usually represented as a human figure wearing a feathered crown, whose cult is first attested at the Upper Nubian site of Musawwarat el-Sufra during the reign of Arnakamani (235–218 BC). He was associated with the Egyptian gods SHU and ONURIS, merg-

ing with the former in the syncretic form Shu-Arensnuphis. The Egyptians interpreted his name as *iry-hemes-nefer* ('the good companion'), although the origins of both the god and his name probably lay much further south in Africa. His absorption into the Egyptian pantheon is also indicated by the fact that he is depicted in the reliefs of the Egyptian temple of Dendur, which originally stood about 75 km to the south of Aswan (now re-erected in the Metropolitan Museum, New York). There was even a KIOSK dedicated to Arensnuphis in the temple of the goddess Isis at PHILAE, which – most unusually – was jointly built and decorated by the Meroitic king Arkamani (218–200 BC) and the Egyptian ruler PTOLEMY IV Philopator (221–205 BC).

E. WINTER, 'Arensnuphis: seine Name und seine Herkunft', *RdE* 25 (1973), 235–50.

Armant (anc. Iunu-Montu)
Upper Egyptian site on the west bank of the Nile, 9 km southwest of Luxor. The excavated features of Armant include extensive cemeteries and many areas of Predynastic settlement. The Predynastic necropolis at Armant, excavated by Robert Mond and Oliver Myers

Sandstone stele from the Bucheum of Armant, on which the Roman emperor Diocletian is depicted in the act of worshipping a mummified Buchis bull. Roman period, AD 288, H. 67 cm. (EA1696)

during the early 1930s, is probably the best-documented site of its date to have been excavated in the first few decades of the twentieth century. There is also a stonebuilt temple of the war-god MONTU – dating from the 11th Dynasty to the Roman period (*c.*2040 BC–AD 200) – which was largely destroyed in the late nineteenth century. To the north of the main site are the remains of the Bucheum, the necropolis of the sacred BUCHIS BULLS (*c.*1350 BC–AD 305), as well as the burial-place of the 'Mother of Buchis' cows. Myers also excavated an A-GROUP cemetery at the site.

R. MOND and O. H. MYERS, *The Bucheum*, 3 vols (London, 1934).

—, *Cemeteries of Armant* I (London, 1937).

—, *Temples of Armant: a preliminary survey* (London, 1940).

W. KAISER, 'Zur inneren Chronologie der Naqadakultur', *Archaeologia Geographica* 6 (1957), 69–77.

K. BARD, 'A quantitative analysis of the predynastic burials in Armant cemetery 1400–1500', *JEA* 74 (1988), 39–55.

army
There was no permanent national army in Egypt during the Old Kingdom (2686–2181 BC), although a small royal bodyguard probably already existed. Groups of young men were evidently conscripted specifically for particular expeditions, ranging from quarrying, mining and trading ventures to purely military campaigns. The inscriptions in the funerary chapel of Weni at Abydos (*c.*2300 BC) describe a campaign in Palestine undertaken by an army of 'tens of thousands of conscripts', whom the king had requisitioned from the various nomarchs (provincial governors).

During the First Intermediate Period (2181–2055 BC) increasing numbers of nomarchs seem to have recruited their own private armies, and it seems likely that the early 12th-Dynasty campaigns in Nubia involved combinations of these local corps rather than a single national force. By the time of Senusret III (1874–1855 BC). however, the reduction in the power of the provinces and the construction of permanent FORTRESSES and garrisons in NUBIA all seem to have contributed to the creation of a large national army. The development of military organization and hierarchy is indicated in the late Middle Kingdom by the emergence of such specific titles as 'soldier of the city corps' and 'chief of the leaders of dog patrols'. Other textual sources, such as the 'Semna dispatches' (see LETTERS), show that there was a considerable military infrastructure, manned by

Soldiers in the reign of Hatshepsut. Important evidence concerning military equipment is derived from reliefs such as this from Hatshepsut's temple at Deir el-Bahri. (P. T. NICHOLSON)

scribes and other bureaucrats, by the end of the 12th Dynasty.

It was in the 18th Dynasty (1550–1295 BC), however, that the military profession came into its own, and it is significant that men with military backgrounds, such as HOREMHEB (1323–1295 BC) and RAMESES I (1295–1294 BC), began to rise to the throne, which had previously been dominated by a more scribal and priestly élite. The New Kingdom army was often led by one of the king's sons; it consisted of a northern and southern corps, each commanded by a 'chief deputy'. When campaigns were launched into western Asia, Libya or Nubia, there were usually four or five large divisions, each comprising about five thousand professional soldiers and conscripts. These divisions were each named after a god, such as Amun or Ptah, perhaps with reference to the deity of the NOME (province) from which the conscripts were drawn. The smallest tactical unit of the army was the 'platoon' of fifty soldiers, generally grouped into 250-strong companies.

From the beginning of the Pharaonic period, mercenaries were used in Egyptian armies: the MEDJAY, for instance, were increasingly used as scouts during desert campaigns. From the Ramesside period onwards, the reliefs depicting military confrontations show that the Egyptian troops had begun to incorporate more and more foreigners, often as branded SLAVES who were able to gain their freedom by enrolling in the Egyptian army. In the Saite period (664–525 BC) the Egyptians became particularly dependent on GREEK and PHOENICIAN mercenaries, who helped to man a fleet of Greco-Phoenician-style war-galleys, enabling Egypt to maintain some control over maritime trade with the Levant. See also CAPTIVES; CHARIOT; SHIPS AND BOATS; STANDARDS.

Y. YIGAEL, *The art of warfare in Biblical lands* (London, 1963).

A. R. SCHULMAN, *Military rank, title and organization in the Egyptian New Kingdom* (Berlin, 1964).

A. J. SPALINGER, *Aspects of the military documents of the ancient Egyptians* (New Haven, 1982).

I. SHAW, *Egyptian warfare and weapons* (Aylesbury, 1991), 25–30.

Arsaphes *see* HERYSHEF

art

Just as the works of the Impressionists or the Cubists can be properly understood only in terms of the particular time and place in which they were made, so the style and purposes of Egyptian art make little real sense without a detailed understanding of ancient Egyptian culture. Egyptian art was essentially functional, in that funerary paintings and sculptures, for instance, were concerned primarily with the continuance of life – the works of art were intended not merely to imitate or reflect reality but to replace and perpetuate it.

Whereas in the modern western world a reasonably clear distinction is usually made between art and craft, the products of ancient Egyptian craftsmen, from faience AMULETS to royal funerary reliefs, were regarded as essentially the same. The level of aesthetic achievement may have varied considerably, but all of these works had the same purpose: to represent, influence and manipulate the real world.

Nothing expresses the nature of Egyptian art more succinctly than the fact that the same religious ritual of 'the OPENING OF THE MOUTH' was performed by Egyptian funerary priests both on the mummy of the deceased and on his or her statuary. The ritual involved touching the face of the statue or mummy with a set of special implements in order to bring it to life and allow the KA (life-force or essence) of the deceased to take up residence there. In the time of the Ptolemies a similar rite was performed each day in the temple of the god Horus at EDFU; its objective was to bring to life every divine figure on the decorated walls, as if the whole temple were a living organism.

Predynastic pottery vessel bearing red painted decoration comprising boats, animals and human figures, including a dancing woman/goddess with raised arms. Early Naqada II period, c.3500 BC, from el-Amra, H. 29.2 cm. (EA35502)

Egyptian art was concerned above all with ensuring the continuity of the universe, the gods, the king and the people – the artists therefore depicted things not as they saw them but as idealized symbols intended to be more significant and enduring than the real day-to-day world. They portrayed each individual element of the subject from the most representative angle: the human torso and eye were clearly both best viewed from the front, whereas the arms, leg and face were best seen from the side. This concern with separate components, at the expense of the overall effect, often causes Egyptian depictions of human figures to appear distorted and internally inconsistent to modern eyes. Even when the figures on the walls of Egyptian tombs and temples are acting out myths, rituals and historical events they are still carved and painted with the stiffness and formulaic appearance of HIEROGLYPHS. In an extreme example of this connection between writing and art, the burial chamber of the tomb of Thutmose III (1479–1425 BC; KV34) has the shape of a CARTOUCHE, thus enabling the body of the king to take the place of the writing of his own name. The Egyptian writing system was based on the precise visual and phonetic meanings of pictures, and in the same way the works of art were intended to be 'read' like an elaborate code. In some tombs, however, hieroglyphs representing animals that might prove dangerous – such as snakes – were sometimes shown mutilated, or with a knife sticking into them, dispelling their power so that they could serve only as symbols.

In most recent western art the artists themselves tend to be as well known as their works: their individual styles – and, in the last resort, their signatures – mark out a body of work as their own. The situation in ancient Egypt, however, was almost the reverse – it was essential for the subject of the art to be identified by name in order that the sculpture or painting could serve its religious purpose; the artists, on the other hand, are only rarely mentioned. Egyptian artists themselves were regularly regarded as anonymous craftsmen, working in teams and according to strict guidelines, although their works might be highly regarded. Surprisingly perhaps, this situation rarely seems to have resulted in inhibited or uninspired art, indeed the most recent studies of tomb-paintings at Thebes have begun to produce evidence for the distinctive styles and approaches of particular groups of craftsmen.

The earliest Egyptian art is quite different from that of the pyramids and temples of the Pharaonic period. As early as the eighth millennium BC the first inhabitants of the Nile valley began to make engraved drawings on the cliffs, particularly in Upper Egypt and Nubia. They depicted the fundamentals of their lives, from wild game and hunting scenes in the earlier times to river-boats and herds of cattle in the early Neolithic period. The art of the Predynastic period (c.5500–3100 BC) has survived mainly in the form of small carved stone and ivory grave goods and painted pot-

tery vessels placed alongside the deceased in simple pit-burials. The small votive figures of people and animals include many female statuettes made of pottery and ivory, whose exaggerated sexual characteristics suggest that they probably related to early fertility cults (see SEXUALITY).

Some of the painted scenes on pottery vessels still reflect the prehistoric rock-carvings, while others foreshadow the styles and preoccupations of the Dynastic period. A painting

Fragment of wall-painting from the tomb of Kynebu at Deir el-Medina, showing the deified ruler Amenhotep I. 20th Dynasty, c.1129–1126 BC, painted plaster, H. 44 cm. (EA37993)

in the late Predynastic Tomb 100 at Hierakonpolis (the first Egyptian example of a decorated tomb chamber), consisting of groups of people, animals and boats, is the only surviving instance of the transferral of the Predynastic pottery paintings on to the plastered wall of a tomb. In addition, a painted linen shroud, preserved in a late Predynastic tomb at GEBELEIN (now in the Museo Egizio, Turin), bears depictions of human figures and a boat, all strongly reminiscent of the scenes on contemporary painted

pottery. This suggests that there were probably many other works of art executed on organic materials, such as linen and leather, which have rarely survived from such early periods.

In the final stages of the Predynastic period a range of unusual ceremonial artefacts – MACES, PALETTES and ivory-handled flint knives – began to play an important role in the emerging religious ritual and social hierarchy. Many of the more elaborate maceheads and palettes, such as those of the kings named SCORPION and NARMER, were discovered in the so-called 'main deposit' of the temple at Hierakonpolis. Although the archaeological circumstances of the discovery are poorly recorded, they were evidently deposited as votive offerings, and their carved decoration appears to summarize the important events of the year in which they were offered to the god. It is not clear whether any of the scenes are depictions of real historical events or simply generalized representations of myth and ritual. The distinction between myth, ritual and history in Egyptian art is a problem that persists throughout the Pharaonic period.

The essential elements of the art of the Old Kingdom (2686–2181 BC) were the funerary sculpture and painted reliefs of the royal family and the provincial élite, along with the remains of the earliest sun temples (see ABU GURAB and HELIOPOLIS) and the shrines of local deities. One of the most impressive statues of the Old Kingdom is the diorite statue of a seated figure of KHAFRA, builder of the second pyramid at Giza, which was found in the valley temple of his funerary complex. On the simplest level the statue is a portrait of a powerful individual, but it is also made up of symbols that relate to the general role of the pharaoh. His head and neck are physically embraced by the wings of a hawk representing HORUS, the divine counterpart of the mortal ruler. His throne is decorated on either side with a complex design consisting of the hieroglyph meaning 'union' tied up with the tendrils of the plants representing Upper and Lower Egypt, the whole symbolizing the unified state over which he rules. In the same way, an alabaster statue of the 6th-Dynasty ruler PEPY I (2321–2287 BC) has the rear of the throne carved to imitate a SEREKH with Horus perched on the top; viewed from the front, on the other hand, Horus stands protectively behind the king, himself the living god. The best Egyptian art achieves a synthesis of the real and the ideal.

At the end of the Old Kingdom the provincial governors' tombs became more richly decorated and the royal tombs grew correspondingly smaller. This decline in the power of the pharaohs resulted in the so-called First Intermediate Period (2181–2055 BC), when no single ruler was strong enough to dominate the whole country. During this comparatively unstable and decentralized period, the provincial workshops at sites such as EL-MOʻALLA and GEBELEIN began to create distinctive funerary decoration and equipment rather than being influenced by the artists at the royal court, as they were in the Old Kingdom and the late Middle Kingdom.

The art of the Middle Kingdom (2055–1650 BC) is exemplified both by the fragments of relief from the royal pyramid complexes at DAHSHUR, EL-LISHT, EL-LAHUN and HAWARA and by the spacious tombs of the governors buried at BENI HASAN in Middle Egypt. In the latter, the traditional scenes of the deceased receiving offerings or hunting and fishing in the marshes are joined by large-scale depictions of wrestling and warfare (perhaps copied from Old Kingdom royal prototypes). The history of the Middle Kingdom is very much characterized by a tension between the artistic styles of the various provincial sites (principally funerary art at Beni Hasan, DEIR EL-BERSHA, MEIR and ASYUT) and the styles of the royal workshops at Itjtawy, a new capital established in the vicinity of el-Lisht. By the late Middle Kingdom the distinctive provincial styles had been eclipsed by the art of the royal Residence, a process which can be traced both in the development of funerary equipment (from coffins to ceramics) and in the quality and locations of provincial governors' tombs.

In the late seventeenth century BC Asiatic rulers (the HYKSOS) gained control of a considerable area of Egypt, which they governed from their strongholds in the Delta. The works of art surviving from the temples and cities of this phase show that they simply re-used and copied traditional Egyptian sculptures and reliefs in order to strengthen their claims to the throne. There were, however, increasing links with the Mediterranean world, and excavations at the Hyksos capital of Avaris (TELL EL-DABʻA) have revealed Minoan-style paintings suggesting close contacts with the people of Crete.

After the expulsion of the Hyksos, Egypt became firmly established as a major power in the Near East; the fruits of conquest and international commerce, from foreign princesses to exotic spices, flowed irresistibly into the Nile valley. The scale and opulence of the temples and tombs of this period could not fail to reflect such an influx of people, commodities and ideas.

Statue of Khaemwaset, a son of Rameses II, holding two standards. The sculptor has had only partial success in carving a difficult band of pebbly stone across the chest. 19th Dynasty, c.1240 BC, sandstone conglomerate, from Karnak. H. 1.46 m. (EA947)

The art of imperial Egypt ranged from the funerary temples of Queen HATSHEPSUT (1473–1458 BC) and RAMESES II (1279–1213 BC) to the more intimate details of the artisans' painted tombs at DEIR EL-MEDINA. The tombs in the VALLEY OF THE KINGS and the temples of KARNAK, LUXOR, MEDINET HABU and DEIR EL-BAHRI have done much to establish the city of Thebes as the centre of the New Kingdom empire. The seat of power, however, was actually the northern city of Memphis, near modern Cairo, where the royal Residence was located. Excavations during the 1970s and 1980s at the New Kingdom necropolis of Memphis (particularly the tombs of the military commander HOREMHEB, the treasurer Maya and the vizier Aper-el) and epigraphic work in the remains of the magnificent temple of Ptah have begun to redress the balance in favour of Memphis.

The style of art that emerged during the so-called AMARNA period, which roughly corresponded to the reign of AKHENATEN (1352–1336 BC), deserves special mention. The painting, relief and statuary of this period were all characterized by an obsessive emphasis on the god ATEN and the royal family, with the king and his family sometimes being shown in unusually intimate scenes. Both the king and his subjects were represented with unusual facial and bodily features, and a new canon of proportions served to exaggerate these physical extremes.

After the end of the New Kingdom, the rapidly changing artistic styles of the first millennium BC demonstrate, above all, that Egyptian art could assimilate new possibilities while retaining its essential character and integrity. The Egyptians of the Late Period (747–332 BC), under attack from all sides, attempted to revive the classic images of the Old and Middle Kingdoms, which must have symbolized a lost sense of stability and certainty amid the political turmoil. The green basalt statue of the naval officer Udjahorresnet demonstrates that the native Egyptian officials were as adaptable as their works of art; it bears a detailed description of his activities both in the reigns of the native Egyptian kings AHMOSE II (570–526 BC) and PSAMTEK III (526–525 BC) and in the ensuing period of Persian rule, when he served under Darius I (522–486 BC) (see PERSIA).

After the conquest of Egypt by ALEXANDER THE GREAT (332–323 BC), the nature of Pharaonic art was adapted to create a compromise between the needs of the native Egyptians and the preferences of the new Ptolemaic (and later Roman) rulers. Some of the largest surviving religious buildings – the temple of Isis at PHILAE and that of Horus at Edfu – were constructed during this period of over seven hundred years, but the reliefs were beginning to appear mass-produced and repetitive. Although such Greco-Roman reliefs were increasingly poorly formulated and executed, suggesting an Egyptian priesthood that was descending into obscurantism and uncertainty, there are nevertheless indications of a skilful patterning of text and iconography which helps to compensate for the apparent aesthetic decline. At the same time, however, there were new cultural elements absorbed into Egypt from the Mediterranean world, from the FAYUM mummy paintings (wooden funerary portraits painted in a mixture of wax and pigment known as encaustic) to the civic architecture of cities such as Alexandria and Antinoopolis.

From the Middle Ages onwards, after centuries in the shadows, Egyptian art was gradually rediscovered by Arab and European travellers. After the sixteenth century there were European revivals of Egyptian artistic and architectural styles. Specific events produced waves of public reaction and interest: the influence of Howard Carter's discovery of the tomb of Tutankhamun on the art and design of

Europe in the 1920s is well known, but comparable levels of interest were also provoked by the re-erection of the Vatican obelisk at St Peter's in 1586. Similarly, the Napoleonic campaigns in Egypt and the publication of the work of his savants (see EGYPTOLOGY) gave rise to Egyptianizing decorative art. The arrival in London of the 'Younger Memnon' (the upper section of a colossal statue of RAMESES II) in 1818 and the opening of the Egyptian Court at Crystal Palace in 1854 were also important events in terms of the western reaction to Egyptian art. For discussion of Egyptian architecture see PALACES; PYRAMIDS; TEMPLES; TOMBS; TOWNS.

K. LANGE and M. HIRMER, *Egypt: architecture, sculpture and painting in three thousand years* (London, 1968).

H. SCHÄFER, *Principles of Egyptian art*, trans. J. Baines (Oxford, 1974).

C. ALDRED, *Egyptian art* (London, 1980).

W. STEVENSON SMITH, *The art and architecture of ancient Egypt*, 2nd ed. (Harmondsworth, 1981).

T. G. H. JAMES and W. V. DAVIES, *Egyptian sculpture* (London, 1983).

T. G. H. JAMES, *Egyptian painting* (London, 1985).

G. ROBINS, *Proportion and style in ancient Egyptian art* (London, 1994).

Ashmunein, el- *see* HERMOPOLIS MAGNA

Asia, western

Geographical area to the east of the SINAI peninsula and the Red Sea, comprising Mesopotamia, Arabia, Anatolia and the Levant. At least as early as the Predynastic period, Egypt was already trading with these areas in order to obtain such raw materials as wood, copper, silver and certain semi-precious stones that were not available in Egypt. The Egyptians' principal export to western Asia appears to have been gold, obtained from mines in the Eastern Desert and Nubia.

The relationship between the two regions was not always an amicable one, and the fertility of the Nile valley made Egypt constantly attractive to settlers from the less prosperous lands of western Asia. The Egyptians' generally contemptuous view of the Asiatics is exemplified by the *Instruction for King Merikara* dating to the First Intermediate Period: 'Lo, the miserable Asiatic, he is wretched because of the place he is in; short of water, bare of wood, its paths are many and painful because of mountains.' The 'miserable Asiatics' comprised not merely the nomadic BEDOUIN (Shasu) but also the more settled peoples of Syria–Palestine, and although Egyptian paintings and sculptures generally portrayed

Fragment of wall-painting from the tomb of Sobekhotep at Thebes, showing Asiatic envoys bringing gifts to Thutmose IV. 18th Dynasty, c.1400 BC, painted plaster, H. 1.14 m. (EA37991O)

the Asiatic as a tribute-bearer or bound captive, the real relationship must have been a more complex amalgam of diplomatic and economic links.

The 18th-Dynasty pharaohs extended the Egyptian 'empire' (perhaps better described as 'sphere of influence') in western Asia as far as the Euphrates, leading to the influx of many foreign materials, goods and ideas, from the introduction of glass to the use of the CUNEIFORM script in diplomatic correspondence (see AMARNA LETTERS). Gradually, however, the Asiatic territories broke away from Egypt and new powers arose such as the HITTITES, ASSYRIANS and PERSIANS, the two latter powers eventually conquering not only the Levant but Egypt itself.

M. ROAF, *Cultural atlas of Mesopotamia and the ancient Near East* (Oxford, 1990).

Assyrians

People inhabiting the north-eastern area of MESOPOTAMIA, centred on the city of Assur overlooking the Tigris. They embarked on a period of imperial expansion between the early second and early first millennia BC, most notably from 883 to 612 BC. In 671 BC, during the reign of Esarhaddon (681–669 BC), they

invaded Egypt, having been stung by the Egyptians' repeated incitement of trouble among the Assyrian vassal-towns in the Levant. On this occasion, however, they soon withdrew, allowing the 25th-Dynasty Kushite pharaoh Taharqo (690–664 BC) to regain power temporarily. In 669 BC the new Assyrian ruler, Ashurbanipal, launched a new campaign into Egypt, culminating in the execution of the rulers of the various small Delta kingdoms, leaving only NEKAU I of Sais to rule the country (or Lower Egypt at least) on Assyria's behalf. In 664 BC Tanutamani, the successor of Taharqo, succeeded to the throne of Kush and immediately laid claim to Egypt. Proceeding north, he was actively welcomed at Aswan and Thebes, and then marched on Memphis which he took, slaying Nekau I in the process.

Ashurbanipal retaliated in 664/3 BC, recapturing Memphis and finally sacking Thebes and looting its temples, although Tanutamani managed to escape to Nubia. PSAMTEK I (664–610 BC), son of Nekau I, was placed in charge of the country, purportedly as an Assyrian vassal, but actually as an independent ruler. He continued his father's delicate policy of encouraging native Egyptian revival while avoiding conflict with his nominal overlords. This period of revitalization ended with the invasion of the PERSIAN king Cambyses in 525 BC. The Assyrian policy of appointing local vassal kings seems to have minimized their impact on the society and economy of the Egyptians, particularly when compared with the effects of the Persian, Ptolemaic and Roman regimes.

D. OATES, *Studies in the ancient history of northern Iraq* (London, 1968), 19–41 [the early development of Assyria].

A. J. SPALINGER, 'Assurbanipal and Egypt: a source study', *JAOS* 94 (1974), 316–28.

—, 'Esarhaddon and Egypt: an analysis of the first invasion of Egypt', *Orientalia* 43 (1974), 295–326.

N. GRIMAL, *A history of ancient Egypt* (Oxford, 1992), 341–5.

A relief block from the palace of Ashurbanipal (c.645 BC), showing the Assyrian army attacking an Egyptian town. H. 1.14 m. (WA124928)

Astarte

War-goddess of Syrian origin, probably introduced into Egypt in the 18th Dynasty (1550–1295 BC), usually portrayed as a naked woman on horseback wearing a headdress consisting of the *atef* crown or bull horns. She was adopted into the Egyptian pantheon as a daughter of RA (or sometimes of PTAH) and one of the consorts of SETH, and she was particularly linked with equestrian and chariotry skills; like ANAT (another Syrian goddess worshipped in Egypt) she was considered to protect the pharaoh's chariot in battle. A stele of Amenhotep II near the Great Sphinx at Giza, recording her delight in the young king's riding skills, is probably the earliest surviving Egyptian textual reference to Astarte.

J. LECLANT, 'Astarte à cheval d'après les représentations égyptiennes', *Syria* 37 (1960), 1–67.

R. STADELMANN, *Syrisch-palästinische Gottheiten in Ägypten* (Leiden, 1967), 101–10.

astronomy and astrology

The Egyptians often decorated the ceilings of their temples, tombs and coffins with depictions of the heavens, since most funerary and religious entities were regarded as microcosms of the universe itself. Just as the sky-goddess NUT was thought to spread her star-studded body over the earth, so she was also considered to stretch herself protectively over mummies and the houses of the gods. In the Old Kingdom, from the reign of the 5th-Dynasty pharaoh Unas (2375–2345 BC) onwards, the belief that mortals could be reborn in the form of the circumpolar stars led to the depiction of large numbers of stars on the ceilings of the corridors and chambers of pyramids. Indeed, one of the utterances in the PYRAMID TEXTS was a request for Nut to spread herself over the deceased so that he might be 'placed among the imperishable stars' and have eternal life.

The astronomical knowledge of the Egyptian priests and architects at this time is indicated by early examples of the ceremony of *pedj shes* ('stretching the cord'), first attested on a granite block of the reign of the 2nd-Dynasty king Khasekhemwy (c.2686 BC). This method relied on sightings of the Great Bear and Orion (see SAH) constellations, using an 'instrument of knowing' (*merkhet*), which was similar in function to an astrolabe, and a sighting tool made from the central rib of a palm leaf, thus aligning the foundations of the pyramids and sun temples with the cardinal points, usually achieving an error of less than half a degree. Although the texts and reliefs in temples of later periods continued to describe the enactment of this procedure (as in the temple of Horus at EDFU), it appears to have become a mere ceremony and in practice the temples were simply aligned in relation to the river.

The earliest detailed texts relating to astronomy are the 'diagonal calendars' or 'star clocks' painted on wooden coffin lids of the early Middle Kingdom and also of the Late Period. These calendars consisted of thirty-six columns, listing the thirty-six groups of stars ('decans') into which the night sky was divided. Each specific decan rose above the horizon at dawn for an annual period of ten days. The brightest of these was the dog star Sirius (known to the Egyptians as the goddess SOPDET), whose 'heliacal rising' on about 19 July coincided with the annual Nile inundation and therefore appears to have been regarded as an astronomical event of some importance. The god SAH, the mythical consort of Sopdet, was the personification of another decan, the constellation of Orion.

The calendrical system based on decans was flawed by its failure to take into account the fact that the Egyptian year was always about six hours short, adding up to a slippage of ten days every forty years. It is therefore unlikely that the Middle Kingdom 'star clocks' were ever regarded as a practical means of measuring time. Nevertheless, the decans were later depicted on the ceilings of tombs and temples, starting with the tomb of SENENMUT in western Thebes (TT353; c.1460 BC). The 'astronomical ceilings' in the Osireion of Sety I at ABYDOS (c.1290 BC), and the tomb of RAMESES IV (KV2) (c.1150 BC) in the Valley of the Kings, include cosmological texts describing the period of seventy days spent in the underworld by each decan.

Interior of the lid of the wooden coffin of Soter, showing Nut flanked by signs of the zodiac and personifications of the 24 hours of the day. Roman period, 2nd century AD, from Abd el-Qurna, Thebes. L. 2.13 m. (EA6705)

From at least as early as the Middle Kingdom the Egyptians recognized five of the planets, portraying them as deities sailing across the heavens in barks. These 'stars that know no rest' were Jupiter (Horus who limits the two lands), Mars (Horus of the horizon or Horus the red), Mercury (Sebegu, a god associated with SETH), Saturn (Horus, bull of the sky) and Venus ('the one who crosses' or 'god of the morning').

The ceilings of many royal tombs in the Valley of the Kings were decorated with depictions of the heavens. In the tombs of Rameses VI, VII and IX (KV9, KV1 and KV6 respectively), dating to the second half of the twelfth century BC, a set of twenty-four seated figures representing stars were transected by grids of horizontal and vertical lines, allowing the passage of time to be measured in terms of the transits of stars through the sky.

The concept of the horoscope (the belief that the stars could influence human destiny) does not seem to have reached Egypt until the Ptolemaic period. By the first century AD the Babylonian zodiac, represented on the ceiling of the chapel of Osiris on the roof of the temple of Hathor at DENDERA, had been adopted. The surviving lists of lucky and unlucky days appear to have had no connection with astrology, deriving instead from the intricacies of religious festivals and mythological events.

Z. ŽÁBA, *L'orientation astronomique dans l'ancienne Égypte, et la précession de l'axe du monde* (Prague, 1953).

O. NEUGEBAUER and R. PARKER, 'Two demotic horoscopes', *JEA* 54 (1968), 231–5.

, *Egyptian astronomical texts*, 3 vols (Providence, 1969).

R. PARKER, 'Ancient Egyptian astronomy', *Philosophical Transactions of the Royal Society of London* 276 (1974), 51–65.

Stele of Senusret III from Elephantine, describing the building of a fortress at the site. 12th Dynasty, c.1871–1855 BC, H. 37 cm. (EA852)

RIGHT *Plan of the Aswan region.*

BELOW *At Aswan the Qubbet el-Hawa (the Dome of the Winds) is actually the Islamic tomb seen on top of this hill on the west bank, but is widely used to refer to the area of Old Kingdom tombs cut into the hillside. The entrances to several of these can be seen midway up the slope. (P. T. NICHOLSON)*

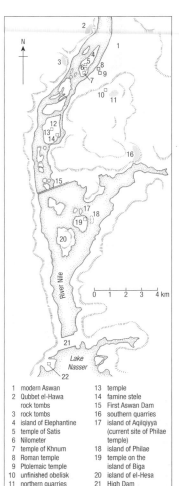

1	modern Aswan	13	temple
2	Qubbet el-Hawa	14	famine stele
	rock tombs	15	First Aswan Dam
3	rock tombs	16	southern quarries
4	island of Elephantine	17	island of Aqilqiyya
5	temple of Satis		(current site of Philae
6	Nilometer		temple)
7	temple of Khnum	18	island of Philae
8	Roman temple	19	temple on the
9	Ptolemaic temple		island of Biga
10	unfinished obelisk	20	island of el-Hesa
11	northern quarries	21	High Dam
12	island of Sehel	22	New Kalabsha

G. R. HUGHES, 'An astrologer's handbook in demotic Egyptian', *Egyptological studies in honor of R. A. Parker*, ed. L. H. Lesko (Hanover and London, 1986), 53–69.

H. BEINLICH, 'Stern', *Lexikon der Ägyptologie* VI, ed. W. Helck, E. Otto and W. Westendorf (Wiesbaden, 1986), 11–14.

Aswan (anc. Swenet, Syene)

Site in Upper Egypt, situated immediately to the north of the first Nile cataract, now at the northern tip of Lake Nasser. It consists of three basic components: the town, temples and granite quarries of Aswan proper on the eastern bank of the Nile; the rock-cut tombs of Qubbet el-Hawa on the western bank; and the town, temples and NILOMETER of Elephantine, an island in the centre of the river. Apart from two small Greco-Roman temples there are few surviving remains of Aswan itself since the area has continued to be occupied up to modern times. The tombs of the governors of Aswan, at Qubbet el-Hawa, which date mainly to the Old and Middle Kingdoms (2686–1650 BC), contain important biographical reliefs and inscriptions. The island of Elephantine has been excavated by a German team since the 1970s; their results show the steady expansion of the settlement from a small Early Dynastic village and temple to the much larger town of the Roman period.

E. EDEL, *Die Felsengräber der Qubbet el-Hawa bei Assuan* (Wiesbaden, 1967–).

E. BRESCIANI and S. PERNIGOTTI, *Assuan: il tempio tolemaico di Isi. I blocchi decorati e iscritti* (Pisa, 1978).

Aswan High Dam

An extensive artificial reservoir was created in Lower Nubia, when the first Aswan dam was constructed (and heightened in three phases) between 1902 and 1933, necessitating a campaign to survey Nubian sites before they were submerged. When work began on the new Aswan High Dam in 1960, the creation of Lake Nasser, one of the largest reservoirs in the world, was initiated. A UNESCO-co-ordinated operation was therefore launched, not only to record the Nubian monuments threatened by this much more extensive flooding but also to dismantle and move certain monuments (including PHILAE, ABU SIMBEL and KALABSHA) to higher ground before the completion of the dam in 1971.

A. E. WEIGALL, *Report on the antiquities of Lower Nubia* (Cairo, 1907).

T. SÄVE-SÖDERBERGH (ed.), *Temples and tombs of ancient Nubia* (London, 1987).

Asyut (anc. Djawty; Lykopolis)

Capital of the thirteenth Upper Egyptian nome (province), located roughly midway between Cairo and Aswan. Despite numerous textual references to the importance of the Pharaonic town of Asyut and its temple of the jackal-god WEPWAWET, the excavated remains are restricted primarily to the rock-tombs of the local élite, dating from the 9th Dynasty to the Ramesside period (*c*.2160–1069 BC). The biographical texts on the walls of the First Intermediate Period and Middle Kingdom rock-tombs provide historical information on the struggle between the rulers of HERAKLEOPOLIS MAGNA and THEBES. The tomb of the

12th-Dynasty nomarch Djefahapy contains uniquely detailed legal texts of endowment and was later re-used as a cult centre of WEPWAWET.

F. L. GRIFFITH, *The inscriptions of Siut and Der Rîfeh* (London, 1889).

G. A. REISNER, 'The tomb of Hepzefa, nomarch of Siût', *JEA* 5 (1919), 79–98.

H. THOMPSON, *A family archive from Siut* (Oxford, 1934).

Aten

Deity represented in the form of the disc or orb of the sun, the cult of which was particularly promoted during the reigns of Amenhotep IV/AKHENATEN (1352–1336 BC)

Akhenaten (left) and Nefertiti (right) worship the Aten (top left), whose rays end in hands, some of them extending to the offerings piled in front of Akhenaten. The figures are heavily damaged, partly due to defects in the stone and partly as a result of the reaction against the so-called heresy of Akhenaten. From the tomb of Tutu (EA8) in the southern group of Amarna. (P. T. NICHOLSON)

and Smenkhkara (1338–1336 BC). The close links between the disc and the sun-god have led to some uncertainty as to whether the Aten was treated as a divine being in its own right. There is also a certain amount of evidence to suggest that Akhenaten may even have equated the Aten with his own father, AMENHOTEP III (1390–1352 BC). Earlier pharaohs had been associated with the Aten, as in the case of

THUTMOSE I (1504–1492 BC), who was portrayed in his temple at Tombos in Nubia wearing the sun-disc and followed by the hieroglyphic sign for 'god'.

The popularity of the Aten slowly grew throughout the New Kingdom and the characteristic iconography of the disc with rays in the form of outstretched arms had already appeared in the time of Amenhotep II (1427–1400 BC). The Aten was particularly favoured by Amenhotep III (1390–1352 BC), during whose reign there is evidence of the presence of priests of Aten at HELIOPOLIS (the traditional centre of the worship of the sun-god RA). He also incorporated references to the Aten in the names he gave to his palace at MALKATA, a division of his army and a pleasure boat.

However, it was under Amenhotep IV that the cult of the Aten reached its peak. On his accession as sole ruler, the Aten became the 'sole' god, and a temple, the Per-Aten, was built on the perimeter of the temple of Amun at KARNAK. This included at least three sanctuaries, one of which was called the Hwt-benben ('mansion of the BENBEN'). Within a short time the cult of Amun appears to have been severely curtailed and eventually proscribed, and the Aten began to be promoted as the sole, exclusive deity.

Around the fifth year of his reign, Amenhotep IV took the next logical step, which was to create a new capital city with its own temples dedicated to the cult of the Aten. He called this new foundation Akhetaten ('the horizon of the disc') and located it in a virgin site in Middle Egypt that was untainted by the worship of other gods (see EL-AMARNA). The king changed his name and titles from Amenhotep to Akhenaten, although elements of his titles which already concerned the sun-god (rather than Amun) were left unchanged. His acknowledgement of the cults of the sun-god included the provision of a burial place for a MNEVIS bull (the physical manifestation of Ra) at el-Amarna, although this tomb remains undiscovered and was perhaps never completed. Although Akhenaten is sometimes regarded as the first proponent of monotheism, his relationship to the cult of the Aten and the rest of the Egyptian pantheon must be regarded firmly in the context of his time. Erik Hornung's view of the cult of the Aten as a form of henotheism, in which one god was effectively elevated above many others, is probably closer to the mark.

Two major temples to the Aten were built at el-Amarna, although, unlike major Theban temples, they were built largely of mudbrick, perhaps with the intention of later rebuilding them in stone. The Per-Aten, described by its excavators as the Great Temple, was an open, unroofed structure covering an area of about 800 × 300 m at the northern end of the central city. The Hwt-Aten (literally 'mansion of the Aten' but usually described by the excavators as the Small Aten Temple) was a smaller building but of similar design; both were strewn with offering tables, and the first court of the small temple contained a massive mud-brick altar, which may have been one of the first monuments to be erected in the new city.

Many of the rock-tombs of the élite at el-Amarna, which were excavated at the northern and southern ends of the bay of cliffs to the east of the city, have prayers to the Aten inscribed on the jambs of their doorways. Most of these prayers appear to be extracts from a longer composition, the *Hymn to the Aten* which some scholars believe to have been composed by Akhenaten himself. The most complete surviving version of this hymn was inscribed in the tomb of AY, 'superintendent of the royal horses', who was probably the brother of Queen TIY (Akhenaten's mother) and later succeeded TUTANKHAMUN on the throne. This hymn, which has several antecedents in earlier 18th-Dynasty hymns to the sun-god, has been compared with the Biblical Psalm 104, although the distinct parallels between the two are usually interpreted simply as indications of the common literary heritage of Egypt and ISRAEL. The hymn also stresses Akhenaten's role as intermediary between the Aten and the populace, by which means he perhaps hoped to avoid the creation of a strong priesthood such as that of Amun. There was rigid official adherence to the cult of the Aten among the élite at el-Amarna, many of whom built shrines dedicated to the new royal family and the Aten in the gardens of their villas. It is clear, however, that traditional religious cults continued to be observed, perhaps covertly, even among the inhabitants of the city at el-Amarna itself. In the 'workmen's village', on the eastern edge of the city, numerous amulets of traditional gods have been found, as well as small private chapels probably dedicated to ancestor worship and showing no traces of the official religion.

On Akhenaten's death there was a reversion to the worship of Amun, and attempts were made to remove all traces of the cult of the Aten. The city at el-Amarna was abandoned and, perhaps as early as the reign of HOREMHEB (1323–1295 BC), it began to be demolished, often leaving only the plaster foundations of the ceremonial buildings. The stone TALATAT blocks from the temples of the Aten were then re-used, primarily as rubble filling the pylons of new temples dedicated to the traditional official cults. In the reliefs at el-Amarna and other sites, the names and faces of Akhenaten, his queen NEFERTITI and all those associated with this 'heresy' were defaced in the aftermath of the Amarna period.

A. PIANKOFF, 'Les grandes compositions religieuses du Nouvel Empire et la reforme d'Amarna', *BIFAO* 62 (1964), 207–18.

D. B. REDFORD, 'The sun-disc in Akhenaten's program: its worship and its antecedents, I', *JARCE* 13 (1976), 47–61.

—, 'The sun-disc in Akhenaten's program: its worship and its antecedents, II', *JARCE* 17 (1982), 21–38.

—, *Akhenaten the heretic king* (Princeton, 1984), 157–84.

C. ALDRED, *Akhenaten, king of Egypt* (London, 1988), 237–48.

Athribis *see* TELL ATRIB

Atrib, Tell (anc. Hwt-Heryib, Athribis)
Town site in the central Delta region near the modern town of Benha, about 40 km north of Cairo. It has been greatly reduced over the years through local farmers' large-scale removal of *sebakh* (ancient mud-brick re-used as fertilizer), although in 1924, in the course of such plundering, a large cache of jewellery dating to the Late Period (747–332 BC) was discovered. A Polish archaeological expedition under the direction of Pascal Vernus excavated part of the post-Pharaonic town during the 1980s and 1990s.

According to surviving texts, Tell Atrib was occupied at least as early as the 4th Dynasty (2613–2494 BC), but no remains earlier than the 12th Dynasty (1985–1795 BC) have been found. The principal god worshipped in the Athribis region was Horus Khenty-khety, represented sometimes as a falcon-headed man and sometimes as a crocodile. The major monuments at the site were a temple dating to the time of AHMOSE II (570–526 BC), the tomb of Queen Takhut (c.590 BC) and a large settlement and cemetery of the Ptolemaic and Roman periods (332 BC–AD 395).

The texts indicate that there was once also an important temple of Amenhotep III (1390–1352 BC) at the site, perhaps because this was the home-town of the influential chief architect, AMENHOTEP SON OF HAPU. Although nothing remains of the temple *in situ*, it would probably have incorporated the statue of a lion now in the collection of the British Museum, which is inscribed with the name of Rameses II (1279–1213 BC), although it originally bore the cartouche of Amenhotep III. This sculpture is similar in appearance to a pair of lions of the reign of Amenhotep III from SOLEB.

A. ROWE, 'Short report on the excavations of the Institute of Archaeology Liverpool at Athribis (Tell Atrib)', *ASAE* 38 (1938), 523–32.

P. VERNUS, *Athribis: textes et documents relatifs à la géographie, aux cultes et à l'histoire d'une ville du Delta égyptien à l'époque pharaonique* (Cairo, 1978).

K. MYSLIWIEC and T. HERBICH, 'Polish archaeological activities at Tell Atrib in 1985', *The archaeology of the Nile Delta: problems and priorities*, ed. E. C. M. van den Brink (Amsterdam, 1988), 177–203.

Atum
Creator-god and solar deity of HELIOPOLIS, where he was gradually syncretized with the sun-god RA, to form the god Ra-Atum. According to the Heliopolitan theology, Atum came into being before heaven and earth were separated, rising up from NUN, the waters of chaos, to form the PRIMEVAL MOUND. His name means 'the all', signifying his CREATION and summation of all that exists.

Atum's creation of the universe was conceptualized in terms of a family of nine gods known as the Heliopolitan ENNEAD. Thus the two offspring of Atum, SHU (air) and TEFNUT (moisture), became the parents of GEB (earth) and NUT (sky), and the grandparents of OSIRIS, ISIS, SETH and NEPHTHYS. Atum was said to have produced Shu and Tefnut by copulating with his hand or, according to other sources, spitting them into being. There has been some debate as to whether Atum's act of procreation constituted masturbation or copulation, in that his hand seems to have represented the female principle. Both Atum and his hand were therefore portrayed as a divine couple on coffins of the First Intermediate Period. Similarly, the title 'god's hand' was adopted by Theban priestesses supposedly married to the god AMUN.

Atum was regarded as a protective deity, particularly associated with the rituals of kingship. It was Atum who lifted the dead king from his pyramid to the heavens in order to transform him into a star-god, and in later times he protected the deceased during the journey through the underworld.

He is usually depicted as an anthropomorphic deity often wearing the double crown. The animals particularly sacred to him were the lion, the bull, the ICHNEUMON and the lizard, while he was also believed to be manifested in the SCARAB, which emerged from its ball of dung just as ATUM appeared from the primeval mound. Sometimes he was portrayed in the essentially primordial form of a snake, which was the appearance that he was expect-

Detail of the funerary stele of Pediamennebnesuttawy, showing the deceased (on the far right) worshipping the sun-god in three separate forms: Ra-Horakhty, Atum (third from the right, wearing the double crown) and Khepri (with a scarab beetle on his head), followed by the funerary deities Osiris, Isis, Nephthys and the jackal-headed Anubis. 30th Dynasty or early Ptolemaic period, 4th–3rd centuries BC, painted plaster on wood, from Thebes, H. 74 cm. (EA8462)

ed to adopt when the cosmos finally collapsed, returning everything to its original primeval state.

K. SETHE, 'Atum als Ichneumon', *ZÄS* 63 (1928), 50–3.

E. BRUNNER-TRAUT, 'Atum als Bogenschütze', *MDAIK* 14 (1956), 20–8.

P. DERCHAIN, 'Le démiurge et la balance', *Religions en Egypte hellénistique et romaine: colloque de Strasbourg* (Paris, 1969), 31–4.

E. HORNUNG, *Idea into image*, trans. E. Bredeck (New York, 1992), 43–7.

autobiographies *see* LITERATURE

Avaris *see* TELL EL-DAB'A

Ay (1327–1323 BC)

Late 18th-Dynasty ruler who came to the throne after the short reign of TUTANKHAMUN (1336–1327 BC). In his earlier career he was an important official during the reign of AKHENATEN (1352–1336 BC). Like YUYA, the father of Queen TIY, he came from AKHMIM and held the titles 'superintendent of the royal horses' and 'god's father'; it has therefore been

argued that he may well have been Tiy's brother, Akhenaten's uncle and perhaps uncle or great-uncle of Tutankhamun. It has even been suggested that the unusual office of 'god's father' could be held only by the king's father-in-law, which might have made Ay the father of NEFERTITI.

Whatever the truth behind these theories, there is good evidence to show that he was closely involved in the events of the Amarna period, and had begun to construct one of the largest tombs at EL-AMARNA, containing the longer of the two surviving versions of the *Hymn to the Aten* (see ATEN). The last decoration in Ay's el-Amarna tomb seems to have taken place in the ninth year of Akhenaten's reign. The progress of his career between then and the end of Akhenaten's reign is known from a number of inscribed funerary items, showing that he rose to the position of VIZIER and royal chancellor, as well as acquiring the unusual epithet, 'doer of right'.

After the reigns of Akhenaten and Smenkhkara both Tutankhamun and Ay began to reform the religious heresies of the Amarna period but, because of Ay's close connections with his predecessors, his reign of four or five years is usually regarded as a continuation of the same grip on the throne. On the wall of the burial chamber of the illustrious smaller tomb in which Tutankhamun was actually buried, Ay is depicted as the loyal heir administering the final rituals to the royal mummy. The real break was to come with the reign of his successor, the general HOREMHEB, who had no family links with the Thutmosid royal family (except possibly through his wife Mutnedjmet).

Abandoning his unfinished tomb at el-Amarna, Ay usurped a second tomb in a western branch of the VALLEY OF THE KINGS (KV23), which had probably been intended for Tutankhamun (and was perhaps originally the tomb of Prince Thutmose, who predeceased his father Amenhotep III). The scenes in the tomb portray him with his first wife Tey rather than Ankhesenpaaten, one of the daughters of Akhenaten, whom he is thought to have married in order to consolidate his claim to the throne. One unique feature of this tomb is the presence of a scene of hunting in the marshes, which was usually found in nobles' tombs rather than the burial place of a pharaoh.

N. DE GARIS DAVIES, *The rock tombs of el-Amarna* VI (London, 1908), 16–24, 28–35.

P. E. NEWBERRY, 'King Ay, the successor of Tutankhamun', *JEA* 18 (1932), 50–2.

K. C. SEELE, 'King Ay and the close of the Amarna period', *JNES* 14 (1955), 168–80.

O. J. SCHADEN, 'Clearance of the tomb of King Ay (WV23)', *JARCE* 21 (1984), 39–64.

C. ALDRED, *Akhenaten: king of Egypt* (London, 1988), 298–301.

B

ba

The Egyptians considered that each individual person was made up of five distinct parts: the physical body, the *ba*, the KA, the NAME and the SHADOW. The *ba* has similarities with our concept of 'personality', in that it comprised all those non-physical attributes which made one human being unique. However, the concept of the *ba* also referred to power, and could be extended to gods as well as inanimate objects. *Ba* was therefore also the term used for what might be described as the physical manifestations of certain gods, so that the Memphite APIS bull was the *ba* of OSIRIS; similarly the four sons of HORUS were his *ba*.

Detail from the Book of the Dead of Hunefer, consisting of the vignette associated with Chapter 17, which shows a ba-*bird on a shrine-shaped plinth. 19th Dynasty, c.1285 BC, painted papyrus, from Thebes. (EA9901)*

It was necessary for the deceased to journey from the tomb to rejoin his *ka* if he was to become transformed into an AKH, and since the physical body could not do this it was the duty of the *ba*. The Egyptian names of the Jabiru stork and the ram both had the same phonetic value as *ba*, therefore the hieroglyphic signs for these creatures were used to refer to it in writing. It is possible that this accidental association with the stork led to the depiction of the *ba* as a bird with a human head and often also with human arms. The Egyptians regarded migratory birds as incarnations of

the *ba*, flying freely between tomb and underworld. However, it was also believed that the *ba* could adopt any form it wished, and there were numerous funerary spells to assist this process of transformation.

In order for the physical bodies of the deceased to survive in the afterlife, they had to be reunited with the *ba* every night, and Spell 89 of the BOOK OF THE DEAD recommended that a golden *ba*-bird should be placed on the chest of the mummy in order to facilitate this reunion. The *ba*-bird was also incorporated into the decoration of private coffins from the 21st Dynasty onwards. Far from corresponding to the modern western concept of a 'spirit' (as it is sometimes translated), the *ba* was closely linked to the physical body, to the extent that it too was considered to have physical needs for such pleasures as food, drink and sexual activity.

E. WOLF-BRINKMANN, *Versuch einer Deutung des Begriffes 'ba' anhand der Überlieferung der Frühzeit und des Alten Reiches* (Freiburg, 1968).
L. V. ZABKAR, *A study of the ba concept in ancient Egyptian texts* (Chicago, 1968).
H. GOEDICKE, *The report about the dispute of a man with his ba (P Berlin 3024)* (Baltimore, 1970).
J. P. ALLEN, 'Funerary texts and their meaning', *Mummies and magic*, ed. P. Lacovara, S. D'Auria, and C. H. Roehrig (Boston, 1988), 38–49.
E. HORNUNG, *Idea into image*, trans. E. Bredeck (New York, 1992), 179–84.

Babylonia

Name given to the southern part of MESOPOTAMIA from the time of Hammurabi (1792–1750 BC) until the Christian era. Its capital was the city of Babylon, the site of which is located about 80 km south of modern Baghdad. The country covered those areas described as SUMER and AKKAD during the third millennium BC, and like them its language (Babylonian) was written in the CUNEIFORM script.

In the late seventh century BC, the expansion of Babylonian power into Syria–Palestine clashed with Egyptian interests there. The Saite pharaoh Nekau II (610–595 BC) opposed the Babylonian advance, but in the battle of Carchemish, the armies of Nabopolassar, led by his son Nebuchadnezzar II, defeated the Egyptian army, thus effectively ending Nekau II's hold on Syria. In 601 BC, however, the armies of Nebuchadnezzar were driven back from the borders of the Delta by an Egyptian army including GREEK mercenaries. In the reign of AHMOSE II (570–526 BC) an alliance was established between Egypt and Babylonia but by then the Egyptians were threatened by the growth of PERSIA.

R. KOLDEWEY, *The excavations at Babylon* (London, 1914).
H. FIGULLA and W. J. MARTIN, *Letters and documents of the Old Babylonian period* (London and Philadelphia, 1953).
J. OATES, *Babylon*, 2nd ed. (London, 1986).
D. B. REDFORD, *Egypt, Canaan and Israel in ancient times* (Princeton, 1992), 430–69.

Badari, el-

Area of Upper Egypt between Matmar and Qau, including numerous Predynastic cemeteries (notably Mostagedda, Deir Tasa and the cemetery of el-Badari itself), as well as at least one early Predynastic settlement at Hammamia. The finds from el-Badari form the original basis for the Badarian period (*c.*5500–4000 BC), the earliest phase of the Upper Egyptian PREDYNASTIC PERIOD. The el-Badari region, stretching for 30 km along the east bank of the Nile, was first investigated by Guy Brunton and Gertrude Caton-Thompson between 1922 and 1931. Most of the cemeteries in the Badarian region have yielded distinctive pottery vessels (particularly red-polished ware with blackened tops), as well as terracotta and ivory anthropomorphic figures, slate palettes, stone vases and flint tools. The contents of the Predynastic cemeteries at el-Badari have been subjected to a number of statistical analyses attempting to clarify the chronology and social history of the Badarian period.

G. BRUNTON et al., *Qau and Badari*, 3 vols (London, 1927–30).
G. BRUNTON and G. CATON-THOMPSON, *The Badarian civilisation and prehistoric remains near Badari* (London, 1928).
G. BRUNTON, *Mostagedda and the Tasian culture* (London, 1937).
—, *Matmar* (London, 1948).
W. KAISER, 'Zur Südausdehnung der vorgeschichtlichen Deltakulturen und zur frühen Entwicklung Oberägyptens', *MDAIK* 41 (1985), 61–87.
D. L. HOLMES, 'Archaeological cultural resources and modern land-use activities: some observations made during a recent survey in the Badari region, Egypt', *JARCE* 29 (1992), 67–80.

Bahariya Oasis

Fertile depression in the northeastern Libyan Desert 200 km west of the Nile. The archaeological remains date primarily from the early New Kingdom to the Roman period (*c.*1550 BC–AD 395). Near the modern town of Bawit are the tombs of several 26th-Dynasty Egyptian governors of the oasis, the 19th-Dynasty tomb of the provincial governor Amenhotep Huy and a necropolis of sacred

birds associated with the worship of THOTH and HORUS, dating to the 26th Dynasty and Greco-Roman period. Also near Bawit are the remains of a Roman triumphal arch and two temples, one dating to the reign of Apries (589–570 BC) and the other to the time of ALEXANDER THE GREAT (332–323 BC). At the southern tip of the oasis is el-Hayz, where a Roman garrison, a basilica and a small settlement dating to the Roman and Christian periods (c.30 BC–AD 641) have been excavated.

A. FAKHRY, *Bahria oasis*, 2 vols (Cairo, 1942–50).
—, *The oases of Egypt* II (Cairo, 1974).
L. GIDDY, *Egyptian oases: Bahariya, Dakhla, Farafra and Kharga during pharaonic times* (Warminster, 1987).

Balat *see* DAKHLA OASIS

Ballana and Qustul

Pair of Nubian élite necropoleis on either side of the Nile some 15 km south of ABU SIMBEL and now submerged beneath Lake Nasser. An A-GROUP cemetery of élite tumulus graves dating to the early third millennium BC was excavated at Qustul by an expedition from the Chicago Oriental Institute.

Ballana is the type-site of the Ballana period (or 'X-Group phase', *c.* AD 350–700), which lasted from the decline of the Meroitic empire to the arrival of Christianity. Many of the distinctive tumulus burials, nearly two hundred of which have been excavated, contained evidence of HUMAN SACRIFICE in the form of the bodies of retainers buried alongside the pre-Christian rulers of Lower Nubia. The drift sand and low scrub covering the tumuli at

Pottery from Qasr Ibrim, including examples of the tall footed goblets that are the most typical vessel forms of the Ballana period. 5th–6th centuries AD, H. of tallest vessel 12.2 cm. (EA66560, 67980, 71821, 71822)

Ballana have helped to preserve the graves from the widespread plundering that affected the earlier élite Kushite cemeteries of MEROE and NAPATA.

W. B. EMERY and L. P. KIRWAN, *The royal tombs of Ballana and Qustul* (Cairo, 1938).
B. G. TRIGGER, 'The royal tombs at Qustul and Ballana and their Meroitic antecedents', *JEA* 55 (1969), 117–28.
—, 'The Ballana culture and the coming of Christianity', *Africa in Antiquity: the arts of ancient Nubia and the Sudan* I, ed. S. Wenig (New York, 1978), 107–11.
W. Y. ADAMS, *Nubia: corridor to Africa*, 2nd ed. (London and Princeton, 1984), 404–13.

B. WILLIAMS, *Excavations between Abu Simbel and the Sudan frontier I: The A-Group royal cemetery at Qustul: cemetery L*, Oriental Institute Nubia Expedition III (Chicago, 1986).
—, *Excavations between Abu Simbel and the Sudan frontier IX: Noubadian X-Group remains from royal cemeteries*, Oriental Institute Nubia Expedition IX (Chicago, 1991).

Ballana culture/period *see* BALLANA AND QUSTUL

bark, bark shrine

Since the principal artery of communication in ancient Egypt was the Nile, and the boat was the most obvious form of transport, it was perhaps inevitable that the 'bark' should have been the accepted vehicle in which Egyptian gods were transported from one shrine to another. These divine barks were similar in shape to Nile boats, except that their prows and sterns were adorned with the AEGIS of the god in question, and the cabin was replaced by a NAOS containing the cult image of the deity. Thus the bark of AMUN, for instance, was decorated with the head of a ram at either end.

These barks were usually kept in the inner sanctuary of the temple, either resting on a plinth before the *naos*, as in the temple of Horus at EDFU, or inside a bark shrine, as at the temples of KARNAK and LUXOR. There were often three such shrines in a row, one for each member of a divine TRIAD (group of three deities). The barks themselves were scale models of genuine boats, and are often depicted in the act of being carried aloft on poles by priests, during FESTIVALS and processions. As well as the principal shrines in the temples, there were also small bark shrines along the routes of ritual processions, usually described as 'resting places', or 'way stations'.

Part of a granite representation of a sacred bark, from the sanctuary of Amun at Karnak. The various elements of the sculpture make up a three-dimensional writing of Mutemwiya, the name of Amenhotep III's mother. 18th Dynasty, c.1360 BC, L. 2.13 m. (EA43)

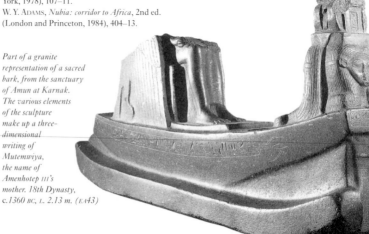

In the case of the festivals of Amun at Thebes, particularly the Valley Festival and the Opet Festival, these model barks were placed on ornate river-going barks to make their journey to the Theban west bank and to Luxor temple respectively. Similarly the bark of HATHOR travelled from her temple at DENDERA to that of Horus at Edfu for the celebration of the 'feast of the beautiful meeting', a divine union.

A more specialized funerary form of ritual boat, with origins stretching back at least as early as the 1st Dynasty at ABYDOS and SAQQARA, is the SOLAR BARK, which may have been intended to carry the deceased through the netherworld. The best surviving example is that of Khufu at GIZA, which was discovered in a pit beside the pyramid and has now been reconstructed *in situ*.

G. LEGRAIN, 'Le logement et transport des barques sacrées et des statues des dieux dans quelques temples égyptiens', *BIFAO* 13 (1917), 1–76.

G. FOUCART, 'Un temple flottant: le vaisseau d'or d'Amon-Ra', *Fondation Eugène Piot: Monuments et mémoires publiés par l'Académie des Inscriptions et Belles Lettres* 25 (1921–2), 143–69.

K. A. KITCHEN, 'Barke', *Lexikon der Ägyptologie* I, ed. W. Helck, E. Otto and W. Westendorf (Wiesbaden, 1975), 619–25.

basketry and cordage

A class of artefacts that have frequently been overlooked by archaeologists in the past, partly because, even in the arid conditions of most Egyptian sites, they are not preserved in the same quantities as pottery and stone vessels. Although such organic materials as basketry, matting (both for floor coverings and roofing) and rope clearly played a significant role in the daily lives of the ancient Egyptians, only a small percentage has survived in the archaeological record, perhaps because discarded baskets would often have been burned, whereas stone and ceramics are difficult to destroy completely.

The Egyptians' uses of baskets ranged from small disposable bags to large decorated storage baskets for clothes, the ancient Egyptian equivalent of the wardrobe or linen closet. The wide variety of uses is partly due to the scarcity of wood in Egypt, whereas the materials used to make baskets and rope were readily available in the Nile valley. Rope was made from tall strong grasses (e.g. *Desmostachya bi-*

Two coiled baskets and a rectangular papyrus-fibre basket. (EA6346, 5918, 5395)

pinnata and *Imperata cylindrica*) or from the rind of the papyrus stem (*Cyperus papyrus*). Baskets were made from the leaves of the dom palm (*Hyphaena thebaica*), and, increasingly from the Late Period onwards, the date palm (*Phoenix dactylifera*). In modern Egypt, virtually all baskets are made from date-palm leaves, while rope and mats are made from the coarse fibres at the bases of the leaves. From the Ptolemaic period onwards, rushes (*Juncus species*) were used for making baskets and mats.

The basket-making techniques employed from the Mesolithic period onwards were coiling, twining and, to a lesser extent, weaving. In the Ptolemaic and Roman periods, a number of other methods and styles emerged, including plaiting and stake-and-strand basketry. Many of these techniques are still used in modern times, therefore the evidence provided by surviving ancient basketry can often be supplemented

and better understood through the ethno-archaeological study of modern basket-makers W. Z. WENDRICH, *Who is afraid of basketry? A guide to recording basketry and cordage for archaeologists and anthropologists* (Leiden, 1991).

Basta, Tell (anc. Per-Bastet, Bubastis)

Site of a temple and town in the eastern Nile Delta, about 80 km to the northeast of Cairo. It flourished from the 4th Dynasty to the end of the Roman period (*c*.2613 BC–AD 395), but the main monument at the site is the red granite temple of the cat-goddess BASTET, which was documented by the Greek historian Herodotus in the fifth century BC. The results of Edouard Naville's excavations in 1887–9 provided archaeological evidence confirming many of the details of this description. The

Plan of the site of Tell Basta.

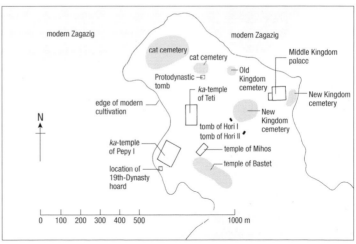

modern Zagazig

modern Zagazig

cat cemetery

cat cemetery

Middle Kingdom palace

Protodynastic tomb

Old Kingdom cemetery

edge of modern cultivation

ka-temple of Teti

New Kingdom cemetery

N

tomb of Hori I
tomb of Hori II

New Kingdom cemetery

ka-temple of Pepy I

temple of Mihos

location of 19th-Dynasty hoard

temple of Bastet

0   100   200   300   400   500   1000 m

Part of a granite temple gateway from Bubastis, showing Osorkon II and Karoma, c.874–850 BC, H. 1.75 m. (EA1077)

site also includes the *ka*-temples of the 6th-Dynasty pharaohs Teti (2345–2323 BC) and Pepy I (2321–2287 BC) and a pair of 'jubilee chapels' built by Amenemhat III (1855–1808 BC) and Amenhotep III (1390–1352 BC) respectively, as well as temples dedicated to the gods ATUM and Mihos. To the north of the city are a series of vaulted mud-brick cat cemeteries and adjacent ateliers. A 19th-Dynasty hoard of gold and silver vessels and jewellery was discovered at the site in 1906 (now in the Egyptian Museum, Cairo).

The city reached its peak when its rulers established the 22nd Dynasty (*c*.945–715 BC). Although the capital during this period was probably still TANIS (and to some extent MEMPHIS), Bubastis must have taken on greater significance as the home city of the new kings of Egypt. OSORKON I (924–889 BC), for instance, appears to have built a hypostyle hall in the temple of Bastet, as well as decorating existing walls with a number of new reliefs and constructing a small temple to Atum outside the main precincts. Osorkon II (874–850 BC) added a new court to the main temple in celebration of his SED FESTIVAL.

E. NAVILLE, *Bubastis (1887–1889)* (London, 1891).

L. HABACHI, *Tell Basta* (Cairo, 1957).

C. C. VAN SICLEN III, 'The city of Basta: an interim report', *NARCE* 128 (1984), 28–39.

Bastet

Cat-goddess and local deity of the town of Bubastis (TELL BASTA), whose name means 'she of the *bast* [ointment jar]'. She was regarded not only as the daughter of the sun-god but also as the more protective aspect of the mother-goddess, in contrast to the aggressive image of the lioness-headed SEKHMET. In her earliest known form, carved on stone vessels of the 2nd-Dynasty ruler Hetepsekhemwy (*c*.2890 BC) at Saqqara, Bastet was represented as a woman with the head of a lioness, frequently holding both the *ankh* sign and a sceptre (as well as, occasionally, a *menat* necklace). By the first millennium BC, however, she was widely portrayed as a cat-headed woman, often carrying a SISTRUM (a form of rattle) and sometimes accompanied by a small group of

Bronze statuette of the cat-goddess Bastet holding an aegis in her left hand and a sistrum in her right; at her feet there are four small kittens. Late Period or Ptolemaic period, c.664–30 BC, H. 26 cm. (EA25565)

kittens. Her name was commonly inscribed on blue glazed ceremonial 'New Year' flasks, perhaps because, like other lioness-goddesses, she would have been linked with the five epagomenal days in the Egyptian CALENDAR. The

festival of Bastet is described by Herodotus.

N. E. SCOTT, 'The cat of Bastet', *BMMA* 17/1 (1958), 1–7.

Z. EL-KORDY, *La déesse Bastet* (Cairo, 1968).

J. MALEK, *The cat in ancient Egypt* (London, 1993).

Bat

Goddess of the seventh Upper Egyptian nome, usually represented by a cow's head with curling horns, perhaps the earliest depiction being the pair of heads at the top of the NARMER palette (*c*.3100 BC). The iconography of Bat was almost completely absorbed into the cult of the more important cow-goddess HATHOR by the Middle Kingdom.

H. G. FISCHER, 'The cult and nome of the goddess Bat', *JARCE* 1 (1962), 7–24.

—, 'Varia Aegyptiaca: II. B3.t in the New Kingdom', *JARCE* 2 (1963), 50–1.

batter

Architectural term denoting the sloping face of a wall in which the foundation courses are wider than the upper courses, thus adding stability. This functional and decorative technique was regularly employed for the walls of MASTABA tombs as well as the enclosure walls of Egyptian temples, where it was associated with PAN BEDDING and sectional construction.

Bawit *see* BAHARIYA OASIS

beard

Facial hair in Egypt has an uneven history. It is clear from certain Predynastic figurines, as well as from the figures depicted on the NARMER palette, that full beards were favoured in the formative stages of Egyptian history. By the beginning of the Dynastic period, however, shaving had become fashionable among the nobility, later spreading throughout the rest of the population. The earliest shaving implements appear to have been sharp stone blades, but in later periods copper or bronze razors were used. The work of the village barber is known from Egyptian literature as well as from tomb scenes such as that of Userhet (TT56) at Thebes, and it seems to have been a mark of poor social status not to shave, except when in mourning or about to depart on an expedition abroad.

None the less, officials and rulers of the Old Kingdom, such as Prince Rahotep, are depicted with moustaches, and full beards are widely shown on mummy masks of the First Intermediate Period and the Middle Kingdom, such as that of a 12th-Dynasty individual named Ankhef. Despite the low status apparently attached to facial hair in life, it was considered to be a divine attribute of the gods, whose closely plaited beards were 'like lapis lazuli'. Accordingly, the pharaoh would express his status as a living god by wearing a 'false beard' secured by cord. Such beards were usually wider toward the bottom (i.e. the end furthest away from the chin), as in the case of the triad statues of MENKAURA. It was usually after their death that kings were portrayed wearing the divine Osirid form of beard with upturned end, as on the gold mask of Tutankhamun. Deceased non-royal individuals are often shown with short, tuft-like beards.

S. QUIRKE and A. J. SPENCER, *The British Museum book of ancient Egypt* (London, 1992), 71–2.

E. STROUHAL, *Life in ancient Egypt* (Cambridge, 1992), 83–4.

bedouin

Nomadic pastoralists of northern and central Arabia and Egypt's Eastern Desert, where their descendants still live today. The ancient bedouin of the Arabian peninsula are thought to have been responsible for domesticating the single-humped Arabian CAMEL at the end of the second millennium BC, but the earliest evidence for the domesticated camel in the Nile valley dates to the ninth century BC.

Organized states have always felt threatened by nomadic peoples, and the Egyptians were no exception. They knew the bedouin as Shasu, or *heryw-sh* ('sand dwellers'), and battles against them are recorded as early as the time of Unas (2375–2345 BC), who depicted them on the causeway of his funerary complex at SAQQARA. In the First Intermediate Period they invaded parts of the Delta, and although they were eventually expelled they continued to be a source of difficulty. During the reign of the 12th-Dynasty pharaoh Amenemhat I

Painted cast of a painted relief in the temple of Rameses II (c.1250 BC) at Beit el-Wali, showing the king trampling bedouin.

(1985–1955 BC) they threatened the TURQUOISE mines at Serabit el Khadim in the Sinai, although defeated, they remained a sufficient threat for defences to be built around the site in the time of AMENEMHAT III (1855–1808 BC).

The military might of the New Kingdom did not deter the bedouin, and Thutmose II (1492–1479 BC) was obliged to campaign against them well beyond Egypt's borders. As before, however, this was not a long-term solution to the problem, and his successors, the warrior pharaohs Thutmose III and Amenhotep II, are also known to have dispatched military expeditions against them. The bedouin's way of life made them almost impossible to eradicate, since they were always on the move and ready to flee into the desert where a conventional army was not able to follow. Occasionally, as under Sety I (1294–1279 BC), they had to be driven from the wells along the Egyptian desert route across Sinai.

Their knowledge of the desert and their ability to move easily across difficult terrain made them valuable military scouts, although their skills were not generally plied on behalf of the Egyptians. When RAMESES II (1279–1213 BC) captured two bedouin before his battle with the HITTITES at QADESH they are said to have misled him into believing that his enemy was still distant, with near-fatal consequences. Similarly, it was the bedouin who guided Cambyses and his PERSIAN army across the wastes of Sinai in their successful invasion of Egypt in 525 BC.

R. GIVEON, *Les bédouins Shosou des documents égyptiens* (Leiden, 1971).

bee

According to one Egyptian myth, bees were the tears of the sun-god RA. They were undoubtedly of great importance in providing honey, which was used both as the principal sweetener in the Egyptian diet and as a base for medicinal unguents thus employing its natural anti-bacterial properties (see

MEDICINE). The Egyptians also collected beeswax for use in metallurgy (i.e. in the moulding of wax images for metal casting by the lost-wax method) as well as in the 'varnishing' of pigments.

Bee-keepers are represented on a relief of Nyuserra (2445–2421 BC) from his sun temple at ABU GURAB, as early as the 5th Dynasty. This record indicates that apiculture, already attested as early as the Neolithic period, was well organized by the middle of the Old Kingdom, and that honey was probably being distributed over large distances. As well as trading honey it is likely that many communities throughout Egypt kept their own bee colonies. Bee-keeping is also shown in the 18th-Dynasty tomb of Rekhmira (TT100). The 26th-Dynasty tomb of Pabasa (TT279) at Thebes clearly shows bees kept in pottery hives, although hives made of mud and other material were probably also used. Honey from wild bees was gathered by professional collectors, known as *bityw*, working along the desert fringes.

The religious significance of the bee also extended to an association with the goddess NEITH, whose temple at Sais was known as *per-bit* ('the house of the bee'). One of the king's names, from the 1st Dynasty onwards, was *nesw-bit*: 'He of the sedge and the bee', which is conventionally translated as 'king of Upper and Lower Egypt' (see KINGSHIP and ROYAL TITULARY).

G. KUÉNY, 'Scènes apicoles dans l'ancienne Égypte', *JNES* 9 (1950), 84–93.

J. LECLANT, 'L'abeille et le miel dans l'Egypte pharaonique', *Traité de biologie de l'abeille (sous la direction de Rémy Chauvin)* v (Paris, 1968), 51–60.

E. CRANE, *The archaeology of beekeeping* (London, 1984), 34–43.

R. DAVID, *The pyramid builders of ancient Egypt* (London, 1986), 155–57.

beer *see* ALCOHOLIC BEVERAGES and FOOD

Begrawiya *see* MEROE

Behbeit el-Hagar (anc. Per-hebyt, Iseum)

Temple town situated in the northern central area of the Nile Delta, which flourished in the 30th Dynasty (380–343 BC) and the Ptolemaic period (332–30 BC). The site is dominated by the remains of a large granite temple of ISIS, the importance of which is indicated by the fact that one of its relief blocks was later incorporated into the temple of Isis in Rome. The plan of the original temple at Behbeit el-Hagar has proved difficult to reconstruct owing to damage caused by quarrying and seismic activity.

A. LEZINE, 'Etat présent du temple de Behbeit el-Hagar', *Kêmi* 10 (1949), 49–57.

B. PORTER and R. L. B. MOSS, *Topographical bibliography* IV (Oxford, 1968), 40–2.

C. FAVARD-MEEKS, *Le temple de Behbeit el-Hagara* (Hamburg, 1991).

Beit el-Wali

Rock-cut temple on the west bank of the Nile in Lower Nubia, which was dedicated to Amun-Ra and founded in the reign of RAMESES II (1279–1213 BC). The reliefs were copied by the German Egyptologist Günther Roeder in 1907, although casts were made by Robert Hay in the 1820s. The site was not comprehensively studied until the work of a joint expedition of the University of Chicago and the Swiss Institute in Cairo during the 1960s. Soon afterwards, the temples at Beit el-Wali and nearby KALABSHA were moved to New Kalabsha, 45 km to the north, in order to save them from the rising waters of Lake Nasser (see ASWAN HIGH DAM). The reliefs include depictions of the siege of a Syrian city, the capture of a Nubian village and the bringing of Nubian tribute into the presence of the king, painted plaster casts of which are displayed in the collection of the British Museum (see illustrations accompanying the entries for BEDOUIN and VICEROY OF KUSH).

G. ROEDER, *Der Felstempel von Beit el-Wali* (Cairo, 1938).

H. RICKE, G. R. HUGHES and E. F. WENTE, *The Beit el-Wali temple of Ramesses II* (Chicago, 1967).

Belzoni, Giovanni (1778–1823)

Italian adventurer, explorer and excavator, who procured large quantities of Egyptian antiquities for European collectors and museums. The son of a barber, Belzoni was born in Padua and at first pursued a career as a circus strong man, travelling throughout Europe. In 1814 he went to Egypt, where his attempts to sell a new type of water wheel proved unsuccessful, leading him to pursue a more lucrative trade in the excavation and transportation of ancient monuments. In 1816 he began to work for Henry Salt, the British Consul-General in Egypt, initially helping him with the transportation of the 'young Memnon', part of a colossal statue of Rameses II, which was to become one of the first major Egyptian antiquities in the collection of the British Museum.

His discoveries were numerous, ranging from the tomb of King SETY I at western Thebes to the Greco-Roman city of Berenice on the Red Sea coast. Although his methods were somewhat unorthodox (and occasionally unnecessarily destructive), judged by modern archaeological standards, he was nevertheless an important pioneer in Egyptology. He did much to encourage European enthusiasm for Egyptian antiquities, not only through his exhibition at the Egyptian Hall in Piccadilly (London) in 1821 but also through the published accounts of his discoveries. In the Great Temple at ABU SIMBEL, for instance, he and James Mangles (a British naval officer) compiled a plan on which they marked the original positions of the items of statuary.

After more than eight years of exploration along the Nile valley, he embarked on an expedition to find the source of the Niger, but died of dysentery at Benin in December 1823.

G. BELZONI, *Narrative of the operations and recent discoveries within the pyramids, temples, tombs and excavations in Egypt and Nubia* (London, 1820).

C. CLAIR, *Strong man Egyptologist* (London, 1957).

S. MAYES, *The great Belzoni* (London, 1959).

benben stone

Sacred stone at HELIOPOLIS that symbolized the PRIMEVAL MOUND and perhaps also the petrified semen of the sun-god Ra-Atum (see ATUM). It served as the earliest prototype for the OBELISK and possibly even the PYRAMID. In recognition of these connections, the gilded cap-stone placed at the very top of each pyramid or obelisk was known as a *benbenet*. The original stone at Heliopolis was believed to have been the point at which the rays of the rising sun first fell, and its cult appears to date back at least as far as the 1st Dynasty. There are strong links between the *benben* and the BENU-BIRD (the Egyptian phoenix), and both terms seem to derive from the word *weben* meaning 'to rise'.

J. R. BAINES, 'Bnbn: mythological and linguistic notes', *Orientalia* 39 (1970), 389–404.

L. HABACHI, *The obelisks of Egypt* (Cairo, 1984), 5, 10.

Beni Hasan

Necropolis located on the east bank of the Nile some 23 km north of el-Minya, dating principally to the 11th and 12th Dynasties (2125–1795 BC) although there are some small tombs dating back to the 6th Dynasty (2345–2181 BC). There are thirty-nine rock-cut tombs at Beni Hasan, several of them belonging to the provincial governors of the 'oryx' nome (province). A number of the 11th- and 12th-Dynasty tombs are decorated with wall-paintings of funerary rituals and daily life, including depictions of Asiatic traders, battle scenes and rows of wrestlers. There is also an extensive cemetery of Middle Kingdom shaft tombs excavated by John Garstang in the early 1900s. The equipment from these undecorated tombs, including painted coffins and models, forms an important corpus with regard to the funerary beliefs of the Middle Kingdom. At the southern end of the site is a New Kingdom rock-cut temple, the SPEOS ARTEMIDOS.

Copy of a scene from the tomb of Khnumhotep at Beni Hasan, showing men picking figs while baboons sit in the tree eating the fruit. Early 12th Dynasty, c.1950 BC.

P. E. NEWBERRY et al., *Beni Hassan*, 4 vols (London, 1893–1900).

S. BICKEL and J.-L. CHAPPAZ, 'Missions épigraphiques du fonds de l'Egyptologie de Genève au Speos Artemidos', *BSEG* 12 (1988), 9–24.

J. D. BOURRIAU, *Pharaohs and mortals* (Cambridge, 1988), 85–109.

benu-bird

The sacred Heliopolitan bird, closely associated with the BENBEN STONE, the OBELISK and the cult of the sun-gods ATUM and RA. Its name probably derived from the Egyptian verb *weben* ('to rise') and it was the prototype for the Greek phoenix. There may well be an etymological connection between the two birds' names, and certainly there are distinct similarities in their respective links with the sun and rebirth, although a number of the other aspects of the phoenix legend are quite distinct.

the desire for transformation might refer to the changing phases of Venus.

R. VAN DEN BROEK, *The myth of the phoenix according to classical and early christian tradition* (Leiden, 1972).

L. KÁKOSY, 'Phönix', *Lexikon der Ägyptologie* IV, ed. W. Helck, E. Otto and W. Westendorf (Wiesbaden, 1982), 1030–9.

G. HART, *Egyptian myths* (London, 1990), 16–17.

R. KRAUSS, 'M–mjtt bnw (pAnastasi I 4.5)', *JEA* 79 (1993), 266–7.

Bes

Dwarf god with grotesque mask-like facial features and a protruding tongue. He is often shown with the ears and mane of a lion, although some scholars have suggested that he is simply wearing a lion-skin cape rather than possessing these physical characteristics. He is commonly portrayed with a plumed headdress and carrying musical instruments, knives or

Painted wooden figure of Bes on a lotus flower. New Kingdom, H. 28 cm. (EA20865)

BELOW *Painted relief figures of Bes and a naked woman or goddess in the 'Bes Chambers' at Saqqara. (REPRODUCED COURTESY OF THE GRIFFITH INSTITUTE)*

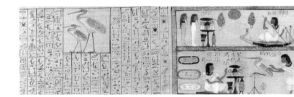

Detail of the Book of the Dead of the scribe Nakht; in the bottom register Nakht is shown adoring the benu-bird. Early 19th Dynasty, c.1280 BC. (EA10471)

The *benu*-bird appears in the PYRAMID TEXTS as a yellow wagtail serving as a manifestation of the Heliopolitan sun-god Atum; in Utterance 600, Atum is said to have 'risen up, as the *benben* in the mansion of the *benu* in Heliopolis'. Later, however, in the BOOK OF THE DEAD, the *benu*-bird was represented as a kind of grey heron (*Ardea cinera*) with a long straight beak and a two-feathered crest, the BA (physical manifestation) of both Ra and OSIRIS. Because of its connections with Osiris, it is sometimes represented wearing the *atef* crown (see CROWNS).

Chapter 83 of the Book of the Dead, the 'spell for being transformed into a *benu*-bird', was usually accompanied by a depiction of the *benu*-bird. In an analysis of the desire to be transformed 'like the *benu*-bird' in Papyrus Anastasi I, Rolf Krauss suggests that the bird symbolized the planet Venus from at least the beginning of the New Kingdom, in which case

the sa hieroglyph representing protection. The name Bes is used to describe a number of similar deities and demons, including the lion-demons known from the Middle Kingdom town of Kahun (see EL-LAHUN and MASKS) and the shaft tombs behind the RAMESSEUM, which are of a similar date. Bes was considered to be capable of warding off snakes from the house, and was sometimes portrayed in the form of the demon Aha strangling two serpents with his bare hands.

Despite his apparent ferocity, he was a beneficent deity, much favoured as a protector of the family, and associated with sexuality and childbirth. His image is therefore found on all of the MAMMISI (birth-houses) associated with Late Period temples, as well as being carved on such everyday objects as cosmetic items. Along with TAWERET he was one of the most popular deities represented in amulets. His image was painted on a frieze in a room of Amenhotep III's palace at MALKATA, as well as on some of the walls of the workmen's villages at EL-AMARNA and DEIR EL-MEDINA, perhaps indicating rooms connected with women and childbirth.

The sexual aspect of the god seems to have become particularly prominent during the Ptolemaic period, when 'incubation' or Bes chambers were built at SAQQARA. Mud-plaster figures of Bes and a naked goddess lined their walls, and it has been suggested that pilgrims probably spent the night there in the hope of experiencing healing DREAMS, perhaps in connection with the renewal of their sexual powers. In the Roman period he was perhaps adopted as a military god since he was often portrayed in the costume of a legionary brandishing a sword.

J. F. ROMANO, 'The origin of the Bes image', *BES* 2 (1980), 39–56.

J. D. BOURRIAU, *Pharaohs and mortals* (Cambridge, 1988), 110–13.

B Group (B Horizon)

Now-discredited cultural term invented by George Reisner to describe the final stages of the Neolithic A GROUP in NUBIA (c.2800–2300 BC), leading up to the beginning of the C-GROUP phase. Two principal reasons have emerged for rejecting the existence of the B Group, at least as Reisner envisaged it. First, there appears to have been great continuity in material culture, settlement patterns and cemetery locations between the A and C Groups and, second, the chronological gap between the two might actually have been no more than three centuries roughly contemporary with the Egyptian 3rd and 4th Dynasties (c.2686–2494 BC). It is therefore possible that

the assemblages usually designated 'B Group' might actually have resulted from the relative impoverishment of Lower Nubia or the depredations of early Egyptian imperialism. It has been suggested that there might have been an enforced reversion to pastoralism or the local Nubian population might even have temporarily abandoned the region, eventually returning in the form of the C Group.

G. REISNER, *Archaeological survey of Nubia: report for 1907–8* I (Cairo, 1910), 18–52.

H. S. SMITH, 'The Nubian B-group', *Kush* 14 (1966), 69–124.

W. Y. ADAMS, *Nubia: corridor to Africa*, 2nd ed. (London and Princeton, 1984), 132–5.

H. S. SMITH, 'The development of the A-Group "culture" in northern Lower Nubia', *Egypt and Africa*, ed. W. V. Davies (London, 1991), 92–111.

Biblical connections

The links between ancient Egypt and the events described in the Old Testament are generally problematic and beset by controversy. There are a number of critical problems with the attempt to correlate Biblical narratives with the Pharaonic textual and archaeological record. Given that most of the events described in the Bible took place many centuries prior to the time that they were written down, it is extremely difficult to know when they are factual historical accounts and when they are purely allegorical or rhetorical in nature.

Because of the vagueness of the Biblical chronological framework, it is usually also difficult to assign events to particular historical periods with any precision. Another major problem is posed by the possibility that those events that were of great significance to the people of Israel cannot be assumed to have had the same importance for the ancient Egyptians, therefore there is no guarantee of any independent Egyptian record having been made (let alone having survived among the small fraction of preserved texts). A great deal of research has therefore tended to concentrate on attempting to date the Biblical stories by means of chance historical clues incorporated in the narratives, although even then there is the danger of encountering anachronisms introduced at the time that the texts were written down.

Most interest has focused on the stories of Joseph and Moses, both of which contain many literary and historical details that suggest at least a knowledge of ancient Egypt on the part of the writers. The episode in the story of Joseph involving his attempted seduction by Potiphar's wife is closely paralleled in an Egyptian story known as the *Tale of the Two*

Brothers, while several of the personal names of characters appear to be authentically Egyptian Late Period forms, such as Asenet ('belonging to the goddess Neith'). However, these literary and linguistic connections with Egypt are of little help in terms of dating the story, which is usually assumed to have taken place during the Egyptian New Kingdom (1550–1069 BC), equivalent to the Late Bronze Age in the Levant), although certain details tie in much more with the political situation of the Saite period (664–525 BC).

The emergence of Moses and the events of the Exodus are thought to have taken place in the early Ramesside period, with RAMESES II (1279–1213 BC) being considered the most likely to have been the pharaoh featuring in the narrative. No texts from his reign make any mention of Moses or the children of Israel, although the name ISRAEL first occurs on the so-called Israel Stele of the time of his successor, MERENPTAH. Attempts have occasionally been made to equate Moses with the pharaoh AKHENATEN, on the grounds that the latter introduced a peculiarly Egyptian form of monotheism, but there are no other aspects of this pharaoh's life, or indeed his cult of the Aten, that remotely resemble the Biblical account of Moses. Akhenaten's *Hymn to the Aten* has been shown to have strong similarities with Psalm 104, but this is probably only an indication that the two compositions belong to a common literary heritage or perhaps even derive from a common Near Eastern original. The same reason is usually given for the very close parallels that have been observed between a Late Period wisdom text known as the *Instruction of Amenemipet son of Kanakht* and the Biblical book of Proverbs, although it has been suggested by some scholars that the writers of Proverbs may even have been influenced by a text of the *Instruction of Amenemipet* itself.

From the Third Intermediate Period (1069–747 BC) onwards, there are more verifiable references to Egypt in the Bible, particularly in terms of the political events involving conflict with the ASSYRIANS and PERSIANS. The 22nd-Dynasty ruler Sheshonq I (945–924 BC), the Biblical Shishak, sacked Jerusalem and the temple of Solomon in 925 BC. Hosea, the ruler of Samaria, is said to have requested military aid from the Egyptian Prince Tefnakht of SAIS, in his attempt to fend off the Assyrians in the late eighth century BC.

P. MONTET, *Egypt and the Bible* (Philadelphia, 1968).

D. B. REDFORD, *A study of the Biblical story of Joseph (Genesis 37–50)* (Leiden, 1970).

S. GROLL (ed.), *Pharaonic Egypt, the Bible and Christianity* (Jerusalem, 1985)

A. F. RAINEY (ed.), *Egypt, Israel, Sinai – archaeological and historical relationships in the Biblical period* (Tel Aviv, 1987).

D. B. REDFORD, *Egypt, Canaan and Israel in ancient times* (Princeton, 1992).

birth-house *see* MAMMISI

Blemmyes

Nomads active in Lower NUBIA during the X-Group phase (*c.*AD 350–700). The Blemmyes are usually identified as the ancestors of the modern Beja people. Both the Blemmyes and the Nobatae (another group of nomads in Lower Nubia) are mentioned in Classical texts, but there is no definite archaeological evidence to connect either of these peoples with the royal cemetery at BALLANA dating to the same period. The situation is summarized by W. Y. Adams: 'We may ... epitomize the riddle of post-Meroitic Nubia by observing that historians tell us of two peoples, the Blemmyes and the Nobatae, where archaeology discloses only one culture, the Ballana; moreover, both history and archaeology leave us in ignorance of the fate of the earlier Meroitic population and culture.'

A. PAUL, *A history of the Beja tribes of the Sudan*, 2nd ed. (London, 1971).

W. Y. ADAMS, *Nubia: corridor to Africa*, 2nd ed. (London and Princeton, 1984), 382–429.

block statue

Type of sculpture introduced in the Middle Kingdom (2055–1650 BC), representing private individuals in a very compressed squatting position, with the knees drawn up to the chin. In some examples the effect is almost to reduce the human body to a schematic block-like shape, while in others some of the modelling of the limbs is still retained. New Kingdom texts suggest that the origin of the style was the desire to represent an individual in the form of a guardian seated in the gateway of a temple. One of the practical advantages of the block statue, which became particularly popular during the Late Period (747–332 BC), was the fact that it provided a very large surface area for inscriptions relating to the funerary cult and the identification of the individual concerned.

C. ALDRED, *Egyptian art* (London, 1980), 133–5.

W. STEVENSON SMITH, *The art and architecture of ancient Egypt*, rev. W. K. Simpson (Harmondsworth, 1981), 181–2.

R. SCHULZ, *Die Entwicklung und Bedeutung des kuboiden Statuentypus* (Hildesheim, 1992)

blue crown *see* CROWNS AND ROYAL REGALIA

board-games *see* GAMES

boats *see* SHIPS AND BOATS

Book of the Dead

Egyptological term used to refer to the funerary text known to the Egyptians as the 'spell for coming forth by day'. It was introduced at the end of the Second Intermediate Period and consisted of about two hundred spells (or 'chapters'), over half of which were derived directly from the earlier PYRAMID TEXTS or COFFIN TEXTS.

Such 'netherworld' texts as the Book of the Dead were usually inscribed on papyri, although certain small extracts were inscribed on AMULETS. Chapter 30A, for example, was known as the 'spell for not letting the deceased's heart create opposition against him in the realm of the dead' and was commonly inscribed on HEART scarabs, while a version of Chapter 6 was inscribed on SHABTI figures so that they might perform corvée work on behalf of the deceased.

Chapter 125, the section of the Book of the Dead that was most commonly illustrated by a vignette, shows the last judgement of the deceased before OSIRIS and the forty-two 'judges' representing aspects of MAAT ('divine order'). The judgement took the form of the weighing of the heart of the deceased against the feather of Maat. An important element of the ritual was the calling of each judge by name, while giving the relevant 'negative confession', such as: 'O Far Strider who came forth from Heliopolis, I have done no falsehood; O Fire-embracer who came forth from Kherarha, I have not robbed; O Nosey who came forth from Hermopolis, I have not been rapacious.' The desired outcome of these negative confessions was that the deceased was declared 'true of voice' and introduced into the realm of the deceased. Although vignettes always optimistically depict a successful outcome, the demon AMMUT ('the devourer of the dead') was usually shown awaiting those who might fail the test.

The Book of the Dead was often simply placed in the coffin, but it could also be rolled up and inserted into a statuette of Sokar-Osiris or even incorporated into the mummy bandaging. The texts could be written in HIEROGLYPHIC, HIERATIC or DEMOTIC scripts. Since most wealthy individuals were provided with Books of the Dead, numerous copies have survived.

R. O. FAULKNER, *The ancient Egyptian Book of the Dead*, ed. C. Andrews (London, 1985).

E. HORNUNG, *Idea into image*, trans. E. Bredeck (New York, 1992), 95–113.

borders, frontiers and limits

The Egyptians used two principal terms to describe a border or limit: *tash*, which refers to a real geographical limit set by people or deities, and *djer*, which appears to describe a fixed and unchanging universal limit. The *tash*, whether field boundary or national border, was therefore essentially an elastic frontier, and, in times of strength and prosperity, such rulers as Senusret I (1965–1920 BC) and Thutmose III (1479–1425 BC) could state an intention to 'extend the borders' (*sewesekh tashw*) of Egypt.

The traditional borders of Egypt comprised the Western Desert, the Sinai Desert, the Mediterranean coast and the Nile CATARACTS south of Aswan. These geographical barriers were sufficient to protect the

Part of a hieratic papyrus inscribed with military dispatches sent from the Egyptian garrison at Semna, on the border with Upper Nubia. Middle Kingdom, c.1841 BC, from Thebes, H. 16 cm. (EA10752 SHEET 3)

Egyptians from outside interference for many centuries. Later on, in the Pharaonic period, these natural borders helped to maintain Egypt's independence during periods of relative weakness. Since, however, the pharaoh's titulary described him as the ruler of the entire known world, the political boundaries of Egypt were theoretically infinite. In practice the greatest extent of the Egyptian empire – achieved during the reign of Thutmos III in the 18th Dynasty – was marked by the Euphrates in the northeast and the KURGUS boundary stele (between the fourth and fifth Nile cataracts) in the south.

The border with Lower Nubia was traditionally marked by the town of Elephantine (ASWAN), naturally defended by its island location and surrounded by a thick defensive wall. The original name of the settlement around the first cataract was Swenet ('trade'), from which the modern name Aswan derives; this place name reflects the more commercial nature of the southern border, representing opportunities for profitable economic activities rather than the threat of invasion. Because the first cataract represented an obstacle to shipping – despite an attempt by the Old Kingdom ruler Merenra (2287–2278 BC) to cut a canal – all trade goods had to be transported along the bank. This crucial land route to the east of the Nile, between Aswan and the region of Philae, was protected by a huge mud-brick wall, almost 7.5 km long, probably built principally in the 12th Dynasty.

The northeastern, northwestern and southern borders of Egypt were more or less fortified from the Middle Kingdom onwards. From at least the reign of Amenemhat I (1985–1955 BC) the eastern Delta was protected by a string of fortresses, known as the Walls of the Prince (*inebw heka*). These were intended to prevent invasion along the coastal route from the Levant, which was known as the Way of Horus during the Middle Kingdom. At about the same time a fortress seems to have been established in the Wadi Natrun, defending the western Delta from the Libyans. The western and eastern Delta defences were well maintained throughout the second millennium BC. The New Kingdom fortresses and garrisons of the Delta borders – including el-Alamein and Zawiyet Umm el-Rakham in the west and Tell Abu Safa (Sile), Tell el-Farama (Pelusium), Tell el-Heir (Migdol) and Tell el-Maskhuta (Pithom) in the east – were intended to prevent any recurrence of the HYKSOS invasion.

S. SCHOSKE and H. BRUNNER, 'Die Grenzen von Zeit und Raum bei den Ägyptern', *Archiv für Orientforschung* 17 (1954–5), 141–5.

D. O'CONNOR, 'Demarcating the boundaries: an interpretation of a scene in the tomb of Mahu, el-Amarna', *BES* 9 (1987–8), 41–51.

S. QUIRKE, 'Frontier or border? The northeast Delta in Middle Kingdom texts', *The archaeology, geography and history of the Delta*, ed. A. Nibbi (Oxford, 1989), 261–74.

E. HORNUNG, *Idea into image*, trans. E. Bredeck (New York, 1992), 73–92.

bread *see* FOOD and OFFERING TABLE

bronze *see* COPPER AND BRONZE

Bubastis *see* TELL BASTA

Buchis

Sacred bull of MONTU at Hermonthis (Armant) south of Luxor. Just as his northern counterpart, the APIS, was considered to be the divine incarnation of the god Ptah, so the Buchis was believed to be the principal physical manifestation (or BA) of RA and OSIRIS. Like the Apis bulls, each Buchis was chosen on the basis of special markings, consisting of a white body and black face, and the Roman writer Macrobius (*c.*AD 400) described the bulls as changing colour with every hour and having hair which grew backwards.

After death, each successive Buchis bull was interred in a great underground catacomb known as the Bucheum (see SERAPEUM), which was discovered in 1927 by Robert Mond and W. B. Emery. As in the case of the Apis, the mothers of the bulls were also interred, and their catacomb at Armant is known as the Baqariyyah. The Buchis bulls' sarcophagi were of sandstone rather than granite, but, as in the case of the Saqqara Serapeum, the site was much plundered. Burials were made from the time of Nectanebo II (360–343 BC) until the reign of Diocletian (AD 284–305). There is evidence for the use of the site from the 18th Dynasty onwards, but burials dating to that time or earlier remain undiscovered.

R. L. MOND and O. H. MYERS, *The Bucheum* (London, 1934).

Buhen

Egyptian site in Lower Nubia, located on the west bank of the Nile, near the second cataract, and about 260 km upstream from

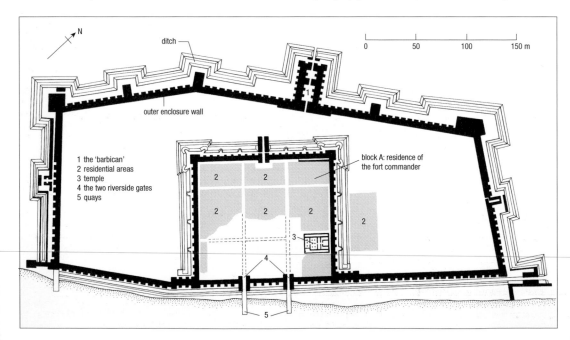

N

ditch

0   50   100   150 m

outer enclosure wall

1 the 'barbican'
2 residential areas
3 temple
4 the two riverside gates
5 quays

block A: residence of the fort commander

View of the 12th-Dynasty ramparts at Buhen.
(REPRODUCED COURTESY OF THE EGYPT
EXPLORATION SOCIETY)

Aswan. The remains were first studied in 1819 but mainly excavated between 1957 and 1964. The settlement at Buhen was founded in the Old Kingdom (2686–2181 BC) as a centre for Egyptian mining expeditions. An impressive array of mud brick fortifications was constructed around the settlement in the 12th Dynasty (1985–1795 BC), thus transforming it into a military garrison controlling the area to the north of the second Nile cataract. The 12th-Dynasty settlement consisted of several regular, rectangular blocks of housing separated by six major streets. The subsequent New Kingdom town was undoubtedly much more of a civilian settlement, as the frontier of Egypt was pushed further south than the fourth Nile cataract, thus considerably reducing Buhen's military importance.

The methods employed by W. B. Emery at Buhen were closer to those of the excavators of EL-AMARNA, AMARA West and SESEBI-SAULA during the 1930s and 1940s than those employed by archaeologists working on settlement sites elsewhere in the world during the 1960s. However, Emery's approach was necessarily *ad hoc* owing to the imminence of the site's flooding by Lake Nasser (see ASWAN HIGH DAM), and the excavations were hampered by considerable post-depositional disturbance of

LEFT *Plan of the Middle Kingdom fortress at Buhen.*

the stratigraphy of the Pharaonic remains at the site.

R. A. CAMINOS, *The New Kingdom temples of Buhen*, 2 vols (London, 1974).
W. B. EMERY et al., *The fortress of Buhen*, 2 vols (London, 1979).

bull

Symbol of strength, masculinity and fertility which, from the earliest historical times, seems to have been regarded as an embodiment of royal might (see NARMER). The heads of bulls, perhaps representing sacrificed animals, were sometimes used in Predynastic and Early Dynastic architecture, as in Mastaba 3504 at Saqqara, dating to the reign of the 1st-Dynasty ruler DJET, where clay heads furnished with real bulls' horns were set in front of the palace-façade-style walls of the tomb.

The epithet 'mighty bull' or 'bull of Horus' was held by several pharaohs of the New Kingdom (1550–1069 BC). The king might also be described as the *ka mutef* ('bull of his mother'), and the royal mother might herself take the form of a COW. Similarly, it was the wild bull which was often depicted as the prey of the king in hunting scenes. The Nile INUNDATION was sometimes depicted as a bull, since both were strongly associated with the renewal of fertility. This connection between fertility, water and bulls probably also explains the occasional representations of the primordial lake NUN with the head of a bull.

Bulls were also associated with solar imagery; the 'bull of RA' is mentioned as early

as the 5th Dynasty (2494–2345 BC) and in the PYRAMID TEXTS, and the cult of the MNEVIS bull of Heliopolis was specifically encouraged by Akhenaten (1352–1336 BC) because of its solar associations. There were, however, also strong links with the moon and the constellation of Ursa Major. A number of bulls enjoyed special status as SACRED ANIMALS, notably the APIS and BUCHIS bulls which were interred in catacombs at SAQQARA and ARMANT respectively.

E. OTTO, *Beiträge zur Geschichte der Stierkulte in Aegypten* (Berlin, 1938).
P. BEHRENS, 'Stierkampf', *Lexikon der Ägyptologie* VI, ed. W. Helck, E. Otto and W. Westendorf (Wiesbaden, 1986), 16–17.
W. HELCK, 'Stiergötter', *Lexikon der Ägyptologie* VI, ed. W. Helck, E. Otto and W. Westendorf (Wiesbaden, 1986), 14–16.
R. WILKINSON, *Reading Egyptian art* (London, 1992), 56–7.

burial *see* CANOPIC JARS; COFFINS AND SARCOPHAGI; FUNERARY BELIEFS; MASTABA; MUMMIFICATION and PYRAMIDS

Buto *see* TELL EL-FARA'IN

Byblos (Gubla, Jubeil)

Ancient coastal town, the site of which is located in modern Lebanon (formerly CANAAN), about 40 km north of Beirut. The principal settlement, known in the Akkadian language as Gubla, has a long history extending from the Neolithic to the Late Bronze Age when the population appears to have moved to a nearby site now covered by a modern village.

The importance of Byblos lay in its function as a port, and from around the time of Egypt's unification it was a source of timber. The famous cedars of Lebanon, and other goods, passed through it, and Egyptian objects are found there from as early as the 2nd Dynasty (2890–2686 BC). Egyptian culture of the Middle Kingdom had an especially strong influence on the court of its Middle Bronze Age rulers, and among the objects found from the royal tombs of this period are several bearing the names of Amenemhat III (1855–1808 BC) and IV (1808–1799 BC) of the 12th Dynasty. Egyptian objects included ivory, ebony and gold while local imitations used other materials and were executed in a less accomplished style.

The site had several religious buildings including the so-called 'Obelisk Temple', dedicated to Ba'alat Gebal, the 'Lady of Byblos', a local form of ASTARTE. One of the obelisks erected to her was inscribed with hieroglyphs. She was identified with HATHOR, a connection which may have helped establish Astarte as a goddess in Egypt.

In the New Kingdom the city features prominently in the AMARNA LETTERS, since its ruler, Ribaddi, sought military assistance from the Egyptian pharaoh. On this occasion Byblos fell into enemy hands, but was later regained. A sarcophagus found with objects of Rameses II (1279–1213 BC) and showing Egyptian influence is important for its later (tenth century BC) inscription for Ahiram, a local ruler, which is in early alphabetic characters. However, by the time of Rameses XI (1099–1069 BC), last king of the New Kingdom, Egypt had become so weak and impoverished that it no longer commanded the respect of cities such as Byblos, and the *Report of Wenamum* tells how an Egyptian official was shabbily treated by a high-handed prince of Byblos, something which would previously have been unthinkable. The importance of Byblos itself gradually declined in favour of the neighbouring ports of Tyre and Sidon.

P. MONTET, *Byblos et l'Egypte*, 2 vols (Paris, 1928).

M. DUNAND, *Fouilles de Byblos* (Paris, 1939–58).

N. JIDEJIAN, *Byblos through the ages* (Beirut, 1968).

J.-F. SALLES, *La nécropole 'k' de Byblos* (Paris, 1980).

C

calendar

The earliest Egyptian calendars were based on lunar observations combined with the annual cycle of the Nile INUNDATION, measured with NILOMETERS. On this basis the Egyptians divided the year into twelve months and three seasons: *akhet* (the inundation itself), *peret* (spring time, when the crops began to emerge) and *shemu* (harvest time). Each season consisted of four thirty-day months, and each month comprised three ten-day weeks. This was an admirably simple system, compared with the modern European calendar of unequal months, and it was briefly revived in France at the time of the Revolution.

The division of the day and night into twelve hours each appears to have been initiated by the Egyptians, probably by simple analogy with the twelve months of the year, but the division of the hour into sixty minutes was

introduced by the Babylonians. The smallest unit of time recognized in ancient Egypt was the *at*, usually translated as 'moment' and having no definite length.

The Egyptian year was considered to begin on 19 July (according to the later Julian calendar), which was the date of the heliacal rising of the dog star Sirius (see ASTRONOMY AND ASTROLOGY and SOPDET). Surviving textual accounts of the observation of this event form the linchpin of the traditional chronology of Egypt. However, even with the addition of five intercalary 'epagomenal' days (corresponding to the birthdays of the deities Osiris, Isis, Horus, Seth and Nephthys), a discrepancy gradually developed between the lunar year of 365 days and the real solar year, which was about six hours longer. This effectively meant that the civil year and the genuine seasonal year were synchronized only once every 1460 years, although this does not seem to have been regarded as a fatal flaw until the Ptolemaic period, when the concept of the 'leap year' was introduced in the Alexandrian calendar, later forming the basis for the Julian and Gregorian calendars.

LEFT *Flask for water from the rising Nile at the beginning of the flood, marking the start of the New Year. This type of 'New Year flask' appears in the Late Period, no earlier than the 7th century BC, perhaps inspired by foreign vessel shapes. Late Period, after 600 BC, green faience of unknown provenance, H. 13 cm. (EA24651, DRAWN BY CHRISTINE BARRATT)*

BELOW *Calendar in which the lucky and unlucky days of the year are marked in black and red respectively. Third Intermediate Period to Late Period, papyrus and pigment, H. 24 cm. (EA10474, SHEET 2)*

As well as the civil calendar there were also separate religious calendars consisting of FES-TIVALS and ceremonies associated with particular deities and temples (e.g. the Feast of Opet at Thebes, celebrated in the second month of *akhet*). The priests often calculated the dates of these according to the lunar month of about 29.5 days rather than according to the civil calendar, since it was essential that many of them should coincide with particular phases of the agricultural or astronomical cycle.

R. A. PARKER, *The calendars of ancient Egypt* (Chicago, 1950).

—, 'Sothic dates and calendar "adjustments"', *RdE* 9 (1952), 101–8.

—, 'The beginning of the lunar month in ancient Egypt', *JNES* 29 (1970), 217–20.

R. KRAUSS, *Sothis- und Monddaten* (Hildesheim, 1985).

E. HORNUNG, *Idea into image*, trans. E. Bredeck (New York, 1992), 57–71.

Cambyses *see* PERSIA, PERSIANS

camel

Although the single-humped Arabian camel (*Camelus dromedarius*, more accurately described as a dromedary) figures prominently in the modern popular image of Egypt, it was very much a late arrival among the domesticated animals of the Nile valley. Remains of the double-humped Bactrian camel have been found at sites such as Shahr-i Sokhta in eastern Iran dating to the third millennium BC, but the earliest evidence for the domestication of the single-humped species in the Near East dates to the ninth century BC. When the ASSYRIAN king Esarhaddon invaded Egypt in 671 BC, he is said to have been aided by camel-using BEDOUIN from the Arabian desert.

It used to be thought that domesticated camels did not appear in the Nile valley until the Ptolemaic period, but the earliest date is now considered to be the late ninth century BC, in the light of the discovery of a camel's mandible and a pellet of camel dung at the Lower Nubian site of QASR IBRIM. The two finds were excavated during the 1980s from separate archaeological contexts dating to the early Napatan period, and both dates were later confirmed by radiocarbon analysis.

I. KÖHLER, *Zur Domestikation des Kamels* (Hanover, 1981).

I. L. MASON, 'Camels', *Evolution of domesticated animals*, ed. I. L. Mason (London, 1984).

P. ROWLEY-CONWY, 'The camel in the Nile valley: new radiocarbon accelerator dates from Qasr Ibrim', *JEA* 74 (1988), 245–8.

Canaan, Canaanites

The region that was occupied by the Canaanite people in the Middle and Late Bronze Ages (part of the area described by the ancient Egyptians as Retenu) roughly corresponds to modern Lebanon, on the northern coast of the Levant. This territory essentially consisted of a number of city-states, including BYBLOS, Lachish, MEGIDDO and Ugarit.

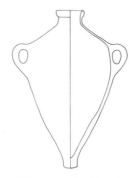

A typical 'Canaanite amphora' from el-Amarna. H. 58.8 cm. Just as the territorial and ethnic connotations of the name 'Canaan' are somewhat ambiguous, so the term 'Canaanite amphora' is conventionally applied to this type of Bronze Age pottery vessel, although it was used for transporting commodities not only in Canaan but throughout the Aegean, Eastern Mediterranean and Egypt. The name reflects the fact that the form clearly originated in Syria-Palestine, although local copies were made elsewhere.

The Canaanites were a Semitic people related to the HYKSOS, who had invaded Egypt in the Second Intermediate Period. They occupied this part of the Levant during the Late Bronze Age from around 2000 to 1200 BC, after which they were displaced by the Israelites and Philistines from the south and PHOENICIANS from the north. Several of their cities, such as Byblos, remained important under their new masters, and much of Canaanite culture is reflected in that of the Phoenicians.

Canaan acted as a kind of 'clearing house' for the trade not only of itself but of its neighbours, the Egyptians, the HITTITES, and the states of MESOPOTAMIA, and was much influenced by them. It may have been the need to develop sophisticated record-keeping or to deal with traders of many nationalities which led to the development here of an alphabetic script around 1700 BC, roughly the same date

as the appearance of alphabetic inscriptions at Serabit el-Khadim in c. 1500. These are known as the Proto-Sinaitic or Proto-Canaanite scripts (see BYBLOS).

K. KENYON, *Amorites and Canaanites* (Oxford, 1966).

A. R. MILLARD, 'The Canaanites', *Peoples of Old Testament times*, ed. D. J. Wiseman (Oxford, 1973), 29–52.

J. F. HEALY, 'The early alphabet', *Reading the past* (London, 1990), 197–257.

D. B. REDFORD, *Egypt, Canaan and Israel in ancient times* (Princeton, 1992), 167–8, 192–213.

canopic jars

Stone and ceramic vessels used for the burial of the viscera removed during MUMMIFICA-TION. The term 'canopic' derives from the misconception that they were connected with the human-headed jars which were worshipped as personifications of the god OSIRIS by the inhabitants of the ancient Egyptian port of Canopus (named after the Homeric character who was Menelaus' pilot). The 'Canopus of Osiris' image appeared on some Roman coins from the Alexandrian mint, and the name was therefore chosen by early Egyptologists to refer to any jar with a stopper in the form of a human head.

The practice of preserving eviscerated organs during mummification is first attested in the burial of HETEPHERES, mother of the 4th-Dynasty ruler Khufu (2589–2566 BC), at GIZA. Her viscera were stored in a travertine ('Egyptian alabaster') chest divided into four compartments, three of which contained the remains of her organs in NATRON, while the fourth held a dry organic material. In later burials, specific elements of the viscera placed under the protection of four anthropomorphic genii known as the SONS OF HORUS, who were themselves protected by tutelary deities guarding the four cardinal points. The human-headed Imsety (linked with ISIS and the south) protected the liver; the ape-headed Hapy (linked with NEPHTHYS and the north) cared for the lungs; the jackal-headed Duamutef (linked with NEITH and the east) guarded the stomach; and the falcon-headed Qebehsenuef (linked with SERKET and the west) looked after the intestines.

During the First Intermediate Period (2181–2055 BC) the jars began to be provided with stoppers in the form of human heads, and at this time the canopic bundles were sometimes also decorated with human-faced masks. By the late Middle Kingdom a set of canopic equipment could comprise two chests (a stone-carved outer container and a wooden inner one) holding four jars furnished with

Wooden dummy canopic jars for an unnamed person. 21st Dynasty, c.1000 BC, H. of human-headed jar 31 cm. (EA9562-5)

stoppers in the form of human heads. In the early 18th Dynasty the stoppers were still human-headed, as in the case of the canopic equipment of TUTANKHAMUN, but from the later 18th Dynasty onwards it became more common for the stoppers to take the form of the characteristic heads of each of the four genii, and by the 19th Dynasty these had completely replaced the human-headed type.

In the Third Intermediate Period (1069–747 BC) mummified viscera were usually returned to the body, sometimes accompanied by models of the relevant genii, but empty or dummy canopic jars were occasionally still included in rich burials. Canopic equipment is found in Ptolemaic tombs but had ceased to be used by the Roman period. The last known royal canopic jars belonged to APRIES (589–570 BC), and one of these survived through its reuse as a vessel containing the body of a mummified hawk at Saqqara.

W. C. HAYES, *Scepter of Egypt* I (New York, 1953), 320–6.

G. REISNER, *Canopics* (Cairo, 1967).

C. DOLZANI, *Vasi canopi* (Milan, 1982).

B. LÜSCHER, *Untersuchungen zu Ägyptischen Kanopenkästen* (Hildesheim, 1990).

A. DODSON, *The canopic equipment of the kings of Egypt* (London, 1994).

captives

The motif of the bound foreign captive is one of the most frequent and potent elements in ancient Egyptian iconography. The NARMER

palette and many other decorated royal arte-facts of the late Predynastic and Early Dynastic periods feature scenes of the king inflicting humiliation on foreign captives. The earliest example of the archetypal scene of the pharaoh striking a bound captive was found on the painted wall of Tomb 100 at HIERAKONPO-LIS in the late fourth millennium BC, and the same 'smiting scene' was still being depicted thousands of years later, on the pylons of Egyptian temples of the Greco-Roman period. On the Narmer macehead (now in the

Ashmolean Museum, Oxford), a depiction of an Early Dynastic royal ritual shows three bound captives running between two sets of three cairns (perhaps symbolizing Egypt's BORDERS).

Limestone and wooden statues of foreign captives have been found in the 5th- and 6th-Dynasty pyramid complexes of Raneferef, Nyuserra, Djedkara-Isesi, Unas, Teti, Pepy I and Pepy II at Saqqara and ABUSIR. The French archaeologist Jean-Philippe Lauer has suggested that there may have been as many as a hundred statues of captives in each pyramid complex, perhaps placed in lines along either side of the causeway linking the valley and mortuary temples. Later in the Pharaonic period, schematic representations of bound captives were used in cursing rituals, as in the case of five early 12th-Dynasty alabaster captive figures (now in the Egyptian Museum, Cairo) inscribed with hieratic EXECRATION TEXTS comprising lists of the names of Nubian princes accompanied by insults.

Throughout the Pharaonic and Greco-Roman periods the depiction of the bound captive continued to be a popular theme of temple and palace decoration. The inclusion of bound captives in the decoration of aspects of the fittings and furniture of royal palaces – particularly contexts where the king might

Detail of the relief decoration on the base of a statue of Rameses II at Luxor temple, showing three foreign captives. 19th Dynasty, c.1250 BC. (I.SHAW)

place his feet, such as painted pavements and footstools — served to reinforce the pharaoh's total suppression of foreigners and probably also symbolized the elements of 'unrule' that the gods required the king to control. There are therefore a number of depictions in Greco-Roman temples showing lines of gods capturing birds, wild animals and foreigners in clap-nets (see HUNTING). REKHYT birds were also sometimes used as symbols of foreign captives and subject peoples.

The captives' role as metaphors for the containment of the forces of chaos is also to be seen in the necropolis seal used in the Valley of the Kings, which consists of a depiction of ANUBIS surmounting nine foreign captives representing the dangers threatening royal tombs. Many of the reliefs in New Kingdom temples list the foreign peoples and cities whom the Egyptians had conquered (or would have liked to conquer), often writing the names of the polities inside schematic depictions of bound captives.

J.-P. LAUER and J. LECLANT, 'Découverte de statues de prisonniers au temple de la pyramide de Pépi Ier', *RdE* 21 (1969), 55–62.

M. VERNER, 'Les statuettes de prisonniers en bois d'Abousir', *RdE* 36 (1985), 145–52.

G. POSENER, *Cinq figures d'envoûtement* (Cairo, 1987).

R. H. WILKINSON, *Reading Egyptian art* (London, 1992), 18–19.

Carter, Howard (1874–1939)

Born in Kensington, the son of Samuel John Carter (an animal painter), it was his talent as a draughtsman that enabled Carter to join the Archaeological Survey of Egypt in 1891, when he was only seventeen. He received his training as an excavator and epigrapher from some of the most important Egyptologists of the late nineteenth century, including Gaston MASPERO and Flinders PETRIE, with whom he worked at EL-AMARNA in 1892. Between 1893 and 1899 he worked as a draughtsman for Edouard Naville at DEIR EL-BAHRI, and in 1899 he was appointed Inspector General of the monuments of Upper Egypt, in which capacity he installed the first electric lights in the VALLEY OF THE KINGS and the temples at ABU SIMBEL. In 1903 he resigned from the Egyptian Antiquities Service after a dispute with French tourists at Saqqara. He then worked for four years as a painter and dealer in antiquities, until the offer of finance from Lord Carnarvon enabled him to return to excavation in the Valley of the Kings. Although he discovered six royal tombs at Thebes, his most famous achievement was undoubtedly the unearthing of the virtually

undisturbed tomb of TUTANKHAMUN, in November 1922, finally rewarding Carnarvon for his support over the preceding fifteen years. Carter spent the remaining seventeen years of his life recording and analysing the funerary equipment from the tomb, a task which is still incomplete.

H. CARTER and P. E. NEWBERRY, *The tomb of Thoutmôsis IV* (London, 1904).

H. CARTER, *The tomb of Tut.Ankh.Amen*, 3 vols (London, 1923–33).

T. G. H. JAMES, *Howard Carter: the path to Tutankhamun* (London, 1992).

N. REEVES and J. TAYLOR, *Howard Carter before Tutankhamun* (London, 1992).

Gilded cartonnage mummy mask of an unnamed woman, whose vulture headdress almost certainly indicates that she was a princess. Middle Kingdom, c.1900 BC, H. 61 cm. (EA29770)

cartonnage

Material consisting of layers of linen or papyrus stiffened with GESSO (plaster) and often decorated with paint or gilding. It was most commonly used for making mummy MASKS, mummy cases, anthropoid coffins and other funerary items. The earliest cartonnage mummy masks date to the First Intermediate Period, although a few surviving examples of Old Kingdom mummies have thin layers of plaster over the linen wrappings covering the face, perhaps representing an earlier stage in the development of the material.

J. H. TAYLOR, 'The development of cartonnage cases', *Mummies and magic*, ed. S. D'Auria, P. Lacovara and C. Roehrig (Boston, 1988), 166–8.

—, *Egyptian coffins* (Princes Risborough, 1989), 23–4, 47–53.

cartouche (Egyptian *shenu*)

Elliptical outline representing a length of knotted rope with which certain elements of the Egyptian ROYAL TITULARY were surrounded. The French word *cartouche*, meaning 'gun cartridge', was originally given to the royal frame by Napoleon's soldiers and savants,

Detail of the façade of the 'great temple' at Abu Simbel, consisting of a cartouche containing the prenomen of Rameses II (User-Maat-Ra). 19th Dynasty, 1279–1213 BC. (I. SHAW)

because of its cartridge-like shape. From the 4th Dynasty (2613–2494 BC) onwards the line was drawn around the king's 'throne name' (prenomen or *nesw-bit*) and 'birth name' (nomen or *sa Ra*). It proved invaluable to early scholars such as Jean-François Champollion who were attempting to decipher the hieroglyphic script, in that it was presumed to indicate which groups of signs were the royal names.

The cartouche was essentially an elongated form of the SHEN hieroglyph, and both signs signified the concept of 'encircling protection' denoted by a coil of rope folded and tied at the end. The physical extension of the original *shen* sign into a cartouche was evidently necessitated by the increasing length of royal names. The symbolic protection afforded by a cartouche, which may have been a diagram of the universe being encircled by the sun, is graphically illustrated by the choice of this sign for the shape of some 18th-and 19th-Dynasty sarcophagi, such as that of Merenptah (1213–1203 BC). Some of the early 18th-Dynasty burial chambers in the Valley of the Kings, as in the tomb of THUTMOSE III (1479–1425 BC) (KV34), were also cartouche-shaped, thus allowing the king's

mummy, like his name, to be physically surrounded by the cartouche.

W. BARTA, 'Der Königsring als Symbol zyklischer Widerkehr', *ZÄS* 98 (1970), 5–16.

P. KAPLONY, 'Königsring', *Lexikon der Ägyptologie* III, ed. W. Helck, E. Otto and W. Westendorf (Wiesbaden, 1980), 610–26.

R. H. WILKINSON, *Reading Egyptian art* (London, 1992), 194–5.

cat

Important both as a domestic pet and as a symbol of deities such as BASTET and RA (the 'great cat of Heliopolis'). There were two indigenous feline species in ancient Egypt: the jungle cat (*Felis chaus*) and the African wild cat

Figure of a cat sacred to the goddess Bastet, wearing protective wedjat-*eye amulet. Late Period, after 600 BC, bronze with gold rings, H. 38 cm. (EA64391)*

(*Felis silvestris libyca*), the former being found only in Egypt and southeastern Asia. The earliest Egyptian remains of a cat were found in a tomb at the Predynastic site of Mostagedda, near modern Asyut, suggesting that the Egyptians were already keeping cats as pets in the late fourth millennium BC.

The Egyptian word for 'cat' was the onomatopoeic term *miw*, which, although not mentioned in the PYRAMID TEXTS, found its way into various personal names from the Old Kingdom onwards, including the 22nd-Dynasty pharaoh known as Pamiu or Pimay, literally 'the tomcat' (773–767 BC). The earliest Egyptian depiction of the cat took the form of three hieroglyphic symbols, each representing seated cats. These formed part of the phrase 'Lord of the City of Cats' inscribed on a stone block from EL-LISHT, which may date as early as the reign of PEPY II (2278–2184 BC). From the 12th Dynasty onwards, cats were increasingly depicted in the painted decoration of private tombs, either participating in the scenes of HUNTING and fowling in the marshes or seated beneath the chair of the owner.

It was in the funerary texts of the New Kingdom that the cat achieved full apotheosis: in the *Amduat* (see FUNERARY TEXTS) it is portrayed as a demon decapitating bound CAPTIVES and in the *Litany of Ra* it appears to be a personification of the sun-god himself, battling with the evil serpent-god APOPHIS. As a result of its connection with the sun-god, the cat was depicted on a number of Ramesside stelae found in the Theban region. From the Late Period onwards, large numbers of sacred cats were mummified and deposited in underground galleries at such sites as Bubastis (TELL BASTA) and SPEOS ARTEMIDOS (see also SACRED ANIMALS), and numerous bronze votive statuettes have also survived, including the 'Gayer–Anderson cat' in the collection of the British Museum.

L. STORK, 'Katze', *Lexikon der Ägyptologie* III, ed. W. HELCK, E. Otto and W. Westendorf (Wiesbaden, 1980), 367–70.

P. L. ARMITAGE and J. CLUTTON-BROCK, 'A radiological and histological investigation into the mummification of cats from ancient Egypt', *Journal of Archaeological Science* 8 (1981), 185–96.

J. MALEK, *The cat in ancient Egypt* (London, 1993).

cataracts, Nile

Rocky areas of rapids in the middle Nile valley, caused by abrupt geological changes. There are six cataracts in the section of the Nile that passes through the area of ancient Nubia, between Aswan and Khartoum.

cattle *see* ANIMAL HUSBANDRY

cavetto cornice

Distinctive form of concave moulding, projecting from the tops of many Egyptian STE-LAE, PYLONS, ALTARS or walls. The characteristic hollow, quarter-circle shape perhaps derives from the appearance of the tops of fronds of vegetation used in Predynastic huts, before the emergence of mud-brick or stone architecture.

S. CLARKE and R. ENGELBACH, *Ancient Egyptian masonry: the building craft* (London, 1930), 5–6.
[reprinted as *Ancient Egyptian construction and architecture* (New York, 1990)]

cemeteries *see* MASTABA and PYRAMIDS

C Group (C Horizon)

Nubian cultural entity roughly synchronous with the period in Egyptian history between the Old and New Kingdoms (*c*.2494–1550 BC). The indigenous C-Group people of NUBIA were subjected to varying degrees of social and economic influence from their powerful northern neighbours. Their princi-

C-Group bowl of polished incised ware from Faras, c.2340–1550 BC, H. 8.1 cm. (EA51230)

pal archaeological characteristics included handmade black-topped pottery vessels bearing incised decoration filled with white pigment, as well as artefacts imported from Egypt.

Their subsistence pattern was dominated by cattle-herding, and their social system was essentially tribal. In the early 12th Dynasty the C-Group territory in Lower Nubia was taken over by the Egyptians, who established a string of FORTRESSES between the 2nd and 3rd Nile cataracts. It has been suggested that one of the effects of the Egyptian occupation in the Middle Kingdom may have been to prevent the C Group from developing contacts with the more sophisticated KERMA culture that was developing in Upper Nubia.

B. TRIGGER, *Nubia under the pharaohs* (London, 1978).
J. H. TAYLOR, *Egypt and Nubia* (London, 1991).

Champollion, Jean-François (1790–1832)

French linguist and Egyptologist who was responsible for the most important achievement in the history of the study of ancient Egypt: the decipherment of HIEROGLYPHS. He is sometimes described as Champollion 'le jeune', because his brother, Jacques-Joseph Champollion-Figeac, was also a scholar. Born at Figeac, he was sent to the Lyceum at Grenoble at the age of eleven and had already delivered a paper on the ancient Egyptian LANGUAGE by the time he left in 1807. He subsequently studied under the pioneering Egyptologist Silvestre de Saçy at the Collège de France in Paris.

Equipped with an excellent knowledge of Hebrew, Coptic, Arabic, Syriac and Chaldaean, he embarked on the task of deciphering hieroglyphs, using the ROSETTA STONE (a Ptolemaic inscription consisting of the same decree written in Greek, DEMOTIC and hieroglyphics) as his principal guide. After examining Egyptian antiquities in various European collections, Champollion undertook a detailed survey of Egypt, along with Ippolito ROSELLINI in 1828–9. Although his *Lettre à M. Dacier* of 1822 is usually regarded as the turning point in his studies, he did not achieve a satisfactory understanding of the language until the completion of his grammar and dictionary shortly before his death from a stroke in 1832.

J.-F. CHAMPOLLION, *Lettre à M. Dacier rélative à l'alphabet des hiéroglyphes phonétiques* (Paris, 1822).
—, *Monuments de l'Egypte et de la Nubie*, 4 vols (Paris, 1835–47).

Fragment of wall-painting from the tomb-chapel of Nebamun at Thebes, showing two chariots. The upper one is pulled by two horses, whereas the lower one appears to be drawn by mules. 18th Dynasty, c.1400 BC, painted plaster, H. 43 cm. (EA37982)

F. LL. GRIFFITH, 'The decipherment of the hieroglyphs', *JEA* 37 (1951), 38–46.
M. POURPOINT, *Champollion et l'énigme égyptienne* (Paris, 1963).

chantress *see* CULT SINGERS AND TEMPLE MUSICIANS

chariot

Although the origins of the horse-drawn chariot have proved difficult to ascertain, its arrival in Egypt can be fairly reliably dated to the Second Intermediate Period (1650–1550 BC). The surviving textual and pictorial evidence suggests that the chariot (*wereret* or *merkebet*) arrived in Egypt at roughly the same time as the HYKSOS. It consisted of a light wooden semicircular, open-backed framework, furnished with an axle and a pair of four- or six-spoked wheels. A long pole attached to the axle enabled the chariot to be drawn by a pair of horses. Its importance as an innovative item of military technology was based on its use as a mobile platform for archers, allowing the enemy to be bombarded by arrows from many different directions. Although the chariot is often portrayed in temple and tomb decoration from the New Kingdom (1550–1069 BC) onwards, only eleven examples have survived, four of which are from the tomb of TUTANKHAMUN. A Ramesside papyrus in the British Museum (P. Anastasi I) provides an insight into the maintenance of chariotry with a description of an Egyptian charioteer's visit to a repair shop in the Levantine coastal city of Joppa.

The chariot was not only used in battle by the *maryannu*, an élite corps of the Egyptian army in the New Kingdom, it was also regarded as an essential part of the royal regalia. Depictions of the king charging enemies in his chariot became a common feature of the exterior walls of temples as symbols of 'the containment of unrule', roughly comparable with the more ancient theme of the king smiting foreigners with a mace (see KINGSHIP).

M. A. LITTAUER and J. H. CROUWEL, *Wheeled vehicles and ridden animals in the Ancient Near East* (Leiden and Cologne, 1979).

A. R. SCHULMAN, 'Chariots, chariotry and the Hyksos', *JSSEA* 10 (1980), 105–53.

M. A. LITTAUER and J. H. CROUWEL, *Chariots and related equipment from the tomb of Tut'ankhamun* (Oxford, 1985).

P. R. S. MOOREY, 'The emergence of the light, horse-drawn chariot in the Near East c.2000–1500 B.C.', *WA* 18/2 (1986), 196–215.

Cheops *see* KHUFU

Chephren *see* KHAFRA

C Horizon *see* C GROUP

children

A great deal of evidence has survived from Egyptian medical and magical documents concerning precautions taken by WOMEN to ensure rapid conception, safe pregnancy and successful childbirth. The graves of children have survived in various cemeteries from the Predynastic period onwards, and attempts have been made to assess the rate of infant mortality on the basis of the ratios of adult to child burials, as well as the study of the human remains themselves. Undoubtedly infant mortality was high, but families were nevertheless fairly large, averaging perhaps at about five children who would actually have reached adolescence (assuming the early death of three or four offspring).

Many surviving reliefs, paintings and sculptures depict women suckling their babies, including the famous depiction of THUTMOSE III being suckled by the goddess ISIS (in the form of a tree) in his tomb in the Valley of the Kings (KV34). The motif of the king being suckled by his mother Isis or HATHOR was an archetypal element of Egyptian religion, perhaps providing some of the inspiration for the image of Madonna and Child in the Christian era. A number of magical spells were evidently intended to restore mother's milk, and a

similar purpose may have been served by the ceramic vessels depicting nursing mothers, which have survived from the Middle Kingdom (2055–1650 BC) onwards. As far as the élite were concerned, wet-nurses were often employed, especially by the women of the royal family; the position of 'royal wetnurse' was evidently a prestigious office, often entitling the individual to be depicted in the tomb of the royal individual whom she had nursed.

From at least the Old Kingdom onwards (2686–2181 BC), both boys and girls often wore a SIDELOCK OF YOUTH, marking them out as pre-pubescent. The sidelock, essentially a tress of hair hanging over the ear, was worn until about the age of ten or more. Both infants and child-gods such as Harpocrates (see HORUS) were regularly depicted with one finger in their mouths as a symbol of their childishness. Nakedness was also particularly common among children, judging from the surviving paintings and reliefs of the Pharaonic period. It is also clear from such funerary art that children, as in all ages, played many GAMES and sports, ranging from dancing and wrestling to ball games and races. A number of balls have survived, but the identification of TOYS has proved more controversial, given the tendency for them to be confused with religious and magical paraphernalia; a 'doll' for instance might equally well have erotic or ritualistic significance (see SEXUALITY).

See also CIRCUMCISION; CLOTHING; EDUCATION; MAMMISI; MEDICINE.

E. FEUCHT, 'Kind', *Lexikon der Ägyptologie* III, ed. W. Helck, E. Otto and W. Westendorf (Wiesbaden, 1980), 424–37.

G. PINCH, 'Childbirth and female figurines at Deir el-Medina and el-Amarna', *Orientalia* 52 (1983), 405–14.

S. WHALE, *The family in the Eighteenth Dynasty of Egypt: a study of the representation of the family in private tombs* (Sydney, 1989).

R. M. and J. J. JANSSEN, *Growing up in ancient Egypt* (London, 1990).

E. STROUHAL, *Life in ancient Egypt* (Cambridge, 1992), 11–29.

G. ROBINS, *Women in ancient Egypt* (London, 1993), 75–91.

chronology

Modern Egyptologists' chronologies of ancient Egypt combine three basic approaches. First, there are 'relative' dating methods, such as stratigraphic excavation, or the 'sequence dating' of artefacts, which was invented by Flinders PETRIE in 1899. Second, there are so-called 'absolute' chronologies, based on calendrical and astronomical records obtained from ancient texts (see ASTRONOMY AND ASTROLOGY and CALENDAR). Finally, there are 'radiometric' methods (principally radiocarbon dating and thermoluminescence), by means of which particular types of artefacts or organic remains can be assigned dates in terms of the measurement of radioactive decay or accumulation. The ancient Egyptians dated important political and religious events not according to the number of years that had elpased since a single fixed point in history (such as the birth of Christ in the modern western calendar) but in terms of the years since the accession of each current king (reg-

King list from the temple of Rameses II at Abydos, the lower register of which repeats the birth and throne names of Rameses II. 19th Dynasty, c.1250 BC, painted limestone, H. 1.38 m. (EA117)

nal years). Dates were therefore recorded in the following typical format: 'day three of the second month of *peret* in the third year of Menkheperra (Thutmose III)'. The situation, however, is slightly confused by the fact that the dates cited in the 5th-Dynasty KING LIST known as the PALERMO STONE appear to refer to the number of biennial cattle censuses (*hesbet*) rather than to the number of years that the king had reigned, therefore the number of 'years' in the date has to be doubled to find out the actual number of regnal years.

The names and relative dates of the various rulers and DYNASTIES have been obtained from a number of textual sources. These range from the *Aegyptiaca*, a history compiled by an Egyptian priest called MANETHO in the early third century BC, to the much earlier KING LISTS, mainly recorded on the walls of tombs and temples but also in the form of papyri (as with the TURIN ROYAL CANON) or remote desert rock-carvings (as with the Wadi Hammamat list). It is usually presumed that Manetho himself used king lists of these types as his sources.

The 'traditional' absolute chronologies tend to rely on complex webs of textual references, combining such elements as names, dates and genealogical information into an overall historical framework which is more reliable in some periods than in others. The 'intermediate periods' have proved to be particularly awkward, partly because there was often more than one ruler or dynasty reigning simultaneously in different parts of the country. The surviving records of observations of the heliacal rising of the dog star Sirius (SOPDET) serve both as the linchpin of the reconstruction of the Egyptian calendar and as its essential link with the chronology as a whole.

The relationship between the calendrical and radiometric chronological systems has been relatively ambivalent over the years. Since the late 1940s, when a series of Egyptian artefacts were used as a bench-mark in order to assess the reliability of the newly invented radiocarbon dating technique, a consensus has emerged that the two systems are broadly in line. The major problem, however, is that the traditional calendrical system of dating, whatever its failings, virtually always has a smaller margin of error than radiocarbon dates, which are necessarily quoted in terms of a broad band of dates (i.e. one or two standard deviations), never capable of pinpointing the construction of a building or the making of an artefact to a specific year (or even a specific decade). The prehistory of Egypt, on the other hand, has benefited greatly from the application of radiometric dating, since it was previously reliant on relative dating methods. The radiometric techniques have made it possible not only to place Petrie's sequence dates within a framework of absolute dates (however imprecise) but also to push the chronology back into the earlier Neolithic and Palaeolithic periods.

R. PARKER, 'The calendars and chronology', *The Legacy of Egypt*, ed. J. R. Harris (Oxford, 1971), 13–26.

R. KRAUSS, *Sothis- und Monddaten: Studien zur astronomischen und technischen Chronologie Altägyptens* (Hildesheim, 1985).
I. M. E. SHAW, 'Egyptian chronology and the Irish Oak calibration', *JNES* 44/4 (1985), 295–317.
K. A. KITCHEN, 'The chronology of ancient Egypt', *WA* 23 (1991), 201–8.

chthonic

Term used to describe phenomena relating to the underworld and the earth, including deities such as GEB, AKER and OSIRIS.

cippus see HORUS

circumcision

The Greek historian Herodotus mentions that the Egyptians practised circumcision 'for cleanliness' sake, preferring to be clean rather than comely'; and the practice may well have been inaugurated purely for reasons of hygiene. Nevertheless, depictions of certain uncircumcised individuals in the decoration of Old Kingdom mastaba tombs suggest that the operation was not universal.

The act of circumcision may have been performed as part of a ceremony akin to the rites of passage in the 'age-grade systems' of many band and tribal societies. A stele of the First Intermediate Period (2181–2055 BC) mentions the circumcision of 120 boys at one time,

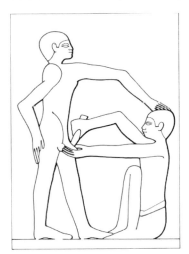

Detail of a relief from the mastaba tomb of Ankhmahor at Saqqara, showing a priest performing an act of circumcision on a boy. 6th Dynasty, c.2300 BC.

which perhaps implies a group of individuals of varying ages. It has been suggested, however, that boys would usually have been about fourteen years old when they were circumcised. The mummy of a young prince aged about eleven, which was found in the tomb of Amenhotep II, is uncircumcised and retains the SIDELOCK OF YOUTH hairstyle, which was therefore perhaps worn by young boys only in the years before circumcision.

The ceremony itself, for which the Egyptian term was *sebi*, was carried out using a curved flint knife similar to those employed by embalmers. On the basis of this archaizing equipment, it has been argued that circumcision was essentially a religious act for the Egyptians. On the other hand, it may have simply been a practical expedient, given the fact that metal knives would hardly have surpassed a newly-knapped flint in terms of sharpness. Moreover, considering the lack of antiseptics, if the cut was as clean and rapid as possible, the healing process would probably have been more likely to be successful.

The 6th-Dynasty mastaba of the vizier Ankhmahor at Saqqara contains a circumcision scene, which appears to show both the cutting and the application of some sort of ointment, although the latter is unclear. From at least the Late Period onwards (747–332 BC) it became compulsory for priests to be circumcised, as part of the purification necessary for the performance of their temple duties, and this further illustrates that it was not compulsory for children to be circumcised at adolescence. In the Roman period, a ban on circumcision (from which only priests were exempt) appears to have been introduced.

The Egyptians themselves may have regarded circumcision as an ethnic 'identifier', judging from depictions of foreigners in battle scenes of the New Kingdom, such as those depicted in the mortuary temple of Rameses III at MEDINET HABU. In enumerating enemy dead, the Egyptians differentiated between the circumcised Semites, whose hands were cut off, and the uncircumcised foes – notably Libyans – whose penises were removed for the counting.

Although Strouhal suggests that some ancient Egyptian texts refer to 'uncircumcised' virgins and the Roman writer Strabo mentions that female circumcision was practised by the Egyptians, no physical evidence of the operation has yet been found on surviving female mummies.

F. JONCKHEERE, 'La circoncision des anciens Egyptiens', *Centaurus* I (1951), 212–34.
O. BARDIS, 'Circumcision in ancient Egypt', *Indiana Journal for the History of Medicine* 12/1 (1967), 22–3.

E. STROUHAL, *Life in ancient Egypt* (Cambridge, 1992), 28–9.

Cleopatra

Name given to seven Ptolemaic queens of Egypt. The last of these, Cleopatra VII (51–30 BC), was the most illustrious. Clearly intelligent and politically astute, she was reputedly the only Ptolemaic ruler to have learnt the Egyptian language. Surprisingly, however, in view of the later eulogies of poets and playwrights such as Shakespeare, her surviving portraits suggest that the historical Cleopatra was not especially beautiful.

Cleopatra VII first shared a COREGENCY with her father Ptolemy XII (80–51 BC) and then with her brother Ptolemy XIII (51–47 BC) who ousted her from power for a time in 48 BC. Her links with Rome were first forged through Pompey, who had been appointed as her guardian on the death of her father, when he had become involved in the financial affairs of the Ptolemaic court. Defeated by Caesar at Pharsalia in 48 BC, Pompey fled to Egypt, where he was assassinated. In the same year Caesar entered Egypt and restored Cleopatra to the throne as coregent with her second brother, Ptolemy XIV (47–44 BC), whom she married.

In 47 BC she bore a son, Ptolemy Caesarion, who she claimed had been fathered by Caesar. She visited Caesar in Rome in 46 BC, returning after his assassination, whereupon she bestowed a similar fate on her brother, replacing him with the young Caesarion; her various political manoeuvres then led to her being summoned to meet with Mark Antony at Tarsus. He spent the winter at Alexandria, after which Cleopatra bore him twins; shortly afterwards they were officially married, and subsequently set about the business of using one another for their own political ends.

In 34 BC, in the so-called 'Donations of Alexandria', Mark Antony divided various parts of the eastern Roman empire between Cleopatra and her children, legitimating this action to the Senate by informing them that he was simply installing client rulers. However, Octavian (later Augustus), who was the brother of Mark Antony's Roman wife, led a propaganda campaign against his brother-in-law and Cleopatra, dwelling on their supposed licentious behaviour in Alexandria, and in 32 BC Rome declared war on Cleopatra. The following year Octavian defeated Mark Antony at the naval battle of Actium, partly because Cleopatra's fleet unexpectedly withdrew from the engagement. Octavian pursued them both into Egypt, but Antony committed suicide and, on 10 August 30 BC, Cleopatra followed

Figures of Cleopatra VII (left) and her son by Julius Caesar, Caesarion (right), making offerings. From the south (rear) wall of the temple of Hathor at Dendera. (P. T. NICHOLSON)

suit, preferring death to the humiliation of a Roman triumph. Octavian then had her eldest son, Ptolemy Caesarion, killed. He appointed himself pharaoh on 30 August, thenceforth treating Egypt as his own private estate.

J. QUAEGEBEUR, 'Cleopatra VII and the cults of the Ptolemaic queens', *Cleopatra's Egypt: Age of the Ptolemies*, ed. R. S. Bianchi (New York, 1988), 41–54.

L. HUGHES-HALLETT, *Cleopatra* (London, 1990).

J. WHITEHORNE, *Cleopatras* (London, 1994).

clepsydra ('water clock')

Device for measuring time, consisting of a water-filled vessel (usually of stone, copper or pottery) with a hole in the base through which the water gradually drained away. The earliest surviving examples date to the 18th Dynasty (1550–1295 BC). There are a variety of fragments of stone clepsydrae in the collection of the British Museum, including part of a basalt vessel dating to the reign of Philip Arrhidaeus (c.320 BC), which is marked with vertical lines of small holes relating to the twelve hours of the night. Part of a cubit rod in the Metropolitan Museum, New York, bears the words 'The hour according to the cubit: a jar(?) of copper filled with water...', thus implying that the rod was dipped into a copper vessel in order to read the time as the water level fell.

B. COTTERELL, F. P. DICKSON and J. KAMMINGA, 'Ancient Egyptian water-clocks: a reappraisal', *Journal of Archaeological Science* 13 (1986), 31–50.

G. HÖLBL, 'Eine ägyptische Wasseruhr aus Ephesus', *Antike Welt* 17/1 (1986), 59–60.

S COUCHOUD, 'Calcul d'un horloge à eau', *BSEG* 12 (1988), 25–34.

clothing

Despite the fact that arid conditions have facilitated the survival of a number of items of clothing, primarily from tombs of the New Kingdom, textiles have so far not been studied in sufficient detail. Modern studies of ancient Egyptian clothing are therefore still largely based on the study of wall-paintings, reliefs and sculptures.

In general Egyptian clothing was very simple: men working in the fields or involved in craftwork often wore little more than a loincloth or short kilt, although shirt-like garments have survived from the Early Dynastic period onwards, the earliest example being a linen dress/shirt from Tarkhan in Lower Egypt (c.2800 BC). Clothing can often be used as a reliable chronological guide in that the Egyptian élite of most periods were generally subject to changes in fashion. The dress of courtiers of Ramesside times, for instance, could be extremely elaborate and the men often wore pleated kilts with unusual apron-like arrangements at the front.

During the Old Kingdom, women (and goddesses) are usually portrayed wearing a kind of sheath-dress with broad shoulder straps, but by the New Kingdom this had evolved into a type of dress with only one strap, and by the reign of Amenhotep III (1390–1352 BC) more diaphanous garments were being worn. Fine clothing became one of the specialist products for which Egypt was known in Roman times. The colourful nature of the fabrics used in daily life (or perhaps the use of bead netting over dresses) is illustrated by the figures of offering bearers from the tomb of Meketra (TT280) dating to the early Middle Kingdom.

The excavation of the Theban tomb of the architect Kha (TT8) led to the discovery of twenty-six knee-length shirts and about fifty loincloths, including short triangular pieces

of material that would have been worn in the context of agricultural or building work. Seventeen heavier linen tunics were provided for winter wear, while two items described as 'tablecloths' were among Kha's wife's clothes. He and his wife each had their own individual laundrymarks, and it is known that there were professional launderers attached to the workmen's village at DEIR EL-MEDINA where Kha and his family lived. A few loincloths made of leather rather than linen have also survived, some particularly fine examples having been excavated from the well-preserved tomb of MAIHERPRI in the Valley of the Kings (KV36).

The tomb of TUTANKHAMUN (KV62) contained a large selection of textiles, including children's clothing. So far little of his wardrobe has been scientifically examined, but some of the linen contains gold thread, and one kilt was made up of colourful beadwork. Decorated textiles became more common in the New Kingdom, but were still not common, some of the best examples deriving from

LEFT *Earliest surviving Egyptian garment: linen shirt or dress, comprising a pleated yoke and sleeves attached to a skirt with weft fringe, excavated in 1912 from mastaba 2050 at Tarkhan. 1st Dynasty, reign of Djet, c.2980 BC, L. of sleeve (neck edge to wrist) 58 cm. (PETRIE MUSEUM, 28614Bi)*

BELOW *Triangular linen loincloths from the tomb of Tutankhamun. 18th Dynasty, c.1330 BC, (CAIRO, NO.50b)*

the tomb of Thutmose IV (1400–1390 BC, KV43) and include crowned *uraei* (see WADJYT). Howard Carter believed these to be ceremonial garments, but more recently it has been suggested that they may have been used as vessel covers.

Priests, viziers and certain other types of officials all marked their status with particular items or styles of dress. The vizier, for instance, was usually depicted wearing a long robe which came up to his armpits, while the *sem*-priest was usually shown wearing a leopard-skin.

R. HALL, *Egyptian textiles* (Princes Risborough, 1986).

G. VOGELSANG-EASTWOOD, *Pharaonic Egyptian clothing* (Leiden, 1993).

cobra

Type of snake that served as the sacred image of WADJYT, patron deity of the town of Buto (TELL EL-FARA'IN) in the Delta, who came to represent Lower Egypt, in contrast to the Upper Egyptian vulture-goddess NEKHBET. As the ruler of the two lands, the king included the cobra (*iaret*) and the vulture among his titles and insignia (see CROWNS AND ROYAL REGALIA and ROYAL TITULARY). The *uraeus* was sometimes described as 'the great enchantress' (*weret hekaw*) and could be depicted as a cobra with a human head (as on the golden shrine of Tutankhamun). Even before its identification with the king, the cobra's protective attributes were recognized, and it was identified as the EYE OF RA, sometimes shown protecting his solar disc by spitting fire and venom. Pairs of cobras also guarded the gates that divided the individual hours of the underworld in the *Book of Gates* (see FUNERARY TEXTS); this is presumed to have been the function of the gilded wooden cobra found in the tomb of Tutankhamun.

H.-W. FISCHER-ELFERT, 'Uto', *Lexikon der Ägyptologie* VI, ed. W. Helck, E. Otto and W. Westendorf (Wiesbaden, 1986), 906–11.

S. JOHNSON, *The cobra goddess of ancient Egypt* (London, 1990).

coffins and sarcophagi

The term 'coffin' is usually applied to the rectangular or anthropoid container in which the Egyptians placed the mummified body, whereas the word 'sarcophagus' (Greek: 'flesh-eating') is used to refer only to the stone outer container, invariably encasing one or more coffins. The distinction made between these two items of Egyptian funerary equipment is therefore essentially an artificial one, since both shared the same role of protecting the corpse. In terms of decoration and shape,

coffins and sarcophagi drew on roughly the same iconographic and stylistic repertoire.

The earliest burials in Egypt contain no coffins and are naturally desiccated by the hot sand. The separation of the corpse from the surrounding sand by the use of a coffin or sarcophagus ironically led to the deterioration of the body, perhaps stimulating developments in MUMMIFICATION. The religious purpose of the coffin was to ensure the well-being of the deceased in the afterlife, literally providing a 'house' for the KA.

The earliest coffins were baskets or simple plank constructions in which the body was placed in a flexed position. From these developed the vaulted house-shaped coffins that remained in use into the 4th Dynasty (2613–2494 BC). At around this time the Egyptians began to bury the corpse in an extended position, perhaps because the increasingly common practice of evisceration (see CANOPIC JARS) made such an arrangement more suitable. By the end of the Old Kingdom (2181 BC) food offerings were being painted on the inside of coffins as an extra means of providing sustenance for the deceased in the event of the tomb chapel being destroyed or neglected. In the Old and Middle Kingdoms, a pair of eyes was often painted on the side of the coffin that faced east when it was placed in the tomb; it was evidently believed that the deceased could therefore look out of the coffin to see his or her offerings and the world from which he or she had passed, as well as to view the rising sun.

Decorated coffins became still more important in the First Intermediate Period (2181–2055 BC), when many tombs contained little mural decoration (see BENI HASAN). It was thus essential that coffins themselves should incorporate the basic elements of the tomb, and by the Middle Kingdom (2055–1650 BC) they often incorporated revised extracts of the PYRAMID TEXTS, known as the COFFIN TEXTS. This change reflects the increased identification of the afterlife with OSIRIS, rather than the sun-god RA (see FUNERARY TEXTS).

Anthropoid coffins first appeared in the 12th Dynasty (1985–1795 BC), apparently serving as substitute bodies lest the original be destroyed. With the New Kingdom (1550–1069 BC), this form of coffin became more popular and the shape became identified with Osiris himself, his BEARD and crossed arms sometimes being added. The feathered, rishi coffins of the 17th and early 18th Dynasty were once thought to depict the wings of the goddess ISIS, embracing her husband Osiris, but are now considered by some scholars to refer to the BA bird. Rectangular coffins were effectively replaced by anthropoid types in the 18th Dynasty, but some of their decorative elements were retained.

In the Third Intermediate Period (1069–747 BC), coffins, papyri and stelae became the main vehicles for funerary scenes that had previously been carved and painted on the walls of tomb chapels. The principal feature of most of the new scenes depicted on coffins was the Osirian and solar mythology surrounding the concept of rebirth (see OSIRIS and RA), including the judgement of the deceased before Osiris and the journey into the underworld, the voyage of the SOLAR BARK and parts of the *Litany of Ra*. Among the new scenes introduced in the decoration of coffins and on funerary papyri was the depiction of the separation of the earth-god Geb from the sky-goddess NUT.

The excavation of the 21st- and 22nd-Dynasty royal tombs at TANIS has provided a number of examples of the royal coffins of the period (although the sarcophagi were sometimes re-used from the New Kingdom). The cache of mummies of high priests of Amun at DEIR EL-BAHRI has also yielded a large number of private coffins of the 21st Dynasty (1069–945 BC). It was also from the end of the New Kingdom onwards that the interiors of coffins began to be decorated again; beneath the lid – especially in the 22nd Dynasty (945–715 BC) – there was often a representation of Nut, while the 'goddess of the west' (HATHOR) or the DJED PILLAR began to be portrayed on the coffin floor. During the Late Period extracts from the BOOK OF THE DEAD were sometimes also inscribed inside the coffin.

In the 25th Dynasty a new repertoire of coffin types, usually consisting of sets of two or three (including an inner case with pedestal, an intermediate anthropoid case and a 'four-poster' or anthropoid outer coffin), was introduced, becoming established practice by the 26th Dynasty. Late Period coffins were also characterized by archaism, involving the re-

Painted wooden coffin and mummy of an unnamed Theban priestess. 21st Dynasty, c.1000 BC, H. 1.83 m. (EA48791–2)

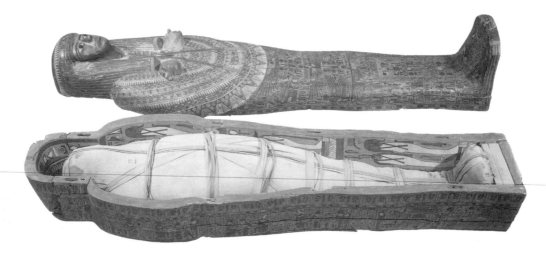

introduction of earlier styles of coffin decoration, such as the provision of the eye panel.

There are comparatively few excavated burials dating from c.525 to 350 BC, but more coffins have survived from the succeeding phase (30th Dynasty and early Ptolemaic period), when they typically have disproportionately large heads and wigs. During the early Ptolemaic period many mummies were provided with cartonnage MASKS and plaques, fixed on to the body by strips of linen.

A. NIWIŃSKI, 'Zur Datierung und Herkunft der altägyptischen Särge', *Bibliotheca Orientalia* 42 (1985), 494–508.

H. WILLEMS, *Chests of life: a study of the typology and conceptual development of Middle Kingdom standard class coffins* (Leiden, 1988).

A. NIWIŃSKI, *21st Dynasty coffins from Thebes* (Mainz, 1988).

J. H. TAYLOR, *Egyptian coffins* (Aylesbury, 1989).

N. A. SILBERMAN, 'Coffins in human shape: a history of anthropoid sarcophagi', *BAR* 16/4 (1990), 52–4.

G. LAPP, *Typologie der Särge und Sargkammern* (Heidelberg, 1993).

Coffin Texts

Term referring to a group of over a thousand spells, selections from which were inscribed on coffins during the Middle Kingdom, particularly the 11th and 12th Dynasties (2055–1795 BC). Many of the Coffin Texts were derived from the PYRAMID TEXTS, a sequence of often-obscure spells carved on the internal walls of the Old Kingdom pyramids.

During the Old Kingdom the afterlife had been the prerogative of the king, who in death was identified with OSIRIS and transformed into a god. For this reason Old Kingdom courtiers sought burial close to the king, hoping for inclusion in his funerary cult so that they too might be granted some form of afterlife, although the best that they could hope for was a continuation of their earthly status. However, with the collapse of the Old Kingdom came greater self-reliance and with it a process which is sometimes described by Egyptologists as the DEMOCRATIZATION OF THE AFTERLIFE. This meant that everyone could have access to the afterlife, without being associated directly with the royal cult. These new aspirations of the deceased are set out in a collection of spells painted in cursive hieroglyphs inside the wooden coffin.

The Coffin Texts were intended to provide a guarantee of survival in the afterworld and some of them are the ancestors of spells found in the New Kingdom BOOK OF THE DEAD. They have titles such as the self-explanatory 'Not to rot and not to do work in the kingdom of the

dead', and 'Spell for not dying a second death', which was designed to prevent the deceased from being judged unfit to enter the kingdom of Osiris and so condemned to oblivion.

Both the Pyramid Texts and the Coffin Texts present more than one version of the destination of the deceased: they might travel the sky with the sun-god RA or, alternatively, might pass down into the underworld of Osiris. This latter view became increasingly common from the time of the Coffin Texts onwards, setting the scene for the funerary beliefs of the New Kingdom.

R. O. FAULKNER, *The Egyptian Coffin Texts*, 3 vols (Warminster, 1973–8).

A. J. SPENCER, *Death in ancient Egypt* (Harmondsworth, 1982), 141–2.

H. WILLEMS, *Chests of life: a study of the typology and conceptual development of Middle Kingdom standard class coffins* (Leiden, 1988), 244–9.

The internal decoration of the coffin of Gua, inscribed with extracts from the Coffin Texts. 12th Dynasty, c.1985–1795 BC, painted wood, from Deir el-Bersha, L. of coffin 2.6 m. (EA30840)

Colossi of Memnon

Two colossal seated statues of AMENHOTEP III (1390–1352 BC), carved from quartzite sandstone, which are located at the eastern end of the site of his much-plundered mortuary temple in western Thebes; each of the figures is flanked by a representation of TIY.

In 27 BC an earthquake damaged the northern statue, and perhaps created some flaw in the stone, causing it to produce a characteristic whistling sound each morning. This has been variously ascribed to the effect of the breeze or the expansion of the stone, although the precise reason remains uncertain. Ancient Greek visitors knew the statue as the 'vocal Memnon', suggesting that the figure was the Homeric character Memnon, singing to his mother Eos, the goddess of the dawn. The Greek writer STRABO at first speculated, some-

The Colossi of Memnon on the west bank at Thebes
are representations in quartzite sandstone of
Amenhotep III. The northern statue (right) is that
known to ancient Greek visitors as the 'vocal
Memnon'. (P.T. NICHOLSON)

what sceptically, that the sound might have
been created by Egyptians standing nearby,
although he claims to have been eventually
convinced of its supernatural origins. In the
third century the Roman emperor Septimius
Severus (AD 193–211) repaired the damaged
colossus, and in doing so seems to have rendered it dumb.

As a result of the identification of the colossi with Memnon, the area of western Thebes
itself became known as Memnonia, and the
RAMESSEUM as the Memnonium. The term
Memnonium was even applied to the Osireion
at ABYDOS. These names were still fashionable
in the early nineteenth century, when
Giovanni BELZONI applied the phrase 'young
Memnon' to a colossal head of Rameses II
which he transported from the Ramesseum to
the British Museum.

A. H. GARDINER, 'The Egyptian Memnon', *JEA*
47 (1961), 91–9.

H. BOWMAN et al., 'The northern colossus of
Memnon: new slants', *Archaeometry* 26/2
(1984), 218–29.

D. KLEMM, R. KLEMM and L. STECLACI, 'Die
pharaonischen Steinbrüche des silifizierten
Sandsteins und die Herkunft der Memnon-
Kolosse', *MDAIK* 40 (1984), 207–20.

A. P. KOZLOFF and B. BRYAN, *Egypt's dazzling
sun: Amenhotep III and his world* (Bloomington,
1992), 138–9.

column

Like much of Egyptian religious architecture,
the shapes of stone columns drew inspiration
from Egyptian native flora and from
Predynastic religious structures made of
reeds, branches and logs. The shaft and capital
were carved in the form of four basic floral
types: PAPYRUS, LOTUS, palm and 'composite'.
In the Greco-Roman period, the composite
capital provided an opportunity for many
more elaborate variations and combinations.
The shafts of columns were also frequently
decorated with scenes and inscriptions in
painted relief.

Wooden columns were used in Egyptian
houses and occasionally also in religious buildings, such as Old Kingdom mortuary chapels,
as decorative supports for the roofs and upper

storeys. But the stone pillars and columns in
Egyptian religious and funerary buildings
served symbolic as well as functional purposes, forming an essential part of the cosmological nature of Egyptian temples.

The earliest stone columns were engaged
papyrus, ribbed and fluted columns in the
entrance and jubilee court of the Step
Pyramid complex at SAQQARA. By the 4th
Dynasty (2613–2494 BC), freestanding
columns of many different stones were being
used in the mortuary and valley temples of
pyramid complexes. In the relief decoration of
the causeway of UNAS (2375–2345 BC), granite
palm columns (some examples of which have
survived in Unas' valley temple) are depicted
in the process of being transported by boat
from the Aswan quarries to Saqqara.

Fluted 'proto-Doric' columns were first
carved in the entrance to the 12th-Dynasty
tombs of Khnumhotep (BH3) and Amenemhat
(BH2) at BENI HASAN, and this unusual form was
used again in the north colonnade of
Hatshepsut's chapel of Anubis at DEIR EL-
BAHRI, where the columns are made to appear
more elegant by tapering them towards the top.

On the most universal level, papyrus
columns represented the reeds growing on the

PRIMEVAL MOUND at the beginning of time, although on a more practical level the forests of columns that make up HYPOSTYLE HALLS were probably also considered essential to avoid the collapse of the roof, especially in the sandstone temples constructed during the New Kingdom. There were two types of papyrus column: the closed form, in which the capital was a papyrus bud, and the 'campaniform' type, in which the flower was shown in full bloom at the top of the column. The lotus column (a relatively rare form except at ABUSIR and BENI HASAN) was also sometimes represented with the capital in flower. Since the PAPYRUS and LOTUS were the plants associated with Upper and Lower Egypt respectively, they could be used as elements of the architectural symbolism surrounding the union of the 'two lands'. An unusual type is the 'tent-pole' column found in the Festival Hall of Thutmose III at KARNAK.

There were also a number of columns pro-

Red granite palm column from the valley temple of Unas at Saqqara. Late 5th Dynasty, c.2345 BC, H. 3.58 m. (EA1385)

vided with capitals that had iconographic associations with the particular religious context in which they stood. Thus, HATHOR-headed (or SISTRUM) columns were erected in religious buildings associated with the goddess Hathor, such as the temple of Hatshepsut at

Deir el-Bahri and the temple of Hathor at DENDERA. Finally, the DJED PILLAR, with four horizontal bars across its capital, is an iconographic motif rather than a physical architectural element, although the meaning of the word *djed* ('stability, duration') was closely linked with the concept of support, and in some instances columns were decorated with *djed* signs, presumably in order to give them greater strength.

S. CLARKE and R. ENGELBACH, *Ancient Egyptian masonry: the building craft* (London, 1930), 136–50.

M. ISLER, 'The technique of monolithic carving', *MDAIK* 48 (1992), 45–55.

D. ARNOLD, *Building in Egypt: pharaonic stone masonry* (New York and Oxford, 1991), 46–7.

concubine of the dead *see* SEXUALITY

copper and bronze

The first metal to be exploited in Egypt, as elsewhere in the ancient world, was copper, the earliest surviving examples of which are small artefacts such as beads and borers of the Badarian period (*c.*5500–4000 BC). By the late PREDYNASTIC PERIOD, however, large items, such as axe- and adze-heads, were being produced, and the knowledge of copper-smelting and working was already highly developed. It has been suggested that the important late Predynastic settlement of MAADI, in Lower Egypt, may have prospered on the basis of its role as intermediary between the sources of copper in Sinai and the Levant and the Upper Egyptian 'proto-states' whose growth and competition produced a demand for metal tools and weapons.

Copper was mined at various localities in the Eastern Desert, Nubia and the Sinai peninsula (such as Wadi Maghara) from at least the early Old Kingdom. The excavation of the Early Dynastic phase of the Egyptian fortress at BUHEN, near the third Nile cataract, revealed traces of copper-smelting, indicating that mining was one of the earliest reasons for the Egyptian presence in Nubia.

The technology of copper-smelting in the Old and Middle Kingdoms (2686–1650 BC) involved the use of crucibles and reed blowpipes. The PALERMO STONE states that copper statues were already being created in the 2nd Dynasty (2890–2686 BC), and the most spectacular surviving examples of copper-working from the Old Kingdom (2686–2181 BC) are the life-size statue of the 6th-Dynasty pharaoh PEPY I and another smaller figure possibly representing his son Merenra, both in the Cairo Museum. These were probably produced by hammering the metal over a wooden core.

The production of bronze, an alloy combining copper and tin, appears to have spread from Western Asia. Among the first known bronze artefacts in Egypt are a pair of ritual vessels from the tomb of the 2nd-Dynasty ruler KHASEKHEMWY at ABYDOS. It was not until the Middle Kingdom that bronze began to be imported regularly from Syria, gradually replacing the use of copper hardened with arsenic. However, the percentage of tin varied considerably, from about 2 to 16 per cent. Tin lowers the melting point of copper, thus increasing its liquidity for casting. Additions of up to 4 per cent make the artefact stronger and harder, but higher levels of tin impair these qualities, unless the artefact is frequently annealed (reheated and allowed to cool).

In the New Kingdom a form of bellows, consisting of a leather-covered clay vessel with a protruding tube, was introduced, making the smelting of copper and bronze easier. From the Saite period (664–525 BC) onwards, large numbers of votive statuettes of deities were cast in bronze using the lost-wax (*cire perdue*) process, which had been known since at least the Old Kingdom. Larger objects could be cast around a core, rather than being made from solid bronze, thus saving valuable metal.

A. LUCAS, *Ancient Egyptian materials and industries*, 4th ed., rev. J. R. Harris (London, 1962), 199–223.

A. RADWAN, *Die Kupfer- und Bronzegefässe Ägyptens: von den Anfängen bis zum Beginn der Spätzeit* (Munich, 1983).

M. COWELL, 'The composition of Egyptian copper-based metalwork', *Science in Egyptology*, ed. A. R. DAVID (Manchester, 1986), 463–8.

M. A. LEAHY, 'Egypt as a bronzeworking centre (1000–539 BC)', *Bronze-working centres of Western Asia*, ed. J. Curtis (London, 1988), 297–310.

Coptic period

Chronological phase in Egypt lasting from the end of the Roman period (*c.* AD 395) until the Islamic conquest (*c.* AD 641). It is now more accurately described as the 'Christian' period and is roughly equivalent to the Byzantine period elsewhere in the Near East. The archaeological and historical definition of 'Coptic' is extremely imprecise, since the term is often applied not only to the art and architecture of the Christian period but also to the culture of the third and fourth centuries AD ('proto-Coptic') and the early medieval period (*c.* AD 700–1200).

The Coptic language and writing system (combining Greek letters with six further signs taken from the DEMOTIC script) were widely used throughout the Christian period

Ostracon bearing eighteen lines of psalms written in the Coptic script. Early Islamic period, 7th–8th centuries AD, pottery with pigment, probably from Thebes, H. 13.2 cm. (EA14030)

in Egypt and are still employed in modern times in the liturgies and Biblical texts of the Coptic church. The earliest surviving Coptic religious establishments include the monasteries of St Anthony, St Catherine and St Samuel.

R. FEDDEN, 'A study of the Monastery of Saint Anthony', *University of Egypt Faculty of Arts Bulletin* 5 (1937), 1–61.

C. C. WALTERS, *Monastic archaeology in Egypt* (Warminster, 1974).

J. KAMIL, *Coptic Egypt* (Cairo, 1987).

G. GABRA and A. ALCOCK, *Cairo, the Coptic Museum and old churches* (Cairo, 1993).

coregency
Modern term applied to the periods during which two rulers were simultaneously in power, usually consisting of an overlap of several years between the end of one sole reign and the beginning of the next. This system was used, from at least as early as the Middle Kingdom, in order to ensure that the transfer of power took place with the minimum of disruption and instability. It would also have enabled the chosen successor to gain experience in the administration before his predecessor died. The discovery that coregencies existed was an important stage in the clarification of the traditional CHRONOLOGY of Egypt.

W. K. SIMPSON, 'The single-dated monuments of Sesostris I: an aspect of the institution of coregency in the Twelfth Dynasty', *JNES* 15 (1956), 214–19.

R. TANNER, 'Bemerkungen zur Sukzession der Pharaonen in der 12., 17. und 18. Dynastie', *ZÄS* 101 (1974), 121–9.

W. J. MURNANE, *Ancient Egyptian coregencies* (Chicago, 1977).

D. LORTON, 'Terms of coregency in the Middle Kingdom', *VA* 2 (1986), 113–20.

corn mummy
Term generally employed to describe a type of anthropomorphic funerary object made of soil mixed with grains of corn, which was usually wrapped up in linen bandages and furnished with a wax face-mask. Most examples measure between 35 and 50 cm in length and were usually placed in small wooden falcon-headed sarcophagi. They are mummiform in shape, and some were provided with a royal sceptre, an erect phallus, an *atef* crown or a white crown; it is therefore usually assumed that they were intended to refer to the god OSIRIS.

Although a few miniature corn mummies have been found encased in Ptah-Sokar-Osiris statues in Late Period burials, most of the fifty or so surviving full-size corn mummies derive from simple pits (rather than tombs) and date to the Ptolemaic or Roman periods. Maarten Raven has pointed out that all those with archaeological provenances appear to derive from only four sites: Wadi Qubbanet el-Qirud (in Thebes), Tihna el-Gebel, el-Sheikh Fadl and the region of Tuna el-Gebel.

The origins of the corn mummy (as well as the OSIRIS BED, an item of New Kingdom royal funerary equipment that probably functioned in a similar way to the corn mummy) can be traced back at least as far as the Middle Kingdom, since it is at this period that links began to be established between the cult of Osiris, fertility and the growth of corn. The COFFIN TEXTS, for instance, include certain spells equating the resurrection of the deceased with the sprouting of barley from the body of Osiris (equated with the corn-god Neper).

Since the corn mummies were not placed in the tombs of individuals, they clearly had a slightly different function from 'Osiris beds' and other such funerary equipment, which were intended simply to aid the resurrection of one deceased individual. Instead, the corn mummies appear to have been connected with the mysteries of the cult of Osiris itself. An inscription in a roof chapel at DENDERA describes rituals relating to Osiris, including the annual ceremonial burial of a corn mummy.

M. J. RAVEN, 'Corn-mummies', *OMRO* 63 (1982), 7–38.

cosmetics
From the earliest times Egyptian men and women included various cosmetic items among their funerary equipment, suggesting that oils, perfumes and eye-paints were regarded as virtual necessities. In the early Predynastic period, stone cosmetic PALETTES, used for grinding eye-paint pigments, were already common. The surfaces of some of these are still stained with traces of black galena or green malachite. The green malachite-based form of paint (*udju*) seems to have been used only until the middle of the Old Kingdom, when it was replaced by the black galena-based form of kohl (*mesdemet*). These ground pigments appear to have been mixed with water to form a paste and were probably applied with the fingers until the introduction of the 'kohl pencil' in the Middle Kingdom.

The types of vessels in which kohl was stored varied from one period to another; in the Middle Kingdom and the 18th Dynasty a small flat-bottomed stone vessel was used whereas in the late New Kingdom a tubular form of vessel (originally a reed) became more common. The purpose of eye-paint was no doubt partly the same as in modern times (i.e. the enhancement and apparent enlargement of eyes, but it probably also had religious and symbolic resonances, as well as being a natural disinfectant and a means of protecting the eyes from bright sunlight. The Egyptians used ochre as a form of 'rouge' on their cheeks (and perhaps also as lipstick) and employed henna to colour their hair. There are many surviving depictions of women applying cosmetics using a MIRROR, which was itself regarded as an important item of funerary equipment.

Throughout Egyptian history, OILS and fats were considered essential both for the preparation of perfumes and INCENSE cones and for the protection of the skin. Tattoos were also used as early as the Predynastic period to decorate the skin, judging from the presence of patterns on some female figurines and the preservation of geometric designs on the mummies of certain dancers, musicians and concubines (as well as in depictions of some women in tomb-paintings); one mummy of a singer had a small tattoo of Bes preserved on the thigh. See also HAIR for discussion of hairstyles and hairdressing.

A. L. LUCAS, 'Cosmetics, perfumes and incense in ancient Egypt', *JEA* 16 (1930), 41–53.

F. JONCKHEERE, 'La "mesdemet": cosmétique et médicaments égyptiens', *Histoire de la Médecine* 2/7 (1952), 1–12.

J. VANDIER and D. ABBADIE, *Catalogue des objets de toilette égyptiens* (Paris, 1972).

M. STEAD, *Egyptian life* (London, 1986), 49–54.

E. STROUHAL, *Life in ancient Egypt* (Cambridge, 1992), 84–9.

cosmogony *see* CREATION; ENNEAD and OGDOAD

cow

Animal which served as the archetypal Egyptian symbol of motherly and domestic qualities. The two goddesses HATHOR and ISIS were often depicted with the horns of the cow, but only Hathor and BAT were depicted with cow's ears. The image of the cow could also symbolize the mother of the Egyptian king; the bovine image of Hathor was therefore depicted suckling King Amenhotep II (1427–1400 BC) at DEIR EL-BAHRI. An association with the sky and the underworld was characteristic of the bovine deities, so that NUT could be depicted as a cow who bore the sun-god RA on her back each morning. Since the sacred APIS bull represented OSIRIS, it was natural that the cow which gave birth to him should be identified with Isis. Thus, from at least the thirty-seventh regnal year of Ahmose II (570–526 BC) onwards, the so-called Mothers of Apis were mummified and had their own catacombs in the SACRED ANIMAL necropolis at Saqqara.

On a more prosaic level the cow was also an important domestic animal, providing milk, meat and hides. The first domestic cattle in Egypt, introduced during the Predynastic period, were probably long-horned, but a short-horned species appeared in the Old Kingdom, and humped Zebu cattle were used from the 18th Dynasty onwards. Wall reliefs depicting scenes of 'cattle counting', for the purpose of TAX-ATION, are common in tombs from the Old Kingdom (2686–2181 BC) onwards, and numerous funerary models of the Middle Kingdom (2055–1650 BC) depict the same activity. Cattle were regarded as status symbols and, as in many other societies, the possession of a large herd was an indication of considerable wealth. The funerary reliefs also indicate that techniques of ANIMAL HUSBANDRY were well developed, much attention being paid to the depiction of the branding of stock and human assistance in the birth of calves. Beef was evidently the food of the wealthy élite, and was often portrayed in religious and funerary offering scenes.

E. HORNUNG, *Der ägyptische Mythos von der Himmelskuh* (Freiburg and Göttingen, 1982).
L. STÖRK, 'Rind', *Lexikon der Ägyptologie* v, ed. W. Helck, E. Otto and W. Westendorf (Wiesbaden, 1984), 257–63.

R. JANSSEN and J. J. JANSSEN, *Egyptian domestic animals* (Aylesbury, 1989), 27–35.
D. J. BREWER, D. B. REDFORD and S. REDFORD, *Domestic plants and animals: the Egyptian origins* (Warminster, 1994), 77–93.

cowroid

Name given to a cowrie-shell-shaped amulet, frequently inscribed and serving a purpose similar to that of a SCARAB. The cowrie shell amulet is known as early as Predynastic times. Its shape was believed to mimic the female genitalia and girdles made from it were used to symbolically protect this area of the body. From the 6th Dynasty (2345–2181 BC) actual shells were imitated in faience and later in cornelian and quartz.

creation

During the Pharaonic period, a great deal of Egyptian thought regarding creation was simply embedded in their iconography, language and ritual. It was only in the Ptolemaic and Roman periods that the process of cosmogony began to be regularly described in explicit narrative accounts. There are, however, three principal surviving Egyptian creation myths, each rooted in the cults of deities associated with particular localities. At HERMOPOLIS

Necklace consisting of cowroids and beads in the form of false beards or sidelocks of youth. 12th Dynasty and New Kingdom, L. 46.3 cm. (EA3077)

MAGNA the myth centred on four pairs of primeval deities (the OGDOAD); at HELIOPOLIS there was a myth involving four generations of deities (the ENNEAD); and at MEMPHIS the account centred on the attributes of the god PTAH.

The myth of the Ogdoad dealt primarily with the first mystery of creation: how did 'being' appear out of 'non-being'? According to the Hermopolitan account, the earliest text of which dates to the Middle Kingdom, the sun-god emerged from a group of four pairs of male and female deities whose names simply describe aspects of the primordial chaos preceding creation: darkness, formlessness, eternity and hiddenness (or, in the earliest version, twilight). The myth of the Ennead, on the other hand, was concerned with the next stage in the process of cosmogony: the question of division and multiplication. How did the creator transform the one into the many? The references to the Ennead in the PYRAMID TEXTS show that, at least as early as the Old Kingdom, the progressive fission and proliferation of life were both seen in terms of divine procreation, resulting in a succession of symmetrical pairs.

In the beginning, according to the myth of the Ennead, there was a mysterious act of creativity or fertility by the creator – the sun-god ATUM, for instance, was considered to have created himself with the aid of such forces as Heka (the Egyptian term for MAGIC), Sia (a personification of 'perception') and Hu ('the divine word'). Having engendered himself, Atum (whose name meant 'completeness') then undertook the first act of division or separation, which he achieved through a combination of 'masturbating', spitting and sneezing, thus producing new life and splitting it into two opposites: air (the god Shu) and moisture (the goddess Tefnut). Shu and Tefnut then procreated to produce NUT and GEB, the heaven and the earth, and a common vignette in the BOOK OF THE DEAD shows Shu

The 'Shabaqo Stone': a basalt slab bearing a text purporting to be a copy of an ancient composition describing the creation of the universe by the god Ptah. 25th Dynasty, c.710 BC, L. 1.37 m. (EA498)

literally separating the personification of the sky from that of the earth.

The myth of the Ennead not only deals with the question of creation but also leads on to the emergence of human society in the form of the myths surrounding the sons and daughters of Geb and Nut: OSIRIS and SETH and their consorts ISIS and NEPHTHYS. These legends, relating principally to Osiris, went beyond cosmogony to deal with such issues as KINGSHIP and human suffering.

The so-called Memphite Theology presents an alternative, but nevertheless compatible, view of creation by means of the spoken word. The text was probably composed in the late New Kingdom and survives in the form of the 25th-Dynasty 'Shabaqo Stone', a basalt slab now in the British Museum bearing a hieroglyphic inscription in which the Memphite god Ptah creates all things by pronouncing their names.

Each local deity – from SOBEK to BASTET –

was, to all intents and purposes, also a creator-god, but their specific characteristics often led to variations on the general theme of creativity. The ram-god KHNUM, who was connected with the fertile Nile silt and the pottery vessels that were formed from it, was considered to have modelled the first humans on a potter's wheel. The fertility god MIN, on the other hand, was portrayed as an icon of male fertility whose erect phallus, combined with an upraised hand thrusting into the V-shape formed by the flail over his shoulder (in apparent simulation of intercourse), served as an unmistakable metaphor for the sexual act itself. In the late New Kingdom the theme of the mound rising out of the waters of Nun was transformed into the myth of the child-like god NEFERTEM, who was thought to have emerged from a lotus floating on the face of the deep. The Book of the Dead describes the sun-god as a 'golden youth who emerged from the lotus'. It was in order to identify himself with Nefertem and the act of creation and rebirth that TUTANKHAMUN (1336–1327 BC) included among his funerary equipment a painted wooden representation of his own youthful head emerging from a lotus.

The Egyptian concepts of creation were closely interlinked with their views concerning rebirth, renewal and life after death, and their religious and funerary imagery is full of metaphors for the first act of creation, from the PRIMEVAL MOUND and the BENBEN stone to the SCARAB beetle emerging from a dunghill. The texts make it clear that they regarded creation not only as a single event at the beginning of the universe but as a phenomenon which constantly recurred with each new day or season and which was intimately connected with the prolonging of life beyond death. The deity most regularly associated with creation was therefore the sun-god, whose appearance at dawn, voyage through the sky during the day and disappearance at the sunset served to epitomize the cyclical nature of the creator.

J. R. ALLEN, *Genesis in Egypt: the philosophy of ancient Egyptian creation accounts* (New Haven, 1988).

B. MENU, 'Les cosmogonies de l'ancienne Egypte', *La création dans l'Orient ancien* (Paris, 1987).

G. HART, *Egyptian myths* (London, 1990), 9–28.

E. HORNUNG, *Idea into image*, trans. E. Bredeck (New York, 1992), 39–54.

crime *see* LAW; MEDJAY and POLICE

Crocodilopolis *see* MEDINET EL-FAYUM

crook and flail *see* CROWNS AND ROYAL REGALIA

crowns and royal regalia

The king can be depicted wearing a number of different head coverings, each corresponding to particular ceremonial situations. The earliest of these to be depicted is a form of tall conical headpiece ending in a bulb. This is the crown of Upper Egypt or white crown (*hedjet*), which is seen as early as the time of the SCORPION macehead and the NARMER palette (*c*.3000 BC). It is sometimes referred to as the NEFER or 'White Nefer'. The Narmer palette also shows the crown of Lower Egypt, or red crown (*deshret*), which comprises a tall 'chair-shaped' arrangement from which protrudes a coil. With unification these two crowns were combined to become the 'Two Mighty Ones', the double crown (*pschent*).

The king might also wear the *nemes* head-cloth. This was a piece of striped cloth pulled tight across the forehead and tied into a kind of tail at the back while at each side of the face two strands or lappets hung down. The brow was decorated with the *uraeus* (see WADJYT) and the VULTURE. This is the head-dress represented in the famous gold mask of TUTANKHAMUN. A plain version of this was the *khat*. From the 18th Dynasty onwards kings also wore the 'blue crown' (*khepresh*), sometimes erroneously described as the 'war

Wooden shabti of Tutankhamun wearing the red crown and holding the crook and flail. 18th Dynasty, c.1330 BC, H. 52 cm. (CAIRO, NO. 330C; REPRODUCED COURTESY OF THE GRIFFITH INSTITUTE)

LEFT *Statue of Thutmose III wearing the* nemes *headcloth, the* uraeus *and the ceremonial 'false beard'. 18th Dynasty, c.1450 BC, greywacke, H. 90.5 cm. (LUXOR MUSEUM, J2, GRAHAM HARRISON)*

cult singers and temple musicians

From the Old Kingdom onwards, 'musical troupes' (*khener*) as well as dancers are attested as elements of the staff of temple cults. They comprised both men and women, the latter sometimes individually named, and clearly of greater importance than their anonymous male counterparts. Female musicians were employed in the cults of both male and female deities.

By the beginning of the New Kingdom the priesthood had become exclusively male, but women of high rank, some of whom were married to the priests, were allowed to serve as musicians (*shemayet*). The role of these women was to play the SISTRUM, as accompaniment to the ritual chants or cult HYMNS, and sometimes even to provide the chants themselves. Usually, however, the chants were performed by male singers or musicians, although these individuals never used the title 'musician' and were probably of a lower status than their élite female colleagues.

G. PINCH, *Votive offerings to Hathor* (Oxford, 1993), 212–13.

G. ROBINS, *Women in ancient Egypt* (London, 1993), 145–9.

cuneiform

Type of script, the name of which derives from the Latin word *cuneus* ('wedge'), referring to the wedge-shaped lines making up the pictographic characters used in the earliest writing. This developed in MESOPOTAMIA during the fourth millennium, and was initially used to record quantities, hence the characters were numerals accompanied by a picture of the thing being quantified. Over time, these pictures became stylized into a series of wedge shapes which could readily be impressed into tablets of wet clay using a cut reed or other stylus. The script could be used for pictographic, logographic and syllabic writing and over time came to incorporate all three.

It was used to write down the SUMERIAN and AKKADIAN languages, but also a host of other western Asiatic tongues, and despite the development of HIEROGLYPHIC writing in Egypt around 3100 BC it was cuneiform which became the language of diplomatic correspondence throughout the Near East. The Egyptian court would have supported scribes fluent in the use of this system. The best-known examples of cuneiform script in Egypt are the AMARNA LETTERS. The script is last

crown', which is shaped like a kind of tall, flanged helmet and made of cloth adorned with golden discs. The '*atef*' crown' is effectively a 'white crown' with a plume on either side and a small disc at the top, which was worn in certain religious rituals.

The most prominent items in the royal regalia were the so-called 'crook' (*heka*), actually a sceptre symbolizing 'government', and the 'flail' or 'flabellum' (*nekhakha*), which may have derived originally from a fly whisk. Before it became part of royal regalia, the flail was associated primarily with the gods OSIRIS and MIN as well as with sacred animals.

G. A. WAINWRIGHT, 'The red crown in early prehistoric times', *JEA* 9 (1923), 25–33.

ABDEL MONEIM ABUBAKR, *Untersuchungen über die altägyptischen Kronen* (Glückstadt, 1937).

E. L. ERTMAN, 'The cap crown of Nefertiti: its function and probable origin', *JARCE* 13 (1976), 63–7.

M. EATON-KRAUSS, 'The *khat* headdress to the end of the Amarna period', *SAK* 5 (1977), 21–39.

A. LEAHY, 'Royal iconography and dynastic change, 750–525 BC: the blue and cap crowns', *JEA* 78 (1992), 223–40.

BELOW *The major types of crown.*

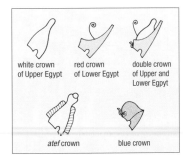

| white crown of Upper Egypt | red crown of Lower Egypt | double crown of Upper and Lower Egypt |

| *atef* crown | blue crown |

used in the first century AD: interestingly these latest texts use Sumerian logograms (word signs) even though the language had long since ceased to be in general use.

The decipherment of cuneiform began with the recognition that a series of brief inscriptions at Persepolis (in PERSIA) were each written out in three forms of the script. By 1802 a German, G. F. Grotefend, had achieved some success with the simplest of these, Old Persian, discovering the names of two kings. This work was carried much further by Henry Rawlinson who, in 1835, deciphered a long inscription of Darius from Behistun in Iran. This site too had three versions of the text and Rawlinson copied all three. Of these the Elamite was deciphered by Edwin Norris in 1855, and Rawlinson himself deciphered the BABYLONIAN text in 1851. This was of great significance since it could be linked to already discovered Babylonian and ASSYRIAN texts from Mesopotamia.

C. WALKER, *Cuneiform* (London, 1987).

J. N. POSTGATE, *Early Mesopotamia: society and economy at the dawn of history* (London and New York, 1992), 51–70.

cynocephalus

Term meaning 'dog-headed', commonly used to refer to a species of baboon (*Papio cynocephalus*), which was one of the principal manifestations of the gods THOTH and KHONS. Typically portrayed in a squatting position, the earliest votive figurines of the cynocephalus baboon have been excavated in the Early Dynastic settlement at ABYDOS, although among the most impressive surviving statues of Thoth are a pair of 18th-Dynasty quartzite colossal figures still standing *in situ* at HERMOPOLIS MAGNA, the main cult-centre of Thoth. The enthusiasm with which wild baboons greeted the rising sun reinforced the association between the baboon form of Thoth and the sun- and moon-gods. The bases of a number of OBELISKS are carved with figures of baboons with their arms raised in characteristic worshipping posture, and a frieze of baboons along the front of the Great Temple at ABU SIMBEL also have their arms raised in adoration of the rising sun.

R. H. WILKINSON, *Reading Egyptian art* (London, 1992), 72–3.

Dab'a, Tell el- (anc. Avaris)

Settlement site in the eastern Delta, covering an area of some two square kilometres on a natural mound partly surrounded by a large lake. The town of Avaris, which has been under excavation since 1966, consists of several strata of occupation dating from the First Intermediate Period to the Second Intermediate Period (2181–1550 BC). There are also considerable remains of a later phase of settlement in the Ramesside period (c.1295–1069 BC) when the city of Piramesse spread across Tellel-Dab'a, although its nucleus was at QANTIR, further to the north.

During the Second Intermediate Period the Hyksos capital of Avaris was effectively an Asiatic colony within Egypt, and Manfred Bietak's excavations suggest that the colonists were allocated rectangular areas of land, the patterning and orientation of which were still occasionally influenced by the preceding Middle Kingdom town plan. Both houses and cemeteries were laid out within the allocated areas, sometimes in close proximity. The deep stratigraphy at Tell el-Dab'a allows the changing settlement patterns of a large Bronze Age community to be observed over a period of many generations.

In the early 1990s the main focus of excavation at Tell el-Dab'a was the substructure of a large palace building of the Hyksos period at Ezbet Helmi on the western edge of the site. In 1991 many fragments of Minoan wall-paintings were discovered among debris covering the ancient gardens adjoining the palace. Several of these derive from compositions depicting 'bull-leapers', like those in the Middle Bronze Age palace at Knossos. Whereas the Minoan and Mycenaean pottery vessels previously found at many New Kingdom sites in Egypt are usually interpreted as evidence of trade with the Aegean (see GREEKS), the presence of Minoan wall-paintings at Tell el-Dab'a suggests that the population of Avaris may actually have included Aegean families. It has been suggested that the frequent use of a red painted background may even mean that the Tell el-Dab'a Minoan paintings predate those of Crete and Thera (Santorini). The existence of Minoan paintings (and therefore presumably Minoan artists) at a site within Egypt itself may help to explain the appearance in early 18th-Dynasty Egyptian tomb-paintings of such Aegean motifs as the 'flying gallop' (i.e. the depiction of animals' fore- and hindlegs outstretched in full flight). Similar fragments of Minoan paintings have been found at two sites in the Levant (Kabri and Alalakh), where they also

Plan of Tell el-Dab'a and Qantir.

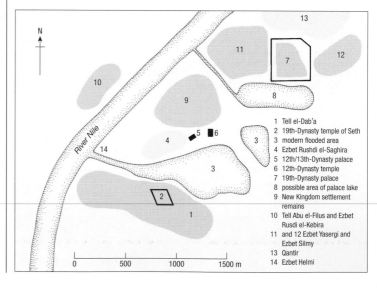

1 Tell el-Dab'a
2 19th-Dynasty temple of Seth
3 modern flooded area
4 Ezbet Rushdi el-Saghira
5 12th/13th-Dynasty palace
6 12th-Dynasty temple
7 19th-Dynasty palace
8 possible area of palace lake
9 New Kingdom settlement remains
10 Tell Abu el-Filus and Ezbet Rusdi el-Kebira
11 and 12 Ezbet Yasergi and Ezbet Silmy
13 Qantir
14 Ezbet Helmi

appear to be associated with the ruling elite, as at Avaris.

In one of the early 18th-Dynasty strata at Ezbet Helmi immediately above those containing the painting fragments Bietak also discovered many lumps of pumice-stone, which may derive from the volcanic explosion on the island of Thera.

M. BIETAK, *Tell el-Dab'a* II–VI (Vienna, 1975–91).

—, *Avaris and Piramesse: archaeological exploration in the eastern Nile delta* (London and Oxford, 1981).

—, 'Tell el-Dab'a', *Archiv für Orientforschung* 32 (1985), 130–5.

Dahshur

Group of pyramid complexes making up the southern end of the Memphite necropolis, the nucleus of which is SAQQARA. The most prominent of the surviving monuments at Dahshur are the two pyramids of the first 4th-Dynasty pharaoh, SNEFERU (2613–2589 BC). The three other major pyramid complexes at Dahshur belong to rulers of the Middle Kingdom, namely AMENEMHAT II (1922–1878 BC), SENUSRET III (1874–1855 BC) and Amenemhat III (1855–1808 BC). The site also includes the remains of one of only three surviving 13th-Dynasty pyramid complexes, containing the sarcophagus and CANOPIC JARS of Amenyqemau (formerly read as Amenyaamu).

The two pyramids of Sneferu were possibly the first such tombs to be designed from the outset as true pyramids rather than step pyramids. The southernmost of the two is the 'bent' or 'rhomboidal' pyramid, so-called because of its marked change of angle from 54° 27′ in the lower part to 43° 22′ in the upper part. The reason for this was probably structural, although the pyramid has other unusual features, notably a western entrance in addition to the usual northern one. It was first investigated by the Egyptian archaeologist Ahmed Fakhry in 1951–5.

Sneferu's other monument at Dahshur is the 'northern' or 'red' pyramid, built from the outset with an angle of 43° 22′, which stands about two kilometres north of the earlier monument. Its base area is second only to the Great Pyramid of his son Khufu at GIZA. Sneferu's construction of two pyramids at Dahshur (as well as his completion of his father's pyramid at MEIDUM) would have necessitated an amount of materials and labour outstripping even the efforts involved in the construction of the Great Pyramid.

Although each of the three 12th-Dynasty pyramids at Dahshur have stone casings, only the 'white pyramid' of Amenemhat II has a stone core, the others being of brick.

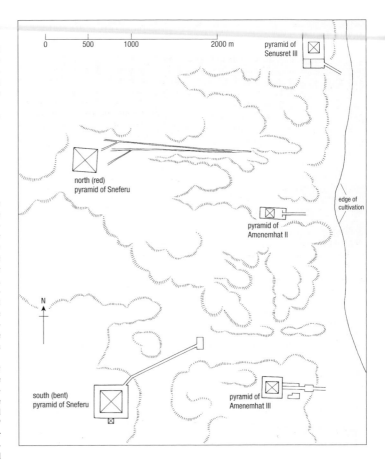

Plan of Dahshur.

Amenemhat II's pyramid is so ruinous that even its exact size is uncertain. The complex was excavated by Jacques de Morgan, who discovered a plundered burial chamber containing a sandstone sarcophagus that is believed to have been part of the original funerary equipment. Nearby are the burials of princesses of the late 12th or early 13th Dynasty.

De Morgan also tunnelled into the pyramid of Senusret III, where he discovered the magnificent granite burial chamber containing a sarcophagus of the same material. This pyramid, the superstructure of which was badly damaged by Maspero's work of 1882–3, was re-examined by Dieter Arnold in the 1980s, revealing that the burial-chamber was painted to resemble limestone, perhaps in order to

allow the sarcophagus to stand out in contrast to its background. The king's remains, however, have not been found in this pyramid, which may have been simply a cenotaph. The nearby MASTABA tombs contained the rich funerary equipment of the daughters of Senusret III and Amenemhat II, including items of jewellery discovered by de Morgan in 1894.

The 'black pyramid' of Amenemhat III also seems to have served as a cenotaph (the actual tomb probably being the pyramid at HAWARA), and work during the 1980s revealed a FOUNDATION DEPOSIT which included pottery, ritual bricks and bull crania. This complex also incorporated the burial of the 13th-Dynasty ruler Awibra Hor, including a fine KA-statue.

J. DE MORGAN, *Fouilles à Dahchour*, 2 vols (Paris and Vienna, 1895–1903).

Interior of the burial chamber of Amenemhat III at Dahshur. (REPRODUCED COURTESY OF DAI, CAIRO)

A. FAKHRY, *The monuments of Sneferu at Dahshur*, 2 vols (Cairo, 1959–61).

V. MARAGIOGLIO and C. A. RINALDI, 'Note sulla piramide di Ameny 'Aamu', *Orientalia* 37 (1968), 325–38.

R. STADELMANN, 'Snofru und die Pyramiden von Meidum und Dahschur', *MDAIK* 36 (1980), 437–49.

D. ARNOLD, *Der Pyramidenbezirk des Königs Amenemhet III in Dahschur* I (Mainz, 1987).

Dakhla Oasis

One of a chain of oases located in the Libyan Desert, 300 km west of the Egyptian city of Luxor. The main pharaonic sites in Dakhla include a town site of the Old Kingdom (2686–2181 BC) and its associated cemetery of 6th-Dynasty MASTABA tombs, near the modern village of Balat; another cemetery dating to the

First Intermediate Period (2181–2055 BC), near modern Amhada; and a temple of the goddess Mut dating to the late Ramesside period (*c.*1130 BC), near Ezbet Bashindi. The Old Kingdom town and cemetery at Balat show that the Egyptians' control extended hundreds of miles into the Libyan Desert from a very early period. The surviving remains of the Greek and Roman periods (332

BC–AD 395) include a necropolis and temple of Thoth at el-Qasr, a temple dedicated to the Theban triad at Deir el-Hagar, Roman tombs at Qaret el-Muzawwaqa and a Roman settlement and temple at Ismant el-Kharab.

H. E. WINLOCK (ed.), *Dakhleh Oasis* (New York, 1936).

L. L. GIDDY and D. G. JEFFREYS, 'Balat: rapport préliminaire des fouilles à 'Ayn Asil, 1979–80', *BIFAO* 80 (1980), 257–69.

L. L. GIDDY, *Egyptian oases: Bahariya, Dakhla, Farafra and Kharga during pharaonic times* (Warminster, 1987).

C. HOPE, 'Excavations at Ismant el-Kharab in the Dakhleh Oasis', *Egyptian Archaeology* 5 (1994), 17–18.

dance

As early as the Predynastic period there were depictions on pottery vessels showing female figures (perhaps goddesses or priestesses) dancing with their arms raised above their heads. The act of dancing was undoubtedly an important component of both ritual and celebration in ancient Egypt. In normal daily life musicians and dancers were a common feature of banquets, but certain ritual dances could also be crucial to the successful outcome of

Quartzite relief block from the Red Chapel at Karnak, showing musicians and dancers. 18th Dynasty, c.1460 BC. (I. SHAW)

Plan of Dakhla Oasis.

Fragment of a wall-painting from the Theban tomb of Nebamun, showing female musicians and dancers at a banquet. 18th Dynasty, c.1400 BC, H. 61 cm. (EA37984)

religious and funerary ceremonies, as in the case of the *muu*-dancers, who wore kilts and reed crowns and performed alongside funeral processions.

The act of dancing appears to have been inseparable from music, therefore the depictions of dancing in pharaonic tombs and temples invariably show the dancers either accompanied by groups of musicians or themselves playing castanets or clappers to keep the rhythm. Little distinction appears to have been made between dancing and what would now be described as acrobatics, with many dancers being depicted in such athletic poses as cartwheels, handstands and back-bends. Detailed study of the depictions of dancers has revealed that the artists were often depicting a series of different steps in particular dances, some of which can therefore be reconstructed. Men and women are never shown dancing together, and the most common scenes depict groups of female dancers, often performing in pairs.

E. BRUNNER-TRAUT, *Der Tanz im alten Ägypten* (Glückstadt, 1958).

H. WILD, Les danse sacrées de l'Egypte ancienne', *Les danses sacrées*, Sources Orientales 6 (Paris, 1963), 33–117.

J. VANDIER, *Manuel d'archéologie égyptienne* IV (Paris, 1964), 391–486.

E. STROUHAL, *Life in ancient Egypt* (Cambridge, 1992), 41–3.

Darius *see* PERSIA, PERSIANS

death *see* FUNERARY BELIEFS

decans *see* ASTRONOMY AND ASTROLOGY

deification

Ancient Egyptian gods were generally 'born' rather than made. As a result it is relatively unusual to find mortals elevated to the status of gods The pharaoh himself was not deified, but was born as the living HORUS, becoming OSIRIS at death. From the 18th Dynasty, however, kings may have been seeking to diminish the power of certain priesthoods, notably that of AMUN, perhaps fearing that they would threaten the position of monarchy. Stress was therefore laid upon the cults of RA and PTAH instead, and in Nubia the reigning king was linked with the official gods, aspects of the ruler's kingship being worshipped in the temples. A similar change took place in Egypt itself, where deified aspects of kingship were worshipped in the form of royal colossal statues in temples. It is possible that, with his promulgation of the worship of the ATEN, the 18th-Dynasty pharaoh AKHENATEN may have taken this process a stage further by effectively declaring himself to be the god incarnate.

Rameses II (1279–1213 BC) identified himself with a local form of Amun at his Theban mortuary temple, the RAMESSEUM. It was his image which replaced that of the god in the portable BARK. Likewise his bark probably rested in front of the statues of Ptah, Amun, Ra and Rameses II in the Great Temple at ABU SIMBEL, where he stressed his identity as a manifestation of the sun-god RA. There were also certain kings who received posthumous cults among the populace, as opposed to their official cults centred on the mortuary temple. Thus Amenhotep I (1525–1504 BC) and his mother Ahmose Nefertari were worshipped by the royal tomb-workers at DEIR EL-MEDINA, in recognition of their supposed role in founding the village.

Private individuals – notably those with a reputation for great wisdom – were also, in a few rare cases, deified. The earliest of these was IMHOTEP, the vizier of the 3rd-Dynasty ruler Djoser (2667–2648 BC) and the architect of the Step Pyramid at SAQQARA. He was deified about two thousand years after his death, and revered as a god of wisdom and medicine whom the Greeks were quick to identify with their own Asklepios. His connection with learning also led to a cultic link with THOTH and hence an association with the cults of SACRED ANIMALS. A number of other Old Kingdom viziers were deified soon after their deaths. AMENHOTEP SON OF HAPU, the architect who built the Theban mortuary temple of AMENHOTEP III (1390–1352 BC) at Kom el-Heitan, was similarly honoured as a god of healing. He was uniquely allowed to build his own mortuary temple among those of the New Kingdom pharaohs, as well as having statues of himself in the temple of Amun at Karnak and a personal shrine at DEIR EL-BAHRI.

The idea that the drowned also became deified was established by the New Kingdom, and features in the *Book of Gates* and *Amduat*, as portrayed in the tomb of Rameses VI (KV9).

By the Late Period, cults began to be established for some of those who drowned in the Nile, as in the case of Pehor and Petiesis at Dendur in Nubia. In the early second century AD the city of Antinoopolis became the cult-centre for the Emperor Hadrian's 'favourite', Antinous, at the spot where he drowned in Middle Egypt.

L. HABACHI, *Features of the deification of Ramesses II* (Glückstadt, 1969).

D. WILDUNG, *Imhotep und Amenhotep: Gottwerdung im alten Ägypten* (Berlin, 1977).

—, *Egyptian saints: deification in pharaonic Egypt* (New York, 1977).

Deir el-Bahri (Deir el-Bahari)

Important Theban religious and funerary site on the west bank of the Nile, opposite Luxor, comprising temples and tombs dating from the early Middle Kingdom to the Ptolemaic period. The site consists of a deep bay in the cliffs containing the remains of the temples of Nebhepetra MENTUHOTEP II (2055–2004 BC), HATSHEPSUT (1473–1458 BC) and THUTMOSE III (1479–1425 BC), as well as private tombs contemporary with each of these pharaohs. The temple of Hatshepsut is the best-preserved of the three, consisting of three colonnaded terraces imitating the architectural style of Mentuhotep's much earlier funerary complex immediately to the south of it. As well as incorporating chapels to Hathor, Anubis and Amun,

the temple is decorated with reliefs depicting the divine birth of the queen and the exploits of her soldiers on a trading mission to the African land of PUNT.

The most important private tombs excavat-

ABOVE *The temple of Hatshepsut at Deir el-Bahri is built into a natural embayment in the cliffs which border the Valley of the Kings. It is better preserved than the earlier temple of Mentuhotep II, the style of which it emulates. (P. T. NICHOLSON)*

LEFT *Fragment of relief from the cult-temple of Mentuhotep II at Deir el-Bahri, showing the king wearing the red crown. 11th Dynasty, c.2030 BC, painted limestone, H. 53.3 cm. (EA1397)*

ed at Deir el-Bahri are those of Meketra (which contained many Middle Kingdom painted wooden funerary models) and SENEN-MUT. An 11th-Dynasty shaft tomb at the southern end of Deir el-Bahri (discovered and robbed in 1871 and finally excavated by Gaston Maspero in 1881) contained a cache of some forty royal mummies from the VALLEY OF THE KINGS reinterred there by 21st-Dynasty priests. The kings whose mummies were found in the 'Deir el-Bahri cache' were SEQ-ENENRA TAA II, AHMOSE I, AMENHOTEP I, THUTMOSE I, II and III, SETY I and RAMESES II, III and IX, Pinudjem I and II and Siamun. Another 'cache'consisting of 153 reburied mummies of the 21st-Dynasty priests themselves was also found in a tomb at Deir el-Bahri in 1891.

E. NAVILLE, *The temple of Deir el-Bahari*, 7 vols (London, 1894–1908).

H. E. WINLOCK, *Excavations at Deir el-Bahari, 1911–31* (New York, 1942).

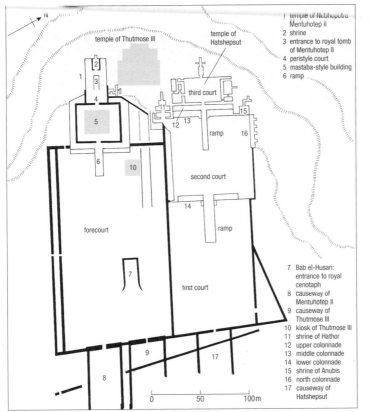

LEFT *Plan of Deir el-Bahri.*

—, *The slain soldiers of Nebhepetre Mentuhotep* (New York, 1945).
J. LIPINSKA, *Deir el-Bahari* II: *The temple of Tuthmosis* III (Warsaw, 1974).
D. ARNOLD, *The temple of Mentuhotep at Deir el-Bahari* (New York, 1979).

Plan of Deir el-Bahri key:

1 temple of Nebhepetre Mentuhotep II
2 shrine
3 entrance to royal tomb of Mentuhotep II
4 peristyle court
5 mastaba-style building
6 ramp

7 Bab el-Husan: entrance to royal cenotaph
8 causeway of Mentuhotep II
9 causeway of Thutmose III
10 kiosk of Thutmose III
11 shrine of Hathor
12 upper colonnade
13 middle colonnade
14 lower colonnade
15 shrine of Anubis
16 north colonnade
17 causeway of Hatshepsut

temple of Thutmose III
temple of Hatshepsut
third court
second court
first court
forecourt
ramp
ramp

Deir el-Ballas

Settlement site on the west bank of the Nile some 45 km north of THEBES, excavated by George Reisner at the turn of the century and subsequently surveyed and re-examined by an expedition from Boston concentrating on the residential areas. Ballas was probably originally a staging post in the reconquest of northern Egypt by KAMOSE (*c*.1555–1550 BC) and AHMOSE I (1550–1525 BC). Peter Lacovara interprets the early New Kingdom phase of Ballas as a prototype of the 'royal city', foreshadowing such later settlements as GUROB, MALKATA and EL-AMARNA.

A major contribution of Lacovara's survey of Ballas is the discussion of the functions of various structures originally excavated by Reisner. Two large ceremonial buildings, the so-called North and South Palaces, lie at either end of a long bay of desert. The South Palace was in fact probably a fortress, while the North Palace may have been a royal residence during the wars against the HYKSOS. The area between these two 'palaces' is occupied by the city itself, a large part of which was excavated by Reisner. Lacovara suggests that a group of New Kingdom houses to the west of the

BELOW *Plan of Deir el-Ballas.*

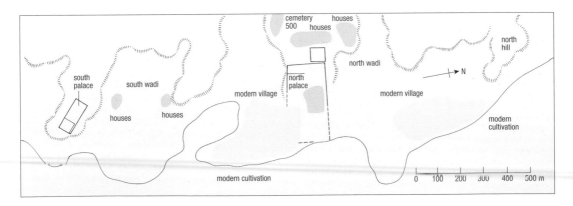

cemetery 500 houses
houses
south palace
south wadi
houses
houses
modern village
north palace
north wadi
north hill
modern village
modern village
modern cultivation
modern cultivation

North Palace were occupied by palace officials, while a large building interpreted by Reisner as a typical el-Amarna-style 'villa' is now thought to have been a set of palace kitchens.
W. STEVENSON SMITH, *The art and architecture of ancient Egypt* (Harmondsworth, 1958, rev. 1981), 278–81.
P. LACOVARA, *Survey at Deir el-Ballas* (Malibu, 1985).

Deir el-Bersha

Funerary site on the east bank of the Nile, 40 km south of modern el-Minya. The major components of the site are a row of tombs in the cliffs at the mouth of the Wadi el-Nakhla, mostly belonging to the Middle Kingdom governors of the fifteenth Upper Egyptian nome. The 12th-Dynasty tomb chapel of Thuthotep contains particularly interesting reliefs and wall-paintings, including a depic-

BELOW *Fragment of painted limestone relief from the tomb of Thuthotep at Deir el-Bersha, showing a procession of servants bearing weapons and, at the right-hand side, a carrying chair. 12th Dynasty. c.1870 BC, H. 33 cm. (EA1147)*

well as a temple dedicated to various gods, which was founded in the reign of Amenhotep III (1390–1352 BC) and almost completely rebuilt in the reign of Ptolemy IV (221–205 BC). Deir el-Medina was excavated by Ernesto Schiaparelli from 1905 to 1909 and by Bernard Bruyère between 1917 and 1947.

The importance of the site to Egyptian archaeology as a whole lies in its unusual combination of extensive settlement remains with large numbers of OSTRACA (used for rough notes and records), providing important evidence of the socio-economic system of Egypt in the 18th to 20th Dynasties. Unfortunately this unrivalled opportunity to synthesize contemporaneous textual and archaeological data from a single site has not been fully realized, primarily because of inadequate standards of excavation.
B. BRUYÈRE, *Rapport sur les fouilles de Deir el Médineh*, 17 vols (Cairo, 1924–53).
E. SCHIAPARELLI, *Relazione sui lavori della missione archaeologica italiana in Egitto* II (Turin, 1927).
M. L. BIERBRIER, *The tomb-builders of the pharaohs* (London, 1982).

ABOVE *Stele of Neferhotep, workman at Deir el-Medina. 19th Dynasty, c.1250 BC, limestone, H. 46 cm. (EA1516)*

tion of the transportation of a colossal statue of the deceased from the HATNUB travertine quarries, some 30 km to the southeast. Closer to the river is a group of Christian monuments, including a church and monastery (Deir Anba Bishuy) which flourished during the sixth and seventh centuries AD.
P. E. NEWBERRY and F. L. GRIFFITH, *El-Bersheh*, 2 vols (London, 1892).

Deir el-Medina

Settlement site on the west bank of the Nile opposite Luxor, situated in a bay in the cliffs midway between the Ramesseum and Medinet Habu. The village of Deir el-Medina was inhabited by the workmen who built the royal tombs in the VALLEY OF THE KINGS between the early 18th Dynasty and the late Ramesside period (c.1550–1069 BC). The site also incorporated the tombs of many of the workmen as

Plan of Deir el-Medina.

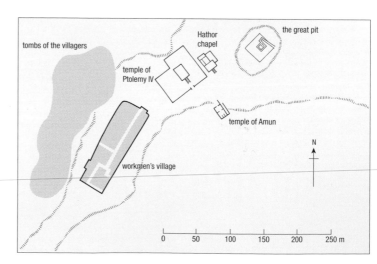

tombs of the villagers

Hathor chapel

the great pit

temple of Ptolemy IV

temple of Amun

workmen's village

N

0   50   100   150   200   250 m

D. VALBELLE, *Les ouvriers de la tombe. Deir el-Médineh à l'époque ramesside* (Cairo, 1985).
L. H. LESKO (ed.), *Pharaoh's workers: the villagers of Deir el-Medina* (Ithaca and London, 1994).

Delta

Term used to describe Lower Egypt, i.e. the region north of ancient MEMPHIS. The name derives from the fact that the Nile fans out into several tributaries as it approaches the Mediterranean, creating a triangular area of fertile land shaped like the Greek letter *delta*. It was this contrast between the narrow Nile valley of Upper Egypt and the broad Delta in the north that perhaps led to the concept of there having originally been 'two lands', united into a single state by the first pharaoh. The modern Delta is intersected by only two branches of the Nile (the Damietta and Rosetta). In the Pharaonic period there were five tributaries, but three of them, the Canopic, Sebennytic and Pelusiac branches, had dried up by the Islamic period, probably because of a combination of canal-digging and a small rise in the ground surface of the eastern Delta.

A. NIBBI (ed.), *The archaeology, geography and history of the Egyptian Delta during the pharaonic period* (Oxford, 1986).
E. C. M. VAN DEN BRINK (ed.), *The Nile Delta in transition: 4th–3rd millennium BC* (Tel Aviv, 1992).

democratization of the afterlife

Phrase used to describe the process of usurping of the pharaoh's funerary prerogatives by private individuals, particularly in terms of the identification of the deceased with the god OSIRIS. The term 'democratization' is, however, to some extent a misnomer, and it has been argued that the usurping of royal formulae and rituals does not necessarily suggest an erosion of belief in the kingship. Instead, it is suggested that the act of imitation might even imply a strengthening belief in the effectiveness of the institution of KINGSHIP.

S. QUIRKE, *Egyptian religion* (London, 1992), 155–8.

demons

In Egyptian religion and mythology, the demons who affected the living were of two main types: the 'Messengers of SEKHMET' and those associated with the netherworld.

The first type of demon represents the goddess Sekhmet in her evil aspect, and this category also includes various other spirits, such as the discontented dead, evil spirits and even sleepwalkers. This type was thought to be especially prevalent at the end of each year and had to be warded off by the benevolent

Resin-covered wooden statuette of a demon (which was placed by its 19th-century discoverer on a Late Period plinth). 19th Dynasty, c.1225 BC, from the Valley of the Kings, H. of figure 42.5 cm, H. of plinth 8.2 cm. (EA61283)

demons of OSIRIS and his followers. This host of demons lived at the edge of the created world, where they formed the forces of chaos which from time to time affected the lives and afterlives of humans.

The demons of the netherworld were still more terrifying, and the best known of these was AMMUT, devourer of the hearts of the unrighteous, who features prominently beside the weighing scale in the vignettes illustrating Chapter 125 of the Book of the Dead. The walls of some tombs, notably those of Rameses VI (KV 9, 1143–1136 BC) and IX (KV 6; 1126–1108 BC), show numerous painted demons from these FUNERARY TEXTS. Like the earthly demons, these too could be warded off by their benevolent counterparts who guarded the tomb and its contents. The 'household gods', such as BES and Aha, are sometimes described as benevolent demons, although this is probably only a reflection of the generally unfocused use of the term 'demon' in Egyptology.

D. MEEKS, 'Génies, anges et démons en Egypte', *Génies, anges et démons*, Sources orientales VIII (Paris, 1971).
G. PINCH, *Magic in ancient Egypt* (London, 1994), 33–46.

demotic (Greek *demotika*: 'popular [script]' or '[script] in common use'; also known as enchorial, 'of the country')

Cursive script known to the Egyptians as *sekh shat* ('writing for documents'), which, except in religious and funerary matters, had replaced the HIERATIC script – from which it was derived – by the 26th Dynasty (664–525 BC). It was at first used only in commercial and bureaucratic documents but by the Ptolemaic period (332–30 BC) it was also being used for religious, scientific and literary texts, including the pseudo-history of the *Demotic Chronicle*, the technical *Apis Embalming Ritual* and the Khaemwaset cycle of stories, and the *Sayings of Ankhsheshonqy* (see WISDOM LITERATURE). Unlike HIEROGLYPHS and HIERATIC, which were intended for mutually exclusive media, demotic could be used as a monumental script, hence its appearance on STELAE and as one of the three texts on the ROSETTA STONE.

Demotic continued in use alongside Greek throughout the Ptolemaic period, its survival being ensured by such features of the administration as the provision of separate Greek and Egyptian lawcourts. The latest surviving business documents written entirely in demotic date to AD 130 and 175–6, and Napthali Lewis has suggested that the demise of demotic stemmed principally from the nature of the new regime imposed at the beginning of the Roman period (c.30 BC), whereby legal and administrative documents began to be written solely in Greek. Non-literary demotic OSTRACA are found as late as AD 232/3, but thereafter the script survived only in the production of literary, religious and scientific texts and in monumental inscriptions (the latest demotic graffito at PHILAE being dated to AD 452). One of the earliest texts containing traces of the COPTIC alphabet (a combination of Greek and demotic) is the demotic

Papyrus from Thebes bearing a demotic inscription describing a loan of wheat and barley. Ptolemaic period, 194 BC, H. 23 cm. (EA10831)

London–Leiden Magical Papyrus, dated to the third century AD.

P. W. PESTMAN, *Receuil de textes démotiques et bilingues* (Leiden, 1977).

S. VLEEMING, 'La phase initiale du démotique ancien', *Chronique d'Egypte* 56 (1981), 31–48.

— (ed.), *Aspects of demotic lexicography* (Louvain, 1987).

N. LEWIS, 'The demise of the demotic document: when and why', *JEA* 79 (1993), 276–81.

Den (Dewen, Udimu) (*c.*2950 BC)

Ruler of the mid 1st Dynasty who probably succeeded his mother MERNEITH on the throne (since she may have acted as regent while he was too young to rule in his own right). He was the first to add the *nesw-bit* name ('he of the sedge and the bee') to his ROYAL TITULARY.

King Den is associated with tombs at ABYDOS and SAQQARA, both of which were constructed with the earliest examples of stairways leading down into them, an architectural refinement that would have allowed the tombs, if necessary, to have been filled up with grave goods during the king's own lifetime (thus perhaps acting as storehouses for surplus produce). The burial chamber of the tomb at Abydos dating to the reign of Den was also paved with granite slabs and some of the wooden roof supports were placed on granite blocks; this is the earliest surviving instance of stone-built architecture in an Egyptian funerary context.

Twenty ivory and ebony labels were excavated from the Abydos tomb, eighteen of them having been found by Flinders Petrie in 1900 among the spoil-heaps left by the earlier excavator, Emile Amélineau. One of the ebony tablets shows a scene from the ritual of the 'appearances of the king of Upper Egypt and the king of Lower Egypt', a ceremony which was probably similar to the SED FESTIVAL (including the earliest depictions of the king wearing the 'double crown' and also running between ritual boundary markers). An ivory label for a pair of sandals (now in the British Museum) shows the king smiting an Asiatic and bears the inscription: 'first time of striking the easterners'; this seems to indicate at least a ritual interest in the control of southern Palestine.

One of the Early Dynastic burials excavated by W. B. Emery in his first season at Saqqara in 1935 was Tomb 3035, which contained jar-sealings referring to a man called Hemaka, who evidently lived in the reign of Den. Emery's first report on Tomb 3035 described it as the tomb of King Den's chancellor in the north, but later, on the basis of the size and wealth of this and other tombs at Saqqara, Emery argued that it must have been the actual burial place of King Den, relegating the tomb of Den at Abydos to the role of a mere cenotaph. However, many Egyptologists now believe that his first theory may have been correct, making Tomb 3035 the burial place of Hemaka, Den's chancellor of Lower Egypt.

W. M. F. PETRIE, *The royal tombs of the first dynasty* I (London, 1900).

W. B. EMERY, *Archaic Egypt* (Harmondsworth, 1961), 73–80.

A. J. SPENCER, *Early Egypt* (London, 1993), 64–6.

Dendera (anc. Iunet, Tantere, Tentyris)

Site of the ancient capital of the sixth Upper Egyptian NOME, located near modern Qena, close to the mouth of the Wadi Hammamat route to the Red Sea, making it an important centre in Dynastic times. The Dendera necropolis ranges in date from the Early Dynastic period to the First Intermediate Period, including MASTABA tombs. There are also burials of sacred animals, especially the cows associated with the cult of Hathor, the local goddess, whose temple dominates the site.

The various surviving buildings making up the temple of Hathor date from the 30th Dynasty to the Roman period and are surrounded by a well-preserved mud-brick enclo-sure wall exhibiting the technique of PAN BEDDING. The main entrance is a comparatively small propylon-style gateway rather than a large pylon as in most other Upper Egyptian temples from the New Kingdom onwards.

The earliest surviving building is a MAMMISI (birth-house) dating to the reign of Nectanebo I (380–362 BC), on the western side of the forecourt. The main temple, of Ptolemaic and Roman date, is dedicated to a local form of Hathor who was closely identified with NUT, as sky-goddess and daughter of RA, as well as being associated with the west and therefore with the dead. Although the present construction is late, a temple has stood on the site from at least the early New Kingdom and texts in the crypt mention a building from the time of Pepy I (2321–2287 BC) of the 6th Dynasty.

A number of unfilled cartouches reflect the uncertain political conditions of the first century BC, while the south exterior wall bears a colossal carving of CLEOPATRA VII and her son Caesarion before the gods. This wall also has a FALSE DOOR, in the form of a Hathor SISTRUM

The first hypostyle hall of the temple of Hathor at Dendera, built in the first century AD by the Emperor Tiberius. The column base shows damage where grains of stone have been ground out for use in folk medicine in post-Pharaonic times.
(P. T. NICHOLSON)

Plan of the temple of Hathor at Dendera

with wooden canopy (now defaced), where those not able to enter the temple might petition the goddess.

The columns of the façade and outer hypostyle hall of the temple have capitals in the form of the head of Hathor surmounted by a NAOS-shaped sistrum. Although most of these columns have been damaged, possibly during the Christian period, some are well preserved. The crypts depict various cult objects stored in them, the most important of which was a BA statue of Hathor. During New Year processions this would visit various parts of the temple including the NUT chapel and the roof chapel where the *ba* was united with the solar disc. The roof also has symbolic mortuary chapels for Osiris, one of which contained a zodiac (now in the Louvre and replaced by a copy), as well as figures of Nut and scenes relating to the rebirth of Osiris.

Outside the main temple, along with the two *mammisis*, were a small temple to Isis and a sanatorium for the accommodation and healing of pilgrims. This may have served as an 'incubation chamber' (where pilgrims slept in order to receive healing DREAMS) but it perhaps principally functioned as a centre for *cippus* healing (see HORUS). Between the two *mammisis* are the remains of a basilica of the Christian period.

A. MARIETTE, *Denderah*, 4 vols (Paris, 1870–3).

W. M. F. PETRIE, *Dendereh* (London, 1900).

E. CHASSINAT and F. DAUMAS, *Le temple de Dendara*, 6 vols (Cairo, 1934–52).

H. G. FISCHER, *Dendera in the 3rd millennium BC* (New York, 1968).

F. DAUMAS, *Dendera et le temple d'Hathor* (Cairo, 1969).

desert

The Egyptians sometimes referred to the desert as *deshret* ('red land') in order to distinguish it from the fertile *kemet* ('black land'), so called because of the black soil that was deposited along the banks of the Nile by the annual INUNDATION. The epithet 'red god' was therefore often applied to SETH, the traditional god of chaos, since he was said to rule over the deserts and the general disorder that they represented, as opposed to the vegetation and fertility associated with his mythical counterpart, OSIRIS. A variety of deities, such as MIN and HATHOR, were considered to watch over the desert routes, affording protection to travellers. The deserts were essentially considered to be places of death: first, in the sense of wildernesses in which wrongdoers might be sent to perish (either as exiles or as forced

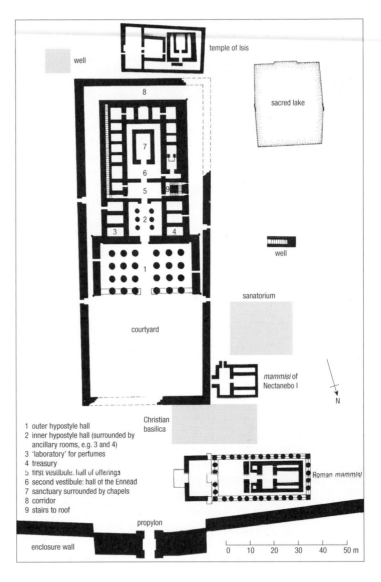

temple of Isis

sacred lake

well

sanatorium

mammisi of Nectanebo I

N

Christian basilica

Roman *mammisi*

1 outer hypostyle hall
2 inner hypostyle hall (surrounded by ancillary rooms, e.g. 3 and 4)
3 'laboratory' for perfumes
4 treasury
5 first vestibule: hall of offerings
6 second vestibule: hall of the Ennead
7 sanctuary surrounded by chapels
8 corridor
9 stairs to roof

propylon

enclosure wall

0 10 20 30 40 50 m

workers in mines or quarries); and, second, as the locations of cemeteries. The Western Desert was regarded as the entrance to the underworld where the sun disappeared each night. Various FUNERARY TEXTS describe the perilous deserts surrounding the kingdom of the dead itself.

The hieroglyph for desert consists of a diagrammatic view of a range of three hills separated by valleys, since the deserts were also mountains, in that they lay at a higher level than the intervening Nile valley. The 'desert' hieroglyph was also used as a 'determinative' sign with reference to any foreign country. Although not impassable, the deserts formed a barrier around Egypt protecting it from its neighbours and probably helping to promote the sometimes introspective tendencies of the Egyptians.

H. KEES, *Ancient Egypt: a cultural topography* (London, 1961).

I. SHAW, 'The black land, the red land', *Egypt: ancient culture, modern land*, ed. J. Malek (Sydney, 1993), 12–27.

didactic literature *see* WISDOM LITERATURE

Diodorus Siculus (*fl. c.*40 BC)

Historian born in the Sicilian town of Agyrium, who is well known for the description of Egypt included in the first book of his *Bibliotheca Historica*, a history of the world from the earliest times until Julius Caesar's conquest of Gaul. Although his own work is considered by scholars to be undistinguished, his writings are often valuable for the fragments reproduced from more important works. His account of the process of MUMMIFI-CATION, for instance, gives details not recorded by HERODOTUS, including the fact that the embalmer's incision was made on the left flank. He also records that the viscera were washed after their removal, and he claims that the man responsible for opening the corpse was usually driven away by his colleagues (an act which is now generally presumed to have been ritual). Few details have survived concerning the life of Diodorus, but he is known to have lived until at least 21 BC.

F. R. WALTON, *Diodorus of Sicily* (London and Cambridge, MA, 1967).

A. BURTON, *Diodorus Siculus I: a commentary* (Leiden, 1972).

Diospolis Parva *see* HIW-SEMAINA REGION

diplomacy *see* AMARNA LETTERS

diseases *see* MEDICINE

divine adoratrice (Egyptian *dwat-netjer*)

Religious title held by women, the precise connotations of which are not fully understood. It was originally adopted by the daughter of the chief priest of the god AMUN in the reign of Hatshepsut (1473–1458 BC). During the time of the sole reign of Thutmose III (1479–1425 BC) it was held by the mother of his principal wife. By the Third Intermediate Period it was held together with the title GOD'S WIFE OF AMUN.

G. ROBINS, *Egyptian women* (London, 1994), 149, 153.

djed pillar

Roughly cruciform symbol with at least three cross-bars. Its origins seem to be among the fetish symbols of the Predynastic period, and it has been suggested that it might represent a pole around which grain was tied. Over the course of time it came to represent the more abstract concept of stability, and, like the ANKH and WAS SCEPTRE hieroglyphs, was commonly used in this sense in decorative friezes. Although the *djed* pillar was originally associated with the god SOKAR, PTAH, the patron deity of Memphis, is sometimes described as 'the noble *Djed*'. It was because of the association of Ptah with Sokar and therefore also with OSIRIS, god of the dead, that the *djed* pillar

Amulet in the form of a djed *pillar. Saite period, faience, H. 11.1 cm. (EA12235)*

eventually became a symbol of Osiris. In the Book of the Dead it is said to represent his backbone, and certain depictions of the pillar portray it with human arms holding the royal regalia.

It was probably at Memphis that kings first performed the ceremony of 'raising the *djed* pillar', the best-known depiction of which is in the Osiris Hall at ABYDOS, although the ritual was also incorporated into one of the SED FES-TIVALS of Amenhotep III (1390–1352 BC) at Thebes. This act not only served as a metaphor for the stability of the monarchy but also symbolized the resurrection of Osiris.

J. VAN DER VLIET, 'Raising the *djed*: a rite de marge', *Akten München 1985* III, ed. S. Schoske (Hamburg, 1989), 405–11.

R. H. WILKINSON, *Reading Egyptian art* (London, 1992), 164–5.

Djer (*c.*3000 BC)

Early king of the 1st Dynasty, who was probably third in the sequence of rulers beginning with NARMER (as listed on a recently excavated clay seal impression from the royal cemetery at ABYDOS). He may also be the same king as Iti, who is mentioned in the KING LIST in the temple of Sety I at ABYDOS. A rock-carving at Gebel Sheikh Suleiman was once interpreted as evidence of a military campaign launched into Nubia at this time, but William Murnane has now shown that it dated earlier than the reign of Djer.

The burial chamber of his tomb at Abydos (which some scholars still interpret as a cenotaph rather than an actual burial-place) was floored with wooden planks. From the reign of Djer onwards, each royal tomb at Abydos contained a number of chambers in which different types of grave goods were placed, ranging from stone vases sealed with golden lids, copper bowls, gold bracelets, food, weapons, tools and furniture made from ivory and ebony. Hidden in the northern wall of Djer's tomb was a linen-wrapped human arm adorned with bracelets of gold and gemstones, perhaps left behind by tomb-robbers. On arrival at Cairo Museum the arm was discarded and only the jewellery was kept, therefore it is still not clear whether the limb was that of Djer himself. At least as early as the Middle Kingdom, his tomb was converted into a cenotaph of the god OSIRIS, and when it was first excavated by Emile Amélineau, the burial chamber contained a stone image of Osiris on a funerary couch.

W. M. F. PETRIE, *The royal tombs of the First Dynasty* I (London, 1900).

W. B. EMERY, *Great tombs of the First Dynasty*, 3 vols (Cairo and London, 1949–58).

W. J. MURNANE, 'The Gebel Sheikh Suleiman monument: epigraphic remarks', *JNES* 46 (1987), 282–5.

Djet (Wadj, 'Serpent') (*c.*2980 BC)

Ruler of the 1st Dynasty who was probably buried in Tomb Z at Abydos, which was excavated by Emile Amélineau and Flinders Petrie at the end of the nineteenth century and re-excavated in 1988 by Werner Kaiser and Gunther Dreyer. His rectangular wood-lined burial chamber is now known to have been surmounted by a brick-cased mound of sand or rubble hidden beneath the main rectangular superstructure. Probably the finest of the 1st-Dynasty funerary stelae (now in the Louvre) was found by Amélineau in the vicinity of the tomb; carved from fine limestone, it bears the serpent hieroglyph (the phonetic value of which is *djet*) framed by a royal SEREKH and surmounted by a HORUS falcon. Both the impressive Tomb 3504 at Saqqara (probably belonging to Sekhemka, an official during Djet's reign) and a large MASTABA tomb at Giza have been dated to Djet's reign by the presence of seal impressions bearing his name.

W. M. F. PETRIE, *The royal tombs of the first dynasty* I (London, 1900).

W. B. EMERY, *Great tombs of the first dynasty* II (London, 1954).

—, *Archaic Egypt* (London, 1961), 69–73.

G. DREYER, 'Umm el-Qaab: Nachuntersuchungen im frühzeitlichen Königsfriedhof 5./6. Vorbericht', *MDAIK* 49 (1993), 57.

Djoser (Zoser; Netjerikhet) (2667–2648 BC)

Second ruler of the 3rd Dynasty, whose architect, IMHOTEP, constructed the Step Pyramid at SAQQARA, which was not only the first pyramidal funerary complex but also the earliest example of large-scale stone masonry in Egypt (see PYRAMIDS). Despite the fame of his tomb, few facts are known concerning Djoser himself or the events of his reign, and most of the 'historical' information concerning his reign takes the form of late sources, such as the Famine Stele at Sehel (see FAMINE and KHNUM). Only the Horus name Netjerikhet was found in 3rd-Dynasty inscriptions associated with the pyramid, and it is only through New Kingdom graffiti that an association has been made between this name and Djoser. A number of fragments of statuary representing Netjerikhet were recovered from the pyramid complex, including an almost life-size seated statue from the SERDAB (now in Cairo), and on the walls of one of the subterranean galleries to the east of the burial chamber were three reliefs depicting the king enacting various rituals.

C. M. FIRTH, J. E. QUIBELL and J.-P. LAUER, *The Step Pyramid*, 2 vols (Cairo, 1935–6).

I. E. S. EDWARDS, *The pyramids of Egypt*, 5th ed. (Harmondsworth, 1993), 34–58.

dog

One ancient Egyptian word for dog is the onomatopoeic *imim*, referring to its barking noise. A number of different types of dogs can be recognized from depictions in tombs, many of them tall sleek breeds suitable for hunting.

The identification of specific breeds from such representations is difficult, since modern breed definitions allow little flexibility. Suffice it to say that breeds closely related to the basenji, saluki and greyhound can be identified, while there is a more general category of dogs apparently related to mastiffs and dachshunds.

As well as having a role in the hunt, some dogs served as domestic pets or guard dogs and even police dogs. Their qualities of faithfulness and bravery are sometimes referred to in the names they were given; these names are known from inscriptions on leather collars as well as from depictions on stelae and reliefs. Thus we know of 'Brave One', 'Reliable' and 'Good Herdsman', as well as simpler names referring to their colour. There were, however, sometimes more negative aspects of the Egyptians' attitude to dogs: their air of domestic subservience could be used as an insult, and some texts include references to prisoners as 'the king's dogs'.

Since the jackal and the dog were not well separated in the Egyptian mind they were both regarded as sacred to ANUBIS, sometimes being buried as SACRED ANIMALS in the Anubieion catacombs at Saqqara, although unfortunately there is little information available concerning the particular species of dog at this site. The term 'Anubis animal', rather than jackal, is sometimes used, since its identification is a matter of debate. Domestic dogs might also receive special burial, either along with their owners – a practice known from the earliest dynasties – or in their own coffins.

M. LURKER, 'Hund und Wolf in ihrer Beziehung zum Tode', *Antaios* 10 (1969), 199–216.

H. G. FISCHER, 'Hunde, Hundestele', *Lexikon der Ägyptologie* III, ed. W. Helck, E. Otto and W. Westendorf (Wiesbaden, 1980), 77–8?

W. BARTA, 'Schakal', *Lexikon der Ägyptologie* V, ed. W. Helck, E. Otto and W. Westendorf (Wiesbaden, 1984), 526–8.

R. JANSSEN and J. J. JANSSEN, *Egyptian domestic animals* (Aylesbury, 1989), 9–13.

D. J. BREWER, D. B. REDFORD and S. REDFORD, *Domestic plants and animals: the Egyptian origins* (Warminster, 1994), 110–18.

donkeys see ANIMAL HUSBANDRY

Dra Abu el-Naga see THEBES

dreams

Dreams played an important role in Egyptian culture, principally because they were thought to serve as a means of communicating the will of the gods and serving as clues to future events. Papyrus Chester Beatty III in the British Museum, an early Ramesside document found at DEIR EL-MEDINA, describes a number of dreams, each of which is followed by an interpretation and an evaluation as to whether it was good or bad. It is suggested, for instance, that if a man dreamed of drinking warm beer, this was bad and he would inevitably undergo suffering. Although the papyrus itself dates to the early thirteenth century BC, the language of the text suggests that this dream-list was originally compiled in the Middle Kingdom (2055–1650 BC).

In royal propaganda (see KINGSHIP), stelae sometimes recount the pseudo-prophetic dreams of pharaohs as a means of justifying their succession to the throne. The classic example of the royal dream stele was erected by THUTMOSE IV (1400–1390 BC) in front of the Great SPHINX at Giza, describing how, as a young prince, he fell asleep in the shade of the sphinx and was then told in a dream that if he cleared the sand away from its flanks he would become king of Egypt. Centuries later, the Kushite pharaoh TANUTAMANI (664–656 BC) set up a similar stele in the temple of Amun at the Napatan capital city Gebel Barkal (see NAPATA), describing a dream in which the throne of Egypt and Nubia was offered to him by two serpents, who presumably symbolized the 'two ladies', the goddesses of Upper and Lower Egypt. Tanutamani's stele thus provides a mythical explanation for the unusual Kushite crowns, which are adorned with double *uraei*: when the king awoke from his dream he was told, 'the two goddesses shine on your brow, the land is given to you in its length and breadth'.

From the Late Period (747–332 BC) onwards it became relatively common for individuals to sleep within temple enclosures so that ORACLES could be communicated to them through divinely inspired dreams (see BES). The Greek term *onirocrites* was used to describe the priests whose role was to interpret these dreams.

J. H. BREASTED, *Ancient records of Egypt* IV (Chicago, 1906), 469.

S. SAUNERON, *Les songes et leur interpretation* (Paris, 1959).

J. D. RAY, *The archive of Hor* (London, 1976), 130–6.

C. ZIVIE, *Giza au deuxième millénaire* (Cairo, 1976), 130–1.

J. D. RAY, 'An agricultural dream: ostracon BM 5671', *Pyramid studies and other essays presented to I. E. S. Edwards*, ed. J. Baines et al. (London, 1988), 176–83.

dress see CLOTHING

duality

The Egyptians believed that unity was emphasized by the complementarity of its parts. Thus the king of a united Egypt still bore the title 'lord of the two lands' (*neb tawy*) and 'he of the sedge and the bee' (*nesw–bit*). Similarly, the country was divided into the black land (*kemet*) and the red land (*deshret*), and split between the east (the land of the living) and the west (the realm of the dead). The earth was distinct from the heavens but the two together were the complementary halves of the created universe, while beyond the BORDERS of the universe was the 'uncreated', the chaos from

The personifications of Lower Egypt (left) and Upper Egypt (right) crown the pharaoh Ptolemy VI Philometer with the double crown. Duality was an important part of Egyptian thought. Temple of Horus at Edfu. (P. T. NICHOLSON)

which man and the gods had emerged (see CREATION and NUN).

   This duality is present at many levels of thought and symbolism, so that there are gods of Upper and Lower Egypt, and gods of the living and the dead. The mythical struggle between HORUS and SETH was essentially regarded as the universal struggle between good and evil, the triumph of light over darkness and the prevailing of order over chaos. In more pragmatic terms the KINGSHIP (personified by the god Horus) and the ordered bureaucracy which it encouraged were seen to be stronger than the powers of anarchy.

H. KEES, *Ancient Egypt: a cultural topography*, ed. T. G. H. James (London, 1961).
B. J. KEMP, *Ancient Egypt: anatomy of a civilization* (London, 1989).

dwarfs and pygmies (Egyptian *deneg, nem*)

Although the same Egyptian term (*deneg*) appears to have been used for both dwarfs and pygmies, the Egyptians' attitudes to each of these categories differed considerably.

   Cases of dwarfism seem to have been fairly common; the condition results from the failure of the bones to ossify properly, resulting in stunted growth (achondroplasia), and several such skeletons have survived, as well as numerous depictions in reliefs and statuary. One particularly striking late 4th- or early 5th-Dynasty 'group statue' depicts the dwarf Seneb and his family. Seneb held several official positions: he was overseer of the palace dwarfs, chief of the royal wardrobe, and priest of the funerary cults of Khufu (2589–2566 BC) and Djedefra (2566–2558 BC). His statue shows him seated cross-legged beside his wife Senetites, who was of normal stature, while his children stand immediately in front of him, apparently conveniently masking the area where his legs would have been if his limbs had been of normal proportions. The wealth and prestige evidently enjoyed by Seneb, to judge from his titles, tomb and funerary equipment, was not unusual for Egyptian dwarfs in general, many of whom appear to have had skilled or responsible occupations. They are depicted as jewellery-makers in the Old Kingdom tomb of MERERU-KA at Saqqara, and they are also shown tending animals, undertaking agricultural work, and sometimes providing entertainment for high officials. Seneb's marriage to a woman who was a lady of the court and a priestess is one of many indications that male dwarfs were not obliged to marry women with similar deformities. The apparent lack of prejudice against dwarfs is perhaps also indicated by the fact that a number of gods, notably BES, show signs of dwarfism.

   Pygmies, however, seem to have received rather less beneficent treatment than dwarfs, no doubt because they were essentially foreigners. They were generally imported into Egypt from tropical Africa, often serving as 'dancers before the god', temple dancers or acrobats in the service of RA. The decoration of the Old Kingdom tomb of Harkhuf (A8) at Qubbet el-Hawa (see ASWAN) includes a copy of a letter from the young 6th-Dynasty ruler PEPY II (2278–2184 BC), urging Harkhuf, who was on his way back from an expedition to the south of Sudan, to take great care of the danc-

Painted limestone group statue of the dwarf Seneb with his wife Senetites and their two children. Late 4th or early 5th Dynasty, c.2500 BC, from Giza, H. 34 cm. (CAIRO, JES1280)

ing pygmy he has acquired. The king is quoted as saying, 'my majesty desires to see this pygmy more than the gifts of the mine-land [Sinai] and of Punt'.

K. R. WEEKS, *The anatomical knowledge of the ancient Egyptians and the representation of the human figure in Egyptian art* (Ann Arbor, 1981).
O. EL-AGUIZY, 'Dwarfs and pygmies in ancient Egypt', *ASAE* 71 (1987), 53–60.
V. DASEN, *Dwarfs in ancient Egypt and Greece* (Oxford, 1993).

dyad (pair-statue)

Pair of statues, often carved from the same block of material, either representing a man and his wife or depicting two versions of the same person. Sometimes the man and wife are accompanied by their children, usually carved next to their legs. There are also occasional groups of two or three identical funerary statues portraying a single individual, one of the earliest examples being the dyad of the 5th-Dynasty priest of RA, Nimaatsed, in MASTABA tomb D56 at Saqqara (now in Cairo). It has been suggested that the intention of such 'pseudo-groups' may have been to represent the body and the spiritual manifestations of the deceased (see KA). It is possible that royal dyads, such as the unusual granite double statue of Amenemhat III from Tanis (also in Cairo), may portray both the mortal and deified aspects of the pharaoh.

M. SALEH and H. SOUROUZIAN, *The Egyptian Museum, Cairo: official catalogue* (Mainz, 1987), cat. nos 48 and 104.

dynasty

The division of the Pharaonic period into dynasties was a chronological system introduced by the priest MANETHO in the early third century BC, when he composed his history of Egypt (the *Aegyptiaca*). The thirty-one dynasties consisted of groups of rulers stretching from the time of the semi-mythical first pharaoh MENES to ALEXANDER THE GREAT. In general Manetho's dynasties appear to correspond quite closely to the grouping of kings suggested by various earlier KING LISTS, such as the TURIN ROYAL CANON, and in modern chronologies the dynasties are usually grouped into 'kingdoms' and 'intermediate periods'. The distinction between one dynasty and another occasionally seems rather arbitrary but two of the most important determining factors appear to have been changes in royal kinship links and the location of the capital.

Because of the tendency to regard the kingship as a unique and indivisible phenomenon, Manetho's dynasties, like the groups of rulers in Pharaonic king lists, tend to be treated as if they occurred in a linear sequence, one after the other, whereas it is now known that some of them (such as the 13th to 17th Dynasties) represented roughly contemporaneous and overlapping sequences of rulers who controlled only certain parts of the country. See also CHRONOLOGY.

W. G. WADDELL, *Manetho* (Cambridge, MA, and London, 1940).

W. HELCK, *Untersuchungen zu Manetho und der ägyptischen Königlisten* (Berlin, 1956).

D. REDFORD, *Pharaonic king-lists, annals and day-books: a contribution to the study of the Egyptian sense of history* (Mississauga, 1986).

S. QUIRKE, *Who were the pharaohs?* (London, 1990).

Early Dynastic period (3100–2686 BC)

Chronological phase, often described as the Archaic period, comprising the first two dynasties of the Pharaonic period, during which many of the major aspects of the culture and society of the Pharaonic period emerged. Some scholars include the 3rd Dynasty (2686–2613 BC) in the Early Dynastic period, but most chronologies treat the 3rd to 6th Dynasties as the OLD KINGDOM.

The transition from the PREDYNASTIC PERIOD to the 1st Dynasty was once regarded as a sudden political event, such as an invasion. The material culture of the period, however, suggests that the emergence of the Early Dynastic monarchy was a very gradual process.

A certain degree of controversy still surrounds the question of the location of the royal tombs of the 1st and 2nd Dynasties, given that there are élite cemeteries of the period at both ABYDOS and SAQQARA, both of which include inscriptions bearing 1st- and 2nd-Dynasty royal names. Current opinion, however, tends more towards Abydos as the royal cemetery and Saqqara as the burial ground of the high officials of the time.

The tombs at Abydos and Saqqara have yielded some of the earliest Egyptian textual evidence, primarily in the form of stone stelae, wooden and ivory labels, inscribed pottery jars and clay seal impressions. On the basis of these documents, together with the evidence of radiocarbon dating, the rough chronological structure of the period has been reconstructed. The sequence of 1st-Dynasty kings, all of whom were probably buried at Abydos, is now widely accepted as NARMER, AHA, DJER, DJET, DEN, ANEDJIB, SEMERKHET and QA'A, with Queen MERNEITH serving as a regent, probably either before or after the reign of Den. The chronology of the early 2nd-Dynasty kings, who were probably buried at SAQQARA, is more nebulous, perhaps taking the form: Hetepsekhemwy, Raneb, Nynetjer, Weneg and Sened. The last two rulers of the 2nd Dynasty were PERIBSEN and KHASEKHEMWY, both buried at Abydos.

B. G. TRIGGER, 'The rise of Egyptian civilization', *Ancient Egypt: a social history*, ed. B. G. Trigger et al. (Cambridge, 1983), 1–70.

I. SHAW, 'The Egyptian Archaic period: a reappraisal of the C-14 dates', *GM* 78 (1984), 79–86.

K. BARD, 'Toward an interpretation of the role of ideology in the evolution of complex society in Egypt', *Journal of Anthropological Archaeology* II (1992), 1–24.

A. J. SPENCER, *Early Egypt: the rise of civilization in the Nile valley* (London, 1993).

B. G. TRIGGER, *Early civilization: ancient Egypt in context* (Cairo, 1993).

economics *see* ADMINISTRATION;

AGRICULTURE; COPPER; GOLD; IRON; SILVER; STONE; TAXATION; TRADE and WOOD.

Edfu (anc. Djeb, Apollonopolis Magna)

Upper Egyptian site dominated by a large, well-preserved temple dedicated to the hawk-god HORUS. The earliest securely dated historical evidence in the region of Edfu is a rock-carving of the name of the 1st-Dynasty king DJET (*c*.2980 BC), in the desert to the east of the main site, as well as a necropolis of the Early Dynastic period (3100–2686 BC).

The main site includes settlement and funerary remains covering the entire Dynastic

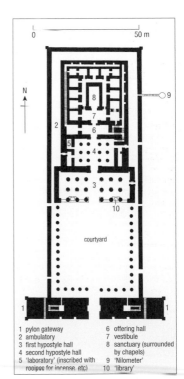

1 pylon gateway
2 ambulatory
3 first hypostyle hall
4 second hypostyle hall
5 'laboratory' (inscribed with recipes for incense, etc)
6 offering hall
7 vestibule
8 sanctuary (surrounded by chapels)
9 'Nilometer'
10 'library'

Plan of the temple of Horus at Edfu.

Pylon of the temple of Horus at Edfu. The south face of the pylon is decorated with reliefs showing Ptolemy XII smiting foreigners. On either side of the gateway are statues of the hawk-god Horus. Ptolemaic period, 71 BC, H. of eastern tower 44 m. (P. T. NICHOLSON)

period, but a substantial proportion of the buildings remain unexcavated. The French and Polish excavators of the 1920s and 1930s examined the temple as well as the Greco-Roman and Byzantine levels of the surrounding settlement. The construction of the Ptolemaic temple of Horus, which was founded on the site of a much earlier Pharaonic temple, dates to the period between the reigns of Ptolemy III and XII (246–51 BC). The reliefs and inscriptions on the walls include the myth of the contendings of Horus and SETH (probably performed annually as a religious drama) and an important account of the ritual foundation of the temple.

M. DE ROCHEMONTEIX and E. CHASSINAT, *Le temple d'Edfou* (Paris, 1892; Cairo, 1918–).

K. MICHALOWSKI et al., *Tell Edfou*, 4 vols (Cairo, 1937–50).

H. W. FAIRMAN, 'Worship and festivals in an Egyptian temple', *Bulletin of the John Rylands Library, Manchester* 37 (1954), 165–203.

—, *The triumph of Horus: an ancient Egyptian sacred drama* (London, 1974).

S. CAUVILLE, *La théologie d'Osiris à Edfou* (Cairo, 1983).

—, *Edfou* (Cairo, 1984).

education

Few ancient Egyptians were given any formal education, and the majority of the people were illiterate. For the latter, training was essentially vocational: practical trades and crafts were passed on from one generation to another, and boys often appear to have served apprenticeships under their fathers. Usually a son would be expected to take over his father's trade or post and eventually to provide the principal means of support for the family. There is little surviving evidence concerning the training or education of women, although daughters generally seem to have acquired domestic skills, such as weaving and cooking, from their mothers.

For the élite members of Egyptian society, education was essentially a matter of scribal training, since the use of writing was the key to Egyptian administration and economic organization, and the sphere of the trained scribe extended beyond writing to the roles of manager and bureaucrat. A document from the fourteenth regnal year of Psamtek I (664–610 BC) contains the individual signatures of fifty high officials, ranging from PRIESTS to VIZIERS, thus indicating the widespread literacy of the members of the ruling élite in the 26th Dynasty at least. Many of the surviving texts from the Pharaonic period were intended to function not only as literary works but also as educational textbooks, such as the *Miscellanies*, and often the very survival of these documents is owed largely to constant copying as a means of acquiring writing skills. The question of the extent of female literacy is still a matter of considerable debate; it is possible that a small proportion of women could read and write, since there are surviving letters to and from women at the New Kingdom workmen's village of Deir el-Medina (c.1500–1100 BC), although it is equally possible that such documents might have been written and read by male SCRIBES on behalf of female patrons.

Written education was very clearly addressed to boys, and many of the so-called 'wisdom texts' are presented in the form of sets of instructions spoken by fathers to sons (see ETHICS and WISDOM LITERATURE). The sons of the élite seem to have been given a broader education involving reading, writing and MATHEMATICS. Such boys would probably have been taught in a scribal school attached to some particular division of the administration, such as the HOUSE OF LIFE in a temple or, in the most privileged cases, at the royal court itself. For most of the Pharaonic period the HIERATIC script would have been the first to be learned, with only a few selected individuals then being instructed in the more elaborate and artistic HIEROGLYPHS. The subject of mathematics was evidently taught by means of numerous examples rather than by the use of abstract formulae, so that problems were usually broken down into a repetitive series of smaller calculations.

Learning was by rote, in that most lessons appear to have taken the form of copying out exercises and committing long passages of text to memory. The exercises took the form of model LETTERS, reports and selections from 'instructions' such as the *Book of Kemyt*. Frequently such instructions presented a distinctly biased view of society, praising the scribal profession and sometimes satirizing other ways of life (see HUMOUR). School discipline was strict, and one text includes the memorable phrase: 'A boy's ear is on his back – he listens when he is beaten'.

T. G. H. JAMES, *Pharaoh's people: scenes from life in ancient Egypt* (Oxford, 1984), 136–51.

E. STROUHAL, *Life in ancient Egypt* (Cambridge, 1992), 31–7.

G. ROBINS, *Women in ancient Egypt* (London, 1993), 111–14.

D. SWEENEY, 'Women's correspondence from Deir el-Medineh', *Sesto Congresso Internazionale di Egittologia, Atti II* (Turin, 1993), 523–9.

Egyptology

Some scholars date the beginning of the discipline of Egyptology to 22 September 1822, the day on which Jean-François CHAMPOLLION wrote his *Lettre à M. Dacier relative à l'alphabet des hiéroglyphes phonétiques*, in which he demonstrated that he had deciphered the HIEROGLYPHIC script. Champollion, however, was undoubtedly already drawing on the work of earlier writers, such as HORAPOLLO, and Thomas YOUNG, and his work was actually the culmination of hundreds of years of earlier 'rediscovery' of ancient Egypt.

The Egyptian civilization was already regarded as a venerable and ancient one by the

Photograph showing 'Cleopatra's needle' in the process of being prepared for transportation by the British engineer James Dixon. The obelisk was placed in a specially-made metal cylinder, towed by boat to England, and eventually erected on the Thames Embankment in 1878, only a year after Dixon had been contracted to bring it from Egypt. (REPRODUCED COURTESY OF THE GRIFFITH INSTITUTE)

time that the Greek historian HERODOTUS (*c*.484–420 BC) compiled the first general account of the culture as a whole. Pharaonic Egypt was also a source of considerable interest to Arabic scholars of the Middle Ages. Many of these early accounts mixed observation with fantasy, and more than a little interest in treasure hunting, but some show a genuine curiosity about the names and histories of the builders of the great monuments. It was obvious to Arabic scholars and early travellers that the tombs and temples were covered in carvings, the mysterious hieroglyphs, and it was this aspect of Egyptian civilization that attracted the attention of European scholars such as the German priest Athanasius Kircher, who undertook important research into Coptic and Arabic manuscripts before turning his attention to the hieroglyphs. Unfortunately, he mistakenly believed these signs to be purely symbolic and non-phonetic, which led him to the fantastic interpretations of texts that in later times have earned him a somewhat unjustified notoriety.

The foundations of Egyptological knowledge were laid by such European 'travellers' as Richard Pococke, Claude Sicard and Frederick Ludwig Norden, whose pioneering accounts of the Pharaonic sites they visited are in some cases the only record of monuments that have long since fallen victim to plundering or natural deterioration. However, the first systematic exploration of Egypt was undertaken at the end of the eighteenth century by a small team of French scholars accompanying Napoleon's military expedition through the Nile valley. The task of these 'savants' was to record all aspects of Egypt's flora, fauna and history, and their results were published between 1809 and 1822 as the twenty-four-volume *Description de l'Egypte*. Napoleon's expedition was brought to an end by the British, but the scholars were allowed to continue their work until 1802. When Alexandria was surrendered to the British, the collections made by the savants were also handed over, including certain objects, such as the ROSETTA STONE, that were to prove crucial to the development of Egyptology.

Large numbers of individual European travellers and collectors began to visit Egypt in the nineteenth century, along with several further large-scale scientific expeditions, most notably the work of Jean-François Champollion and Ippolito ROSELLINI between 1828 and 1829, as well as the ambitious and wide-ranging researches of the German scholar Karl Richard LEPSIUS between 1842 and 1845. Lepsius' expedition undertook extensive mapping and a certain amount of excavation, recording some sites not visited by the French as well as adding further details to the accounts of known sites; his work was published under the title of *Denkmaeler aus Aegypten und Aethiopien*. In the English-speaking world, the first comprehensive and reliable description of Egyptian antiquities and culture was Sir John Gardner WILKINSON's monumental *Manners and customs of the ancient Egyptians*, published in three volumes in 1837, after twelve years of continuous fieldwork in Egypt and Nubia.

These scientific expeditions unfortunately took place against a background of looting and collecting by such pioneers as Bernardino Drovetti and Giovanni BELZONI. The antiquities acquired by such men eventually formed the nuclei of important national collections, such as the British Museum, the Louvre, the Berlin museums and the Museo Egizio in Turin. In 1858 the Pasha appointed a Frenchman, Auguste MARIETTE, to oversee all future excavation in Egypt. Not only did this mark the beginning of more orderly study but it also reflected an increasing involvement in the conservation and detailed analysis of the monuments.

Gradually the subject gained respectability, partly through the establishment of a number of important academic posts in Egyptology, and scholars such as Flinders PETRIE and George REISNER were able to develop increas-

Portrait in oils of Howard Carter, painted by his elder brother William in 1924. (REPRODUCED COURTESY OF THE GRIFFITH INSTITUTE)

ingly meticulous techniques of field recording and excavation. As a result, from the 1890s onwards the subject became increasingly professional in nature. Mariette's overseeing of excavations developed into the Egyptian Antiquities Service (the modern incarnation of which is the Supreme Council for Antiquities), which is now responsible for granting excavation permits to foreign missions, as well as co-ordinating their work in the best interests of the Egyptian people. This increasingly involves the rescue of sites and monuments endangered by construction works, such as the ASWAN HIGH DAM in the 1960s, the Cairo 'waste-water project' in the

1980s, and the el-Salaam canal in northern Sinai during the 1990s. In terms of the popular conception of Egyptology, however, these rescue projects have been distinctly overshadowed by Howard CARTER's discovery of the tomb of Tutankhamun in 1922, which was the first great 'media event' in the history of Egyptology, capturing the imagination of subsequent generations of scholars.

Modern Egyptologists draw on a huge diversity of techniques and disciplines, including sophisticated geophysical survey, meticulous excavation and recording in plans and photographs, computer-generated reconstructions, as well as the more traditional fields of epigraphy (copying of inscriptions, paintings and reliefs) and papyrology.

See Appendix 1 for a list of the names and dates of the major early travellers and Egyptologists mentioned in the text.

K. R. LEPSIUS, *Denkmaeler aus Aegypten und Aethiopien*, 12 vols (Berlin, 1849–59).

B. M. FAGAN, *The rape of the Nile: tomb robbers, tourists and archaeologists in Egypt* (London, 1977).

J. VERCOUTTER, *The search for ancient Egypt* (London, 1992).

D. O'CONNOR, 'Egyptology and archaeology: an African perspective', *A history of African archaeology*, ed. P. Robertshaw (London, 1990), 236–51.

W. R. DAWSON, E. P. UPHILL and M. BIERBRIER, *Who was who in Egyptology*, 3rd ed. (London, 1995).

el- All site names beginning with 'el-' (Arabic 'the') are alphabetized under the second part of the name, e.g. Kurru, el-.

Elephantine *see* ASWAN

Elkab (anc. Nekheb)

Upper Egyptian site on the east bank of the Nile at the mouth of Wadi Hillal, about 80 km south of Luxor, consisting of prehistoric and Pharaonic settlements, rock-cut tombs of the early 18th Dynasty (1550–1295 BC), remains of temples dating from the Early Dynastic period (3100–2686 BC) to the Ptolemaic period (332–30 BC), as well as part of the walls of a COPTIC monastery. First scientifically excavated by James Quibell at the end of the nineteenth century, the site has been investigated primarily by Belgian archaeologists since 1937.

The walled Pharaonic settlement of Nekheb was one of the first urban centres of the Early Dynastic period, and for a short time

Setau and his wife seated before a table of offerings. Tomb of Setau at Elkab. (P. T. NICHOLSON)

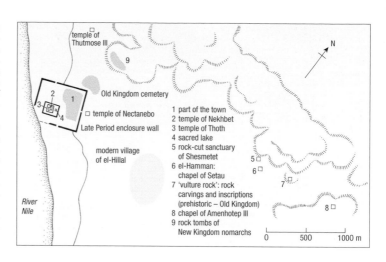

Plan of Elkab.

in the New Kingdom (1550–1069 BC) it eclipsed the city of Nekhen (HIERAKONPOLIS) on the opposite bank, becoming the capital of the third nome of Upper Egypt. Its massive mud-brick walls, dating to the Late Period (747–332 BC) and still largely preserved, enclosed an area of about 250,000 sq. m. Near the centre of the town are the remains of sandstone temples dedicated to the deities NEKHBET and THOTH, which date primarily to the 18th to 30th Dynasties (1550–343 BC), but the original foundation of the temple of Nekhbet

almost certainly dates back to the late fourth millennium BC.

The rock-tombs of the provincial governors of Elkab in the New Kingdom include those of Ahmose son of Ibana (EK5), an admiral in the wars of liberation against the Hyksos rulers (c.1550 BC), and Setau (EK4), a priest during the reign of Rameses III (1184–1153 BC). The style of the early 18th-Dynasty wall-paintings anticipates that of the first New Kingdom nobles' tombs at Thebes.

In 1967 Paul Vermeersch discovered a series of well-stratified EPIPALAEOLITHIC campsites. Radiocarbon-dated to c.6400–5980 BC, these

In the map:

temple of Thutmose III
9
Old Kingdom cemetery
temple of Nectanebo
Late Period enclosure wall
modern village of el-Hillal
River Nile
N

1 part of the town
2 temple of Nekhbet
3 temple of Thoth
4 sacred lake
5 rock-cut sanctuary of Shesmetet
6 el-Hamman: chapel of Setau
7 'vulture rock': rock carvings and inscriptions (prehistoric – Old Kingdom)
8 chapel of Amenhotep III
9 rock tombs of New Kingdom nomarchs

0   500   1000 m

are the type sites of the Elkabian microlithic industry, filling a gap in the prehistoric cultural sequence of Egypt, between the Upper Palaeolithic period (c.10,000 BC) and the earliest Neolithic phase (c.5500 BC).

J. E. QUIBELL, El-Kab (London, 1898).

—, 'L'Elkabien. Une nouvelle industrie epipaléolithique à Elkab en Haute Egypte, sa stratigraphie, sa typologie', CdE 45 (1970), 45–68.

P. DERCHAIN and P. VERMEERSCH, Elkab, 2 vols (Brussels and Louvain, 1971–8).

encaustic

Painting technique, employing a heated mixture of wax and pigment, which was particularly used for the Fayum mummy-portraits of Roman Egypt (see ART and HAWARA).

enchorial see DEMOTIC

ennead (Egyptian pesedjet)

Term used to describe a group of nine gods. The earliest and most significant instance of such a grouping was the Great Ennead of HELIOPOLIS, consisting of ATUM (the so-called

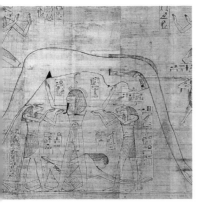

Vignette from the Book of the Dead papyrus of Nesitanebtashru, showing three of the members of the Heliopolitan Ennead: Geb, Nut and Shu, symbolizing heaven and earth separated by the sky. 21st Dynasty, c.1025 BC. (EA10554, SHEET 87)

'bull of the Ennead') and three generations of his progeny: his children SHU and TEFNUT, his grandchildren GEB and NUT, and his four great-grandchildren OSIRIS, ISIS, SETH and NEPHTHYS. These nine deities participated in the Heliopolitan CREATION myth, whereby the sun-god emerged from the primeval waters of NUN.

E. HORNUNG, Conceptions of God in ancient Egypt; the one and the many (London, 1983).

N. GRIMAL, A history of ancient Egypt (Oxford, 1992), 41–5.

E. HORNUNG, Idea into image, trans. E. Bredeck (New York, 1992), 39–54.

Epipalaeolithic

Poorly defined chronological phase between the Palaeolithic and Neolithic periods, characterized in Egypt by a subsistence pattern midway between HUNTING and AGRICULTURE. In cultural terms, it was roughly equivalent to the European Mesolithic period.

erotica

Since the definition of 'erotica' or 'pornography', as opposed to the honest portrayal of SEXUALITY, is a culturally biased exercise, much of the possible erotic significance of Egyptian art and literature may well be in the eye of the beholder. The line between erotic art and religion is not easily drawn, particular-

So-called 'Naukratic figure', from the Greek settlement at Naukratis. Ptolemaic period, c.300 BC, H. 5.7 cm. (EA54893)

ly in the case of the ancient Egyptian culture, in which sexuality and fertility were often important elements of divine cults, such as those of BES, HATHOR and MIN. The so-called 'incubation chambers' of Bes at Saqqara appear to have been rooms in which 'pilgrims' hoped to receive erotic dreams leading to greater fertility. The walls of the chambers were lined with figures of the dwarf-god Bes accompanied by nude females. Similarly, symplegmata (pottery artefacts depicting entangled groups of individuals engaged in sexual acts) were clearly depicting sexual intercourse, but it is not clear whether they were purely erotica or votive in function. A relatively uncontentious example of erotica has survived from the 19th Dynasty (1295–1186 BC), in the form of the celebrated Turin erotic papyrus (Turin, Museo Egizio), which appears to portray the adventures of a comic character during a visit to a brothel. A number of ostraca also depict men and women engaged in sexual acts.

The genre of love poetry appears to have flourished in the more cosmopolitan atmosphere of the New Kingdom, when Egypt was exposed to new peoples and exotic ideas from abroad. The poems, written on papyri or ostraca and dating primarily to the 19th to 20th Dynasties, seem to have been read out loud with musical accompaniment from harpists, and so might be regarded as a form of song. They would perhaps have provided part of the entertainment at the lavish banquets of the nobility, and were unlikely to have been spontaneous compositions. In such poems it was usual for the couple to refer to one another as 'brother' and 'sister', sometimes taking turns to describe their feelings of joy or loss at their particular romantic situation, or delivering monologues addressed to their own hearts.

Feasts and banquets in the 18th Dynasty often appear to have included elements of erotica, and both men and women are depicted wearing diaphanous clothing at such occasions, when they are depicted on the walls of tomb chapels. Their entertainment often consisted of naked or semi-naked dancing girls, some of whom may have been prostitutes. It is possible, however, that the erotic overtones in these tomb paintings may have been deliberately intended to emphasize sexuality and fertility in order to enhance the potency of the funerary cult. Naked women, sometimes associated with cats and ducks, were often used as decorative elements on toilet objects, particularly during the reign of AMENHOTEP III (1390–1352 BC). See SEXUALITY for a discussion of the possible relationships between erotica and fertility, including the production of so-called 'fertility figurines'.

J. OMLIN, 'Der papyrus 55001 und seine satirisch-erotischen Zeichnungen und Inschriften', Catalogo del Museo Egizio di Torino III (Turin, 1973).

P. DERCHAIN, 'La perruque et le cristal', SAK 2 (1975), 55–74.

M. LICHTHEIM, Ancient Egyptian literature II (Berkeley, 1976), 181–93.

L. MANNICHE, Sexual life in ancient Egypt (London, 1987).

E. STROUHAL, Life in ancient Egypt (Cambridge, 1992), 11–19, 39–49.

Esna (anc. Iunyt, Ta-senet, Latopolis)

Site on the west bank of the Nile in Upper Egypt, 50 km south of Luxor. The main surviving archaeological remains are the sacred necropolis of the Nile perch (Lates niloticus) and the Greco-Roman temple dedicated to the ram-god KHNUM as well as the goddesses NEITH and Heka (see MAGIC), which was built on the site of a temple mentioned by texts at least as early as the reign of Thutmose III

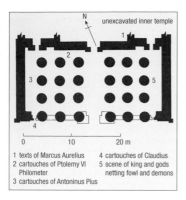

1 texts of Marcus Aurelius
2 cartouches of Ptolemy VI Philometer
3 cartouches of Antoninus Pius
4 cartouches of Claudius
5 scene of king and gods netting fowl and demons

Plan of the Temple of Khnum at Esna.

(1479–1425 BC). Only the HYPOSTYLE HALL was excavated by Auguste Mariette, and the rest of the temple remains buried under the surrounding buildings of the modern town. The building was probably connected originally with the Nile by a processional way leading to a quay, traces of which, bearing cartouches of the Roman emperor Marcus Aurelius (AD 161–180), have been preserved *in situ.* According to some of the inscriptions in the temple, there were originally four other temples in the region (one of which was recorded by Napoleon's savants), but none of these has survived into modern times.

Important late Palaeolithic remains have also been found in the vicinity of Esna. Together with contemporaneous material at NAQADA, Dishna and Toshka, they make up the main sources of evidence for the 'Esnan' lithic industry which flourished alongside the Qadan, Afian and Sebilian industries during the Sahaba–Darau period (*c.*13,000–10,000 BC). The remains at Esnan sites include grinding stones and sickle blades associated with the cultivation of domesticated plants, as well as the stone points and scrapers associated with hunting and gathering.

S. SAUNERON, *Esna,* 5 vols (Cairo, 1959–67).

D. DOWNES, *The excavations at Esna 1905–1906* (Warminster, 1974).

F. WENDORF and R. SCHILD (ed.) *Prehistory of the Nile valley* (New York, 1976), 289–91.

ethics

The accepted code of social behaviour and the distinction between right and wrong during the Pharaonic period both tend to be closely intertwined with FUNERARY BELIEFS and cultic requirements. The concept of MAAT (often translated as 'truth' or 'harmony') was central

to ancient Egyptian ethics, representing the original state of tranquillity at the moment of the CREATION of the universe. It was the feather of the goddess Maat that was weighed against the heart of the deceased to determine whether he or she was worthy of resurrection in the afterlife. The so-called 'negative confession' – a list of sins that had not been committed by the deceased – was intended to be recited in this 'hall of judgement' in order to ensure a successful outcome.

A number of practical statements of Egyptian ethics have survived in the form of the *sebayt* (see WISDOM LITERATURE), mainly written on papyrus and dating from the Old Kingdom to the Roman period (*c.*2686 BC–AD 395). The earliest of these documents describe the qualities required of a person in order to ensure success both in his or her lifetime and in the afterlife. Individuals were expected both to satisfy their superiors and to protect those who were poorer. From the second millenni-

Two fragments of a papyrus inscribed with sections of the Instruction of Ptahhotep. *12th Dynasty, c.1900 BC, H. 15 cm. (EA10371, 10435)*

um BC, the code of ethics described in the *sebayt* was less worldly, tending to measure virtue more in terms of piety to the gods than in terms of material success. See also LAW.

T. G. H. JAMES, *Pharaoh's people* (Oxford, 1984), 73–99.

E. STROUHAL, *Life in ancient Egypt* (Cambridge, 1992), 31–4.

execration texts

Type of document listing places, groups of people or individuals regarded as hostile or inherently evil. These texts occur from the late Old Kingdom onwards and were inscribed on statuettes of prisoners or pottery jars, which were often broken and buried as part of a magical process of triumphing over the persons or places listed. Most of the surviving examples were found in the vicinity of tombs at Thebes and Saqqara, but a large number were also excavated at the Middle Kingdom FORTRESS of Mirgissa in Nubia (including texts inscribed on a human skull), no doubt comprising mag-

ical defences to back up the physical military fortifications.

The execration texts have helped Egyptologists to identify those who were considered to be enemies of Egypt at different periods in their history, although the historical value of such lists is reduced by the tendency to repeat stock lists of names, which are often obviously anachronistic. Sometimes the names

Line-drawing of an 'execration figure' consisting of a schematic statuette of a bound captive inscribed with a hieratic cursing ritual, one of five similar figures that are thought to have been found at Helwan. The text lists various Nubians and Libyans as well as two Egyptian rebels. 12th Dynasty, c.1920 BC, travertine, H. 15 cm. (CAIRO, JE63955, DRAWN BY RICHARD PARKINSON)

of the hostile forces are listed in great detail, while in other instances the enemies are the stereotypical NINE BOWS, the figure 'nine' representing three times three, which was the 'plurality of pluralities', thus designating the entirety of all enemies. A related example of the magic involved in the execration texts is the ceremony of 'breaking red jars' as part of temple ritual designed to ward off evil, the jars being the colour of blood.

G. POSENER, 'Achtungstexte', *Lexikon der Ägyptologie* I, ed. W. Helck, E. Otto and W. Westendorf (Wiesbaden, 1975), 67–9.

—, *Cinq figures d'envoûtement* (Cairo, 1987).

D. B. REDFORD, *Egypt, Canaan and Israel in ancient times* (Princeton, 1992), 87–93.

R. K. RITNER, *The mechanics of ancient Egyptian magical practice* (Chicago, 1993).

eye of Ra

Term used to describe the eye of the sun-god,

which was considered to exist as a separate entity, independent of the god himself. The symbolism of the eye of RA, associated with a number of goddesses, was complex and diverse. In the myth identifying HATHOR as the eye, she was regarded as having travelled to Nubia, whence she had to be lured back. The SEKHMET version of the eye, on the other hand, took the form of a savage goddess who revelled in the slaughter of humans as the instrument of the sun-god's wrath. These two versions of the eye were essentially the two sides of the personality of the goddess. The eye was also closely identified with the cobra-goddess WADJYT, the divine personification of the *uraeus* (*iaret* or *nesret* in Egyptian) which was worn on the brow of the king in order to spit venom at his enemies (see COBRA).

H. te VELDE, 'Mut, the eye of Re', *Akten Munchen 1985* III, ed. S. Schoske (Hamburg, 1989), 395–403.

eye-paint *see* COSMETICS

F

faience

Ceramic material composed of crushed quartz, or quartz sand, with small amounts of lime and plant ash or natron. This body material is usually coated with a bright blue or green glaze of soda–lime–silica type. It was used from the Predynastic period to the Islamic period; typical products include small figurines and amulets, architectural ornaments and inlays, vessels, and such funerary artefacts as SHABTI figures.

The material was known to the Egyptians as *tjehenet*, the literal meaning of which was 'brilliant' or 'dazzling'. Like GLASS, which was introduced in the New Kingdom (1550–1069 BC), its main purpose was probably to imitate gem-stones such as TURQUOISE and LAPIS LAZULI. Although blue and green are the most common colours, many others could also be achieved, and polychrome pieces were very popular at certain periods, not least during the New Kingdom when elaborate inlays and pieces of jewellery were being produced. Black decoration was sometimes added to monochrome pieces by painting in manganese.

The technology for producing faience may have developed from the process of glazing quartz and steatite stones. The material is more properly called 'Egyptian faience', in order to distinguish it from the tin-glazed earthenware originally made at Faenze in Italy from late medieval times. Because the bright colours of the Egyptian material reminded early Egyptologists of European 'faience' (now more correctly called *majolica*), they used this somewhat misleading name.

The body material of faience was mixed with water and then moulded or hand-modelled to the required shape. Difficult shapes were sometimes abraded from rough-outs when partly dried, thus allowing very delicate pieces to be produced if necessary. Many hundreds of clay moulds for producing rings, amulets and other items of faience have

Egyptian faience bowl from Thebes. New Kingdom. (EA4790)

survived, particularly from urban sites such as EL-AMARNA and QANTIR.

Glazing was achieved in three ways. The first of these was 'efflorescence', whereby the glazing material was mixed with the quartz body and effloresced on to its surface as the piece dried; when fired, this coating melted to become a glaze. The second method was 'cementation', in which the artefact to be glazed was surrounded by glazing powder, which bonded with its surface during firing. The finished piece was then removed from the unused glazing powder, which could be easily crumbled away. In the third method, known as 'application glazing', the object was coated in slurry (or in powder of glazing material) and then fired.

A. KACZMARCZYK and R. E. M. HEDGES, *Ancient Egyptian faience* (Warminster, 1983).

P. VANDIVER and W. D. KINGERY, 'Egyptian faience: the first high-tech ceramic', *Ceramics and civilization* III, ed. W. D. Kingery (Columbus, Ohio, 1987), 19–34.

P. T. NICHOLSON, *Egyptian faience and glass* (Princes Risborough, 1993).

falcon

One of a number of birds which figured among the SACRED ANIMALS of ancient Egypt. The falcon (Egyptian *bik*) or hawk was frequently regarded as the BA of HORUS, the hawk-headed god and son of OSIRIS (to whom the bird was also sacred). Excavations at HIERAKONPOLIS ('city of the falcon'), the ancient Egyptian Nekhen, revealed a fine gold falcon head with two plumes and *uraeus* (Cairo, Egyptian Museum), which was once part of a composite statue. The Horus-falcon was the guardian deity of the ruler and is frequently depicted with its wings outstretched protectively behind the head of the king, as on the famous statue of the 4th-Dynasty ruler KHAFRA. It was also the falcon that surmounted the royal SEREKH, where it served a similar protective function, an extension of the role it seems to have adopted as early as the beginning of the Pharaonic period, when it was depicted on the palette of NARMER. The bird was also sacred to the gods MONTU and SOKAR, and occasionally also associated with the goddess HATHOR. A falcon on a plumed staff was one of the symbols of the west and the necropoleis, and the BA was sometimes represented as a human-headed falcon.

At least as early as the Late Period (747–332 BC) at SAQQARA there was a catacomb constructed specifically for mummified hawks sacred to Horus. Recent examination of a number of these mummies has shown them to comprise a number of different types of birds

of prey. Thus, the Horus-falcon image may have been regarded as interchangeable with a whole range of other birds of prey.

L. STÖRK and H. ALTENMÜLLER, 'Falke', *Lexikon der Ägyptologie* II, ed. W. Helck, E. Otto and W. Westendorf (Wiesbaden, 1977), 93–7.

R. WILKINSON, *Reading Egyptian art* (London, 1992), 82–3.

false door

Elaborate stone or wooden architectural element inside Egyptian tombs and mortuary temples, in front of which funerary offerings were usually placed. The false door, west-orientated and serving as a link between the living and the dead, was a rectangular imitation doorway which first appeared in tombs of the Old Kingdom (2686–2181 BC). The typical form of the false door evolved out of the 'palace-façade' external architecture of the MASTABA tombs of the élite in the Early Dynastic period (3100–2686 BC), the external sides of which consisted of a series of alternate panels and recessed niches. The false door was effectively a narrow stepped niche surmounted by a rectangular stone slab-stele,

Limestone false door of Ptahshepses from his tomb at Saqqara. 5th Dynasty. c.2450 BC, H. 3.66 m. (EA682)

usually carved with a figure of the deceased seated before an OFFERING TABLE and inscribed with the traditional OFFERING FORMULA and the name and titles of the tomb-owner. Some surviving false doors incorporate a life-size relief figure of the *ka* (spiritual 'double') of the deceased stepping out of the niche.

S. WIEBACH, *Die ägyptische Scheintür* (Hamburg, 1981).

N. STRUDWICK, *The administration of Egypt in the Old Kingdom* (London, 1985).

M. SALEH and H. SOUROUZIAN, *The Egyptian Museum, Cairo: official catalogue* (Mainz, 1987), cat. nos. 57–8.

G. HAENY, 'Scheintür', *Lexikon der Ägyptologie* V, ed. W. Helck, E. Otto and W. Westendorf (Wiesbaden, 1984), 563–71.

family *see* CHILDREN

famine

Egypt's agricultural prosperity depended on the annual INUNDATION of the Nile. For crops to flourish it was desirable that the Nile should rise about eight metres above a zero point at the first cataract near Aswan. A rise of only seven metres would produce a lean year, while six metres would lead to a famine. That such famines actually occurred in ancient Egypt is

The Famine Stele on the island of Sehel, south of Aswan. The rock bears a carved inscription which refers to a seven-year famine and purports to date to the time of the 3rd-Dynasty ruler Djoser, but actually belongs to the Ptolemaic period.
(P. I. NICHOLSON)

well documented from a number of sources, both literary and artistic.

On the island of Sehel, immediately south of Aswan, is the Famine Stele. This purports to be a decree of Djoser (2667–2648 BC) of the 3rd Dynasty recording his concern over a seven-year famine, which is supposed to have been eventually ended by the ram-god KHNUM, who controlled the rising of the waters. In fact the text dates to Ptolemaic times, and may simply be designed to reinforce the claims of the temple of Khnum on Elephantine to tax local produce (although some scholars believe that it is a copy of an authentic document).

That famines took place during the Old Kingdom is not in doubt, and the surviving visual evidence includes several fragments of relief from the walls of the 5th-Dynasty causeway of the pyramid complex of UNAS (2375–2345 BC) at Saqqara. These reliefs depict numerous emaciated figures, their ribcages clearly visible, seated on the ground and apparently weak from hunger. It has been argued by some scholars, partly on the basis of these reliefs, that the Old Kingdom (2686–2181 BC) ended largely because of prolonged drought and increasing desertification. The 'autobiographical' inscriptions in the tomb of the provincial governor Ankhtifi (c.2100 BC), at EL-MO'ALLA, describe how he saved his people from 'dying on the sandbank

of hell'; the phrase 'on the sandbank' (*em tjes*) perhaps refers to a low inundation and hence to famine. The inscriptions in the tomb of Hetepi at Elkab also describe a famine during the reign of INTEF II (2112–2063 BC).

Prolonged periods of famine, caused by poor inundation, may indeed sometimes have led to political turmoil and helped to bring about a temporary end to the established order. The Biblical story of Joseph may itself have taken place during the Second Intermediate Period (1650–1550 BC), and it has been suggested that it was a HYKSOS king of Egypt whom Joseph saved from the effects of famine (but see also BIBLICAL CONNECTIONS).

The building of canals and irrigation ditches did much to alleviate the suffering caused by low floods, but such stratagems were not always sufficient. At lean times people appear to have turned to the black market or to theft in order to feed themselves, and certain papyri indicate that the royal tomb-robberies of the 20th Dynasty (1186–1069 BC) may have been prompted by the need for gold to buy food during the so-called 'year of the hyenas'.

J. VANDIER, *La famine dans l'Egypte ancienne* (Cairo, 1936).

S. SCHOTT, 'Aufnahmen vom Houngersnotrelief aus dem Aufweg der Unaspyramide', *RdE* 17 (1965), 7–13.

D. B. REDFORD, *A study of the Biblical story of Joseph* (Leiden, 1970), 91–9.

B. BELL, 'The dark ages in ancient history. I: The first dark age in Egypt', *American Journal of Archaeology* 75 (1971), 1–26.

W. STEVENSON SMITH, *The art and architecture of*

ancient Egypt, 2nd ed. (Harmondsworth, 1981), 133–4

Farafra Oasis (anc. Ta-iht)

Fertile depression in the Western Desert, about 300 km west of the modern town of Asyut. The smallest of the major Egyptian oases, it is first mentioned in texts dating to the Old Kingdom (2686–2181 BC), and by the 19th Dynasty (1295–1186 BC) it was said to have been inhabited by Libyans. However, no archaeological traces of the Pharaonic phase of occupation have yet been discovered, the earliest known sites being the settlements and cemeteries at Ain el-Wadi and Wadi Abu Hinnis in the northern part of the oasis, which date to the Roman period (30 BC–AD 395). At Ain Dallaf, on the northwestern edge of the Farafra depression, are the remains of a town of the early Christian period (c. AD 450).

H. J. L. BEADNELL, *Farafra Oasis* (Cairo, 1901).

L. GIDDY, *Egyptian oases, Bahariya, Dakhla, Farafra and Kharga during pharaonic times* (Warminster, 1987).

Fara'in, Tell el- (anc. Pe and Dep, Per-Wadjyt, Buto)

Cluster of three mounds (comprising two towns and a temple complex) in the northwestern Delta, which was occupied from late Predynastic times until the Roman period (c.3300 BC–AD 395). The site was identified as ancient Buto by Flinders Petrie, and in 1904 C. T. Currelly undertook trial excavations. The site was subsequently not properly examined until the 1960s when the survey and excavations of Veronica Seton-Williams and Dorothy Charlesworth revealed Late Period, Ptolemaic and Roman remains, including cemeteries, houses, baths and temples. Textual sources have identified Buto with 'Pe and Dep', the semi-mythical Predynastic twin capitals of Lower Egypt. The Predynastic strata at the site were first located in the 1980s by Thomas von der Way, whose excavations appear to have revealed a stratigraphic level in which Lower Egyptian Predynastic pottery types were gradually being replaced by Upper Egyptian Early Dynastic wares (see PREDYNASTIC PERIOD).

W. M. F. PETRIE and C. T. CURRELLY, *Ehnasya* (Cairo, 1904).

T. VON DER WAY, 'Tell el-Fara'in 83–85: Probleme – Ergebnisse – Perspektiven', *Problems and priorities in Egyptian archaeology*, ed. J. Assmann et al. (London, 1987), 299–304.

—, 'Excavations at Tell el-Fara'in/Buto in 1987–1989', *The Nile Delta in transition: 4th–3rd millennium BC*, ed. E. C. M. van den Brink (Tel Aviv, 1992), 1–10.

Faras (anc. Pachoras)

Settlement on the border between modern Egypt and Sudan, which was first established as a small Egyptian fortress in the Middle Kingdom (2055–1650 BC) and continued in use in the 18th to 19th Dynasties (1550–1186 BC) with the construction of five Egyptian temples. W. Y. Adams argues that the importance of Faras owed more to indigenous Nubian traditions than to any military significance that it might have had for the Egyptian colonists. It continued to function as a religious centre after the departure of the Egyptians, and during the Christian period (c.AD 600–1500) it was one of the most important bishoprics in Nubia.

The episcopal cathedral (founded c.AD 650) and the bishop's palace were discovered in exceptionally good condition when Polish excavators examined a large mound in the centre of the modern village that had previously been erroneously interpreted as a typical stratified TELL-site. Although the site is now submerged under the waters of Lake Nasser the Polish archaeologists were able to transfer 169 painted murals from the cathedral to the museums at Warsaw and Khartoum. The stratified pottery from the site, as well as the paint-layers and stylistic development of the cathedral murals, have contributed significantly to the development of a chronological framework for Christian Nubia.

K. MICHALOWSKI, *Faras* I–II (Warsaw, 1962–5).

—, *Faras: centre artistique de la Nubie chrétienne* (Leiden, 1966).

J. VANTINI, *The excavations at Faras* (Bologna, 1970).

S. JAKOBIELSKI, *Faras* III (Warsaw, 1972).

J. KUBINSKA, *Faras* IV (Warsaw, 1974).

W. Y. ADAMS, *Nubia: corridor to Africa* (London and Princeton, 1984), 226, 472–84.

Sandstone block of decorative frieze from the first cathedral at Faras. 7th century AD, H. 25 cm. (EA606)

farm animals *see* AGRICULTURE *and* ANIMAL HUSBANDRY

Fayum region (anc. Ta-she, She-resy, Moeris)

Large fertile depression covering 12,000 sq. km in the Libyan Desert about 60 km to the southwest of Cairo. The region incorporates archaeological sites dating from the late Palaeolithic to the late Roman and Christian periods (c.8000 BC–AD 641). Until the Palaeolithic period a vast salt-water lake lay at the heart of the depression, but this was gradually transformed into the smaller, fresh-water Lake Moeris, linked to the Nile by the Bahr

Yussef channel. The earliest inhabitants of the Fayum were the EPIPALAEOLITHIC 'Fayum B' culture, which was succeeded by the Neolithic 'Fayum A' culture in c.5500 BC. Traces of both groups were first found by Gertrude Caton-Thompson and Elinor Gardner in the northern Fayum.

The region flourished from the Middle Kingdom (2055–1650 BC) onwards, when the Egyptian capital was relocated at Itjtawy, somewhere in the region of EL-LISHT, but most of the surviving archaeological remains date to the Ptolemaic and Roman periods, when such towns as Karanis (Kom Aushim), Tebtunis (Tell Umm el-Breigat) and Bacchias (Kom el-Atl) were at their height.

K. S. SANDFORD and W. J. ARKELL, *Prehistoric survey of Egypt and Western Asia: Paleolithic man and the Nile–Fayum divide* (Chicago, 1929).

G. CATON-THOMPSON and E. O. GARDNER, *The Desert Fayum* (London, 1934).

F. WENDORF and R. SCHILD (eds), *Prehistory of the Nile Valley* (New York, 1976), 155–61.

E. HUSSELMAN, *Karanis: excavations of the University of Michigan in Egypt*, 1928–35 (Michigan, 1979).

A. K. BOWMAN, *Egypt after the pharaohs* (London, 1986), 142–55.

fecundity figures *see* HAPY

fertility figurines *see* SEXUALITY

festivals

The Egyptian religious calendar was punctu-

Plan of the Fayum region.

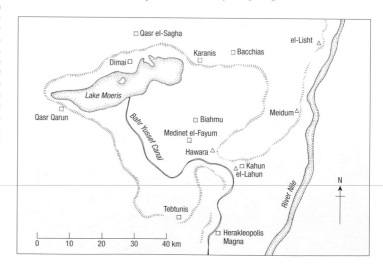

ated by numerous festivals, often consisting of a procession in which the cult image of a deity was moved from one temple to another (usually providing opportunities for ORACLES along the route). In the Festival Hall of Thutmose III (1479–1425 BC) at KARNAK there is a list of fifty-four feast-days in one year. A similar text in the mortuary temple of Rameses III (1184–1153 BC) at MEDINET HABU lists sixty festivals. Some of the most important national events of this type were the New Year Festival, the Festival of SOKAR, the Raising of the Sky and the Festival of the Potter's Wheel, but there would also have been many purely local festivals associated with the smaller provincial temples.

Two of the best-known annual religious events were the Festival of Opet and the Beautiful Festival of the Valley, both of which took place at Thebes from the early 18th Dynasty onwards. The Beautiful Festival of the Valley involved an annual procession taking the cult statues of the Theban triad (Amun, Mut and Khons) from Karnak to DEIR EL-BAHRI, which are located almost exactly opposite one another, on either side of the Nile. A later version of this festival involved a more complex processional route via one of the mortuary temples that lined the edge of the cultivation on the west bank. A similar festival linked Luxor temple with the temple of Thutmose III at MEDINET HABU (immediately to the northeast of Rameses III's mortuary temple).

The Festival of Opet also took place annually (in the second month of the season of *akhet*), lasting for a period that varied from two to four weeks. The main event in this festival was the ritual procession of the divine images from Karnak to LUXOR, which is depicted on the walls of the colonnade at Luxor, built by Amenhotep III (1390–1352 BC) and decorated by Tutankhamun (1336–1327 BC). The temple at Luxor was in fact constructed largely as a suitable architectural setting for the Festival of Opet.

The divine images in their sacred BARKS were initially carried to Luxor overland, along a sphinx-lined route broken at intervals by 'bark-shrines' or way-stations, within which the barks would be temporarily placed en route. By the late 18th Dynasty, however, the divine images were taken to and from Luxor in a series of ceremonial boats. The religious purpose of this festival was to celebrate the sexual intercourse between Amun and the mother of the reigning king, thus allowing her to give birth to the royal KA (spiritual essence or double). At the culmination of the festival, the king himself entered the inner sanctum, enabling his physical form to coalesce with the eternal form of the *ka*, so that he could emerge from the temple as a god.

According to the 'calendar of feast and offerings' at Medinet Habu, such festivals required the provision of amounts of loaves varying from eighty-four in a standard monthly festival to nearly four thousand in the Festival of Sokar. Each festival therefore incorporated a ceremony known as the 'reversion of offerings', in which the extra food offerings brought to the temple were redistributed to the masses.

See also SED FESTIVAL.

G. FOUCART, 'Etudes thébaines: la Belle Fête de la Vallée', *BIFAO* 24 (1924), 1–209.

W. WOLF, *Das schöne Fest von Opet* (Leipzig 1931).

S. SCHOTT, *Das schöne Fest vom Wüstentale* (Wiesbaden, 1952).

H. W. FAIRMAN, 'Worship and festivals in an Egyptian temple', *Bulletin of the John Rylands Library, Manchester* 37 (1954), 165–203.

C. J. BLEEKER, *Egyptian festivals: enactments of religious renewal* (Leiden, 1967).

B. J. KEMP, *Ancient Egypt: anatomy of a civilization* (London, 1989), 205–17, fig. 71.

Field of Reeds (Fields of Offerings, Fields of Iaru)

To 'pass through the field of reeds' was an Egyptian metaphor for death, since the 'field of reeds' was a term used to describe the domain of OSIRIS. According to Chapter 145 of the BOOK OF THE DEAD, it was here that the deceased would gather the abundant crops of emmer and barley; Chapter 109, meanwhile, describes the gigantic sizes of these crops.

The field was so synonymous with fertility and abundance that the hieroglyph for field (*sekhet*) sometimes replaced the *hetep*-sign that was usually employed to denote the act of offering. Similarly, reed-shaped loaves of bread depicted on offering tables were occasionally portrayed as actual reeds, thus

Detail of wall-painting in the tomb of Sennedjem at Deir el-Medina, western Thebes, depicting the deceased in the Field of Reeds. 19th Dynasty, c.1200 BC. (GRAHAM HARRISON)

symbolizing not only the offerings of bread but a general abundance of other offerings. See also FUNERARY BELIEFS.

L. LESKO, 'The Field of Hetep in Egyptian coffin texts', *JARCE* 9 (1971–2), 89–101.

R. H. WILKINSON, *Reading Egyptian art* (London, 1992), 124–5.

First Intermediate Period (2181–2055 BC)

Chronological phase between the OLD KING-DOM (2686–2181 BC) and the MIDDLE KINGDOM (2055–1650 BC), which appears to have been a time of relative political disunity and instability. The period corresponds to MANETHO'S 7th to 10th Dynasties and the early part of the 11th Dynasty. It begins with the death of Queen Nitiqret, the last ruler of the 6th Dynasty, and ends in the reign of Nebhepetra MENTUHOTEP II.

According to Manetho, the 7th and 8th Dynasties still governed Egypt from the Old Kingdom capital, MEMPHIS, but the apparently rapid succession of rulers and the comparative lack of major building works are both likely indications of a decline in royal authority. The general lack of information concerning the political developments during this period also highlights the extent to which the knowledge of other periods in Egyptian history is founded on the evidence provided by the survival of élite funerary monuments. The presence of the pyramid complex of the 8th-Dynasty ruler Qakara Iby at SAQQARA suggests that Memphis at least lay within the control of the 7th- and 8th-Dynasty kings. Although most of the rulers of the First Intermediate Period used the ROYAL TITULARY, it seems likely that they actually governed only a small part of the country.

W. C. Hayes suggested that the pharaohs of the 8th Dynasty, perhaps lasting about thirty years, were the successors of the 6th- and 7th-Dynasty pharaohs through the female line; hence the frequent use of the name Neferkara, which was the throne name, or prenomen, of PEPY II. If there were, as the KING LISTS suggest, about twenty-five kings in thirty years, they must either have reigned simultaneously or some of them must have been impostors (or perhaps both). This hypothesis, however, is at odds with the listing of seventeen names in cartouches in the ABYDOS king list, since this list was part of the celebration of the royal cult; therefore theoretically only legitimate rulers would have been considered eligible.

The 9th and 10th Dynasties may have lasted for as long as a hundred years. They comprised a series of rulers originating from HERAKLEOPOLIS MAGNA, the first of these probably being Meribra Khety I (*c.*2160 BC). It is not clear where the seat of power lay during this period, and it is even possible that Memphis still continued to be the principal administrative centre, but the territory was largely restricted to northern Egypt. The Herakleopolitan rulers came into conflict with the early Theban 11th Dynasty, beginning with Sehertawy INTEF I (2125–2112 BC). During this period the artistic production of provincial sites such as GEBELEIN, EL-MO'ALLA and ASYUT was flourishing, and the funerary inscriptions of the governors of these areas describe both their own achievements and their allegiance to either the Herakleopolitan or Theban rulers. Eventually the Theban king Mentuhotep II (2055–2004 BC) succeeded in gaining control of the entire country, although the lack of textual sources for the middle of his reign means that it is not clear whether he did so by the military conquest of Herakleopolis or by some form of diplomatic arrangement. It is noticeable, for instance, that relations between Thebes and Herakleopolis in the early Middle Kingdom do not seem to be characterized by any lingering resentment or hostility.

H. E. WINLOCK, *The rise and fall of the Middle Kingdom in Thebes* (New York, 1947).

B. G. TRIGGER, B. J. KEMP, D. O'CONNOR and A. B. LLOYD, *Ancient Egypt: a social history* (Cambridge, 1983), 112–16.

S. SEIDLMAYER, 'Wirtschaftliche und gesellschaftliche Entwicklung im Übergang vom Alten zum Mittleren Reich', *Problems and priorities in Egyptian archaeology*, ed. J. Assmann, G. Burkard and V. Davies (London, 1987), 175–218.

N. GRIMAL, *A history of ancient Egypt* (Oxford, 1992), 137–54.

fish

Fish enjoyed a somewhat ambiguous position in ancient Egypt: sometimes sacred, sometimes scorned; eaten by some, denied to others. According to the Greek writer Plutarch (AD 46–126), when the body of the god OSIRIS

A polychrome glass fish vessel, which would have been used as a container for cosmetics. 18th Dynasty, c.1350 BC, from el-Amarna, L. 14.5 cm. (EA55193)

was cut into pieces by SETH his phallus was eaten by three species of Nile fish – the Nile carp (*Lepidotus*), the Oxyrynchus (*Mormyrus*) and the *Phagrus*. Despite this apparently inauspicious action, the Oxyrynchus fish was regarded as sacred at the town of that name in the Fayum region, since one tradition held that this fish came forth from the wounds of Osiris himself. In the tomb of Kabekhnet at Deir el-Medina (TT2) a fish is depicted in the position where the mummy of the deceased would usually be shown, apparently being embalmed by the god ANUBIS.

Various provinces of Egypt regarded particular fish as sacred (see SACRED ANIMALS), so that a fish which was TABOO in one area could be eaten in another, something which is said to have led to occasional conflict. The Delta city of MENDES was the principal cult centre of the goddess HAT-MEHIT, the 'chief of the fishes', who was worshipped in the form of either a fish or a woman wearing a fish emblem (sometimes identified as a dolphin but probably a *Lepidotus* fish). The *Tilapia* (or *Chromis*) fish, with its colourful fins, and the *abdju* (i.e. Abydos) fish, with its lapis blue colour, both acted as pilots for the boat of the sun-god RA, warning of the approach of the snake APOPHIS during the voyage through the netherworld.

The Nile, the marshy Delta, the Red Sea and the Mediterranean coast are all rich in edible fish, and for the poor people of ancient Egypt these would have served as a substitute for the more costly meat. Wealthier people frequently kept fish in ponds both for ornament and as a source of food. It is known from records excavated at DEIR EL-MEDINA that fishermen were employed to provide some of the rations for the royal tomb-workers, and that temples also employed them to provide food for lesser officials. However, the king, priests and the 'blessed dead' (see AKH) were not allowed to eat fish, since it was identified particularly with the evil god SETH. In the text of the Victory Stele of PIY (747–716 BC) the Kushite leader describes his unwillingness to meet all but one of the defeated Lower Egyptian princes, on the grounds that they were fish-eaters.

Fish were usually caught in traps or nets, some of which might be dragged along the river channel either by teams of men or between two boats; Chapter 153 of the BOOK OF THE DEAD, for instance, is concerned with helping the deceased to avoid being captured in a kind of trawling net. Fishing using hooks on a line is also recorded, as is harpooning from papyrus skiffs, although this was presumably regarded more as a sport than as a means of subsistence.

I. GAMMER-WALLERT, *Fische und Fischkult im alten Ägypten* (Berlin, 1970).

I. DANNESKIOLD-SAMSOE, 'The abomination of the fish in Egyptian religion', *Karl Richard Lepsius: Akten der tagung anlässlich seines 100. Todestag*, ed. E. Freier and W. F. Reinecke (Berlin, 1988), 185–90.

D. J. BREWER and R. F. FRIEDMAN, *Fish and fishing in ancient Egypt* (Warminster, 1989).

flail *see* CROWNS AND ROYAL REGALIA

flies

The fly was considered to have apotropaic and prophylactic properties, and stone amulets were being created as early as the Naqada II period (*c.*3500–3100 BC), already depicting it in the form that the hieroglyphic 'determinative' sign denoting the fly (*aff*) was later to assume. The image of the fly was also depicted on various ritual artefacts during the Old and Middle Kingdoms (2686–1650 BC),

Golden necklace of Ahhotep I with three pendants in the form of 'flies of valour'. New Kingdom, c.1550 BC, L. (chain) 59 cm, (fly) 9 cm. (CAIRO, JE4694)

including the so-called MAGIC 'wands'. Although the precise symbolism of fly amulets remains obscure, the iconographic significance of flies is best known during the New Kingdom (1550–1069 BC), when the military decoration known as the 'order of the golden fly' (or 'fly of valour') was introduced, perhaps because of flies' apparent qualities of persistence in the face of opposition. Ahmose Pennekhbet, a military official in the reign of Thutmose I (1504–1492 BC), records that he was awarded six of these honorific flies. The best-known example is a gold chain and three fly pendants from the Theban tomb of Queen AHHOTEP I (*c.*1550 BC). In addition, the tomb ascribed to three of the wives of Thutmose III (1479–1425 BC) contained a necklace adorned with thirty-three small flies.

A. HERMANN, 'Fliege', *Reallexikon für Antike und Christentum* VII (Stuttgart, 1968–9), 1110–24.

M. WEBER, 'Fliege', *Lexikon der Ägyptologie* II, ed. W. Helck, E. Otto and W. Westendorf (Wiesbaden, 1977), 264–5.

M. SALEH and H. SOUROUZIAN, *The Egyptian Museum, Cairo: official catalogue* (Mainz, 1987), 120.

C. ANDREWS, *Ancient Egyptian amulets* (London, 1994), 62–3.

A pair of golden 'flies of valour', a form of honorific award. New Kingdom, c.1500–1250 BC, L. 2 cm. (EA59416–7)

food

A great deal of information has survived concerning the diet of the ancient Egyptians, both through depictions of food processing and consumption in their funerary art, and in the form of food remains from funerary, religious and domestic contexts. The poorest people in ancient Egypt seem to have subsisted on bread, beer (see ALCOHOLIC BEVERAGES) and a few vegetables, notably onions; according to the Greek writer Herodotus it was with these very commodities that the builders of the Great Pyramid were paid. Similarly, the OFFERING FORMULA, inscribed in Egyptian tombs from the Old Kingdom onwards, usually included a request for 'a thousand of bread, a thousand of beer...'.

Bread was made from emmer-wheat (*Triticum dicoccum*, see AGRICULTURE), which was laboriously ground on an arrangement of stones known as a saddle quern, replaced in Ptolemaic and Roman times (332 BC–AD 395) by the more efficient rotary quern. Stoneground flour inevitably contained fragments of stone and occasional sand grains, which, judging from surviving human skeletal material, inflicted considerable wear on the teeth. Numerous types of loaf were produced, and some of these were made in moulds, especially if they were intended for ritual use rather than everyday consumption. It was bread that formed the centrepiece of offering scenes in tombs, where it was usually portrayed in rows of long slices on the table. Similarly it was the loaf of bread on a slab that the hieroglyphic sign *hetep* ('offering') was actually depicting.

Beer was usually made from barley

(*Hordeum vulgare*), and seems to have been a thick, soupy liquid, which, although not always strongly alcoholic, was nutritious. In a scene in the New Kingdom tomb of Intefiqer (TT60) a child is shown holding a bowl and the accompanying lines of speech read: 'Give me some ale, for I am hungry', thus emphasizing the nature of beer as food rather than simply a drink. Beer was also sometimes sweetened with dates or flavoured with other fruits.

Funerary offerings consisting of bread and fowl placed on a reed offering-stand. 18th Dynasty, c.1450 BC, from Thebes, H. of stand 21.8 cm. (EA5340)

The texts on ostraca excavated at the workmen's village of DEIR EL-MEDINA indicate that the workers' payments took the form of food rations. Although these men and their families were clearly more affluent than agricultural labourers, the lists of rations give some idea of the foodstuffs commonly available in the New Kingdom (1550–1069 BC). Emmer and barley were the most prized items, since they were part of the staple diet. Beans, onions, garlic, lettuces and cucumbers were among the most regular supplies of vegetables, but salted FISH also formed an important element of the villagers' diet. Meat was usually provided in the form of complete cattle from the temple stock-yards, or simply as individual portions. Outside Deir el-Medina, meat would have been regarded as a considerable luxury for

most Egyptians, something to be eaten primarily at FESTIVALS or on other special occasions.

The wealthy would have eaten oxen, and the evidence from the Middle Kingdom (2055–1650 BC) pyramid-town of Kahun (EL-LAHUN) as well as the New Kingdom 'workmen's village' at EL-AMARNA shows that pigs were raised for their meat. Hares, gazelle and other wild animals would have provided a supplement to the diet of poorer people, as well as providing HUNTING quarry for the élite.

Animals were also used as a source of fat, and in order to provide milk for cheese making. Ducks and, from the New Kingdom onwards, hens were kept for eggs and meat, and wild-fowl were hunted for sport and food.

Various fruits (such as dates, figs, grapes, pomegranates, dom-palm nuts and, more rarely, almonds) were available both to the inhabitants of the workmen's village at Deir el-Medina and to the population at large. Grapes were also used in the making of wine, and there are numerous tomb scenes of vintners at work. Wine, however, appears to have been generally consumed by the wealthier groups in Egyptian society, and the jars in which it was kept frequently state its place of origin and year of vintage (see ALCOHOLIC BEVERAGES).

Honey was obtained both from wild and domesticated BEES, and, in the absence of sugar, it was used to transform bread into cakes and to sweeten beer. At Deir el-Medina it is recorded that confectioners were

employed to prepare honey-cakes for the gang of workmen.

W. B. EMERY, *A funerary repast in an Egyptian tomb of the Archaic period* (Leiden, 1962).

W. DARBY, *Food: the gift of Osiris* (London, 1977).

D. J. CRAWFORD, 'Food: tradition and change in Hellenistic Egypt', *WA* 11 (1979–80), 136–46.

B. J. KEMP, *Ancient Egypt: anatomy of a civilization* (London, 1989), 117–28.

P. T. NICHOLSON and I. SHAW (ed.), *Ancient Egyptian materials and technology* (Cambridge, 2000). [chapters by S. Ikram, D. Samuel and M. A. Murray]

fortresses

The first representations of fortresses in ancient Egypt take the form of late Predynastic schematic depictions of circular and rectangular fortified towns, but the earliest surviving archaeological remains of fortifications are the roughly circular walls at two Early Dynastic settlement sites in Upper Egypt: Kom el-Ahmar (HIERAKONPOLIS) and ELKAB.

Egyptian towns were apparently only fortified at times of political instability, such as the Early Dynastic phase (3100–2686 BC) and the three 'intermediate periods'. Military fortresses and garrisons, as opposed to fortified settlements, were essential to the defence of Egypt's frontiers (see BORDERS, FRONTIERS AND LIMITS). In the reign of Amenemhat I (1985–1955 BC), a row of forts, known as the Walls of the Prince (*inebw heka*), was established across the northeastern Delta in order to protect Egypt against invasion from the Levant. The same border was later protected by a number of fortresses set up by Rameses II (1279–1213 BC).

During the Middle Kingdom (2055–1650 BC) the area of Lower Nubia from the first to the third cataract, which had probably been peacefully exploited by Egyptian mineral prospectors during the Old Kingdom, became part of the Egyptian empire. A group of at least seventeen fortresses were built, mainly between the reigns of Senusret I and III (c.1965–1855 BC), apparently serving both practical and symbolic purposes. On the one hand they were intended to control and protect the king's monopoly on the valuable trade route from the lands to the south. On the other hand their large scale – perhaps disproportionate to the task – must have served as physical propaganda in an increasingly militaristic age.

The designs of these fortresses, stretching from Aswan to Dongola, incorporate many ingenious architectural devices which would be more readily associated with medieval architecture. Ten of the fortresses (south to north: Semna South, Kumma, Semna, Uronarti, Shelfak, Askut, Mirgissa, Dabenarti, Kor and Buhen) were constructed in the area of the second cataract where the Nile valley is at its narrowest. Although they share many common architectural features (such as bastions, walls, ditches, internal grid-plans and walled stairways connecting with the Nile), their various shapes and sizes were each designed to conform to differing local topographical and strategic requirements.

In the New Kingdom (1550–1069 BC), the Nubian fortresses were substantially rebuilt, but the role of the fortifications appears to have become much more symbolic. Temples began to be built outside the fortress walls and new towns were established with relatively perfunctory defences. Essential fortresses and garrisons continued to be built on the western and eastern borders of the Delta during the New Kingdom (such as the Ramesside fortifications at Zawiyet Umm el-Rakham in the west and Tell el-Heir in the east), and the Victory Stele of the 25th-Dynasty ruler PIY (747–716 BC) mentions nineteen fortified settlements in Middle Egypt. However, only a small number of fortified structures of the Third Intermediate Period (1069–747 BC) and Late Period (747–332 BC) have been preserved, such as the 'palace' of Apries (589–570 BC) at MEMPHIS and the fortress of Dorginarti in Lower Nubia. See also WARFARE.

D. DUNHAM and J. M. A. JANSSEN, *Second cataract forts*, 2 vols (Boston, 1961–7).

Y. YADIN, *The art of warfare in Biblical lands in the light of archaeological discovery* (London, 1963).

A. W. LAWRENCE, 'Ancient Egyptian fortifications', *JEA* 51 (1965), 69–94.

W. B. EMERY et al., *The fortress of Buhen*, 2 vols (London, 1977–9).

foundation deposits

Buried caches of ritual objects, usually placed at crucial points in important buildings such as pyramids, temples and tombs, from the Old Kingdom to the Ptolemaic period (2686–30 BC). It was believed that the offering of model tools and materials would magically serve to maintain the building for eternity. The pits in which the deposits were buried, sometimes brick-lined and occasionally in excess of two metres in width, were generally located in the vicinity of the corners, axes or gateways.

In the mortuary temple of the 11th-Dynasty ruler Nebhepetra Mentuhotep II (2055–2004 BC) at DEIR EL-BAHRI, a series of pits marked the axis of the building. Each contained a loaf of bread, while the corners were marked with larger pits containing food offerings, including parts of a sacrificed ox and miniature vessels for wine or beer. The tops of these deposits were marked by four mud bricks, three of which contained tablets of stone bearing the ROYAL TITULARY of Mentuhotep. The tablets were made from stone, wood and metal, thus symbolizing, along with the mud bricks themselves, the four principal materials used in building the temple. Other foundation deposits, such as those of Amenemhat I (1985–1955 BC) at EL-

Reconstructed foundation deposit from the temple of Queen Hatshepsut at Deir el-Bahri. D. c. 1 m.
(ROGERS FUND 1925, METROPOLITAN MUSEUM NEW YORK, 25.3.39)

LISHT, incorporated more bricks and a wider range of building materials, including FAIENCE.

Probably the best-known foundation deposits are those from the temple of Hatshepsut (1473–1458 BC) at DEIR EL-BAHRI. Fourteen brick-lined pits, measuring c.1 m in diameter and 1.5–1.8 m in depth, were each placed at a crucial juncture in the plan of the temple. The contents of the pits included food offerings and materials used in the construction of the temple, as well as SCARABS, COWROIDS, AMULETS, travertine jars and model tools (such as crucibles and the copper ore, lead ore and charcoal for smelting). The particular selections of model tools and vessels in foundation deposits can sometimes provide insights into the technology of the Pharaonic period, while the study of the food offerings has contributed to the knowledge of ancient agriculture and diet.

Apart from their ritual significance, these deposits have proved invaluable to archaeologists from a chronological point of view, since they often include large numbers of plaques inscribed with the name of the ruler responsible for the construction of the building in question. The foundation deposits associated with a temple of Rameses IV (1153–1147 BC), near Deir el-Bahri, for instance, contained several hundred inscribed plaques. Many Late Period foundation deposits, such as those excavated at Tell Balamun in the Delta, have proved essential to the dating of temple complexes.

G. A. REISNER, 'The Barkal temples in 1916', *JEA* 4 (1917), 213–27. [comparison of foundation deposits from Gebel Barkal with those from Egyptian sites]

W. C. HAYES, *The scepter of Egypt* II (New York, 1959), 84–8.

B. LETELLIER, 'Gründungsbeigabe', *Lexikon der Ägyptologie* II, ed. W. Helck, E. Otto and W. Westendorf (Wiesbaden, 1977), 906–12.

frog

The Egyptians referred to frogs by several names, the most common being the onomatopoeic *kerer*. This attention to the frog's call was extended to familiarity with its habits, including aspects of its life-cycle. As a result, it became a symbol of fertility, creation and regeneration. The image of the tadpole (*hefner*) became the hieroglyph for 100,000 and is commonly found decorating the SHEN ring or the notched staff representing years, thus wishing the king a reign of 100,000 years.

The deity most commonly associated with the frog was HEKET, the consort of the creator god KHNUM. Just as he created the human race on his potter's wheel, so she often served as a personification of childbirth, particularly the final stages of labour. In the Middle Kingdom (2055–1650 BC) Heket was often shown on magical objects which were probably used in the rituals surrounding conception and birth.

The connection of the frog with creation is also demonstrated by the fact that HEH, KEK,

Egyptologists to explore the complexity and gradual elaboration of this belief system, although far more research is required before the full nature of Egyptian views on the afterlife can be understood, particularly during the formative period of the Predynastic, before the emergence of writing.

The Egyptians believed that each human individual comprised not only a physical body but also three other crucial elements, known as the KA, BA and AKH, each of which was essential to human survival both before and after

in both royal and private funerary texts and rituals.

Just as the royal mortuary cult involved the transformation of the dead king into Osiris, so the funerary equipment of private individuals was designed to substitute the deceased for Osiris, so that they could re-enact the myth of resurrection and obtain eternal life for themselves (see DEMOCRATIZATION OF THE AFTERLIFE). In order to be assimilated with Osiris, however, the deceased first had to prove that his or her earthly deeds had been worthy and

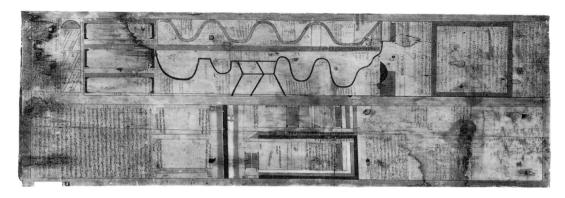

NUN and AMUN, four of the eight members of the OGDOAD associated with the Hermopolitan CREATION myth, were said to be frog-headed. Frog amulets were sometimes included in the wrappings of mummies, or carried as talismans. Even in the reign of AKHENATEN (1352–1336 BC), when most traditional religious beliefs were discouraged, frog amulets were still carried, many being manufactured at Akhenaten's new capital (el-Amarna). With the official arrival of Christianity in Egypt in the fourth century AD, the frog was retained as a Coptic symbol of rebirth.

L. STÖRK, 'Frosch', *Lexikon der Ägyptologie* II, ed. W. Helck, E. Otto and W. Westendorf (Wiesbaden, 1977), 334–6.

funerary beliefs

During the Pharaonic period, the Egyptians' attitudes to life and death were influenced by two fundamental beliefs: first, that death was simply a temporary interruption rather than a complete cessation of life; and, second, that eternal life could be ensured by various means, including piety to the gods, the preservation of the body through MUMMIFICATION, and the provision of statuary and other funerary equipment. The survival of numerous TOMBS and FUNERARY TEXTS has enabled

death. They also considered that the NAME and SHADOW were living entities, crucial to human existence, rather than simply linguistic and natural phenomena. The essence of each individual was contained in the sum of all these parts, none of which could be neglected. The process of ensuring any individual's enjoyment of the afterlife was therefore a delicate business whereby all of these separate elements (the body, *ka*, *ba*, *akh*, shadow and name) were sustained and protected from harm. At the most basic level this could be achieved by burying the body with a set of funerary equipment, and in its most elaborate form the royal cult could include a number of temples complete with priests and a steady flow of offerings, usually financed by gifts of agricultural land and other economic resources.

The surviving funerary texts present an often conflicting set of descriptions of the afterlife, ranging from the transformation of humans into circumpolar stars to the continuation of normal life in an afterworld sometimes described as the FIELD OF REEDS. The identification of the deceased with OSIRIS, the god of Abydos who was murdered by his brother SETH and brought back to life through the efforts of his wife ISIS, played a crucial part

Interior detail of the coffin of Gua, decorated with a map showing two different routes to the underworld (part of the Book of Two Ways). 12th Dynasty, c.1985–1795 BC, painted wood, from Deir el-Bersha, L. of coffin 2.6 m. (EA30839)

virtuous. Since the individual's HEART was regarded as the physical manifestation of their intelligence and personality, the judgement scene depicted on many BOOK OF THE DEAD papyri shows the heart being weighed against the feather of the goddess MAAT, symbol of the universal harmony and ethical conduct to which all Egyptians aspired (see ETHICS).

A. H. GARDINER, *The attitude of the ancient Egyptians to death and the dead* (Cambridge, 1935).

A. J. SPENCER, *Death in ancient Egypt* (Harmondsworth, 1982), 139–64.

E. HORNUNG, *Idea into image*, trans. E. Bredeck (New York, 1992), 167–84.

funerary cones

Clay cones of 10–15 cm in length which were placed at the entrances of tombs, particularly those in the Theban area. They are first recorded from the 11th Dynasty (2125–1985 BC) and continue into the Late Period (747–332 BC), although most belong to the

Funerary cone of Merymose, c.1350 BC, pottery, from Thebes, H. 16.7 cm, D. 7.1 cm. (EA9649)

Each tomb-owner had about three hundred identical cones, and the owners of many decorated tombs of the New Kingdom have been readily matched with surviving cones. However, there is no evidence of cones from over three hundred other known tombs. More significant, on the other hand, is the fact that no tombs are known for a further four hundred or so cones, suggesting that the tombs to which they belonged have been destroyed or re-used, or else await discovery.

N. DE G. DAVIES and F. L. MACADAM, *A corpus of inscribed funerary cones* I (Oxford, 1957).

H. M. STEWART, *Mummy cases and inscribed funerary cones in the Petrie collection* (Warminster, 1986).

J. KONDO, 'Inscribed funerary cones from the Theban necropolis', *Orient* 23 (1987).

also found in eight pyramids dating from the 6th to 8th Dynasties (2345–2125 BC), comprise some eight hundred spells or 'utterances' written in columns on the walls of the pyramid chambers, but apparently not arranged in any specific order. No single pyramid contains the whole collection of spells, the maximum number being the 675 utterances inscribed in the pyramid of PEPY II (2268–2184 BC). The words spoken at the ceremony of OPENING OF THE MOUTH are first

Part of the Book of the Dead papyrus of the royal scribe Ani, consisting of the vignette associated with Chapter 125, in which the heart of the deceased is weighed against the feather of the goddess Maat. 19th Dynasty, c.1250 BC, painted papyrus. (EA470, SHEET 3)

New Kingdom and the bulk of them to the 18th Dynasty (1550–1295 BC).

The broadest end of the cone is usually stamped with hieroglyphs bearing a name, title and sometimes a short inscription or genealogy. The earliest, however, are uninscribed. They were once thought to represent loaves of bread, roofing poles, MUMMY LABELS or boundary stones but current opinion suggests a more likely explanation. The pointed end allowed them to be set in plaster as a frieze above the tomb entrance, while the broad end would be clearly visible. It may be that this broad circular end represented the sun's disc, and was part of the solar iconography of rebirth.

D. P. RYAN, 'The archaeological analysis of inscribed funerary cones', *VA* 4/2 (1988), 165–70.

funerary texts

The Egyptians' composition of texts relating to death and the afterlife probably stretched back to an original preliterate oral tradition, traces of which have survived only in the form of poorly understood funerary artefacts and sculptures. The earliest such writings are known as the PYRAMID TEXTS, the first examples of which were inscribed in the 5th-Dynasty pyramid of UNAS (2375–2345 BC) at Saqqara. These texts, versions of which are

recorded in these funerary texts, along with offering lists.

In the political and social turmoil of the First Intermediate Period (2181–2055 BC) the practice of inscribing funerary writings on private coffins developed. These private funerary documents, which were effectively compressed and edited versions of the Pyramid Texts, have become known as the COFFIN TEXTS, although they were sometimes also inscribed on papyri or the walls of private tombs. They are often said to reflect a DEMOCRATIZATION OF THE AFTERLIFE, whereby individuals were no longer dependent on the ruler for their afterlife, perhaps as a direct result of the gradual decline in the ambitions of royal funerary complexes. However, it might also be argued that, in their derivation from the Pyramid Texts, they simply re-emphasize the crucial role still played by the pharaoh in private funerary rituals.

The Coffin Texts often included utterances forming 'guide-books' to the netherworld, known as the *Book of Two Ways*. The 'guiding' function of the funerary texts became increasingly important from the Second Intermediate Period (1650–1550 BC) onwards, eventually culminating in the appearance of the so-called BOOK OF THE DEAD (or 'spell for coming forth by day'), made up of around two hundred spells (or 'chapters'), over half of which were derived directly from either the Pyramid Texts or the Coffin Texts. Such 'netherworld texts' were usually written on papyri, although certain sections were inscribed on AMULETS.

The netherworld texts comprise a number of related funerary writings, which together were known to the Egyptians as *Amduat* or 'that which is in the netherworld'. They included the *Book of Caverns*, *Book of Gates* and the *Writing of the Hidden Chamber*. The theme of all of these works is the journey of the sun-god through the realms of darkness during the twelve hours of the night, leading up to his triumphant re-birth with the dawn each morning. Many copies of these books have been discovered, often with elaborate vignettes illustrating the text. During the New Kingdom (1550–1069 BC) they were virtually confined to royal burials, although from the Third Intermediate Period (1069–747 BC) onwards they began to appear in private burials. They were frequently portrayed on the walls of the royal tombs in the VALLEY OF THE KINGS, just as the Pyramid Texts had decorated the funerary complexes of the Old Kingdom. Their placing is significant: for example in the tomb of Rameses VI (KV9; 1143–1136 BC) the *Book of Gates* is at the entrance to the upper level, the *Book of Caverns* follows, and in the lower level, furthest from the entrance, is the *Book of that which is in the Netherworld*.

During the Ptolemaic period (332–30 BC) these 'netherworld books' continued to be produced, including such remarkable texts as the *Book of Spending Eternity* and the *Book of Breathing*, which were apparently designed to protect the deceased and facilitate safe passage to the underworld. These later texts reflect the essential continuity of belief throughout ancient Egyptian history. The differences between the texts of different periods tend to result from changes in funerary practice, such as the shift from regarding the afterlife as being

Various items of domestic furniture: a box of cosmetics, linen, a bed, a headrest, a jar and a jar-stand. New Kingdom, c.1300 BC from Thebes, H. of chest 61 cm. (EA2470, 6526, 6639, 18196, 24708)

achievable only via the king to a situation in which individuals increasingly made their own provisions. There was also a gradual move towards the concept of righteous living as a qualification for the enjoyment of an afterlife.
R. O. FAULKNER, *The ancient Egyptian Pyramid Texts* (Oxford, 1969).
—, *The ancient Egyptian Coffin Texts*, 3 vols (Oxford, 1973–8).
—, *The ancient Egyptian Book of the Dead*, ed. C. Andrews (London, 1985).
J. P. ALLEN, 'Funerary texts and their meaning', *Mummies and Magic*, ed. S. D'Auria, P. Lacovara and C. H. Roehrig (Boston, 1988), 38–49.
E. HORNUNG, *Idea into image*, trans. E. Bredeck (New York, 1992), 95–113.

furniture

The best ancient Egyptian furniture was beautifully made and elegantly proportioned, and it is not surprising that some of their designs were adopted for European furniture of the early nineteenth century (often with less success than their prototypes). By modern standards, however, Egyptian houses, particularly those of the poor, would have had little furniture. The most common items were beds, chairs, stools and boxes (which served the purpose of the modern sideboard or wardrobe). Low tables were also used, two wooden examples being known from Tarkhan as early as the 1st Dynasty (3100–2890 BC).

The vast majority of the surviving furniture is made of wood, although at sites such as EL-AMARNA numerous limestone stools are found. Beds are recorded from the 1st Dynasty, and comprised a wooden frame, jointed at the corners, and upholstered with matting or leather. Chairs were used only by the most wealthy people, and could be very elaborate. The length of the back support varied greatly, as did the standard of workmanship: the most elaborate could have elegant LION's paw feet and might be inlaid. Most chairs are of a simple type with no arms, but throne-like versions are known, including the famous example from TUTANKHAMUN's tomb (KV62), which is gilded and inlaid.

Most people would have used low stools, and by the Middle Kingdom a folding stool had been developed. Some of these are finely crafted, as in the example from the tomb of Tutankhamun, the legs of which end in ducks' heads, each grasping a rail in their bills. The Egyptians had a great facility for making such light or prefabricated furniture for use when travelling or on military expeditions. As early as the 4th Dynasty a complete travelling bedroom set, including a tent and carrying chair, has survived among the funerary equipment of Queen HETEPHERES, mother of KHUFU (2589–2566 BC). A series of poles and rails make up a frame which could be fitted inside a tent or room to add extra warmth or privacy, serving as a sort of portable boudoir.

The Theban tomb of the architect Kha (TT8) contains a representative range of New Kingdom furniture (now in the Museo Egizio,

Wooden chair. 18th Dynasty, H. 73 cm. (EA2479)

Turin), including a toilet box, a chair and a stand for a pottery vessel.

C. ALDRED, 'Fine woodwork', *A history of technology* I, ed. C. Singer, E. J. Holmyard, and A. R. Hall (Oxford, 1954), 684–703.

E. WANSCHER, *Sella curulis, the folding stool: an ancient symbol of dignity* (Copenhagen, 1980).

G. KILLEN, *Egyptian furniture*, 2 vols (Warminster, 1980–94)

—, *Egyptian woodworking and furniture* (Princes Risborough, 1994).

G

games

The most popular board game known to the Egyptians was *senet*, the game of 'passing', which was played either on elaborate inlaid boards or simply on grids of squares scratched on the surface of a stone. The two players each had an equal number of pieces, usually seven, distinguished by shape or colour, and they played on a grid of thirty squares known as *perw* ('houses') and

ABOVE *Ivory-covered game box from the tomb of Tutankhamun, with ivory playing pieces and knuckle-bones. 18th Dynasty c.1330 BC, L. of box 27.5 cm. (CAIRO, NO. 593, REPRODUCED COURTESY OF THE GRIFFITH INSTITUTE)*

RIGHT *Detail of the Satirical Papyrus, in which animals imitate figures in funerary scenes. A lion and an antelope are shown playing a game of senet. Late New Kingdom, c.1150 BC, painted papyrus, H. 9 cm. (EA10016)*

arranged in three rows of ten. Moves were determined by 'throw-sticks' or 'astragals' (knuckle-bones). The object was to convey the pieces around a snaking track to the finish, via a number of specially marked squares representing good or bad fortune. Sometimes the wall-paintings in private tomb chapels depict the deceased playing a board-game, but it is not clear whether this activity, when portrayed in a funerary context, was regarded simply as entertainment or as a symbolic contest intended to replicate the journey through the netherworld.

A less popular board game was 'twenty

squares', which is thought to have been introduced from western Asia. Although several boards have survived and it is known to have been played by two players using five pieces, the rules of the game, as with *senet*, have not been preserved.

J. VANDIER, *Manuel d'archéologie égyptienne* IV (Paris, 1964), 486–527.

E. B. PUSCH, *Das Senet Brettspiel im Alten Ägypten* I (Berlin, 1979).

T. KENDALL, 'Games', *Egypt's golden age*, ed. E. Brovarski, S. K. Doll and R. E. Freed (Boston, 1982), 263–72.

W. J. TAIT, *Game boxes and accessories from the tomb of Tutankhamun* (Oxford, 1982).

gardens

In an essentially arid land such as Egypt, the cultivated strip of the Nile valley represented an area of fertile green fields and watery irrigation channels. This same lush vegetation, often accompanied by a pool, was a highly desirable asset for houses and temples too. Secular gardens were mainly cultivated for vegetables, and were set close to the river or canal, but by the New Kingdom (1550–1069 BC) they had developed into more luxurious areas, often of a semi-formal plan, and sometimes surrounded by high walls.

Attached to temples there were often gar-

Scene from the Book of the Dead papyrus of Nakht, showing the deceased and his wife Tjuiu approaching Osiris and Maat in their garden. 19th Dynasty, c.1300 BC. (EA10471, SHEET 21)

den plots for the cultivation of specific kinds of vegetable; the growing of 'cos lettuces' (sacred to MIN) is frequently portrayed in reliefs and paintings. Similar small plots, made up of squares of earth divided by walls of mud, are known from the 'workmen's village' at EL-AMARNA, where vegetables may have been grown for use in the rituals performed at the chapels there. Ornamental trees were sometimes planted in pits in front of temples, such as that of HATSHEPSUT (1473–1458 BC) at Deir el-Bahri, where pits for two trees were found, unlike the whole grove of sycamore and tamarisk which stood in front of the 11th-Dynasty temple of Nebhepetra MENTUHOTEP II (2055–2004 BC).

The houses of the wealthy often had large and elaborate gardens centred on a pool, which in the New Kingdom was sometimes T-shaped. Pools of this shape are known also from Hatshepsut's temple at Deir el-Bahri, and the shape may therefore have had religious connotations. Such pools were stocked with ornamental fish, and served as havens for waterfowl. Flowers, such as white and blue lotuses (a kind of water lily), grew in some of these pools, and papyrus is attested in the pools at Deir el-Bahri.

The provision of shade was an important element of the Egyptian garden, and from the paintings in the Theban tomb chapel of Kenamun (TT93) it is known that wooden columns were sometimes used to support a pergola arrangement of vines. As well as providing shady arbours, trees were used as a source of fruit, such as dates, figs and dom-palm nuts. Grapes might be used for the production of raisins or even home-made wine. The sacred persea tree was grown in both religious and secular gardens. Nineteen species of tree were represented in the garden of Ineni, architect to Thutmose I (1504–1492 BC), and among the most popular species were the pink-flowered tamarisk, the acacia and the willow.

Cornflowers, mandrakes, poppies, daisies and other small flowers were grown among the trees and, like the lotus flowers and some of the tree foliage, could be used in the making of garlands for banquets or other occasions. The pomegranate, introduced in the New Kingdom, became a popular shrub, and its flowers added to the colour of the garden. The overall effect would be one of cool shade, heavy with the fragrance of the flowers and trees; gardens are therefore one of the most frequent settings of Egyptian romantic tales.

Unfortunately, given the aridity of the Egyptian climate, gardens required constant attention, not least irrigation, and representations such as that from the tomb of Ipuy (TT217) show a SHADUF in use. The gardeners employed by temples and wealthy households had several responsibilities, including the watering and weeding of plants, as well as the artificial propagation of date palms, a process that evidently required considerable skill.

G. GOOD and P. LACOVARA, 'The garden', *Egypt's golden age*, ed. E. Brovarski, S. K. Doll and R. E. Freed (Boston, 1982), 37–9.

J.-C. HUGONOT, *Le jardin dans l'Egypte ancienne* (Frankfurt, 1989).

A. WILKINSON, *Gardens in ancient Egypt: their location and symbolism* (London, 1990).

gazelle *see* ANTELOPE.

Geb

God of the earth, whose sister and wife was NUT the sky-goddess. In the doctrine of Heliopolis he was the son of SHU (god of the air) and TEFNUT (goddess of moisture), who were themselves the children of ATUM (see CREATION).

The offspring of Geb and Nut were OSIRIS, ISIS, SETH and NEPHTHYS, and these nine gods made up the Heliopolitan ENNEAD. In the myth of HORUS and Seth, Geb acted as judge between them. Since Osiris was the rightful ruler of the world, and had been murdered by his brother Seth, Geb automatically favoured Horus, son of Osiris and avenger of his father, making him ruler of the living. The pharaoh was therefore sometimes described as 'heir of Geb', in recognition of Geb's protective role.

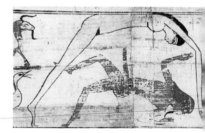

Scene from the Book of the Dead papyrus of Tameniu, showing an ithyphallic figure of the earth-god Geb beneath the sky-goddess Nut. Third Intermediate Period, c.950 BC, painted papyrus from Thebes, H. (as cut and framed today) 9.5 cm. (EA10008)

Geb is usually depicted as reclining on his side with one arm bent. As a god of the earth, responsible for vegetation, he was sometimes coloured green, and might actually be portrayed with vegetation springing from him. He was also sometimes shown with the white-fronted goose, his emblem, on his head, although in some other instances he wore the Lower Egyptian crown. Isis, as his daughter, might be described as the 'egg of the goose'. In funerary contexts he was a malevolent force, imprisoning the buried dead within his body, and it was in this context that he was often mentioned in the PYRAMID TEXTS. Earthquakes were believed to be the 'laughter of Geb'. In his benevolent aspect he was a god of fertility, sometimes emphasized by his erect phallus pointing skyward towards his wife. In the Ptolemaic period (332–30 BC) he became identified with the Greek god Kronos.

W. HELCK, 'Rp't auf dem Thron des Geb', *Orientalia* 19 (1950), 416–34.

H. TE VELDE, 'Geb', *Lexikon der Ägyptologie* II, ed. W. Helck, E. Otto and W. Westendorf (Wiesbaden, 1977), 427–9.

C. TRAUNECKER, *Coptos: hommes et dieux sur le parvis de Geb* (Leuven, 1992).

Gebel el-Arak knife-handle

Decorated ivory handle of a ripple-flaked flint knife dating to the late Predynastic period (*c.*3200 BC), which was purchased in 1894 by the French archaeologist Georges Bénédite at Gebel el-Arak in Middle Egypt, and is now in the collection of the Louvre. Like the Protodynastic palettes and maceheads from ABYDOS and HIERAKONPOLIS, it provides important evidence relating to the early development of the Egyptian state.

Both sides of the hippopotamus tusk handle are engraved in a style which is thought to be Levantine or Mesopotamian rather than Egyptian. The decoration on one side consists of a depiction of several wild beasts, including the Mesopotamian or Elamite motif of two lions separated by a man. The other side of the handle bears scenes of hand-to-hand fighting between foot-soldiers as well as a naval conflict between three crescent-shaped papyrus skiffs and two unusual vertical-prowed boats possibly representing foreigners. The style of the Gebel el-Arak knife-handle constitutes part of the growing body of evidence for the influence of Western Asia on late Predynastic Egypt.

G. BÉNÉDITE, 'Le couteau de Gebel el Arak', *Fondation Eugène Piot, Monuments et Mémoires* 22 (1916), 1–34.

J. VANDIER, *Manuel d'archéologie égyptienne* 1/1 (Paris, 1952), 533–9.

H. ASSELBERGHS, *Chaos in beheersing* (Leiden, 1961), pls xxxviii–lxi.

A. L. KELLEY, 'A review of the evidence concerning early Egyptian ivory knife handles', *The Ancient World* 6 (1983), 95–102.

Gebel Barkal *see* NAPATA

Gebelein (anc. Per-Hathor, Pathyris, Aphroditopolis)

The distinctive topography of this site, about 30 km south of Thebes, is indicated by its Arabic name, which means 'two hills'. The eastern hill is dominated by the remains of a temple of Hathor, the decoration of which dates primarily from the 11th to 15th Dynasties (2055–1550 BC), although the survival of a number of Gerzean artefacts suggests that the much-plundered cemeteries were already in use by the late Predynastic period. The temple of Hathor was certainly established by the end of the Early Dynastic period (2686 BC) and was still in existence during the Roman period (30 BC–AD 395). Many demotic and Greek papyri have been found at the site, providing a detailed picture of daily life at Gebelein in the Ptolemaic period. On Gebelein's western hill are a number of tombs, some of which, although much plundered, have been able to be dated to the late Predynastic. Most date to the First Intermediate Period (2181–2055 BC), including the tomb of Iti, whose wall-paintings are now in the Museo Egizio, Turin. The remains of the unexcavated town-site are located at the foot of the eastern hill.

G. W. FRASER, 'El Kab and Gebelein', *PSBA* 15 (1893), 496–500.

G. STEINDORFF, *Grabfunde des Mittleren Reiches* II (Berlin, 1901), 11–34.

E. SCHIAPARELLI, 'La missione italiana a Ghebelein', *ASAE* 21 (1921), 126–8.

B. PORTER and R. L. B. MOSS, *Topographical bibliography* V (Oxford, 1937), 162–3.

H. G. FISCHER, 'The Nubian mercenaries of Gebelein during the First Intermediate Period', *Kush* 9 (1961), 44–80.

P. W. PESTMAN, 'Les archives privées de Pathyris à l'époque ptolémaïque' *Studia Papyrologica Varia* (Pap. Lugd. Bat XIV), ed. E. Boswinkel et al. (Leiden, 1965), 47–105.

Gebel el-Silsila (anc. Khenw, Kheny)

Pharaonic and Greco-Roman sandstone quarries, rock-cut shrines and stelae on both sides of the Nile about 65 km north of Aswan. The quarries, primarily on the east bank, were in use from the 18th Dynasty onwards, but there are also petroglyphs and graffiti in the cliffs dating back to the late Predynastic period

View of the Gebel el-Silsila sandstone quarries. (I. SHAW)

(*c.*3400–3100 BC). Most of the shrines, including the Great SPEOS of Horemheb, are located along the west bank and date primarily to the New Kingdom (1550–1069 BC).

B. PORTER and R. L. B. Moss, *Topographical bibliography* V (Oxford, 1937), 208–18, 220–1.

R. A. CAMINOS and T. G. H. JAMES, *Gebel el Silsilah* I (London, 1963).

Gerzean *see* PREDYNASTIC PERIOD

gesso

Material consisting of a layer of fine plaster to which gilding was often attached using an adhesive, particularly in the decoration of CARTONNAGE. The term derives from the Italian word for a chalky substance used in preparing panels for painting during the Renaissance, although it can also be traced back to a term used for gypsum in ancient Mesopotamia.

Giza

Necropolis located in the immediate vicinity of the southwestern suburbs of modern Cairo, where a group of pyramid complexes of the 4th Dynasty (2613–2494 BC), comprising those of KHUFU, KHAFRA and MENKAURA, are located. The Giza plateau cannot be regarded as fully explored, as MASTABA V, which probably dates to the reign of the 1st-Dynasty ruler DJET (*c.*2980 BC). The name of the owner of the tomb is unknown, although the presence of the graves of fifty-six retainers suggests that he or she was an important member of the Early Dynastic élite. Jar-sealings bearing the name of the 2nd-Dynasty ruler Nynetjer (*c.*2800 BC)

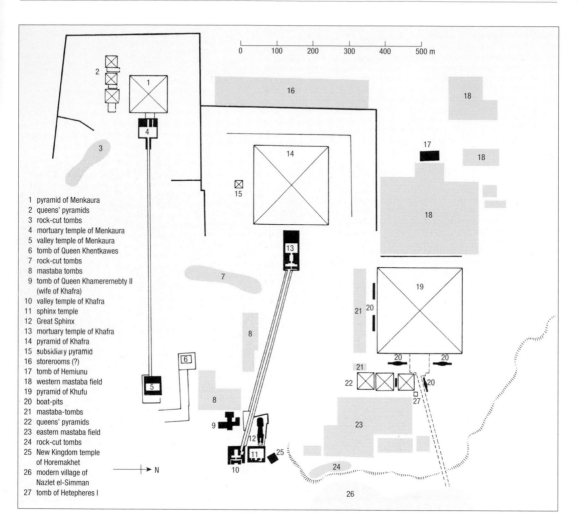

1 pyramid of Menkaura
2 queens' pyramids
3 rock-cut tombs
4 mortuary temple of Menkaura
5 valley temple of Menkaura
6 tomb of Queen Khentkawes
7 rock-cut tombs
8 mastaba tombs
9 tomb of Queen Khamerernebty II
  (wife of Khafra)
10 valley temple of Khafra
11 sphinx temple
12 Great Sphinx
13 mortuary temple of Khafra
14 pyramid of Khafra
15 subsidiary pyramid
16 storerooms (?)
17 tomb of Hemiunu
18 western mastaba field
19 pyramid of Khufu
20 boat-pits
21 mastaba-tombs
22 queens' pyramids
23 eastern mastaba field
24 rock-cut tombs
25 New Kingdom temple
   of Horemakhet
26 modern village of
   Nazlet el-Simman
27 tomb of Hetepheres I

Plan of the Giza necropolis.

have also been found in a tomb to the south of
the main necropolis.

Khufu (2589–2566 BC) – whose father SNE-
FERU (2613–2589 BC) had erected the first
true pyramid – built the largest surviving
pyramid, now usually described as the Great
Pyramid but originally called 'Khufu is the
one belonging to the horizon'. It was constructed from some 3,200,000 blocks of limestone, each weighing an average of 2.5 tons,
and it differs from most pyramids in having
two burial chambers within the built structure and a third unfinished chamber below

ground. From each of the two upper chambers, narrow sloping tunnels were constructed; these so-called 'air shafts' probably had
little to do with ventilation, and for some
time it has been accepted that they may have
some astronomical function. In 1993 a
German team led by Rudolf Gantenbrink
and Rainer Stadelmann, using a robot cam-
era, discovered a sealed door in one of the
shafts from the Queen's chamber, which has
led to speculation that a fourth chamber
might be located there.

It has been suggested that in the original
design of the Great Pyramid there was to have
been a subterranean burial chamber, but that

this must have been abandoned at an early
stage of the work, since it is only partly hewn.
When first recorded the chambers were found
empty, perhaps having been robbed as early as
the First Intermediate Period (2181–2055 BC)
when the central authority, which had been
responsible for their construction, collapsed.

Like all pyramids, that of Khufu was part
of a complex, of which the three subsidiary
pyramids (the so-called queens' pyramids)
are the most obvious part. The temple on the
east side is ruined, and the causeway leading
to the valley temple has been robbed out and
lost beneath the modern settlement of Nazlet
el-Simman. Several boat-pits surrounded the

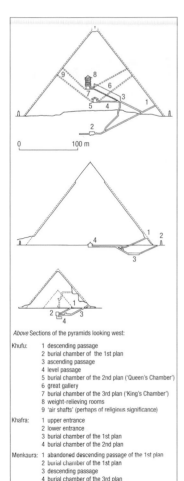

Above Sections of the pyramids looking west:

Khufu:
1 descending passage
2 burial chamber of the 1st plan
3 ascending passage
4 level passage
5 burial chamber of the 2nd plan ('Queen's Chamber')
6 great gallery
7 burial chamber of the 3rd plan ('King's Chamber')
8 weight-relieving rooms
9 'air shafts' (perhaps of religious significance)

Khafra:
1 upper entrance
2 lower entrance
3 burial chamber of the 1st plan
4 burial chamber of the 2nd plan

Menkaura:
1 abandoned descending passage of the 1st plan
2 burial chamber of the 1st plan
3 descending passage
4 burial chamber of the 3rd plan

Section drawings of the three Giza pyramids.

pyramid, and boats have been found in two of these. One has been reconstructed and is currently displayed close to the site of its discovery. It has been argued that these boats were used in the funerary ceremonies, and that perhaps one of them bore the king's body to the valley temple. However, it is equally likely that they performed a more symbolic role, as part of the funerary equipment provided for the travels of the deceased king with the sun-god.

Like the other true pyramids, at this site and elsewhere, the superstructure of the Great Pyramid would not originally have been uneven but covered by a layer of smooth white Tura limestone, probably crowned by gold sheet at the apex. This covering was stripped away in medieval and later times. The burial of HETEPHERES, the mother of Khufu, lies just to the east of the pyramid and gives some indication of the riches which might have accompanied a pharaoh of this period.

Although Khufu's immediate successor,

The pyramids of Giza. The Great Pyramid of Khufu (left) appears smaller than that of Khafra (centre), since this latter is built on a slight eminence. The smallest is that of Menkaura.
(P. T. NICHOLSON)

Djedefra (2566–2558 BC), began to construct a pyramid complex at ABU ROASH 8 km north of Giza, he may have been responsible for some quarrying at Giza, and some scholars have attributed work on the Great SPHINX to him, although this sculpture is usually assigned to the reign of Khafra (2558–2532 BC), builder of the second of the Giza pyramids. The sphinx is carved from a knoll of rock in a quarry beside Khafra's causeway, which leads from his well-preserved granite valley temple to the mortuary temple on the eastern side of his pyramid. Statues of the king, his head symbolically protected by HORUS (now in the Egyptian Museum, Cairo), were discovered by Auguste Mariette's workmen in 1860, during the excavation of the valley temple (see KHAFRA illustration).

The site of the pyramid itself is on a slight eminence; and for this reason, and by virtue of its still preserving some of its limestone casing at the apex, it appears larger than that of Khufu. In ancient times the monument was known as 'Great is Khafra', and is more typical of Old Kingdom pyramid design, with its

subterranean burial chamber. On the north and west sides it shows clear evidence of the quarrying necessary to level the site, the removed stone being used for the construction itself.

The smallest of the three pyramid complexes at Giza is that of Menkaura (2532–2503 BC). Unlike its predecessor, the valley temple was not of granite but finished in mud brick. However, it was here that a series of superb schist triad statues were discovered by the Harvard/Boston expedition in 1908. They represent the king with HATHOR, goddess of MEMPHIS, and NOME deities. Like the pyramid of Khafra, that of Menkaura had its lowest courses cased in red granite, and like its predecessor had the chambers below the built structure. Unlike the other pyramids at Giza, however, 'Menkaura is Divine' had palace-façade carving on its interior walls. This pyramid was the subject of SAITE interest in the 26th Dynasty (664–525 BC), when a new wooden coffin was inserted. In 1838 the original granite sarcophagus was lost at sea while being transported to England, although the wooden coffin lid is in the British Museum.

The pyramid complexes are surrounded by groups of MASTABA tombs, in which members of the royal family and high officials were buried. The most extensive mastaba cemeteries are arranged in regular 'streets' to the west, south and east of the pyramid of Khufu, each tomb being of a similar size. The earliest private tombs at Giza are cut into the quarry faces surrounding the pyramids of Khafra and Menkaura.

During the New Kingdom there was renewed activity at Giza. In the 18th Dynasty Amenhotep II (1427–1400 BC) built a temple to Horemakhet ('Horus of the Horizon') near the Great Sphinx, and this was later enlarged by

Sety I (1294–1279 BC) in the 19th Dynasty. During the Third Intermediate Period (1069–747 BC) the southernmost of the subsidiary queens' pyramids in the Khufu complex was converted into a temple of Isis. In the 26th Dynasty the pyramid of Menkaura was restored, the temple of Isis was enlarged and a number of tombs were constructed along the causeway of Khafra, an area which continued to be used as a cemetery as late as the Persian period.

W. M. F. PETRIE, *The pyramids and temples of Gizeh* (London, 1883).

H. JUNKER, *Giza*, 12 vols (Vienna, 1929–55).

G. A. REISNER and W. STEVENSON SMITH, *A history of the Giza necropolis*, 2 vols (Cambridge, MA, 1942–55).

N. BARAKAT et al., *Electromagnetic sounder experiments at the pyramid of Giza* (Berkeley, 1975).

M. LEHNER, 'A contextual approach to the Giza pyramids', *Archiv der Orientforschung* 32 (1985), 136–58.

I. E. S. EDWARDS, *The pyramids of Egypt*, 5th ed. (Harmondsworth, 1993), 98–151.

glass

Although the glazing of stones such as quartz and steatite, as well as the making of FAIENCE, had been known since Predynastic times (*c.*5500–3100 BC), glass is extremely rare before *c.*1500 BC, and not certainly attested in Egypt before the late Middle Kingdom.

It is possible that the craft of glass-making was first introduced into Egypt following the campaigns of Thutmose III (1479–1425 BC), when captive glass-makers may have been brought to Egypt from MITANNI, where the technology was already available. Glass is certainly one of the materials mentioned in lists of tribute in the *Annals of Thutmose III* at Karnak, and even by the time of Akhenaten (1352–1336 BC) glass was still of sufficient importance to merit inclusion in diplomatic correspondence. In the AMARNA LETTERS the Hurrian and Akkadian terms *ehlipakku* and *mekku* were used, and these loan-words perhaps point to the eastern origins of the earliest glass.

A distinction should be made between glass-*making* from its raw materials (silica, alkali and lime) and glass-*working* from ready-prepared ingots or scrap glass (cullet). The first of these is considerably more difficult than the second, and recent analyses suggest that some of the earliest glass in Egypt was made using materials from abroad, so that either finished items or raw glass were imported for use by workers (captive or otherwise) in Egypt. It is likely that, even when the industry became better established, there were workshops which worked only glass, obtaining their supplies in the form of ingots from more sophisticated installations.

Perhaps because of an importation of craftsmen from abroad, there are no surviving

Glass containers for unguents and cosmetics, all coreformed apart from the gold-rimmed solid cast example on the left. The jug, which bears the name of Thutmose III, is one of the earliest datable Egyptian glass vessels. 18th Dynasty, c.1450–1336 BC, L. of fish 14.5 cm. (EA24391, 47620, 2589, 55193, 4741)

instances of trial stages in the making of glass in Egypt, which instead appears as a fully fledged industry. Consequently, technologically difficult pieces, such as clear decolorized glass, are known from as early as the reign of Hatshepsut (1473–1458 BC) and colourless glass inlays occur in the throne of Tutankhamun (1336–1327 BC).

As well as being used for inlays, beads and amulets, glass was used also in attempts at more ambitious pieces, including vessels. The latter were not made by blowing, which was introduced only in Roman times, but by core-forming. A core of mud and sand in the shape of the vessel interior was formed around a handling rod. This core would then be dipped into the viscous molten glass (or the glass be trailed over it) and evened out by rolling the whole on a flat stone (marver). The rims and feet of the vessels could be shaped using pincers, but the process was usually more complicated than this. Coloured threads were added to the base colour of the vessel (commonly blue or blue-green) so that strands of yellow, white, red etc. decorated the piece. These were sometimes pulled with a needle to make swag or feather patterns, and then rolled on the marver to impress them into the still soft body glass.

The finished vessel was then allowed to cool slowly in an oven in a process known as annealing, which allowed the stresses developed in the glass to be released gradually. Once cold the core could be broken up and removed through the vessel opening. It was frequently difficult to remove the core entirely, especially in the shoulders of narrow-necked vessels, and the remains of the core often added to the opacity of these pieces, while those with broader necks appear more translucent.

Glass might also be moulded. At its simplest this involved the making of plain glass forms, but it could also be much more complex, with sections of glass cane of different colours fused together in a mould to make multicoloured vessels, such as those with yellow eyes on a green background, or the conglomerate glass pieces with angular fragments of many colours fused into bowls.

It was also possible to work glass by cold cutting. In this process, lumps of glass, sometimes moulded to roughly the shape desired, were worked as though they were pieces of stone and so carved to shape. This is an extremely difficult process requiring great skill. None the less some fine pieces, including two headrests made for Tutankhamun, were produced in this way.

Glass seems to have been regarded as an artificial precious stone, and like such stones is sometimes imitated in painted wood. Perhaps because of this connection it never developed forms of its own but rather copied those traditionally made in stone, faience or other materials. It seems that for much of the New Kingdom it was a costly novelty material, probably under royal control, and given as gifts to favoured officials. Until recently the production of glass was thought to have declined after the 21st Dynasty (1069–945 BC), not to be revived on any scale until the 26th Dynasty (664–525 BC), but J. D. Cooney has suggested that it persisted on a much reduced scale. In Ptolemaic times, Alexandria became a centre for glass craftsmanship, with the production of core-formed vessels and, in Roman times, items of cameo glass, probably including the famous Portland Vase (now in the British Museum).

The best evidence for glass production comes from Flinders Petrie's excavations at EL-AMARNA, where he found a great deal of glass waste, but there are still enormous areas of technology that are not properly understood, and excavations at that site during the 1990s have produced new evidence based primarily on the detailed study of kilns. It seems increasingly likely that glass-making was carried on alongside faience production, and possibly other pyrotechnical crafts. As well as the remains at el-Amarna, there are glass-working sites at EL-LISHT and MALKATA.

B. NOLTE, *Die Glasgefässe im alten Ägypten* (Berlin, 1968).

J. D. COONEY, *Catalogue of Egyptian Antiquities in the British Museum* IV: *Glass* (London, 1976).

C. LILYQUIST and R. H. BRILL, *Studies in early Egyptian glass* (New York, 1993).

P. T. NICHOLSON, *Egyptian faience and glass* (Aylesbury, 1993).

goats *see* ANIMAL HUSBANDRY

god's wife of Amun *(hemet netjer nt Imen)*
The title of 'god's wife of Amun' is first attested in the early New Kingdom in the form of a temple post endowed by AHMOSE I (1550–1525 BC) for his wife AHMOSE NEFERTARI. It later became closely associated with the title of DIVINE ADORATRICE *(dwat-netjer)* which was held by the daughter of the chief priest of Amun under Hatshepsut (1473–1458 BC), and by the mother of the 'great royal wife' (see QUEENS) in the sole reign of Thutmose III (1479–1425 BC), although its importance at this time was much reduced. From the time of Amenhotep III (1390–1352 BC) until the end of the 18th Dynasty there appears to have been no royal holder of the office of god's wife of Amun.

The function of the god's wife was to play the part of the consort of AMUN in religious ceremonies, thus stressing the belief that kings were descended from the union between Amun and the great royal wife. The title 'god's hand' was also sometimes used, referring to the act of masturbation by ATUM by which he produced SHU and TEFNUT. Atum's hand was thus regarded as female. In the 19th Dynasty (1295–1186 BC), the title was reintroduced, but its importance was slight compared with earlier periods. In the late 20th Dynasty, however, Rameses VI (1143–1136 BC) conferred on his daughter Isis a combined title of both god's wife of Amun and divine adoratrice, thus creating what was largely a political post. This office was from then on bestowed on the king's daughter who, as a priestess, would have held great religious and political power in the city of Thebes. She was barred from marriage, remaining a virgin; therefore she had to adopt the daughter of the next king as heiress to her office. In this way the king sought to ensure that he always held power in Thebes and also prevented elder daughters from aiding rival claimants to the throne. The god's wife was in fact the most prominent member of a group of 'Amun's concubines', all virgins and all with adopted successors.

In the 25th and 26th Dynasties (747–525 BC), the god's wife and her adopted successor

Granite statuette of the god's wife Amenirdis I, daughter of the Kushite ruler Kashta. Late 8th century BC, H. 28.3 cm. (EA46699)

played an important role in the transference of royal power. This office was sometimes combined with that of chief of the priestesses of Amun. Some measure of the wealth and influence of these women is seen by the building of a 'tomb with chapel' by Amenirdis I, sister of King Shabaqo (716–702 BC) of the 25th Dynasty, within the temple enclosure at MEDINET HABU.

U. HÖLSCHER, *The excavation of Medinet Habu* V: *Post-Ramessid remains* (Chicago, 1954).

M. GITTON, *L'épouse du dieu, Ahmès Néfertary* (Paris, 1975).

E. GRAEFE, *Untersuchungen zur Verwaltung und Geschichte der Institution der Gottesgemahlin des*

*Amun vom Begin des Neuen Reiches bis zur
Spätzeit* (Wiesbaden, 1981).
M. GITTON, *Les divines épouses de la 18e dynastie*
(Paris, 1984).
G. ROBINS, *Women in ancient Egypt* (London,
1993), 149–56.

gold

That gold was a precious commodity in Egypt
is undoubted, although it was outranked by
SILVER when this was first introduced. By the
Middle Kingdom (2055–1650 BC), however,
gold had become the most precious material,
and was eagerly sought. It is no surprise that
the oldest known geological map is a diagram
of the gold mines and *bekhen*-stone (siltstone)
quarries in the Wadi Hammamat. The late
Predynastic town at NAQADA, near the mouth of
Wadi Hammamat, was known as Nubt ('gold
town'), perhaps indicating that it grew rich
from the gold trade.

Gold was mined both from the Eastern
Desert and from Nubia, where there are
Egyptian inscriptions from Early Dynastic
and Old Kingdom times (3100–2181 BC). New
Kingdom private tombs, such as that of
Sobekhotep (TT63), sometimes include depictions of Nubians bringing gold as tribute.
During the New Kingdom (1550–1069 BC) it
was obtained also from Syria–Palestine by way
of tribute, despite the fact that Egypt was
already much richer in gold than the
Levantine city-states. The Egyptians' prodi-
gious wealth in gold made them the envy of
their neighbours in the Near East, and finds
frequent mention in the AMARNA LETTERS. For
example letter EA19 from Tushratta of Mitanni
reads: 'May my brother send me in very great
quantities gold that has not been worked, and
may my brother send me much more gold than
he did to my father. In my brother's country
gold is as plentiful as dirt ...'

Mining and quarrying expeditions were
carried out under military control, and many
of the labourers were convicts (see STONE AND
QUARRYING). The laborious and dangerous
work may have ensured that for many it was a
death sentence. The gold-bearing rock had to
be laboriously crushed and washed to extract
the metal which was then carried off for refin-
ing and working.

Gold was regarded as the flesh of RA and the
other gods, a divine metal that never tar-
nished. As such it was used in the making of

RIGHT *Part of a floral collar formed from gold,
cornelian and blue glass inlaid elements, which
illustrates the use of the cloisonné technique of
goldworking. New Kingdom, c.1370–1300 BC,
H. (as strung) 12.2 cm. (EA3074)*

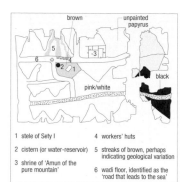

1 stele of Sety I   4 workers' huts

2 cistern (or water-reservoir) 5 streaks of brown, perhaps
                                  indicating geological variation

3 shrine of 'Amun of the   6 wadi floor, identified as the
  pure mountain'   'road that leads to the sea'

images of the god, or as gilt for divine statues;
it also adorned temples and the pyramidions
surmounting obelisks and pyramids. The
ROYAL TITULARY included the 'Golden Horus'
name, associating the king with the sun, while
the goddess Hathor was sometimes described
as 'the golden one'.

This connection with the gods made it the
ideal metal in funerary contexts, as spectacu-
larly witnessed by the mask and coffins of
Tutankhamun (1336–1327 BC), although lesser
individuals aspired to gilded or yellow-painted
masks. The sarcophagus chamber in the royal
tomb was known as the 'house of gold', while
at the ends of sarcophagi or coffins ISIS and
NEPHTHYS were often shown kneeling on the
hieroglyphic sign for gold (*nebu*). In the 5th-
Dynasty tomb of Iy-Mery at Giza (G6020) an

LEFT *Copy of part of the 'Turin mining papyrus',
the earliest surviving geological map, which
documents a quarrying expedition in the vicinity of
a gold-mining settlement in the Wadi Hammamat.
Reign of Rameses IV, c.1153–1147 BC. (TURIN,
MUSEO EGIZIO, CAT.1879)*

BELOW *Part of a wall-painting from the tomb-
chapel of Sobekhotep (TT63), showing Nubians
presenting gold as tribute to the Egyptian king. The
gold has been cast into rings for ease of transport.
18th Dynasty, c.1400 BC, from Thebes. (EA921)*

inscription points out that the shape of the
nebu sign was being imitated by pairs of
dancers in the funerary dance known as the
tcheref.

In times of unrest the golden funerary
equipment acted as a lure for tomb-robbers,
as recorded in Papyrus Abbot which deals with
the desecration of the tomb of King Sobekem-
saf II of the 17th Dynasty (1650–1550 BC):

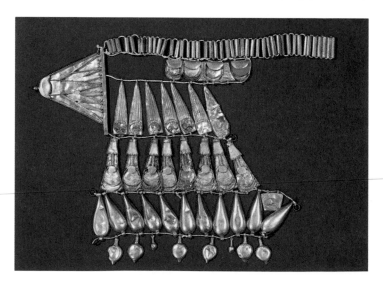

'We opened their sarcophagi and their coffins… and found the noble mummy of this King equipped with a falchion [curved sword] … amulets and jewels of gold were upon his neck, and his headpiece of gold was upon him. The noble mummy of this King was completely bedecked with gold, and his coffins were adorned with gold … We collected the gold we found on the mummy of this god … and we set fire to their coffins … '

Gold could also serve the living, and the material melted down by the robbers would have been used in exchanges, since there was no actual coinage. The high value of gold made it a suitable reward for eminent individuals, and there are representations of favoured New Kingdom officials such as Maya and HOREMHEB being rewarded with golden collars by the pharaoh. There are many surviving examples of the 'FLY of valour', a military honour usually made of gold.

The gold of ancient Egypt became legendary and eventually passed into medieval folklore. With the discovery of the tomb of Tutankhamun, the imagination of the twentieth-century press became particularly obsessed with the 'gold of the pharaohs', often at the expense of discoveries that are archaeologically more significant.

J. ČERNY, 'Prices and wages in Egypt in the Ramesside period', *Cahiers d'Histoire Mondiale* 1 (1954), 903–21.
R. KLEMM and D. D. KLEMM, 'Chronologischer Abriss der antiken Goldgewinnung in der Ostwüste Ägyptens', *MDAIK* 50 (1994), 29–35.

great green (Egyptian *wadj wer*)
Term used to refer to a fecundity figure (see HAPY) who appears to have personified either the lakes within the Nile Delta or the Mediterranean sea. The latter interpretation is a matter of considerable debate; it has been pointed out, for instance, that certain texts (such as Papyrus Ramesseum VI) describe the crossing of the 'great green' by foot, and other documents use a determinative sign for the term that suggests dry land rather than water.
J. BAINES, *Fecundity figures: Egyptian personification and the iconology of a genre* (Warminster, 1986).
C. VANDERSLEYEN, 'Le sens de Ouadj-Our (W'*d*-Wr)', *Akten München 1985* IV, ed. S. Schoske (Hamburg, 1991), 345–52.

great royal wife see QUEENS

Greeks
Egypt did not develop close contacts with

Copy of a wall-painting from the tomb of Menkheperraseneb at Thebes, showing foreign rulers from the Aegean and the Near East bringing tribute to the pharaoh. The prostrate figure on the left is described as the 'chief of the Keftiw' (usually assumed to be a reference to Crete) and the figure on the far right wears Aegean clothing and carries a Minoan-style bull's head. 18th Dynasty, c.1450 BC.

Greece until well into the Pharaonic period, although various economic and political links gradually developed over the centuries. By the 12th Dynasty (1985–1795 BC) the TOD treasure shows Greek influence, but it was in the New Kingdom (1550–1069 BC) that contacts become most clear. In Egyptian tombs of 1500–1440 BC there are representations of cups of the type found at Vapheio in mainland Greece, which were brought to Thebes as tribute by Cretans. Paintings in the tomb of Senenmut (TT71) show not only a giant Vapheio cup but also a bull-headed rhyton, while Cretans are also shown in the tomb of Menkheperraseneb (TT86). It may be that Cretans and other Greeks visited Egypt during this time and took away with them notions of Egyptian architecture, since some Minoan frescos portray papyrus columns. The goddess TAWERET was modified to become the so-called Cretan 'genius', losing her hippopotamus form until she more closely resembled a donkey. Thoth, in his baboon manifestation, was also imported into Crete. Similarly, Mycenaean pottery reached Egypt in the New Kingdom, perhaps as containers for a particular valued commodity, and has been found in large quantities at sites such as EL-AMARNA. Cyprus was also important as a source of copper, imported as ox-hide ingots. Certain resins may also have been imported from Cyprus (and elsewhere in Greece) and Cypriot pottery is also attested in Egypt.

Psamtek I (664–610 BC) allowed Greeks from Miletus to found a commercial centre at NAUKRATIS, and under Ahmose II (570–526 BC) their trade was limited to this city. The Egyptians levied a duty on commerce there, and this was sent to the temple of Neith at SAIS. The city struck its own coinage, the only type of coin known from Pharaonic Egypt.

Mercenary soldiers, including some from the Mediterranean, had been used increasingly from the New Kingdom, but by the SAITE period (664–525 BC) Egypt had come to depend ever more heavily on Greek mercenary troops, who were settled in Memphis. The rising power of PERSIA inevitably led to the conquest of Egypt in 525 BC, making Egypt a natural ally of the Greek city-states. In 465 BC, following the death of Xerxes I (486–465 BC), there was a revolt by Psamtek of Sais, and with Athenian help he besieged the Persians at Memphis, although he was eventually killed in 454 BC. Through the last decades of the fifth century BC, his supporters survived in the Delta marshes, retaining their contacts with Athens. It was at some time during this period that the Greek historian HERODOTUS made his visit to Egypt, recording recent political events and local curiosities.

In 405 BC Darius II of Persia (424–405 BC) died and in the following year Amyrtaios (404–399 BC) seized power in Egypt, becoming the only ruler of the 28th Dynasty. Egypt had been drawn ever more into the Greek world, and Nepherites I (399–393 BC) supported the Cypriots against the Persians. Later, revolts in Persia led Teos (362–360 BC) to attempt to regain those provinces that had been lost; in this campaign he depended heavily on the Greek mercenaries provided by the Spartan king Agesilaus and the Athenian admiral Chabrias. The power of the Greek mercenaries at this time is indicated by the fact that a subsequent revolt in favour of Nectanebo II (360–343 BC), nephew of Teos, succeeded primarily because of the support of Agesilaus. In 343 BC the Persians attacked again, but the Greek mercenaries were once more disloyal, and Egypt fell.

It was the coming of Macedonian Greeks

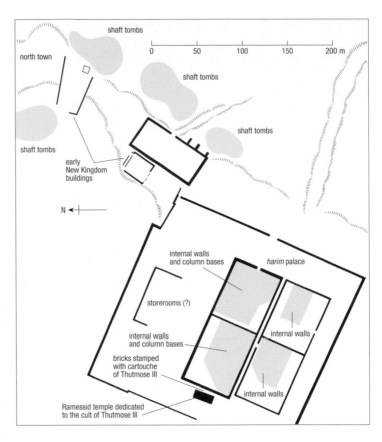

under ALEXANDER THE GREAT (332–323 BC), ousting the Persians in 332 BC, that brought Egypt fully into the Hellenistic world. New cities such as ALEXANDRIA and Ptolemais were established and settled by Greeks, while the FAYUM REGION became an important agricultural centre. Greek was adopted as the official language, and numerous papyri of the period have been discovered at OXYRYNCHUS and elsewhere. This mixing of Greeks and Egyptians led to new artistic developments, with traditional subjects depicted in innovative ways, as in the scenes from the tomb of PETOSIRIS at Tuna el-Gebel.

The Greeks, and through them the Romans, held Egypt in high regard as a font of ancient wisdom, and in this way Egyptian civilization exerted a strong influence on the Classical world. The ancient Greek *kouros*-figures, for example, derived their characteristic appearance from the Greeks' observation of

Plan of Gurob.

Egyptian statues. The roots of western civilization owe considerably more to Egypt than is commonly realized.

H.-J. THISSEN, 'Griechen in Ägypten', *Lexikon der Ägyptologie* III, ed. W. Helck, E. Otto and W. Westendorf (Wiesbaden, 1977), 898–903.

B. J. KEMP and R. MERRILEES, *Minoan pottery from second millennium Egypt* (Mainz, 1981).

A. K. BOWMAN, *Egypt after the pharaohs* (London, 1986).

N. LEWIS, *Greeks in Ptolemaic Egypt* (Oxford, 1986).

D. J. THOMPSON, *Memphis under the Ptolemies* (Princeton, 1988).

Gurob (Medinet el-Ghurob; anc. Mi-wer) Settlement site at the southeastern end of the Fayum region, occupied from the early 18th Dynasty until at least the time of Rameses V

(1147–1143 BC). Excavated between 1888 and 1920, Gurob has been identified with the town of Mi-wer, which was established by Thutmose III (1479–1425 BC) as a royal HARIM, and appears to have flourished in the reign of Amenhotep III (1390–1352 BC). Flinders Petrie excavated part of the New Kingdom town, as well as a building identified as a temple, and cemeteries dating to the New Kingdom and the Ptolemaic period (332–30 BC). The work of subsequent British archaeologists concentrated primarily on the cemeteries and temple, although W. L. S. Loat mentions the remains of a small 18th-Dynasty village close to a fortified building, which may have been an early New Kingdom settlement similar to that beside the South Palace at DEIR EL-BALLAS.

In 1905 the town was examined by the German archaeologist Ludwig Borchardt, who suggested that the main enclosure-wall contained not a temple – as Petrie had argued – but a late 18th-Dynasty palace and *harim* as well as the town itself. More recently, Barry Kemp has synthesized the results of the various excavations to construct an impression of the New Kingdom *harim*-town which must have superseded the earlier village. The main town, contained within an enclosure wall and divided into three blocks (each with its own enclosure walls and gateways), appears to focus on a central limestone building, dating to the reign of Thutmose III, which was eventually dismantled by Rameses II (1279–1213 BC).

Many of the finds from the town are in the collection of the Petrie Museum, London, and have been catalogued in the course of a reassessment of the site as a whole. It might be argued that the combination of artefactual material from town, temple and cemeteries constitutes a more representative set of evidence than the material at the better-documented and better-preserved urban site of EL-AMARNA, which includes very few artefacts from funerary contexts.

W. M. F. PETRIE, *Kahun, Gurob and Hawara* (London, 1890).

—, *Illahun, Kahun and Gurob* (London, 1891).

W. L. S. LOAT, *Gurob* (London, 1905).

L. BORCHARDT, *Der Porträtkopf der Königin Teje: Ausgrabungen der Deutschen Orient-Gesellschaft in Tell el-Amarna* I (Leipzig, 1911).

G. BRUNTON and R. ENGELBACH, *Gurob* (London, 1927).

B. J. KEMP, 'The harim-palace at Medinet el-Ghurab', *ZÄS* 15 (1978), 122–33.

A. P. THOMAS, *Gurob: a New Kingdom town*, 2 vols (Warminster, 1981).

H

hair

The style, presence or absence of hair were all of great importance to the Egyptians, not only as a matter of personal appearance but also as symbols or indications of status. The act of ritual humiliation and subjection was demonstrated by the king's action of seizing his enemies by the hair before smiting them.

The Egyptians took great care of their hair, and were concerned to avoid greying and baldness, judging from the survival of texts including remedies for these conditions, none of which seems likely to have been very effective. Nevertheless, hair was usually washed and scented, and wealthy individuals employed hairdressers. The 11th-Dynasty sarcophagus of Queen Kawit from Deir el-Bahri (*c.*2040 BC; now in the Egyptian Museum, Cairo) shows such a hairdresser at work. Children wore

their hair at the side of the head sometimes as one or two tresses or a plait, and were otherwise shaven. This characteristic SIDELOCK OF YOUTH was regularly depicted, even in the portrayals of deities such as the infant HORUS (Harpocrates).

Hair-pieces in the form of false plaits and curls were sometimes added to the existing hair, even in the case of relatively poor individuals. One of the slain soldiers of Mentuhotep II (2055–2004 BC) buried at Deir el-Bahri was found to be wearing a hair-piece of this type. More common, however, were full wigs, which were not confined to those who had lost their hair but served as a regular item of dress for the élite, as in eighteenth-century Europe.

Many Egyptian wigs were extremely complex and arranged into careful plaits and strands. Women often wore very long, heavy wigs and these were considered to add to their

sexuality. Men generally wore shorter wigs than women, although their styles were sometimes even more elaborate. Wigs were worn on public occasions and at banquets, and, like

ABOVE *Elaborate wig made from about 120,000 human hairs. It consists of a mass of light-coloured curls on top of plaits, designed to allow ventilation, and would probably have been worn on a festive occasion. New Kingdom, from Deir el-Medina, H. 50.5 cm. (EA2560)*

LEFT *Detail from the relief decoration of the sarcophagus of Queen Kawit (a wife of Nebhepetra Mentuhotep II, shown having her hair arranged by a servant. 11th Dynasty, c.2055–2004 BC, L. of entire sarcophagus 2.62 m (CAIRO JE47397)*

hair, would often have been scented (see INCENSE). In 1974 a team of Polish archaeologists discovered the remains of a wig-maker's workshop dating to the Middle and New Kingdoms in a rocky cleft at Deir el-Bahri. The objects included a sack and jars containing hair, as well as a model head with the outline of the wig's attachments.

Wigs were usually made of genuine human hair, although vegetable fibres were sometimes used for padding beneath the surface. Date palm is known to have been used for this purpose in the 21st Dynasty (1069–945 BC). Two Roman wigs made entirely of grass have also survived, but the use of this material seems to have been wholly exceptional. Contrary to persistent references in the archaeological literature, there is no evidence for the use of wool or other animal hair in wigs.

From at least as early as the New Kingdom, the heads of PRIESTS were completely shaven during their period of office, to signify their subservience to the deity, and to reinforce their cleanliness, according to the Greek historian Herodotus. Times of mourning were often marked by throwing ashes or dirt over the head, and sometimes even removing locks of hair. The hieroglyphic determinative sign for mourning consists of three locks of hair, perhaps alluding to the myth of Isis cutting off one of her locks as a symbol of her grief for Osiris, an act hinted at in Papyrus Ramesseum XI and described in detail by the Greek writer Plutarch (c.AD 46–126).

E. LASKOWSKA-KUSZTAL, 'Un atelier de perruquerier à Deir el-Bahari', *ET* 10 (1978), 83–120.

G. POSENER, 'La légende de la tresse d'Hathor', *Egyptological studies in honor of R. A. Parker*, ed. L. H. Lesko (Hanover and London, 1986), 111–17.

J. FLETCHER, 'A tale of hair, wigs and lice', *Egyptian archaeology* 5 (1994), 31–3.

—, 'Hair and wigs', *Ancient Egyptian materials and technology*, ed. P. T. Nicholson and I. Shaw (Cambridge, 2000).

Hapy (baboon-god) *see* CANOPIC JARS

Hapy (god of the inundation)
The Egyptians made an important distinction between the Nile itself – which was simply known as *iterw*, 'the river' – and the Nile INUNDATION, which they deified in the form of Hapy. He was usually represented as a pot-bellied bearded man with pendulous breasts and a headdress formed of aquatic plants. These attributes were designed to stress his fertility and fecundity, and in this sense he was interchangeable with a number of other 'fecundity figures' whose depictions draw on the same reservoir of characteristics. It has also been suggested that the androgynous features of the pharaoh AKHENATEN (1352–1336 BC) – and, to some extent, AMENHOTEP III (1390–1352 BC) – may reflect a similar desire to present an image of the body that drew on both male and female aspects of fertility.

Hapy's major cult centres were at GEBEL EL-SILSILA and ASWAN, where he was thought to dwell in the caverns among the rocks of the first cataract. The lower registers of many temple walls, from the 5th-Dynasty mortuary temple of Sahura (2487–2475 BC) at ABUSIR to the Greco-Roman temple of Horus and Sobek at KOM OMBO, were decorated with depictions of processional fecundity figures bearing tráys of offerings. From the 19th Dynasty (1295–1186 BC) onwards there were occasionally reliefs portraying two fecundity figures, one wearing the papyrus of Lower Egypt and

Quartzite statue of the inundation-god Hapy, shown with the facial features of Osorkon I, whose son, Sheshonq II, is depicted in relief on the left side of the statue. 22nd Dynasty, c.910 BC, H. 2.2 m. (EA8)

the other wearing the Upper Egyptian lotus, in the act of binding together the wind-pipe hieroglyph (*sema*) signifying the unity of the southern and northern halves of Egypt.

D. BONNEAU, *La crue du Nil, divinité égyptienne à travers mille ans d'histoire (332 av.–641 ap. J.C)* (Paris, 1964).

J. BAINES, *Fecundity figures: Egyptian personifications and the iconology of a genre* (Warminster, 1985).

D. VAN DER PLAS, *L'hymne à la crue du Nil*, 2 vols (Leiden, 1986).

harim (Egyptian *ipet, per-khener*)
Term used by Egyptologists to describe an administrative institution connected with royal women and probably attached to Pharaonic palaces and villas during the New Kingdom. However, the use of this evocative term in the ancient Egyptian context is con-

fusing both because it had none of the erotic connotations of the Ottoman *harim* and because the texts and archaeological remains are difficult to reconcile.

On the one hand, the surviving texts describe an important economic institution supported from taxation, and receiving regular supplies of rations, and on the other hand the archaeological remains at GUROB are clearly identified as the remains of an independent establishment relating to royal women (a '*harim*-palace'), founded in the reign of Thutmose III (1479–1425 BC) and occupied throughout the rest of the 18th Dynasty. The inscriptions on stelae, papyri and various other inscribed artefacts from the main buildings at the site repeatedly include the titles of officials connected with the royal *harim* (or *per-khener*) of Mi-wer. There was evidently a similar establishment at MEMPHIS, but that site has not survived.

Although other *harims* have in the past been identified among the remains at such sites as MALKATA and EL-AMARNA, which incorporated the palaces of Amenhotep III (1390–1352 BC) and Akhenaten (1352–1336 BC) respectively, they are unlikely to have had any connection with the *harim* described in the texts and usually in fact derive more from the imaginations of the excavators than from any hard evidence (although the so-called North Palace at el-Amarna, which ironically was not identified as a *harim* by its excavators, bears some compari-

Copy of a relief showing Rameses III with one of the princesses in his harim. *Eastern Gate, Medinet Habu.*

son with the buildings at Gurob. As far as the textual version of the institution is concerned, the women are said to have undertaken such tasks as the weaving of linen (an activity that is well attested at Gurob). The *harim* was administered by such male officials as tax-collectors and scribes, whose titles have been preserved on numerous surviving documents.

When the pharaoh took a new wife or

concubine she was added to the *harim*, along with her entourage of maidservants, so that as time went by, literally dozens of women might be attached to it. Children, including occasional young foreign captives, were brought up in the royal *harim*, a practice that may have fostered the Biblical story of Moses. Given the details of the Moses narrative, it is perhaps not surprising to find that the women of the *harim* occasionally became involved in political intrigue. From the Turin Judicial Papyrus it is known that Tiy, a wife of Rameses III (1184–1153 BC), plotted with other women and some of the male officials to overthrow him in favour of her son. In the event the plot was discovered and the prince was forced to commit suicide, along with several of the other conspirators, although the fate of Tiy and the other women is not known.

A. DE BUCK, 'The judicial papyrus of Turin', *JEA* 23 (1937), 152–64.

E. REISER, *Der königliche Harim im alten Ägypten und seine Verwaltung* (Vienna, 1972) [reviewed by B. J. Kemp, *JEA* 62 (1976), 191–2]

B. J. KEMP, 'The harim-palace at Medinet el-Ghurab', *ZÄS* 15 (1978), 122–33.

D. NORD, 'The term *hnr.* "harem" or "musical performers"?', *Studies in ancient Egypt, the Aegean and the Sudan*, ed. W.K. Simpson and W. M. Davis (Boston, 1981), 137–45.

G. ROBINS, *Women in ancient Egypt* (London, 1993), 38–40.

Harpocrates *see* HORUS

Harsomtus *see* HORUS

Hathor

Important bovine goddess worshipped in three forms: as a woman with the ears of a cow, as a cow, and as a woman wearing a headdress consisting of a wig, horns and sun disc. Her associations and cult centres were among the most numerous and diverse of any of the Egyptian deities. In her vengeful aspect she sometimes also shared the leonine form of the goddess SEKHMET, and in this guise she was regarded as one of the 'eyes' of the sun-god RA. She was also described as 'lady of the sky', and her role as the daughter of RA was reinforced in the temple of HORUS at EDFU by references to her marriage to Horus of Edfu, a falcon-god associated with the heavens.

The literal meaning of her name was 'house of Horus', and was written in the form of a falcon contained within a hieroglyph representing a rectangular building. Since the pharaoh was identified with Horus, Hathor was correspondingly regarded as the divine mother of each reigning king, and one of the royal titles

was 'son of Hathor'. Her role as royal mother is well illustrated by a statue of Hathor in the form of a cow suckling the pharaoh Amenhotep II (1427–1400 BC) from a chapel at DEIR EL-BAHRI (now in the Egyptian Museum, Cairo). The king, however, was also regularly described as the son of ISIS, who appears to have usurped Hathor's role when the legend of Isis, SETH and OSIRIS was conflated with that of the birth of Horus.

In one myth Hathor was said to have been sent to destroy humanity (see EYE OF RA), but

Faience sistrum decorated with the face of the goddess Hathor, with cow's ears and distinctive curling wig. 26th Dynasty, after 600 BC. (EA34190)

she was more usually associated with pleasurable aspects of life as SEXUALITY, joy and MUSIC. Her connection with music was particularly represented by the SISTRUM, ceremonial examples of which were often endowed with Hathor heads, sometimes surmounted by a NAOS, and frequently shaken by the priestesses of the cult of Hathor. She was also regularly portrayed on the *menat* counterpoise attached to necklaces.

In her funerary aspect, most notably at western Thebes, she was known as 'lady of the West' or 'lady of the western mountain'. Each evening she was considered to receive the set-

ting sun, which she then protected until morning. The dying therefore desired to be 'in the following of Hathor' so that they would enjoy similar protection in the netherworld. Hathor was also one of the deities who was thought to be able to determine the destinies of newborn children.

She was the goddess most often associated with the desert and foreign countries, and as such was worshipped as 'lady of BYBLOS'. At the TURQUOISE mines of Serabit el-Khadim in Sinai a temple was built to her in her role as 'lady of turquoise'. By extension she was also known as 'lady of FAIENCE' (the latter being an artificial substance designed to imitate certain precious stones).

The city of Memphis was an important centre of Hathor worship, and she was described there as 'lady of the sycamore', but from as early as the Old Kingdom (2686–2181 BC) her principal cult centre was at DENDERA, where a temple of the Ptolemaic and Roman periods dedicated to the triad of Hathor, Horus and Ihy is still preserved (on the site of an earlier foundation). The sanatorium associated with this temple probably relates to the healing properties that were associated with the goddess because of the myth in which she restored the sight of Horus after his eye had been put out by Seth.

S. ALLAM, *Beiträge zum Hathorkult (bis zum Ende des MR)* (Berlin, 1963).

P. DERCHAIN, *Hathor Quadrifons* (Istanbul, 1972).

S. QUIRKE, *Ancient Egyptian religion* (London, 1992), 126–30.

G. PINCH, *Votive offerings to Hathor* (Oxford, 1993).

Hat-Mehit

Fish-goddess of the Delta, who served as the symbol of the sixteenth nome of Lower Egypt, the capital of which was the city of MENDES, her principal cult centre. Her worship at Mendes became less important with the rise of the ram-god Banebdjedet, who came to be regarded as her consort. She was usually represented either as a Nile carp (*Lepidotus*) or as a woman with a FISH emblem (once misidentified as a dolphin) on her head.

Hatnub

'Egyptian alabaster' (travertine) quarries and associated seasonally occupied workers' settlement in the Eastern Desert, about 65 km southeast of modern el-Minya. The pottery, hieroglyphic inscriptions and hieratic graffiti at the site show that it was in use intermittently from at least as early as the reign of Khufu until the Roman period (c.2589 BC–AD 300). The Hatnub quarry settlements, associated

View of the Old Kingdom travertine quarry at Hatnub. (I. SHAW)

with three principal quarries, like those associated with gold mines in the Wadi Hammamat and elsewhere, are characterized by drystone windbreaks, roads, causeways, cairns and stone alignments.

G. W. FRASER, 'Hat-Nub', *PSBA* 16 (1894), 73–82.

R. ANTHES, *Die Felseninschriften von Hatnub* (Leipzig, 1928).

I. M. E. SHAW, 'A survey at Hatnub', *Amarna reports* III, ed. B. J. Kemp (London, 1986), 189–212.

Hatshepsut (1473–1458 BC)

Daughter of THUTMOSE I (1504–1492 BC) and Queen AHMOSE NEFERTARI, who was married to her half-brother Thutmose II (1492–1479 BC), the son of a secondary wife, perhaps in order to strengthen his claim to the throne. She had a daughter, Neferura, by Thutmose II, but the heir to the throne, the future Thutmose III was the son of one of Thutmose II's concubines. Since Thutmose III (1479–1425 BC), was the only male child, he was married to his half-sister Neferura in order to reinforce his position. Because Thutmose III was still young when his father died, Hatshepsut was appointed regent, and she took the further step of having herself crowned king, allowing her to continue to enjoy a long COREGENCY with the young Thutmose, thus effectively blocking him from full power. In this she appears to have had the support of the priests of Amun, and some of the reliefs in her mortuary temple at DEIR EL-BAHRI reinforced her claim by emphasizing her divine birth, the result of a

union between Amun and her mother Queen Ahmose. She was probably never the chosen heir of her father Thutmose I, although she claimed to have been given the kingship during her father's lifetime. It is likely, however, that these reliefs and inscriptions concerning her legitimacy were simply part of the usual paraphernalia of KINGSHIP rather than self-conscious propaganda on her part.

During her reign there was renewed build-

Relief block from the Red Chapel of Hatshepsut at Karnak, showing the queen performing a religious ceremony associated with the kingship. 18th Dynasty, c.1470 BC, quartzite. (GRAHAM HARRISON)

ing activity at Thebes and elsewhere, in which she was assisted by SESENMUT, architect, chief courtier and tutor to Neferura. It is possible that his political skills had already helped to gain Hatshepsut her elevated position. Her temple at Deir el-Bahri, influenced by the earlier temple of Nebhepetra MENTUHOTEP II (2055–2004 BC), was the finest of her buildings. Here she recorded other aspects of her reign, most notably her trading expeditions to PUNT, BYBLOS and SINAI as well as the transport of two enormous granite obelisks from the quarries at Aswan to the temple of Amun-Ra at KARNAK. It has, in the past, been suggested that the reign of Hatshepsut was an unusually peaceful period in Egyptian history, but evidence has gradually emerged for the continued dispatch of military expeditions during her reign, despite the apparent emphasis on trade in the reliefs at Deir el-Bahri.

Her monuments at Deir el-Bahri and elsewhere frequently show her in kingly costume, including the royal beard, and they often refer to her with masculine pronouns and adjectives as though she were male (although, once again, it is likely that this was simply a case of adhering to the accepted decorum of kingship rather than deliberate deception). In practice, there must have been some sense of conflict between her sex and the masculine role of the pharaoh, but only the occasional grammatical slips in the texts (and, more importantly, the posthumous attempts to remove her name from monuments) have survived as indications of such feelings of inappropriateness.

When Thutmose III reached maturity, he eventually became sole ruler, but it is by no means clear whether Hatshepsut simply died or was forcibly removed from power. It has been argued that the apparent disappearance both of Neferura and Senenmut (who is not attested after Thutmose III's nineteenth regnal year) may perhaps have eased the transfer of power. It used to be thought that Thutmose immediately set about removing his step-mother's name from her monuments, as retribution for her seizure of power, but it is now known that these defacements did not take place until much later in his reign. This re-dating perhaps calls into question the motive of pure vengeance or anger, as opposed to a feeling that her reign had simply been contrary to tradition. On the other hand her two massive obelisks at Karnak appear to have been deliberately concealed behind masonry, and her name was among those omitted from subsequent KING LISTS.

She had prepared a tomb for herself in the Valley of the Kings (KV20), which was discovered by Howard Carter in 1903. There is no evidence that KV20 was ever used for her burial, although it contained an empty quartzite sarcophagus originally intended for Thutmose I (now in the Museum of Fine Arts, Boston). She may have been laid to rest in an earlier tomb, the so-called 'south tomb' in the Wadi Sikket Taqa el-Zeid in the cliffs to the south of Deir el-Bahri, which had been constructed before her rise to the throne.

H. CARTER and T. M. DAVIES, *The tomb of Hâtshopsîtû* (London, 1906).

H. CARTER, 'A tomb prepared for Queen Hatshepsuit and other recent discoveries at Thebes', *JEA* 4 (1917), 107–18.

W. F. EDGERTON, *The Thutmosid succession* (Chicago, 1933).

P. DORMAN, *The monuments of Senenmut* (London, 1988).

P. DER MANUELIAN and C. E. LOEBEN, 'New light on the recarved sarcophagus of Hatshepsut and Thutmose I in the Museum of Fine Arts, Boston', *JEA* 79 (1994), 121–56.

J. TYLDESLEY, *Hatchepsut: the female pharaoh* (Harmondsworth, 1996).

Hawara

Royal necropolis in the southeastern Fayum region, the most important element of which was the pyramid complex of AMENEMHAT III

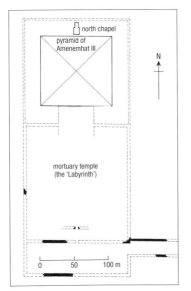

Plan of the pyramid complex of Amenemhat III at Hawara.

ABOVE *View of the pyramid at Hawara. (I. SHAW)*

RIGHT *Mummy case of Artemidorus, incorporating an encaustic portrait of the deceased. Roman period, early 2nd century AD, painted and gilded stucco, from Hawara, H. 1.67 m. (EA21810)*

(1855–1808 BC). The mortuary temple constructed immediately to the south of the pyramid was known to Classical authors as the 'Labyrinth'. It was visited by the Greek historian Herodotus, who described a complex of three thousand rooms connected by winding passages. The site subsequently became part of the itinerary of Greek and Roman travellers. Although only a few traces of the mortuary temple have survived, it has been suggested that it may originally have had some similarities to the complex surrounding the Step Pyramid of Djoser (2667–2648 BC) at SAQQARA. Hawara was first identified by Lepsius in 1843 and later excavated by Flinders Petrie in 1889–9 and 1910–11. In the vicinity of Hawara Petrie also discovered a cemetery incorporating a number of Fayum mummy-portraits executed in ENCAUSTIC or tempera and dating to the Roman period (30 BC–AD 395).

W. M. F. PETRIE, *Hawara, Biahmu and Arsinoe* (London, 1889).

—, *Kahun, Gurob and Hawara* (London, 1890).

W. M. F. PETRIE, G. A. WAINWRIGHT and E. MACKAY, *The Labyrinth, Gerzeh and Mazguneh* (London, 1912).

A. B. LLOYD, 'The Egyptian Labyrinth', *JEA* 56 (1970), 81–100.

D. ARNOLD, 'Das Labyrinth und seine Vorbilder', *MDAIK* 35 (1979), 1–9.

Hawawish, el- *see* AKHMIM

hawk *see* FALCON

headdresses

The insignia and regalia of Egyptian rulers and deities included a wide variety of headdresses. The pharaoh invariably wore headgear of some kind, ranging from the double crown to the simple *nemes* headcloth (see CROWNS AND ROYAL REGALIA).

The deities' headdresses were often extremely distinctive, and from an Egyptological point of view often serve as the principal clue to the identity of the deity concerned. Occasionally such attributes as the headdress are transferred from one deity to another in order to reflect the adoption of particular characteristics. The commonest headdresses are listed below:

Amentet (personification of the West): standard surmounted by a feather and bird.

Amun: crown with two tall plumes, also combined with a sun disc.
Anuket: crown or cap of feathers.
Atum: double crown of Upper and Lower Egypt.
Geb: either a goose or the crown of Lower Egypt combined with the *atef* crown.
Ha (god of the Western Desert): the hieroglyph for desert or hills.
Hathor: cow's horns and solar disc.
Heh: notched palm frond.
Horus: double crown or triple *atef* crown.
Iabet (personification of the East): spear standard.
Isis: the hieroglyphic sign for throne, a pair of cow's horns and a solar disc, or a vulture headdress.
Khons: lunar disc and crescent.
Maat: feather.
Min: double-plumed crown with ribbon or streamer hanging from the back.
Mut: vulture headdress sometimes surmounted by double crown.
Nefertem: lotus flower.

Neith: shield with two crossed arrows and crown of Lower Egypt.
Nekhbet: vulture headdress or crown of Upper Egypt.
Nephthys: hieroglyphs denoting 'mistress of the house', consisting of a rectangle surmounted by a basket shape.
Nut: ceramic vessel.
Osiris: *atef* crown.
Ptah: skull-cap.
Satet: white crown with antelope horns.
Serket: scorpion.
Seshat: star of five or seven points.
Shu: ostrich feather.
Waset/Wosret (goddess of the Theban nome): WAS SCEPTRE with a ribbon, placed above the hieroglyphic sign for nome (a field marked out with irrigation channels).

heart

To the Egyptians the heart (*haty* or *ib*), rather than the brain, was regarded as the source of human wisdom and the centre of the emotions and memory. Its function in the circulation of the blood was not understood, although one religious treatise states that the movement of all parts of the body was determined by the heart. Because of its supposed links with intellect, personality and memory, it was considered to be the most important of the internal organs.

Since it was felt that the heart could reveal a person's true character, even after death, it was left in the body during MUMMIFICATION, and if accidentally removed would be sewn back into place. There was some concern that the heart might testify against its owner and so condemn him or her at the judgement; in order to prevent this, a heart SCARAB was commonly wrapped within the bandages. The inscription on this scarab usually consisted of Chapter 30 from the BOOK OF THE DEAD: 'O my heart which I had from my mother; O my heart which I had upon earth, do not rise up against me as a witness in the presence of the lord of things; do not speak against me concerning what I have done, do not bring up anything against me in the presence of the great god of the west . . .'

In the portrayal of the final judgement – a popular vignette in copies of the Book of the Dead – the heart of the deceased was shown being weighed against the feather of MAAT (the symbol of universal truth and harmony), and the god Anubis was sometimes to be seen adjusting the balance slightly in favour of the deceased to ensure a safe entry into the underworld. The heart was thought to be given back to the deceased in the afterlife; Chapters 26–9 of the Book of the Dead were therefore

Amentet   Iabet   Isis   Nephthys   Ha   Neith

Neith, Hemsut   Meskhent   Wadjyt   Nut   Heh   Lower Egypt, Hapy

Upper Egypt, Hapy   Maat, Shu   Atum, Horus   Osiris   Seshat

Khnum   Sobek   Nekhbet, Mut, Isis   Hathor, Isis   Ra-Horakhty, Sekhmet

Khons   Satet   Reshef   Amun, Horus   Onuris   Anuket

A selection of heart scarabs and amulets: TOP LEFT *green faience scarab inscribed with Chapter 30B of the Book of the Dead, 3rd Intermediate Period, L. 6.7 cm.* (EA66817) TOP RIGHT *steatite, very flat, human-headed heart scarab inscribed on the underside with Chapter 30B of the Book of the Dead for the woman Isis, New Kingdom, L. 6.8 cm.* (EA38073) BOTTOM LEFT *green-glazed steatite scarab inlaid with cornelian and blue glass. The underside bears Chapter 30B of the Book of the Dead, New Kingdom, L. 4.3 cm.* (EA66814) BOTTOM CENTRE *polychrome glass heart amulet with slightly convex faces, 18th Dynasty, H. 2.1 cm.* (EA29265) BOTTOM RIGHT *light turquoise-blue glass, flat-backed, convex-faced heart, New Kingdom, H. 2.6 cm.* (EA8128)

intended to ensure that the heart was restored and could not be removed.

From the New Kingdom (1550–1069 BC) onwards, 'heart amulets', taking the form of a vase with lug handles (perhaps representing the blood vessels), were introduced into the funerary equipment. The heading of Chapter 29b in the Book of the Dead stated that such amulets should be made of *seheret* stone (cornelian), but there are many surviving examples which are made from other materials, such as glass.

R. O. FAULKNER, *The ancient Egyptian Book of the Dead*, ed. C. Andrews (London, 1972), 52–6. C. ANDREWS, *Amulets of ancient Egypt* (London, 1994), 72–3.

Heh

God of infinity, usually represented as a kneeling man either holding a notched palm-rib (hieroglyphic symbol for 'year') in each hand or wearing a palm-rib on his head. Occasionally he is also shown carrying an ANKH sign over his arm. The primary meaning of the term *heh* was 'millions', but he was transformed into the god of eternal life by such symbolic associations with the concepts of 'year' and 'life'. His image was consequently incorporated into royal iconography as a means of ensuring the king's longevity. With typical Egyptian attention to DUALITY, the alternative word for eternity, *djet*, was represented as a female deity.

Along with his consort Hauhet, Heh was also one of the OGDOAD, a group of eight primeval deities whose main cult centre was at HERMOPOLIS MAGNA. The motif of Heh was often incorporated into the decoration of royal regalia as a means of ensuring longevity. Heh was also connected with the myth of the 'celestial COW', who was said to have been supported by a group of eight Heh deities; in the

Lid of a mirror-case from the tomb of Tutankhamun, bearing a figure of the god Heh, H. 27 cm. (CAIRO NO. 271C–D, REPRODUCED COURTESY OF THE GRIFFITH INSTITUTE)

same way, Heh is often represented as holding up the SOLAR BARK and finally lifting it back into the heavens at the end of its voyage through the netherworld.

H. ALTENMÜLLER, 'Heh', *Lexikon der Ägyptologie* II, ed. W. Helck, E. Otto and W. Westendorf (Wiesbaden, 1977), 1082–4.

J. F. BORGHOUTS, 'Heh, Darreichen des', *Lexikon der Ägyptologie* II, ed. W. Helck, E. Otto and W. Westendorf (Wiesbaden, 1977), 1084–6.

heiress theory *see* AHMOSE NEFERTARI and QUEENS

Heka *see* MAGIC

Heket (Heqat)

Goddess represented in the form of a frog, a typical primordial creature which, at certain times of the year, was observed to emerge from the Nile, apparently reborn and thus perhaps emphasizing the coming of new life. She is first attested in the PYRAMID TEXTS where she is said to have assisted in the journey of the dead king to the sky. The remains of a temple of Heket have been excavated at Qus, and in the tomb of PETOSIRIS (c.300 BC) at Tuna el-Gebel there is a text dealing with a procession in her honour, in which she requests that her temple at Her-wer (a still-unlocated site) be restored and protected from the inundation.

Heket's strongest association was with childbirth, particularly the final stages of labour. During the Middle Kingdom (2055–1650 BC), she was depicted or named on such magical artefacts as ivory daggers and clappers, in her role as protector of the household and guardian of pregnant women: The term 'servant of Heket' may have been applied to midwives. Just as the ram-god KHNUM was considered to have been responsible for fashioning the first humans on a potter's wheel, so Heket was portrayed as his

Diorite-gneiss amulet in the form of the frog-goddess Heket. New Kingdom–3rd Intermediate Period, H. 1.4 cm. (EA14758)

female complement in that she was credited with fashioning the child in the womb and giving it life.

Although amulets of Heket were less popular than those of BES or TAWERET, they are not uncommon, even during the reign of AKHENATEN (1352–1336 BC), when many other traditional cults were proscribed. Her life-giving powers associated her with the myths surrounding OSIRIS, the god of the dead, and in this capacity she was depicted as receiving offerings from Sety I (1294–1279 BC) in his temple at Abydos.

C. ANDREWS, *Amulets of ancient Egypt* (London, 1994), 63.

heliacal rising *see* CALENDAR and SOTHIC CYCLE

Heliopolis (Tell Hisn; anc. Iunu, On)
One of the most important cult-centres of the Pharaonic period and the site of the first known sun temple, dedicated to the god Ra-Horakhty (see RA), which was probably first constructed in the early Old Kingdom (c.2600 BC). Although little remains of the site now, its importance in the Pharaonic period was such that ARMANT was sometimes described as the 'southern Heliopolis'.

The 5th-Dynasty sun temple of Nyuserra (2445–2421 BC) at ABU GURAB is thought to have been modelled on the prototypical Heliopolitan sun-temple complex. Because a great deal of the original temple at Heliopolis is now buried beneath the northwestern suburb of Cairo, the only significant monument still standing *in situ* is a pink granite OBELISK dating to the time of Senusret I (1965–1920 BC). There are a number of surviving monuments and fragments of relief from Heliopolis

that have been moved elsewhere, including the obelisks re-erected in New York and London, which both date to the reign of Thutmose III (1479–1425 BC).

The site also incorporates a Predynastic cemetery and the tombs of the chief priests of Heliopolis during the 6th Dynasty (2345–2181 BC). In an area now known as Arab el-Tawil there was a necropolis of sacred MNEVIS bulls of the Ramesside period (1295–1069 BC).

W. M. F. PETRIE and E. MACKAY, *Heliopolis, Kafr Ammar and Shurafa* (London, 1915).

L. HABACHI, 'Akhenaten in Heliopolis', *Festschrift Ricke: Beiträge zur Ägyptischen Bauforschung und Altertumskunde 12* (Cairo, 1971), 35–45.

F. DEBONO, *The predynastic cemetery at Heliopolis* (Cairo, 1988).

Heqat *see* HEKET

Herakleopolis Magna (Ihnasya el-Medina; anc. Henen-nesw)
Site located 15 km to the west of modern Beni Suef, which reached its peak as the capital of the 9th and 10th Dynasties during the First Intermediate Period (2181–2055 BC). It was renamed Herakleopolis Magna in the Ptolemaic period (332–30 BC), when the Greeks identified the local deity, a ram-god called HERYSHEF, with their own god Herakles. The surviving remains include two Pharaonic temples, one of which was dedicated to Heryshef, and the nearby necropolis of

Granite column with a palm-leaf capital, from the temple of Heryshef at Herakleopolis Magna. Reign of Rameses II c.1250 BC, H. 5.28 m. (EA1123)

Sedment el-Gebel, which incorporates a cemetery of the First Intermediate Period and rock-tombs of the Ptolemaic and Roman periods (332 BC–AD 395). The main temple of Heryshef was founded at least as early as the Middle Kingdom (2055–1650 BC) and significantly enlarged during the reign of Rameses II (1279–1213 BC), when a HYPOSTYLE HALL was constructed.

The site also flourished during the Third Intermediate Period (1069–747 BC), and the surviving remains of this date include a cemetery, a large temple and part of the settlement. When the temple was excavated by a Spanish team during the 1980s, the finds included a libation altar and a pair of inlaid eyes thought to derive from a cult statue. The same team has also excavated parts of the First Intermediate Period and Third Intermediate Period cemeteries.

E. NAVILLE, *Ahnas el Medineh (Heracleopolis Magna)* (London, 1894).

W. M. F. PETRIE, *Ehnasya 1904* (London, 1905).

J. LÓPEZ, 'Rapport préliminaire sur les fouilles d'Hérakleopolis (1968)', *Oriens Antiquus* 13 (1974), 299–316.

J. PADRÓ and M. PÉREZ-DIE, 'Travaux récents de la mission archéologique espagnole à Hérakleopolis Magna', *Akten München 1985* II, ed. S. Schoske (Hamburg, 1989), 229–37.

M. PÉREZ-DIE, 'Discoveries at Heracleopolis Magna', *Egyptian Archaeology* VI (1995), 23–5.

Herihor (fl. 1080–1070 BC)
High priest of Amun at Thebes during the reign of the last 20th-Dynasty ruler RAMESES XI (1099–1069 BC). Inscriptions in the last decade of the Dynasty refer to a 'renaissance era', during which, although Rameses was still nominally the only legitimate ruler, the administration of Egypt was effectively divided between three men: the pharaoh himself, whose power-base was in Memphis and Middle Egypt, SMENDES (his eventual successor) who controlled most of Lower Egypt from the Delta city of TANIS, and Herihor, who dominated Upper Egypt and Nubia.

The origins of Herihor are poorly known, but it is thought likely that his parents were Libyan. The textual studies of Jansen-Winkeln increasingly suggest that Piankhi, once thought to be Herihor's son and successor, was the father-in-law of Herihor (see NEW KINGDOM). By the last decade of Rameses XI's reign, Herihor had acquired the titles of high priest of Amun at Thebes, generalissimo and VICEROY OF KUSH, a combination of offices that must have brought him to the brink of ruling as a pharaoh in his own right. Indeed, in one relief in the temple of

Detail of the Book of the Dead papyrus of Herihor, showing the deceased and his wife. Late New Kingdom, c.1070 BC. (EA10541)

Khons at KARNAK, his name is written in a cartouche and he is explicitly portrayed as equal in status to the king, while in another relief elsewhere in the temple he is shown wearing the double crown.

Both Herihor and his wife Nodjmet were given cartouches in the inscriptions on their funerary equipment, but this 'kingship' seems to have been limited to a few relatively restricted contexts within the confines of Thebes, and it was Rameses XI's name that appeared in administrative documents throughout the country. Apart from the reliefs at Karnak, the only significant surviving monuments of Herihor are a statue (Egyptian Museum, Cairo) and a stele (Rijksmuseum van Oudheden, Leiden), and no traces of his tomb have been found in western Thebes.

His rule over the Theban region was the chronological setting for the *Report of Wenamun* (the text of which is preserved on a single papyrus now in the Pushkin Museum, Moscow). This literary classic, which may possibly be based on a true account, narrates the difficulties encountered by an Egyptian diplomat sent by Herihor to bring back timber from SYRIA at a time when Egyptian influence in the Levant was on the wane.

G. LEFÉBVRE, *Histoire des grands prêtres d'Amon de Karnak jusqu'à la XXIe dynastie* (Paris, 1929).

M. LICHTHEIM, *Ancient Egyptian literature* II (Berkeley, 1976), 224–30 [translation of the *Report of Wenamun*]
M.-A. BONHÊME, 'Hérihor, fut-il effectivement roi?', *BIFAO* 79 (1979), 267–84.
K. A. KITCHEN, *The Third Intermediate Period in Egypt (1100–650 BC)*, 2nd ed. (Warminster, 1986), 16–23, 248–52, 535–41.
K. JANSEN-WINKELN, 'Das Ende des Neuen Reiches', *ZÄS* 119 (1992), 22–37.

Hermopolis Magna (el-Ashmunein; anc. Khmun)

Ancient Pharaonic capital of the 15th Upper Egyptian NOME and cult-centre of Thoth, located to the west of the Nile, close to the modern town of Mallawi. The site was badly plundered during the early Islamic period but there are still surviving traces of temples dating to the Middle and New Kingdoms, including a pylon constructed by Rameses II (1279–1213 BC) which contained stone blocks quarried from the temples of Akhenaten (1352–1336 BC) at EL-AMARNA, a few kilometres to the southeast. There are also substantial remains of a COPTIC basilica constructed from the remains of a Ptolemaic temple built entirely in a Greek architectural style. The nearby cemetery of TUNA EL-GEBEL includes two of the rock-cut 'boundary stelae' of Akhenaten, the tomb-chapel of PETOSIRIS (c. 300 BC), a temple of Thoth and extensive catacombs dating mainly from the 27th Dynasty to the Roman period (c.525 BC–AD 395).

G. ROEDER, *Hermopolis 1929–39* (Hildesheim, 1959).
J. D. COONEY, *Amarna reliefs from Hermopolis in American collections* (Brooklyn, 1965).
G. ROEDER and R. HANKE, *Amarna-reliefs aus Hermopolis*, 2 vols (Hildesheim, 1969–78).
A. J. SPENCER and D. M. BAILEY, *Excavations at el-Ashmunein*, 4 vols (London, 1983–93).
A. J. SPENCER, 'Ashmunein 1980–1985: a practical approach to townsite excavation', *Problems and priorities in Egyptian archaeology*, ed. J. Assmann et al. (London, 1987), 255–60.

ABOVE *One of the colossal statues of the god Thoth as a baboon, at Hermopolis Magna. Reign of Amenhotep III, c.1370 BC. (I. SHAW)*

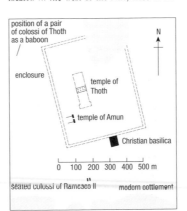

position of a pair of colossi of Thoth as a baboon

N

enclosure

temple of Thoth

temple of Amun

Christian basilica

0 100 200 300 400 500 m

seated colossi of Rameses II

modern settlement

LEFT *Plan of Hermopolis Magna.*

Herodotus (*c*.484–*c*.420 BC)

Greek traveller and historian born at Halicarnassus in Asia Minor, whose works are a particularly valuable source for the later history of Egypt. Some scholars have described him as the 'father of history', although others have called him 'father of lies', because of his supposedly fantastic tales. Nevertheless, a number of his stories have subsequently been vindicated by archaeology (see TELL BASTA).

The nine books of Herodotus' *Histories* were written between 430 and 425 BC, and principally describe the struggles between the GREEKS and the Persians, although the second book is devoted to Egypt, apparently drawing heavily on personal experiences.

His travels in Egypt, which took place in about 450 BC, may have extended as far south as Aswan, although he gives no detailed account of Thebes, concentrating instead on the Delta. His information was largely provided by Egyptian priests, many of whom probably held only minor offices and would perhaps have been anxious to take advantage of an apparently gullible visitor in order to show off their assumed knowledge. Nevertheless, his account of Egypt in the fifth century BC has been largely substantiated, and his astute observations included the identification of the pyramids as royal burial places. A major source of information on MUMMIFICATION and other ancient Egyptian religious and funerary customs, he attracted numerous ancient imitators, including STRABO (who visited Egypt in *c*.30 BC) and DIODORUS SICULUS.

W. G. WADDELL, *Herodotus, Book II* (London, 1939).

J. WILSON, *Herodotus in Egypt* (Leiden, 1970).

A. B. LLOYD, *Herodotus Book II.1: an introduction* (Leiden, 1975).

—, *Herodotus Book II.2: commentary 1–98* (Leiden, 1976).

—, *Herodotus Book II.2: commentary 99–182* (Leiden, 1988).

Heryshef (Arsaphes)

Fertility god usually represented in the form of a ram or ram-headed man, who was worshipped in the region of HERAKLEOPOLIS MAGNA, near modern Beni Suef, from at least as early as the 1st Dynasty (3100–2890 BC), according to the PALERMO STONE. The etymology of Heryshef's name, which literally means 'he who is upon his lake', suggests that he was considered to be a creator-god who emerged from the primeval waters of the sacred lake. The first-century Greek historian Plutarch rendered the name as Arsaphes and translated it as 'manliness', but he was probably simply taking an Egyptian pun at face value. Heryshef was at various times associated with the sun-god Ra and the god of the dead OSIRIS: he is therefore sometimes portrayed with either the sun-disc headdress or the *atef* crown (see CROWNS AND ROYAL REGALIA).

G. HART, *A dictionary of Egyptian gods and goddesses* (London, 1986), 85–7.

Hesyra (Hesy) (*c*.2660 BC)

Official of the time of the 3rd-Dynasty ruler DJOSER (2667–2648 BC), whose titles included the posts of 'overseer of the royal scribes, greatest of physicians and dentists'. His MASTABA tomb (S2405 [A3]), located to the north of the Step Pyramid at SAQQARA, was discovered by Auguste Mariette in the 1880s, and re-excavated, about thirty years later, by James Quibell.

The tomb has an elaborate corridor chapel with palace-façade decoration (see SEREKH) along its west wall consisting of eleven niches, each of which would originally have been brightly painted in matting patterns. At the back of each niche stood a carved wooden panel, only six of which had survived at the time of discovery (now in the Egyptian Museum, Cairo). The panels are sculpted

ABOVE *Detail of a wooden stele from the tomb of Hesyra at Saqqara, 3rd Dynasty, c.2650 BC, H. of complete stele 114 cm. (CAIRO JE28504, I. SHAW)*

with the figure of Hesyra in various costumes, while the beautifully carved hieroglyphs present his name and titles. The eastern wall of this corridor was decorated with delicately painted carvings of furniture and offerings, carefully set out as if arranged in a shelter of matting. In an outer corridor was the earliest representation of a crocodile awaiting unwary cattle as they crossed a stream, a theme that was to be repeated many times in later mastabas. The burial itself was located in a subterranean chamber connected with the superstructure by a shaft. The tomb was one of the first to incorporate a SERDAB (statue chamber).

A. MARIETTE, *Les mastabas de l'Ancien Empire* (Paris, 1882–9).

J. E. QUIBELL, *The tomb of Hesy: excavations at Saqqara* (Cairo, 1913).

W. WOOD, 'A reconstruction of the reliefs of Hesy-re', *JARCE* 15 (1978), 9–24.

M. SALEH and H. SOUROUZIAN, *The Egyptian Museum, Cairo: official catalogue* (Mainz, 1987), no. 21.

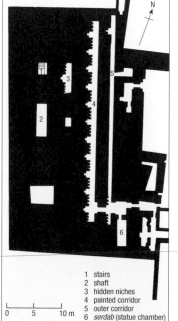

1 stairs
2 shaft
3 hidden niches
4 painted corridor
5 outer corridor
6 serdab (statue chamber)

0   5   10 m

LEFT *The mastaba tomb of Hesyra (SAQQARA 2405).*

Hetepheres I (c.2600 BC)

Early 4th-Dynasty queen, who was the principal wife of SNEFERU (2613–2589 BC), the mother of KHUFU (2589–2566 BC) and probably also the daughter of Huni, last ruler of the 3rd Dynasty. Little is known of her life, but her well-preserved burial at GIZA (G7000x) was discovered in 1925 by the staff photographer of the Harvard–Boston expedition, led by George Reisner.

The excavation of an area of unexplained white plaster on the eastern side of the Great Pyramid revealed a tomb shaft leading to a small empty room, deep below which was a concealed burial chamber. This contained a

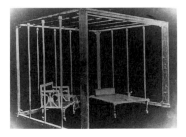

Canopy, bed and chair from the tomb of Queen Hetepheres. 4th Dynasty, c.2600 BC. (EGYPTIAN MUSEUM, CAIRO)

sealed sarcophagus, a mass of gilded wood in a very poor state of preservation, and a number of items of metalwork. Inscriptions on some of the objects indicated that the tomb belonged to Hetepheres, the mother of Khufu, whose funerary equipment had apparently been hastily reburied. Although the sarcophagus was empty, a concealed niche was found to contain an alabaster CANOPIC box, with residues believed to derive from the MUMMIFICATION of her body.

Reisner believed that the remains of Hetepheres' funerary equipment had been reburied by Khufu after her original tomb, perhaps located near that of Sneferu at DAHSHUR, was robbed. However no tomb of Hetepheres has yet been found at Dahshur, and indeed the only evidence for her existence derives from Tomb G7000x. This has led Mark Lehner to suggest that the Giza shaft tomb was in fact the queen's original place of burial but that her body and the majority of the equipment were reburied under GI-a, the first of the 'satellite pyramids' to the east of Khufu's main pyramid. This theory might also explain the damage inflicted on the sarcophagus, pottery and furniture of the original tomb. It is still not clear, however, why the

canopic chest was not removed, although it is possible that G7000x was felt to be so close to the satellite pyramid as not to require the transfer of canopic equipment. Ironically, it was probably the lack of a superstructure that helped to preserve the original burial, whereas pyramid GI-a was robbed in ancient times.

The careful restoration of the finds (now in the Egyptian Museum, Cairo) has yielded some of the best evidence for funerary equipment during the Old Kingdom, providing insights into the likely wealth of a full royal burial of the period. The items of gilded wooden FURNITURE included a carrying chair, a bed and an elaborate canopy that would probably have been erected over the bed.

G. A. REISNER and W. S. SMITH, *A history of the Giza necropolis II: The tomb of Hetepheres, the mother of Cheops* (Cambridge, MA, 1955).
M. LEHNER, *The pyramid tomb of Hetep-heres and the satellite pyramid of Khufu* (Mainz, 1985).

Hiba, el- (anc. Teudjoi; Ankyropolis)

Settlement site incorporating a poorly preserved temple of 'Amun of the crag' (or 'Amun great of roarings'), constructed by Sheshonq I (945–924 BC). From the late 20th to the 22nd Dynasty (1100–715 BC), the town of Teudjoi functioned as an important frontier fortress between the zones controlled by the cities of Herakleopolis Magna and Hermopolis Magna. Large numbers of bricks from the enclosure wall were stamped with the names of Pinudjem I and Menkheperra, who were powerful Theban chief priests of Amun-Ra in the early 21st Dynasty (c.1050 BC) who presumably established a residence at el-Hiba.

After a period of decline during the Late Period (717–??? BC) the town regained its importance under the name of Ankyronpolis in the Greco-Roman period (c.304 BC–AD 395), when it once more developed into a military settlement. The earliest excavations at el-Hiba concentrated either on the cemeteries, where there were caches of Greek and demotic papyri, or on the Greco-Roman areas of the town. In 1980, however, the American archaeologist Robert Wenke conducted a surface survey of the entire site, including test excavations within the settlement, which indicate that Teudjoi was founded at least as early as the New Kingdom.

B. GRENFELL and A. HUNT, *The Hibeh papyri I* (London, 1906).
H. RANKE, *Koptische Friedhöfe bei Karara und der Amontempel Scheschonks I. bei el Hibe* (Berlin, 1926).
E. G. TURNER, *The Hibeh papyri II* (London, 1955).
R. J. WENKE, *Archaeological investigations at el-Hibeh 1980: Preliminary report* (Malibu, 1984).

Hierakonpolis (Kom el-Ahmar; anc. Nekhen)

Settlement and necropolis, 80 km south of Luxor, which was particularly associated with the hawk-god HORUS, the Greek name of the town meaning 'city of the hawk/falcon'. It flourished during the late Predynastic and Early Dynastic periods (c.4000–2686 BC). One

Plan showing the location of the principal settlement and cemetery areas of Hierakonpolis.

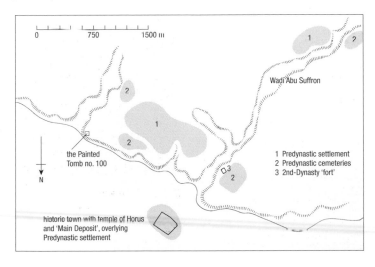

of the most important discoveries in the Predynastic cemetery is Tomb 100, a late Gerzean brick-lined burial which was the first Egyptian tomb to be decorated with wall-paintings (see ART), but the location of this so-called Painted Tomb is no longer known. The poorly recorded excavation of the town of Hierakonpolis undertaken by James Quibell and F. W. Green included the discovery of the 'Main Deposit', a stratum between two walls relating to an Old Kingdom temple complex within the settlement. The Main Deposit seems to have consisted primarily of ceremonial objects dating to the Protodynastic period (c.3000 BC), including the NARMER palette and SCORPION macehead. However, because of a lack of accurate published plans and stratigraphic sections, the true date and significance of this crucial Protodynastic assemblage remain unclear. Further survey and excavations at Hierakonpolis took place in the 1970s and 1980s, not only identifying a range of Predynastic sites in the desert surrounding the town but also shedding further light on socioeconomic patterning of the Early Dynastic town and identifying the only known example of a Predynastic shrine. The so-called 'fort' of KHASEKHEMWY has now been identified as a 'funerary enclosure' like the Shunet el-Zebib at ABYDOS.

J. E. QUIBELL and F. W. GREEN, *Hierakonpolis*, 2 vols (London, 1900–2).

B. J. KEMP, 'Photographs of the decorated tomb at Hierakonpolis', *JEA* 59 (1973), 36–43.

B. ADAMS, *Ancient Hierakonpolis* (Warminster, 1974).

M. A. HOFFMAN et al., 'A model of urban development for the Hierakonpolis region from predynastic through Old Kingdom times', *JARCE* 23 (1986), 175–87.

B. ADAMS, *The fort cemetery at Hierakonpolis (excavated by John Garstang)* (London, 1988).

hieratic (Greek *hieratika*: 'sacred')
Script dating from the end of the Early Dynastic period (c.2686 BC) onwards. The essentially cursive hieratic script was based on the hieroglyphic symbols that had emerged some five centuries earlier, but it should not be confused with 'cursive hieroglyphs', which were used for most of the Pharaonic period in such religious writings as the COFFIN TEXTS and the BOOK OF THE DEAD. Hieratic was always written from right to left, whereas the orientation of cursive hieroglyphs varied. Until the 11th Dynasty (2055–1985 BC) hieratic documents were arranged mainly in columns, but most texts from the 12th Dynasty (1985–1795 BC) onwards consisted of horizontal lines. It was also in the Middle Kingdom (2055–1650

One sheet of the Great Harris Papyrus, a hieratic document consisting of a list of temple endowments and a short summary of the reign of Rameses III. It is the longest surviving papyrus roll, measuring 41 m. Reign of Rameses IV. c.1150 BC, from Thebes, H. 42.5 cm. (EA9999, SHEET 75)

BC) that hieratic began to be written in different styles, ranging from the rapid 'business' hand to the more aesthetically pleasing 'literary' hand.

With the development of hieratic, scribes were able to write more rapidly on papyri and ostraca, and this script – rather than the more cumbersome hieroglyphs – became the preferred medium for scribal tuition (see EDUCATION). There was also an even more cursive form of the script known as 'abnormal hieratic', which was used for business texts in Upper Egypt during the Third Intermediate Period (1069–747 BC). By the 26th Dynasty (664–525 BC) the DEMOTIC script had emerged out of the so-called 'business hieratic' of Lower Egypt.

G. MÖLLER, *Hieratische Lesestücke*, 3 vols (Leipzig, 1909–10).

—, *Hieratische Paläographie*, 3 vols (Leipzig, 1909–12).

R. J. WILLIAMS, 'Scribal training in ancient Egypt', *JAOS* 92 (1972), 214–21.

W. V. DAVIES, *Egyptian hieroglyphs* (London, 1987), 21–3.

hieroglyphs (Greek: 'sacred carved [letters]')
The Egyptian hieroglyphic script, consisting of three basic types of sign (phonograms, logograms and 'determinatives') arranged in horizontal and vertical lines, was in use from the late Gerzean period (c.3200 BC) to the late fourth century AD. The last known datable hieroglyphic inscription, on the gate of Hadrian at Philae, was carved on 24 August AD 394. The apparently low level of literacy in Pharaonic Egypt (estimated at perhaps as low as 0.4 per cent of the population) has led to the suggestion that hieroglyphic texts were employed by the élite as a means of restricting knowledge and power.

The decipherment of hieroglyphs by Jean-François CHAMPOLLION, primarily through his examination of the trilingual decree inscribed on the ROSETTA STONE, was undoubtedly the single greatest event in the development of Egyptology, providing the key to an understanding of the names, history and intellectual achievements of the ancient Egyptians.

Painted hieroglyphs on the interior of the outer coffin of the physician Seni. Middle Kingdom, c.2000 BC, painted wood, from Deir el-Bersha, H. 15 cm. (EA30841)

Hieroglyphs were primarily used as descriptive components of the carved reliefs decorating temples and funerary monuments. It was felt that the hieroglyphic names of gods, people and animals were as capable of posing a threat as the living entity itself – for this reason many of the signs in the PYRAMID TEXTS and some COFFIN TEXTS were deliberately abbreviated and mutilated in order to neutralize any potential dangers within the royal tomb.

Although a total of more than six thousand hieroglyphic signs have been identified, the majority of these were introduced during the Ptolemaic and Roman periods. In the Pharaonic period fewer than a thousand symbols are attested, and an even smaller number were in regular use. There was a nucleus of frequent basic signs, and others were evidently invented and introduced as they became necessary, sometimes providing an indication of changes in material culture. The signs were written in continuous lines without any punctuation or spaces to show where words or sentences began or ended. The orientation of the letters was usually towards the right, so that the text was read from right to left and top to bottom, although in certain instances (such as the engraving of two symmetrical inscriptions on either side of a stele or relief) the orientation was from left to right.

As in Egyptian art, the individual signs of the hieroglyphic script are essentially diagrams of the phenomenon or entity in question; whether the sign is representing a loaf of bread, an owl or a human figure, it was intended that the ideogram should consist of the most characteristic and visually familiar elements of its physical appearance – thus most birds are shown completely in profile, but one exception is the owl, which, because of its distinctive eyes, has its face shown frontally.

The logograms and determinatives in hieroglyphic script were both essentially depictions of the things that they represented: thus logograms were individual signs whose meaning was broadly equivalent to their appearance (i.e. a shorthand diagram of the sky meant 'sky'). Determinatives were pictures of *types* of things, placed at the ends of words made up of phonograms in order to indicate what types of words they were (i.e. the verb *wesheb*, meaning 'to answer', was followed by a sign consisting of a man holding his hand to his mouth). The phonograms consist of three types: twenty-six uniconsonantal signs (each representing a single consonant, e.g. the quail-chick sign, pronounced *w*), about a hundred biconsonantal signs (pairs of consonants, such as the diagram of a house-

plan, which was pronounced *pr*), and forty to fifty triconsonantal signs (e.g. the logogram representing the adjective 'good', which was pronounced *nfr*).

The main problem encountered in pronouncing a section of hieroglyphic text is that there were no vowels in the written form of ancient Egyptian, only consonants. The study of the COPTIC language (which evolved out of the ancient Egyptian language), as well as various surviving transliterations of Egyptian words into other ancient scripts (such as ASSYRIAN, BABYLONIAN and Greek), has enabled the 'vocalization' of many Egyptian words to be at least partially reconstructed. However, the conventional method of making the consonants pronounceable is to read the signs ʿ and з as if they were the letter *a*, and to insert the letter *e* wherever necessary: thus the words *sʿ*, *pr* and *nfr* are conventionally pronounced as *sa*, *per* and *nefer*.

There were three basic stages in the development of the hieroglyphic script: early, middle and late; it was highly conservative and continually lagged behind the spoken LANGUAGE in both vocabulary and syntax. A crucial distinction therefore needs to be made between the stages in the development of the language and the various phases of its written form. The language has one distinct break, in the Middle Kingdom (2055–1650 BC), when 'synthetic' Old and Middle Egyptian, characterized by inflected verb endings, was replaced, in the spoken language at least, by the 'analytical' form of Late Egyptian, with a verbal structure consisting of articulated elements. Egyptian is the only 'language of aspect' for which the change from the 'synthetic' stage to 'analytical' can actually be studied in its written form.

The hieroglyphic system was used for funerary and religious texts while the cursive

HIERATIC script was used primarily for administrative and literary texts. By the 26th Dynasty (664–525 BC) DEMOTIC had replaced hieratic, and for a number of centuries the Greek and demotic scripts were used side by side, eventually being superseded by COPTIC. See LANGUAGE for chart of hieroglyphs.

See also FUNERARY TEXTS; LIBRARIES; LITERATURE; PAPYRUS and SCRIBES.

A. H. GARDINER, *Egyptian grammar, being an introduction to the study of hieroglyphs*, 3rd ed. (Oxford, 1957).

C. A. ANDREWS, *The Rosetta Stone* (London, 1981).

J. R. BAINES, 'Literacy and ancient Egyptian society', *Man* 18 (1983), 572–99.

J. D. RAY, 'The emergence of writing in Egypt', *WA* 17/3 (1986), 390–8.

W. V. DAVIES, *Egyptian hieroglyphs* (London, 1987).

H. G. FISCHER and R. A. CAMINOS, *Ancient Egyptian epigraphy and palaeography*, 3rd ed. (New York, 1987).

hippopotamus

Riverine mammal that flourished in Egypt until well into Dynastic times. The date of its disappearance in Egypt is debatable, but it was certainly still present during the New Kingdom (1550–1069 BC). Like the crocodile, the male hippopotamus was regarded as a nuisance and a doer of evil, because it often trampled and devoured crops; a New Kingdom school text makes this clear: 'Do you not recall the fate of the farmer when the harvest is registered? The worm has taken half the grain, the hippopotamus has devoured the rest...' It was probably for this reason that hippopotamus hunts were organized as early as the prehistoric period. Many of the mastaba tombs of the Old Kingdom, such as that of the 5th-Dynasty official TY at Saqqara (no. 60), included depictions of the spearing of hippopotami.

Faience statuette of a hippopotamus, 12th–13th Dynasties, H. 9.2 cm. (EA35044)

Such hunts might have given rise to a royal ceremony in which the king's ritual killing of a hippopotamus was symbolic of the overthrow of evil, as in the myth of HORUS and SETH. In this myth, Horus was often portrayed in the act of harpooning Seth as a hippopotamus (although in other contexts Seth was depicted as a crocodile, an ass or a typhonian animal). This scene was frequently repeated on the walls of temples, most notably that of Horus at EDFU, as well as in tomb scenes and in the form of royal funerary statuettes such as those showing Tutankhamun with his harpoon and coils of rope.

However, the female hippopotamus had a beneficent aspect, in the form of TAWERET ('the great [female] one'), the pregnant hippopotamus-goddess who was among the most popular of the household gods, and particularly associated with women in childbirth. In PLUTARCH's version of the myth of Horus and Seth, Taweret was the consort of Seth, who deserted him for Horus.

During the Middle Kingdom (2055–1650 BC), large numbers of blue faience figurines of hippopotami were created, probably for funerary use, although their popularity with art collectors is such that few have been obtained from archaeological excavation, therefore their provenances are poorly known. It is usually assumed, however, that these statuettes, whose bodies are frequently decorated with depictions of vegetation, were associated with fertility and the regenerative effect of the Nile.

T. SÄVE-SÖDERBERGH, *On Egyptian representations of hippopotamus hunting as a religious motive* (Uppsala, 1953).

H. KEES, 'Das "Fest der Weissen" und die Stadt *Sm', ZÄS* 83 (1958), 127–9.

A. BEHRMANN, *Das Nilpferd in der Vostellungswelt der Alten Ägypten* I (Frankfurt, 1989).

history and historiography

Defining Egyptian history is as difficult a task as defining Egyptian 'literature'; in both cases, modern scholars are inevitably attempting to impose upon the Egyptian sources modern concepts and categories that would often have had no real meaning or relevance to the ancient writers. The types of ancient Egyptian texts that are usually described as 'historical' would have had a very different function when they were originally composed (see, for instance, KING LISTS); they therefore have to be carefully interpreted if genuinely 'historical' data are to be extracted from them.

The Canadian Egyptologist Donald Redford defines true history as 'the telling of events involving or affecting human beings

(not necessarily, though usually, in narrative form), which took place prior to the time of composition, the chief aim of which is to explain those events for the benefit, predilection and satisfaction of contemporaries, and not for the enhancement of the writer's personal reputation'. In fact William Hayes suggests, in the *Cambridge Ancient History*, that there are only four surviving Egyptian historical texts that would conform to a definition such as that given by Redford: these are the stelae of KAMOSE (*c.*1555–1550 BC), describing his battles against the Hyksos; the *Annals of Thutmose III* (1479–1425 BC), describing his campaigns in Syria–Palestine; and the Victory Stele of PIY (747–716 BC), describing his conquest of Egypt. Redford adds to these Hatshepsut's speech inscribed in the SPEOS ARTEMIDOS rock-temple, a possibly fictional speech made by RAMESES III (1184–1153 BC) at the end of the Great Harris Papyrus and Osorkon's description of the Theban rebellions in the Third Intermediate Period (1069–747 BC). A further text which may now be added to this list is a fragment of the annals of AMENEMHAT II (1922–1878 BC), discovered at Memphis in the mid-1950s but not published until 1980, which shows that something approximating to the modern concept of a historical record (although lacking any analytical component) was already being compiled in the Middle Kingdom (2055–1650 BC), in the form of detailed records of the political and religious events from each year of a king's reign.

However, notwithstanding the few exceptions listed above, the vast majority of such narrative-structured and ceremonial texts surviving from Egypt were concerned much more with preserving and transmitting national traditions or with performing a particular religious or funerary role, rather than being attempts to present objective accounts of the past. Even the supposedly historical fragments of Egyptian texts such as the Kamose stelae, the Speos Artemidos 'speech' and the *Annals of Thutmose III* are effectively components of the temples in which they were found: they therefore differ considerably from the true historical tradition inaugurated by the Greek historian HERODOTUS (*c.*484–*c.*420 BC) in that they incorporate a high degree of symbolism and pure ritual. In their cult of the king's personality they are closer to the *Res gestae* glorifying the deeds of the Roman emperor Augustus than the more 'journalistic' histories written by Thucydides or Tacitus, in which the stated aim at least is to present the objective truth about past events.

The contents of most of the monumental texts and reliefs on the walls of Egyptian tombs and temples are much closer to the symbolic and static world of myth than to history. There is a common tendency to regard myth as a form of 'primitive history', but this is rarely the case. Redford makes a good distinction between myth and history: 'The meaning of myths has nothing to do with their having occurred in the past, but rather with their present significance…Horus's championing of his father, the upliftings of Shu, the murder of Osiris – these are all primordial events, timeless and ever-present; and neither king nor priest who re-enacts them can be said to fulfil an historic role, or to be commemorating "history"'.

L. BULL, 'Ancient Egypt', *The idea of history in the Ancient Near East*, ed. J. Obermann (New Haven and London, 1955).

D. B. REDFORD, *Pharaonic king-lists, annals and day-books: a contribution to the study of the Egyptian sense of history* (Mississauga, 1986).

E. HORNUNG, *Idea into image*, trans. E. Bredeck (New York, 1992).

J. MALEK, 'The annals of Amenemhat II', *Egyptian Archaeology* 2 (1992), 18.

Hittites

People of somewhat obscure origins, described by the Egyptians as Kheta, who settled in Anatolia in the third millennium BC. Although they themselves were speakers of an Indo-European language, in time their empire absorbed the Hurrian-speaking people of MITANNI, and the AKKADIAN language was frequently used for diplomatic and commercial correspondence.

During the Hittite Old Kingdom (*c.*1750–1450 BC), the nucleus of the state was established in central Anatolia, with its capital initially at Kussara and later at the better-known site of Boghazköy (ancient Hattusas). By the sixteenth century BC they had conquered Syria, and at one stage the empire stretched as far south as BABYLON.

During this period of imperial expansion (*c.*1450–1200 BC) the Hittites appear to have concentrated on reinforcing their grip over northern Syria, thus displacing the Mitannians and bringing them into direct conflict with ASSYRIA and Egypt.

The most famous of their military confrontations with Egypt took place during the early reign of Rameses II (1279–1213 BC), culminating in the BATTLE OF QADESH in 1274 BC, which was commemorated on many of Rameses' temples. The stalemate that resulted from this battle, in which both Rameses and the Hittite king Muwatallis appear to have claimed victory, eventually led to the signing of a peace treaty in the twenty-first year of Rameses' reign. This document is preserved both on Egyptian monuments and on Akkadian cuneiform tablets from Boghazköy. Rameses cemented the alliance by marrying a Hittite princess, an act that was celebrated by the Hittite marriage stele at Abu Simbel. This was not, however, the first attempt to link the two great powers. A letter discovered in the Hittite archives is believed to have been sent by a royal woman of the late Amarna period (perhaps Ankhesenamun, widow of TUTANKHAMUN), requesting the Hittite king Suppiluliumas I to send one of his sons to be her husband. The prince in question, however, was murdered *en route* to Egypt and the proposed marriage seems never to have taken place.

It was also during the Hittite imperial phase that a closely guarded technique for smelting IRON was discovered, and iron is certainly one of the commodities mentioned in the ARMARNA LETTERS as being imported into Egypt in small quantities. An iron dagger in the tomb of Tutankhamun no doubt derived from the same source. Even among the Hittites themselves, iron seems to have been regarded as an extremely precious metal, suitable only for prestige goods.

The Anatolian heartland of the Hittite empire finally began to disintegrate in the late thirteenth century BC, perhaps as a result of the appearance of the SEA PEOPLES whose migrations also threatened Egypt. This left only the rump of their empire in Syria, consisting of a group of 'Neo-Hittite' city-states which were finally absorbed by ASSYRIA in the eighth century BC.

J. VERGOTE, *Toutankhamon dans les archives hittites* (Istanbul, 1961).

K. A. KITCHEN, *Suppiluliuma and the Amarna pharaohs* (Liverpool, 1962).

—, *Pharaoh triumphant: the life and times of Rameses II* (Warminster, 1982), 74–95.

J. G. MACQUEEN, *The Hittites and their contemporaries in Asia Minor*, 2nd ed. (London, 1986).

O. R. GURNEY, *The Hittites*, 2nd ed. (Harmondsworth, 1990).

Hiw-Semaina region (Diospolis Parva)

Group of PREDYNASTIC, Pharaonic and Roman-period sites on the east bank of the Nile in Upper Egypt. The Hiw–Semaina region, which was surveyed and excavated by Flinders Petrie in 1898–9, stretches for about 15 km along either side of the modern el-Ranan canal, from the village of Hiw in the southwest to Semaina in the northeast. It was

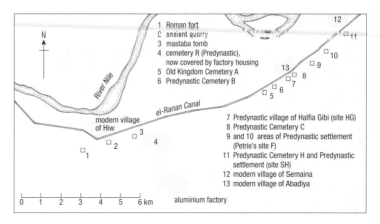

1 Roman fort
2 ancient quarry
3 mastaba tomb
4 cemetery R (Predynastic), now covered by factory housing
5 Old Kingdom Cemetery A
6 Predynastic Cemetery B
7 Predynastic village of Halfia Gibi (site HG)
8 Predynastic Cemetery C
9 and 10 areas of Predynastic settlement (Petrie's site F)
11 Predynastic Cemetery H and Predynastic settlement (site SH)
12 modern village of Semaina
13 modern village of Abadiya

modern village of Hiw

River Nile

el-Ranan Canal

0 1 2 3 4 5 6 km   aluminium factory

The Hiw–Semaina region.

the excavation report on the Predynastic cemeteries of Abadiya and Hiw that formed the basis for Petrie's compilation of the first relative chronology of the late PREDYNASTIC PERIOD (Naqada I–II), which is still largely valid.

In 1989 Kathryn Bard conducted a new survey of the area, relocating some of these cemeteries and finding that the Predynastic Cemeteries U and R and the Old Kingdom MASTABA at Cemetery A had been destroyed. She also re-examined a few surviving patches of Predynastic settlement that Petrie had mentioned only briefly in his report. At site 'SH', an area of late Predynastic settlement which Bard discovered near Semaina and beside Petrie's Cemetery H, another surface survey revealed widespread traces of stone-working, suggesting that the Hiw–Semaina region may have been a Predynastic centre for stone vessel manufacture.

W. M. F. PETRIE, *Diospolis Parva: the cemeteries of Abadiyeh and Hu* (London, 1901).

K. BARD, 'Predynastic settlement patterns in the Hiw-Semaineh region, Upper Egypt', *Nyame Akuma* 32 (1989), 2–4.

Horapollo (fourth century AD)

Supposedly a native of Upper Egypt, whose work, the *Hieroglyphica*, claimed to be an explanation of the symbolic meaning of various hieroglyphic signs, derived directly from ancient Egyptian sources. The original was probably written in COPTIC, although the work is known only from Greek translations. Although the meanings of many signs were correctly identified by Horapollo, the allegorical reasons that he gives for their meanings are

often fantastic. The *Hieroglyphica* was rediscovered in the fourteenth century AD and exerted great influence on the scholars of Renaissance Europe, forming the basis of G. P. Valeriano Bolzoni's *Hieroglyphica*, which first appeared in 1556 and was reprinted and enlarged on several occasions. Unfortunately it was the allegorical and symbolic aspects of Horapollo's work that led scholars such as Athanasius Kircher (1602–80) to regard hieroglyphs as a symbolic language, a view which retarded the decipherment of the script for many years. Even in the nineteenth century a number of scholars, such as Gardner WILKINSON, were still being misled by Horapollo and thus frustrated in their attempts at decipherment.

H. R. HALL, 'Letters to Sir William Gell from Henry Salt, (Sir) J. G. Wilkinson, and Baron von Bunsen', *JEA* 2 (1915), 133–67.

Horemakhet *see* HORIZON and HORUS

Horemheb (1323–1295 BC)

General and 18th-Dynasty pharaoh, whose rule represented a return to comparative normality after the AMARNA period. His military career probably began during the reign of AKHENATEN (1352–1336 BC), when he was perhaps known by the earlier name of Paatenemheb, although this is disputed by many Egyptologists. Little is known of his background apart from the fact that his family came from Herakleopolis. His wife Mutnedjmet may possibly have been NEFERTITI's sister, in which case she may have bolstered his claims to the throne. By the reign of TUTANKHAMUN (1336–1327 BC) he had risen to a position of great power as generalissimo and began work on his tomb at SAQQARA, the

LEFT *Door-jamb from the tomb of Horemheb, with carved relief showing the king in an attitude of adoration. 18th Dynasty, c.1300 BC, H. (inc. restoration) 1.83 m. (EA550)*

BELOW *Scribe statue of Horemheb. 18th Dynasty, c.1300 BC. H. 1.17 m. (NEW YORK, METROPOLITAN MUSEUM, 23.10.1)*

horizon was also considered to be protected by AKER, a god personified by a pair of LIONS sometimes replacing the mountains in amulets depicting the horizon. It was perhaps this link between the lions and the horizon which led to the Great Sphinx at Giza being regarded as the principal manifestation of Horemakhet.

The appearance of the horizon was often

Amulet in the form of the akhet hieroglyph representing the horizon. (EA8300)

imitated in the iconography and forms of Egyptian art and architecture, from the goddess of the horizon, whose two breasts sometimes replaced the mountains on either side of the sun, to the twin towers of PYLONS, which formed part of the transformation of temples into metaphors for the cosmos.
R. H. WILKINSON, *Reading Egyptian art* (London, 1992), 134–5.

Memphite necropolis. This tomb was first located by the German archaeologist Richard Lepsius in the nineteenth century and excavated by an Anglo Dutch expedition during the late 1970s. Its painted relief scenes, fragments of which are spread through the collections of many different museums, depict scenes of his triumphant return from military campaigns, as he attempted to restore the Egyptian empire in Nubia and the Levant. When he succeeded AY (1327–1323 BC) on the throne he undertook numerous construction works at the temples of KARNAK and LUXOR, and at GEBEL EL-SILSILA he created a SPEOS (rock-temple).

On an administrative level he introduced numerous reforms designed primarily to decentralize the government, and he erected a stele in the temple of Mut at Karnak bearing an inscription outlining his plans for the restoration of order after the depredations of the Amarna period. It was during Horemheb's reign that the dismantling of Akhenaten's temples to the ATEN began, although it is possible that the destruction of the royal tomb at el-Amarna took place slightly later, in the early Ramesside period.

He usurped Ay's mortuary temple in the vicinity of MEDINET HABU in western Thebes and constructed a new royal tomb for himself in

the Valley of the Kings, abandoning his virtually completed private tomb at Saqqara. The Theban tomb (KV57) was innovative both in its decoration (sunk relief scenes from the *Book of Gates*) and in its architectural style, consisting of a single straight corridor with side-chambers, rather than the bent-axis style of the previous 18th-Dynasty royal tombs. In the burial chamber his red granite sarcophagus remains *in situ*, but the mummy has not survived.
R. HARI, *Horemheb et la reine Moutnedjmet, ou la fin d'une dynastie* (Geneva, 1965).
E. HORNUNG and F. TEICHMANN, *Das Grab des Haremhab im Tal der Könige* (Berne, 1971).
J.-M. KRUCHTEN, *Le décret d'Horemheb: traduction, commentaire épigraphique, philologique et institutionnel* (Brussels, 1981).
G. T. MARTIN, *The Memphite tomb of Horemheb* (London, 1989).

horizon
The Egyptian hieroglyph denoting the horizon (*akhet*) was essentially a schematic depiction of the two mountains between which the sun rose, indicating that the horizon was regarded as the home of the sun-god. One aspect of the god HORUS, who was closely associated with the sun cult, was therefore described as Horemakhet ('Horus in the horizon'). As the place of sunrise and sunset the

horse
The domesticated horse was introduced into Egypt from western Asia in the Second Intermediate Period (1650–1550 BC) at roughly the same time as the CHARIOT, although a horse skeleton excavated at BUHEN may date as early as the Middle Kingdom (2055–1650 BC). Several horse burials have been excavated at TELL EL-DAB'A, the site of the HYKSOS capital Avaris.

Unlike donkeys, which were used for agricultural work from at least the beginning of the Pharaonic period (c.3100 BC), horses were essentially status symbols, used for such activities as HUNTING, WARFARE and ceremonial processions. They were almost always used to pull chariots rather than being ridden, although battle scenes in the New Kingdom (1550–1069 BC) occasionally show individual soldiers mounted on them. On the basis of surviving chariot yokes it has been calculated that the average height would have been around 1.35 m, although some surviving examples were evidently taller, such as the 1.5-m-high skeleton found in front of the tomb of SENENMUT (TT71). By the end of the 18th Dynasty (1550–1295 BC), horses were firmly established as prestige gifts between rulers in north Africa and the Near East, but they seem to have been particularly prized by the Kushite kings of the

RIGHT Relief block from el-Amarna bearing a depiction of a pair of horses, which probably originally formed part of a depiction of a royal chariot procession. 18th Dynasty, c.1350 BC, H. 23 cm. (METROPOLITAN MUSEUM, NEW YORK, L. 1979.8.19)

25th Dynasty (747–656 BC), who had several horses interred beside their pyramidal tombs at EL-KURRU and NURI.

A. R. SCHULMAN, 'Egyptian representations of horsemen and riding in the New Kingdom', *JNES* 10 (1957), 267–70.

M. A. LITTAUER and J. H. CROUWEL, *Wheeled vehicles and ridden animals in the Ancient Near East* (Leiden and Cologne, 1979).

L. STORCK, 'Pferd', *Lexikon der Ägyptologie* IV, ed. W. Helck, E. Otto and W. Westendorf (Wiesbaden, 1982), 1009–13.

R. and J. JANSSEN, *Egyptian household animals* (Aylesbury, 1989), 38–43.

C. ROMMELAERE, *Les chevaux du Nouvel Empire Égyptien* (Brussels, 1991).

Horus (Haroeris, Harpocrates, Harsomtus, Horemakhet, Ra-Horakhty)

FALCON-god whose name is attested from at least as early as the beginning of the Dynastic period (c.3100 BC). Although not actually named as such, it is probably the Horus-falcon who was depicted on the 'Battlefield' and 'Narmer' ceremonial PALETTES, apparently subjugating his enemies in the battles leading to the unification of Egypt. In addition, the TURIN ROYAL CANON (a 19th-Dynasty king list) describes the Predynastic rulers of Egypt as 'followers of Horus'.

Usually depicted as a hawk or as a man with the head of a hawk, Horus was not only a god of the sky but the embodiment of divine KINGSHIP and protector of the reigning pharaoh. Gradually the cults of other hawk-gods merged with that of Horus, and a complex array of myths became associated with him. According to one of the most common myths, he was the child of the goddess ISIS, and in this role (later known as Harpocrates) he was usually depicted in human form with the SIDELOCK OF YOUTH and a finger to his mouth, often being seated on his mother's lap (particularly in amulets and bronze votive statuettes).

From the Late Period to the Roman period (747 BC–AD 395) a new vehicle for the image of Horus, the *cippus*, became popular. This was a form of protective stele or amulet showing the naked child-god Horus standing on a crocodile and holding snakes, scorpions, lions or other animals in his outstretched arms. On such *cippi* Horus was also sometimes associat-ed with other deities. The purpose of the *cippus* seems to have been to provide healing powers to combat such problems as snake bites or scorpion stings.

As a son of Isis and OSIRIS, Horus was also worshipped under the name of Harsiese, the god who performed the rite of OPENING OF THE MOUTH on his dead father, thus legitimizing his succession to the throne as earthly ruler. In a similar vein, as Horus Iun-mutef, priests or eldest sons wearing panther-skin costumes would ritually purify the path of the deceased's coffin.

Cippus or 'Horus stele', showing Horus as a child with the power to overcome harmful forces. Like New Kingdom examples, this item is of wood, but the prominent Bes head and three-dimensional representation of the child Horus point to the Late Period, when most examples were of stone. Late Period, after 600 BC, wood, from Memphis (?), H. 39 cm. (EA60958)

The mythology of the Osirian Horus (rather than any of the other aspects of Horus) was principally concerned with his struggles to avenge the murder of his father Osiris and to claim his rightful inheritance, the throne of Egypt, by defeating the evil god SETH. The latest narratives of the myth tend to combine several different traditions. In the first version, Seth was Horus' uncle, whereas in the second version he was his brother. There are also differing accounts of their struggles or 'contendings', which were associated with the myth of Horus even before the contendings became linked with the Osiris myth. The Shabaqo Stone (c.705 BC, now in the British Museum), a 25th-Dynasty inscription purporting to be a copy of an Old Kingdom text, describes the story of the earth-god GEB judging between the two and eventually awarding the throne to Horus. However, a more lively version is provided by the Ramesside Papyrus Chester Beatty I (Chester Beatty Library, Dublin), which details the varied, sometimes ludicrous, rivalry of Horus and Seth, including a race in boats of stone. In this version it is the sun-god RA who adjudicates at the end of an eighty-year contest, although as usual it is Horus who finally becomes king of Egypt. It is possible that these mythological contendings, an even later account of which is given by the Greek writer PLUTARCH, may reflect a distant memory of the struggles of the 'two lands' before unification, although few prehistorians would now attempt to use such comparatively recent documents to interpret the late Predynastic archaeological material (c.3200–3100 BC).

During his contendings with Seth, Horus is said to have lost his left eye (which represented the moon), although fortunately the goddess HATHOR was able to restore it. The *udjat*- or *wedjat*-eye (the 'eye of Horus') therefore came to symbolize the general process of 'making whole' and healing, the term *udjat* literally meaning 'sound'. It also represented the waxing and waning of the moon, and served as a metaphor for protection, strength and perfection; *wedjat*-eye amulets are extremely common.

Since Horus was a sky-god and a cosmogonic deity, his eyes were interpreted as the sun and moon, and he was frequently described in the Old Kingdom (2686–2181 BC) as a god of the east, and hence of the sunrise. In this guise he became known as Horemakhet ('Horus in the HORIZON') and he was also merged with Ra, to become Ra-Horakhty. There were numerous forms of Horus throughout Egypt, but he is particularly associated with EDFU, the site of the ancient city of Mesen. There was a temple of Horus at Edfu from at least as early as the New Kingdom, and in the well-preserved Ptolemaic temple he was worshipped as part of a triad with Hathor and their child Harsomtus. From at least as early as the 4th Dynasty Horus Khenty-Irty was worshipped at Letopolis (Kom Ausim) in the western Delta.

Horus was also closely associated with HIER-AKONPOLIS (literally 'town of the hawk') which was known as Nekhen during the Pharaonic period. From the temple at this site was excavated the golden falcon head (now in the Egyptian Museum, Cairo) which probably formed part of a cult image. In his role as Horus of Behdet, a town in the Delta, he was also portrayed as a winged sun-disc, an image that constantly recurred in the decoration of many other temples, harking back to his original manifestation as a god of the sky.

See also KOM OMBO and SONS OF HORUS.

G. DARESSY, *Textes et dessins magiques* (Cairo, 1903), 1–2.

A. H. GARDINER, *The Chester Beatty papyri* I (London, 1931).

—, 'Horus the Behdetite', *JEA* 30 (1944), 23–60.

J. G. GRIFFITHS, *The conflict of Horus and Seth from Egyptian and Classical sources* (Liverpool, 1960).

H. W. FAIRMAN, *The triumph of Horus: an ancient Egyptian sacred drama* (London, 1974).

S. QUIRKE, *Ancient Egyptian religion* (London, 1992), 61–7.

C. ANDREWS, *Amulets of ancient Egypt* (London, 1994), 43–4.

House of Life (Egyptian *per ankh*)

Temple institution sometimes compared with a medieval scriptorium. Although usually associated with a religious institution, the House of Life differed from its monastic counterpart in that it was not simply a place where PRIESTS were trained in the reading and copying of sacred texts but apparently also a school for SCRIBES and the children of the élite (see EDUCATION). It is also likely that copies of such funerary texts as the BOOK OF THE DEAD were produced for sale to private individuals. ASTRONOMY, geography, MATHEMATICS and LAW, as well as the interpretation of DREAMS, would have been taught in the House of Life, while priests would have had ample theological material to study. They would probably also have utilized the temple LIBRARY, or House of Books (*per medjat*), which would no doubt have been the principal source of the original documents copied by the pupils. The personnel of the House of Life also appear to have been concerned with MEDICINE, and it may be that the sanatoria associated with a number of later temples were connected in some way with the Houses of Life.

The priests of the House of Life may also have been concerned with overseeing the work of temple craftsmen, and were perhaps involved in the design of new pieces for manufacture. Houses of Life are recorded at Memphis, Akhmim, Abydos, Koptos, Esna and Edfu and there must certainly have been examples at Thebes and elsewhere. The House of Life at EL-AMARNA, a complex of mud-brick buildings in the centre of the city of Akhetaten, midway between the main temple and palace, was clearly indentifiable when excavated in the 1930s because the bricks were stamped with the words *per ankh*. In most other respects, however, these buildings were undistinctive, although significantly it was in these rooms that one of the rare fragments of papyrus at el-Amarna (part of a funerary text) was found.

A. H. GARDINER, 'The House of Life', *JEA* 24 (1938), 157–79.

A. VOLTEN, *Demotische Traumdeutung* (Copenhagen, 1942), 17–44.

J. D. S. PENDLEBURY, *City of Akhenaten* III/1 (London, 1951), 115, 150.

E. STROUHAL, *Life in ancient Egypt* (Cambridge, 1992), 235–41.

houses *see* TOWNS

Hu *see* HIW–SEMAINA REGION

human sacrifice

There is no certain evidence of the practice of human sacrifice in Egypt from the Old Kingdom (2686–2181 BC) onwards, although the practice is known from KERMA in Nubia at a time roughly contemporary with the Second Intermediate Period (1650–1550 BC).

In the Protodynastic and Early Dynastic period (*c*.3200–2686 BC), there may be archaeological indications of the funerary sacrifice of servants. It has been argued that the apparent shared roof covering many 'subsidiary burials' surrounding the tombs of certain 1st-Dynasty rulers at Abydos and Saqqara (3100–2890 BC) is an indication that large numbers of royal retainers were killed simultaneously in order to accompany the pharaoh into the afterlife. This practice would no doubt later have been superseded by the more widespread use of representations of servants at work (in the form of wall decoration and three-dimensional models), and the eventual provision of SHABTI figures, whose role appears to have been to undertake agricultural work on behalf of the deceased.

From the late Predynastic period onwards, votive objects and temple walls were frequently decorated with scenes of the king smiting his enemies while gripping them by their hair, but these acts of ritual execution are usually depicted in the context of warfare. The actual sacrifice of prisoners at temples – as opposed to the depiction of foreigners as bound captives – is attested by textual evidence from the reign of Amenhotep II (1427–1400 BC). He claims to have executed seven Syrian princes in the temple of Amun at Karnak, displaying the bodies of six of them on its walls, and hanging the body of the seventh on the walls of NAPATA.

The tale of the 4th-Dynasty ruler Khufu (2589–2566 BC) and the magician Djedi, composed in the Middle Kingdom (2055–1650 BC) and preserved on Papyrus Westcar (Berlin), provides a good illustration of the Egyptians' apparent abhorrence of human sacrifice. Khufu is portrayed as a stereotypical tyrant who asks for a prisoner to be decapitated so that Djedi can demonstrate his magical ability to restore severed heads, but, according to the story, the magician insists that the demonstration be made on a goose rather than a human.

It is also worth noting that the PYRAMID TEXTS include possible references to cannibalism in the form of the so-called 'cannibal hymn' (Utterances 273–4), which describes the king 'eating the magic' and 'swallowing the spirits' of the gods. However, it is difficult to know in this instance whether the concept of the king eating the gods was purely metaphorical or based on some early sacrificial act.

M. LICHTHEIM, *Ancient Egyptian literature* I (Berkeley, 1975), 36–8, 217–20. ['cannibalism hymn' and Papyrus Westcar]

A. J. SPENCER, *Early Egypt* (London, 1993), 63–97.

humour

Since humour and satire are both concerned with the subversion and undermining of the normal decorum of society, they are notoriously difficult to analyse or dissect in modern times, let alone in an ancient culture such as Pharaonic Egypt, when even the most basic framework of the system of decorum (or social mores) is not fully understood. Notwithstanding this basic problem, there are a few relatively unambiguous surviving examples of visual humour, such as the scene, among the reliefs in the temple of Hatshepsut (1473–1458 BC) at DEIR EL-BAHRI, that portrays the overweight figure of the queen of PUNT followed by a small donkey, whose caption reads 'the donkey that had to carry the queen'. The comic impact of this scene on ancient Egyptians is perhaps indicated by the survival of an OSTRACON bearing a rough sketch of the queen clearly copied from the original.

Such titles as *Satire on the trades* and *Be a scribe* are used by Egyptologists to describe particular types of text from the Middle and New Kingdoms that poured scorn on all trades and professions other than that of the scribe. Although the Egyptian scribe's superiority complex was so highly developed that parts of the 'satires' may even have been regarded as factual rather than ironic, there is undoubtedly a considerable element of comical exaggeration and caricature in the descriptions of the various trades, providing a literary counterpart for the gentle visual mockery of some of the labourers depicted in private tomb-paintings.

On the whole, there seem to have been relatively few outlets for humour within the confines of official funerary and religious art and literature; therefore most of the more light-hearted aspects of Egyptian culture tend to be restricted to the arena of rough sketches and OSTRACA, depicting such TABOO subjects as a pharaoh with unseemly stubble on his chin. A large number of such sketches, however, fall into the category of 'animal fables', in which animals – particularly cats and mice – are depicted engaged in typical human activities such as beating captives, driving chariots or making obeisance to a ruler. In a few instances these scenes are portrayed on papyrus, as in the case of the so-called Satirical Papyrus (now in the British Museum), which dates to the late New Kingdom and includes scenes of a lion and antelope playing a board-game (see GAMES for illustration) and a cat herding geese. It has been suggested that these images of animals may be all that survive of 'beast fables', although no literary counterparts have survived, and there is currently no sure way of determining whether the pictures were either intended to be humorous or connected in some way with such didactic writings as the *Discourse*

of *N, ferty*, in which the disintegration of society is described in terms of deliberate reversals and inversions of the natural world.

S. CURTO, *La satira nell'antico Egitto* (Turin, 1965).

B. VAN DE WALLE, *L'humour dans la littérature et dans l'art de l'ancienne Egypte* (Leiden, 1969).

Huni *see* MEIDUM *and* SNEFERU

hunting

Although hunting in the Pharaonic period was relatively unimportant as a means of subsistence, it still retained a great deal of ritualistic and religious significance. Two basic types of hunting were regularly represented on the walls of tombs and temples throughout the Pharaonic period: 'fowling and fishing' and 'big-game', the former consisting primarily of small-scale fishing and bird-snaring on the banks of the Nile, and the latter consisting of the hunting of wild deer and lions in desert terrain, and bulls, crocodiles and HIPPOPOTAMI in the marshes. These two categories also correspond roughly to the private and royal domains, with scenes of 'fowling and fishing in the marshes' being a common component of private tomb decoration but only in one case appearing in a royal tomb (that of King AY, KV23 in the Valley of the Kings).

By the New Kingdom (1550–1069 BC), descriptions of the pharaoh's exploits as a hunter of such beasts as wild bulls, LIONS, elephants and rhinoceroses formed an essential part of the characteristic Egyptian style of KINGSHIP. Two series of commemorative SCARABS of AMENHOTEP III (1390–1352 BC) were

inscribed with detailed descriptions of his hunting of wild bulls and lions, and the decoration of the first pylon of the mortuary temple of Rameses III (1184–1153 BC) at MEDINET HABU includes a detailed depiction of the king and his soldiers hunting bulls. Such royal hunts appear to have taken place within deliberately enclosed areas, so that the animals would have no escape, and the excavation of the New Kingdom settlement at SOLEB in Nubia has yielded traces of post-holes which may well indicate the presence of an enclosure surrounding a large hunting park covering an area of 600 m × 300 m. There are also a few private tombs that show the deceased hunting wild game in the desert, thus providing the artists with a rare opportunity to depict the distinctive savanna and desert landscapes in which the hunt occurred.

Conversely, the simple netting of birds became an important part of temple decoration, with the king and various gods often being depicted hauling clap-nets containing both birds and beasts. Whereas the depictions of fowling in private tombs no doubt reflected the actual activities of the élite, the temple scenes are usually interpreted as allegories of the preservation of harmony by hunting down and suppressing evil and unstable phenomena (symbolized by the birds and animals struggling in nets).

In the Old Kingdom, the pyramid com-

Wall-painting from the tomb-chapel of Nebamun, showing the deceased with his family hunting birds in the marshes. 18th Dynasty, c.1400 BC, painted plaster, from Thebes, H. 81 cm. (EA37977)

Relief decoration on the back of the first pylon of the mortuary temple of Rameses III (1184–1153) at Medinet Habu, showing the king hunting wild bulls. Rameses is portrayed standing in his chariot and thrusting a long hunting spear at one of the bulls. The leading group of soldiers in the lower register are shown firing arrows, apparently engaged only in the more mundane pursuit of the birds and fish of the marsh-lands. (I. SHAW)

plexes of Sahura (2487–2475 BC) and Pepy II (2278–2184 BC) contained depictions of the king hunting a hippopotamus rendered at a larger-than-life scale; the allegorical nature of these scenes, in terms of the king's containment of chaos, is demonstrated by the reliefs in the temple of HORUS at EDFU, which transform the act of binding and spearing a hippopotamus into a dramatic re-enactment of the mythical conflict between the gods Horus and SETH.

T. SÄVE-SÖDERBERGH, *On Egyptian representations of hippopotamus hunting as a religious motive* (Uppsala, 1953).

J. LECLANT, 'Un parc de chasse de la Nubie pharaonique', *Le sol, la parole et l'écrit: 2000 ans d'histoire africaine: mélanges en hommage à Raymond Manny* (Paris, 1981), 727–34.

W. DECKER, *Sports and games of ancient Egypt*, trans. A. Guttmann (New Haven, 1992), 147–67.

E. STROUHAL, *Life in ancient Egypt* (Cambridge, 1992), 118–22.

husbandry *see* AGRICULTURE *and* ANIMAL HUSBANDRY

Hyksos (Egyptian *heka khaswt*: 'rulers of foreign lands')

Term used to refer to a Palestinian group (or perhaps only their rulers) who migrated into Egypt during the late Middle Kingdom (*c.*1800–1650 BC) and rose to power in Lower Egypt during the Second Intermediate Period (1650–1550 BC). It used to be assumed that the Hyksos conquered Egypt at the end of the 13th Dynasty, but it is now recognized that the process was probably far more gradual and peaceful; according to Donald Redford, 'it is not unreasonable to assume that with the gradual weakening of royal authority, the Delta defenses were allowed to lapse, and groups of transhumants found it easy to cross the border and settle in Lower Egypt... Having persuaded oneself of this, the Hyksos assumption of power reveals itself as a peaceful takeover from within by a racial element already in the majority.'

The Semitic names of such 15th-and 16th-Dynasty Hyksos rulers as Khyan, Joam and Jakbaal (*c.*1650–1550 BC) clearly indicate their non-Egyptian origins. A number of New Kingdom texts, including the Ramesside Papyrus Sallier I (*c.*1220 BC), suggest that the Hyksos interlude was essentially the ruthless imposition of Asiatic culture on that of the native Egyptians, but these were undoubtedly biased accounts, and the archaeological evidence is considerably more ambiguous.

The cemeteries, temples and stratified settlement remains at such eastern Delta sites as TELL EL-DAB'A, TELL EL-MASKHUTA and TELL EL-YAHUDIYA include considerable quantities of Syro-Palestinian material dating to the Middle Bronze Age II period (*c.*2000–700 BC), but the Hyksos kings themselves have left few distinctively 'Asiatic' remains. The small number of royal sculptures of the Hyksos period largely adhere to the iconographic and stylistic traditions of the Middle Kingdom There is some evidence to suggest that the rulers supported the traditional forms of government and adopted an Egyptian-style ROYAL TITULARY, although Manfred Bietak has discovered a door jamb at Tell el-Dab'a bearing the name of the Hyksos king Sokarher with the title *heka khaswt*. Their major deity was SETH but they also worshipped other Egyptian gods as well as ANAT and ASTARTE, two closely related goddesses of Syro-Palestinian origin. Conventional forms

A selection of scarabs dating to the Hyksos period. (NEW YORK, METROPOLITAN MUSEUM)

of Egyptian literature, such as the Rhind Mathematical Papyrus (see MATHEMATICS) continued to be composed or copied.

Having established their capital at Avaris, they appear to have gradually spread westward, establishing centres such as TELL EL-YAHUDIYA, and taking control of the important Egyptian city of Memphis. The discovery of a small number of objects inscribed with the names of Hyksos kings at sites such as Knossos, Baghdad and Boghazköy (as well as the remains of Minoan frescos at 15th-Dynasty Avaris) suggest that the new rulers maintained trading links with the Near East and the Aegean.

Seals at the Nubian site of KERMA bear the name Sheshi, apparently a corrupted form of Salitis, the earliest known Hyksos king. The presence of these seals probably indicates that there was an alliance between the Hyksos and the kingdom of Kerma, which would have helped them both to counter opposition in Upper Egypt, where a rival group, the 17th Theban Dynasty, were violently opposed to foreign rule. The Second Stele of KAMOSE, describing one of the Theban campaigns against the Hyksos, includes clear references to a Nubian–Hyksos alliance by the end of the 17th Dynasty.

During the Hyksos period, greater use was made of HORSES, and their use in warfare was developed through the introduction of the CHARIOT, which facilitated the development of new military techniques and strategies. The curved sword (*khepesh*) was introduced, along with body armour and helmets. Ironically, it was probably the adoption of such new military technology by the Thebans that helped their rulers to defeat the Hyksos, and to establish AHMOSE I (1550–1525 BC) as the first king of the 18th Dynasty, and founder of the New Kingdom (1550–1069 BC).

The grave goods in Upper Egyptian private cemeteries of the Hyksos period (such as Abydos and Qau) show great continuity with the pre-Hyksos period, suggesting that the cultural impact of the Hyksos rulers may have been restricted to the Delta region. Even sites in the Memphite region and the western Delta show few indications of Palestinian influence. It has also been suggested by Barry Kemp that the apparent 'cultural hiatus' in the Fayum region during the Second Intermediate Period may simply be an indication of political disruption in those areas which had previously had a strong association with the Middle Kingdom central administration.

J. VON BECKERATH, *Untersuchungen zur politischen Geschichte der zweiten Zwischenzeit in Ägypten* (Glückstadt and New York, 1965).

J. VAN SETERS, *The Hyksos: a new investigation* (New Haven, 1966).

B. J. KEMP, 'Old Kingdom, Middle Kingdom and Second Intermediate Period', *Ancient Egypt: a social history*, B. G. Trigger et al. (Cambridge, 1983), 71–182.

D. B. REDFORD, *Egypt, Canaan and Israel in ancient times* (Princeton, 1992), 98–129.

hymns and litanies

One of the most common types of religious text in ancient Egypt was the hymn, usually consisting of a eulogy incorporating the names, titles and epithets of a deity. The mythological details included in many hymns help to compensate for the general dearth of narrative-style myths in Egyptian literature.

Hymns could be inscribed on the walls of both tombs and temples as well as on papyri; although they were generally intended to be recited as part of the ritual of a cult – Papyrus Chester Beatty IX (recto, now in the British Museum), for instance, includes hymns to be sung by the worshippers in a temple – but they were sometimes composed simply as 'literary' documents in their own right, as in the case of the *Hymn to the Nile Inundation* (one version of which is recorded on Papyrus Chester Beatty V). Often the function of the hymn can be difficult to ascertain: a cycle of five hymns to SENUSRET III (1874–1855 BC) were found in the town associated with his pyramid at EL-LAHUN, but it is not clear when they would have been recited, whether as part of the regular cult at the pyramid complex or on a special occasion such as the visit of the reigning king.

Numerous funerary stelae were inscribed with hymns to OSIRIS, the god of the dead, and the *Litany of Ra*, a hymn to the sun-god, was inscribed in many Ramesside royal tombs in the VALLEY OF THE KINGS. Among the most poetic of the hymns to the sun was the *Hymn to the Aten*, the longest version of which was inscribed in the tomb of AY at EL-AMARNA. Its description of the role of the ATEN in the sustenance of the world from dawn to sunset has often been compared with Psalm 104, although the undoubted similarities between the two compositions almost certainly result from a common literary heritage rather than – as some scholars have argued – from any connection between the worship of the Aten and the origins of Jewish monotheism. In addition, it has often been pointed out that there is little in the *Hymn to the Aten* that does not already appear in earlier Egyptian hymns to the sun-god.

A. BARUCQ and F. DAUMAS, *Hymnes et prières de l'Egypte ancienne* (Paris, 1980).

M. LICHTHEIM, *Ancient Egyptian literature* II (Berkeley, 1976), 81–118.

P. AUFFRET, *Hymnes d'Egypte et d'Israel: études de structures littéraires* (Freiburg, 1981).

hypaethral

Term used to describe a building that has no roof and is therefore open to the sky, as is the case in the Kiosk of Trajan at PHILAE.

hypocephalus

Amuletic discs inscribed with extracts from Chapter 162 of the BOOK OF THE DEAD and occasionally bearing vignettes representing certain deities. They were intended to 'warm' the head of the deceased. The earliest examples simply consisted of pieces of inscribed papyrus, but the hypocephali proper consist of

Hypocephalus of Neshorpakhered, a temple musician, decorated with the profile figures of four baboons worshipping the sun. Late Period or Ptolemaic period, 4th–3rd centuries BC, plastered linen and pigment, from Thebes, D. 14 cm. (EA36188)

papyrus sheets mounted on small CARTONNAGE discs, which have been discovered in a few tombs from the 26th Dynasty (664–525 BC onwards). There are also a few surviving examples made from metal. In keeping with their intended function, they were usually placed between the head of the mummified body and the funerary headrest.

hypostyle hall

Large temple court filled with columns, forming an essential element in Egyptian religious architecture, the name deriving from the Greek for 'resting on pillars'. There was a distinct transition from the PYLON into the open courtyard and then into the hypostyle hall. The hall was crowded with pillars and lit only by clerestory windows in the uppermost part of the walls. The columns could be of varying diameter and height, although those lining the axis route of the temple were usually the tallest and broadest. It was not uncommon for a single temple to have two hypostyle halls.

The symbolism expressed by the hypostyle hall is that of the reed swamp growing at the fringes of the PRIMEVAL MOUND, since the entire TEMPLE was regarded as a microcosm of the process of CREATION itself. Beyond the hall, the roof of the temple invariably became lower and the floor higher, while the dimensions of the rooms grew smaller, until the sanctuary itself was reached. This cosmogonic symbolism is well illustrated in the temple of Amun at KARNAK, where a dense forest of 134 columns spring from bases reminiscent of the earth around the roots of papyrus plants. The great columns along the axis route are each 23 m in height, and end in massive open papyrus flowers, while the rest of the columns have closed papyrus bud capitals.

In the temple of Khnum at ESNA, the 'swamp' symbolism is reinforced by the carving of insects on the column capitals. The architraves above the columns, as well as the ceiling itself, are representative of the sky (see ASTRONOMY AND ASTROLOGY), while the lowest parts of the enclosing walls often bear scenes of rows of offering bearers walking along the ground surface.

P. A. SPENCER, *The Egyptian temple: a lexicographical study* (London, 1984).

E. HORNUNG, *Idea into image*, trans. E. Bredeck (New York, 1992), 115–29.

Part of the Great Hypostyle Hall of the temple of Amun at Karnak. These are the smaller, closed papyrus bud columns: the open papyrus columns along the axial route stand 23 m high.
(P. T. NICHOLSON)

I

ibis

The sacred ibis (*Threskiornis aethiopicus*) is the best known of the principal species of ibis in Egypt; its distinctive features include a white body, a dark curved bill and a black neck, wing-tips, hindquarters and legs. Until the nineteenth century it was relatively common in Egypt but by 1850 it had almost disappeared. This bird was regarded as an incarnation of THOTH, and in the Late Period (747–332 BC) and Ptolemaic times (332–30 BC) sacred ibises were mummified in vast numbers and buried in catacombs at TUNA EL-GEBEL, SAQQARA and elsewhere (see SACRED ANIMALS).

The Greek historian HERODOTUS states that in his time it was an offence to kill an ibis. However, it is known from examination of the

A mummified ibis from the Sacred Animal Necropolis at north Saqqara. Ptolemaic period, c.150 BC. (EA68219)

mummified remains of these birds that some must have been hastened to their death; in addition it seems that they were being deliberately bred for the purpose of votive mummification. It has been suggested that their eggs were artificially incubated in ovens; both mummified eggs and the remains of other species of ibises are known from the catacombs at Saqqara.

The cult of Thoth led to the production of numerous ibis amulets and statuettes, many of which have survived at Tuna el-Gebel and Saqqara. The mummification of ibises and the production of votive items must have played an important part in the economy, and a variety of fraudulent practices are recorded in the archive of a priest called Hor at Saqqara.

The 'glossy ibis' (*Plegadis falcinellus*) has a characteristic curved bill, as well as long legs and an iridescent bronze-coloured gloss on its upper back and wings. Like the sacred ibis, it was frequently depicted in tomb reliefs from the Old Kingdom (2686–2181 BC), usually being painted as if it were completely black. According to Herodotus it fought with winged serpents which flew to Egypt from Arabia. The 'hermit ibis' (*Geronticus eremita*) has a long neck, long legs and a distinctive ruff, leading some scholars to describe it as the 'crested ibis'. Its image served as the hieroglyph meaning 'to shine' (see AKH). In modern Egypt it is a rare accidental migrant, but it may have been more common in ancient times. Since it is not a waterside bird, it features less commonly in ancient scenes set on the banks of the Nile, which usually include the sacred and glossy varieties.

J. D. RAY, *The archive of Hor* (London, 1976).

G. T. MARTIN, *The sacred animal necropolis at North Saqqara* (London, 1981).

P. F. HOULIHAN, *The birds of ancient Egypt* (Warminster, 1986), 26–32, 146–7.

ichneumon

Type of mongoose common in Africa, which is larger than a domestic cat, and thus bigger than its Indian counterpart. The creature is realistically portrayed in a number of Old Kingdom tombs such as that of the 5th-Dynasty noble TY (*c.*2400 BC; Tomb 60 at Saqqara), and less realistically depicted in some of the New Kingdom tombs, such as that of Menna (TT69) at Thebes.

By the Middle Kingdom (2055–1650 BC) the ichneumon was included among the SACRED ANIMALS and by Ramesside times (1295–1069 BC) it served as a symbol of the spirits of the underworld. Its skill in despatching snakes led to the myth that the sun-god RA once took the form of an ichneumon in order to fight APOPHIS, the great serpent of the underworld. This solar identification is responsible for the sun disc surmounting some ichneumon figures. Sometimes this disc is accompanied by a *uraeus*, which serves to identify the creature with WADJYT, the goddess traditionally associated with Lower Egypt. The mongoose emblem of the goddess Mafdet suggests that she may have originally adopted this manifestation, which would have been particularly suitable given her supposed power over snakes and scorpions.

Many bronze figurines of ichneumons have survived, although most date from the Late Period (747–332 BC) or Ptolemaic period (332–30 BC), when its depiction can be difficult to differentiate from that of the shrew.

E. BRUNNER-TRAUT, 'Spitzmaus und ichneumon als Tiere des Sonnengottes', *Nachrichten der Akademie der Wissenschaften in Göttingen* (1965), 123–63.

—, 'Ichneumon', *Lexikon der Ägyptologie* III, ed. W. Helck, E. Otto and W. Westendorf (Wiesbaden, 1980), 122–3.

J. MALEK, *The cat in ancient Egypt* (London, 1993), 32–9

Illahun *see* EL-LAHUN

Imhotep

Vizier and architect of the first pyramid, the Step Pyramid of DJOSER (2667–2648 BC) of the 3rd Dynasty. MANETHO credits him (under the Greek form of his name, Imouthes) with the invention of building in dressed stone. He is also said to have written a number of 'instructions' (*sebayt*, see WISDOM LITERATURE), although none has survived. It was for his great learning that he was most respected and, some two thousand years after his death, the first evidence appears of his deification, a great rarity for non-royal individuals in ancient Egypt. He was considered to be a god of wisdom, writing and MEDICINE, and as a result became linked with the cults of the gods THOTH and PTAH.

Votive bronze statuette of the deified architect, Imhotep. Late Period, 6th–4th centuries BC. (EA63800)

The Greeks identified him with their own god of medicine, Asklepios, and his cult centre at Saqqara, the 'Asklepion', became a centre for pilgrimage by those seeking healing. Many worshippers left a mummified IBIS as a votive offering to him in the great underground catacombs nearby, and some of these birds bear appliqués of Imhotep on their wrappings. Pilgrims also left clay models of diseased limbs and organs in the hope of being healed by Imhotep. Bronze figurines of the deified Imhotep are common from the Late Period onwards. He is usually represented as a seated scribe unrolling a papyrus across his knees. The base of the statuette sometimes bears the names and titles of its donor.

The Saqqara catacombs extend beneath the 3rd-Dynasty MASTABA tombs, a fact which led the British archaeologist W. B. Emery to search the area for the tomb of Imhotep himself, a process which inadvertently led to the discovery of the SACRED ANIMAL necropolis. The tomb of Imhotep has still not been discovered, although some have argued that it may be the large uninscribed mastaba 3518 at Saqqara.

As well as having a cult centre at Saqqara, Imhotep was also worshipped at KARNAK, DEIR EL-BAHRI, PHILAE and in the Ptolemaic temple to Hathor at DEIR EL-MEDINA, where he was venerated alongside AMENHOTEP SON OF HAPU, another important deified official.

D. WILDUNG, *Imhotep und Amenhotep: Gottwerdung im alten Ägypten* (Berlin, 1977).
—, *Egyptian saints: deification in pharaonic Egypt* (New York, 1977).

imiut

Fetish symbol consisting of the stuffed, headless skin of an animal (often a feline) tied to a pole which was mounted in a pot. It is recorded as early as the 1st Dynasty (3100–2890 BC), but is best known through its assimilation with the worship of Anubis, being depicted in the chapel of Anubis at DEIR EL-BAHRI and elsewhere. As a result, the *imiut* is sometimes described as the 'Anubis fetish' and serves as one of the epithets of the god. Models of the emblem were sometimes included among funerary equipment, as in the case of the tomb of TUTANKHAMUN (1336–1327 BC).

C. N. REEVES, *The complete Tutankhamun* (London, 1990), 135.

incense

The most common Egyptian word for the product used as incense is *senetjer* (meaning 'to make divine'). However, the term incense has

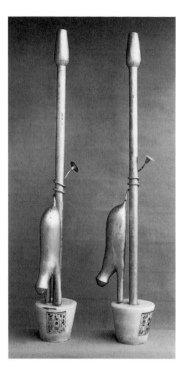

Two imiut *fetishes (or 'Anubis fetishes') from the tomb of Tutankhamun. 18th Dynasty, c. 1330 BC, H. 167 cm. (CAIRO, NOS 194 AND 202, REPRODUCED COURTESY OF THE GRIFFITH INSTITUTE)*

been somewhat vaguely used by Egyptologists to describe a range of aromatic substances used for burning in temples and for scenting the person. 'Incense trees' were one of the commodities brought to Egypt by Hatshepsut (1473–1458 BC) as a result of the expedition that she sent to the African land of PUNT, and aromatics were also imported from the Mediterranean. *Senetjer*, however, is now known to come from a species of *Pistacia*.

The function of 'incense cones' is a matter of some debate. There are numerous representations of guests at banquets and public functions, as in the tomb of Nebamun, wearing their heavy wigs, on top of which a cone of incense mixed with fat was placed. Traditionally it has been assumed that these cones would gradually melt in the warm atmosphere and run down the wig and clothing of the guest to leave them fragrant and cool. No such cones have been discovered archaeo-

BELOW *Fragment of wall-painting from the tomb of Nebamun, showing guests wearing incense cones at a banquet. 18th Dynasty, c.1400 BC, painted plaster, from Thebes, H. 61 cm. (EA37984)*

logically, however, and Joann Fletcher has put forward an argument that the depiction of the cone is used simply as a hieroglyphic symbol to depict the fact that the wigs were scented. It seems unlikely that guests would have wished to have their very elaborate and expensive wigs matted with congealed fat or their fine linen garments marked and stained (although some paintings perhaps suggest that this did happen). The view that the cone illustrates something that would otherwise be impossible to represent seems a plausible one.

A. M. BLACKMAN, 'The significance of incense and libations in funerary and temple rituals', *ZÄS* 50 (1912), 69–75.

J. FLETCHER, *Ancient Egyptian hair: a study in style, form and function* (unpublished dissertation, Manchester University, 1995).

M. SERPICO and R. WHITE, 'The botanical identity and transport of incense during the Egyptian New Kingdom', *Antiquity* 74 (2000), 884–97.

instructions *see* WISDOM LITERATURE

Intef (Inyotef)
Name taken by three rulers of the Theban 11th Dynasty (2125–1985 BC), who were all buried in rock-cut SAFF TOMBS, in the el-Tarif region of western Thebes. They called themselves after an 8th-Dynasty Theban nomarch (provincial governor) and chief priest, listed as a ruler in the so-called Table of Karnak (an 18th-Dynasty Theban KING LIST), who was the father of MENTUHOTEP I (*c.*2125 BC), the founder of the 11th Dynasty.

Intef I Sehertawy (2125–2112 BC), the son of Mentuhotep I, initially took the title 'supreme chief of Upper Egypt', but later in his reign he conquered the rival cities of KOPTOS, DENDERA and HIERAKONPOLIS and adopted a ROYAL TITULARY.

Intef II Wahankh (2112–2063 BC), the son of Intef I Sehertawy, succeeded in consolidating the military successes to achieve genuine control over Upper Egypt. The inscriptions in the tomb of Hetepi at Elkab describe a FAMINE during his reign. In addition, the lower portion of a stele (Egyptian Museum, Cairo) was found in 1860 by Auguste Mariette, outside Intef II's tomb at el-Tarif, describing his conquests and portraying him with five named dogs at his feet.

Intef III Nakhtnebtepnefer (2063–2055 BC) is thought to have restored the funerary chapel of the deified nomarch Heqaib at Elephantine. His reign is generally more poorly documented than his predecessors, although he is usually described as Intef the Great. His son, Nebhepetra MENTUHOTEP II, was to become the first ruler of both Upper

and Lower Egypt since the end of the Old Kingdom.

The name Intef was also taken by three Theban rulers of the 17th Dynasty, who ruled Upper Egypt during a period of instability immediately preceding the emergence of rulers (in this case KAMOSE and AHMOSE I) who reunited the two halves of the country.

P. E. NEWBERRY, 'On the parentage of the Intef kings of the Eleventh Dynasty', *ZÄS* 72 (1936), 118–20.

H. E. WINLOCK, *The rise and fall of the Middle Kingdom in Thebes* (New York, 1947).

W. SCHENKEL, *Memphis, Herakleopolis, Theben: die epigraphischen Zeugnisse der 7.–11. Dynastie Ägyptens* (Wiesbaden, 1965).

D. ARNOLD, *Gräber des Alten und Mittleren Reiches in El-Tarif* (Mainz, 1976).

inundation
Term used to describe the annual flooding of the Nile in Egypt, which has not taken place since the completion of the ASWAN HIGH DAM in 1971. Such was the importance of the Nile inundation to the ancient Egyptians that they worshipped HAPY, a personification of the floods and the ensuing fertility. The Egyptian seasons were based on the annual Nile cycle, and named accordingly: *akhet* the inundation, *peret* the growing season, and *shemu* the drought season. However, the inundation only occasionally occurred in the calendrical season of *akhet*, since the civil CALENDAR itself became gradually more and more out of step with the seasonal and lunar measurements of time.

Each year between June and September the Nile and its tributaries, the Blue Nile and the Atbara, receive the heavy summer rains of the Ethiopian highlands. These rivers greatly increase their volume and flood along the Nile's course. For thousands of years, prior to the construction of the High Dam, the flood would have become noticeable at Aswan by the last week of June, and would have reached its full height in the vicinity of Cairo by September. The floods would begin to subside about two weeks later. The flooding of the land led to the deposition of a new layer of fertile silt every year, so that fertilizer was not generally necessary, the soil being replaced each year. The importance of recording the level of the inundation, in terms of predicting soil fertility and crop yields, led to the devising of methods for the recording of the Nile's height, using NILOMETERS (although there is no evidence for them in the earliest periods). However, there is no firm evidence that such records were used to calculate crop yields as a basis for TAXATION.

The first crops could be planted in October and November and would ripen in March or April, at which time the river had reached its lowest level (see AGRICULTURE). During this time little watering would have been necessary. The water could be retained longer on the land by the use of basins and canals, and it could be raised from the river by irrigation devices such as the SHADUF. The extensive flooding of the land also produced an unavoidable 'slack period' in the agricultural year, during which certain corvée tasks could be undertaken. In the Old Kingdom (2686–2181 BC), PYRAMID building was one such task, and the high water levels could be used to ship stone closer to construction sites than would otherwise have been possible.

The inundation was also a time of celebration, and offerings were made to HAPY, the god who personified the Nile flood. The *Hymn to the Nile Inundation*, probably composed in the Middle Kingdom (2055–1650 BC), praises the river for the renewed life it brings to Egypt each year.

B. H. STRICKER, *De overstroming van de Nijl* (Leiden, 1956).

D. BONNEAU, *La crue du Nil* (Paris, 1964).

K. BUTZER, *Early hydraulic civilization in Egypt* (Chicago, 1976).

W. SCHENKEL, *Die Bewässerungsrevolution im alten Ägypten* (Mainz, 1978).

J. J. JANSSEN, 'The day the inundation began', *JNES* 46/2 (1987), 129–36.

Inyotef *see* INTEF

iron
Although iron was introduced into western Asia by the third millennium BC, the first evidence of iron smelting in Egypt, dating to the sixth century BC, was excavated by Flinders Petrie at the Delta city of NAUKRATIS. There are a number of earlier examples of iron artefacts in Egypt, stretching back to the early Old Kingdom (*c.*2600 BC), but most of these are assumed to have involved naturally occurring meteoric rather than smelted iron. A fragment of iron found in the pyramid complex of Khufu at GIZA has been shown to be much later in date than the Old Kingdom.

Until the 22nd Dynasty (945–715 BC) iron artefacts were primarily restricted to ritual contexts, such as royal tombs, as in the case of the small iron dagger found in the tomb of TUTANKHAMUN (KV62; 1336–1327 BC). The AMARNA LETTERS include references to gifts of iron sent from western Asiatic rulers to Amenhotep III (1390–1352 BC) and Akhenaten (1352–1336 BC), indicating the prestigious nature of the metal at this date (see HITTITES).

It was only during the Roman period (30 BC–AD 395) that iron tools and weapons became relatively common in Egypt. For the use of iron in Nubia, see MEROE.

A. LUCAS, *Ancient Egyptian materials and industries*, 4th ed., rev. J. R. Harris (London, 1962), 235–43.

R. MADDIN, 'Early iron metallurgy in the Near East', *Transactions of the Iron and Steel Institute of Japan* 15/2 (1975), 59–68.

R. F. TYLECOTE, 'The origin of iron smelting in Africa', *West African Journal of Archaeology* 5 (1975), 1–9.

B. SCHEEL, *Egyptian metalworking and tools* (Princes Risborough, 1989), 17–18.

irrigation *see* AGRICULTURE; INUNDATION; SCORPION and SHADUF

ished tree *see* TREES

Isis

Goddess who encapsulated the virtues of the archetypal Egyptian wife and mother. She was the sister-wife to OSIRIS and mother to HORUS, and as such became the symbolic mother of the Egyptian king, who was himself regarded as a human manifestation of Horus. The association between Isis and the physical royal throne itself is perhaps indicated by the fact that her name may have originally meant 'seat', and the emblem that she wore on her head was the hieroglyphic sign for throne. From the New Kingdom (1550–1069 BC) onwards, she was closely connected with HATHOR and so sometimes wore a solar disc between cow horns. Her maternal role included that of the 'Isis-cow', mother to the APIS bull, and 'great white sow of Heliopolis'. Her origins are uncertain, although she seems to have been first worshipped in the Delta; in the Heliopolitan theology she was regarded as a daughter of the deities GEB and NUT.

She is best known mythologically as the devoted wife of Osiris, whose body she sought after his murder by SETH. She is said to have made the first mummy from the dismembered limbs of Osiris, using her wings to breathe life into him and magically conceiving her son Horus in the process. In the temple of Hathor at DENDERA, there are reliefs depicting this necrophiliac act of conception, showing Isis hovering over the mummy in the form of a kite. In reference to this role, she is often depicted in the form of a woman with long elegant wings, often embracing the pharaoh or, in private funerary scenes, the deceased. According to the myths, Osiris became ruler of the underworld, while Isis gave birth to her son at Khemmis in the Delta. Numerous bronzes and

reliefs show her suckling Horus in the form of the young king seated on her lap.

As 'Isis great in magic' she could be called upon to protect the young, and would be invoked at times of injury. She was also able to combine her medicinal skills with great cunning. When the sun-god RA was bitten by a snake (fashioned by Isis from earth mixed with Ra's saliva) she is said to have offered to cure him in return for knowledge of his secret name. Having found out this name, she became 'mistress of the gods who knows Ra by his own name' and passed on her knowledge to Horus, thus enabling him to acquire great powers. Her great cunning was also described in the story of the contendings of Horus and

Gilt, bronze and wood statuette of Isis suckling Horus. The wooden chair and pedestal are original and the face of the goddess is gilt. Late Period, after 600 BC, from north Saqqara, H. 23 cm. (EA67186)

Seth, in which she was instrumental in having Seth condemn himself, so that her son would become the earthly ruler of Egypt.

Her most famous and long-lived sanctuary was on the island of PHILAE near Aswan, but as a universal goddess she was widely worshipped, with significant cults at Egyptian sites such as DENDERA as well as at BYBLOS in Syria–Palestine. The great importance attached to her cult by the Nubians is demonstrated by the survival of her worship at Philae (on the border between Egypt and Nubia) until the sixth century AD, by which time virtually all of Egypt had become Christianized.

In post-Pharaonic times her cult was adopted as one of the Classical 'mystery' cults, gradually spreading through the Hellenistic world and the Roman empire. There were temples erected to her in Rome itself, including a substantial complex at the Campus Martius. The Classical writer Apuleius (*c.*AD 140) described a ceremony of initiation into the cult of Isis in his *Metamorphoses*, although the final rite in the ceremony was not disclosed. In Greco–Roman times, her cult began to surpass that of Osiris in popularity, seriously rivalling both the traditional Roman gods and early Christianity.

H. W. MÜLLER, 'Isis mit dem Horuskinde', *MJK* 14 (1963), 7–38.

M. MÜNSTER, *Untersuchungen zur Göttin Isis vom Alten Reich bis zum Ende des Neuen Reiches* (Berlin, 1968).

J. G. GRIFFITHS, *Plutarch's De Iside et Osiride* (Swansea, 1970).

R. E. WITT, *Isis in the Graeco-Roman world* (London, 1971).

J. LECLANT, *Inventaire bibliographique des Isiaca*, 2 vols (Leiden, 1972–4).

F. DUNAND, *Le culte d'Isis dans le bassin orientale de la Méditerranée*, 3 vols (Leiden, 1973).

R. A. WILD, *Water in the cultic worship of Isis and Sarapis* (Leiden, 1981).

Israel

The Israelites are attested in Syria–Palestine from the late Bronze Age onwards. Their cultural and ethnic origins are difficult to clarify, partly because the archaeological and Biblical sources of evidence are difficult to reconcile. The Biblical accounts of the origins of the people of Israel, which are principally described in the books of Numbers, Joshua and Judges, are often at odds both with other ancient textual sources and with the archaeological evidence for the settlement of CANAAN in the late Bronze Age and early Iron Age (*c.*1600–750 BC).

Israel is first textually attested as a political entity in the so-called Israel Stele, an inscription of the fifth year of the reign of MERENPTAH (1213–1203 BC), which includes a list of defeated peoples: 'Their chiefs prostrate themselves and beg for peace, Canaan is devastated, Ashkelon is vanquished, Gezer is taken, Yenoam annihilated, Israel is laid waste, its seed exists no more, Syria is made a widow for Egypt, and all lands have been pacified.'

Donald Redford has suggested that the Israelites were probably emerging as a distinct

The so-called 'Israel Stele' or 'victory stele of Merenptah', which is inscribed with a list of defeated peoples, including the first known mention of Israel (DETAIL ABOVE). The stele was erected by Merenptah in his funerary temple at Thebes. 19th Dynasty, 1213–1203 BC, grey granite, H. 3.18 m. (CAIRO JE31408)

element of Canaanite culture during the century or so prior to this. Some authorities have argued that the early Israelites were an oppressed rural group of Canaanites who rebelled against the Canaanite cities along the coast, while others have hypothesized that they were the survivors of a decline in the fortunes of Canaan who established themselves in the highlands at the end of the Bronze Age. Redford, however, makes a good case for equating the very earliest Israelites with the semi-nomadic people in the highlands of central Palestine, known to the Egyptians as the Shasu (see BEDOUIN), who constantly disrupted the Ramesside pharaohs' sphere of influence in Syria–Palestine. This theory is bol-

stered by the fact that the hieroglyphic determinative written in front of the name Israel on the Israel Stele indicates that it was regarded as a group of people rather than a city.

Although, unlike Israel, the Shasu are often mentioned in Egyptian texts, their pastoral lifestyle has left few traces in the archaeological record. By the end of the thirteenth century BC the Shasu/Israelites were beginning to establish small settlements in the uplands, the architecture of which closely resembled contemporary Canaanite villages.

In the tenth century BC Solomon ruled over an Israelite kingdom that had overcome both Canaanites and Philistines, emerging as the dominant state in the Levant. At the capital, Jerusalem, only the barest ruins of Solomon's temple and palace have survived. After his reign, the territory was split between the kingdoms of Israel and Judah, which survived until 722 and 587 BC respectively. In the Egyptian Third Intermediate Period (1069–747 BC) and Late Period (747–332 BC) there are a number of references in Egyptian texts to Egyptian political dealings with Israel, Judah and other Syro-Palestinian polities, particularly in the forging of alliances to hold back the threats posed by the ASSYRIANS and PERSIANS.

See also BIBLICAL CONNECTIONS.

W. M. F. PETRIE, *Six temples at Thebes* (London, 1897), 13.

E. HORNUNG, 'Die Israelstele des Merenptah', *Ägypten und Altes Testament* 5 (1983), 224–33.

G. W. AHLSTRÖM, *Who were the Israelites?* (Winona Lake, IN, 1986).

M. SALEH and H. SOUROUZIAN, *The Egyptian Museum, Cairo* (Mainz, 1987), no. 212.

D. B. REDFORD, *Egypt, Canaan and Israel in ancient times* (Princeton, 1992), 257–82.

ithyphallic

Not specifically an Egyptological term, but generally used to refer to deities or human figures having an erect penis, particularly the gods AMUN and MIN.

iuwen (Egyptian *iwn*: 'pillar')

Pillar-shaped fetish of the city of HELIOPOLIS which was a symbol of the moon, in the same way that the OBELISK was associated with the sun-god. The name was also applied to the moon-god manifestation of OSIRIS.

K. MARTIN, *Ein Garantsymbol des Lebens* (Hildesheim, 1977), 16–18.

—, 'Iun-Pfeiler', *Lexikon der Ägyptologie* III, ed. W. Helck, E. Otto and W. Westendorf (Wiesbaden, 1980), 213–14.

J

jackal *see* ANUBIS, DOG and WEPWAWET

jewellery

From the earliest times in ancient Egypt, jewellery was used as a means of self-adornment and also as an indication of social status. Thus, it is not surprising to find that jewellery is among the first types of artefact known from Egypt. During the Badarian period (*c.*5500–4000 BC) broad belts or 'girdles' of green glazed stone beads were made. Later in the PREDYNASTIC PERIOD necklaces of faience beads were worn, along with bracelets and amulets of shell and ivory.

In the 1st-Dynasty tomb of DJER at Abydos a dismembered arm decorated with four bracelets was discovered by Flinders Petrie. These early examples of jewellery show considerable sophistication, and such precious materials as GOLD, LAPIS LAZULI, TURQUOISE and amethyst were already being used. Although the actual burial was not preserved in the 3rd-Dynasty tomb of SEKHEMKHET at Saqqara, the excavations did reveal items of spectacular jewellery, including a delicate bracelet of gold ball-beads. The 4th-Dynasty tomb of Queen HETEPHERES I at Giza contained numerous pieces of royal jewellery, including silver bangles inlaid with butterfly designs. In certain periods the Egyptians seem to have regarded SILVER as more valuable than gold, and this find gives some indication of the rich jewellery that must have accompanied the burials of the pharaohs during the Old Kingdom (2686–2181 BC).

The peak of Egyptian jewellery-making was undoubtedly the Middle Kingdom (2055–1650 BC), when works of great elegance and refinement were produced, as in the case of the jewellery of Princess Khnemet, who was buried at DAHSHUR during the reign of the 12th-Dynasty ruler Amenemhat II (1922–1878 BC). Her equipment included two beautifully made openwork diadems inlaid with semi-precious stones, and the famous Cretan-influenced 'bull mosaic' pendant, which, until recently, was widely believed to be GLASS. The Dahshur treasure was rivalled only by the late 12th-Dynasty jewellery of Sithathoriunet from a shaft-tomb at EL-LAHUN, which included a diadem, a gold collar and two pectorals, as well as necklaces and bead-girdles (now in the Metropolitan Museum, New York and the Egyptian Museum, Cairo).

From the royal necropolis at EL-LISHT came

Egyptian royal jewellery of the Middle Kingdom and Second Intermediate Period (c.1880–1590 BC). TOP *electrum winged scarab, inlaid with cornelian, green feldspar and lapis lazuli. (EA54460)* ABOVE CENTRE *ajouré gold plaque showing Amenemhat IV offering unguent to Atum. (EA59194)* CENTRE *gold finger-ring with lapis lazuli bezel. (EA57698)* LEFT AND RIGHT *two bracelet spacer-bars crowned by reclining cats, with twelve threading tubes; the inscription on the base of each names Nubkheperra Intef and his wife Sobkemsaf. (EA57699, 57700)* BOTTOM *human-headed green jasper heart scarab of Sobkemsaf II, a roughly-incised verse of Chapter 30B from the Book of the Dead around the gold plinth. (EA7876) L. of heart scarab 3.6 cm.*

the fine jewellery of a 12th-Dynasty noblewoman named Senebtisy, whose 'broad collar' incorporates faience, turquoise and gold leaf. However, the fact that this piece has no fastenings suggests that it may have been made specifically for funerary use. The same tomb contained gold hair ornaments in the form of flowers, a bead belt with a gold buckle decorated with Senebtisy's name, and a further broad collar with falcon terminals. The jewellery of this period was to influence products in neighbouring lands, and excavations at the Syro-Palestinian city of Byblos have revealed numerous Egyptianizing items, including a gold 'breast-plate' bearing the pattern of an Egyptian broad collar.

The earliest significant finds of jewellery in the New Kingdom derive from the tomb of Queen AHHOTEP II, whose equipment included magnificent inlay work, and an extremely fine chain made from looped six-ply gold wire. The jewellery of Menwi, Merti and Menhet, three foreign wives of Thutmose III (1479–1425 BC), was discovered in a much-plundered rock tomb at Wadi Gabbanet el-Qurud, about three kilometres to the west of Deir el-Bahri in western Thebes. The finds (now in the Metropolitan Museum of Art, New York) include glass elements among the gemstones and gold. Although glass was precious

a son of Rameses II (1279–1213 BC) whose funerary chapel was attached to the SERAPEUM at Saqqara. Two of the Apis bull burials made by the prince also contained jewellery, although this is generally regarded as clumsy and poorly made.

have revealed large quantities of fired clay moulds used for the making of faience amulets, beads and finger rings. Blue faience disc beads were evidently produced (and lost) in their thousands at such 18th-Dynasty town sites as el-Amarna and Malkata.

H. E. WINLOCK, *The treasure of three Egyptian princesses* (New York, 1948).

C. ALDRED, *Jewels of the pharaohs* (London, 1971).

C. A. R. ANDREWS, *Catalogue of Egyptian antiquities in the British Museum* VI: *Jewellery (London, 1981).*

J. OGDEN, *Jewellery of the ancient world* (London, 1982).

C. A. R. ANDREWS, *Ancient Egyptian jewellery* (London, 1990).

judgement of the dead *see* FUNERARY BELIEFS

Fragment of wall-painting from the tomb of Sobekhotep (TT63), showing jewellery-makers and metal-workers making beads and precious objects. Several of the men are using quadruple and triple bow drills to pierce hard-stone beads. 18th Dynasty, reign of Thutmose IV, c. 1395 BC, painted plaster, from Thebes, H.66 cm. (EA920)

at this time, the Wadi Qubbanet el-Qirud finds mark the beginning of a trend whereby New Kingdom jewellery became increasingly elaborate and garish, making more use of artificial stones, and gradually becoming less delicate.

The fabulous jewellery of TUTANKHAMUN (1336–1327 BC) is sometimes described as expensive costume jewellery, lacking the refinement of the Middle Kingdom and early New Kingdom work. The major find of the 19th Dynasty is the jewellery of Khaemwaset,

During the New Kingdom ear ornaments became relatively common, and a variety of earrings were produced, particularly in stone and glass. Pierre Montet's excavations at TANIS in 1939–40 led to the discovery of royal jewellery of the Third Intermediate Period (1069–747 BC), which, although less accomplished than some of the earlier work, is clearly of a generally similar type to the New Kingdom material.

The scientific and aesthetic study of the surviving items of jewellery has been supplemented by pictorial evidence, from tombs such as those of REKHMIRA (TT100), Amenemopet (TT276) and Sobekhotep (TT63), as well as the debris of FAIENCE workshops such as those at EL-AMARNA. The jewellery worn by poorer people was mostly made from less valuable gemstones or faience. The excavations of the 18th-Dynasty city at el-Amarna

K

ka

Almost untranslatable term used by the Egyptians to describe the creative life-force of each individual, whether human or divine. The *ka*, represented by a hieroglyph consisting of a pair of arms, was considered to be the essential ingredient that differentiated a living person from a dead one, and is therefore sometimes translated as 'sustenance'. It came into existence at the same moment that the individual was born, subsequently serving as his or her 'double' and sometimes being depicted in funerary art as a slightly smaller figure standing beside the living being (see DYAD). Sometimes the creator-god KHNUM was shown modelling the *ka* on a potter's wheel at the same time as he was forming the bodies of humanity.

When any individual died, the *ka* continued to live, and so required the same sustenance as the human being had enjoyed in life. For this reason it was provided either with genuine food offerings or with representations of food depicted on the wall of the tomb, all of which were activated by the OFFERING FORMULA, addressed directly to the *ka*. It appears that the *ka* was thought not to eat the offerings physically but simply to assimilate their life-preserving force. In giving food or drink to one another in normal daily life, the Egyptians therefore sometimes used the formula 'for your *ka*' in acknowledgement of this life-giving force. Consequently the offerings themselves came to be known as *kaw* and were sometimes replaced in representations of the OFFERING TABLE by the *ka* sign – two outstretched arms that magically warded off the forces of evil. It was to the *ka* that offerings were made before the FALSE DOORS set up in tombs.

Funerary statues were regarded as images of the *ka* of the deceased, and sometimes these too incorporated the *ka* symbol, as in the case of the image of the 13th-Dynasty ruler Awibra Hor from DAHSHUR (*c*.1750 BC; Egyptian Museum, Cairo), which depicts the deceased with the *ka* hieroglyph in the form of a headdress. It was thought that the reunion of the BA and *ka* in the underworld effectively transformed the deceased into an AKH (one of the 'blessed dead').

J. P. ALLEN, 'Funerary texts and their meaning', *Mummies and magic*, ed. P. Lacovara, S. D'Auria and C. H. Roehrig (Boston, 1988), 38–49.

Ka-statue of King Awibra Hor, discovered within its naos in a tomb to the north of the pyramid of Amenemhat III at Dahshur. 13th Dynasty, c.1700 BC, H. naos 2.07 m, H. of statue 1.7 m. (CAIRO JE30948)

E. HORNUNG, *Idea into image*, trans. E. Bredeck (New York, 1992), 167–84.

Kalabsha (anc. Talmis)

Site of an unfinished, free-standing temple in Lower Nubia, about 50 km south of Aswan. The complex was built in sandstone masonry and consisted of a pylon, forecourt, hypostyle hall, two vestibules and a sanctuary. It was dedicated to the local god Mandulis and dates primarily to the early Roman period (*c*.30 BC), but the colony at Talmis evidently dates back to at least the reign of Amenhotep II (1427–1400 BC), who is depicted in the painted wall reliefs of the hypostyle hall. In 1962–3 the buildings were dismantled, in order to save them from the waters of Lake Nasser, and in 1970 they were reassembled at a new location 750 m to the south of the ASWAN HIGH DAM.

K. G. SIEGLER, *Kalabsha. Architektur und Baugeschichte des Tempels* (Berlin, 1970).

Kamose (1555–1550 BC)

Last ruler of the Theban 17th Dynasty, successor of SEQENENRA TAA II (*c*.1560 BC) and predecessor of AHMOSE I (1550–1525 BC), the first 18th-Dynasty ruler. The principal documents relating to his reign are two large stelae at Karnak (both recounting his campaigns against the HYKSOS rulers), as well as the Carnarvon Tablet, which appears to be a later scribal copy of the stelae. The text derived from these three documents begins by describing the war between Seqenenra Taa II and the Hyksos king Aauserra APEPI (1585–1542 BC) and goes on to narrate Kamose's continuation of the conflict after his father's death. He was buried in a pyramidal-style tomb at Dra Abu el-Naga (see THEBES), where the earlier 17th-Dynasty royal tombs are located, and it appears that his tomb had still not been robbed over four hundred years later when the necropolis was inspected during the reign of Rameses IX (1126–1108 BC). His coffin was discovered at Dra Abu el-Naga in 1857, but his mummified body disintegrated as soon as it was opened.

A. H. GARDINER, 'The defeat of the Hyksos by Kamose', *JEA* 3 (1917), 95–110.

H. WINLOCK, 'The tombs of the kings of the Seventeenth Dynasty at Thebes', *JEA* 10 (1924), 217–77.

H. GAUTHIER, 'Les deux rois Kamose (XVIIe dynastie)', *Studies Griffith*, ed. S. R. K. Glanville (Oxford, 1932), 3–8.

L. HABACHI, *The second stele of Kamose and his struggle against the Hyksos ruler and his capital* (Glückstadt, 1972).

Kamutef

Divine epithet meaning 'bull of his mother', which was used from the New Kingdom onwards to refer to the combined ithyphallic form of AMUN and MIN. Amun-Min-Kamutef is frequently depicted receiving offerings of lettuces, or standing beside them as they grow.

H. RICKE, *Das Kamutef-Heiligtum Hatschepsuts und Thutmoses III* (Cairo, 1939).

H. JARITZ, 'Kamutef', *Lexikon der Ägyptologie* III, ed. W. Helck, E. Otto and W. Westendorf (Wiesbaden, 1980), 308–9.

G. HAENY, 'Zum Kamutef', *GM* 90 (1986), 33–4.

Karanog

Large town-site and necropolis located in Lower Nubia about 60 km south of Aswan, which flourished in the Meroitic and post-Meroitic periods (*c.*300 BC–AD 550). By at least as early as the third century BC, Karanog had developed into a major town; the unusually scattered settlement was unique among Meroitic administrative centres (e.g. FARAS, Gebel Adda and QASR IBRIM) in being protected by a huge three-storey mud-brick 'castle' rather than a surrounding enclosure wall. Whereas Meroitic sites in Upper Nubia consist principally of temples and tombs, the remains of Karanog and other surviving Lower Nubian Meroitic settlements are dominated by palaces and fortifications, and there is a distinct lack of royal sculptures and inscriptions. In view of this discrepancy W. Y. Adams has proposed that Lower Nubian towns such as Karanog may have been governed by local feudal rulers rather than being under the direct control of the Meroitic kings in the south.

C. L. WOOLLEY and D. RANDALL-MACIVER, *Karanog, the Romano-Nubian cemetery* (Philadelphia, 1910).

C. L. WOOLLEY, *Karanog, the town* (Philadelphia, 1911).

W. Y. ADAMS, 'Meroitic north and south, a study in cultural contrasts', *Meroitica* 2 (1976), 11–26.

—, *Nubia: corridor to Africa*, 2nd ed. (London and Princeton, 1984), 356–7, 371–8.

Karnak (anc. Ipet-isut)

Huge complex of religious buildings covering over a hundred hectares in the northeastern area of modern Luxor, consisting of three major sacred precincts dedicated to the deities AMUN-RA, MUT and MONTU, each surrounded by trapezoidal mud-brick enclosure walls. The enclosures also encompassed several smaller temples dedicated to PTAH, Opet and KHONS respectively. The main temples were continu-

Plan of the temple complex at Karnak.

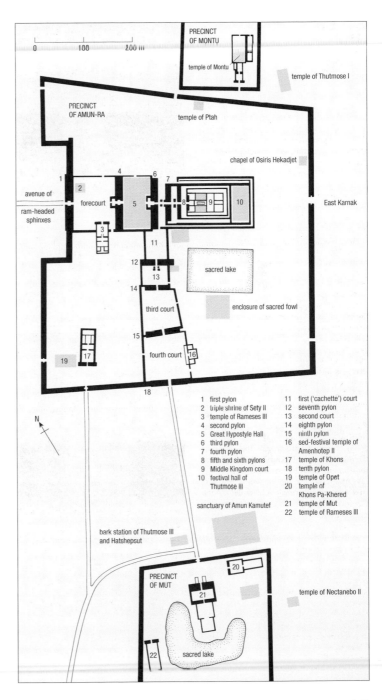

1 first pylon
2 triple shrine of Sety II
3 temple of Rameses III
4 second pylon
5 Great Hypostyle Hall
6 third pylon
7 fourth pylon
8 fifth and sixth pylons
9 Middle Kingdom court
10 festival hall of Thutmose III

11 first ('cachette') court
12 seventh pylon
13 second court
14 eighth pylon
15 ninth pylon
16 sed-festival temple of Amenhotep II
17 temple of Khons
18 tenth pylon
19 temple of Opet
20 temple of Khons Pa-Khered
21 temple of Mut
22 temple of Rameses III

sanctuary of Amun Kamutef

ally extended and embellished by the rulers of Egypt from at least the Middle Kingdom (2055–1650 BC) until the Roman period (30 BC–AD 395), but most of the surviving remains date to the New Kingdom (1550–1069 BC).

The principal temple at Karnak, dedicated to Amun-Ra, the pre-eminent god of the New Kingdom, consisted of two axes, each comprising a succession of pylons and courtyards interspersed with obelisks, smaller temples, shrines and altars. The earliest axis stretches from west to east, incorporating the Great Hypostyle Hall of Rameses II (1279–1213 BC), which is over 0.5 hectares in area. The second axis extends the temple southwards towards the nearby precinct of the goddess Mut. To the south of the junction between the two axes is a vast rectangular SACRED LAKE. The first court on the north–south axis is also known as 'cachette court', since an impressive collection of thousands of fragments of royal and private statuary (mostly now in the Egyptian Museum, Cairo) was discovered here in 1902, buried under the temple floor.

Although Karnak has been subject to numerous excavations since the late nineteenth century, the vast majority of resources have been devoted to the conservation and re-erection of the standing monuments. It is the largest and best preserved temple complex of the New Kingdom, and its reliefs and inscriptions incorporate valuable epigraphic data concerning the political and religious activities of imperial Egypt.

Karnak was surrounded by the growing city of Thebes (anc. Waset), which was the religious centre of Egypt for most of the Dynastic period. In c.667 BC the temple and town were sacked by the ASSYRIAN ruler Ashurbanipal and from then on the city centre gradually moved two kilometres southwards to the area around LUXOR temple. Much of the ancient Theban settlement therefore lies underneath modern Luxor, rendering it largely inaccessible to archaeologists.

G. LEGRAIN, *Les temples du Karnak* (Brussels, 1929).
CENTRE FRANCO-ÉGYPTIEN D'ÉTUDE DES TEMPLES DE KARNAK, *Cahiers de Karnak*, 6 vols (1943–82).
P. BARGUET, *Le temple d'Amon-Re à Karnak: essai d'exégèse* (Cairo, 1962).

Kawa

Temple site located opposite Dongola in the heartland of the Nubian KERMA culture. The temple complex was founded by AMENHOTEP III (1390–1352 BC) but it had been virtually abandoned by the reign of Rameses VII (1136–1129 BC). Eventually, with the emergence of the Kushite 25th Dynasty (747–656 BC), the site

Bronze statuette of a Kushite king (perhaps Taharqo) from Temple T at Kawa. 25th Dynasty, c.690 BC, H. 11.2 cm. (EA63595)

regained its importance and SHABAQO (716–702 BC), Shabitqo (702–690 BC) and TAHARQO (690–664 BC) all contributed new buildings, reliefs and statuary. Taharqo effectively created a new sanctuary of AMUN comparable with that at Gebel Barkal, after which the Kushite kings were obliged to carry out important rituals at Kawa. Taharqo's work was commemorated by a stele, still *in situ*, dating to the sixth year of his reign.

M. F. L. MACADAM, *The temples of Kawa*, 2 vols (Oxford, 1949–55).

Kematef *see* AMUN

Kemet

The name that the ancient Egyptians used to describe Egypt itself. The literal meaning of Kemet is 'black land', a reference to the fertile Nile silt which was annually spread across the land by the INUNDATION. The Egyptians referred to themselves as the *remetch en Kemet* ('the people of the black land'). For the Egyptians, therefore, black was essentially the colour of rebirth and regeneration, probably having none of the western connotations of death and decay.

The fertile, black landscape of Kemet was surrounded, in stark contrast, by the desert, known to the Egyptians as Deshret ('the red land'). This sense of natural DUALITY was deeply ingrained in the Egyptian world-view, in that their land was that of the LOTUS and the PAPYRUS, of the red crown and the white, of Upper and Lower Egypt.

H. KEES, *Ancient Egypt: a cultural topography*, ed. T. G. H. James (London, 1961).

Kenamun (Qenamun) (c.1450–1400 BC)

High official of the 18th Dynasty, whose well-preserved Theban tomb (TT93) was never properly excavated since it was already known to early travellers in the eighteenth century AD. He was chief steward to AMENHOTEP II (1427–1400 BC) and superintendent of the dockyard of Peru-nefer near Memphis. The fact that he was the son of the royal nurse Amenemopet is perhaps an indication that high administrative posts could be gained during the New Kingdom even by individuals with relatively indirect links to the royal family. A SHABTI of Kenamun, probably given to him by the king, is the first known piece of three-dimensional Egyptian sculpture to be formed from GLASS (although a glass sculpture of the head of Amenhotep II, now in the Corning Museum of Glass, New York, would have been roughly contemporary). This Kenamun should not be confused with his namesake, who was Mayor of the Southern City (Thebes) in the reign of Amenhotep III (1390–1352 BC), and owner of another Theban tomb (TT162).

N. de G. DAVIES, *The tomb of Ken-Amun at Thebes*, 2 vols (London, 1930).
J. D. COONEY, 'Glass sculpture in ancient Egypt', *Journal of Glass Studies* 2 (1960), 12–14.

Kerma

Town-site of the early second millennium BC, near the third Nile cataract in Upper Nubia, which was almost certainly the capital of the Kushite Kingdom during the Egyptian Old and Middle Kingdoms (2686–1650 BC) – it is therefore the type-site for the Kerma culture (c.2500–1500 BC), probably to be identified with the Egyptians' 'land of Yam'. The site of Kerma incorporates a large settlement of the Second Intermediate Period (1650–1550 BC), a cemetery of late Kerma-culture tumulus-graves (including the tombs of rulers). These élite burials also incorporated large numbers of sacrificed retainers.

The site is dominated by two enigmatic mud-brick structures, known as the *deffufa*, dating to the seventeenth century BC. The L-shaped western *deffufa*, almost certainly a temple, is in the centre of the town, while the east-

Handmade 'Kerma ware' beaker from Tumulus K at Kerma. Classic Kerma phase, c.1750–1550 BC, H. 11.6 cm. (EA55424)

ern *deffufa*, a type of funerary chapel, is part of the cemetery at the southern end of the site. Each of the *deffufas* was originally an almost solid block of mud bricks covering an area of roughly 1500 sq. m.

G. REISNER, *Excavations at Kerma* I–IV, 2 vols (Cambridge, MA, 1923).

B. GRATIEN, *Les cultures Kerma: essai de classification* (Lille, 1978).

C. BONNET, 'La deffufa occidentale à Kerma: essai d'interprétation', *BIFAO* 81 Supp. (1981), 205–12.

—, 'Excavations at the Nubian royal town of Kerma: 1975–91', *Antiquity* 66 (1992), 611–25

Khafra (Chephren, Rakhaef; 2558–2532 BC) Son of KHUFU (2589–2566 BC), fourth ruler of the 4th Dynasty and builder of the second pyramid at GIZA. He succeeded to the throne after the death of his half-brother Djedefra (2566 2558 BC), who had constructed his pyramid at ABU ROASH rather than Giza (leading to suggestions from some scholars that there was a temporary religious schism between the younger and elder branches of Khufu's successors). Khafra's ROYAL TITULARY included the new *sa Ra* ('son of Ra') epithet, which Djedefra had used for the first time.

His pyramid complex at Giza was similar to that of Khufu, although slightly smaller and currently better preserved. It is usually assumed that the head of the Great Sphinx was carved into the appearance of Khafra, since it is situated immediately next to his causeway and valley temple. There have been suggestions that the geological condition of the sphinx indicates that it was carved at a somewhat earlier date, but the archaeological and circumstantial evidence appear to support

its synchronicity with the 4th-Dynasty pyramid complexes.

Khafra's granite-lined valley temple, excavated by Auguste Mariette in 1860, was found to contain several royal statues, including a magnificent monolithic seated statue of the king with a Horus falcon embracing the back of his head, which is one of the masterpieces of Old Kingdom sculpture (now in the Egyptian Museum, Cairo). The diorite-gneiss from which the statue was carved was obtained by an expedition sent to the so-called 'Chephren quarries' in Lower Nubia, some 240 km south-west of modern Aswan. The head of a pink granite statue of a similar type, representing Khafra, has also been discovered more recently.

M. SALEH and H. SOUROUZIAN, *The Egyptian Museum, Cairo: official catalogue* (Mainz, 1987), cat. no. 31.

Diorite-gneiss seated statue of Khafra from his pyramid complex at Giza. 4th Dynasty, c.2500 BC, H. 1.68 m. (CAIRO JE10062)

C. VANDERSLEYEN, 'Une tête de Chéfren en granite rose', *JdE* 38 (1907), 94–7.

N. GRIMAL, *A history of ancient Egypt* (Oxford, 1992), 72–4.

I. E. S. EDWARDS, *The pyramids of Egypt*, 5th ed. (Harmondsworth, 1993), 121–37.

Kharga Oasis

The southernmost and, at around 100 sq. km, the largest of the major Egyptian western oases, which is located in the Libyan Desert about 175 km east of Luxor. There are traces of Middle Palaeolithic (Mousterian) occupa-

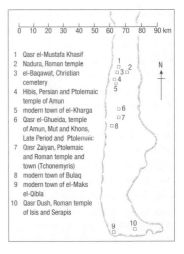

1 Qasr el-Mustafa Khashif
2 Nadura, Roman temple
3 el-Baqawat, Christian cemetery
4 Hibis, Persian and Ptolemaic temple of Amun
5 modern town of el-Kharga
6 Qasr el-Ghueida, temple of Amun, Mut and Khons, Late Period and Ptolemaic
7 Qasr Zaiyan, Ptolemaic and Roman temple and town (Tchonemyris)
8 modern town of Bulaq
9 modern town of el-Maks el-Qibla
10 Qasr Dush, Roman temple of Isis and Serapis

Plan of Kharga Oasis.

tion at Kharga and its material culture was clearly closely connected with that of the Nile valley throughout the Pharaonic period.

However, most of the surviving architectural remains (including settlements, stone temples and cemeteries) date from the Ptolemaic period to Coptic times (c.332 BC–AD 500).

G. CATON-THOMPSON, *Kharga Oasis in prehistory* (London, 1952).

L. GIDDY, *Egyptian oases: Bahariya, Dakhla, Farafra and Kharga during pharaonic times* (Warminster, 1987).

Khasekhemwy (Khasekhem) (c.2686 BC) Late 2nd-Dynasty ruler, whose reign is particularly important because he was the last Abydene ruler (see ABYDOS). The reign of DJOSER (perhaps his son) was marked by the transfer of power to MEMPHIS, the introduction of large-scale stone masonry and the official transfer to a new royal cemetery at SAQQARA.

One of Khasekhemwy's wives, Nimaathep, was later worshipped as the ancestress of the 3rd Dynasty (2686–2613 BC).

The name Khasekhemwy was usually written inside a SEREKH frame surmounted by depictions of a SETH animal alongside the usual HORUS falcon. Since the *serekh* of his predecessor PERIBSEN was surmounted by a Seth animal alone, it has been suggested that Khasekhemwy's reign represented a return to religious (and perhaps also political) normality, after a period of turmoil under his predecessor. This, however, is probably an excessively historical explanation for what may essentially have been an iconographic phenomenon. The debate about the political events at the end of the 2nd Dynasty hinges partly on the question of whether the myth of the struggle of Horus and Seth had any historical antecedents. The picture was once believed to be further complicated by the existence of the name Khasekhem, which was thought to refer to another ruler reigning between Peribsen and Khasekhemwy. However, the name is now generally considered to be an alternative spelling for Khasekhemwy.

The principal surviving monuments from Khasekhemwy's reign are Tomb v in the Early Dynastic cemetery at Umm el-Qa'ab and the Shunet el-Zebib, both of which are at ABYDOS, as well as the so-called 'fort' of Khasekhemwy at HIERAKONPOLIS. Two statues of the king, as well as an inscribed granite door jamb (bearing his name and a depiction of the temple foundation ceremony), decorated stone vessels (both bearing depictions of the goddess NEKHBET) and a fragment of a stele, were all excavated from the Early Dynastic temple at Hierakonpolis. The depictions of slain enemies on the two statues have been interpreted as evidence of military activities during his reign.

His tomb, nearly 70 m in length, is not only the last royal tomb in cemetery B at Umm el-Qa'ab but also the largest and most unusual. The substructure consists of a central corridor, flanked by thirty-three store-rooms for funerary offerings, leading to a stone-lined burial chamber which is then followed by a continuation of the corridor flanked by ten further magazines.

The Shunet el-Zebib, a huge double-walled mud-brick enclosure located at the desert edge, is the best surviving example of a group of 'funerary enclosures', probably the forerunners of the valley temples in pyramid complexes, each of which was erected by one of the rulers buried in cemetery B. The Hierakonpolis 'fort', a large mud-brick enclosure also located close to the floodplain, is now generally considered to have been a mortuary monument comparable with the Shunet el-Zebib, although the poor standard of Emile Amélineau's excavation in 1897–9 and 1905 has hindered any more definite statement regarding its function.

P. E. NEWBERRY, 'The Set rebellion of the second dynasty', *Ancient Egypt* (1922), 40–6.

R. ENGELBACH, 'A foundation scene of the second dynasty', *JEA* 20 (1934), 183–4.

M. HOFFMAN, *Egypt before the pharaohs* (London, 1980), 348–54.

kheker frieze

Decorative motif commonly employed in ancient Egyptian architecture from at least as early as the 3rd Dynasty (2686–2613 BC). The earliest shrines and temples were constructed from reeds tied into bundles or matting, and sometimes the tops of these were elaborately knotted. As techniques of stone architecture developed, these rows of knots were translated into decorative carved or painted friezes around the upper edges of buildings, thus constantly alluding to the idea of the first shrines built on the PRIMEVAL MOUND as it arose from the waters of NUN.

Khenty-khety *see* TELL ATRIB

Khepri

Creator-god principally manifested in the form of the SCARAB or dung beetle, although he was sometimes depicted in tomb paintings and funerary papyri as a man with a scarab as a head or as a scarab in a boat held aloft by NUN. In the tomb of PETOSIRIS at Tuna el-Gebel (*c*.300 BC), he is depicted wearing the *atef* CROWN of the god Osiris.

Because the Egyptians observed that scarab beetles emerged, apparently spontaneously, from balls of dung, it was perhaps not surprising that they came to believe that the scarab was associated with the process of CREATION itself. Khepri is attested from at least as early as the 5th Dynasty (2494–2345 BC), when one of the spells in the PYRAMID TEXTS invoked the sun to appear in his name of Khepri (the literal meaning of which was 'he who is coming into being'). Because he was self-created, he was identified with the creator-god ATUM, and because the movement of the sun from east to west was believed to be the result of being physically pushed like a dung-ball, he was also identified with the sun-god RA. As a deity closely associated with resurrection, Khepri was also believed to be swallowed by his mother NUT each evening, and passed through her body to be reborn each morning. He appears in this guise in Chapter 83 of the BOOK OF THE DEAD: 'I have flown up like the primeval ones, I have become Khepri…'

From the Middle Kingdom (2055–1650 BC) onwards, the scarab form of amulet was being produced in very large quantities. On a more monumental scale, it is considered likely that each temple originally incorporated a colossal

Granite colossal statue of a scarab beetle, probably representing the god Khepri, the form taken by the sun-god at the time of his birth in the morning. It was found in Constantinople, where it had probably been taken in Roman times. Date and provenance unknown, H. 89 cm. (EA74)

stone scarab on a plinth, representing the temple as the PRIMEVAL MOUND from which the sun-god emerged to begin the process of cosmogony. Such a scarab is still preserved *in situ* beside the sacred lake in the temple of Amun at KARNAK.

J. ASSMANN, 'Chepre', *Lexikon der Ägyptologie* I, ed. W. Helck, E. Otto and W. Westendorf (Wiesbaden, 1975), 934–40.

Khnum

Ram-god whose principal cult centre was on the island of Elephantine at ASWAN, where he was worshipped, probably from the Early Dynastic period (3100–2686 BC) onwards, as part of a triad with the goddesses SATET and ANUKET. In his earliest form he appears to have

principal creator-gods (see CREATION). This creative role stemmed inevitably from the combination of the creative symbolism of moulding pottery, the traditional potency of the ram and the fact that the Egyptian word for ram, BA, also had the meaning of 'spiritual essence' (although the latter was usually written with the stork hieroglyph). Perhaps partly because of this punning connection with the concept of the *ba*, Khnum was regarded as the quintessential *ba* of the sun-god RA, who was therefore depicted with a ram's head as he passed through the netherworld in the solar bark.

The best-preserved temple of Khnum is the Greco-Roman construction at ESNA, where his consort was Menhyt, a relatively unknown

to Khnum at a time of famine caused by low inundations.

A. M. BADAWI, *Der Gott Chnum* (Glückstadt, 1937).

L. HABACHI, 'Was Anukis considered as the wife of Khnum or as his daughter?', *ASAE* 50 (1950), 501–7.

P. BARGUET, *La stèle de la famine à Séhel* (Cairo, 1953).

P. BEHRENS, 'Widder', *Lexikon der Ägyptologie* VI, ed. W. Helck, E. Otto and W. Westendorf (Wiesbaden, 1986), 1243–5.

Khons

Moon-god, whose name means 'wanderer', typically represented as a mummiform human figure (occasionally hawk-headed) holding

Votive stele, the upper register of which depicts a seated figure of the god Khons receiving a libation and offerings. 18th Dynasty, c.1550–1295 BC, limestone, H. 38.1 cm. (EA1297)

been portrayed as the first type of ram domesticated in Egypt (*Ovis longipes*), which had corkscrew horns extending horizontally outwards from the head, as opposed to the later species (*Ovis platyra*), which had horns curving inwards towards the face and was more often associated with the god AMUN.

Khnum's strong association with both the Nile INUNDATION and the fertile soil itself contributed to his role as a potter-god and therefore also to his cosmogonic role as one of the

Fragment of sandstone wall-relief decorated with a representation of the god Khnum as a ram-headed man. 18th Dynasty, c. 1300 BC, H. 45 cm. (EA63544)

lioness-goddess, although the goddess NEITH also features prominently in the reliefs. The texts on the walls of the Esna temple celebrate his creation of the entire universe including gods, humans, animals and plants. The so-called FAMINE Stele at Sehel describes appeals

sceptre and flail and wearing the SIDELOCK OF YOUTH with a headdress consisting of a horizontal crescent moon surmounted by a full moon. Like THOTH (another lunar deity), he was also portrayed as a CYNOCEPHALUS baboon. He appears to have originally been associated with childbirth, and in the Theban region he was considered to be the son of AMUN and MUT. In the 20th Dynasty (1186–1069 BC) a temple of Khons was built within the precincts of the temple of Amun at KARNAK. At KOM OMBO, however, he was regarded as the son of the deities SOBEK and HATHOR.

One manifestation of Khons, known as 'the provider', was credited with the ability to drive out evil spirits. The Bentresh Stele (now in the Louvre) is an inscription composed in the fourth century BC but purporting to date to the reign of Rameses II (1279–1213 BC). It claims that the pharaoh sent a statue of Khons to a Syrian ruler in order to facilitate the cure of an ailing foreign princess called Bentresh.

P. DERCHAIN, 'Mythes et dieux lunaires en Egypte', *Sources orientales 5: La lune, mythes et rites* (Paris, 1962), 19–68.

G. POSENER, 'Une réinterprétation tardive du nom du dieu Khonsou', *ZÄS* 93 (1966), 115–19.

H. BRUNNER, 'Chons', *Lexikon der Ägyptologie* I, ed. W. Helck, E. Otto and W. Westendorf (Wiesbaden, 1975), 960–3.

Khufu (Cheops) (2589–2566 BC)

Second ruler of the 4th Dynasty, whose name is an abbreviation of the phrase *Khnum-kuefui* ('KHNUM protects me'). He was the son of SNEFERU (2613–2589 BC) and the builder of the Great Pyramid at GIZA. His own burial chamber was found to contain only an empty sarcophagus, but part of the funerary equipment of his mother, HETEPHERES I, survived in a MASTABA tomb near his pyramid. Despite the fame of his funerary complex, the only surviv-

Ivory statuette of Khufu, whose Horus name is inscribed on the right side of the throne; his cartouche, inscribed on the other side, is partly broken. This is the only surviving representation of the builder of the Great Pyramid at Giza. 4th Dynasty, c.2570 BC, from Abydos, H. 7.5 cm (CAIRO JE36143)

ing complete representation of Khufu himself is a small ivory statuette of a ruler wearing the red crown of Lower Egypt and seated on a throne carved with Khufu's Horus-name, which was excavated from the temple of Khentimentiu at ABYDOS by Flinders Petrie, and is now in the Egyptian Museum, Cairo. Several rock-carved texts at remote quarrying sites such as HATNUB and Wadi Maghara suggest that his reign, not unexpectedly, was marked by considerable quarrying and mining activity.

In later tradition he was reputed to have been a tyrannical ruler, although these traditions cannot be substantiated by contemporary evidence and perhaps relate simply to the imposing scale of his pyramid.

W. M. F. PETRIE, *Abydos* II (London, 1903), 30, pls 13–14.

Z. HAWASS, 'The Khufu statuette: is it an Old Kingdom sculpture?', *Mélanges Gamal Moukhtar* I (Cairo, 1985), 379–94.

I. E. S. EDWARDS, *The pyramids of Egypt*, 5th ed. (Harmondsworth, 1993), 98–121.

Khyan (Seuserenra, c.1600 BC)

A 15th-Dynasty HYKSOS ruler of Lower Egypt, whose 'throne name' was Seuserenra. Unlike the other Hyksos pharaohs, who commissioned very few architectural or sculptural monuments, Khyan was responsible for the decoration of religious structures at GEBELEIN (along with his successor Aauserra APEPI) and Bubastis (TELL BASTA). The international influence of Khyan is perhaps indicated by the discovery of a number of objects bearing his name at sites outside Egypt, including scarabs and seal impressions in the Levant, a travertine vase lid at Knossos, part of an obsidian vessel at the Hittite capital of Hattusas (Boghazköy). Although the two latter items were presumably prestige gifts or trade goods, it is possible that the seals indicate a degree of Hyksos control over southern Palestine. The granite lion bearing Khyan's name that was found built into a house wall at Baghdad and is now in the collection of the British Museum is usually assumed to have been removed from Egypt some time after the Hyksos period.

R. GIVEON, 'A sealing of Khyan from the Shephela of southern Palestine', *JEA* 51 (1965), 202–4.

W. C. HAYES, 'Egypt from the death of Ammenemes III to Seqenenre II', *Cambridge Ancient History* II/1, ed. I. E. S. Edwards et al., 3rd ed. (Cambridge, 1973), 42–76.

king lists

Term used by Egyptologists to refer to surviv-

ing lists of the names and titles of rulers of Egypt, some of which also incorporate information concerning the length and principal events of individual reigns. Virtually all of the surviving examples derive from religious or funerary contexts and usually relate to the celebration of the cult of royal ancestors, whereby each king established his own legitimacy and place in the succession by making regular offerings to a list of the names of his predecessors. The lists are often surprisingly accurate, although they are also noticeably selective, regularly omitting certain rulers, such as AKHENATEN (1352–1336 BC), who were considered to have been in any way illegitimate or inappropriate.

Several such lists exist, although only that in the temple of Sety I (1294–1279 BC) at ABYDOS, listing seventy-six kings from MENES to Sety himself, remains in its original context. A second list, from the nearby temple of Rameses II (1279–1213 BC), is now in the British Museum, and an earlier example from the temple of Amun at KARNAK, listing sixty-two kings from Menes to Thutmose III (1479–1425 BC), is now in the Louvre.

The Saqqara Tablet, an example of a private funerary cult of the royal ancestors, was found in the tomb of a scribe called Tenroy; it lists fifty-seven rulers from the 1st Dynasty until the reign of Rameses II. Another private example of a king list was found in the tomb of Amenmessu at Thebes (TT373; c.1300 BC), where the deceased is shown worshipping the statues of thirteen pharaohs.

The hieratic papyrus known as the TURIN ROYAL CANON, compiled in the 19th Dynasty, and the basalt stele known as the PALERMO STONE, dating from the end of the 5th Dynasty, are valuable records, although both are incomplete, much of the Turin Canon having been lost in modern times. There are also a few much briefer king lists, such as a graffito at the mining and quarrying site of Wadi Hammamat, dated palaeographically to the 12th Dynasty (1985–1795 BC), which consists of the names of five 4th-Dynasty rulers and princes.

The historian MANETHO must have used such king lists, presumably in the form of papyrus copies in temple LIBRARIES, when he was compiling his account of the history of Egypt, which is known only from the sometimes contradictory fragments preserved in the works of other ancient authors.

W. B. EMERY, *Archaic Egypt* (Harmondsworth, 1961), 21–4.

D. B. REDFORD, *Pharaonic king-lists, annals and day-books: a contribution to the study of the Egyptian sense of history* (Mississauga, 1986).

B. J. KEMP, *Ancient Egypt: anatomy of a civilization* (London, 1989), 21–3.

kingship

The concept of kingship and the divinity of the pharaoh were central to Egyptian society and religion. At the very beginning of Egyptian history, the evidence from such sites as ABYDOS, NAQADA and SAQQARA suggests that the basic nature of Egyptian ADMINISTRATION and the strong association between the king and the falcon-god HORUS had already become well established. A great deal of the ideology surrounding Egyptian kingship can be deduced to some extent from the development of the ROYAL TITULARY, which fulfilled a number of roles, including the establishment of the relationships between the king and the gods, and the explanation of how each reign related to the kingship as a whole.

The title *nesw-bit* (literally 'he of the sedge and the bee') is usually translated as 'King of Upper and Lower Egypt' but its true meaning is quite different, and considerably more complex, in that *nesw* appears to mean the unchanging divine king (almost the kingship itself), while *bit* seems to be a more ephemeral reference to the individual holder of the kingship. Each king was therefore a combination of the divine and the mortal, the *nesw* and the *bit*, in the same way that the living king was linked with Horus and the dead kings, the royal ancestors (see KING LISTS), were associated with OSIRIS.

Ideally the kingship passed from father to son, and each king was usually keen to demonstrate his filial links with the previous ruler. On a practical level, the ruler could demonstrate the continuity of the kingship by ensuring that his predecessor's mortuary temple and tomb were completed, and on a more political level he would do his best to demonstrate that he was the chosen heir whose right to rule was ensured by his own divinity. Sometimes the attempts of certain rulers to demonstrate their unquestioned right to the kingship have been misinterpreted as 'propagandist' efforts to distort the truth by means of the various reliefs and inscriptions depicting such events as their divine birth and the bestowal of the kingship by the gods.

Although there may have been a certain amount of political (rather than religious) impetus behind the works of such unusual rulers as Queen HATSHEPSUT (1473–1458 BC), most of the surviving references to the kingship belong much more within the overall role of the king in imposing order and preventing chaos. The function of the king as the representative of the gods was to preserve and

Detail of a section of wall-relief in the temple of Hathor at Dendera, showing the writing of the word 'pharaoh' (per-aa) in a cartouche. The inscriptions in temples of the Ptolemaic and Roman periods often include cartouches inscribed with this generic term for the king, rather than with a specific ruler's name. (I. SHAW)

restore the original harmony of the universe, therefore a great deal of the iconography in Egyptian temples, tombs and palaces was concerned much more with this overall aim than with the individual circumstances of the ruler at any particular point in time. Just as it was essential to stress the king's divine birth, so the celebration and depiction of each SED FESTIVAL (royal jubilee) was intended to ensure that the king was still capable of performing his ritual role.

The term *per-aa* ('great house') – which was eventually transformed, via Greek, into the word *pharaoh* – was initially used to describe the royal court or indeed the state itself, in the sense that the 'great house' was the overarching entity responsible for the TAXATION of the lesser 'houses' (*perw*), such as the temple lands and private estates. By extension, from the late 18th Dynasty onwards, the term began to be used to refer to the king himself.

H. FRANKFORT, *Kingship and the gods* (Chicago, 1948).

H. W. FAIRMAN, 'The kingship rituals of Egypt', *Myth, ritual and kingship*, ed. S. H. Hooker (Oxford, 1958), 74–104.

G. POSENER, *De la divinité du pharaon* (Paris, 1960).

B. G. TRIGGER et al., *Ancient Egypt: a social history* (Cambridge, 1983), 52–61, 71–6, 204–25, 288–99.

N. GRIMAL, *Les termes de la propagande royal égyptienne de la xixe dynastie à la conquête d'Alexandre* (Paris, 1986).

M. A. BONHÉME and A. FOGEAU, *Pharaon, les secrets du pouvoir* (Paris, 1988).

J. D. RAY, 'The pharaohs and their court', *Egypt: ancient culture, modern land*, ed. J. Malek (Sydney, 1993), 68–77.

kiosk

Type of small openwork temple with supporting pillars, the best known examples being that of Senusret I (1965–1920 BC) at KARNAK, and that of Trajan (AD 98–117) at PHILAE. The term is sometimes also employed to refer to a small sun-shade or pavilion for the use of a king or official.

kohl *see* COSMETICS

kom

Term which has entered Arabic from the Coptic word *xwμ* ('village') and is generally used to refer to the mounds made up of the ruins of ancient settlements. Its meaning is therefore similar to the Arabic word *tell*, although the latter is more commonly applied to the higher settlement mounds of the Levant and Mesopotamia.

Kom Abu Billo (Terenuthis)

Site of a Pharaonic and Greco-Roman town situated in the western Delta, which derives its Greek name from that of the snake-goddess RENENUTET, whose cult was celebrated in the area. The early Ptolemaic temple remains, excavated by F. Ll. Griffith in 1887–8, were dedicated to the goddess HATHOR in her manifestation of 'mistress of turquoise', and there are nearby burials of sacred cows presumably relating to the cult of Hathor. The importance of this temple rests primarily on the fact that it is one of the few monuments constructed during the reign of the first PTOLEMY (Ptolemy I Soter; 305–285 BC). During the Roman period the economic importance of Terenuthis rested on the role it played in the procurement and trading of NATRON and salt, owing to the proximity of the road leading to Wadi Natrun.

The nearby cemetery spans a much broader period, ranging from the Old Kingdom to the late Roman period. Some of the New Kingdom graves contained 'slipper-coffins' made of pottery and decorated with ugly facial features, while many of the Roman-period tombs were marked by unusual stelae consisting of relief representations of the deceased either standing or lying on a couch and accompanied by an inscription in DEMOTIC or Greek.

A. HERMANN, 'Die Deltastadt Terenuthis und ihre Göttin', *MDAIK* 5 (1934), 169–72.

B. PORTER and R. L. B. MOSS, *Topographical bibliography* IV, 1st ed. (Oxford, 1934), 67–9.

J. G. GRIFFITHS, 'Terenuthis', *Lexikon der Ägyptologie* VI, ed. W. Helck, E. Otto and W. Westendorf (Wiesbaden, 1986), 424.

Detail of a section of wall-relief in the temple of
Horus and Sobek at Kom Ombo, showing Ptolemy
IV Philopator making offerings to the crocodile-god
Sobek. Ptolemaic period, c.221–205 BC (I. SHAW)

Plan of the double temple of Horus and Sobek at
Kom Ombo.

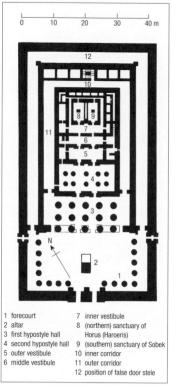

1	forecourt	7	inner vestibule
2	altar	8	(northern) sanctuary of
3	first hypostyle hall		Horus (Haroeris)
4	second hypostyle hall	9	(southern) sanctuary of Sobek
5	outer vestibule	10	inner corridor
6	middle vestibule	11	outer corridor
		12	position of false door stele

Kom el-Ahmar see HIERAKONPOLIS

Kom el-Hisn (anc. Imu)

Site of the town of Imu, located in the western Delta, about 12 km south of NAUKRATIS. When it was first surveyed by F. Ll. Griffith, in 1885, a large proportion of the mound was still in existence, but it is now much reduced by the work of *sebakhin* (farmers quarrying ancient mud-brick for use as fertilizer). The principal mound is dominated by the ruins of a temple dedicated to the local goddess, SEKHMET-HATHOR, which was established by SENUSRET I (1965–1920 BC) in the early 12th Dynasty.

When the large rectangular temple enclosure was excavated in 1943–6 by the Egyptian archaeologists A. Hamada and M. el-Amir, it was found to contain various items of Middle and New Kingdom sculpture, including statues of Amenemhat III (1855–1808 BC) and Rameses II (1279–1213 BC).

In the New Kingdom (1550–1069 BC), the town of Imu replaced the earlier (still undiscovered) town of Hwt-ihyt as the capital of the third Lower Egyptian nome. The nearby cemetery contains hundreds of graves, most of which date from the First Intermediate Period (2181–2055 BC) to the New Kingdom.

According to the brief report describing a Canadian survey of the site in 1980, the most impressive surviving architectural feature at Kom el-Hisn is the painted, stone-built Middle Kingdom tomb of Khesuwer, 'overseer of prophets'.

E. A. GARDNER, *Naukratis* II (London, 1888), 77–80.

G. DARESSY, 'Rapport sur Kom el-Hisn', *ASAE* 4 (1903), 281–3.

B. PORTER and R. L. B. MOSS, *Topographical bibliography* IV, 1st ed. (Oxford, 1934), 51–2.

A. HAMADA and S. FARID, 'Excavations at Kom el-Hisn, season 1945', *ASAE* 46 (1947), 195–205.

—, 'Excavations at Kom el-Hisn, 1946', *ASAE* 48 (1948), 299–325.

P. BRODIE et al., 'Kom el-Hisn', *Cities of the Delta I: Naukratis* (Malibu, 1981), 81–5.

Kom Medinet Ghurob see GUROB

Kom Ombo (anc. Ombos)

Temple and associated settlement site located 40 km north of Aswan, with surviving structural remains dating from at least as early as the 18th Dynasty (1550–1295 BC), although there are also a number of Upper Palaeolithic sites scattered over the surrounding region.

The surviving temple buildings, first cleared of debris by Jacques de Morgan in 1893, were dedicated to the deities Sobek and Haroeris (see HORUS) and date mainly to the Ptolemaic and Roman periods (332 BC–AD 395), most of the relief decoration having been completed in the first century BC. The architectural plan of the temple is unusual in that it effectively combines two traditional cult temples into one, each side having its own individual succession of gateways and chapels.

J. DE MORGAN et al., *Kom Ombos*, 2 vols (Vienna, 1909).

Kom el-Shuqafa *see* ALEXANDRIA

Koptos (Qift, anc. Kebet)

Temple and town site located about 40 km north of Luxor, at the entrance to the Wadi Hammamat. This valley contained gold mines and breccia quarries and also served as the principal trade-route between the Nile valley and the Red Sea. The benefits of the town's location, on the east bank of the Nile, are considered to have been the primary reason for the foundation and subsequent prosperity of the Pharaonic settlement at Koptos. To the east of the main site there are cemeteries dating to the late Predynastic period (*c*.3300–3100 BC), when NAQADA, situated almost opposite Koptos on the west bank, was the dominant town in the region.

The surviving settlement remains at Koptos date back to the beginning of the historical period (*c*.3000 BC), including three colossal

B. J. KEMP, *Ancient Egypt: anatomy of a civilization* (London, 1989), 64–91.
C. TRAUNECKER and L. PANTALACCI, 'Le temple d'Isi à El Qal'a près de Coptos', *Akten München 1985* III, ed. S. Schoske (Hamburg, 1989), 201–10.

Kumma *see* SEMNA

Kurgus

Site in the fifth-cataract region of Nubia, where Thutmose I (1504–1492 BC) and Thutmose III (1479–1425 BC) both carved inscriptions on boulders marking the southern frontier of Egypt. The choice of this spot for the erection of the stelae, close to the southern end of the so-called Korosko Road, suggests that an important overland trade-route, passing through the gold-bearing region of the Wadis Allaqi and Gabgaba, was probably already being used in the early New Kingdom.

the royal tombs at el-Kurru were built in the style of miniature Egyptian pyramids, starting with that of PIY (747–716 BC), the founder of the 25th Dynasty. Undecorated rectangular funerary chapels were located immediately beside the east faces of each of the superstructures. The subterranean burial chambers could be entered down long flights of steps leading from shafts also situated to the east of each pyramid. Adjacent to the pyramidal tombs, which include those of SHABAQO (716–702 BC), Shabitqo (702–690 BC) and TANUTAMANI (664–656 BC), are twenty-four roughly contemporary horse burials. After the mid seventh century BC, el-Kurru was effectively abandoned and Nuri became the site of the new cemetery of the Napatan rulers.

D. DUNHAM, *The royal cemeteries of Kush*, I: *El-Kurru* (Boston, 1950).

Kush *see* KERMA; NUBIA and VICEROY OF KUSH

UC 14786

Limestone sunk relief depicting Senusret I engaged in a sed-festival ritual in the presence of the fertility-god Min. The king is shown running between boundary stones symbolizing the limits of his kingdom; in front of him are his throne name and Horus name. The line of vertical text below the names reads 'hastening by boat to Min, the great god who is in the midst of his city'. 12th Dynasty, c.1950 BC, H. 1.11 m. (PETRIE MUSEUM, 14786)

limestone statues of the local fertility-god MIN and various other items of 'preformal' sculpture, which were excavated by Flinders Petrie in an Early Dynastic context at the temple of Min. The visible remains of the temple date mainly from the New Kingdom onwards. The Greek and Roman monuments at Koptos, including a small temple of ISIS at the nearby site of el-Qal'a, have been studied by Claude Traunecker and Laure Pantalacci.

W. M. F PETRIE, *Koptos* (London, 1896).

A. J. REINACH, *Rapports sur les fouilles de Koptos* (Paris, 1910).

W. Y. ADAMS, *Nubia: corridor to Africa*, 2nd ed. (London and Princeton, 1984), fig. 33.

Kurru, el-

Royal necropolis of the Napatan period (*c*.1000–300 BC), situated in Upper Nubia on the Dongola reach of the Nile. The site was first used from *c*.1000 BC onwards for the tumulus-burials of the rulers of the kingdom of Kush, the political focus of which was NAPATA, which also includes the sites of Gebel Barkal, NURI and Sanam.

In the later Napatan period (*c*.750–653 BC),

L

Lahun, el-

Necropolis and town-site, located at the eastern edge of the FAYUM REGION, about 100 km southeast of Cairo. The principal monument is the pyramid complex of Senusret II (1880–1874 BC). The internal arrangement of the superstructure consisted of a knoll of rock, surmounted by a network of stone-built retaining walls stabilizing the mud-brick matrix of the building. One of the most unusual features of Senusret II's monument is the fact that, unlike most other pyramids, the entrance is from the south rather than the north, perhaps because he was more concerned with the security of the tomb than its alignment with the circumpolar stars. The burial chamber contains an exquisite red granite sarcophagus and a travertine offering table. In one of the four shaft-tombs on the south side of the pyramid, Flinders Petrie and Guy Brunton discovered the JEWELLERY of Sithathoriunet, including items bearing the

The pyramid of Senusret II at el-Lahun is constructed of mud-brick around a series of limestone walls, some of which can be seen at the base of the pyramid. The structure has lost its outer casing and so has weathered to a rounded profile. (P. T. NICHOLSON)

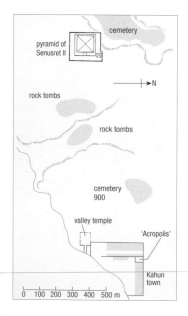

Plan of the pyramid complex of Senusret II at el-Lahun and the associated settlement.

cartouches of Senusret II and Amenemhat III (1855–1808 BC).

Beside Senusret II's Valley Temple are the remains of Kahun, a rectangular, planned settlement, measuring about 384 m × 335 m, which is thought to have originally housed the officials responsible for Senusret's royal mortuary cult but was later regarded as a town in its own right, having a *haty-* '(mayor). Small surviving areas of such settlements have been found at other sites in the immediate vicinity of Old and Middle Kingdom pyramids. A large number of HIERATIC papyri, dating to the late Middle Kingdom (*c*.1850–1650 BC) and ranging from religious documents to private correspondence, were discovered by Flinders Petrie in 1889–90 (now in the Petrie Museum, University College London). Further documents were later discovered as a result of illicit excavations; these papyri, the business letters of the temple scribe Horemsaf, are now in Berlin and have not yet been fully published.

W. M. F. PETRIE, *Kahun, Gurob and Hawara* (London, 1890).

—, *Illahun, Kahun and Gurob* (London, 1891).

F. LL. GRIFFITH, *Hieratic papyri from Kahun and Gurob* (London, 1898).

W. M. F. PETRIE, G. BRUNTON and M. A. MURRAY, *Lahun II* (London, 1923).

H. E. WINLOCK, *The treasure of El-Lahun* (New York, 1934).

B. GUNN, 'The name of the pyramid town of Sesostris II', *JEA* 31 (1945), 106–7.

U. LUFT, 'Illahunstudien', *Oikumene* 3 (1982), 101–56; 4 (1983), 121–79; 5 (1986), 117–53. [the papyri]

B. J. KEMP, *Ancient Egypt: anatomy of a civilization* (London, 1989), 149–57.

U. LUFT, *Das Archiv von Illahun (Hieratische Papyri)* (Berlin, 1992).

I. E. S. EDWARDS, *The pyramids of Egypt*, 5th ed. (Harmondsworth, 1993), 212–13.

language

Ancient Egyptian is probably the second oldest written language in the world, being preceded only by SUMERIAN in western Asia. It forms one of the five branches of a family of languages spoken in north Africa and the ancient Near East, known as Afro-Asiatic (or Hamito-Semitic). Because of various common elements of vocabulary and grammar, these five linguistic branches are thought to derive from an earlier 'proto-language'. Ancient Egyptian therefore includes certain words that are identical to those in such languages as Hebrew, Berber and Tuareg.

Egyptian is also the earliest written language in which verbs have different 'aspects' rather than tenses, which means that the emphasis is placed on whether an action has been completed or not, rather than whether it occurred in the past, present or future. A crucial distinction needs to be made between the stages in the development of the Egyptian language and the various phases of its written

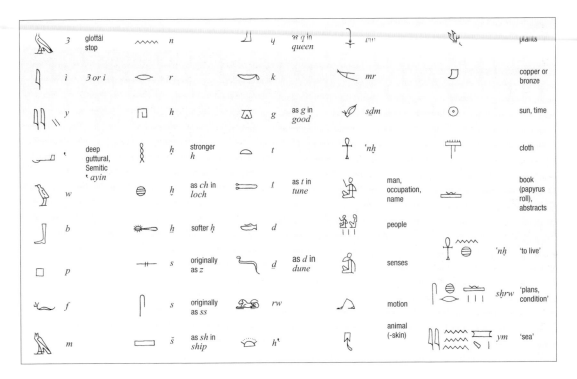

3	glottal stop	n		y	as g in queen			plants
i	3 or i	r		k		mr		copper or bronze
y		h		g	as g in good	sdm		sun, time
ʿ	deep guttural, Semitic ʿayin	ḫ	stronger h	t		ʿnḫ		cloth
w		ḫ	as ch in loch	t	as t in tune	man, occupation, name		book (papyrus roll), abstracts
b		ẖ	softer ḫ	d		people		
p		s	originally as z	d	as d in dune	senses		ʿnḫ 'to live'
f		s	originally as ss	rw		motion		sḫrw 'plans, condition'
m		š	as sh in ship	hʿ		animal (-skin)		ym 'sea'

Chart showing the different types of hieroglyphic characters.

form. The language has one distinct break, in the Middle Kingdom (2055–1650 BC), when 'synthetic' Old and Middle Egyptian, characterized by inflected verb endings, was replaced, in the spoken language at least, by the more complex 'analytical' form of Late Egyptian, with a verbal structure consisting of articulated elements. Egyptian is the only 'language of aspect' for which the change from the 'synthetic' stage to 'analytical' can actually be studied in its written form.

The written form of Egyptian, on the other hand, passed through several phases. In the first stage, the stone-carved HIEROGLYPHIC system was used for funerary and religious texts while the cursive HIERATIC script was used for administrative and literary texts. By the 25th to 26th Dynasties (747–525 BC) DEMOTIC emerged, and for a number of centuries the Greek and demotic scripts were used side by side.

The demotic and hieroglyphic writing systems began to be replaced in the third century AD by COPTIC, which consisted of the Greek alphabet combined with six demotic signs. This was actually a less suitable means of rendering the Egyptian language, but it was introduced for purely religious and cultural reasons: Egypt had become a Christian country and the hieroglyphic system and its derivatives were considered to be fundamentally 'pre-Christian' in their connotations. Nevertheless, the Egyptian language itself, despite being written in an adaptation of the Greek alphabet, has survived in a fossilized form in the liturgy of the Coptic church even after the emergence of Arabic as the spoken language of Egypt.

Since the pre-Coptic Egyptian writing systems consisted purely of consonants, Coptic texts (as well as occasional instances of Greek, Akkadian and Babylonian documents that transcribe Egyptian words and names into other scripts) have proved extremely useful in terms of working out the vocalization of the Egyptian language.

A. H. GARDINER, *Egyptian grammar, being an introduction to the study of hieroglyphs*, 3rd ed. (Oxford, 1957).

T. C. HODGE, *Afroasiatic: a survey* (The Hague, 1971).

J. and T. BYNON (eds), *Hamito-Semitica: proceedings of a colloquium held by the historical section of the Linguistics Association (Great Britain), March 1970* (The Hague, 1975).

C. C. WALTERS, *An elementary Coptic grammar of the Sahidic dialect*, 2nd ed. (Oxford, 1983).

lapis lazuli (Egyptian *khesbed*)

Metamorphosed form of limestone, rich in the blue mineral lazurite (a complex feldspathoid), which is dark blue in colour and often flecked with impurities of calcite, iron pyrites or gold. The Egyptians considered that its appearance imitated that of the heavens, therefore they considered it to be superior to all materials other than gold and silver. They used it extensively in JEWELLERY until the Late Period (747–332 BC), when it was particularly popular for amulets. It was frequently described as 'true' *khesbed*, to distinguish it from imitations made in FAIENCE or GLASS. Its primary use was as inlay in jewellery, although small vessels are also known, and it could also be used as inlay in the eyes of figurines.

Unlike most other stones used in Egyptian jewellery, it does not occur naturally in the deserts of Egypt but had to be imported

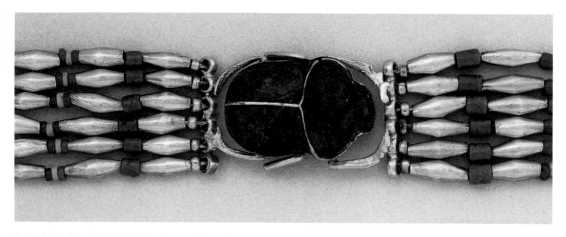

Detail of a bracelet consisting of a lapis lazuli scarab set in gold. The beads are of gold, cornelian and faience. L. of scarab 2.8 cm. (EA65616)

either directly from Badakhshan (in north-eastern Afghanistan) or indirectly, as tribute or trade goods from the Near East. Despite its exotic origin it was already in use as early as the Predynastic period, showing that far-reaching exchange networks between north Africa and western Asia must have already existed in the fourth millennium BC. It is represented in temple scenes at MEDINET HABU and at KARNAK.

A. LUCAS, *Ancient Egyptian materials and industries*, 4th ed. (London, 1962), 398–400.

G. HERRMANN, 'Lapis lazuli: the early phases of its trade', *Iraq* 30 (1968), 21–57.

J. C. PAYNE, 'Lapis lazuli in early Egypt', *Iraq* 30 (1968), 58–61.

E. PORADA, 'A lapis lazuli figurine from Hierakonpolis in Egypt', *Iranica Antiqua* 15 (1980), 175–80.

lapwing *see* REKHYT BIRD

Late Period (747–332 BC)

Phase of Egyptian history comprising the 25th to 31st Dynasties, stretching from the end of the THIRD INTERMEDIATE PERIOD (1069–747 BC) to the arrival of ALEXANDER THE GREAT (332 BC). The Third Intermediate Period was dominated by simultaneous dynasties of rulers in the Delta and the Theban region, but SHABAQO (716–702 BC), the second ruler of the Kushite 25th Dynasty, exerted Nubian influence over the north both by military conquest and by moving the administrative centre back from Thebes to Memphis.

Despite the fact that the 25th-Dynasty

kings ruled over a larger territory than in the preceding period, the state does not seem to have been truly unified during this period, with local princes apparently maintaining considerable independence. Nevertheless, the combined kingdom of Egypt and Nubia was a formidable one, rivalled only by the rising empire of the ASSYRIAN rulers. The Egyptian kings attempted to thwart the spread of Assyria into the Levant by joining forces with some of the Palestinian rulers. Not only did they fail to overthrow the Assyrians, but in 674 BC they were themselves threatened, when Esarhaddon (681–669 BC) mounted an invasion of Egypt. This attack failed, and although his second campaign, in 671 BC, was more successful, he was still unable to suppress all opposition. The Egyptian king TAHARQO (690–664 BC), who had fled to Nubia, was therefore able to reoccupy Memphis. However, the Assyrians attacked again, this time under Ashurbanipal (669–627 BC), who was aided by two local rulers from SAIS – NEKAU I (672–664 BC) and his son Psamtek – and was thus able finally to establish Assyrian rule over Egypt. Nekau I was left as governor, but was killed by the armies of TANUTAMANI (664–656 BC), the son and successor of Taharqo.

The constant breaking of Assyrian rule led to severe reprisals, and Ashurbanipal returned to Egypt at some point after 663 BC, laying waste to great areas of the country and forcing Tanutamani to flee back to Nubia. However, this by no means put paid to Egyptian independence: a rebellion in BABYLONIA caused Ashurbanipal to withdraw, and, with Tanutamani also gone, Nekau I's son, PSAMTEK I (664–610 BC), was able to appoint himself king

as the first full ruler of the 26th SAITE Dynasty (664–525 BC).

Psamtek was an astute ruler and sought to establish a sense of national identity while at the same time making use of foreign mercenaries, notably Greeks and Carians, to suppress those local rulers who might oppose him. From this time onwards Egypt was increasingly drawn into the Classical and Hellenistic sphere. Later in the dynasty, a trading colony of GREEKS was established; the Greek writer Herodotus credits this act to AHMOSE II (570–526 BC), although it is more probable that Ahmose simply reorganized one of a number of existing Greek settlements. Foreign policy in the 26th Dynasty had largely been concerned with attempting to preserve the balance of power, but by the time that Ahmose II's son, Psamtek III (526–525 BC), succeeded to the throne, PERSIA had become the dominant power.

In 525 BC Cambyses (525–522 BC) invaded Egypt, establishing the Persian 27th Dynasty (525–404 BC). He appears to have been an unpopular ruler, but his successor Darius I (522–486 BC) undertook major building works, including the completion of projects that had been initiated by Saite rulers. The Egyptians, however, presumably inspired by Greek victories over the Persians, embarked on a course of rebellion, supported by military aid from the Greeks.

In 404 BC Egyptian unrest reached a climax in the revolt by Amyrtaios of Sais which resulted in the expulsion of the Persians, first from the Delta, and within four years from the whole country. But Amyrtaios (404–399 BC) proved to be the only king of the 28th Dynasty: in 399 BC the throne was usurped by Nefaarud (Nepherites) I (399–393 BC), ruling from another Delta city, MENDES. He and his successors of the 29th Dynasty (399–380 BC) relied heavily upon foreign mercenaries for their military power, and in this way were able to stave off further Persian incursions. Finally they were themselves displaced by the 30th-Dynasty rulers, beginning with NECTANEBO I (380–362 BC).

This new line continued the 'nationalistic' air of the 25th and 26th Dynasties, particularly in terms of the renewal of building activity and increased devotion to traditional cults. The cults of SACRED ANIMALS were particularly important at this time, and it is possible that the various industries and priesthoods associated with the sacred animal necropoleis became an important part of the economy.

Persian attempts at re-conquest were thwarted until 343 BC when Nectanebo II (360–343 BC), the last native pharaoh, was defeated by Artaxerxes III Ochus (343–338 BC) who established the 31st Dynasty or Second Persian Period (343–332 BC). This short second phase of Persian domination was particularly unwelcome; therefore the conquering armies of Alexander the Great (332–323 BC) in 332 BC appear to have encountered little opposition. With the Macedonian conquest, Egypt became established as part of the Hellenistic and Mediterranean world, under the control of Alexander's successors the Ptolemies (see PTOLEMAIC PERIOD).

F. K. KIENITZ, *Die politische Geschichte Ägyptens vom 7. bis zum 4. Jahrhundert vor der Zeitwende* (Berlin, 1953).

E. R. RUSSMANN, *The representation of the king, XXVth Dynasty* (Brussels, 1974).

A. J. SPALINGER, 'Esarhaddon and Egypt: an analysis of the first invasion of Egypt', *Orientalia* 43 (1974), 295–326.

A. LLOYD, 'The Late Period, 664–323 BC', *Ancient Egypt: a social history*, ed. B. G. Trigger et al. (Cambridge, 1983), 279–348.

N. GRIMAL, *A history of ancient Egypt* (Oxford, 1992), 334–82.

J. H. JOHNSON (ed.), *Life in a multi-cultural society: Egypt from Cambyses to Constantine and beyond* (Chicago, 1992).

law

A Greek writer states that there was a Pharaonic legal code set out in eight books, but this is known only from the Late Period (747–332 BC); therefore the situation in earlier times is more difficult to assess. The law is a particularly difficult area of study because the translation of ancient terms into modern legal language tends to give them a misleading air of precision.

Egyptian law, like the codes of ETHICS, was essentially based on the concept of MAAT ('decorum' or 'correctness'), in other words the common-sense view of right and wrong as defined by the social norms of the day. Since the pharaoh was a living god, ruling by divine right, it was clearly he who was the supreme judge and law-giver (see KINGSHIP). However, as with his priestly duties, it was often found necessary to delegate his authority.

The principles of the Pharaonic legal system are thought to have been codified to some extent, but no such documents have survived. There are, however, a number of funerary texts outlining the duties of such high officials as the VIZIER, which can shed some indirect light on the legal practices. In theory, anyone with a grievance could take a case to the vizier, although actually gaining an audience would

Detail from the Salt Papyrus, which contains the petition of the workman Amennakhte denouncing the crimes of the foreman Paneb. Late 19th Dynasty, c.1200 BC, from Deir el-Medina. (EA10055)

no doubt often have been difficult. That some cases were clearly dealt with in this way is reflected in the popular Middle Kingdom (2055–1650 BC) narrative known as the *Tale of the Eloquent Peasant*.

Definitions of official roles probably existed for all important offices, thus allocating them places in the overall administrative hierarchy. The Egyptians do not appear to have differentiated between administrative and legal functions, so that any person in authority might, in certain circumstances, make legal judgements. However, the title 'overseer of the six great mansions' seems to have been held by the ancient equivalent of a 'magistrate' and the term 'mansions' probably referred to the main

law court in Thebes (although there must surely have been other such courts). It is thought that a gold MAAT pendant (now in the British Museum) may have been the official 'badge' held by legal officials. Some surviving statues of high officials from the Late Period are shown wearing such a chain and pendant. The cases that they examined would be reported to the pharaoh, who may have been responsible for deciding the punishment in the most serious cases.

Verdicts and punishments were probably based loosely on precedent with variations being introduced where appropriate. Since the records of cases were archived at the temple or vizierate offices, references to past cases were no doubt usually possible. It was thanks to this practice of automatically archiving such documents that the famous trial of tomb-robbers, recorded on the Leopold II–Amherst Papyrus, was preserved. Unfortunately, this papyrus does not record the sentences of the accused. It seems, however, that Egyptian law issued similar punishments to all those who had committed similar offences, irrespective of variations in wealth or status (except in the case of SLAVES). Judgements and decisions were evidently recorded by official scribes.

In cases where individuals were sentenced to exile, their children were automatically outlawed along with them. Similarly, families could suffer imprisonment if a relative deserted from military service, or defaulted on the corvée labour demanded by the state. Papyrus Brooklyn 35.1446, dating to the 13th Dynasty (c.1795–1650 BC), records the punishment duties imposed on labour defaulters.

Minor cases were tried by councils of elders, each town having its own local *kenbet* in charge of the judiciary. For example, a number of cases survive from the New Kingdom (1550–1069 BC), in the form of the records of the workmen at DEIR EL-MEDINA, mostly dealing with small matters such as non-repayment of loans. Individuals frequently kept their own notes of such cases on OSTRACA, presumably so that if repayments were not made in the agreed time they could remind those present at the judgement and receive redress.

Cases were sometimes judged by divine ORACLES rather than by human magistrates. It is known from Deir el-Medina, for instance, that the deified founder of the village, Amenhotep I (1525–1504 BC), was often asked to decide on particular cases. It is unclear how this divine judgement was actually given, but it seems that ostraca for and against the accusation would be put at each side of the street and the god's image would incline toward whichever verdict was deemed appropriate.

A national variant on this was the giving of the law through the oracle of Amun, which was practised during the 21st Dynasty (1069–945 BC).

In the Ptolemaic period (332–30 BC), Egyptian law existed alongside that of the Greeks, although only certain cases could be tried under it. Greeks were favoured by the law, and cases against them were generally heard in the state courts. The Romans introduced a system of law that was common throughout the empire, with only summary modifications.

J. WILSON, 'Authority and law in ancient Egypt', *Journal of the American Oriental Society Supplement* 17 (1954), 1–7.

S. P. VLEEMING, 'The days on which the *Knbt* used to gather', *Gleanings from Deir el-Medina*, ed. R. J. Demarée and J. J. Janseen (Leiden, 1982), 183–92.

J. SARRAF, *La notion du droit d'après les anciens égyptiens* (Vatican City, 1984).

I. HARARI, 'Les decrets royaux: source du droit', *DE* 8 (1987), 93–101.

J. TYLDESLEY, *The judgement of the pharaoh: crime and punishment in ancient Egypt* (London 2000).

Leontopolis *see* TELL EL-MUQDAM

Lepsius, Karl Richard (1810–84)

German Egyptologist who led the Prussian expedition to Egypt in 1842–5. He was born in Naumburg-am-Saale and educated at the universities of Leipzig, Göttingen and Berlin, completing a doctorate in 1833. It was after the completion of this dissertation that he began to study Egyptology in Paris, using Jean-François CHAMPOLLION's newly published grammar to learn the ancient Egyptian language. Like Champollion, he spent several years visiting European collections of Egyptian antiquities before making his first visit to Egypt in 1842. He took with him a team of Prussian scholars, including a skilled draughtsman, and his main aim was to record the major monuments and collect antiquities, in the same way as the earlier Napoleonic expedition (see EGYPTOLOGY). He also worked in Sudan and Palestine, sending some fifteen thousand antiquities and plaster casts back to Prussia in the course of his travels.

In 1849–59 he published the results of the expedition in the form of an immense twelve-volume work, *Denkmaeler aus Aegypten und Aethiopien*, which, like the Napoleonic *Description de l'Egypte*, still provides useful information for modern archaeologists (many of the sites and monuments having severely deteriorated since the mid nineteenth century). In 1865, Lepsius was appointed as

Keeper of the Egyptian collections in the Berlin Museum, and the following year he returned to Egypt with an expedition to record the monuments of the eastern Delta and Suez region, in the course of which he discovered the Canopus Decree at TANIS, a bilingual document that provided a useful linguistic comparison with the ROSETTA STONE.

His career continued with numerous further publications as well as the editing of the principal German Egyptological journal (*Zeitschrift für ägyptische Sprache und Altertumskunde*), and in 1869 he visited Egypt for the last time in order to witness the inauguration of the Suez Canal. He died in Berlin in 1884, having made one of the greatest individual contributions in the history of Egyptology.

K. R. LEPSIUS, *Denkmaeler aus Aegypten und Aethiopien*, 12 vols (Leipzig, 1849–59).

—, *Discoveries in Egypt* (London, 1852).

—, *Königsbuch der alten Aegypter*, 2 pts (Leipzig, 1858).

—, *Das bilingue Dekret von Kanopus in der Originalgrösse mit übersetzung beider Texte* (Leipzig, 1886).

G. EBERS, *Richard Lepsius*, Eng. trans. (New York, 1887).

letters

There are two ways in which Egyptian letters have been preserved in the archaeological record: sometimes the originals themselves have survived (in the form of papyri, ostraca and wooden boards), but in many other cases such commemorative documents as stelae, inscriptions or temple archives incorporate transcriptions of letters, whether real or imagined. The earliest known letters belong to the latter category, being hieroglyphic copies of letters sent by King Djedkara-Isesi (2414–2375 BC) to the officials Senedjemib and Shepsesra at ABUSIR. Only a few other letters have survived from the Old Kingdom (2686–2181 BC), such as Harkhuf's record of a letter sent to him by the young PEPY II (2278–2184 BC). Most of those from the Middle Kingdom (2055–1650 BC) are made up of an archive of eighty-six letters from Kahun (see EL-LAHUN) and a set of eleven items of correspondence between Hekanakhte and his family, although an important specialized form of letter from this period has survived in the form of the so-called 'SEMNA dispatches' (12th-Dynasty military communications between Thebes and the Nubian FORTRESSES).

Many items of private and royal correspondence from the New Kingdom have survived, including the simple hieratic notes on ostraca sent by the workmen at DEIR EL-MEDINA,

numerous late Ramesside private letters, and the royal diplomatic correspondence from el-Amarna (see AMARNA LETTERS), which was written in cuneiform on clay tablets. A large number of actual items of correspondence written on papyri have survived, such as the two letters written by an oil-boiler at el-Amarna. One of the most important texts used in scribal teaching during this period was the satirical *Letter of Hori* in which one official writes to a colleague, ridiculing his abilities and setting tests of his bureaucratic knowledge. This document would have educated scribes in the protocol of letter-writing.

G. MASPERO, *Du genre épistolaire chez les égyptiens de l'époque pharaonique* (Paris, 1872).

T. G. H. JAMES, *The Hekanakhte papers and other early Middle Kingdom documents* (New York, 1962).

E. WENTE, *Letters from ancient Egypt* (Atlanta, 1990).

J. JANSSEN, *Late Ramesside letters and communications (hieratic papyri in the British Museum)* (London, 1991).

R. B. PARKINSON, *Voices from ancient Egypt* (London, 1991), 89–95, 142–5.

letters to the dead

The Egyptians believed that the worlds of the living and the dead overlapped (see FUNERARY BELIEFS), so that it was possible for the dead to continue to take an interest in the affairs of their families and acquaintances, and perhaps even to wreak vengeance on the living. The relatives of the deceased therefore often sought to communicate with them by writing letters, invariably requesting help or asking for forgiveness. Fewer than twenty of these letters

A letter to the dead written on the interior (RIGHT) and exterior (LEFT) of the 'Cairo Bowl', a rough red pottery vessel which would probably have been filled with food offerings and placed in a tomb. The letter is from a woman called Dedi to her dead husband, informing him that their servant-girl is ill and appealing to him for help in warding off the illness. Early 12th Dynasty, c.1900 BC, D. 40 cm. (DRAWN BY R. PARKINSON)

have survived, but it has been pointed out that their extensive geographical distribution probably indicates a widespread sense of the need to communicate with the dead because of the magical powers that they were thought to have acquired in the afterlife. The letters date from the Old Kingdom to the New Kingdom (2686–1069 BC), but they appear to have been replaced in the Late Period (747–332 BC) by letters addressed directly to deities.

Some letters to the dead were simply written on papyrus but a number of shrewder individuals adopted the ploy of inscribing the texts on the bowls in which food was offered to the deceased in the tomb-chapel. One of the best-known such letters was sent from a Ramesside military officer to his dead wife, whom he addressed as 'the excellent spirit, Ankhiry', asking her why she had abandoned him and threatening to complain to the gods about the unhappiness that her untimely death had caused.

A. H. GARDINER and K. SETHE, *Egyptian letters to the dead* (London 1928).

W. K. SIMPSON, 'The letter to the dead from the tomb of Meru (N3737) at Nag' ed-Deir', *JEA* 52 (1966), 39–52.

—, 'A late Old Kingdom letter to the dead from Nag' ed-Deir N3500', *JEA* 56 (1970), 58–64.

M. GUILMOT, 'Lettre à une épouse défuncte (Pap. Leiden I, 371)', *ZÄS* 99 (1973), 94–103.

R. PARKINSON, *Voices from ancient Egypt* (London, 1991), 142–5.

libraries

The general question of the nature of ancient Egyptian libraries is overshadowed by the loss of the Great Library at ALEXANDRIA, which was burned to the ground in the late third century AD. The Alexandria library had probably been established by PTOLEMY I Soter (305–285 BC), who also founded the Museum ('shrine of the Muses'), initially creating both institutions as annexes to his palace. Later in the Ptolemaic period, another large library was created, probably within the Alexandria SERAPEUM, but this too was destroyed in AD 391. Although the papyri themselves have not survived, the legacy of the Alexandria libraries can be measured also in terms of the scholarship undertaken by such writers as Apollonius of Rhodes and Aristophanes of Byzantium, who both served as directors of the Great Library.

As far as the libraries of the Pharaonic period are concerned, there is certainly evidence that the Alexandrian institutions stood at the end of a long tradition of Egyptian archivism. The HOUSE OF LIFE (*per ankh*), where Egyptian SCRIBES generally worked and learned their trade, has been identified at such cities as

MEMPHIS and EL-AMARNA, but temple libraries and official archives have generally proved more difficult to locate. The term *per medjat* ('house of papyrus rolls') is used to describe the repositories of papyri associated with government buildings and temple complexes.

A number of temples, such as those at ESNA and PHILAE, have lists of texts written on certain walls, but the only definitely identified temple library is a niche-like room in the southern wall of the outer hypostyle hall of the Greco-Roman temple of Horus at EDFU (*c*.80 BC). An inscription over the entrance to this room describes it as the 'library of Horus', although it is possible that it simply contained the few rolls necessary for the daily rituals. The location (or indeed the very existence) of a library in the RAMESSEUM (*c*.1250 BC) at Thebes has proved a more contentious question, with most modern Egyptologists failing to identify any room that equates with the 'sacred library' mentioned by the Greek historian Diodorus (*c*.300 BC), although archives of the late New Kingdom administration were found in the immediate vicinity of the mortuary temple of Rameses III at MEDINET HABU (*c*.1170 BC). The existence of royal libraries is indicated by the survival of three faience 'bookplates' bearing the names of AMENHOTEP III, two of which are also inscribed with the names of the literary works written on the papyrus rolls to which they were attached.

A small temple library of the Roman period, excavated from a room in the Fayum city of Tebtunis, contained a number of literary and medical works along with the purely religious texts that had no doubt dominated most earlier temple libraries in the Pharaonic period. A list of the texts used by Egyptian priests was compiled by Clement, bishop of Alexandria in the late second century AD.

In 1896 James Quibell excavated shaft-tomb no. 5 under the Ramesseum, discovering a wooden chest containing a set of papyri belonging to a lector-priest of the 13th Dynasty (*c*.1795–1650 BC). This collection of texts – the most valuable single find of Middle Kingdom papyri – is often referred to as a 'library', but in this context the term refers more loosely to an assemblage of documents rather than an actual institution or building. Nevertheless, the texts provide a good idea of the wide variety of texts which might have been included in a Middle Kingdom library, including literary narratives, military dispatches from SEMNA fortress (see LETTERS), an ONOMASTICON, medical remedies, magical spells, a hymn to Sobek and fragments of a dramatic or ritualistic composition. The word 'library' is also used to describe the large col-

lection of papyri owned by a succession of scribes at DEIR EL-MEDINA, including the Chester Beatty papyri.

J. E. QUIBELL, *The Ramesseum* (London, 1898).

H. R. HALL, 'An Egyptian bookplate: the *ex-libris* of Amenophis III and Teie', *JEA* 12 (1926), 30–3.

V. WESSETZKY, 'Die ägyptische Tempelbibliothek', *ZÄS* 100 (1973), 54–9.

—, 'Die Bücherliste des Tempels von Edfu und Imhotep', *GM* 83 (1984), 85–90.

G. BURKARD, 'Bibliotheken in alten Ägypten', *Bibliothek: Forschung und Praxis* 4 (1980), 78–115.

J. D. BOURRIAU, *Pharaohs and mortals* (Cambridge, 1988), 79–80, 110.

L. CANFORA, *The vanished library*, trans. M. Ryle (London, 1989), 147–60.

Libyans (Tjehenu, Tjemehu, Meshwesh, Libu)

In the Old and Middle Kingdoms, the Western Desert, beyond Egypt's frontiers, was home to the Tjehenu, usually translated as 'Libyans'. They were regularly depicted by the Egyptians as bearded and light-skinned, but they were also occasionally shown as fair-haired and blue-eyed. They seem to have been semi-nomadic pastoralists, and they make occasional appearances in Egyptian art from early times, although they are often difficult to distinguish satisfactorily from the inhabitants of the western Delta of Egypt itself. It is thought likely, however, that the defeated enemy depicted on the late Predynastic Battlefield Palette (*c*.3100 BC) were Libyans.

King DJER (*c*.3000 BC) of the 1st Dynasty is said to have sent an expedition against the Libyans, and other campaigns are recorded under SNEFERU (2613–2589 BC) of the 4th Dynasty and Sahura (2487–2475 BC) of the 5th Dynasty. Sahura's mortuary temple contained reliefs showing the dispatching of a Libyan chief by the king, a scene repeated in the mortuary temple of Pepy II (2278–2184 BC) of the 6th Dynasty, and still current in later times.

Until the New Kingdom (1550–1069 BC), action against the Libyans was generally little more than punitive raiding. By the time of Sety I (1294–1279 BC), a people known as the Meshwesh and Libu had settled in the territory previously occupied by the Tjehenu and were attempting to settle in the Delta. They were held at bay by Sety and his son Rameses II (1279–1213 BC), but it was left to MERENPTAH (1213–1203 BC) to repulse them. He faced a force comprising not only Meshwesh and Libu but also Ekwesh, Shekelesh, Teresh, Sherden and various Aegean groups. This confederation became known as the SEA PEOPLES. They attacked Egypt in Merenptah's

Stele showing a Libu chief offering the hieroglyph for 'countryside' to the Egyptian deities Sekhmet and Heka, a donation dated in the hieratic text below to year 7 of Sheshonq V and specified as ten arouras (about seven acres). 22nd Dynasty, c.760 BC, limestone, H. 30.5 cm. (EA73965)

fifth regnal year, and although the initial response was slow the king eventually drove them back, supposedly killing six thousand and taking nine thousand prisoners. But the victory was not final and they returned under Rameses III (1184–1153 BC), only to be defeated in a bloody naval battle.

Ironically, many of the prisoners taken in such actions were forcibly settled in Egypt and gradually became a powerful group, at first serving the generals ruling Thebes in the 21st Dynasty (1069–945 BC), who were probably themselves of Libyan ancestry. Ultimately the Libyans came to power in their own right, as the 22nd and 23rd Dynasties (945–715 BC), ruling from Bubastis (TELL BASTA) and TANIS respectively (see OSORKON and SHESHONQ). This so-called 'Libyan period' was beset by rivalries between different claimants to the throne, and some scholars argue that the existence of contemporaneous lines of rulers was characteristic of Libyan society. The aggressive and anarchic spirit of these times is perhaps reflected in the demotic *Cycle of Pedubastis* (see LITERATURE). Despite this political uncertainty, particularly during the 23rd Dynasty, certain crafts such as bronze work flourished, although there seems to have been little monumental construction taking place. The reunification of Egypt under the Kushite 25th Dynasty and Saite 26th Dynasty put an end to the period of Libyan

anarchy, and the motif of the smiting of a Libyan chief reappeared in the temple of Taharqo (690–664 BC) at KAWA.

O. BATES, *The eastern Libyans* (London, 1914).
G. WAINWRIGHT, 'The Meshwesh', *JEA* 48 (1962), 89–99.
N. K. SANDARS, *The Sea Peoples: warriors of the eastern Mediterranean* (London, 1978), 114–19.
A. SPALINGER, 'Some notes on the Libyans of the Old Kingdom and later historical reflexes', *JSSEA* 9 (1979), 125–60.
M. A. LEAHY, 'The Libyan period in Egypt: an essay in interpretation', *Libyan Studies* 16 (1985), 51–65.
—, *Libya and Egypt, c.1300–750 BC* (London, 1990).

lion

By the Pharaonic period the number of lions in Egypt had declined compared with prehistoric times, when their symbolic and religious associations first became established. It is possible that the connection between the king and the lion stemmed from the hunting of these animals by the tribal chiefs of the Predynastic period. A Greek papyrus mentions lion burials at Saqqara in the SACRED ANIMAL necropolis, but these have not yet been located.

Since lions characteristically lived on the desert margins, they came to be considered as the guardians of the eastern and western horizons, the places of sunrise and sunset. In this connection they sometimes replaced the eastern and western mountains, symbolic of past and future, on either side of the HORIZON hieroglyph (*akhet*). Headrests sometimes took the form of this *akhet* hieroglyph, supported by two lions; on an example from

Tutankhamun's tomb they flank SHU, god of the air, who supports the head of the king, representing the sun. Since the sun itself could be represented as a lion, Chapter 62 of the BOOK OF THE DEAD states: 'May I be granted power over the waters like the limbs of Seth, for I am he who crosses the sky, I am the Lion of Ra, I am the Slayer who eats the foreleg, the leg of beef is extended to me...' The lion-god AKER guarded the gateway to the underworld through which the sun came and went each day. Since the sun was born each morning and died each evening on the horizons, so the lion was also connected with death and rebirth and was thus portrayed on funerary couches or biers, as well as embalming tables.

The beds and chairs of the living were sometimes also decorated with lions' paws or heads, perhaps in order that the occupant too would rise renewed after sleep or rest. The gargoyle rainspouts of temples were often made in the form of lions' heads because it was imagined that the lion stood on the temple roof absorbing the evil rainstorms of SETH and then spitting them out down the sides of the building.

The Delta site of Leontopolis (TELL EL-MUQDAM) in the Delta was sacred to the lion god Mihos (Greek Mysis), and Shu and TEFNUT were also venerated in leonine form at

Statue of a lion, probably sculpted in the reign of Amenhotep III but bearing a dedicatory text of Tutankhamun and an inscription of the Meroitic ruler Amanislo. 18th Dynasty, c.1350 BC, granite, from Gebel Barkal, originally from Soleb, H. 1.17 m. (EA2)

the site since they were sometimes regarded
as lion cubs created by ATUM. Most leonine
deities were female; the most important of
these was SEKHMET, whose cult was eventually
merged with those of BASTET and MUT. She
was regarded as one of the 'EYES OF RA', and in
one myth she was almost responsible for the
annihilation of mankind.

See also SPHINX.

U. SCHWEITZER, *Löwe und sphinx im alten Ägypten*
(Glückstadt, 1948).

C. DE WIT, *Le rôle et le sens du lion dans l'Egypte
ancienne* (Leiden, 1951).

U. RÖSSLER-KÖHLER, 'Löwe–Köpfe;
Löwe-Statuen', *Lexikon der Ägyptologie* III, ed.
W. Helck, E. Otto and W. Westendorf
(Wiesbaden, 1980), 1080–90.

R. H. WILKINSON, *Reading Egyptian art*
(London, 1992), 68–9.

Lisht, el-

Necropolis including the pyramid complexes
of the two earliest 12th-Dynasty rulers, AMEN-
EMHAT I and SENUSRET I (*c.*1985–1920 BC),
located on the west bank of the Nile, about 50
km south of Cairo. The establishment of a
royal necropolis at el-Lisht was a direct result
of the founding of a new royal residence,
Itjtawy, which appears to have temporarily
replaced MEMPHIS as the seat of government.
Itjtawy is often mentioned in texts of the period and probably lay a short distance to the east
of el-Lisht. The actual town-site has not yet
been located, because, like many Egyptian settlements, it has probably been covered by cultivated land.

The pyramid of Amenemhat I, at the northern end of the site, was originally about 58 m
high; its core included limestone blocks taken
from Old Kingdom buildings at SAQQARA. Its
mortuary temple was located on its east side. A
stone causeway leads down from the mortuary
temple towards the valley temple excavated by
the Antiquities Inspectorate. The complex of
Senusret I is similar in basic plan to that of his
father, comprising a limestone pyramid, originally 61 m high, surrounded by nine small
subsidiary pyramids. Just to the north of the
mortuary temple, ten seated life-size statues of
the king were found (now in the Egyptian
Museum, Cairo).

The pyramids are surrounded by the
remains of numerous MASTABA tombs of

*Statuette of a god or king (possibly Senusret I)
from the tomb of Imhotep in the south pyramid
cemetery at el-Lisht. 12th Dynasty, c.1950 BC,
gessoed and painted wood, H. 58 cm.*
(METROPOLITAN MUSEUM, NEW YORK 14.3.17)

courtiers, including that of Senusret-ankh,
chief priest of Ptah, located about 200 m to the
east of the outer enclosure wall of Senusret I.
Senusret-ankh's burial chamber contains
extracts from the PYRAMID TEXTS executed in
sunk hieroglyphs.

W. K. SIMPSON, 'The residence of It-towy',
JARCE 2 (1963), 53–64.

D. ARNOLD, *The south cemeteries of Lisht I: The
pyramid of Senwosret I* (New York, 1988).

—, *The south cemeteries of Lisht II: The control
notes and team marks* (New York, 1990).

—, *The south cemeteries of Lisht III: The pyramid
complex of Senwosret I* (New York, 1992).

literature

The term 'Egyptian literature' is often
employed to refer to the entire surviving corpus of texts from the Pharaonic period (usually excluding such practical documents as LET-
TERS or administrative texts), rather than
being used in its much more restricted sense to
describe overtly 'literary' output. However, the
individual documents can, like other
ancient texts, be variously grouped and cate-
gorized on the basis of such diverse criteria as
physical media (e.g. OSTRACA, PAPYRI or STE-
LAE), script (HIEROGLYPHICS, HIERATIC, DEMOT-
IC, Greek or COPTIC) and the precise date in the
history of the language. Although many texts
have been assigned to particular genres (such
as WISDOM LITERATURE or love poems), they are
usually best understood in terms of the specific historical and social context in which they
were written. Inscriptions listing the contents
of temple archives and LIBRARIES, as well as a
few surviving caches of papyri and ostraca
owned by individuals or institutions, provide a
good sense of the range of texts that were
deliberately collected and preserved during
the Pharaonic period, including technical
manuals such as medical and mathematical
documents.

Within particular periods of Egyptian history, there were many different genres of
texts. The Old Kingdom literary record was
dominated by religious FUNERARY TEXTS, particularly the PYRAMID TEXTS, used in royal
tombs, and the 'funerary autobiography',
used in private tombs to provide a poetic
description of the virtues of the deceased.
There is also some evidence of the composition of such technical texts as medical trea-
tises, although no actual documents have
survived. Although a form of verse was used
for many 'non-practical' writings, there was
no literature in the narrowest sense of the
term. As far as HISTORY AND HISTORIOGRAPHY is
concerned, a few fragments of annals have
survived (see KING LISTS).

The Middle Kingdom was particularly characterized by the introduction of such fictional literature as the *Tale of the Shipwrecked Sailor*, the *Tale of the Eloquent Peasant*, the *Tales of Wonder* (Papyrus Westcar) and the *Tale of Sinuhe*, all of which purport to be historical accounts, although many of the details of their plots indicate that they were fantasies designed to entertain and edify rather than to record actual events. Many of these fictional narratives

Wooden board, prepared with gesso to provide a reasonably good writing surface. It was probably suspended from a peg by passing a cord through the hole on the right. The text is the only surviving version of the Discourse of Khakheperraseneb, *a literary discourse concerning social and personal chaos. Early 18th Dynasty, c.1500 BC, painted wood, provenance unknown, H. 30 cm. (EA5645A)*

(sometimes described, rather misleadingly and anachronistically, as 'propaganda') provide a good counterpoint to official texts, in that they present a much more ambivalent view of ancient Egypt, showing the subtle shades of distinction between good and evil. In the religious sphere, the COFFIN TEXTS, based on the Pyramid Texts, began to be used in private tombs. Manuscripts have survived more plentifully from the 12th and 13th Dynasties, including a much wider range of types of text, from HYMNS AND LITANIES TO ONOMASTICA.

In the New Kingdom (1550–1069 BC) many of the existing genres were augmented and expanded, including such categories as annals, offering lists, prayers, hymns, journals, 'funerary biographies', funerary texts (e.g. the BOOK OF THE DEAD), mathematical and diagrammatic texts, king lists, onomastica, decrees and treaties. It is noticeable that literary texts began to be composed in Late Egyptian, whereas official inscriptions continued to be written in Middle Egyptian (see LANGUAGE). The style of New Kingdom narratives, such as the *Tale of the Predestined Prince* and the *Tale of the Capture of Joppa*, is generally considered to be more light-hearted and episodic. A new form of text is the so-called 'miscellany', consisting of collections of prayers, hymns or didactic

texts, similar to the modern anthology. In addition, many more 'personal' types of document began to be composed, including love poems, written in hieratic from the Ramesside period onwards and usually consisting of dramatic monologues spoken by one or both of the lovers. There are also numerous surviving records of economic transactions from the New Kingdom (e.g. deeds of sale, tax documents, census lists, see TAXATION and TRADE), as well as many legal records (e.g. trials and wills, see LAW), magical spells and medical remedies (see MAGIC), 'day-books' (daily scribal accounts of royal activities) and LETTERS.

Although the demotic script, introduced in the Late Period, was initially used only for commercial and administrative texts, it began to be used for literary texts from at least the early Ptolemaic period onwards. The range of demotic literary genres was just as wide as in hieroglyphs and hieratic, although no love poetry has yet been attested. The two outstanding examples of demotic narrative fiction are the *Tales of Setne/Khaemwaset* and the *Cycle of Inaros/Pedubastis*, each consisting of a set of stories dealing with the exploits of a heroic individual. It has been suggested that some of the themes and motifs in these demotic tales were borrowed from, or at least influenced by, Greek works such as the Homeric epics or Hellenistic novels and poetry.

Throughout the Pharaonic period it is often difficult to distinguish between fictional narratives and accounts of actual events, and part of this problem stems from a general inability to recognize the aims and contexts of particular texts. Two late New Kingdom documents, the *Report of Wenamun* and the *Literary Letter of Woe*, exemplify this problem, in that we cannot be sure whether they are official accounts of actual individuals or simply stories with comparatively accurate historical backgrounds. Many such documents are perhaps best regarded as semi-fictional works and their original function and intended audience may never be properly clarified.

The related question of the extent of literacy is also controversial. Many scholars have argued that the percentage of literate members of Egyptian society may have been as low as 0.4 per cent of the population, although others have suggested, on the basis of the copious written records from DEIR EL-MEDINA (admittedly an atypical community), that the ability to read and write was considerably more widespread. It is noticeable, however, that virtually all of the surviving 'literary' texts were primarily aimed at (and written by) a small élite group. See also EDUCATION; HOUSE OF LIFE; LETTERS TO THE DEAD; SCRIBES.

J. H. BREASTED, *Ancient records of Egypt*, 4 vols (Chicago, 1906).

G. POSENER, *Littérature et politique dans l'Egypte de la XIIe dynastie* (Paris, 1956).

J. ASSMANN, 'Der literarische Texte im Alten Ägypten: Versuch einer Begriffbestimmung', *OLZ* 69 (1974), 117–26.

—, 'Egyptian Literature', *The Anchor Bible Dictionary*, vol. 2, ed. D. N. Freedman (New York, 1992), 378–90.

M. LICHTHEIM, *Ancient Egyptian literature*, 3 vols (London, 1975–80).

J. BAINES, 'Literacy and ancient Egyptian society', *Man* n.s. 18 (1983), 572–99.

R. B. PARKINSON, *Voices from ancient Egypt: an anthology of Middle Kingdom writings* (London, 1991).

livestock *see* AGRICULTURE and ANIMAL HUSBANDRY

lotus

Botanical term used by Egyptologists to refer to the water lily (*seshen*), which served as the emblem of Upper Egypt, in contrast to the Lower Egyptian PAPYRUS plant. The lotus and papyrus are exemplified by two types of granite pillar in the Hall of Records at KARNAK.

During the Pharaonic period there were essentially two kinds of lotus: the white *Nymphaea lotus*, whose petals are bluntly pointed and which has very large flowers, and the blue *Nymphaea caerulea*, which has pointed petals and a slightly smaller flower. In later times, however, probably after 525 BC, a third type, *Nelumbo nucifera*, was introduced from India. It is the blue lotus which is most commonly depicted in art, frequently held to the noses of banqueters in tomb scenes, although the fragrance may not be very strong. The Greek historian Herodotus states that parts of the plant were sometimes eaten, and recent researchers have suggested that the lotus had hallucinogenic properties.

The lotus was symbolic of rebirth, since one of the CREATION myths describes how the newborn sun rose out of a lotus floating on the waters of NUN. The buds form under water and gradually break the surface before opening suddenly a few days later. The centre of the flowers is yellow, and the blooms generally last only a single day, and certainly no more than four, before closing and sinking beneath the water, from which they do not re-emerge.

Chapter 81 of the BOOK OF THE DEAD is concerned with the act of being transformed into such a lotus: 'I am the pure one who issued from the fen... Oh Lotus belonging to the semblance of Nefertem...' The blue lotus was also the emblem of the god NEFERTEM, 'lord of perfumes'. A painted wooden sculpture from the tomb of Tutankhamun (1336–1327 BC) appears to depict the head of the king in the

The head of Tutankhamun emerging out of a lotus, from his tomb in the Valley of the Kings. 18th Dynasty, c.1330 BC, painted wood, H. 30 cm.
(CAIRO, NO. 8, REPRODUCED COURTESY OF THE GRIFFITH INSTITUTE)

form of Nefertem emerging from a lotus (see illustration).

W. B. HARER, 'Pharmacological and biological properties of the Egyptian lotus', *JARCE* 22 (1985), 49–54.

A. NIBBI, 'The so-called plant of Upper Egypt', *DE* 19 (1991), 53–68.

C. OSSIAN, 'The most beautiful of flowers: water lilies and lotuses in ancient Egypt', *KMT* 10 (1) (1999), 48–59.

love poems *see* EROTICA *and* SEXUALITY

Luxor

Modern name for a Theban religious site dedicated to the cult of AMUN Kamutef, consisting of the *ipet-resyt* ('temple of the southern private quarters' or 'southern *harim*'), which was founded in the reign of AMENHOTEP III (1390–1352 BC) and augmented by successive pharaohs, including RAMESES II (1279–1213 BC) and ALEXANDER THE GREAT (332–323 BC). The primary function of the original temple was as a setting for the FESTIVAL of Opet, in which the cult statue of the god Amun was carried

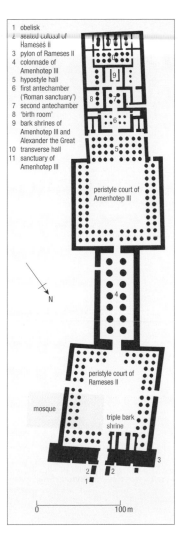

1 obelisk
2 seated colossi of Rameses II
3 pylon of Rameses II
4 colonnade of Amenhotep III
5 hypostyle hall
6 first antechamber ('Roman sanctuary')
7 second antechamber
8 'birth room'
9 bark shrines of Amenhotep III and Alexander the Great
10 transverse hall
11 sanctuary of Amenhotep III

peristyle court of Amenhotep III

peristyle court of Rameses II

mosque

triple bark shrine

0   100 m

Plan of the temple of Amun-Kamutef at Luxor.

annually along an avenue of sphinxes leading from the temple of Amun at KARNAK to Luxor.

One of the purposes of the Opet festival was to enable the human king to 'merge' with his divine royal KA in the presence of Amun, and then to reappear with his royal and divine essence rejuvenated. The inscriptions in the temple describe him as 'Foremost of all the living kas' when he emerges from the inner sanctuary.

The processional colonnade at Luxor, constructed by Amenhotep III and later usurped by

HOREMHEB (1323–1295 BC), is flanked by a frieze depicting the celebration of the Festival of Opet, which is one of the few surviving examples of temple relief from the reign of TUTANKHAMUN (1336–1327 BC). The peristyle court, the pylon entrance and two OBELISKS were added by Rameses II. The pylon contained TALATAT BLOCKS deriving from a now-destroyed temple to the ATEN. Only one of the obelisks remains *in situ*; the other, given to the French in 1819, now stands in the Place de la Concorde in Paris. The main sanctuary of the temple, which had perhaps fallen into disrepair by the Late Period (747–332 BC), was reconstructed in the late fourth century BC by Alexander the Great, who claims to have restored it to its original state 'in the time of Amenhotep'.

The temple was transformed into a shrine of the imperial cult in the Roman period and eventually partially overbuilt by the mosque of Abu Haggag. In 1989 a cachette of exquisitely carved stone statuary (similar to the KARNAK cachette) was excavated from beneath the floor of the court of Amenhotep III. The statues, dating mainly to the 18th Dynasty (1550–1295 BC), had perhaps been buried there by the priesthood in order to protect them from the pillaging of invaders.

A. GAYET, *Le temple de Louxor* (Cairo, 1894).

C. KUENTZ, *La face sud du massif est du pylone de Ramsès II à Louxor* (Cairo, 1971).

L. BELL, 'Luxor temple and the cult of the royal *ka*', *JNES* 44 (1985), 251–94.

M. ABDEL-RAZIQ, *Das Sanktuar Amenophis III im Luxor-Tempel* (Tokyo, 1986).

M. EL-SAGHIR, *The discovery of the statuary cachette of Luxor temple* (Mainz, 1991).

M

Maadi

Late Predynastic settlement-site of about 18 hectares, located 5 km to the south of modern Cairo. The settlement, consisting of wattle-and-daub oval and crescent-shaped huts, as well as large subterranean houses, flourished from Naqada I to II; recent excavations suggest that the eastern part was occupied earlier than the western. At the northern edge of the settlement there were one-metre-high pottery storage jars buried up to their necks. There were also large numbers of storage pits containing carbonized grain, cornelian beads and other valuable items at the southern end of the site. The bodies of foetuses and children were sometimes buried within the settlement, but there were also three cemeteries nearby, that at Wadi Digla being the richest.

There was less evidence of hunting and gathering at Maadi than at earlier Lower Egyptian Predynastic sites. As well as agricultural remains, there was also extensive evidence of craft specialization, including the processing and trading of copper, the analysis of which suggests that it probably derived from mines at Timna and the Wadi Arabah, in southeastern Sinai. Over eighty per cent of the pottery is of a local ware (not known from Upper Egyptian sites), but the presence of Gerzean pottery and stone artefacts also implies that there was increasing contact with Upper Egypt. It should be noted that the remains of cemeteries at el-Saff and Harageh (in Middle Egypt) contain items that are characteristic of the 'Maadian' culture, suggesting that there may also have been a certain amount of cultural expansion southwards in the late Predynastic period.

The excavation of Maadi has revealed large quantities of imported pottery from Palestine dating to the Early Bronze Age I phase (including thirty-one complete jars); these mainly consisted of a globular jar with a broad, flat base, high shoulders and long cylindrical neck. The imported ceramics also included the so-called Ware V pottery, made with unusual manufacturing techniques and, according to petrographic analysis, from Palestinian clay. The combination of Palestinian products found at Maadi (including copper pins, chisels, fishhooks, basalt vessels, tabular-like flint tools, bitumen and cornelian beads) and the presence of typical Maadian and Gerzean products at such Palestinian sites as Wadi Ghazzeh (Site H)

and Tel el-Erani suggest that Maadi was functioning as an entrepot in the late Predynastic period. The means by which the trade goods were transported has perhaps been confirmed by the discovery of bodies of donkeys at Maadi.

M. AMER, 'Annual report of the Maadi excavations, 1935', *CdE* II (1936), 54–7.

M. A. HOFFMAN, *Egypt before the pharaohs* (New York, 1979), 200–14.

I. RIZKANA and J. SEEHER, 'New light on the relation of Maadi to the Upper Egyptian cultural sequence', *MDAIK* 40 (1984), 237–52.

I. CARERA, M. FRANGIPARE and A. PALMIERI, 'Predynastic Egypt: new data from Maadi', *African Archaeological Review* 5 (1987), 105–14.

I. RIZKARA and J. SEEHER, *Maadi*, 4 vols (Mainz, 1987–90).

J. SEEHER, 'Maadi – eine prädynastische Kulturgruppe zwischen Oberägypten und Palestina', *Praehistorische Zeitschrift* 65 (1990), 123–56.

Maat

Goddess personifying truth, justice and the essential harmony of the universe, who was usually portrayed as a seated woman wearing an ostrich feather, although she could sometimes be represented simply by the feather itself or by the plinth on which she sat (probably a symbol of the PRIMEVAL MOUND), which is also sometimes shown beneath the throne of OSIRIS in judgement scenes. On a cosmic scale, Maat also represented the divine order of the universe as originally brought into being at the moment of CREATION. It was the power of Maat that was believed to regulate the seasons, the movement of the stars and the relations between men and gods. The concept was

therefore central both to the Egyptians' ideas about the universe and to their code of ETHICS.

Although the figure of Maat is widely represented in the temples of other deities, only a few temples dedicated to the goddess herself have survived, including a small structure in the precinct of Montu at KARNAK. Her cult is attested from the Old Kingdom (2686–2181 BC) onwards and by the 18th Dynasty (1550–1295 BC) she was being described as the 'daughter of Ra', which was no doubt an expression of the fact that the pharaohs were considered to rule through her authority. The image of Maat was the supreme offering given by the king to the gods, and many rulers held the epithet 'beloved of Maat'. Even AKHENATEN (1352–1336 BC), whose devotion to the cult of the ATEN was later reviled as the antithesis of Maat, is described in the Theban tomb of the vizier RAMOSE (TT55) as 'living by Maat'.

Since the goddess effectively embodied the concept of justice, it is not surprising to find that the VIZIER, who controlled the LAW courts of Egypt, held the title 'priest of Maat', and it has been suggested that a gold chain incorporating a figure of the goddess may have served as the badge of office of a legal official. Maat was also present at the judgement of the dead, when the HEART of the deceased was weighed against her feather or an image of the goddess, and sometimes her image surmounts the balance itself. The place in which the judgement took place was known as the 'hall of the two truths' (*maaty*).

R. ANTHES, *Die Maat des Echnaton von Amarna* (Baltimore, 1952).

V. A. TOBIN, 'Ma'at and Síkn: some comparative considerations of Egyptian and Greek thought', *JARCE* 24 (1987), 113–21.

J. ASSMANN, *Ma'at: Gerechtigkeit und Unsterblichkeit im alten Ägypten* (Munich, 1990).

E. TEETER, *The presentation of Maat: the iconography and theology of an ancient Egyptian offering ritual* (Chicago, 1990).

E. HORNUNG, *Idea into image*, trans. E. Bredeck (New York, 1992), 131–46.

mace

Early weapon consisting of a stone head attached to a shaft of wood (or sometimes of ivory or horn), often tapering towards the end that was gripped. Many maceheads have been excavated from Predynastic and Early Dynastic cemeteries. The earliest examples, dating to the Naqada I period (*c.*4000–3500 BC), were disc-shaped, although many of these appear to have been either too light or too small to have been actually used in battle. The discovery of a clay model macehead at Mostagedda suggests that they may often have

Golden chain with a gold foil pendant in the form of the goddess Maat, which may have served as a judge's insignia. 26th Dynasty or later, after c.600 BC, H. 2.8 cm. (EA48998)

A diorite disc-shaped Predynastic macehead from el-Mahasna, dating to the Naqada I period (4000–3500 BC), D. 8.8 cm, and a red breccia pear-shaped macehead of the Naqada II period (c.3500–3100 BC), H. 6.9 cm. (EA49003 AND 32089)

been intended as ritualistic or symbolic objects.

In the Naqada II period (c.3500–3100 BC), the discoid form was superseded by the pear-shaped head (as well as a narrow, pointed form that may have been introduced from western Asia). By the late Predynastic period both ceremonial PALETTES and maceheads had become part of the regalia surrounding the emerging KINGSHIP. In Tomb 100 at HIERAKONPOLIS the painted decoration includes a scene in which a warrior, who may even be an early pharaoh, threatens a row of CAPTIVES with a mace.

The image of the triumphant king brandishing a mace had already become an enduring image of kingship by the time the NARMER palette (Egyptian Museum, Cairo) was carved. This ceremonial mudstone palette, showing King Narmer (c.3100 BC) wearing the white CROWN and preparing to strike a foreigner with his mace, was found in the 'Main Deposit' (probably incorporating a cache of votive items) in the Old Kingdom temple at Hierakonpolis. The same deposit included two limestone maceheads carved with elaborate reliefs, one belonging to King SCORPION and the other to Narmer (Oxford, Ashmolean Museum), showing that the macehead itself had become a vehicle for royal propaganda. The archetypal scene of the mace-wielding pharaoh was of such iconographic importance that it continued to be depicted on temple walls until the Roman period.

The mace was associated with the healthy eye of the god HORUS, whose epithets included the phrase 'lord of the mace, smiting down his foes', and its importance in terms of the kingship is re-emphasized by the presence of two gilt wooden model maces among the funerary equipment of TUTANKHAMUN (1336–1327 BC).

W. WOLF, *Die Bewaffnung des altägyptischen Heeres* (Leipzig, 1926).

B. ADAMS, *Ancient Hierakonpolis* (Warminster, 1974), 5–13.

W. DECKER, 'Keule, Keulenkopf', *Lexikon der Ägyptologie* III, ed. W. Helck, E. Otto and W. Westendorf (Wiesbaden, 1980), 414–15.

magic

The Egyptians used the term *heka* to refer to magical power, in the sense of a divine force (sometimes personified as the god Heka) that could be invoked both by deities and humans to solve problems or crises. In modern times a clear distinction is usually made between the use of prayers, MEDICINE or 'magic', but in ancient Egypt (and many other cultures) these three categories were regarded as overlapping and complementary. Thus, a single problem, whether a disease or a hated rival, might be solved by a combination of magical rituals or treatments (*seshaw*), medicinal prescriptions (*pekhret*) and religious texts (*rw*).

A somewhat artificial distinction is usually made between the religious texts in tombs and temples and the 'magical texts' or 'spells' that were intended to solve the everyday problems of individuals. These texts range from the *Book of Gates* in New Kingdom royal tombs to curses inscribed on OSTRACA, or even spells to cure nasal catarrh, but all of them would have been regarded by the Egyptians as roughly comparable methods of gaining divine assistance. All employed *heka*, the primeval potency that empowered the creator-god at the beginning of time. Whereas magic, in the modern sense of the word, has become relatively peripheral to the established religions, in ancient Egypt it lay at the very heart of religious ritual and liturgy. Magic was the means by which the restoration of all forms of order and harmony could be ensured. The royal *uraeus* (see COBRA and WADJYT), perhaps the most vivid symbol of the pharaoh's power, was sometimes described as *weret hekaw*: 'great of magic'.

Probably the best-known literary description of the practice of magic in Egypt is a fictional narrative composed in the Middle Kingdom (2055–1650 BC) and preserved on the 18th-Dynasty Papyrus Westcar. This text describes various marvels performed by the magicians Djadjaemankh and Djedi at the courts of SNEFERU and KHUFU in the 4th Dynasty (2613–2494 BC).

As in many other cultures the techniques employed by Egyptian magicians were based largely on the concept of imitation – the belief that the replication of a name, image or mythical event could produce an effect in the real world. The imitation of names meant that verbal trickery, such as puns, metaphors and acrostics, were regarded as powerful forms of magic rather than simply literary skills. In the

Curved 'magic' wand, incised with figures of deities and mythical beasts, probably intended to protect the owner from harm. Middle Kingdom, c.1800 BC, hippopotamus ivory, L. 36 cm. (EA18175)

case of the EXECRATION TEXTS, the act of smashing ostraca or figurines bearing the names of enemies was considered to be an effective way of thwarting them. Similarly, the creation of statuettes or figurines of gods or enemies, which could then be either propitiated or mutilated, was regarded as an effective way of gaining control over evil forces. In a sophisticated combination of verbal, visual and physical imitation, it was believed that water poured over *cippi* of HORUS (stelae depicting Horus the child defeating snakes, scorpions and other dangers) would confer healing on those who drank it.

The shaft tomb of a priest of the late Middle Kingdom (*c.*1700 BC) excavated from beneath the Ramesseum in western Thebes contained a mixture of 'religious' and 'magical' artefacts, including a statuette of a woman wearing a lion MASK and holding two snake-wands, an ivory clapper, a section of a magic rod, a female fertility figurine, a bronze cobra-wand, and a box of papyri inscribed with a wide range of religious, literary and magical texts (see LIBRARIES). This single collection of equipment clearly demonstrates the vast spectrum of strategies which would have been involved in Egyptian magic, enabling an individual priest to draw on the power of the gods with a wide variety of means and for a number of different purposes.

M. LICHTHEIM, *Ancient Egyptian literature* (Berkeley, 1973), 215–22. [Papyrus Westcar]

J. F. BORGHOUTS, *Ancient Egyptian magical texts* (Leiden, 1978).

M. RAAVEN, 'Wax in Egyptian magic and symbolism', *Oudheidkundige Mededelingen uit het Rijksmuseum van Oudheden te Leiden* 64 (1983), 7–47.

C. JACQ, *Egyptian magic*, trans. J. M. Davis (Warminster, 1985).

A. M. BLACKMAN, *The story of King Kheops and the magicians, transcribed from Papyrus Westcar (Berlin Papyrus 3033)*, ed. W. V. Davies (Reading, 1988).

J. F. BORGHOUTS, 'Magical practices among the villagers', *Pharaoh's workers: the villagers of Deir el-Medina*, ed. L. H. Lesko (Ithaca and London, 1994), 119–30.

R. K. RITNER, *The mechanics of ancient Egyptian magical practice* (Chicago, 1993).

G. PINCH, *Magic in ancient Egypt* (London, 1994).

magic bricks

Set of four mud bricks that were often placed on the four sides of the tomb during the New Kingdom (1550–1069 BC) in order to protect the deceased from evil. Surviving examples date from at least as early as the reign of

Magic brick with shabti*-like human figure, from the north wall of the burial chamber in the tomb of Tutankhamun. 18th Dynasty, c.1330 BC, H. 15.1 cm. (CAIRO, NO. 259, REPRODUCED COURTESY OF THE GRIFFITH INSTITUTE)*

Thutmose III (1479–1425 BC) until the time of Rameses II (1279–1213 BC). A socket in each brick supported an AMULET, the form of which depended on the cardinal point where the brick was placed: thus the brick beside the western wall included a faience DJED pillar, that beside the eastern wall incorporated an unfired clay ANUBIS, and those beside the southern and northern walls contained a reed with a wick resembling a torch and a mummiform SHABTI-like figure respectively. The amulets themselves usually faced towards the opposite wall. The bricks were inscribed with sections of the hieratic text of Chapter 151 of the BOOK OF THE DEAD, describing the role they played in protecting the deceased from the enemies of OSIRIS.

E. THOMAS, 'The four niches and amuletic figures in Theban royal tombs', *JARCE* 3 (1964), 71–8.

S. QUIRKE and J. SPENCER, *The British Museum book of ancient Egypt* (London, 1992), 94–5.

Maiherpri (Mahirpra) (*c.*1450 BC)

Military official of the early 18th Dynasty, whose small intact tomb (KV36) was found in western Thebes by Victor Loret in 1899. It was the first unplundered tomb to be discovered in the VALLEY OF THE KINGS in modern times, although the poor records of its excavation mean that little is known about the original

disposition of the items within the burial chamber, and there is not even a definitive list of the objects themselves.

Because of the fine quality of the burial and its location among the royal tombs of the New Kingdom, it has been suggested that Maiherpri, who held the titles 'fan bearer on the right hand of the king' and 'child of the [royal] nursery', must have enjoyed considerable royal favour, perhaps being a foster-brother or son of one of the early New Kingdom rulers, while his physical features (dark complexion and curly hair) indicate that he was of Nubian descent. There are few clues as to the ruler under whom he served; possible candidates are Hatshepsut (1473–1458 BC), whose name was inscribed on a piece of linen in the tomb, Thutmose III (1479–1425 BC), Amenhotep II (1427–1400 BC) and Thutmose IV (1400–1390 BC).

The funerary equipment included a large black resin-covered wooden sarcophagus containing two smaller coffins, both of which were empty. The body itself lay in a second set of coffins to one side of the sarcophagus. The funerary equipment included an impressive BOOK OF THE DEAD papyrus, as well as leather quivers full of arrows (some tipped with flint) which reinforce his identification as a standard-bearer in the Egyptian army (perhaps even a royal bodyguard). Other leather items preserved among his funerary equipment were two dog collars, one of which was inscribed with the animal's name (Tantanuet), as well as a box containing leather loincloths, which Howard Carter later discovered buried under a rock outside the tomb.

H. CARTER, 'Report on general work done in the southern inspectorate I: Biban el-Molouk', *ASAE* 4 (1903), 46.

M. SALEH and H. SOUROUZIAN, *The Egyptian Museum, Cairo: official catalogue* (Mainz, 1987), no. 142.

C. N. REEVES, *The Valley of the Kings* (London, 1990), 140–7.

Malkata

Settlement and palace site at the southern end of western Thebes, opposite modern LUXOR, dating to the early fourteenth century BC. Essentially the remains of a community that grew up around the Theban residence of Amenhotep III (1390–1352 BC), it was excavated between 1888 and 1918, but only a small part of this work has been published, and the more recent re-examination of the site by David O'Connor and Barry Kemp in the early 1970s has only partially remedied this situation. The excavated area of the site comprises several large official buildings (including four probable palaces), as well as kitchens, store-rooms, residential areas and a temple dedicated to the god Amun

To the east of Malkata are the remains of a large artificial lake (the Birket Habu) evidently created at the same time as Amenhotep III's palaces, probably in connection with his SED FESTIVAL. The southern end of the site (Kom el-Samak) was surveyed and excavated during the 1970s and 1980s by a Japanese expedition from Waseda University, revealing an unusual ceremonial painted platform-kiosk approached by a stair and ramp.

R. DE P. TYTUS, *A preliminary report on the pre-excavation of the palace of Amenhotep III* (New York, 1903).

W. HAYES, 'Inscriptions from the palace of Amenhotep III', *JNES* 10 (1951), 35–40.

B. J. KEMP and D. O'CONNOR, 'An ancient Nile harbour: University Museum excavations at the Birket Habu', *International Journal of Nautical Archaeology and Underwater Exploration* 3/1 (1974), 101–36.

Y. WATANABE and K. SEKI, *The architecture of Kom El Samak at Malkata South: a study of architectural restoration* (Tokyo, 1986).

mammisi (Coptic: 'birth-place', 'birth-house') Artificial Coptic term invented by the nineteenth-century Egyptologist Jean-François Champollion to describe a particular type of

The mammisi *of Horus at Edfu was constructed by Ptolemy VII and XIII and was the setting for annual 'mystery plays' concerning the birth of the god. (P. T. NICHOLSON)*

building attached to certain temples, such as EDFU, DENDERA and PHILAE, from the Late Period to the Roman period (747 BC–AD 395), often placed at right angles to the main temple axis. The Ptolemaic *mammisi* usually consisted of a small temple, surrounded by a colonnade with intercolumnar screen walls, in which the rituals of the marriage of the goddess (Isis or Hathor) and the birth of the child-god were celebrated. There appear to have been earlier counterparts of the *mammisi* in the form of 18th-Dynasty reliefs describing the divine birth of Hatshepsut (1473–1458 BC) at DEIR EL-BAHRI and that of Amenhotep III (1390–1352 BC) at LUXOR.

The temple complex at Dendera includes two *mammisis* in front of the main temple. One of these dates to the Roman period, while the other is a much earlier construction of Nectanebo I (380–362 BC) in which 'mystery plays' concerning the births of both the god Ihy (see HATHOR) and the pharaoh are said to have been enacted, comprising thirteen acts and two intervals. It is highly likely that similar dramas and rituals took place in other birth-houses, with the intention of ensuring agricultural success and the continuation of the royal line.

E. CHASSINAT, *Le mammisi d'Edfou*, 2 vols (Cairo, 1939).

—, *Les mammisi des temples égyptiens* (Paris, 1958).

F. DAUMAS, *Les mammisis de Dendara* (Cairo, 1959).

J. JUNKER and E. WINTER, *Das Geburtshaus des Tempels der Isis in Philä* (Vienna, 1965).

Manetho (*c.*305–285 BC)

Egyptian priest and historian. Little is known of his life, and it is disputed whether he was born at MENDES or HELIOPOLIS. It is clear, however, that he was Egyptian and could read Egyptian scripts, although he wrote in Greek. His major work, a HISTORY of Egypt called the *Aegyptiaca*, was probably prepared during his time at the temple of Sebennytos, which is near the modern town of Samannud in the Delta. It has been tentatively suggested that his priestly duties included a role in the establishment of the cult of SERAPIS under Ptolemy I Soter (305–285 BC). As a priest he would have had access to the archives of Egypt's temples (see LIBRARIES), and with his ability to read hieroglyphs he was able to produce a valuable study, which he dedicated to Ptolemy II (285–246 BC).

Unfortunately his history has not survived intact, but is preserved in a series of sometimes contradictory fragments in the works of other writers, notably the Jewish historian Josephus (first century AD), and the Christian writers Julius Africanus (*c.* AD 220), Eusebius (*c.* AD 320) and George called Syncellus (*c.* AD 800). Nevertheless, his division of the earthly rulers into thirty DYNASTIES (with the later addition of a thirty-first) has been a major influence on modern perceptions of the outline of Egyptian history, and the system was used by Jean-François Champollion in ordering the sequence of CARTOUCHES he discovered from his decipherment of the hieroglyphs.

Manetho is credited with a further seven works: *The Sacred Book, An Epitome of Physical Doctrines, On Festivals, On Ancient Ritual and Religion, On the Making of Kyphi* (the latter being a type of incense), *Criticisms of Herodotus* and *The Book of Sothis*. The last of these was certainly not the work of Manetho, and it is equally possible that some of the other works were never even written.

MANETHO, *Aegyptiaca*, ed. and trans. W. G. Wadell, Loeb Classical Library (London, 1940).

A. LLOYD, 'Manetho and the Thirty-First Dynasty', *Pyramid studies and other essays presented to I. E. S. Edwards*, ed. J. Baines et al. (London, 1988), 154–60.

maps and plans

The question of ancient Egyptian use of maps, plans and diagrams is complicated by the differences between modern conceptions of art and representation and those that prevailed in the Pharaonic period. There are therefore Egyptian depictions of such phenomena as landscapes and architectural features that might be described – in modern terms – as 'diagrammatic', in the sense that they combine

several different perspectives. For instance, in Rameses II's depictions of the Battle of QADESH (c.1274 BC), there is a bird's-eye view of the immediate context of Qadesh (i.e. a tract of land bounded by two branches of the River Orontes), but the city itself is depicted as if seen from the side.

There are also, however, a small number of surviving drawings on ostraca and papyri that differ from mainstream Egyptian works of art in that they appear to have had various practical uses as diagrams, whether as the working drawings of architects or, on a more metaphysical level, as a means of navigating through the afterlife. The earliest surviving Egyptian maps are of the latter type, consisting of schematic depictions of the route to the netherworld (the *Book of Two Ways*) painted on coffins of the Middle Kingdom (2055–1650 BC).

The earliest surviving Egyptian map of an actual geographical region is the so-called Turin Mining Papyrus, an annotated pictorial record of an expedition to the *bekhen*-stone (greywacke or siltstone) quarries of Wadi Hammamat in the Eastern Desert. The Turin Mining Papyrus, now in the Museo Egizio, Turin, dates to the mid-twelfth century BC; it was evidently a document either created to assist in a *bekhen*-stone quarrying expedition in the reign of Rameses IV (1153–1147 BC), or, at the very least, composed in order to commemorate the details of the event. The map identifies the essential elements of a group of gold mines (at a site now known as Bir Umm Fawakhir) as well as the principal quarries, which are located further to the east.

The textual and pictorial details of the papyrus have recently been re-analysed, and its meaning and archaeological context reassessed. It incorporates colour-coded geological zones, the locations of the mines and quarries, a miners' settlement, a cistern (or 'water-reservoir'), three ancient roads, two locations associated with the processing and transportation of minerals, a shrine dedicated to 'Amun of the pure mountain' and a commemorative stele from the time of SETY I (1294–1279 BC).

An ostracon of the Ramesside period in the British Museum bears a rough architectural plan annotated with measurements and accompanied by a hieratic text describing the orientation of the drawing in relation to an actual building, which remains unidentified. Two other architectural drawings have been recognized as plans of specific royal tombs in the VALLEY OF THE KINGS. A papyrus in Turin bears part of a detailed ink plan of the tomb of Rameses IV, while a less detailed plan on an

ostracon in the Egyptian Museum, Cairo has been identified as the tomb of Rameses IX (1126–1108 BC).

H. CARTER and A. H. GARDINER, 'The tomb of Ramesses IV and the Turin plan of a royal tomb', *JEA* 4 (1917), 130–58.
E. HORNUNG, 'Zum Turiner Grabplan', *Pyramid studies and other essays presented to I. E. S. Edwards*, ed. J. Baines et al. (London, 1988), 138–42.
R. B. PARKINSON, *Voices from ancient Egypt* (London, 1991), 134–6. [plan of the netherworld]
J. A. HARRELL and V. M. BROWN, 'The oldest surviving topographical map from ancient Egypt: Turin Papyri 1879, 1899 and 1969', *JARCE* 29 (1992), 81–105.

Mariette, Auguste (1821–81)

French Egyptologist who excavated many of the major Egyptian sites and monuments and founded the Egyptian Antiquities Service. He was born and educated in Boulogne-sur-Mer and in 1839–40 he lived in England, teaching French and drawing in Stratford and working unsuccessfully as a designer in Coventry. In 1841 he returned to Boulogne to complete his education, and the following year he developed an enthusiasm for Egyptology when he examined the papers bequeathed to his family by his cousin Nestor L'Hôte, who produced huge numbers of drawings as a draughtsman on CHAMPOLLION's expedition to Egypt in 1828–9.

Between 1842 and 1849 Mariette taught himself hieroglyphics (using Champollion's grammar and dictionary) and studied Coptic, eventually obtaining a post in the Louvre, where he made an inventory of all of the Egyptian inscriptions in the collection. In 1850 he was sent to Egypt to acquire papyri for the Louvre, but instead embarked on the excavation of the Saqqara SERAPEUM; the ensuing four years were probably the most successful of his archaeological career. In 1855 he became Assistant Conservator at the Louvre and two years later he returned to Egypt. With the financial support of Said Pasha, the viceroy of Egypt, he undertook several simultaneous excavations, including work at Giza, Thebes, Abydos and Elephantine. In June 1858 he was appointed as the first Director of the newly created Egyptian Antiquities Service, which enabled him to gather together sufficient antiquities to establish a national museum at Bulaq, near Cairo. His subsequent excavations at thirty-five different sites, regularly using large numbers of relatively unsupervised workers, were criticized by later, more scientific, exca-

vators such as Flinders PETRIE and George REISNER, but he is nevertheless deservedly honoured by modern archaeologists as the creator of the Egyptian Antiquities Service and the Egyptian Museum, without which the plundering of Egypt would have carried on at a far greater pace in the late nineteenth century. He died at Bulaq in 1881 and was buried in a sarcophagus which was later moved to the forecourt of the modern Egyptian Museum in Cairo.

A. MARIETTE, *Le Sérapéum de Memphis* (Paris, 1857).
—, *Notice des principaux monuments exposés dans les galeries provisoires du Musée…à Boulak* (Cairo, 1864).
—, *The monuments of Upper Egypt* (London, 1877).
E. MARIETTE, *Mariette Pacha* (Paris, 1904).
G. DANIEL, *A hundred years of archaeology*, 1st ed. (London, 1950), 160–4.

marriage

Although many current descriptions of ancient Egypt tend to assume that marriage in the Pharaonic period was similar to the modern institution, there is surprisingly little evidence either for marriage ceremonies or for the concept of the married couple (as opposed to a man and woman simply living together).

The word *hemet*, conventionally translated as 'wife', is regularly used to identify a man's female partner, but it is not clear what the social or legal implications of the term were. In addition, it has been pointed out that the equivalent male term *hi* ('husband') is only rarely encountered. This is one of the most obvious results of the fact that most of the surviving sculptures and texts relate to male funerary cults; therefore women are primarily identified in terms of their relationships with men (rather than the men being defined by their links with women).

The word *hebswt* seems to have been used to refer to another category of female partner, which is occasionally translated as 'concubine', but the situation is confused by the existence of some texts of the New Kingdom (1550–1069 BC) that describe a woman as both *hemet* and *hebswt* at the same time. *Hebswt* is therefore sometimes taken to refer to a man's second or third wife, if he remarried after the death or divorce of an earlier spouse.

Very few documents describing the act of marriage have survived from the Pharaonic period, although a number of legal texts, often described as 'marriage contracts', have survived from the period spanning the Late and Ptolemaic periods (747–30 BC). These texts, frequently incorporating the phrase *shep en schemet* ('price for [marrying] a woman'), appear to lay down the property rights of each of the partners in a marriage, rather than specifically documenting or endorsing the act of marriage itself.

The actual ceremony of marriage is poorly documented, but there are more frequent records of divorces. Both remarriage and multiple marriages were possible, but it is not clear how common it was for men to take more than one wife. It has been pointed out that the numbers of rooms in the New Kingdom tomb-workers' community of DEIR EL-MEDINA appear to conform with monogamous rather than polygamous arrangements. However, from at least as early as the 13th Dynasty (*c*.1795–1650 BC), polygamy was certainly practised by the Egyptian kings, with one consort usually being cited as the 'great royal wife' (*hemet nesw meret*, see QUEENS). The custom of brother–sister and father–daughter marriage appears to have been confined to the royal family, perhaps partly because the deliberate practice of incest, commonly occurring in the myths of Egyptian deities, was regarded as a royal prerogative, effectively setting the king apart from his subjects.

In the New Kingdom, many pharaohs also took foreign wives in so-called 'diplomatic marriages', which were used either as a means of consolidating alliances with the kingdoms of the ancient Near East or as an indication of the complete subjugation of a foreign prince, who would have been obliged to send his daughter to the king both as an act of surrender and as a means of ensuring his subsequent loyalty.

P. PESTMAN, *Marriage and matrimonial property in ancient Egypt* (Leiden, 1961).

W. K. SIMPSON, 'Polygamy in Egypt in the Middle Kingdom', *JEA* 60 (1974), 100–5.

A. R. SCHULMAN, 'Diplomatic marriage in the Egyptian New Kingdom', *JNES* 38 (1979), 177–94.

S. ALLAM, 'Quelques aspects du mariage dans l'Egypte ancienne', *JEA* 67 (1981), 116–35.

E. STROUHAL, *Life in ancient Egypt* (Cambridge, 1992), 51–8.

G. ROBINS, *Women in ancient Egypt* (London, 1993), 56–74.

Maskhuta, Tell el- (anc. Per-Temu, Tjeku)

Town-site and capital of the eighth nome of Lower Egypt during the Late Period (747–332 BC), located at the eastern edge of the Delta, 15 km west of modern Ismailiya and the Suez Canal. The site was first excavated by Edouard Naville in 1883 on behalf of the newly established Egypt Exploration Fund.

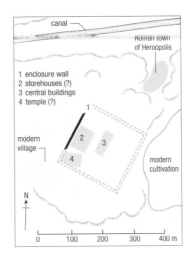

Plan of Tell el-Maskhuta.

Black granite votive falcon of Rameses II. 19th Dynasty, 1279–1213 BC, from Tell el-Maskhuta, H 95 cm. (EA1006)

On the basis of its ancient name, Per-Temu, the site was identified with the Biblical city of Pithom, but more recent excavations by a team from the University of Toronto have disproved this theory, demonstrating that there was a HYKSOS level below the remains of the city founded by Nekau II (610–595 BC) which was still flourishing in the Roman period (30 BC–AD 395). The fluctuating importance of the site appears to have been closely linked to the fortunes of the Wadi Tumilat, through which an ancient canal connected the apex of the Delta with the Red Sea.

H. E. NAVILLE, *The store-city of Pithom and the route of the Exodus* (London, 1885).

J. S. HOLLADAY, Jr, *Cities of the Delta III: Tell el-Maskhuta* (Malibu, 1982).

masks

The question of the extent to which masks were used in Egyptian religious and funerary rituals has not yet been satisfactorily resolved. Paintings, reliefs and statuary throughout the Pharaonic period regularly include depictions of human figures with the heads of various creatures, from jackals to falcons. It is uncertain, however, whether these depictions are always intended to represent physical manifestations of the gods themselves, or whether, as seems possible in some instances, the figures are masked priests representing the deity in question. Some of the ceremonial PALETTES of the late Predynastic and Early Dynastic periods (*c*.3300–2900 BC) are carved with depictions of bird- and animal-headed humans, sometimes described as masked figures, although they are not necessarily any more likely to be masked than equivalent depictions of the Pharaonic period.

Studies concerning priests' use of masks are hampered by the fact that only two examples have survived. In the Römer-Pelizaeus Museum at Hildesheim there is a painted ceramic bust of Anubis of unknown provenance, nearly 50 cm high and dated to the fifth or sixth century BC. A pair of holes were bored through the pottery below the snout, presumably in order to allow the priest to see out; the 'mask' also had notches on either side of the base to fit over the wearer's shoulders. A relief in the Ptolemaic temple of Hathor at Dendera shows a priest apparently wearing a similar jackal-head mask, with his own head visible inside the outline of the jackal's head.

At one of the houses in the town of Kahun (see EL-LAHUN), Flinders Petrie excavated a CARTONNAGE lion's head mask provided with eye-holes, which would probably have allowed the wearer to assume the identity of the magical demon Aha. This mask, dating to the

Middle Kingdom (2055–1650 BC), is now in the collection of the Manchester Museum. The unusual set of late Middle Kingdom objects found in shaft-tomb 5 under the Ramesseum included a wooden figurine representing either a lion-headed goddess or a woman wearing a similar kind of mask, which was probably connected in some way with the performance of MAGIC. It is possible that many other masks were made of organic materials such as cartonnage, linen or leather, which, even in Egypt's climate, would not necessarily have survived in the archaeological record.

Profile view of the funerary mask of Tutankhamun, from his tomb in the Valley of the Kings. The characteristic beard has been removed in this photograph. 18th Dynasty, c.1330 BC, gold, lapis lazuli, cornelian, quartz, obsidian, turquoise and coloured glass, H. 54 cm. (CAIRO JE60672, REPRODUCED COURTESY OF THE GRIFFITH INSTITUTE)

The use of masks in funerary contexts is much better documented, ranging from the famous golden masks of TUTANKHAMUN (1336–1327 BC) and PSUSENNES I (1039–991 BC) to the humbler painted cartonnage masks that were introduced in the First Intermediate Period (2181–2055 BC) to assist in the identification of the linen-wrapped mummy. The cartonnage mummy mask was used in the First Intermediate Period, the Middle Kingdom, the 18th and 26th Dynasties and the Greco-Roman period (32 BC–AD 395), when hollow painted plaster heads and the so-called 'Fayum portraits' (depicting the face of the deceased in ENCAUSTIC or tempera on a wooden board) began to be used alongside the traditional cartonnage masks.

The forerunners of mummy-masks date to the 4th to 6th Dynasties (2613–2181 BC), taking the form of thin coatings of plaster moulded either directly over the face or on top of the linen wrappings, perhaps fulfilling a similar purpose to the 4th-Dynasty RESERVE HEADS. A plaster mould, apparently taken directly from the face of a corpse, was excavated from the 6th-Dynasty mortuary temple of TETI (2345–2323 BC), but this is thought to be of Greco-Roman date. The superficially similar plaster 'masks' that were excavated in the house of the sculptor Thutmose at EL-AMARNA were probably not death-masks at all but copies of sculptures, intended to aid the sculptors in making accurate representations of the el-Amarna élite.

W. M. F. PETRIE, *Kahun, Gurob and Hawara* (London, 1890), 30, pl. VIII.27.

J. E. QUIBELL, *Excavations at Saqqara (1907–1908)* (Cairo, 1909), 112, pl. lx.

C. L. BLEEKER, 'Die Maske: Verhüllung und Offenbarung', *The sacred bridge* (Leiden, 1963), 236–49.

C. A. ANDREWS, *Egyptian mummies* (London, 1984), 27–30.

A. WOLINSKI, 'Ancient Egyptian ceremonial masks', *DE* 6 (1986), 47–53.

P. PAMMINGER, 'Anubis-Maske', *Ägyptens Aufstieg zur Weltmacht*, exh. cat. Hildesheim, ed. A. Eggebrecht (Mainz, 1978), 312–13.

W. DAVIS, *Masking the blow: the scene of representation in late prehistoric Egyptian art* (Berkeley, 1992), 38–40, 72–82.

D. SWEENEY, 'Egyptian masks in motion', *GM* 135 (1993), 101–4.

J. H. TAYLOR, 'Masks in ancient Egypt: the image of divinity', *Masks: the art of expression*, ed. J. Mack (London, 1994), 168–89.

Maspero, Gaston (1846–1916)

French Egyptologist who succeeded Auguste MARIETTE as Director of the Egyptian Museum at Bulaq and edited the first fifty volumes of the immense catalogue of the collection there. He was born in Paris and educated at the Lycée Louis le Grand and the Ecole Normale, eventually becoming Professor of Egyptology at the Ecole des Hautes Etudes in 1869, at the age of only twenty-three, having studied with both Mariette and Olivier de Rougé. In 1880 he made his first trip to Egypt at the head of a French archaeological mission that was eventually to become the Institut Français d'Archéologie Orientale. From 1881 onwards, as Director of the Egyptian Antiquities Service and the Bulaq Museum, he excavated at numerous sites from Saqqara to the Valley of the Kings. His distinguished career, which included the first publication of the PYRAMID TEXTS and the discovery of the cache of royal mummies at DEIR EL-BAHRI, was eventually brought to an end through illness, which forced him to return to France in 1914. He died two years later, just before he was about to address a meeting of the Academy in Paris.

G. MASPERO, *Les momies royales de Deir el-Bahari* (Cairo, 1889).

—, *Etudes de mythologie et d'archéologie égyptienne*, 8 vols (Paris, 1893–1916).

—, *Les inscriptions des pyramides de Saqqarah* (Paris, 1894).

—, *Histoire ancienne des peuples de l'Orient*, 3 vols (Paris, 1895–9).

G. MASPERO and A. BARSANTI, *Fouilles autour de la pyramide d'Ounas* (Cairo, 1900)

G. MASPERO, *New light on ancient Egypt* (London, 1908).

—, *Guide du visiteur au musée du Caire*, 4th ed. (Cairo, 1915).

W. R. DAWSON, 'Letters from Maspero to Amelia Edwards', *JEA* 33 (1947), 66–89.

mastaba (Arabic: 'bench')

Arabic term applied to style of Egyptian tomb in which the superstructure resembles the low mud-brick benches outside Egyptian houses. Mastaba tombs have sloping walls, so that the roof area is smaller than that of the base.

The mastaba tomb was used for both royal and private burials in the Early Dynastic period (3100–2686 BC) but only for private burials in the Old Kingdom (2686–2181 BC). It comprises a substructure, usually consisting of the burial chamber and magazines, surmounted by a mud-brick or stone superstructure. Ancillary buildings, notably chapels, were originally attached to the superstructure but were gradually incorporated into it. The best evidence for mastabas of the Early Dynastic period derives from ABYDOS and SAQQARA, supplemented by those at NAQADA. For the Old Kingdom, GIZA, SAQQARA, ABUSIR and MEIDUM are all important mastaba cemeteries.

Early Dynastic mastabas comprise a pit cut into the rock and divided by brick partitions. The central chamber, that for the burial, was sometimes decorated. In the earliest examples, the underground rooms did not have connecting doors, and all were roofed over with timber. As a result the burial had to be made before the brick superstructure was completed. From the mid 1st Dynasty onwards a stairway was incorporated into the design allowing easier access to the tomb, and completion of the

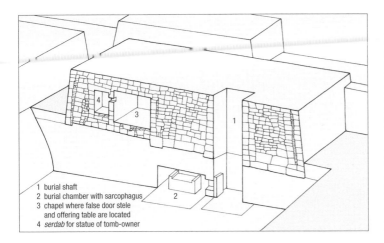

1 burial shaft
2 burial chamber with sarcophagus
3 chapel where false door stele
  and offering table are located
4 *serdab* for statue of tomb-owner

Cut-away drawing of an Old Kingdom private mastaba tomb.

superstructure before burial was made. This stairway was blocked by portcullises in an attempt to prevent robbery of the burial and magazines, some of which began to be incorporated into the superstructure. By the late 2nd Dynasty a series of rock-cut chambers sometimes led from a central corridor beneath the superstructure. Tombs were surrounded by an enclosure wall, which, like the superstructure, took the form of a palace-façade design (see SEREKH) during the 1st Dynasty. Some of these tombs were accompanied also by boat pits. Superstructures of the 2nd Dynasty were plainer, except for niches at the north and south ends of the eastern wall.

During the 3rd Dynasty (2686–2613 BC), the PYRAMID complex developed as the royal burial monument, but the mastaba continued to be used by the rest of the élite, although the number of subterranean rooms was gradually reduced until, by the 4th Dynasty (2613–2494 BC), only a burial chamber remained, connected to the superstructure by a vertical shaft which could be blocked with rubble. This type of mastaba was built throughout the rest of the Old Kingdom. Panelled façades regained popularity during the 3rd Dynasty, although not always on all sides of the tomb, and by the 4th Dynasty stone had become the preferred building material. Similarly, the southern offering niche, which had evolved into a simple chapel, became larger, developing into a distinct room within the superstructure, and by the 5th and 6th Dynasties (2494–2181 BC) a whole series of rooms had developed in the superstructure,

transforming it into a funerary chapel. These often bore elaborate decoration, including scenes of daily life which are valuable for the understanding of agricultural and craft activities (see MERERUKA and TY).

The chapel contained the FALSE DOOR stele and altar, usually located in an offering chamber above the burial. Here the family would come to make their offerings to the deceased. An OFFERING FORMULA carved on the walls would also magically ensure sustenance for the deceased, statues of whom were walled up in a SERDAB and visible only through small openings in the masonry. During the Old Kingdom, the afterlife of officials depended on royal favour, and their tombs, granted by the king, clustered around his monument, as in the 'streets' of tombs at GIZA and SAQQARA.

Mastaba tombs continued to be constructed for private individuals at sites such as ABUSIR, EDFU, Qatta and Qubaniya during the Middle Kingdom, sometimes copying the pyramids of the 12th Dynasty (1985–1795 BC) in their use of elaborate open-excavation corridors. At most other sites, the rock-cut tomb had essentially replaced the mastaba as the principal form of private funerary architecture. In the New Kingdom (1550–1069 BC), however, the so-called 'chapel-tombs', particularly exemplified by the Memphite tomb of HOREMHEB at Saqqara, have been likened by some scholars to the mastaba form. The superstructure of these chapel-tombs usually had the appearance of a shrine or temple consisting of a set of rooms arranged along an axis, in contrast to the relatively solid mass of the Old and Middle Kingdom mastabas. Shafts led down to the burial chamber from the courtyards of the superstructure.

Chapel-tombs were also common after the end of the New Kingdom, as in the case of the royal tombs of the 21st and 22nd Dynasties (1069–715 BC) in the precincts of the temple of Amun at TANIS, which probably originally had superstructures of this type (although only the substructures have survived). The Late Period tombs of the GOD'S WIVES OF AMUN at MEDINET HABU were also in the same architectural tradition.

W. B. EMERY, *Archaic Egypt* (Harmondsworth, 1961).
J. BRINKS, 'Mastaba und Pyramidentempel – ein struktureller Vergleich', *GM* 39 (1980), 45–60.
A. J. SPENCER, *Death in ancient Egypt* (Harmondsworth, 1982), 45–111.
P. WATSON, *Egyptian Pyramids and mastaba tombs* (Aylesbury, 1987).
S. D'AURIA, P. LACOVARA and C. H. ROEHRIG (eds), *Mummies and magic* (Boston, 1988).
N. CHERPION, *Mastabas et hypogées d'Ancien Empire: le problème de la datation* (Brussels, 1989).

mathematics and numbers

The Egyptian numerical system was a combination of the decimal and the repetitive. It lacked a symbol for zero, but scribes occasionally left a gap between numbers as though such a sign existed. The following signs were used to represent numbers:

$\mid$	1
$\cap$	10
	100
	1000
	10,000
	100,000
	1,000,000 [often meaning 'more than I can count'].

Numbers were written from the largest to the smallest, so that 1,122 (reading from right to left) would be: as shown.

Unlike the Greeks, the Egyptians did not develop abstract formulae, but proceeded by a series of smaller calculations. The state of mathematical knowledge in the Pharaonic period has been deduced from a small number of mathematical texts, comprising four papyri (the Moscow, Berlin, Kahun and, most famously, Rhind), a leather scroll and two wooden tablets. A number of mathematical papyri written in the DEMOTIC script have also survived from the Ptolemaic period (332–30 BC).

The modern surveys of monuments have enabled much to be deduced concerning the Egyptians' practical use of mathematics, and –

Section of the Rhind Mathematical Papyrus, written in the Hyksos period, but claiming to be a copy of a 12th-Dynasty work. This part of the text consists of a series of problems concerning the volumes of rectangles, triangles and pyramids. 15th Dynasty, c.1550 BC, papyrus, from Thebes, H. 32 cm. (EA10057, SHEET 8)

at least since the time of Flinders Petrie's survey of GIZA – it has been clear that the methods involved in setting out the pyramid complexes (2686–1650 BC) were pragmatic rather than mystical.

The Egyptians' calculation of whole numbers was relatively simple: to multiply by ten, for example, the appropriate hieroglyphs were changed for the next highest, so that ten, for instance, could become one hundred. In other calculations, a sum equal to the desired multiplier was reached by a process of doubling, while the multiplicand was itself doubled as many times as necessary for the multiplier. Thus the sum 17×19 would be calculated by first deriving the multiplier from the table below, in which $16 + 2 + 1 = 19$:

MULTIPLIER	MULTIPLICAND
1*	17*
2*	34*
4	68
8	136
16*	272*

Once a number was reached which was equal to half or more of that desired, no further doubling was needed. Thus, in the case cited above, 16

is more than half of 19. All that was now necessary was to read across the table and add the relevant figures (marked above by an asterisk), $272 + 34 + 17 = 323$, which is the product of 17×19. Hence there was no need for multiplication tables, simply tables of duplication. Division was achieved by reversing this process.

The use of fractions appears to have caused more difficulties, particularly as the Egyptians recognized only those in which the numerator was one, all of which were written by placing the hieroglyph 'r' above the relevant number: thus one-third would have been rendered as ⌐ ⌐ ⌐. There were, however, also some special signs for such commonly used fractions as two-thirds, three-quarters, four-fifths and five-sixths, and the Rhind Papyrus is exceptional in presenting a table of fractions in which the numerator is two. Complicated fractions were written by reducing them to two or three separate fractions, the first of which had the smallest possible denominator. Thus two-fifths was written as one-third + one-fifteenth. In calculations fractions were broken down and thus treated as whole numbers.

The Egyptians used the observation of practical situations to develop geometrical knowledge early in their history. They knew that the area of a rectangle was equal to its length multiplied by its width. They had also found that if a triangle was drawn inside the rectangle, having the same length as its sides and the same height as its width, then its area would be half that of the rectangle.

However, the Egyptians' major achievement in geometry was the calculation of the area of a circle according to the length of its diameter. This was done by squaring eight-ninths of the diameter's length, which gives an approximate value for *pi* of 3.16. With their knowledge of area, they were also able to calculate volume, including that for a cylinder and pyramid, even when truncated. This again was achieved by a series of smaller calculations, which, although they lack the elegance of formulae, are nevertheless correct.

In the absence of formulae, scribes learned their mathematics by copying out set examples, replacing the figures with their own. Unlike the Mesopotamian mathematicians the Egyptians were more interested in practicalities than in theory. Nevertheless, certain calculations in the Rhind Mathematical Papyrus end with the short phrase *mitt pw* ('it is equal'), which is used where calculations could not be exactly matched to proofs.

C. F. NIMS, 'The bread and beer problems of the Moscow Mathematical Papyrus', *JEA* 44 (1958), 56–65.

R. J. GILLINGS, *Mathematics in the time of the pharaohs* (Cambridge, MA, 1972).

R. A. PARKER, *Demotic mathematical papyri* (London, 1972).

J. SVASTAL, 'Beitrag zur Erforschung der Geschichte der Vermessungskunde im alten Ägypten', *Acta Polytechnica, Práce CVUT v Praze* 13 (1983), 69–80.

G. ROBINS and C. SHUTE, *The Rhind mathematical papyrus* (London, 1987).

measurement

Knowledge of weights and measures was fundamental to the smooth running of the Egyptian bureaucracy. This is evident from tomb scenes showing scribes recording the amount of grain or counting cattle (see TAX-ATION), and from the measured rations and weights of copper issued at DEIR EL-MEDINA, as well as vignettes of the weighing of the heart in the BOOK OF THE DEAD.

The main unit of measurement was the royal cubit (52.4 cm), approximately the length of a man's forearm and represented by the hieroglyph ⌐⌐. The royal cubit comprised 7 palm widths each of 4 digits of thumb width (thus 28 digits to the cubit). Artists generally used a grid to lay out their drawings, and until the end of the Third Intermediate Period (1069–747 BC) they used the 'short cubit' of 6 palms (44.9cm) which was roughly the length from elbow to thumb tip, conventionally 45 cm. From the SAITE PERIOD (664–525 BC) onwards, however, the royal cubit was used by artists. During the Persian occupation, on the other hand, the royal Persian cubit of 64.2 cm was sometimes used, although a reference cubit for this measure at Abydos is actually 63.85 cm long.

The length of the double *remen* was equal to that of the diagonal of a square with sides of 1 royal cubit (74.07 cm). The double *remen*, divided into forty smaller units of 1.85 cm each, was the measurement used in land surveying, long with the *ta* (or *meh-ta*) of 100 royal cubits. Area was measured by *setjat* (100 cubic square), later called the *aroura*.

A number of measuring rods, including the wooden examples used by craftsman and surveyors, have survived. The most detailed knowledge of the cubit derives not from workaday measures, which could vary considerably, but from ceremonial cubit-rods cut in stone and deposited in temples, or occasionally buried with officials. These were also inscribed

the *kite* measured silver or gold only. They were used to describe the equivalent value of a wide variety of non-metallic goods, thus forming a rudimentary price system in the non-monetary economy of the Pharaonic period (see TRADE).

Measures of capacity also existed, notably the *hin* (about 0.47 l): ten *hinw* making one *hekat* of about 4.77 l, and one *khar* making 160 *hinw* (75.2 l). The *hin* could be subdivided into units as small as $1/32$, as well as into thirds, known as *khay*. Scribes measuring grain are depicted in the tomb of Menna.

A. WEIGALL, *Weights and balances* (Cairo, 1908).

J. CERNY, 'Prices and wages in Egypt in the Ramesside period', *Cahiers d'Histoire Mondiale* I (1954), 903–21.

F. G. SKINNER, 'Measures and weights', *A history of technology* I, ed. C. Singer, E. J. Holmyard and A. R. Hall (Oxford, 1954), 774–84.

the main temple, a much earlier phase, dated by pottery to the late Old Kingdom (c.2300–2181 BC), was uncovered in 1939. This consisted of a polygonal enclosure wall containing a grove of trees surrounding a small, roughly rectangular mud-brick temple. At the rear of the small temple there were two winding corridors, each leading to a small chamber, and each chamber being covered by an oval mound of soil, perhaps symbolizing the PRIMEVAL MOUND. This early 'shrine' appears to lie outside the normal conventions of Pharaonic temple design.

C. ROBICHON and A. VARILLE, 'Médamoud: fouilles du Musée du Louvre, 1938', *CdE* 14/27 (1939), 82–7.

—, *Description sommaire du temple primitif de Médamoud* (Cairo, 1940).

B. J. KEMP, *Ancient Egypt: anatomy of a civilization* (London, 1989), 66–9.

23078

ABOVE *Wooden cubit-rod. Late period, L. 53.3 cm. (EA23078)*

RIGHT *Fragment of schist cubit-rod. New Kingdom. L. 15.2 cm. (EA36656)*

with other useful information such as INUNDATION levels or references to nomes (provinces), forming a kind of compendium of the sort once found in school exercise books in Europe. A knotted rope was used in surveying land, the boundaries of which could be marked with stones, as portrayed in the tomb of Menna at Thebes (TT69, c.1400 BC).

Weights were also commonly used, and a large number in stone, pottery and bronze have survived; the earliest, excavated at Naqada, date to the Predynastic period (c.3500–3100 BC). Many weights in the Dynastic period are inscribed, while others are in the shape of bulls' heads, cattle or other animals. Weights were traditionally made in units known as *debens*, weighing about 93.3 g, but after the 12th Dynasty (1985–1795 BC) this unit was supplemented by the *kite* of 9–10 g, and the *deben* itself was increased to weigh 10 *kite*. The *deben* was a measure of copper, silver or gold, whereas

Medamud (anc. Madu)

Site of an ancient town located 5 km northeast of KARNAK temple, at the northernmost edge of Thebes. The modern site is dominated by a temple of the falcon-god MONTU which dates back at least to the Middle Kingdom (2055–1650 BC), although the nucleus of the complex is of the 18th Dynasty (1550–1295 BC) and the outer sections are Greco-Roman in date (332 BC–AD 395). The temple is dedicated to the local triad comprising Montu, Ra'ttawy and Harpocrates (the child-like form of HORUS). Next to the main Greco-Roman temple was a SACRED LAKE and behind it was a smaller temple dedicated to the bull manifestation of Montu, similar to the Bucheum at ARMANT.

The ground-plan of the Middle Kingdom phase of the temple of Montu has been obliterated by the later phases superimposed on it, but numerous stone architectural elements such as columns and royal statues have survived, re-used elsewhere on the site. Beneath

medicine

Egyptian medicine was a mixture of magical and religious spells with remedies based on keen observation of patients, and any attempt to impose the modern distinction between MAGIC and medicine usually only confuses the picture. The most common cure for maladies was probably the AMULET or the magic spell rather than medical prescriptions alone, since many illnesses tended to be regarded as the result of malignant influences or incorrect behaviour.

However, at least as early as the 3rd Dynasty (2686–2613 BC), there were already individuals corresponding roughly to the modern concept of a doctor, for whom the term *sinw* was used. There were also surgeons (called 'priests of Sekhmet') as well as the ancient equivalents of dental and veterinary practitioners. The Greek historian HERODOTUS, writing in the fifth century BC, claimed that Egyptian doctors each had their own specializations, such as

Detail of the London Medical Papyrus. New Kingdom, c.1300–1200 BC. (EA10059).

gynaecology or osteopathy, but there is no evidence that this was so in the Pharaonic period. Egyptian doctors appear to have been mainly men, given the fact that only one woman doctor is definitely attested, although this evidence may well be biased, in that the principal sources are inscriptions on funerary monuments, most of which were created for men rather than women.

A number of surviving medical papyri provide information concerning the Egyptians' knowledge of medicine and the composition of the body. Such medical texts may have been housed in temple archives (see LIBRARIES), although the only evidence for this is the assertion of the Greek physician Galen (c.AD 129–99) that the ancient temple archives at Memphis were being consulted by Greek and Roman doctors of his own time.

The Edwin Smith Medical Papyrus (c.1600 BC) was once thought to be the work of a military surgeon, but recent opinion suggests that its author may have been a doctor associated with a pyramid-building workforce. The text deals mainly with such problems as broken bones, dislocations and crushings, dividing its forty-eight cases into three classes: 'an ailment which I will treat', 'an ailment with which I will contend' and an 'ailment not to be treated'. The symptoms of each case are described and where possible a remedy prescribed. Although it cannot be claimed that the writer fully understood the concept of the circulation of the blood, he clearly recognized that the condition of the heart could be judged by the pulse: 'The counting of anything with the fingers [is done] to recognize the way the heart goes. There are vessels in it leading to every part of the body . . . When a Sekhmet priest, any *sinw* doctor . . . puts his fingers to the

head . . . to the two hands, to the place of the heart . . . it speaks . . . in every vessel, every part of the body.'

The Kahun Medical Papyrus (c.2100–1900 BC), which may also be the original source for the Ramesseum IV–V and Carlsberg VIII papyri, deals with the ailments of women and is particularly concerned with the womb and the determination of fertility. It also describes such methods of contraception as the consumption of 'excrement of crocodile mixed with sour milk' or the injection of a mixture of honey and natron into the vagina. The Berlin Papyrus (c.1550 BC), on the other hand, contains the earliest known pregnancy test: 'Barley and emmer'. 'The women must moisten it with urine every day . . . if both grow, she will give birth. If the barley grows, it means a male child. If the emmer grows it means a female child. If neither grows she will not give birth.' Modern experiments have shown that the urine of a woman who is not pregnant will actually prevent the growth of barley, suggesting surprising scientific support for this test.

The Ebers Medical Papyrus (c.1555 BC) was originally over 20 m long and consisted simply of a list of some 876 prescriptions and remedies for such ailments as wounds, stomach complaints, gynaecological problems and skin irritations. Prescriptions were made up in proportions according to fractions based on parts of the eye of HORUS, each part symbolizing a fraction from $\frac{1}{64}$ to $\frac{1}{2}$. The Hearst Papyrus (c.1550 BC) is inscribed with over 250 prescriptions, a number of which deal with broken bones and bites (including that of the hippopotamus).

The Brooklyn Papyrus deals with snakebites at great length, while the Chester Beatty VI Papyrus (c.1200 BC) is concerned only with diseases of the anus. The London Papyrus is one of the best examples of the Egyptian three-pronged approach to healing,

which might be described as holistic in modern terms. It consists of a combination of magical spells, rituals and practical prescriptions, all of which would have been considered equally essential to the recovery of the patient.

It is clear from these works that it would be incorrect to suppose that the dissection involved in mummification provided the Egyptians with a good knowledge of the workings of the human body. The purpose of numerous organs remained unknown; for example, although it was known that brain damage could cause paralysis, it was not realized that the brain had anything to do with the act of thinking, an activity which the Egyptians ascribed to the heart. The purpose of the kidneys was also unknown, and it was believed that all bodily fluids, such as blood, urine, excrement and semen, were constantly circulating around the body.

In the Ptolemaic period (332–30 BC) Greek forms of medicine were combined with those of the Egyptians, just as the local deities were assimilated with those of the Greeks. Thus the deified IMHOTEP become identified with the Greek god Asklepios, and the Asklepieion at Saqqara became a centre for medicine. Patients sometimes also stayed overnight in so-called incubation chambers at such temples, as in the cult-place of BES at Saqqara, in the hope of receiving a cure through divinely inspired DREAMS. From the Late Period (747–332 BC) onwards, sanatoria were often attached to major temples such as the cult-centre of Hathor at DENDERA.

J. H. BREASTED, *The Edwin Smith Papyrus*, 2 vols (Chicago, 1930).

A. GARDINER, *The Ramesseum Papyri* (Oxford, 1955).

P. GHALIOUNGUI, *The physicians of pharaonic Egypt* (Cairo, 1983)

A.-P. LECA, *La médecine égyptienne au temps des pharaons* (Paris, 1983).

J. NUNN, *Ancient Egyptian medicine* (London, 1995)

Medinet el-Fayum (Kiman Fares; anc. Shedyet, Crocodilopolis)

Site of the cult centre of the crocodile-god SOBEK, located in the centre of the FAYUM REGION. It is not clear when the settlement of Shedyet was founded, but the earliest known architectural remains derive from a temple of Sobek constructed in the 12th Dynasty (1985–1795 BC) and restored by Rameses II (1279–1213 BC). The settlement and the temple must have particularly flourished during the late Middle Kingdom, when several rulers of the 13th Dynasty (1795–1650 BC) took names including references to Sobek. Most of the surviving remains (including another temple, a sacred lake and some baths) date to the Greco-Roman period (332 BC–AD 395), when the town was the capital of the province of Arsinoe. In the early twentieth century AD the site still covered an area of some three hundred acres, but it has now diminished considerably because of the northwestward expansion of the modern city.

L. KÁKOSY, 'Krokodilskulte', *Lexikon der Ägyptologie* III, ed. W. Helck, E. Otto and W. Westendorf (Wiesbaden, 1980), 801–11.

Medinet Habu (anc. Djamet; Djeme)

Temple complex dating from the New Kingdom to the Late Period (*c*.1550–332 BC) at the southern end of the Theban west bank, opposite modern Luxor. Most of the archaeological and epigraphic work at the site was undertaken by the Chicago Epigraphic Survey in the 1920s and 1930s.

The earliest section of the complex was a small temple built by Hatshepsut (1473–1458 BC) and Thutmose III (1479–1425 BC), but this was later eclipsed by the construction of the mortuary temple of Rameses III (1184–1153 BC). The latter is aligned roughly southeast to northwest, but conventionally the side facing the Nile is described as east. The whole complex is surrounded by massive mud-brick walls, with a copy of a Syrian fortress, known as a *migdol*, serving as its eastern gateway (sometimes called the 'pavilion gate'). The heads of foreign captives are displayed below windows in the eastern passage of the gateway. In rooms above the gate are scenes showing Rameses III at leisure, playing draughts with the women of his HARIM. It is possible that it was in this private suite of rooms that an unsuccessful attempt to assassinate Rameses III took place. Nearby was a landing stage where boats could moor, having reached the site by a canal from the Nile.

The exterior walls of the temple are decorated with scenes from the various campaigns of Rameses III, notably his wars with the LIBYANS and the SEA PEOPLES, who are also depicted in the first court of the temple. The first PYLON shown the king smiting his enemies, while rows of human-headed 'name rings' depict the conquered lands. The second court is devoted to scenes of religious processions, notably those of MIN and SOKAR. Despite the generally good state of preservation of the temple, the HYPOSTYLE HALL has suffered greatly, the columns being reduced to only a few metres. However, in the southwest corner is a treasury building with scenes depicting some of the temple

1	courtyard of Antoninus Pius	8	first court	15	Gate of Rameses III
2	Ptolemaic pylon	9	second pylon	16	palace
3	eastern (fortified or 'Migdol') gateway	10	second court	17	western gateway
4	tomb chapels of god's wives of Amun	11	hypostyle hall	18	residential areas
5	temple of Amun (of Hatshepsut/Thutmose III)	12	first vestibule	19	magazines
6	sacred lake	13	second vestibule	20	indicates position of
7	first pylon	14	sanctuary		the house of Butehamun

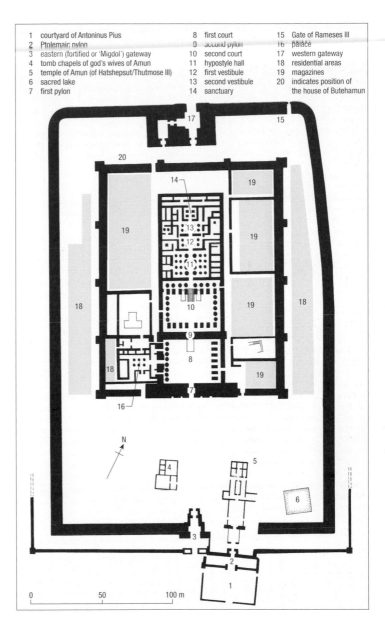

The temple complex of Rameses III at Medinet Habu.

equipment. Other temple valuables were probably kept in a better concealed building immediately in front of the north wall of the sanctuary. The focus of the main axis of the temple is the sanctuary of Amun, behind which lies a false door for 'Amun-Ra united with eternity', namely the divine form of Rameses III.

The temple of Medinet Habu. Set within mud-brick enclosure walls (left and right) is the mortuary temple of Rameses III, the first pylon of which is shown here, as well as other buildings. In the foreground (left) the chapels of the god's wives of Amun can be seen. (P. T. NICHOLSON)

On the southeastern side of the temple are the remains of a royal PALACE, which was probably much smaller than the king's main residence, serving as a spiritual palace as well as for occasional royal visits. It was originally decorated with glazed tiles, many of which are now in the Cairo Museum, and its bathrooms were lined with limestone to protect the mudbrick. From the palace the king could enter the first court, or peruse it from a 'window of appearances' on its southern side

Because of its strong fortifications, Medinet Habu became a refuge in unsettled times, and the residents of the workmen's village at DEIR EL-MEDINA moved there during the late 20th Dynasty (c.1100–1069 BC); the remains of the house of one of the village scribes, Butehamun, are at the western end of the temple. At some later time, however, the temple defences were overwhelmed and the west gate demolished. Near the eastern gate are a group of 'chapel-tombs', beneath which several of the 25th- and 26th-Dynasty GOD'S WIVES OF AMUN (Shepenwepet II, Amenirdis I, Shepenwepet III and Mehitenwesekhet) were buried.

The route to the Amun temple of Hatshepsut and Thutmose III underwent modifications in the 25th Dynasty (747–656 BC), and in Ptolemaic and Roman times. In the Ptolemaic period the town of Djeme was built within the main walled compound. It derived its name from the ancient Egyptian term for the site, Tjamet or Djamet, and took advantage

of the protection offered by the site. During this time the second court of Rameses III's temple was used as a church. For a discussion of the archaeological significance of New Kingdom mortuary temples, see RAMESSEUM (on which the basic plan of Rameses III's mortuary temple was modelled).

EPIGRAPHIC SURVEY, CHICAGO, *Medinet Habu*, 8 vols (Chicago, 1930–70).

U. HÖLSCHER, *The excavation of Medinet Habu*, 5 vols (Chicago, 1934–54).

W. J. MURNANE, *United with eternity: a concise guide to the monuments of Medinet Habu* (Chicago and Cairo, 1980).

Medinet Maadi (anc. Dja; Narmouthis)

Site in the southwestern Fayum region where a temple of the cobra-goddess RENENUTET (a harvest deity) was founded during the reigns of AMENEMHAT III and IV (1855–1799 BC). It was later expanded and embellished during the Greco-Roman period. The dark sandstone inner part of the temple consists of a small papyrus-columned hall leading to a sanctuary comprising three chapels, each containing statues of deities. The central chapel incorporated a large statue of Renenutet, with Amenemhat III and IV standing on either side of her. The Ptolemaic parts of the temple comprise a paved processional way passing through an eight-columned KIOSK leading to a portico and transverse vestibule. It has been suggested that the unusually good preservation of this temple complex, excavated by a team of archaeologists from the University of Milan in the 1930s, may have been due simply to its relative seclusion.

A. VOGLIANO, *Primo (e secondo) rapporto degli scavi condetti della R. Universita di Milano nella zona di Madinet Maadi*, 1935–6 (Milan, 1936–7).

R. NAUMANN, 'Der Tempel des Mittleren

Reiches in Medinet Madi', *MDAIK* 8 (1939), 185–9.

Medjay

Nomadic group originally from the eastern deserts of Nubia, who were commonly employed as scouts and light infantry from the Second Intermediate Period (1650–1550 BC) onwards. They have been identified with the archaeological remains of the so-called PAN-GRAVE CULTURE, although some scholars disagree with this association.

E. ENDESFELDE (ed.), *Ägypten und Kusch* (Berlin, 1977), 227–8.

B. J. KEMP, 'Old Kingdom, Middle Kingdom and Second Intermediate Period', *Ancient Egypt: a social history*, B. G. Trigger et al. (Cambridge, 1983), 71–182 (169–71).

Megiddo, Battle of

Conflict between the armies of the 18th-Dynasty ruler THUTMOSE III (1479–1425 BC) and those of the prince of the Syro-Palestinian city of Qadesh. The latter was no doubt backed by the military might of the state of MITANNI, which had created a network of vassal city-states in Syria during the early 15th century BC. The 'annals' of the reign of Thutmose III, compiled by the military scribe Tjaneni and inscribed on the walls of the Hall of Annals in the temple of Amun at KARNAK, have provided the details of the Battle of Megiddo, as well as sixteen further campaigns in the Levant.

Less than a year after assuming sole rule of Egypt (i.e. after the death of HATSHEPSUT), Thutmose embarked on a campaign to deal with an uprising of Syro-Palestinian city-states. A council of war between the king and his generals revealed that there were three possible strategies for attacking the prince of Qadesh, whose armies were encamped near the city of Megiddo: to take a southerly route via a town called Taanach, which lay about eight kilometres southeast of Megiddo; to march northwards to the town of Djefty, emerging to the west of Megiddo; or to head directly across the ridge, which would allow them to appear from the hills about two kilometres from Megiddo. In time-honoured fashion, the pharaoh chose the direct approach, against the advice of his generals and dismissed the dangers involved in a three-day march single-file through a narrow pass. This route, however, was negotiated successfully, allowing them to launch a surprise frontal attack on the enemy. In the ensuing slaughter, the Asiatics fled into the city, leaving behind the kings of Qadesh and Megiddo, who had to be hauled on to the battlements by their clothing. After a seven-month siege, Megiddo was captured, bringing the campaign to a successful conclusion.

H. H. NELSON, *The battle of Megiddo* (Chicago, 1913).

H. GRAPOW, *Studien zu den Annalen Thutmosis des dritten und zu ihnen verwandten historischen Berichten des Neuen Reiches* (Berlin, 1949).

A. J. SPALINGER, 'Some notes on the Battle of Megiddo and reflections on Egyptian military writing', *MDAIK* 30 (1974), 221–9.

—, 'Some additional remarks on the battle of Megiddo', *GM* 33 (1979), 47–54.

Meidum

Funerary site of an unusual early pyramid complex and associated private cemetery, situated close to the Fayum region. The pyramid

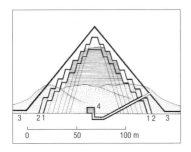

Cross-section through the pyramid at Meidum, showing how the original stepped profiles (1, 2) were infilled to give the smooth profile (3). The burial chamber is labelled 4.

is usually ascribed to Huni (2637–2613 BC), last king of the 3rd Dynasty, although his name does not appear anywhere on the monument and it is perhaps more likely that his funerary monument would have been located at SAQQARA (possibly in an unexcavated enclosure to the west of the step pyramids of DJOSER and SEKHEMKHET). The Meidum pyramid may have belonged to his son SNEFERU, whose name is mentioned in graffiti dating to the New Kingdom (1550–1069 BC) in the passage and chamber of a small mortuary temple at the site. Alternatively it may have been completed by Sneferu but begun by Huni, since Sneferu himself appears to have had two pyramid complexes at DAHSHUR.

The modern appearance of the Meidum pyramid is that of a stepped tower, but it was originally constructed as a seven-stepped pyramid, amended to eight steps, and finally provided with a smooth outer casing to transform it into the earliest true pyramid

(although Sneferu's 'north' pyramid at Dahshur may have been the earliest to have been designed as such from the outset). It was once suggested that the outer casing of the Meidum pyramid collapsed early in the 4th Dynasty, and thus inspired the change of angle in the final stages of Sneferu's 'bent' pyramid at Dahshur, assuming that both were being built simultaneously. However, the presence of a well-established cemetery of early 4th-Dynasty MASTABA tombs surrounding the pyramid, as well as the New Kingdom graffiti in the mortuary temple, all make it more likely that the collapse came much later, and certainly no earlier than the New Kingdom.

The corbelled burial chamber was built into the superstructure of the pyramid at the level of the old ground surface, and, in its architec-

The pyramid of Meidum now presents a tower-like appearance due to the loss of its original casing. It was probably constructed by either Huni or his son, Sneferu. (P. T. NICHOLSON)

tural sophistication, it is regarded as second only to the 'grand gallery' in the Great Pyramid of Khufu (2589–2566 BC) at GIZA. The building interpreted as a mortuary temple on the east side of the pyramid was found to incorporate two enormous uninscribed round-topped stone stelae probably forming part of an offering chapel. An open causeway led to the valley temple, which has not yet been excavated.

The mastaba cemeteries, located north and east of the pyramid, have provided some of the best examples of early 4th-Dynasty paintings,

reliefs and statuary. The internal walls of the superstructure of the tomb of Nefermaat and his wife Atet were decorated with painted scenes of daily life, including the celebrated depiction of the 'Meidum Geese'. The same tomb also includes an innovative, but apparently short-lived, form of wall decoration using coloured paste inlays. The painted limestone statues of Rahotep and Nofret (Egyptian Museum, Cairo), probably a son and daughter-in-law of Sneferu, were discovered by Auguste Mariette in 1871 in a mastaba to the north of the pyramid. The earliest surviving mummy, dating to the 5th Dynasty, was excavated by Flinders Petrie at Meidum in 1891, but it was later destroyed when the Royal College of Surgeons was bombed during the Second World War.

W. M. F. PETRIE, *Meydum* (London, 1892).

W. M. F. PETRIE, E. MACKAY and G. A. WAINWRIGHT, *Meydum and Memphis III* (London, 1910).

K. MENDELSSOHN, 'A building disaster at the Meidum pyramid', *JEA* 59 (1973), 60–71.

I. E. S. EDWARDS, 'The collapse of the Meidum pyramid', *JEA* 60 (1974), 251–2.

R. STADELMANN, 'Snofru und die Pyramiden von Meidum und Daschur', *MDAIK* 36 (1980), 437–9.

M. SALEH and H. SOUROUZIAN, *The Egyptian Museum, Cairo* (Mainz, 1987), nos 25–7.

I. E. S. EDWARDS, *The pyramids of Egypt*, 5th ed. (Harmondsworth, 1993), 71–8.

Meir

Group of decorated rock-cut tombs in Middle

Egypt, about 50 km northwest of modern Asyut. The tombs, dating to the 6th and 12th Dynasties (2345–2181 and 1985–1795 BC respectively), were badly pillaged during the nineteenth century and eventually excavated and recorded by Aylward Blackman between 1912 and 1950. They contained the funerary remains of the governors of Cusae and members of their families, while the shaft-tombs of their servants were cut into the surrounding cliffs. Among the most important tombs are those of Niankhpepykem, a chancellor of Pepy I (AI; 2321–2287 BC), and Senbi, a nomarch (provincial governor) during the reign of Amenemhat I (BI; 1985–1955 BC). There are few remaining traces of the town of Cusae (Qis), the capital of the fourteenth province of Upper Egypt, which was situated about eight kilometres to the east.

A. M. BLACKMAN, *The rock tombs of Meir*, 6 vols (London, 1914–53).

Memnon *see* COLOSSI OF MEMNON

Memphis (Men-nefer)

Capital city of Egypt for most of the Pharaonic period, the site of which is centred on the modern village of Mit Rahina, some 24 km south of modern Cairo. It was capital of the first Lower Egyptian NOME and the administrative capital during the Early Dynastic period (3100–2686 BC) and Old Kingdom (2686–2181 BC). It is said to have been founded by the Ist-Dynasty ruler MENES.

The 'Memphite necropolis', located to the west of the city, includes (north to south) ABU ROASH, GIZA, ZAWIYET EL-ARYAN, ABUSIR, SAQQARA and DAHSHUR, covering a distance of approximately 35 km. Saqqara, however, is both the largest and nearest section of the necropolis. Very few tombs are actually located at Memphis itself, although a few from the First Intermediate Period (2181–2055 BC) have been discovered close to Mit Rahina, while at Kom Fakhry there are tombs of 22nd-Dynasty high priests (945–715 BC).

The name Memphis seems to derive from the pyramid town associated with the pyramid of Pepy I (2321–2287 BC) at Saqqara, which was called Men-nefer (meaning 'established and beautiful'). A more ancient name for the city was Ineb-hedj ('White Walls' or 'White Fortress'), which probably referred to the appearance of the fortified palace of one of the earliest kings. It has been suggested that this original town may have been located near the modern village of Abusir and that the settlement gradually shifted southwards toward modern Mit Rahina. The location of the site at the apex of the Delta made it well suited for

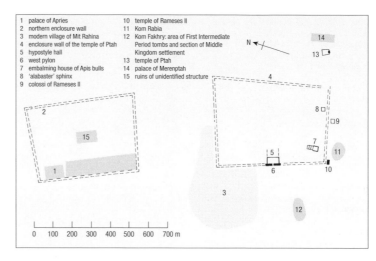

1 palace of Apries
2 northern enclosure wall
3 modern village of Mit Rahina
4 enclosure wall of the temple of Ptah
5 hypostyle hall
6 west pylon
7 embalming house of Apis bulls
8 'alabaster' sphinx
9 colossi of Rameses II
10 temple of Rameses II
11 Kom Rabia
12 Kom Fakhry: area of First Intermediate Period tombs and section of Middle Kingdom settlement
13 temple of Ptah
14 palace of Merenptah
15 ruins of unidentified structure

0 100 200 300 400 500 600 700 m

Plan of Memphis.

the control of both this and the Nile valley, so that it was sometimes also known as the 'balance of the two lands'.

The remains of early Memphis lie beneath thick deposits of Nile alluvium, and much is below the water table. However, a survey directed by David Jeffreys on behalf of the Egypt Exploration Society is attempting to locate an early settlement in an area of ancient higher ground by means of a series of drill corings forming the basis for a map of the subsurface topography.

The most obvious monuments at the site belong to the New Kingdom, the time when THEBES had become the religious and administrative centre of Egypt. Nevertheless, Memphis retained a great deal of importance, and continued to serve as the northern capital. Indeed many scholars see it as the 'real' administrative capital for most of Pharaonic history. The visible New Kingdom monuments comprise the temple of PTAH, patron of the city, much of which dates to the time of Rameses II (1279–1213 BC). However, Ptah, who at Memphis formed a TRIAD with SEKHMET and NEFERTEM, was one of the most ancient deities of Egypt, and earlier temples to him clearly existed. Part of the Ramesside temple re-uses pyramid casing blocks, perhaps brought from Saqqara, and earlier elements, including a lintel of Amenemhat III (1855–1808 BC), have been found there, indicating that older structures remain to be discovered. A fallen colossus of Rameses II and

an 'alabaster' sphinx of the New Kingdom are those features of the site most commonly visited in modern times, since the temple is often flooded owing to the high water table.

The Kom Qala area of the site contains the remains of a palace of Merenptah (1213–1203 BC), successor to Rameses II, along with a smaller Ptah temple. Nearby Petrie discovered the remains of an industrial site of the Roman period, where FAIENCE was being produced. The Kom Rabia area was the focus of a British excavation during the 1980s, yielding a valuable ceramic chronological sequence for the New Kingdom, as well as giving greater insights into a small part of the ancient city.

An embalming house for the APIS bull, living manifestation of Ptah, was built by Sheshonq I (945–924 BC) of the 22nd Dynasty, probably replacing an earlier structure, and traces of this, including enormous travertine embalming tables, are still visible. This too has been the subject of recent excavation. North of the precinct of Ptah is an enclosure of the Late Period, best known for the impressive 26th-Dynasty palace mound of Apries (589–570 BC). Perhaps intentionally, this mound would have provided Apries with a clear view of the Saqqara necropolis, which was a source of inspiration for artistic revival during the SAITE PERIOD.

In Ptolemaic times the city dwindled in importance, losing out to the new sea-port at ALEXANDRIA, while the founding of Fustat, ultimately to become part of Cairo (after the Arab conquest in 641), dealt the final blow to the city. Its remains were still clearly visible in the twelfth century AD, but like the stone buildings of the [...] they have suffered from 'quarrying' and the activities of *sebakhin* (farmers using ancient mud-brick as fertilizer).

W. M. F. PETRIE, *Memphis* I (London, 1909).

R. ANTHES, *Mitrahina 1956* (Philadelphia, 1965).

B. PORTER and R. L. B. MOSS, *Topographical bibliography* III/2 (Oxford, 1978), 830–75.

D. G. JEFFREYS, *The survey of Memphis* (London, 1985).

D. G. JEFFREYS and A. TAVARES, 'The historic landscape of Early Dynastic Memphis', *MDAIK* 50 (1994), 143–74.

Mendes (anc. Per-banebdjedet)

Tell el-Rub'a is the site of Per-banebdjedet, the capital of the sixteenth Lower Egyptian NOME. The chief deity here was originally the goddess HAT-MEHIT, but from the 2nd Dynasty (2890–2686 BC) onwards she was increasingly replaced by her consort, the ram-god Banebdjedet (*ba* [manifestation] of the Lord of Djedet). Their son Harpocrates (see HORUS) completed the Mendesian triad. The earliest surviving structures at the site are MASTABA tombs of the late Old Kingdom, and a granite NAOS of the time of Ahmose II (570–526 BC) is the earliest of the temple remains. The associated city may have been the home-town, and perhaps also the capital, of some of the rulers of the 29th Dynasty (399–380 BC). The Greek historian Herodotus, who visited Egypt around 450 BC, noted the sacrifice of goats at Mendes, in contrast to the use of sheep elsewhere in Egypt. It is possible, however, that he mistook the sacred ram for a goat. There are

also traces of minor Ramesside buildings at the site. Fresh fieldwork during the 1990s has revealed settlement remains of the late Predynastic and Early Dynastic periods.

H. DE MEULENAERE and P. MACKAY, *Mendes* II (Warminster, 1976).

D. J. BREWER and R. J. WENKE, 'Transitional late Predynastic–Early Dynastic occupations at Mendes: a preliminary report', *The Nile Delta in transition: 4th–3rd millennium BC*, ed. E. C. M. van den Brink (Tel Aviv, 1992), 191–7.

Menes (c.3000 BC)

According to the Egyptian historian MANETHO (c.305–285 BC), Menes was the founder of the Egyptian state, responsible for

Inscription on an ivory label for an oil jar, with a record of events in the reign of King Aha. At the right-hand side of the top register is the hieroglyph men, *which has been interpreted as the name of* Menes. *Early Dynastic Period, c.3100 BC, ivory, from the mastaba tomb of Neithhotep at Naqada, H. 4.8 cm. (CAIRO JE31773)*

the Unification of the Two Lands. Unfortunately it is not clear whether Menes is to be identified with the historical figures NARMER or AHA. An ivory plaque from NAQADA bears the name of both Menes (Men) and Aha, although it has been argued that it probably records a visit by the latter to a place connected with Menes. Many scholars now believe that Narmer is the legendary Menes, since the two names are linked on jar-sealings from ABYDOS. However, the identification remains uncertain. In either case we know virtually nothing of the reign of this ruler. His great achievement, the unification of Egypt, now stands as his only memorial. The Greek writer Herodotus credits him with draining the plain of MEMPHIS, but without any evidence. To the ancient Egyptians he was the first human ruler, whereas earlier kings were regarded as demi-gods.

W. B. EMERY, *Archaic Egypt* (Harmondsworth, 1961).

Menkaura (2532–2503 BC)

Penultimate king of the 4th Dynasty, and builder of the third pyramid at GIZA. He was the son of KHAFRA (2558–2532 BC) and grandson of KHUFU (2589–2566 BC), the builders of the two other pyramids at the site. The surviving details of his life are largely anecdotal and derive principally from the Greek historian HERODOTUS, who describes him as a pious and

Wooden coffin from the pyramid of the 4th-Dynasty ruler Menkaura at Giza. 26th Dynasty, c.664–525 BC. (E46647)

just ruler. When told by the oracle of BUTO that he had only six years to live, he is said to have effectively doubled his remaining life by banqueting through the hours of each night.

His pyramid complex was excavated by George REISNER, although the pyramid itself had been entered previously by a number of early nineteenth-century Egyptologists, including Colonel Vyse, who removed a fine sarcophagus (decorated in the palace-façade style; see SEREKH) and attempted to send it back to England by boat. Unfortunately it was lost when the merchant vessel *Beatrice* sank in October 1838. However, part of an anthropoid coffin bearing the name of the king was safely removed to London along with bones from the burial chamber. It is now known that the date of the coffin cannot be any earlier than SAITE

The 'ram of Mendes'. 26th Dynasty, c.600 BC, glass, L. of base 9 cm. (EA63772)

Greywacke triad statue of Menkaura,
accompanied by the goddess Hathor (on his right)
and the personification of the 17th nome of Upper
Egypt (on his left). It was excavated by the
Harvard-Boston expedition from the valley temple
of Menkaura at Giza in 1908, along with three
other triads in perfect condition and a fragment of
a fifth. 4th Dynasty, c.2500 BC, H. 92.5 cm.
(CAIRO JE40679)

times (664–525 BC), and was probably a later
reburial of remains believed to be those of the
king, although the associated bones have been
dated to the Coptic period.

The pyramid, which covers less than a
quarter of the area of the Great Pyramid,
underwent several changes of plan, and was
probably never finished. Its lowest sixteen
courses are of red granite, and it is possible
that the whole was to be covered in this way;
some of the passages are also lined with granite, occasionally carved into palace-façade decoration. From the complex comes a statue of
the king and his wife, Queen Khamerernebty
II, while a number of fine TRIAD statues have
also been discovered. These are among the
finest examples of Old Kingdom sculpture
and are now in the Egyptian Museum, Cairo.
Menkaura was succeeded by Shepseskaf
(2503–2498 BC) who chose to be buried in a
large mastaba-shaped tomb (the Mastabat
Fara'un) midway between SAQQARA and
DAHSHUR.

G. A. REISNER, *The temples of the third pyramid at*
Giza (Cambridge, MA, 1931).
I. E. S. EDWARDS, *The pyramids of Egypt*, 5th ed.
(Harmondsworth, 1993), 137–51.

Menna (*c*.1400 BC)

An 'estate inspector' in the reign of Thutmose
IV (1400–1390 BC), whose Theban tomb (TT
69) at Sheikh Abd el-Qurna included important scenes depicting land survey. The wall
decorations also include the agricultural activities overseen by Menna, as well as religious
and funerary scenes, including the weighing of
the HEART.

B. PORTER and R. L. B. MOSS, *Topographical*
bibliography 1/1 (Oxford, 1960), 134–9.

Mentuemhat (*c*.700–650 BC)

'Prince of the city' and 'fourth prophet of
Amun', who rose to power in the Theban
region during the reign of the Kushite
pharaoh TAHARQO (690–664 BC), on whose
behalf he constructed various additions to the
temple at KARNAK. His career spanned the
transition between the 25th and 26th
Dynasties, surviving the turmoil of the mid
seventh century BC, during which Egypt was

twice conquered by the ASSYRIANS and Taharqo's successor, Tanutamani, struggled for several years against the Saite pharaohs, NEKAU I (672–664 BC) and PSAMTEK I (664–610 BC). Despite the fact that the first Assyrian invasion involved the sacking of Thebes by Esarhaddon's armies, Mentuemhat appears

Grey granite statue of Mentuemhat, from the Cachette Court in the temple of Amun at Karnak. 25th–26th Dynasties, c.670 BC, H. 1.37 m. (CAIRO CG12236)

to have maintained a tight grip over the Theban region, and a cylinder-seal of Ashurbanipal described him as 'king of Thebes'. At the death of Tanutamani in c.656 BC, he controlled a large area, sometimes described as a 'temple state', stretching from Aswan in the south to perhaps as far north as Hermopolis Magna.

Mentuemhat's tomb in western Thebes (TT34) consisted of a decorated subterranean burial chamber and a huge stone and mud-brick superstructure with tall papyrus columns in its forecourt. The reliefs are typical of the archaizing tendencies of the 25th and 26th Dynasties, drawing extensively on the styles and subject-matter of scenes in Old and New Kingdom tombs.

J. LECLANT, *Mentouemhat, quatrième prophète d'Amon, prince de la ville* (Cairo, 1961).

D. EIGNER, *Die monumentalen Grabbauten der Spätzeit in der thebanischen Nekropole* (Vienna, 1984).

Mentuhotep

'Birth name' (meaning 'MONTU is content'), held by a series of three Theban kings of the 11th Dynasty (2055–1985 BC) and one of their ancestors. Their reigns (particularly that of Mentuhotep II) heralded a return to political stability after the comparative confusion and decentralization of the First Intermediate Period (2181–2055 BC). Very little is known

about *Mentuhotep I*, who was the father of *Intef I* (2125–2112 BC), the first recognized ruler of the Theban region. Most chronologies therefore list Intef I, rather than Mentuhotep I, as the earliest 11th-Dynasty ruler of the Theban region. In the reign of Senusret I, however, both Mentuhotep I and Intef I were given their own religious cults and the fictitious Horus name Tepy-aa ('ancestor') was invented for Mentuhotep I, since he and Intef I were both recognized as the founders of the Middle Kingdom.

The most important of the four 11th-

Painted sandstone head of a statue of Mentuhotep II Nebhepetra, from his cult temple at Deir el-Bahri. 11th Dynasty. c.2055–2004 BC, H. 38 cm. (EA720)

Dynasty rulers of Egypt was *Mentuhotep II Nebhepetra*. He assumed control of the country as a whole, primarily by overthrowing the Herakleopolitan 10th Dynasty, who had been the principal rivals of the early 11th-Dynasty rulers. He subsequently moved the capital to Thebes, re-established the post of VIZIER, launched military campaigns against the LIBYANS and the Sinai BEDOUIN, and regained a certain degree of control over NUBIA. At DEIR EL-BAHRI, in western Thebes, he built an unusual terraced funerary complex, the precise reconstruction of which is a matter of debate, although it appears to have been an ingenious combination of elements of the SAFF

TOMB, the Old Kingdom MASTABA and the symbolism of the PRIMEVAL MOUND. Six hundred years later its plan was copied and elaborated by HATSHEPSUT (1473–1458 BC) in the design of her mortuary temple, which is located immediately to the north. Mentuhotep II's complex incorporated a cenotaph containing a seated statue of the king as well as the tombs of six of his queens, including a magnificent set of limestone sarcophagi. His successor, *Mentuhotep III Sankhkara* (2004–1992 BC), was buried in another valley a short distance to the south of Deir el-Bahri, but his funerary complex, consisting of a similar combination of ramp and podium, was unfinished and uninscribed. He rebuilt the fortresses along the border of the eastern Delta, where a cult was later dedicated to himself and the Herakleopolitan ruler Khety III at the site of el-Khatana. The name of the final 11th-Dynasty ruler, *Mentuhotep IV Nebtawyra* (1992–1985 BC), is recorded on a stone bowl from EL-LISHT, but would otherwise be practically unknown if it were not for the rock-carved records of his quarrying expeditions to the Wadi el-Hudi amethyst mines and the Wadi Hammamat siltstone quarries, the latter venture being led by a VIZIER named Amenemhat, who may have later become AMENEMHAT I (1985–1955 BC), the founder of the 12th Dynasty (1985–1795 BC).

E. NAVILLE, *The XIth Dynasty temple at Deir el-Bahari*, 3 vols (London, 1907–13).

H. E. WINLOCK, *The slain soldiers of Nebhepetre Mentuhotep* (New York, 1945).

—, *The rise and fall of the Middle Kingdom in Thebes* (New York, 1947).

D. ARNOLD, *Der Tempel des Königs Mentuhotep von Deir el-Bahari*, 2 vols (Mainz, 1974).

N. GRIMAL, *A history of ancient Egypt* (Oxford, 1992), 154–8.

Merenptah (1213–1203 BC)

The extraordinary length of the reign of RAMESES II (1279–1213 BC) meant that at least twelve of his sons died before him, including Khaemwaset, who was for several years the appointed heir. Merenptah, the fourth pharaoh of the 19th Dynasty, was therefore probably already in his fifties by the time he came to the throne. Apart from an incident in which he sent food supplies to the ailing HITTITE empire, the major event of his reign was an attempted invasion by the LIBYANS and SEA PEOPLES, which he managed to fend off in the fifth year after his accession. Just as Rameses II had recorded the Battle of QADESH in both prose and poetry, so Merenptah described his victory in prose form on a wall beside the sixth pylon at KARNAK and in poetic form on a large granite stele (Egyptian Museum, Cairo), which was discovered by Flinders Petrie in 1896 in the first court of Merenptah's mortuary temple at western THEBES. This monument is usually described as the Israel Stele because it is the earliest surviving Egyptian text to mention the people of ISRAEL (in a list of cities and states defeated by Merenptah). Little of the mortuary temple now remains *in situ* and it mostly consisted of re-used stone blocks, columns and stelae from the nearby mortuary temple of AMENHOTEP III.

Unusually, given the generally poor preservation of PALACES, the best surviving structure from Merenptah's reign is the royal residence that he built next to the temple of Ptah at MEMPHIS. It was excavated in 1915–19 by Clarence Fisher, and many fragments of masonry are now in the collection of the University Museum of Philadelphia. His other major surviving monument is tomb KV8 in the VALLEY OF THE KINGS, which still contains fragments of his stone sarcophagi, although the magnificent granite lid of the outer sarcophagus was excavated from an intact royal burial at TANIS, where it had been re-used to cover the coffins and mummy of PSUSENNES (Pasebakhaenniut) I (1039–991 BC). The body of Merenptah himself was found among the cache of mummies reinterred in the tomb of Amenhotep II (KV35). Following the brief reign of a usurper called Amenmessu, he was succeeded by his son SETY II (1200–1194 BC).

W. M. F. PETRIE, *Six temples at Thebes* (London, 1897).

G. E. SMITH, 'Report on the unwrapping of the mummy of Menephtah', *ASAE* 8 (1907), 108–12.

G. A. WAINWRIGHT, 'Merneptah's aid to the Hittites', *JEA* 46 (1960), 24–5.

M. LICHTHEIM, *Ancient Egyptian literature* II (Berkeley, 1976), 73–8.

D. G. JEFFREYS, *The survey of Memphis* I (London, 1985), 19–20.

Mereruka (*c.*2350 BC)

Vizier, chief justice and inspector of the prophets and tenants of the pyramid of Teti (2345–2323 BC) of the early 6th Dynasty. Also known by the nickname 'Mera', he was the son of Nedjetempet, a royal acquaintance. His wife was the Princess Watetkhethor (nicknamed Seshseshet) and, in keeping with the practice of the Old Kingdom, it was due to his connections with the royal family that he held high office.

His MASTABA tomb at SAQQARA is the largest known at the site, with some thirty-two rooms, and incorporated the burial of his wife and son, Meri-Teti, as well as himself. The tomb is

elegantly decorated with numerous daily-life scenes, including depictions of attempts to domesticate gazelles and hyenas (see ANIMAL HUSBANDRY), and craft activities which are a valuable source of information on the society and economy of the 6th Dynasty. The funerary statue of Mereruka is situated at the northern side of his six-columned hall. The mastaba also incorporated a number of SERDABS (statue chambers).

G. E. J. DARESSY, *Le mastaba de Mera* (Cairo, 1898).

P. DUELL, *The mastaba of Mereruka* (Chicago, 1938).

B. PORTER and R. L. B. MOSS, *Topographical bibliography* III/2 (Oxford, 1978), 525–37.

meret chest

Ceremonial chests containing linen or clothing of four different colours, which symbolized the cloth that was used to wrap up the body of OSIRIS. Each of the four chests was bound up on the outside and decorated with four upright ostrich feathers. From the 17th Dynasty (1650–1550 BC) to the Roman period a ritual called 'consecration of the *meret* chests' or 'dragging the *meret* chests' was celebrated by the pharaoh and often depicted in temple reliefs. The four chests symbolized the four corners of the earth and therefore the whole of Egypt, and the ritual involved the presentation of each chest four times before a god. The symbolic link between Egypt and the chests appears to have derived at least partly from the phonetic similarity between the term *ta meret* (*meret* chest) and the phrase *ta mery* (beloved land). Since the dismemberment, reassembly and revival of the dead god was a crucial element in the myth of Osiris, the presentation of the chests also symbolized resurrection and renewal.

A. EGBERTS, 'Consecrating the *meret*-chests: some reflections on an Egyptian rite', *Akten München, 1985*, ed. S. Schoske (Hamburg, 1989), 241–7.

R. H. WILKINSON, *Symbol and magic in Egyptian art* (London, 1994), 175–6.

Meretseger

Theban cobra-goddess, the literal meaning of whose name is 'she who loves silence'. Her cult is primarily attested during the New Kingdom (1550–1069 BC). She was thought to live on the mountain overlooking the VALLEY OF THE KINGS, which in ancient times bore her name; as a result of this topographic connection, she was also sometimes known as 'the peak of the west'. Her realm encompassed the whole of the Theban necropolis, and she was especially revered by the workmen of DEIR EL-MEDINA

Ostracon showing the workman Khnummose worshipping the serpent form of the goddess Meretseger. 19th Dynasty, c.1200 BC, painted limestone, from Deir el-Medina, Thebes, H. 16.5 cm. (EA8510)

who dedicated many stelae to her. She was believed to punish by blindness or venom those who committed crimes, and the stelae frequently seek to make atonement for such wrongdoings in the hope of a cure. The cult of Meretseger began to decline from the 21st Dynasty (1069–945 BC) onwards, at roughly the same pace as the abandonment of the Theban necropolis itself.

B. BRUYÈRE, *Mert Seger à Deir el Médineh* (Cairo, 1930).

M. LICHTHEIM, *Ancient Egyptian literature* II: *The New Kingdom* (London, 1976), 107–9.

Merimda Beni Salama

Predynastic settlement site in the western margin of the Delta, about 60 km northwest of Cairo, where excavations by German archaeologists in 1928–39 and the 1980s have revealed the earliest evidence for fully sedentary village life in the Nile valley. The 'Merimda' phase of the Lower Egyptian PREDYNASTIC PERIOD appears to have been roughly contemporary with the late Badarian and Amratian phases in Upper Egypt. The total extent of the site is estimated at 180,000 sq. m, and some areas of debris are up to 2 m deep. Radiocarbon dates suggest that it was inhabited between about 5000 and 4500 BC. Karl Butzer has estimated the population at about sixteen thousand, but this may be an overestimate, since Barry Kemp argues that the entire site may have been one small but gradually shifting community rather than a large set of simultaneously occupied villages. The graves within the settlement are largely those of children and are entirely lacking in grave goods.

The pottery and lithics are similar to those

of the Fayum A culture (see ... DEGION) but the shapes and decoration of the pottery are more elaborate and varied at Merimda. Polished black pottery has been found in the upper strata, as well as pear-shaped stone maceheads possibly deriving from Asiatic examples, which have been interpreted as prototypes for the Upper Egyptian Gerzean maceheads (see MACE). The presence of fish bones, hooks, net weights and harpoons suggests that fishing was an important subsistence activity.

The earliest houses at Merimda Beni Salama were simple wind-breaks and pole-framed huts, while the later strata include the remains of mud-brick huts (probably with pitched roofs), measuring no more than 3 m in diameter. The high level of organization within the villages is indicated by the presence of numerous 'granaries', taking the form of jars or baskets, and by the fact that a number of the mud huts were laid out in rough rows as if arranged along streets.

H. JUNKER, *Vorläufer Bericht über die Grabung der Akademie der Wissenschaften in Wien auf der neolitischen Siedlung von Merimde-Beni Salâme*, 6 vols (Vienna, 1929–40).

B. J. KEMP, 'Merimda and the theory of house burial in prehistoric Egypt', *CdE* 43 (1968), 22–33.

M. A. HOFFMAN, *Egypt after the pharaohs* (New York, 1979), 167–81.

J. EIWANGER, *Merimde-Benisalâme*, 2 vols (Mainz, 1984–8).

merkhet *see* ASTRONOMY AND ASTROLOGY

Merneptah *see* MERENPTAH

Meroe

Type-site of the Meroitic period (c.300 BC–AD 350), located on the east bank of the Nile in the Butana region of Sudan, excavated by John Garstang, George Reisner and Peter Shinnie. To the east of the town of Meroe, which became the centre of the Kushite kingdom in the fifth century BC, and adjacent to the modern village of Begarawiya is a cemetery of small pyramidal royal tomb chapels of the Meroitic period, the earliest of which were located at the southern end.

The city includes a number of palaces (possibly two-storeyed), a temple of Isis dating to the NAPATAN period (c.1000–300 BC) and a temple of Amun which was established in the seventh century BC and elaborated in the first century AD. To the east of the town there was also a temple of APEDEMAK, the Nubian lion-god, founded in the third century BC. One of the most striking features of the site is the

presence of large slag heaps deriving from the smelting of IRON, which may well have been one of the mainstays of the city's prosperity. It was once suggested that the Meroitic kingdom supplied iron to the rest of Africa, but iron artefacts do not appear to have been unusually prominent in Meroitic settlements or graves and it was not until the post-Meroitic period that iron became crucial to the economy of Nubia.

New insights into the end of the Meroitic

ABOVE *Fragment of relief from the south wall of the funerary chapel of pyramid N 11 at Meroe, which probably belonged to Queen Shakdakhete (c. 2nd century BC), the first female ruler of Meroe. She is here shown enthroned with a prince and protected by the wings of the goddess Isis. H. 2.52 m. (EA719)*

LEFT *Gold ornament representing some form of canine animal, perhaps a jackal. Although it is said to have been found near Cyrene in Libya, it is clearly of Meroitic work and is closely paralleled by other examples found in the pyramid of Queen Amanishakheto. 1st century BC, H. 3.1 cm. (EA68502)*

period – suggesting that there was no dramatic collapse of the civilization but simply a process of cultural change – have been provided by the excavation of a 'post-Meroitic' tumulus burial at the site of el-Hobagi, about 60 km southwest of Meroe.

D. DUNHAM and S. CHAPMAN, *The royal cemeteries of Kush*, III –V (Boston, 1952–63).

P. L. SHINNIE, *Meroe: a civilization of the Sudan* (London, 1967).

P. L. SHINNIE and F. J. KENSE, 'Meroitic iron

working', *Meroitic studies*, ed. N. B. Millet and
A. L. Kelley (Berlin, 1982), 17–28.

P. LENOBLE and N. D. M. SHARIF, 'Barbarians at
the gates? the royal mounds of el-Hobagi and the
end of Meroë', *Antiquity* 66 (1992), 626–35.

L. TÖRÖK, *Meroe city: an ancient African capital*
(London, 1997).

Meroitic *see* MEROE

Mersa Matruh (anc. Paraetonium)
Harbour-site on the Egyptian Mediterranean
coast, about 200 km west of Alexandria, which
was the site of the Ptolemaic city of
Paraetonium. In the late second millennium
BC colonists from the eastern Mediterranean
appear to have founded the first small settle-

*Basalt vessel of a type thought to be of Libyan
origin; similar stone vessels have been excavated
from graves in the vicinity of Mersa Matruh.
Early 3rd millennium BC, H. 27.5 cm. (EA64354)*

ment at Mersa Matruh on an island in the
lagoon. The excavated artefacts from the
island include large quantities of Syro-
Palestinian, Minoan, Cypriot and Mycenaean
pottery vessels, indicating a wide range of
trade links between the Aegean region and the
north African coast during the New Kingdom
(1550–1069 BC). The earliest traces of
Egyptian occupation in the area are the ruins
of a fortress of Rameses II (1279–1213 BC) at
Zawiyat Umm el-Rakham, about 20 km to the
west of the site of Paraetonium.

D. WHITE, 'Excavations at Mersa Matruh,
summer 1985', *NARCE* 131 (1985), 3–17.

—, 'The 1985 excavations on Bates' Island,
Marsa Matruh', *JARCE* 23 (1986), 51–84.

—, 'University of Pennsylvania expedition to
Marsa Matruh, 1987', *NARCE* 139 (1987), 8–12.

Meskhent
Goddess of childbirth, who is represented in
the form of a female-headed birth-brick (on
which ancient Egyptian women delivered their
children) or as a woman with a brick on her
head. At the time of a child's birth she also
determined its destiny. However, from the
New Kingdom (1550–1069 BC) onwards this
role could be taken by the male god SHAY.
Papyrus Westcar describes how she told each
of the first three kings of the 5th Dynasty
(2494–2345 BC), all of whom were buried at
ABUSIR, that they would eventually come to
rule Egypt. She was also a funerary goddess
and was present at the judgement of the
deceased to aid in their rebirth into the afterlife, just as she had in life itself.

See also BES; HEKET; TAWERET.

G. PINCH, *Magic in ancient Egypt* (London,
1994), 127–8.

Mesopotamia
Term used to describe the area covered by
modern Iraq, encompassing at various times
the ancient Kingdoms of AKKAD, SUMER, BABY-
LONIA and ASSYRIA. The word derives from the
Greek term meaning '[the land] between the
rivers', the rivers being the Tigris and
Euphrates.

M. ROAF, *Cultural atlas of Mesopotamia* (New
York and Oxford, 1990).

metals and metalworking *see* COPPER;
GOLD; IRON and SILVER

Middle Kingdom (2055–1650 BC)
Chronological phase that began with the reign
of the Theban ruler MENTUHOTEP II
Nebhepetra (2055–2004 BC) and ended with
the demise of the 13th Dynasty (c.1650 BC); it
is usually divided into two phases, the early
Middle Kingdom (consisting of the late 11th
and early 12th Dynasties) and the late Middle
Kingdom (from the reign of SENUSRET III to
the end of the 13th Dynasty). The diverse literary output of the Middle Kingdom, including the proliferation of WISDOM LITERATURE,
provides some insights into the social and
political concerns of the period, although
many of the classic texts, such as the *Tale of
Sinuhe* and the *Discourse of Neferty*, are difficult to analyse because of uncertainty as to
their original functions, audience and intent.

In the New Kingdom the KING LISTS suggest
that Mentuhotep II was regarded as the
founder of the Middle Kingdom, and at this
period his funerary monument at DEIR
EL-BAHRI was evidently considered to be one of
the finest achievements of the period. Little
textual evidence has survived concerning

Mentuhotep IV Nebtawyra, the last 11th-
Dynasty ruler, but it is possible that his vizier,
Amenemhat, may be the same individual as the
first king of the 12th Dynasty, AMENEMHAT I,
who established a new capital called
Amenemhatitjtawy ('Amenemhat takes possession of the two lands'), often abbreviated to
Itjtawy. The archaeological remains of this city,
where the Residence (royal court) was situated
until the end of the Middle Kingdom, have not
yet been located. It is usually assumed to have
been on the west bank of the Nile in the vicinity of the pyramid complexes of Amenemhat I
and his successor Senusret I at EL-LISHT, midway between Memphis and Meidum.

The early 12th Dynasty was characterized
by the clarification of the boundaries of
nomes, the agricultural development of the
FAYUM and the gradual annexation of Lower
NUBIA. The principal sources of evidence for
the royal court of the 12th Dynasty derive
from the pyramid complexes located at el-
Lisht, EL-LAHUN (Senusret II), DAHSHUR
(Amenemhat II, Senusret III and Amenemhat
III) and HAWARA (Amenemhat III), but élite
provincial cemeteries at sites such as ASYUT,
DEIR EL-BERSHA, MEIR and BENI HASAN also continued to flourish during the early 12th
Dynasty at least. By the late 12th Dynasty the
royal pyramid complexes began to be surrounded by more substantial remains of the
tombs of courtiers, perhaps indicating
stronger links between the nomarchs (provincial governors) and the Residence.

As far as the non-funerary architecture of
the period is concerned, a few examples of
religious buildings have survived, including
the earliest known phases of the temple of
Amun at KARNAK and the temple of Sobek and
Amenemhat III at MEDINET MAADI, but many
appear to have been dismantled and re-used in
the course of the foundation of the temples of
the New Kingdom. ABYDOS became particularly important as a centre of pilgrimage as a
result of the increasing significance of the god
OSIRIS, whose burial place was identified with
that of DJER, in the Umm el-Qa'ab region of
the site.

The reign of Senusret III seems to have constituted a watershed in the Middle Kingdom,
both in terms of the administrative system and
the nature of the surviving funerary remains.
It was during his reign that the string of
FORTRESSES in Nubia were strengthened, thus
consolidating the Egyptian grip on the
resources of Nubia. At the same time, the
excavation of a channel through the first Nile
cataract at Aswan would have had the effect of
allowing boats to travel unhindered from the
second cataract to the Mediterranean coast.

Although Manetho's 13th Dynasty evidently continued to rule from Itjtawy, there appear to have been a large number of rulers with very short reigns, none of whom were in power for long enough to construct funerary complexes on the same scale as their 12th-Dynasty predecessors. In other respects, however, the material culture and political and social systems of the late 12th and 13th Dynasties were relatively homogeneous. W. C. Hayes argued that the real central power during the 13th Dynasty resided largely with the VIZIERS, but it is now considered more likely that royal authority was maintained, despite a general lack of political continuity. The fragmented nature of the 13th Dynasty undoubtedly had a damaging effect on the control of Egypt's borders, resulting in a relaxation of the grip over Nubia and an influx of Asiatics in the Delta (particularly apparent in the archaeological remains at TELL EL-DAB'A in the eastern Delta). The end of the Middle Kingdom was marked by the abandonment of Itjtawy at roughly the same time that the minor rulers of parts of the Delta were supplanted by the *heka-khaswt* ('rulers of foreign lands'), rendered in Greek as the HYKSOS.

See also BUHEN; C GROUP; COFFIN TEXTS; MIRGISSA and SEMNA.

H. E. WINLOCK, *The rise and fall of the Middle Kingdom in Thebes* (New York, 1947).

W. C. HAYES, *A papyrus of the late Middle Kingdom in the Brooklyn Museum* (Brooklyn, 1955).

G. POSENER, *Littérature et politique dans l'Egypte de la XII dynastie* (Paris, 1956).

I. E. S. EDWARDS, C. J. GADD and N. G. L. HAMMOND (ed.), *Cambridge Ancient History* 1/2: *Early history of the Middle East*, 3rd ed (Cambridge, 1971), 464–531.

J. BOURRIAU, *Pharaohs and mortals: Egyptian art in the Middle Kingdom* (Cambridge, 1988).

D. FRANKE, 'Zur Chronologie des Mittleren Reiches: I & II', *Orientalia* 57 (1988), 113–38, 245–74.

R. B. PARKINSON, *Voices from ancient Egypt: an anthology of Middle Kingdom writings* (London, 1991).

S. QUIRKE (ed.), *Middle Kingdom studies* (New Malden, 1991).

Min

ITHYPHALLIC fertility god and symbol of male potency, who served also as the protector of mining areas in the Eastern Desert. He was associated first with the site of KOPTOS and later with AKHMIM, which became known as Panopolis in the Ptolemaic period, because of the Greeks' association of Min with the god Pan. Characteristic Pharaonic depictions show

him as a mummiform figure holding his erect phallus with his left hand, while his right arm is raised in a smiting gesture, with a flail simultaneously poised above his hand. He

Ceremonial palette carved in the form of schematic birds' heads at the top and bearing the symbol of the fertility-god Min in raised relief. Late Predynastic, c.3100 BC, schist, from el-Amra, H. 29.5 cm. (EA35501)

usually wore a low crown surmounted by two plumes and with a long ribbon trailing down behind him. At least as early as the 6th Dynasty (2345–2181 BC), he was particularly associated with the long (or 'cos') lettuce (*lactuca sativa*), probably because of a perceived link between the milky sap of lettuces and human semen, and the depictions of Min often show a set of lettuces placed on an offering table beside him.

He was already being worshipped in the late Predynastic period (*c*.3100 BC), when his emblem – a strange shape consisting of a horizontal line embellished with a central disc flanked by two hemispherical protrusions (variously interpreted as a door-bolt, barbed arrow, lightning bolt or pair of fossil shells) – was depicted on pottery vessels, maceheads and palettes. This emblem, often placed on a standard, later became part of the hieroglyphic representation of the god's name and also that of the ninth Upper Egyptian nome, of which Akhmim was the capital.

An ink drawing on a stone bowl from the tomb of the late 2nd-Dynasty king Khasekhemwy (*c*.2686 BC) is probably the earliest example of the anthropomorphic, ithyphallic portrayal of Min, but there are also

three limestone colossal statues excavated by Flinders Petrie at the site of Koptos. If these figures (now in the Ashmolean Museum, Oxford) date to the Early Dynastic period (3100–2686 BC), as many scholars have suggested on art-historical grounds, they would be the earliest surviving three-dimensional versions of the anthropomorphic aspect of Min. This was evidently the form taken by a statue of the god which, according to the PALERMO STONE, a KING LIST dating to the 5th Dynasty (2494–2345 BC), was carved by royal decree in the 1st Dynasty.

In a 5th-Dynasty tomb at Giza a 'procession of Min' is mentioned, and it has been suggested that he may have featured in the PYRAMID TEXTS as 'the one who raises his arm in the east'. In the Middle Kingdom (2055–1650 BC) the cult of Min–like that of SOPED, another deity of the Eastern Desert–was often assimilated with the myth of HORUS, and he was sometimes described as the son of ISIS. At other times, however, he was considered to be part of a TRIAD, with Isis as his consort and Horus as their son.

By the New Kingdom (1550–1069 BC), Min

Fragment of a basalt clepsydra ('water clock') carved with scenes of offering involving the Macedonian king, Philip Arrhidaeus, and (on the left) an ithyphallic figure of Min. Macedonian period, c.320 BC, H. 35 cm. (EA938)

had effectively become the primeval creator-god manifestation of AMUN. The ceremonies surrounding the coronations and jubilees of Egyptian kings (see SED FESTIVAL) therefore usually incorporated a festival of Min designed to ensure the potency of the pharaoh. Senusret I (1965–1920 BC) is portrayed in the act of performing certain jubilee rituals in front of Min on a limestone relief

now in the Petrie Museum, London (see KOP-
TOS for illustration). A Min festival is also
depicted among the reliefs in the second court
of the temple of Rameses III (1184–1153 BC) at
MEDINET HABU, where the king is shown scyth-
ing a sheaf of wheat in recognition of Min's
role as an agricultural god.

W. M. F. PETRIE, *Koptos* (London, 1896), pls
III–IV

R. GERMER, 'Die Bedeutung des Lattichs als
Pflanze des Min', *SAK* 8 (1980), 85–7.

J. R. OGDON, 'Some notes on the iconography of
Min', *BES* 7 (1985–6), 29–41.

B. J. KEMP, *Ancient Egypt: anatomy of a
civilization* (London, 1989), 79–81, 85, fig. 28.

R. H. WILKINSON, 'Ancient Near Eastern raised-
arm figures and the iconography of the Egyptian
god Min', *BES* II (1991–2), 109–18.

Minshat Abu Omar

Predynastic and Early Dynastic cemetery site
located in the eastern Delta, about 150 km
northeast of Cairo, which, like the roughly
contemporary settlement at MAADI, shows evidence of trade with southern Palestine.
Excavations in the late 1970s and 1980s
revealed a sequence of nearly four hundred
graves stretching from Naqada II to the 1st
Dynasty. Out of a total of about two thousand
pottery vessels, twenty were definitely identified as Palestinian imports. The dates of these
imported vessels (mainly wavy-handled and
loop-handled jars) suggest that the Minshat
Abu Omar trade links with the Levant began
slightly later than those of Maadi but continued until a slightly later date. There is also a
larger proportion of Gerzean pottery at
Minshat Abu Omar than at Maadi, suggesting
much stronger links with Upper Egyptian late
Predynastic sites. An auger-bore survey of the
surrounding region has indicated the presence
of late Predynastic and Early Dynastic settlement about 500 m from the cemetery.

K. KROEPER and D. WILDUNG, *Minshat Abu
Omar: Münchner Ostdelta-Expedition Vorbericht
1978–1984* (Munich, 1985).

K. KROEPER, 'The excavations of the Munich
East-Delta expedition in Minshat Abu Omar',
*The archaeology of the Nile Delta: problems and
priorities*, ed. C. M. van den Brink (Amsterdam,
1988), 11–19.

L. KRZYŻANIAK, 'Recent archaeological evidence
on the earliest settlement in the eastern Nile
delta', *Late prehistory of the Nile Basin and the
Sahara*, ed. L. Krzyżaniak and M. Kobusiewicz
(Poznan, 1989), 267–85.

Mirgissa (anc. Iken?)

Fortified site of the Middle Kingdom
(2055–1650 BC), located in Lower Nubia,

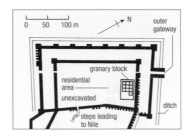

The Middle Kingdom fortresses at Mirgissa.

immediately to the west of the southern end of
the second Nile cataract, 350 km south of
modern Aswan. The site has been submerged
beneath Lake Nasser since the completion of
the ASWAN HIGH DAM in 1971, but the surviving
remains consisted of a pair of 12th-Dynasty
fortresses (one on the desert plateau and one
on the valley floor) as well as two cemeteries.
The plateau fortress was surrounded by a
ditch and inner and outer enclosure walls.
Covering a total area of some four hectares, it
was the largest of eleven fortresses built in the
reign of Senusret III (1874–1855 BC) between
the second and third cataracts, protecting the
royal monopoly on trade from the south. The
site included granaries, an armoury (where
spears, javelins and shields were manufactured
and stored), an extensive quayside and a mud-
lined slipway (so that boats could be dragged
along the bank, thus avoiding the Kabuka
rapids). These factors suggest that Mirgissa
was not only a garrison but also a depot for the
warehousing of trade goods.

On the island of Dabenarti, about a kilometre east of Mirgissa, are the remains of an
unfinished fortified mud-brick outpost, apparently of similar date. The presence of only four
potsherds at this smaller site suggests that it
was never actually occupied; it may perhaps
have been intended as a temporary outpost to
which the Mirgissa garrison could be transferred in an emergency.

S. CLARKE, 'Ancient Egyptian frontier
fortresses', *JEA* 3 (1916), 155–79.

J. W. RUBY, 'Preliminary report of the University
of California expedition to Dabenarti, 1963',
Kush 12 (1964), 54–6.

D. DUNHAM, *Second cataract forts* II: *Uronarti,
Shalfak, Mirgissa* (Boston, 1967), 141–76.

J. VERCOUTTER, *Mirgissa*, 3 vols (Paris and Lille,
1970–6).

mirror

As might be expected of an implement which
reflects an image, the mirror had both functional and symbolic uses. Mirrors occur from
at least as early as the Old Kingdom
(2686–2181 BC). They consist of a flat disc,
usually of polished bronze or copper, attached
to a handle. From the Middle Kingdom
(2055–1650 BC) onwards they take the form of
a sun-disc, and the handle is frequently represented as a PAPYRUS stalk, or as the goddess
HATHOR, to whom two mirrors might be
offered as they were to the goddess MUT.
Handles could also take the form of female figures, probably carrying erotic overtones and
serving as an extension of the Hathor theme. A
greater diversity of types of handle is known
from the New Kingdom (1550–1069 BC), perhaps because metal was commonly used for
the handles of this time, while wood and ivory
were more common in earlier periods.
Occasional representations show mirrors in
use, such as a lady applying kohl in the Turin
Erotic Papyrus (see EROTICA).

H. SCHÄFER, 'Die Ausdeutung der Spiegelplatte
als Sonnenscheibe', *ZÄS* 68 (1932), 1–7.

C. EVRARD-DERRIKS, 'A propos des miroirs
égyptiens à manche en forme de statuette
féminine', *Revue des Archéologiques et Historiens
d'Art de Louvain* 5 (1972), 6–16.

H. SCHÄFER, *Egyptian mirrors from the earliest
times through the Middle Kingdom* (Berlin, 1979).

C. LILYQUIST, 'Mirrors', *Egypt's golden age*, ed.
E. Brovarski et al. (Boston, 1982), 184–8.

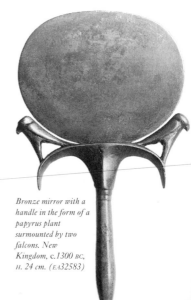

*Bronze mirror with a
handle in the form of a
papyrus plant
surmounted by two
falcons. New
Kingdom, c.1300 BC,
H. 24 cm. (EA32583)*

Mitanni

One of Egypt's most powerful rivals in western Asia, the Mitannian state developed in the area of the Tigris and Euphrates rivers some time before 1500 BC, and was overthrown by the HITTITES and ASSYRIANS around 1370 BC, having formerly been their equal.

The capital of Mitanni was Washshukanni, which has tentatively been identified with the site of Tell el-Fakhariyeh in Turkey. The country was probably known to the Egyptians as Nahrin, while the Assyrians referred to it as Hanigalbat, and the Hittites described it as 'the land of the Hurrians'. The names of the Mitannian rulers suggest that they were Indo-Europeans, although the mass of the population were Hurrian, a people whose language is unrelated to other main groups. This people seem to have originated around the Caspian Sea during the third millennium BC, and gradually moved south into Syria.

The campaigns of THUTMOSE III (1479–1425 BC) took him beyond the vassal cities of Syria (see BATTLE OF MEGIDDO) and into the Mitanni heartland itself. In the reign of Thutmose IV (1400–1390 BC) there were diplomatic marriages between the two countries, with Mitannian princesses entering the Egyptian HARIM. Such alliances probably sought to offset the threat from the Hittite empire. That friendly relations between Egypt and Mitanni followed is witnessed by the sending, on two occasions, of the Ninevite goddess Ishtar (the Mesopotamian name for ASTARTE) to Egypt, in order to help cure Amenhotep III (1390–1352 BC) of an illness. The AMARNA LETTERS contain references to Mitanni at this time and during the reign of Akhenaten (1352–1336 BC).

G. CONTENAU, La civilisation des Hittites et des Mitannienes (Paris, 1934).

M. LIVERANI, 'Hurri e Mitanni', Oriens Antiquus 1 (1962), 253–7.

H. KLENGEL, 'Mitanni: Probleme seiner Expansion und politische Struktur', Revue hittite et asianique 36 (1978), 94–5.

M. ROAF, Cultural atlas of Mesopotamia (New York and Oxford, 1990), 132–40.

D. B. REDFORD, Egypt, Canaan and Israel in ancient times (Princeton, 1992), 159–74.

Mnevis (Mer-wer)

Sacred bull regarded as the BA ('power' or physical manifestation) of the sun-god at HELIOPOLIS. Whereas many sacred birds and animals, such as ibises, cats and baboons, were slaughtered and mummified in large numbers as votive offerings, there was only one APIS, BUCHIS or Mnevis bull at any one time. When the sacred bull died it was usually buried with great ceremony and a new bull with similar

being placed in its place. While the Apis was usually a black bull selected because of the diamond-shaped patch of white hair on its forehead, the Mnevis bull was required to be totally black and was usually represented with a sun-disc and uraeus (see WADJYT) between its horns.

The historian PLUTARCH claimed that the Mnevis bull was second only to the Apis in rank, and that, like the Apis, he gave ORACLES to his worshippers. Just as the mothers of the Apis and Buchis bulls were given separate cults, so also the mother of the Mnevis bull was revered in the guise of the cow-goddess Hesat. Ramesside burials of Mnevis bulls are known from Arab el-Tawil, to the northeast of the destroyed temple of Heliopolis. Eventually the cult of the Mnevis bull became subsumed into that of the creator-god Ra-ATUM.

Because of his close connections with the sun-god, the Mnevis was one of the few divine beings recognized by Akhenaten (1352–1336 BC), who stated on one of the 'boundary stelae' at EL-AMARNA: 'Let a cemetery for the Mnevis bull be made in the eastern mountain of Akhetaten that he may be buried in it'. However the location of this burial, possibly close to Akhenaten's tomb, is unknown.

W. J. MURNANE and C. C. VAN SICLEN III, The boundary stelae of Akhenaten (London, 1993), 41, 169.

L. KÁKOSY, 'Mnevis', Lexikon der Ägyptologie IV, ed. W. Helck, E. Otto and W. Westendorf (Wiesbaden, 1982), 165–7.

Mo'alla, el-

Rock-cut cemetery of the First Intermediate Period (2181–2055 BC), located on the east bank of the Nile, about 24 km south of Luxor. The only two decorated tombs belong to the provincial governors Ankhtifi and Sobekhotep; the biographical texts on the walls of Ankhtifi's tomb provide important historical information concerning the complicated political events in the immediate aftermath of the end of the Old Kingdom (see FAMINE).

J. VANDIER, Mo'alla, la tombe d'Ankhtifi et la tombe de Sébekhotep (Cairo, 1950).

D. SPANEL, 'The date of Ankhtifi of Mo'alla', GM 78 (1984), 87–94.

modius

Term for a tall cylindrical container, which is usually employed to refer to a Roman measure of capacity. However, in Classical art and Egyptology the term is used also to describe a cylindrical headdress (of variable height), commonly worn by such deities as the hippopotamus-goddess TAWERET.

Montu (Month, Monthu)

Falcon-headed god of war, usually represented with a headdress consisting of a sun-disc and two plumes. His cult is first attested at various sites in the Theban region, and major temples, dating from the Middle Kingdom (2055–1650 BC) to the Roman period, were constructed at ARMANT, KARNAK, MEDAMUD and TOD. His two consorts were the goddesses Tjenenyet and Ra'ttawy, both also associated with the Theban district. The sacred BUCHIS (bekh) bulls, buried in the so-called Bucheum at Armant, were regarded as physical manifestations of Montu, just as the APIS bulls were associated with PTAH (see SERAPEUM) and the MNEVIS bulls linked with Ra at HELIOPOLIS.

Montu played an important role in the 11th

A red granite four-sided monument of unknown purpose from the temple complex at Karnak. The monument is carved with six high-relief figures, comprising two of Montu-Ra (one of which is shown on the far left in the illustration), two of Thutmose III, and two of the goddess Hathor. 18th Dynasty, reign of Thutmose III, c.1450 BC, H. 1.78 m. (EA12)

Dynasty (2125–1985 BC), when four of the kings held the 'birth name' MENTUHOTEP ('Montu is content'). But the emergence of the 12th Dynasty (1985–1795 BC), including a number of rulers named AMENEMHAT ('Amun is in the forefront'), clearly indicated that Montu was being overshadowed by another Theban deity, AMUN. Nevertheless Montu retained a considerable degree of importance as a personification of the more aggressive aspects of the kingship, particularly in the conquest of neighbouring lands during the New Kingdom and, like Amun, he eventually became fused with the sun-god as Montu-Ra.

G. LEGRAIN, 'Notes sur le dieu Montou', *BIFAO* 12 (1912), 75–124.

F. BISSON DE LA ROQUE, 'Notes sur le dieu Montou', *BIFAO* 40 (1941), 1–49.

E. K. WERNER, *The god Montu: from the earliest attestations to the end of the Old Kingdom* (Ann Arbor, 1986)

—, 'Montu and the "falcon ships" of the Eighteenth Dynasty', *JARCE* 23 (1986), 107–23.

mourning *see* FUNERARY BELIEFS

mummification

The preservation of the body was an essential part of ancient Egyptian funerary practice, since it was to the body that the KA would return in order to find sustenance. If the body had decayed or was unrecognizable the *ka* would go hungry, and the afterlife be jeopardized. Mummification was therefore dedicated to the prevention of decay.

It has often been stated that the practice grew from observing that the hot, dry sand preserved those bodies buried in it; and that, having seen the effect on Predynastic corpses, the Egyptians sought to improve upon nature. This seems an inadequate and flawed explanation, and it is probably best to assume that the practice evolved simply to preserve the image of the body, and as techniques became more sophisticated so more of the actual body was retained. Some support for this is found in the fact that mummies from the Old Kingdom (2686–2181 BC) seem to have had their form and features preserved in plaster and paint, while the actual body decayed away beneath.

The Greek historian HERODOTUS (*c.*450 BC) provides the best literary account of the mummification process, although the technique would have been well past its peak by the time he observed it. He states:

There are those who are established in this profession and who practise the craft. When a corpse is brought to them they show the bearers wooden models of mummies, painted in imitation of the real thing. The best method of embalming is said to be that which was practised on one whose name I cannot mention in this context [i.e. OSIRIS]. The second method they demonstrate is somewhat inferior and costs less. The third is cheapest of all. Having indicated the differences, they ask by which method the corpse is to be prepared. And when the bearers have agreed a price and departed, the embalmers are left to begin their work.

In the best treatment, first of all they draw out the brains through the nostrils with an iron hook. When they have removed what they can this way they flush out the remainder with drugs. Next they make an incision in the flank with a sharp Ethiopian stone [i.e. obsidian blade] through which they extract all the internal organs. They then clean out the body cavity, rinsing it with palm wine and pounded spices, all except frankincense, and stitch it up again. And when they have done this they cover the corpse with natron for seventy days, but no longer, and so mummify it. After the seventy days are up, they wash the corpse and wrap it from head to toe in bandages of the finest linen anointed with gum, which the Egyptians use for the most part instead of glue. Finally they hand over the body to the relatives who place it in a wooden coffin in the shape of a man before shutting it up in a burial chamber, propped upright against a wall. This is the most costly method of preparing the dead.

Those for whom the second and less expensive way has been chosen are treated as follows: the embalmers fill their syringes with cedar oil which they inject into the abdomen, neither cutting the flesh nor extracting the internal organs but introducing the oil through the anus which is then stopped up. Then they mummify the body for the prescribed number of days, at the end of which they allow the oil which has been injected to escape. So great is its strength that it brings away all the internal organs in liquid form. Moreover the natron eats away the flesh, reducing the body to skin and bone. After they have done this the embalmers give back the body without further ado. The third method of embalming, which is practised on the bodies of the poor, is this: the embalmers wash out the abdomen with a purge, mummify the corpse for seventy days then give it back to be taken away.

Embalmers evidently took some pride in their work, and were more highly organized than Herodotus implies. The overseers held priestly titles, stemming from the distant past when only royalty and the highest nobility were embalmed. It should be remembered that for most of Egyptian history the poorest people must have been interred in simple graves in the sand and relied on natural preservation. In charge of mummification was the 'overseer of the mysteries' (*hery seshta*) who took the part of the jackal-god ANUBIS. His assistant

Coffin and wrapped mummified body of Irethoreru. The mummy is furnished with a gilt mask and covered in a bead netting decorated with a figure of the sky-goddess Nut over the breast. 26th Dynasty, c.600 BC (?), from Akhmim, H. 1.65 m. (EA20745).

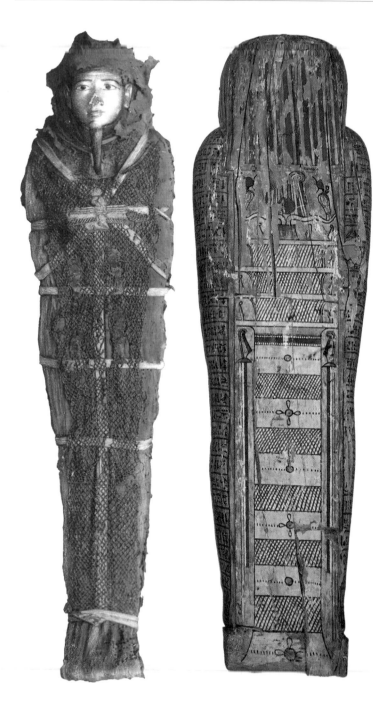

was the 'seal-bearer of the god' (*hetemw net-jer*), a title formerly borne by priests of Osiris. It was the lector priest (*ḥery ḥeb*) who read the magical spells. Together these men oversaw the 'bandagers' (*wetyw*) who undertook most of the actual evisceration and bandaging.

As these titles indicate, mummification was not only a technical process but also a ritualized one, the whole act seeking to repeat the stages in the making of the original mummy, that of Osiris. We know from two papyri of the first century AD describing 'the ritual of embalming' (copied from earlier sources) that very specific rituals accompanied every stage of the work.

Shortly after death a body would be taken to a tent known as the *ibw* or 'Place of Purification' where it would be washed in NATRON solution, before being taken to another area enclosing a further tent and known as the 'House of Beauty' (*per nefer*), where the actual mummification took place. In the first method described by Herodotus the body would be eviscerated, except for the heart and kidneys. This was achieved by making an incision in the left flank, which would later be covered by an embalming plate. Prior to the New Kingdom (1550–1069 BC), however, evisceration was not always practised, and the brain was usually discarded.

When the viscera were removed, they were dried, rinsed, bandaged and placed in CANOPIC JARS or parcels, which were placed with the body or, in the Third Intermediate Period (1069–717 BC), returned to the body cavity, decorated on the exterior with the images of the four SONS OF HORUS. Wax figures of the latter were also frequently included in the visceral packages. Natron would then be piled over the corpse to desiccate it. Until quite recently scholars believed that the body was placed in a liquid natron solution, but experimental work has shown that dry natron is more effective. From the discovery of a wooden embalming table at Thebes, and from the travertine embalming tables of the APIS bulls at Memphis, it is clear that the natron was mounded over the body. Packets of natron might also be inserted into the body cavity during this period, to assist in the dehydration process. During this time up to 75 per cent of the body weight would be lost.

After some forty days the temporary stuffing would be removed (although it contained part of the deceased and was therefore retained for the burial), and the body cavity was packed with bags of clean natron, resin-soaked bandages and various aromatics in such a way as to give the body a more natural shape. In the 21st Dynasty (1069–945 BC), subcutaneous packing was sometimes used to model the musculature of arms and legs and fill out the face. This was attempted, somewhat over-enthusiastically, on the mummy of the 21st-Dynasty priestess Henuttawy (wife of the chief priest of Amun, Pinudjem I), whose cheeks cracked as the skin shrank and dried. The brain cavity was also filled with resin or linen, the openings to the skull were packed, and artificial eyes were often added.

The whole body was then coated in resin, thus adding to the already darkened colour of the skin. The Arabs mistook this blackening for the effects of bitumen, and it is from their word for this – *mummiya* – that the word 'mummy' derives. In fact bitumen is rarely found on mummies, although many have the appearance of being coated with it. Cosmetics were sometimes added, in order to give the body its final life-like appearance, and the whole was then bandaged, AMULETS being wrapped among the layers in the appropriate places dictated by their function. The type, material, and placing of such amulets is described in the BOOK OF THE DEAD. The bandaging took some fifteen days, and used many metres of linen, much of it from old clothing. In the cheaper methods evisceration was undertaken through the anus, much as Herodotus states, and the body desiccated.

The entire process – from death to burial – usually took seventy days, a period of time probably connected with the phases of the dog star Sirius (see SOTHIC CYCLE). In the Old Kingdom, the deceased was believed to return as a star, and the period of mummification coincided with the time during which the star was invisible. At the end of the process the deceased was renewed, and one of the embalming spells concludes with the assurance: 'You will live again, you will live for ever. Behold, you are young again for ever.'

Less is known about the mummification of animals, although research into the mummification of cats and ibises has recently been undertaken. A demotic papyrus in Vienna records the procedures that accompanied mummification of the Apis bull. See also OPENING OF THE MOUTH CEREMONY.

G. E. SMITH, *A contribution to the study of mummification in ancient Egypt with special reference to the measures adopted during the 21st Dynasty for moulding the form of the body* (Cairo, 1906).

A. and E. COCKBURN, *Mummies, disease and ancient cultures* (Cambridge, 1980).

J. HARRIS and E. F. WENTE, *An X-ray atlas of the royal mummies* (Chicago, 1980).

B. ADAMS, *Egyptian mummies* (Aylesbury, 1984).

C. ANDREWS, *Egyptian mummies* (London, 1984).

A. F. SHORE, 'Human and divine mummification', *Studies in pharaonic religion and society presented to J. Gwyn Griffith*, ed. A. B. Lloyd (London, 1992), 226–8.

L. TROY, 'Creating a god: the mummification ritual', *BACE* 4 (1993), 55–81.

F. DURAND and R. LICHTENBERG, *Mummies: a journey into eternity* (London, 1994).

R. PARTRIDGE, *Faces of pharaohs: royal mummies and coffins from ancient Thebes* (London, 1994).

mummy label (Greek *tabla*)

During the Greco-Roman period, when corpses were regularly being transported from the home to the cemetery (and sometimes, if the death occurred away from home, back to their village), they were usually identified by tags made of wood, and occasionally stone. Mummy labels were inscribed with short ink texts in Greek or demotic (or occasionally in both languages), giving such vital information as the name, age, home-town and destination of the deceased, although some bear more elaborate inscriptions ranging from the cost of transport to short funerary prayers. In the case of poorer individuals, it appears that the labels might even have served as cheap STELAE or tombstones in the graves themselves.

W. SPIEGELBERG, *Ägyptische und griechische Eigennamen auf Mummienetiketten der römischen Kaiserzeit* (Leipzig, 1901).

J. C. SHELTON, 'Mummy tags from the Ashmolean Museum, Oxford', *CdE* 45 (1970), 334–52.

F. BARATTE and B. BOYAVAL, 'Catalogue des étiquettes de momies du Musée du Louvre', *CRIPEL* 2 (1974), 155–264.

J. QUAEGEBEUR, 'Mummy labels: an orientation', *Textes grecs, démotiques et bilingues (P. L. Bat. 19)*, ed. E. Boswinkel and P. W. Pestman (Leiden, 1978), 232–59.

Muqdam, Tell el- (anc. Taremu; Leontopolis)

Large settlement site in the central Delta, which was probably the power-base of the 23rd Dynasty (818–715 BC). The eastern sector of the site of the ancient town of Taremu is still dominated by the remains of the temple of the local LION-god Mihos. The large-scale removal and re-use of relief blocks from the temple has made the building difficult to date precisely, although surviving stelae and statuary indicate that there was already a temple at Taremu in the 18th Dynasty (1550–1295 BC). The site is usually assumed to have incorporated the royal cemetery of the 23rd Dynasty, although it has recently been argued that the capital at this time may actually have been at Khemenu (HERMOPOLIS MAGNA). Only the tomb of Queen Kama(ma), mother of OSORKON III (777–749 BC), has so far been locat-ed at Leontopolis (to the west of the main ruins). During the Ptolemaic period Taremu became known as Leontopolis ('lion city') and was capital of the eleventh Lower Egyptian nome (province).

E. NAVILLE, *Ahnas el Medineh (Heracleopolis Magna)* (London, 1894), 27–31.

K. A. KITCHEN, *The Third Intermediate Period in Egypt (1100–650 BC)*, 2nd ed. (Warminster, 1986), 128–30.

P. A. SPENCER and A. J. SPENCER, 'Notes on late Libyan Egypt', *JEA* 72 (1986), 198–201.

C. A. REDMOUNT and R. FRIEDMAN, 'The 1993 field season of the Berkeley Tell el-Muqdam project: preliminary report', *NARCE* 164 (winter 1994), 1–10.

music, musical instruments

A great deal of Egyptian religious and secular celebration was marked by the performance of both music and DANCE. The depiction of musicians on such late Predynastic artefacts as ceremonial palettes and stone vessels indicates the importance accorded to music even in prehistoric times. A wide variety of instruments were played, ranging from pairs of simple ivory clappers (probably already depicted on Predynastic pottery vessels of the mid fourth millennium BC) to the harps and lutes that were frequently played at banquets during the New Kingdom (1550–1069 BC).

The importance of music in ancient Egypt is attested by the large number of instruments in museum collections. Ancient Egyptian musical instruments consisted of four basic types: idiophones, membranophones, aerophones and cordophones. The idiophones, including clappers, sistra, cymbals and bells, were particularly associated with religious worship. The membranophones included the tambourine, usually played by girls at banquets or in outdoor ceremonies, and also the drum, a military instrument that was sometimes used in religious processions. The earliest Egyptian aerophone was the flute, but there were also double 'clarinets', double 'oboes' and trumpets or bugles (mostly connected with the army). The chordophones consisted of three types: the harp (an indigenous Egyptian instrument) and the lute and lyre (both Asiatic imports). Perhaps the best indication of the ancient Egyptians' sheer enjoyment of music is to be found in a 'satirical' papyrus (Museo Egizio, Turin) depicting an ass with a large arched harp, a lion with a lyre, a crocodile with a lute and a monkey with a double 'oboe'.

H. HICKMANN, *45 siècles de musique dans l'Egypte ancienne* (Paris, 1956).

R. D. ANDERSON, *Musical instruments* (London, 1976).

Detail of a fragment of wall-painting from a Theban tomb-chapel, showing female musicians singing and playing various instruments (lutes, a double oboe and a tambourine). 18th Dynasty, c.1400 BC, painted plaster, from Thebes, H. 61 cm. (EA37981)

C. ZIEGLER, *Les instruments de musique égyptiens au Musée du Louvre* (Paris, 1979).

L. MANNICHE, *Music and musicians in ancient Egypt* (London, 1991).

Mut

Vulture goddess who usurped the role of Amaunet in the Theban TRIAD as consort of AMUN and mother of KHONS. She was usually

Detail of a sandstone stele recording repaired flood damage, showing the Roman Emperor Tiberius offering a figure of the goddess Maat to the deities Mut and Khonsu. Roman period, AD 14–37, H. 66.3 cm. (EA398)

depicted as a woman wearing a long brightly coloured (sometimes feather-patterned) dress and a vulture headdress surmounted by the 'white crown' or 'double crown' (see CROWNS). She usually also held a long PAPYRUS sceptre symbolizing Upper Egypt. Like ISIS and HATHOR she essentially played the role of divine mother to the reigning king; therefore many amulets representing Mut show her as a seated woman suckling a child, often only distinguishable as Mut rather than Isis because of the presence of a crown or an inscription naming the figure. The royal women holding the title of GOD'S WIFE OF AMUN were all portrayed with iconographic features linking them with Mut. She also, however, had a more aggressive aspect as a feline goddess closely linked with SEKHMET, and many of the statues in her temple at KARNAK represent her in this lioness-headed form. Sekhmet, Mut and TEFNUT were all daughters of the sun-god, or 'EYES OF RA', sent to terrorize the peoples of the earth.

H. TE VELDE, 'Towards a minimal definition of the goddess Mut', *JEOL* 8/26 (1979–80), 3–9.

H. DE MEULENAERE, 'Isi et Mout des mammisi', *Studia Naster* II, ed. J. Quaegebeur (Leuven, 1982).

H. TE VELDE, 'The cat as sacred animal of the goddess Mut', *Studies in Egyptian religion dedicated to Professor Jan Zandee*, ed. M. Heerma van Voss et al. (Leiden, 1982), 127–37.

—, 'Mut, the eye of Re', *Akten München 1985* III, ed. S. Schoske (Hamburg, 1989), 395–403.

Mycerinus *see* MENKAURA

mythology

The activities of the gods of the Pharaonic period, as well as their interactions with humans, are largely encapsulated in divine 'attributes' (such as epithets and iconographic features) or such genres as HYMNS, spells and rites, rather than being expressed in conventional narrative forms. On the basis of these scattered fragments of information, however, it has proved possible to reconstruct versions of a variety of 'myths' of the Pharaonic period, associated with such issues as CREATION, KINGSHIP and life after death (see FUNERARY BELIEFS and OSIRIS). There are, however, also a number of surviving literary texts that more closely approximate to the Classical concept of a narrative-style myth, such as the *Tale of Horus and Seth* and the *Tale of Isis and the Seven Scorpions*. In addition, the reliefs and inscriptions in the ambulatory of the Ptolemaic temple of HORUS at EDFU (as well as the Middle Kingdom 'Ramesseum Dramatic Papyrus') have been interpreted by many scholars as the texts of a mythological 'drama', consisting of the enactment of the triumph of the god Horus over his rival SETH.

See also AMUN; BOOK OF THE DEAD; COFFIN TEXTS; FUNERARY TEXTS; PYRAMID TEXTS and RELIGION.

H. FRANKFORT, *Kingship and the gods: a study of Near Eastern religion as the integration of society and nature* (Chicago, 1948).

H. W. FAIRMAN, *The triumph of Horus* (London, 1974).

H. ALTENMÜLLER, 'Dramatischer Ramesseumspapyrus', *Lexikon der Ägyptologie* I, ed. W. Helck, E. Otto and W. Westendorf (Wiesbaden, 1975), 1132–40.

J. ASSMANN, 'Die Verborgenheit des Mythos in Ägypten', *GM* 25 (1977), 7–44.

E. BRUNNER-TRAUT, 'Mythos', *Lexikon der Ägyptologie* IV, ed. W. Helck, E. Otto and W. Westendorf (Wiesbaden, 1982), 277–86.

J. R. ALLEN, *Genesis in Egypt – the philosophy of ancient Egyptian creation accounts* (New Haven, 1988).

G. HART, *Egyptian myths* (London, 1990).

N

Nag el-Deir (Naga-el-Der)

Cemetery in northern Upper Egypt situated on the east bank of the Nile south of AKHMIM and spanning the Predynastic period to the Middle Kingdom (*c*.4000–1650 BC). Its excavation was begun in 1901 by the American scholar George REISNER, whose team recorded the excavation in meticulous detail and excavated the cemetery as a whole, rather than concentrating only on individual, potentially rich tombs, as had been the case with the work of many late nineteenth-century excavators. As a result, it has proved possible to gain some idea of the development of the cemetery and to examine the burial practices closely. Reisner made a full publication of each Predynastic tomb, rather than simply publishing those that he considered to be significant. With this comprehensive style of publication, he surpassed his predecessors (and indeed many later excavators of Egyptian sites). His careful excavations revealed such details as the clothing and position of the bodies, which would have otherwise been lost information. Among the finds from the Dynastic period is a 6th-Dynasty LETTER TO THE DEAD from the tomb of Meru (N3737).

The work conducted by Reisner and Albert Lythgoe at the N7000 Predynastic cemetery was sufficiently detailed to allow recent re-analysis of the remains. Their excavation records included unusually detailed descriptions of the skeletons themselves, provided by the anatomist Grafton Elliot Smith, thus supplying modern biological anthropologists with a good database for further research.

G. A. REISNER and A. MACE, *The Early Dynastic cemeteries of Naga-ed-Dêr* (Boston, 1908–9).

G. A. REISNER, *A provincial cemetery of the pyramid age: Naga-ed-Dêr* (Oxford, 1932).

A. LYTHGOE, *The Predynastic cemetery* N7000, *Naga-ed-Der*, Part IV, ed. D. Dunham (Berkeley, 1965).

P. V. PODZORSKI, *Their bones shall not perish: an examination of Predynastic human skeletal remains from Naga-ed-Dêr in Egypt* (New Malden, 1990).

—,'The correlation of skeletal remains and burial goods: an example from Naga-ed-Der N7000', *Biological anthropology and the study of ancient Egypt*, ed. W. V. Davies and R. Walker (London, 1993), 119–29.

Nakht

Scribe and astronomer of AMUN who probably lived during the reign of Thutmose IV (1400–1390 BC). He is best known for his well-preserved tomb (TT52) in the Theban cemetery of Sheikh 'Abd el-Qurna, which is decorated with many paintings depicting scenes from daily life, including agricultural activities, as well as the entertainment of guests at a banquet. The name of the god Amun was excised from this tomb during the time of Akhenaten (1352–1336 BC) as part of the ATEN 'heresy'.

N. DE G. DAVIES, *The tomb of Nakht at Thebes* (New York, 1917).

B. PORTER and R. L. B. MOSS, *Topographical bibliography* 1/1 (Oxford, 1960), 99–102.

names

Egyptians set great store by the naming of people and objects, and the name was regarded as an essential element of every human individual, just as necessary for survival as the KA, BA or AKH. Fashions in personal names often follow those of the rulers of the time, and often incorporate the name of a deity chosen either because they were pre-eminent

Limestone 'name-stone' of Hatshepsut from the vicinity of her Valley Temple at Deir el Bahri. Such stones are especially common at the temple and seem to have served a votive purpose. The other side of this example bears an ink inscription mentioning Senenmut and the date 'second month of the summer season, day 9'. Thebes, H. 28 cm. (EA52882)

at that period or locally important in the place where the individual was born. The name of an individual is therefore often a clue as to date or geographical origins. Although some names are simply nouns or adjectives, such as Neferet ('beautiful woman'), others take the form of statements such as Rahotep ('Ra is satisfied') or Khasekhemwy ('the two powers appear').

The importance of words and names, not merely as abstract symbols but as physical manifestations of the named phenomena themselves, is re-emphasized by the so-called Memphite Theology, inscribed on the SHABAQO Stone, in which the god PTAH creates everything in the universe by pronouncing each of the names (see CREATION). In the same way, the Egyptian reference works known as ONOMASTICA simply consisted of lists of names for such things as people, professions and places, without any description or definition, since it was presumably felt that the name or word was in itself a perfect expression of the phenomenon concerned.

Like the SHADOW, the name was regarded as a living part of each human being, which had to be assigned immediately at birth, otherwise it was felt that the individual would not properly come into existence. In the case of KING LISTS inscribed on the walls of temples and tombs, the cult of the royal ancestors was celebrated by writing out the CARTOUCHES of past rulers, and in a sense it was the list of names on which the cultic rituals focused rather than the individual rulers themselves.

The symbolic importance of the name also meant that the removal of personal or royal names from monuments or statuary was considered to be equivalent to the destruction of the very memory and existence of the person to whom the name referred. Conversely, the addition of a new name to a relief or statue (an act usually described by Egyptologists as the 'usurping' of a work) was considered to imbue it with the essence and personality of the new owner, regardless of its actual physical appearance.

See also ROYAL TITULARY.

P. LACAU, 'Suppressions des noms divins dans les textes de la chambre funéraire', *ASAE* 26 (1926). 69–81.

H. RANKE, *Die ägyptische Personennamen*, 3 vols (Hamburg, 1932–77).

G. POSENER, 'Sur l'attribution d'un nom à un enfant', *RdE* 22 (1970), 204–5.

S. QUIRKE, *Who were the pharaohs?* (London, 1990), 9–19.

E. HORNUNG, *Idea into image*, trans. E. Bredeck (New York, 1992), 177–8.

naophorous *see* NAOS

naos

Ancient Greek term for the innermost part of a temple or shrine, which is used by Egyptologists to refer to a type of shrine containing the cult-image or sacred BARK of a deity kept in the sanctuary. Generally taking the form of a rectangular chest or box hewn from a single block of wood or stone, the *naos* could also be used as a container for a funerary statue or a mummified animal. Egyptian 'naophorous' statues portrayed the subject holding a shrine, sometimes containing a divine image.

G. ROEDER, *Naos*, 2 vols (Leipzig, 1914).

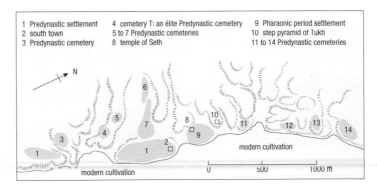

Standing naophorous (naos-bearing) statue of a man in traditional Egyptian posture; the naos contains a figure of the god Atum wearing the double crown. Roman period, 1st century AD, basalt, H. 46 cm. (EA65443)

Napata

District of NUBIA on the Dongola reach of the Nile, about 30 km southwest of the fourth cataract, which has given its name to the Napatan period. The area was settled in the mid-fifteenth century BC as a southern outpost of the Egyptian empire. When the empire declined, however, Napata emerged as the political centre of the kingdom of Kush (c.1000–300 BC), which had previously been dominated by the KERMA culture. The location of Napata would have allowed the Kushite kings of the Napatan period to control trade along two important desert routes: the northern road to the town of KAWA and the southern to MEROE (which gradually replaced Napata as political centre from the early sixth century BC onwards). It is clear, however, that Napata was still an area of

considerable importance throughout the Meroitic period (300 BC–AD 300).

The main site of Napata, located to the south of the Nile (which at this point is flowing from east to west), incorporates a cemetery, a possible palace building and a partially excavated settlement. To the north of the river are the remains of an unusual temple of AMUN at Gebel Barkal ('pure mountain') and probably also another settlement, although the latter has not yet been satisfactorily examined.

The district of Napata in its wider sense includes the royal cemeteries at EL-KURRU and NURI and an extensive settlement and cemetery at Sanam, where F. Llewellyn Griffith excavated about fifteen hundred non-royal graves. Although the Napatan religious and funerary remains have been used to construct a detailed chronology for the Napatan period, there has still been very little excavation of Napatan settlements, therefore little is known of the economic and social aspects of Kush in the first millennium BC.

F. LL. GRIFFITH, 'Oxford excavations in Nubia', *Liverpool Annals of Archaeology and Anthropology* 9 (1922), 67–124.

D. DUNHAM, *The royal cemeteries of Kush*, 4 vols (Boston, 1950–7).

B. G. HAYCOCK, 'Towards a better understanding of the Kingdom of Cush (Napata-Meroë)', *Sudan Notes and Records* 49 (1968), 1–16.

D. DUNHAM, *The Barkal temples* (Boston, 1970).

T. KENDALL, *Gebel Barkal epigraphic survey 1986: preliminary report to the Visiting Committee of the Department of Egyptian Art* (Boston, 1986).

Naqada (anc. Nubt, Ombos)

One of the largest Predynastic sites in Egypt, located about 26 km north of Luxor on the west bank of the Nile. The Predynastic cemeteries of Tukh and el-Ballas, about 7 km north of the modern village of Naqada, were

excavated by Flinders Petrie and James Quibell in 1895. Petrie initially misinterpreted the contents of over two thousand graves as the remains of foreigners dating to the First Intermediate Period (2181–2055 BC), whom he described as the 'New Race'. Eventually, primarily as a result of Jacques de Morgan's identification of Predynastic remains at ABYDOS, Petrie recognized that the material he had excavated at Naqada and HIW–SEMAINA, including pottery, pressureflaked flints and ivory combs, was prehistoric, forming the basis for the chronological phases Naqada I and II, c.4000–3100 BC, now more commonly described as the Amratian and Gerzean periods (see PREDYNASTIC PERIOD). Cemetery T at Naqada is a collection of fifty-seven brick-built and richly equipped graves which are thought to have belonged to the ruling élite of the late Naqada II (Gerzean) period.

The site also includes the remains of a Predynastic walled town (the 'South Town') founded at least as early as 3600 BC. The historical name for Naqada was Nubt, meaning 'Gold[-town]', suggesting that the inhabitants may well have benefited from their location opposite KOPTOS and the Wadi Hammamat, through which they would have been able to exploit the precious minerals of the Eastern Desert. The South Town at Naqada continued to flourish up to the beginning of the Early Dynastic period, when it appears to have been eclipsed by the growing political power of the settlements at HIERAKONPOLIS and ABYDOS. The site also incorporates a town and temple of the Dynastic period.

An Early Dynastic mud-brick MASTABA tomb with palace-façade walls surrounding its superstructure – which closely resembles those at SAQQARA and Abydos – was discovered about

Plan of Naqada

1 Predynastic settlement	4 cemetery T: an élite Predynastic cemetery	9 Pharaonic period settlement
2 south town	5 to 7 Predynastic cemeteries	10 step pyramid of Tukh
3 Predynastic cemetery	8 temple of Seth	11 to 14 Predynastic cemeteries

ABOVE *A pot of the Naqada II period (c.3500 BC), painted with designs of boats and human figures. This type of decoration disappears in pharaonic times. H. 30.5 cm. (EA36327)*

J. DE MORGAN, *Recherches sur les origines de l'Egypte*, 2 vols (Paris, 1896–7).

E. BAUMGARTEL, *Petrie's Naqada excavation: a supplement* (London, 1970).

J. J. CASTILLOS, 'An analysis of the tombs in the Predynastic cemeteries at Nagada', *JSSEA* 10 (1981), 97–106.

W. DAVIS, 'Cemetery T at Naqada', *MDAIK* 39 (1983), 17–28.

C. BAROCAS, 'Fouilles de l'Istituto Universitario Orientale (Naples) à Zawaydah (Naqadah, "South Town" de Petrie): campagne 1984', *Akten München* 1985 II, ed. S. Schoske (Hamburg, 1989), 299–303.

K. BARD, 'The evolution of social complexity in predynastic Egypt: an analysis of the Nagada cemeteries', *JMA* 2/2 (1989), 223–48.

Narmer (c.3100 BC)

Early Egyptian ruler who is sometimes identified with MENES, the semi-mythical founder of MEMPHIS. He is thought to have been buried in Tomb B17–18 in the Umm el-Qa'ab royal cemetery at ABYDOS. He is primarily known, however, from a mudstone ceremonial palette (Egyptian Museum, Cairo) and a limestone macehead (Ashmolean, Oxford), both of which were excavated at HIERAKONPOLIS in Upper Egypt. The archaeological contexts of the two artefacts were poorly documented but

BELOW *The Narmer Palette from the so-called 'Main Deposit' at Hierakonpolis. On one side (left) Narmer, wearing the crown of Upper Egypt, smites a foreigner. On the other side (right) he wears the crown of Lower Egypt. Protodynastic, c.3000 BC, mudstone, H. 64 cm. (CAIRO JE32169)*

three kilometres northwest of Naqada village by Jacques de Morgan in 1897. It contained fragments of stone vases and ivory labels as well as clay sealings bearing the names of the 1st-Dynasty ruler AHA (c.3100 BC), and a woman called Neithhotep (perhaps his wife), to whom the tomb may have belonged. Another monument in the vicinity is a small stone-built step pyramid near the village of Tukh. This is one of at least seven small step pyramids of unknown function erected at different sites from Seila down to Aswan, possibly in the reign of the 3rd-Dynasty ruler Huni (2637–2613 BC).

W. M. F. PETRIE and J. E. QUIBELL, *Naqada and Ballas* (London, 1896).

the macehead appears to have been one of a set of Protodynastic votive items (described as the 'Main Deposit') buried beneath the floor of the temple building of the Old Kingdom (2686–2181 BC), while the palette was discovered a few metres away. Both have been dated stylistically to the Protodynastic period (c.3100–2950 BC).

Only fragments of the macehead were recovered, whereas the palette has survived intact and in virtually perfect condition. Both faces are carved with reliefs showing an Egyptian ruler who is identified as 'Narmer' by two early hieroglyphic characters carved in front of him. On one side he is shown as a king wearing the white CROWN of Upper Egypt smiting a foreigner (possibly a LIBYAN) in the presence of the hawk-god, while on the reverse he is depicted in the red crown of Lower Egypt apparently taking part in a procession with standard-bearers, moving towards rows of decapitated prisoners perhaps suggesting a victory celebration.

Until the 1980s, the Narmer palette was widely regarded as a memorial relating to a set of specific military successes over Libyans and/or northern Egyptians, accomplished by the king of Upper Egypt in the course of unifying Egypt, and there are still some adherents to this view. However, it now seems less likely that the decorations on the Narmer palette and other contemporary votive objects (such as the Narmer macehead, Libyan palette and SCORPION macehead) are documents of specific historical events. Nicholas Millet argues that the depictions are instead iconographic summaries of the particular year in which the object concerned was presented to the temple, and warns against construing the events shown on these objects as 'in themselves necessarily important and "historical"'. Whitney Davis interprets the images on the Protodynastic palettes, including that of Narmer, as visual metaphors for the process by which the king/artist/hunter creeps up on his prey and delivers the death-blow.

J. E. QUIBELL, *Hierakonpolis* I (London, 1900), pl. XXIX.

W. B. EMERY, *Archaic Egypt* (Harmondsworth, 1961), 42–7.

M. SALEH and H. SOUROUZIAN, *Official catalogue: the Egyptian Museum, Cairo* (Mainz, 1987), cat. no. 8.

B. WILLIAMS, 'Narmer and the Coptos colossi', *JARCE* 25 (1988), 93–101.

N. MILLET, 'The Narmer macehead and related objects', *JARCE* 27 (1990), 53–9.

W. A. FAIRSERVIS Jr, 'A revised view of the Na'rmr palette', *JARCE* 28 (1991), 1–20.

W. DAVIS, *Masking the blow* (Berkeley, 1992).

natron

Naturally occurring compound largely consisting of sodium carbonate and sodium bicarbonate. It was important principally for its use in purification rituals, not least during MUMMIFICATION, and was subject to a royal monopoly

Bag of natron from Deir el-Bahri. Natron is a common constituent of caches of embalmers' materials, well known from Thebes. 18th Dynasty. (EA47807)

in the Ptolemaic period (332–30 BC). It was often used in daily cleansing, serving those purposes for which soap or toothpaste would now be used. It had a variety of 'industrial' uses, the most important of which was the making of GLASS and glazes, although it does not seem to have been widely used as an alkali source in glass-making before the Ptolemaic and Roman periods.

The best-known source of natron is the Wadi Natrun in Lower Egypt, although deposits are also known at ELKAB in Upper Egypt, as well as in the Beheira province of Lower Egypt. In all of these regions, the substance has accumulated on the shores and beds of ancient lakes. The deposits at Wadi Natrun and Elkab are mentioned in textual sources from the Pharaonic period, and the historians Strabo (c.64 BC–AD 21) and Pliny (AD 23–79) both mention the presence of natron in Egypt.

A. LUCAS, *Ancient materials and industries*, 4th ed. (London, 1962), 263–7.

A. T. SANDISON, 'The use of natron in mummification in ancient Egypt', *JNES* 22 (1963), 259–67.

Naukratis (Kom Gi'eif)

Site of a Greek settlement on the CANOPIC branch of the Nile in the western Delta. It was located only about 16 km from SAIS, the

capital of the 26th-Dynasty rulers, under whom Naukratis was reorganized. The modern name of the site itself is Kom Gi'eif, although the ancient name appears to have survived in the name of the nearby village of el-Niqrash.

According to the Greek historian Herodotus, the site was given to the Greeks by Ahmose II (570–526 BC), along with a monopoly on seaborne TRADE to Egypt, although it is more likely that Ahmose II simply reorganized an existing settlement of foreigners, giving them new trading privileges. It is clear from such finds as Corinthian 'transitional' pottery that the Greek settlement at the site dates back to c.630 BC. The levy on trade was directed to the temple of NEITH at Sais.

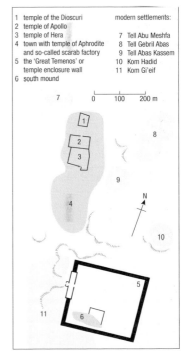

		modern settlements:
1	temple of the Dioscuri	
2	temple of Apollo	
3	temple of Hera	7 Tell Abu Meshfa
4	town with temple of Aphrodite and so-called scarab factory	8 Tell Gebril Abas
5	the 'Great Temenos' or temple enclosure wall	9 Tell Abas Kassem
6	south mound	10 Kom Hadid
		11 Kom Gi'eif

Plan of Naukratis.

The earliest Greeks at the site seem to have been Corinthians, but it was the Milesians and a number of other groups who were most influential in Saite times. The Hellenion building served the communal needs of these various Greek communities.

There were temples to various deities, including Chian Aphrodite and Samian Hera (whose name is known from votive pottery) as well as the Milesian Apollo.

The site was excavated by Flinders Petrie in 1884–5, when it was found to be in poor condition. It was also later investigated by F. Ll. Griffith and D. G. Hogarth, and, during the 1980s, by an American team of archaeologists. In the southern part of the town, Petrie discovered a FAIENCE workshop which produced such typically Egyptian items as SCARABS, as well as various Greek and Egyptianizing products. Evidence for pottery production has also been discovered at the site.

Silver and bronze coins, comprising the only coinage known from Pharaonic Egypt, were struck at Naukratis, and it is likely that coins struck elsewhere in the Greek world entered Egypt via this important settlement. Under the Ptolemies the importance of Naukratis declined in favour of ALEXANDRIA.

W. M. F. PETRIE and E. A. GARDNER, *Naukratis* I (London, 1886).

D. G. HOGARTH, 'Excavations at Naucratis', *Annual of the British School at Athens* 5 (1898–9), 26–97.

D. G. HOGARTH, H. L. LORIMER and C. C. EDGAR, 'Naukratis 1903', *Journal of Hellenic Studies* 25 (1905), 105–36.

J. BOARDMAN, *The Greeks overseas* (Harmondsworth, 1964).

W. DAVIS, 'The Cypriotes at Naukratis', *GM* 41 (1980), 7–19.

W. D. E. COULSON and A. LEONARD Jr, *Cities of the Delta* I: *Naukratis: preliminary report on the 1977–1978 and 1980 seasons* (Malibu, 1981).

—, 'The Naukratis project 1983', *Muse* 17 (1983), 64–71.

navy *see* ARMY; SEA PEOPLES and SHIPS AND BOATS

Necho *see* NEKAU

Nectanebo

Name employed by the Egyptian historian MANETHO to refer to two Egyptian rulers of the 30th Dynasty (380–343 BC), who actually held two different 'birth names': Nakhtnebef (Nectanebo I) and Nakhthorheb (Nectanebo II).

Nectanebo I Kheperkara (380–362 BC) of Sebennytos seized the throne after the deaths of the 29th-Dynasty rulers Hakor (393–380 BC) and Nepherites II (380 BC). Six years later the Persian satrap Pharnabazes launched an invasion of Egypt, sending a fleet manned mainly by GREEK soldiers from northern Palestine to the mouth of the Mendesian tributary of the Nile. Although the Persians were initially very successful, they were eventually delayed in their victorious march south as a result of dissension between Pharnabazes and the Greek general Iphikrates, thus allowing Nectanebo to reassemble his armies and expel the Persians from the Delta. The rest of his reign was relatively peaceful, although the Egyptians appear to have been virtually alone in their defiance of the Persians. Towards the end of the reign, his son Teos (362–360 BC) even led a campaign into Syria–Palestine.

Nectanebo undertook programmes of construction and decoration at virtually all of the major Egyptian temples, including the building of the First Pylon in the temple of Amun at KARNAK. He built the earliest surviving section of the temple of Isis at PHILAE (although blocks of the reign of Taharqo have been found beneath the temple floor) and awarded new endowments and tax exemptions to a number of religious institutions. During his reign there was also a growth in the popularity of the cults of SACRED ANIMALS, reflected in new constructions at HERMOPOLIS MAGNA, MENDES and Saft el-Hinna. It has been suggested that the cultivation of the animal cults by the 30th-Dynasty rulers was part of a concerted effort to emphasize the native culture of Egypt, thus making a stand against increasing foreign influences and incursions. In 362 BC Nectanebo was succeeded by Teos.

Nectanebo II Senedjemibra (360–343 BC) was enthroned through the machinations of his father Tjahepimu, who declared him king while he was campaigning in Syria–Palestine with his uncle Teos. Having the general support of the armies, Nectanebo II was able to depose Teos, who then fled to the court of the Persian king. The ensuing reign was to be the last period of rule by a native Egyptian king until modern times. As well as constructing a huge temple to Isis at BEHBEIT EL-HAGAR, he continued the support of the cults of sacred animals by undertaking new works and restoration at ARMANT, Bubastis (TELL BASTA), the Saqqara SERAPEUM and the nearby complex associated with the Mother of Apis.

After an unsuccessful invasion in 351 BC Artaxerxes III eventually reincorporated Egypt into the Persian empire in 343 BC, reputedly plundering many temples and slaughtering APIS and BUCHIS bulls in the process. Nectanebo II appears to have temporarily held on to Upper Egypt (and was briefly succeeded by an Egyptian or Nubian pharaoh named Khababash). Egypt, however, had effectively been absorbed into the Persian empire once more, and was to remain a satrapy until the arrival of ALEXANDER THE GREAT.

J.-J. CLÈRE, 'Une statuette du fils ainé du roi Nectanebo', *EdE* (1951), 135–56.

H. JENNI, *Das Dekorationsprogramma des Sarkophages Nektanebos II* (Geneva, 1986).

N. GRIMAL, *A history of ancient Egypt* (Oxford, 1992), 375–81.

Nefaarud (Nepherites) *see* LATE PERIOD

nefer

Hieroglyphic sign with many meanings, the most common being 'beautiful' and 'good', although 'happy' can also be meant. These positive associations made it a popular element

Turquoise-blue faience jewellery element in the form of a nefer *sign. New Kingdom, H. 2.3 cm. (EA71390)*

in personal names, perhaps the best known in modern times being NEFERTITI ('the beautiful one is come'), wife of Akhenaten (1352–1336 BC).

The *nefer* sign is usually said to depict the stomach and windpipe of an animal, although it is more likely that the heart and windpipe were intended. As an AMULET it occurs only as an element of bracelets or necklaces, rather than as an individual piece. It was particularly popular in jewellery of the 18th Dynasty (1550–1295 BC), and is well represented among pieces from the tomb of the foreign wives of Thutmose III (1479–1425 BC) in the Wadi Qubbanet el-Qirud at Thebes (see JEWELLERY). Occasionally the white CROWN of Upper Egypt was referred to as the 'Nefer', and depicted in such a way as to emphasize this association by making it resemble the *nefer* sign.

R. H. WILKINSON, *Reading Egyptian art* (London, 1992), 78–9.

C. Andrews, *Amulets of ancient Egypt* (London, 1994), 87–8.

Nefertari (*c.*1300–1250 BC)

Principal wife of RAMESES II (1279–1213 BC), often depicted at his side for at least the first twenty years of his reign. Her unusual prominence is indicated by the fact that the smaller temple at ABU SIMBEL was dedicated both to her and to the goddess Hathor. Nefertari was thus probably the only royal wife, apart from the 18th-Dynasty (1550–1295 BC) Queen TIY, to be deified during her lifetime (see QUEENS). A CUNEIFORM tablet from the HITTITE city of Boghazköy appears to be inscribed with a letter from Nefertari to the Hittite king Hattusilis, although the preservation of letters from Rameses II to Hattusilis' wife Pudukhepa suggests that Nefertari's Hittite counterpart may have been even more influential in the politics of the time.

Nefertari's elaborate rock-tomb was the largest and most beautifully decorated tomb in the VALLEY OF THE QUEENS (QV66); its magnificent wall-paintings began to seriously deteriorate in the mid-twentieth century, but they have now been largely restored by the Getty Conservation Institute.

C. Desroches Noblecourt and C. Kuentz, *Le petit temple d'Abou Simbel*, 2 vols (Cairo, 1968).
W. Helck, 'Nofretere', *Lexikon der Ägyptologie* IV, ed. W. Helck, E. Otto and W. Westendorf (Wiesbaden, 1982), 518–19.
M. A. Corzo (ed.), *Wall paintings of the tomb of Nefertari* (Cairo and Malibu, 1987).
M. A. Corzo and M. Afshar (ed.), *Art and eternity: the Nefertari wall paintings conservation project* (Malibu, 1993).

Nefertari, Ahmose (1570–1505 BC) *see*
AHMOSE NEFERTARI

Nefertem

God of the primeval LOTUS blossom, who is represented by the blue lotus (*nymphaea cerulea*). He was usually depicted as a man with a lotus-flower HEADDRESS, sometimes with the addition of two plumes and two necklace counterpoises, which are symbols of fertility through their connection with HATHOR. Since the sun was believed to have risen from a lotus, Nefertem was linked with the sun-god, and is therefore described in the PYRAMID TEXTS (Utterance 266) as the 'lotus blossom which is before the nose of RA', probably an allusion to the use of this scented flower by guests at banquets.

At Memphis he was regarded as the son of SEKHMET, the lioness-goddess, and PTAH. As a result he was sometimes depicted as LION-

headed and occasionally it was suggested that the cat-goddess BASTET was his mother. At BUTO in the Delta he was regarded as the son of the Lower Egyptian cobra-goddess, WADJYT. His epithet *khener tawy* ('protector of the two lands') perhaps suggests a role as guardian of the unified state of Egypt.

S. Morentz and J. Schubert, *Der Gott auf der Blume: ein ägyptische Kosmogonie und ihre weltweite Bildwirkung* (Ascona, 1954).
H. Schlögl, *Der Sonnengott auf der Blüte* (Basel, 1977).
—, 'Nefertem', *Lexikon der Ägyptologie* IV, ed. W. Helck, E. Otto and W. Westendorf (Wiesbaden, 1982), 378–80.

Nefertiti (*c.*1380–1340 BC)

Principal wife of the 18th-Dynasty ruler AKHENATEN (1352–1336 BC) during the 'Amarna period'. She may also have been the daughter of AY (1327–1323 BC), one of Akhenaten's important officials, who was later to succeed TUTANKHAMUN (1336–1327 BC) on the throne; this blood link would probably have made her Akhenaten's cousin. She had six daughters by Akhenaten, but there is no mention of any male heir, and the princesses are given an unusual degree of prominence in the temple and palace reliefs at the new capital city of EL-AMARNA, often being shown processing behind the king and queen as they brought offerings to the ATEN, or playing on the laps of the royal pair in scenes of extraordinary intimacy.

In Akhenaten's sixth year he built a new temple to the Aten which seems to have been associated with his SED FESTIVAL, and the reliefs and statuary surrounding its walls are surprisingly dominated by figures of Nefertiti. She is regularly portrayed officiating in religious ceremonies alongside the king, often

ABOVE *Column fragment bearing a relief depiction of Nefertiti. The extended arm with hand touching the* uraeus *on her crown is one of the rays of the Aten to whom she offers flowers. One of her daughters stands behind her with a sistrum. 18th Dynasty, c.1350 BC, H. 36.2 cm. (GRIFFITH INSTITUTE NO. 1893.1.41, REPRODUCED COURTESY OF THE GRIFFITH INSTITUTE)*

LEFT *Bronze statuette of Nefertem inlaid with silver and gold. Late Period, H. 37 cm. (EA464880)*

wearing a unique type of crown, and on one TALATAT BLOCK from an el-Amarna temple, reused at HERMOPOLIS MAGNA, she is shown in the traditional pose of the pharaoh smiting a foreigner. Even by the standards of 18th-Dynasty royal women, who included among their ranks the powerful figures of AHHOTEP I (c.1560 BC) and HATSHEPSUT (1473–1458 BC), she seems to have achieved unusual power and influence. It is possible that she was able to build on the achievements of her predecessor Queen TIY, who lived on after the death of AMENHOTEP III (1390–1352 BC) and even appears to have visited the new court at el-Amarna.

In the workshop of the sculptor THUTMOSE at el-Amarna, the German excavator Ludwig Borchardt discovered the famous painted limestone bust of Nefertiti. The circumstances of its subsequent export to the Berlin museum, however, were a source of some controversy at the time.

In the twelfth year of Akhenaten's reign, Nefertiti receded into comparative obscurity, her place apparently being filled by another queen, Kiya, and probably also by one of her daughters, Meritaten. By the fourteenth year, she appears to have died, although it has been suggested that she herself may have assumed the role of a coregent in order to succeed her husband on the throne, simply taking the name Smenkhkara (whose second name, Neferneferuaten, she shared). As with many aspects of the Amarna period, there is insufficient evidence either to prove or to discount this theory completely. However, there is a reasonably good case for identifying as Smenkhkara the body of a young man buried with various items of Amarna-period royal funerary equipment (some of which were originally intended for the queens Tiy and Kiya) in the enigmatic tomb KV55 in the Valley of the Kings.

Queen Nefertiti was probably buried in the royal tomb in a wadi to the east of el-Amarna, along with her husband, although no traces of royal mummies have survived at the site, and the wall decoration provides evidence only of the funeral of princess Meketaten.

R. ANTHES, Die Büste der Königin Nofretete (Berlin, 1968).

D. REDFORD, Akhenaten, the heretic king (Princeton, 1984).

J. SAMSON, Nefertiti and Cleopatra: queen-monarchs of ancient Egypt (London, 1985).

C. ALDRED, Akhenaten, king of Egypt (London, 1988), 219–30.

Neith

Creator-goddess of great antiquity whose cult centre was at SAIS in the Delta. Her most ancient symbol was a warlike motif consisting of a shield and crossed arrows which is attested as early as the 1st Dynasty (3100–2890 BC), in the form of inscribed funerary stelae and labels from the Early Dynastic graves at ABYDOS and an inlaid amulet from a tomb at NAG EL-DEIR. Two of the most important 1st-Dynasty royal women, Neithhotep (see NAQADA) and Merneith, had names referring to Neith, and a wooden label from Abydos appears to depict a visit made by King AHA (c.3100 BC) to a sanctuary of Neith (or possibly the foundation of her temple).

She was usually shown wearing the red CROWN of Lower Egypt, the region with which she was most closely associated. By the time of the Old Kingdom (2686–2181 BC), however, she had also come to be regarded as the consort of the god SETH and the mother of the crocodile-god SOBEK. This association with crocodiles may have stemmed from her connections with the Delta region. The maternal aspect of her cult led to a link with the sky, under the epithet 'Great Cow', thus leading to potential confusion with the sky-goddesses NUT and HATHOR. In Roman times, inscriptions in the temple of Khnum at ESNA sought to identify Neith as an Upper Egyptian creator-goddess who had only later settled at Sais. In this cosmogonic role, Neith was sometimes depicted as a sexless being, equated with the

Bronze statuette of Neith. Late Period, from the Fayum, H. 20.5 cm. (EA11011)

lake of NUN, the primordial waters of chaos that preceded creation.

From the Old Kingdom onwards Neith was associated with funerary rituals. Utterance 606 in the PYRAMID TEXTS speaks of her watching over the deceased OSIRIS alongside ISIS, NEPHTHYS and SERKET. Each of these four goddesses was depicted on one particular side of the COFFIN and took care of one of the four SONS OF HORUS (the genii associated with the CANOPIC JARS), Neith being depicted on the east side of coffins and serving as protectress of Duamutef. As the mythical inventor of weaving, she was also linked with the mummy bandages.

She became particularly important during the 26th Dynasty (664–525 BC), when Sais was capital of Egypt. From the reign of Ahmose II (570–526 BC) onwards some of her temple revenue derived from the Greek-dominated trading settlement at NAUKRATIS. The Greeks identified her with Athena, probably because of her warlike aspect.

D. MALLET, Le culte de Neit à Saïs (Paris, 1888).

W. C. HAYES, Scepter of Egypt I (New York, 1953), 321.

R. EL-SAYED, La déesse Neith de Sais (Cairo, 1982).

Nekau (Necho)

The 'birth name' held by two rulers of the 26th Dynasty (664–525 BC).

Nekau I (672–664 BC) was nominally the first of the SAITE pharaohs. When the ASSYRIAN king Esarhaddon conquered Egypt in 671 BC he appointed 'Nekau of Sais and Memphis', one of the Delta princes, as vassal ruler of Egypt. It seems likely that Nekau was killed by the Kushite pharaoh TANUTAMANI in 664 BC, leaving the throne of Lower Egypt to his son, Psamtek I (664–610 BC), whom Esarhaddon had placed in charge of the city of Athribis (TELL ATRIB). Few monuments of Nekau I have survived, although a glazed statuette of Horus is inscribed with his full royal titulary.

Nekau II Wehemibra (610–595 BC) was the third Saite pharaoh and successor to PSAMTEK I. Within a year of his accession he had capitalized on the decline of the Assyrian empire by seizing control over the kingdoms of ISRAEL and Judah. He therefore re-established the Egyptian empire in the Levant for about four years, but by 601 BC his own eastern borders were threatened by Babylonian armies.

Nekau II encouraged Greek traders and sailors to establish colonies in the Delta and created the first full Egyptian navy, manned by Greek mercenaries. He also ordered the excavation of a new canal along the Wadi Tumilat, thus linking the Pelusiac branch of the Nile with the northern end of the Red Sea. It was in connection with this new activity in the Wadi Tumilat that Nekau founded the new city of Per Temu Tjeku ('the house of Atum of Tjeku') at the site now known as TELL EL-MASKHUTA.

J. YOYOTTE, 'Néchao', *Supplement au Dictionnaire de la Bible* VI (Paris, 1960), 363–94.

N. GRIMAL, *A history of ancient Egypt* (Oxford, 1992), 145–6, 359–61.

Nekhbet

Vulture-goddess whose iconographic significance was firmly rooted in the DUALITY of the Egyptian kingship. She and the cobra-goddess WADJYT represented dominion over Upper and Lower Egypt respectively. In recognition of this, the king's five names therefore included the *nebty* ('two ladies') title from at least as early as the reign of ANEDJIB (*c.*2925 BC) in the 1st Dynasty; this name was written with depictions of the vulture and cobra beside it. Occasionally both goddesses were represented as cobras, as in the two *uraei* worn on the head-dresses of QUEENS from the 18th Dynasty (1550–1295 BC) onwards, but the Nekhbet cobra is sometimes distinguished from Wadjyt by wearing the white CROWN of Upper Egypt. Most commonly, however, Nekhbet took the form of a vulture with wings outspread and talons holding SHEN signs (symbols of eternity), and it was this form that she usually assumed on royal pectorals and regalia. In paintings and reliefs she was frequently depicted in a protective posture with one wing outstretched as she hovered over the scene below.

Nekhbet's cult was first celebrated in the ancient city of Nekheb (ELKAB), which derived its name from her. In the PYRAMID TEXTS she is described as the 'white crown' and associated with the principal shrine of Upper Egypt, but her maternal aspects are also emphasized: she is described as 'the great white cow that dwells in Nekheb' and is said to have had pendulous breasts. Because she was also considered to serve as nurse to the pharaoh she was later identified with Eileithyia, the Greek goddess of childbirth.

M. HEERMA VAN VOSS, 'Nechbet', *Lexikon der Ägyptologie* IV, ed. W. Helck, E. Otto and W. Westendorf (Wiesbaden, 1982), 366–7.

nemes *see* CROWNS AND ROYAL REGALIA

nemset vessel

Form of spouted vase or lustration vessel usually employed in ritual contexts such as the OPENING OF THE MOUTH CEREMONY, which was a ritual intended to instil life into funerary statues or mummies.

Nepherites *see* LATE PERIOD

Nephthys

Goddess of the Heliopolitan ENNEAD, who appears to have possessed no cult centre or temple of her own. Her name means 'Lady of the Mansion' and her emblem, worn on her head, comprised the hieroglyphs for this phrase. She was usually said to have been the wife of the evil god SETH and, in later tradition, she was regarded as the mother of ANUBIS from a union with OSIRIS. More important, however, was her role as sister of ISIS, and this positive connection apparently freed her from any of the negative associations that might have been expected through her relationship with Seth.

She was usually represented alongside Isis,

Detail from a coffin of painted cartonnage belonging to a woman named Tentmutengebtiu. At the top Isis (left) and Nephthys (right), both carrying ankh signs, flank Osiris in the form of a djed pillar. In the lower register Horus (left) and Thoth (right) purify the dead woman with water represented by ankh *and* was *symbols. Third Intermediate Period, c.900 BC, from Thebes. (EA22939)*

and the two could both take the form of kites at either end of the bier of the deceased. She was a protector of the dead, and on New Kingdom royal sarcophagi she was depicted on the external northern wall (next to the head of the deceased), while Isis was portrayed at the southern end, by the feet. Although Nephthys continued to be associated with the head of the coffin throughout the Pharaonic period, there are a few private coffins on which she and Isis were both portrayed at the 'head'. The two goddesses often appeared in judgement scenes illustrating copies of the BOOK OF THE DEAD.

Nephthys was also the protectress of the baboon-headed Hapy, guardian of the lungs (see CANOPIC JARS). Mummy wrappings, themselves a gift of NEITH in her mortuary aspect, were likened to the tresses of her HAIR, from which the deceased king had to free himself in order to attain the afterlife. In the Late Period (747–332 BC) she was associated with the goddess ANUKET, and worshipped alongside her at Kom Mer, between ESNA and ELKAB, in Upper Egypt.

B. ALTENMÜLLER, *Synkretismus in den Sargtexten* (Wiesbaden, 1975), 92–4.

E. GRAEFE, 'Nephthys', *Lexikon der Ägyptologie* IV, ed. W. Helck, E. Otto and W. Westendorf (Wiesbaden, 1982), 457–60.

New Kingdom (1550–1069 BC)

With the expulsion of the HYKSOS at the end of the SECOND INTERMEDIATE PERIOD (1650–1550 BC), the Egyptian army pushed beyond the traditional frontiers of Egypt into Syria–Palestine. The Theban conquerors established the 18th Dynasty (1550–1295 BC), creating a great empire under a succession of rulers bearing the names THUTMOSE and AMENHOTEP. The newly reunified land had a stronger economy than previously, and this was supplemented by the resources of the empire in NUBIA and western Asia.

The empire was a source not only of foreign tribute but of exotic influences and ideas. It is possible that the cosmopolitan atmosphere of the court of Amenhotep III (1390–1352 BC) served as part of the inspiration for the radical religious changes instituted under his son Amenophis IV / AKHENATEN (1352–1336 BC). The loosely defined period around Akhenaten's reign is sometimes referred to as the 'Amarna period', named after EL-AMARNA, the modern site of Akhenaten's new capital. After this period of religious heresy the old order was re-established under TUTANKHAMUN (1336–1327 BC), AY (1327–1323 BC) and HOREMHEB (1323–1295 BC). The latter is variously regarded as the last ruler of the 18th Dynasty, or, less commonly, the first of the 19th (1295–1186 BC).

The 19th Dynasty was dominated by a succession of kings, mostly called RAMESES or SETY. Rameses II (1279–1213 BC) evidently campaigned vigorously and his many battles are depicted on temples throughout Upper Egypt and Nubia. Notable among his exploits was the BATTLE OF QADESH against the HIT-

TITES. He also moved the capital from THEBES to Piramesse (QANTIR), where it remained for the rest of the New Kingdom. The succeeding 20th Dynasty (1186–1069 BC) comprised ten reigns, nine of whose rulers also took the name Rameses. These, however, were troubled times, and Rameses III (1184–1153 BC) had to defend himself against the incursions of the SEA PEOPLES and LIBYANS. Under subsequent pharaohs the country became prey to regular raiding. The Theban region became so unsafe that the inhabitants of the tomb-workers' village at DEIR EL-MEDINA were moved into the precinct of the temple of MEDINET HABU, protected by its great enclosure walls.

Although the 20th-Dynasty kings ruled from the Delta, they were buried in the VALLEY OF THE KINGS at Thebes. Their overall weakness and distance from Thebes, a traditional seat of royal power, left the way open for rival powers to emerge. Panehsy, VICEROY OF KUSH, attempted to seize Thebes but was defeated and retreated into Nubia. The Libyan general, HERIHOR, however, came to power in year nineteen of Rameses XI (1099–1069 BC). He effectively ruled Upper Egypt, establishing his own dating system and assuming the ROYAL TITULARY, and was eventually succeeded by Pinudjem I (who also held both the royal titulary and the office of High Priest).

There is some debate, however, concerning the figure of Piankhi, who was once thought to have been Herihor's son and successor. According to Jansen-Winkeln's study of inscriptions and papyri of the late 20th and early 21st Dynasties, Piankhi – often described simply as 'the general' (*imy-r mesha*) and apparently never holding the royal titulary – must have actually preceded Herihor, who would probably have been his son-in-law. If Piankhi, rather than Herihor, was the immediate successor of Panehsy (the Viceroy of Kush), it would therefore have been Piankhi who effectively established the new line of Libyan generals who were to dominate events in the 21st Dynasty. Herihor himself should probably therefore be seen simply as the first of the Libyan generals to assume the royal titulary.

C. NIMS, *Thebes of the pharaohs* (London, 1965).

C. REDFORD, *History and chronology of the Eighteenth Dynasty of Egypt: seven studies* (Toronto, 1967).

B. J. KEMP, 'Imperialism and empire in New Kingdom Egypt (*c*.1575–1087 BC)', *Imperialism in the ancient world*, ed. P. D. A. Garnsey and C. R. Whittaker (Cambridge, 1978), 7–57, 284–97, 368–73.

D. O'CONNOR, 'New Kingdom and Third Intermediate Period, 1552–664 BC', *Ancient*

Egypt: a social history, ed. B. G. Trigger et al. (Cambridge, 1983), 183–278.

T. G. H. JAMES, *Pharaoh's people: scenes from life in imperial Egypt* (Oxford, 1984).

G. T. MARTIN, *A bibliography of the Amarna period and its aftermath* (London, 1991).

N. GRIMAL, *A history of ancient Egypt* (Oxford, 1992), 199–292.

Nile

The longest river in the world, stretching for 6741 km from East Africa to the Mediterranean, which is unquestionably the single most important element of the geography of both ancient and modern Egypt. Without the waters and fertile flood-plain of the Nile, it is highly unlikely that Egyptian civilization would have developed in the deserts of north-eastern Africa.

The study of the topography and geology of the Nile valley has revealed a complex sequence of phases, whereby the river gradually changed its location and size over the course of millions of years. Even in recent millennia, the course of the river has continued to shift, resulting in the destruction or submer-

LEFT *View of the Nile valley, looking north from the cliffs of Beni Hasan.* (GRAHAM HARRISON)

BELOW *The steps of the Nilometer on the island of Elephantine at Aswan measured the height of the Nile. This example dates to the Roman period.* (P. T. NICHOLSON)

sion of archaeological remains, particularly of the PREDYNASTIC PERIOD.

Three rivers flowed into the Nile from the south: the Blue Nile, the White Nile and the Atbara. The southern section of the Nile proper, between ASWAN and Khartoum, was interrupted by six 'cataracts' each of which consists of a series of rapids produced by changes in the type of rock forming the river bed. This section of the Nile valley corresponds to the land of NUBIA, conventionally divided into Lower Nubia (the northern half), between the first and second cataracts, and Upper Nubia, between the second and sixth cataracts. The border between the modern states of Egypt and Sudan is located just to the north of the second cataract.

From the earliest times, the waters of the Nile, swollen by monsoon rains in Ethiopia, flooded over the surrounding valley every year between June and September – an event known as the INUNDATION – and new layers of fertile soil were thus annually deposited on the flood-plain. From the early nineteenth century onwards, however, the Nile was subject to a series of dams and sluices, culminat-

ing in the completion of the ASWAN HIGH DAM in 1971. After more than a decade of rescue work, Lower Nubia was largely flooded by Lake Nasser. Since then, the Egyptian section of the Nile valley has ceased to be subject to the inundation, thus allowing thousands of acres of new land to be cultivated through irrigation schemes, as well as the production of electricity from a hydroelectric plant attached to the dam. See also AGRICULTURE; DELTA; HAPY; INUNDATION; NILOMETER and SHADUF.

J. H. SPEKE, *Journal of the discovery of the source of the Nile*, 2nd ed. (London, 1906).

D. BONNEAU, *La crue du Nil: divinité égyptienne, à travers mille ans d'histoire* (Paris, 1964).

K. W. BUTZER, *Early hydraulic civilization in Egypt: a study in cultural ecology* (Chicago, 1976).

D. BONNEAU, *Le régime administratif de l'eau du Nil dans l'Egypte greque, romaine et byzantine* (Leiden, 1993).

Nilometer

Device for measuring the height of the Nile, usually consisting of a series of steps against which the increasing height of the INUN-

DATION, as well as the general level of the river, could be measured. Records of the maximum height of the inundation were kept, although there is no firm evidence that these records were used in any systematic way in the determination of TAXATION on the amount of agricultural land flooded.

There are surviving Nilometers associated with the temples at Philae, Edfu, Esna, Kom Ombo and Dendera, but one of the best-known examples is located on the island of Elephantine at ASWAN. The Elephantine Nilometer was rebuilt in Roman times, and the markings still visible at the site date from this later phase. It was also repaired in 1870 by the Khedive Ismail. At Geziret el-Rhoda in Cairo there is an Islamic Nilometer dating back to AD 705–15, although it was possibly built on the site of an earlier Pharaonic example. The Islamic Nilometer worked on the same principles as its ancient counterparts, except for the use of an octagonal pillar (rather than steps) as the measure.

W. POPPER, *The Cairo Nilometer* (Los Angeles, 1951).

P. HEILPORN, 'Les nilomètres d'Elephantine et la date de la crue' *CdE* 64/127–8 (1989), 283–5.

V. SETON-WILLIAMS and P. STOCKS, *Blue guide: Egypt*, 3rd ed. (London, 1993), 220, 635.

Nine Bows

Ancient term used to refer to the enemies of Egypt, presumably both because of their use of bows and arrows in warfare and because of the ritual of physically 'breaking the bows' as a metaphor for military defeat and surrender. The particular enemies designated by the term were a matter of choice, but the selection generally included Asiatics and Nubians (see EXECRATION TEXTS). The Nine Bows were usually represented in the form of rows of bows (although the actual number varies), and they were regularly used to decorate such royal furniture as footstools and throne bases, so that the pharaoh could symbolically tread his enemies underfoot. On monuments they often appeared as a series of bound CAPTIVES, and were even depicted on the inner soles of the sandals of Tutankhamun (1336–1327 BC). The depiction of nine bound captives surmounted by a jackal, on the seal of the necropolis of the VALLEY OF THE KINGS, was evidently intended to protect the tomb from the depredations of foreigners and other sources of evil.

D. TOMIMURA, 'A propos de l'origine du mot égyptien "Neuf-Arcs"', *Oriento, Bulletin of the Society for Near Eastern Studies in Japan* 24 (1981), 114–24.

D. VALBELLE, *Les neufs arcs* (Paris, 1990).

R. H. WILKINSON, *Reading Egyptian art* (London 1992), 184–5.

nomarch *see* ADMINISTRATION and NOME

nome, nome symbols

In the Ptolemaic period the Greek term *nome* began to be used to refer to the forty-two traditional provinces of Egypt, which the ancient Egyptians called *sepat*. A system of division into provinces had been in existence since at least the beginning of the Pharaonic period (*c*.3100 BC). In the late 3rd Dynasty, probably during the reign of Huni (2637–2613 BC), a set of seven non-sepulchral step pyramids was erected at certain sites perhaps corresponding to proto-capitals of nomes: Zawiyet el-Mayitin, Abydos, Naqada, el-Kula, Edfu, Seila and the island of Elephantine (ASWAN). The capitals of some nomes shifted over time, while the location of others remains uncertain.

For most of the Dynastic period, there were twenty-two Upper Egyptian nomes, each governed by a nomarch and having its own symbol, usually represented in the form of a standard, thus leading to provinces being described by such names as the 'hare nome' or the 'ibis nome'. The twenty Lower Egyptian nome signs are much later in date, and did not incorporate standards. The reliefs in many temples and shrines include a lower register along which groups of personifications of estates or nomes processed around the temple, bearing food offerings to the cult. See map on page 6 for nome symbols and boundaries.

G. STEINDORFF, *Die ägyptischen Gaue und ihre politische Entwicklung* (Leipzig, 1909).

P. MONTET, *Géographie de l'Egypte ancienne*, 2 vols (Paris, 1957).

H. KEES, *Ancient Egypt: a cultural topography* (London, 1961).

W. HELCK, *Die altägyptische Gaue* (Wiesbaden, 1974).

—, 'Gau', *Lexikon der Ägyptologie* II, ed. W. Helck, E. Otto and W. Westendorf (Wiesbaden, 1977).

Nubia (anc. Yam, Irem, Ta-sety, Kush)

In terms of modern political boundaries the land of Nubia encompasses both northern Sudan and the southern end of Egypt, although most of the Egyptian section of Nubia has been submerged under Lake Nasser since the completion of the ASWAN HIGH DAM in 1971. Aptly defined by W. Y. Adams as the 'corridor to Africa', Nubia has served as a crucial trading conduit, channelling the resources of tropical Africa northwards to the civilizations of the Mediterranean and western Asia from at least the fourth millennium BC until the Middle Ages. This traditional image, however, has been challenged by John Alexander and Mark Horton, who argue instead that Nubia was primarily controlled from the south, with the periods of Egyptian influence being short interludes compared with the many centuries during which it was essentially an autonomous African civilization.

The area occupied by Nubia is the narrow strip of cultivated land surrounding the Middle Nile between ASWAN and Khartoum, which is punctuated by the six Nile cataracts, a series of rocky areas of rapids marking the abrupt geological changes in this section of the Nile valley. Although the climate of Nubia is more extreme than that of Egypt, ranging from the dry arid north to the tropical south, the ancient agricultural base of both countries was fairly similar (and remains so in modern times), being characterized primarily by cereal crops, cattle, sheep and goats.

The earliest Egyptian activities in Nubia date back at least to the late Predynastic period (*c*.3500–3100 BC) and a number of surviving rock-drawings from the Early Dynastic period (3100–2686 BC) probably indicate the earliest incursions by the newly unified Egyptian state into territories occupied by the Nubian A GROUP (*c*.3500–2800 BC). In the Old Kingdom (2686–2181 BC) the involve-

BELOW *Fragment of a wall-painting from the Theban tomb-chapel of Sobekhotep, showing Nubians presenting exotic gifts to Tuthmose IV. H. 80 cm. (EA922)*

ABOVE *Section of relief in the second court of the temple of Horus and Sobek at Kom Ombo, depicting a female personification of the 18th nome of Lower Egypt (the capital of which was Bubastis) bringing offerings to Hathor. Reign of Augustus, c.30 BC–AD 14. (I. SHAW)*

ment of the Egyptians in Nubia was restricted primarily to trading and mining activities. At this period the term Yam seems to have been used by the Egyptians to refer to Nubia. Just to the north of the second cataract, at the site which was later occupied by the Middle Kingdom fortress of BUHEN, there appears to have been a small walled settlement containing traces of copper smelting, dating to the 4th and 5th Dynasties (2613–2345 BC). By the early 12th Dynasty (c.1950 BC) the Egyptians had begun to establish a string of FORTRESSES between the second and third cataracts. The purpose of these military establishments appears to have been to gain a stranglehold on the economic resources of Lower Nubia and the countries further to the south, (including

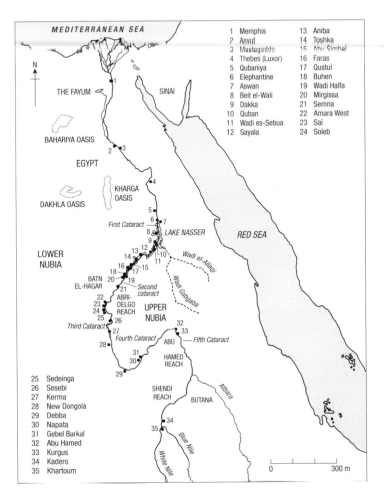

1	Memphis	13	Aniba
2	Asyut	14	Toshka
3	Mostagedda	15	Abu Simbel
4	Thebes (Luxor)	16	Faras
5	Qubaniya	17	Qustul
6	Elephantine	18	Buhen
7	Aswan	19	Wadi Halfa
8	Beit el-Wali	20	Mirgissa
9	Dakka	21	Semna
10	Quban	22	Amara West
11	Wadi es-Sebua	23	Saï
12	Sayala	24	Soleb

25	Sedeinga
26	Sesebi
27	Kerma
28	New Dongola
29	Debba
30	Napata
31	Gebel Barkal
32	Abu Hamed
33	Kurgus
34	Kadero
35	Khartoum

Egypt and Nubia: the principal sites from the Neolithic to the New Kingdom.

CHRONOLOGICAL TABLE: NUBIA

Lower Palaeolithic	700,000–100,000 BC
Middle Palaeolithic	100,000–26,000 BC
Upper Palaeolithic	26,000–10,000 BC
Final Palaeolithic (Arkinian)	10,000–6000 BC
Khartoum Mesolithic	6000–3500 BC
Khartoum Neolithic	4000–3000 BC
Cataract Tradition (Gemaian, Qadan and Abkan industries)	
A Group (A Horizon)	3500–2800 BC
C Group (A Horizon)	2300–1500 BC
Kerma	2500–1500 BC
New Kingdom (Egyptian occupation)	1550–1069 BC
Napatan period	1000–300 BC
25th Dynasty (Nubian rule over Egypt)	747–656 BC
Meroitic period	300 BC–AD 350
X Group (X Group, Noba, Ballana)	AD 350–550
Christian period	AD 550–1500
Islamic period	AD 1500–

such important commodities as GOLD, ivory, ebony, animals and slaves). The boundary STELE erected by Senusret III (1874–1855 BC) at SEMNA, near the third cataract, clearly states this policy: 'southern boundary... in order to prevent that any negro should cross it, by water or by land, with a ship or any herds of the negroes; except a negro who shall come to do trading in Iken [probably MIRGISSA] or with a commission'. The fortresses not only served as important symbols of Egyptian military strength as far as the local C-GROUP people were concerned, but, in the case of Buhen, Mirgissa and Askut in particular, acted as temporary depots for the imported materials.

At the end of the Middle Kingdom (c.1650 BC), when Lower Egypt fell under the control of the HYKSOS, Lower Nubia became dominated instead by an indigenous Kushite culture centred on the site of KERMA in the comparatively fertile terrain of the Dongola reach. The Egyptians of the late Middle Kingdom had already been aware of a rising power in Upper Nubia which they still described as the land of Yam. The Kerma culture reached its height during the years of the Second Intermediate Period (1650–1550 BC) but was eventually forced into retreat by the resurgence of a

united Egypt at the beginning of the 18th Dynasty (1550–1295 BC).

The archaeological remains clearly indicate that the socio-economic strength of the Kerma culture was gradually and inexorably eclipsed by the empire of New Kingdom Egypt (1550–1069 BC). The Egyptians appear to have consolidated their control over Nubia as far south as the fourth cataract, establishing such new towns as AMARA West and SESEBI-SUDLA, where the emphasis moved away from fortifications towards the building of temples, a clear indication that most of Nubia had begun to be considered as part of Egypt itself rather than alien territory. By the beginning of the 18th Dynasty the post of VICEROY OF KUSH (or

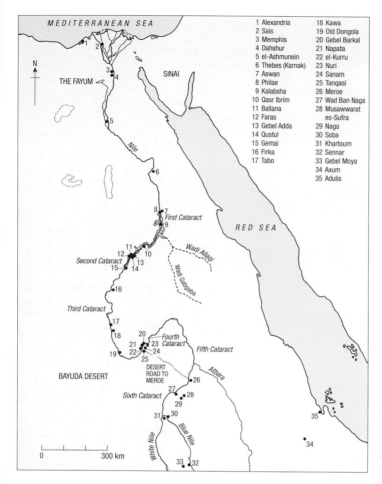

1	Alexandria	18	Kawa
2	Sais	19	Old Dongola
3	Memphis	20	Gebel Barkal
4	Dahshur	21	Napata
5	el-Ashmunein	22	el-Kurru
6	Thebes (Karnak)	23	Nuri
7	Aswan	24	Sanam
8	Philae	25	Tanqasi
9	Kalabsha	26	Meroe
10	Qasr Ibrim	27	Wad Ban Naga
11	Ballana	28	Musawwarat
12	Faras		es-Sufra
13	Gebel Adda	29	Naga
14	Qustul	30	Soba
15	Gemai	31	Khartoum
16	Firka	32	Sennar
17	Tabo	33	Gebel Moya
		34	Axum
		35	Adulis

Egypt and Nubia: the principal sites from the Napatan to the Christian period.

King's son of Kush) had been created, enabling Nubia to be governed as a separate region (consisting of the two provinces of Wawat and Kush), just as the Egyptian-dominated areas of Syria–Palestine were transformed into three administrative units under Egyptian control.

By the eleventh century BC, however, the Egyptian grip over Nubia had diminished, and the local rulers at NAPATA were able to assume control, just as their Kerma-culture predecessors had. The Napatan rulers, however, capitalized on the divisions within Egypt during the Third Intermediate Period (1069–747 BC) to create a new kingdom that was eventually able to absorb Egypt itself, inaugurating the reigns of the 'Kushite' 25th Dynasty (747–656 BC; see PIY; SHABAQO; SHABITQO; TAHARQO and TANUTAMANI). From the Late Period (747–332 BC) onwards the Nubians were able to continue to develop separately from Egypt, during the Meroitic (see MEROE), BALLANA (X Group) and Christian periods, although inevitably there were continued religious, political and social influences from their northern neighbours.

See also ANIBA; APEDEMAK; ARENSNUPHIS; B GROUP; BEIT EL-WALI; BLEMMYES; CAPTIVES; FARAS; KALABSHA; KAWA; KURGUS; EL-KURRU;

MAIHERPRI; MEDJAY; NURI; PAN-GRAVE CULTURE; SEDEINGA; SLAVES; SOLEB.

A. J. ARKELL, *A history of the Sudan from the earliest times to 1821*, 2nd ed. (London, 1961).
W. B. EMERY, *Egypt in Nubia* (London, 1965).
B. G. TRIGGER, *History and settlement in Lower Nubia* (New Haven, 1965).
F. WENDORF (ed.), *The prehistory of Nubia*, 2 vols (Dallas, 1968).
B. G. TRIGGER, *Nubia under the pharaohs* (London, 1976).
F. HINTZE, 'The Meroitic period', *Africa in antiquity*, ed. S. Wenig (Brooklyn, 1978), 89–105.
W. Y. ADAMS, *Nubia: corridor to Africa*, 2nd ed. (London and Princeton, 1984).
D. O'CONNOR, 'The locations of Yam and Kush and their historical implications', *JARCE* 23 (1986), 27–50.
J. ALEXANDER, 'The Saharan divide in the Nile valley: the evidence from Qasr Ibrim', *African Archaeological Review* 6 (1988), 73–90.
M. HORTON, 'Africa in Egypt: new evidence from Qasr Ibrim', *Egypt and Africa*, ed. W. V. Davies (London, 1991), 264–77.

Nun

God who personified the original formless ocean of chaos from which the PRIMEVAL MOUND of the sun-god ATUM arose. The mass of negative forces represented by Nun was considered to have continued to exist at the edges of the universe, even after the first act of creation had taken place. Nun was therefore the dwelling place of all that lay outside the

Detail of the Book of the Dead papyrus of the priestess Anhai showing Nun, the god of the primeval waters, lifting up the solar bark. 20th Dynasty, c.1100 BC. (EA10472)

bounds of the universe, such as stillborn babies or condemned souls (see TABOO).

It has been suggested that the PAN BEDDING (alternation of convex and concave courses of bricks) used in the enclosure walls of many Egyptian TEMPLES, such as KARNAK and DENDERA, was intended to symbolize the undulations of the waters of Nun. The watery chaos was thus effectively being held back at the margins of the temple, which was itself a metaphor for the universe. Since Nun also symbolized the depths of the netherworld, he was often portrayed as a bearded figure holding up the SOLAR BARK. Along with his consort Naunet he was one of the eight creator deities of the Hermopolitan OGDOAD.

E. HORNUNG, *Idea into image*, trans. E. Bredeck (New York, 1992), 95–113.

Nuri

Napatan funerary site located in Upper Nubia, about 25 km southwest of the fourth Nile cataract and a few kilometres to the northeast of NAPATA (one of the principal political centres of the kingdom of Kush). It was the burial site of the Kushite royal family from the mid seventh to the early third century BC (i.e. after the tombs at EL-KURRU and before those at southern MEROE). According to the site's principal excavator, George Reisner, there were at least nineteen Napatan royal burials at Nuri, including that of the 25th-Dynasty pharaoh TAHARQO (690–664 BC), each of which was covered by a small pyramidal superstructure built of the local sandstone. In the substructure of the kings' tombs, usually consisting of three chambers, the mummified body of the deceased was placed in a wooden coffin or stone sarcophagus surrounded by funerary offerings including many luxury items imported from Egypt. The stylistic changes in the Napatan royal tombs were used by Reisner as a basis for his relative chronology of Kushite kings. As at el-Kurru, the Napatan queens were buried in a separate section of the cemetery comprising more than fifty tombs.

D. DUNHAM, *The royal cemeteries of Kush*, II: *Nuri* (Boston, 1955).

W. Y. ADAMS, *Nubia: corridor to Africa* (London and Princeton, 1984), 278–85.

Nut

Sky-goddess, whose body symbolized the vault of the sky. In the Heliopolitan doctrine of the ENNEAD, she was considered the daughter of SHU, sister-wife of GEB and mother of OSIRIS, ISIS, SETH and NEPHTHYS. She was usually shown in human form, but more rarely

ABOVE *Pyramids covering the burials of the kings of Kush at Nuri in Upper Nubia.* (DEREK WELSBY)

RIGHT *The sky-goddess Nut, her body arched over the earth, is seen swallowing the sun each evening and giving birth to it each morning. The scene is shown on the ceiling of a kiosk-like chapel in the temple of Hathor at Dendera, hence the image of Hathor on which the sun's rays fall.*
(P. T. NICHOLSON)

she was also portrayed as a cow, thus leading to occasional confusion with the bovine images of another sky-goddess, HATHOR. The Greek writer Plutarch adds Apollo (the Greek equivalent of HORUS) to the list of her progeny, in a story which relates how the sun-god Helios (RA) cursed Rhea (Nut) preventing her from giving birth on any of the 360 days of the calendar. The five children were able to be born only through the intervention of Hermes (THOTH) who provided five extra days of light. This myth was therefore used to explain the existence of the five epagomenal days in the Egyptian CALENDAR.

Nut's body, each limb at a cardinal point, was thought to be arched over the earth. Every evening she swallowed the setting sun, Ra, and every morning gave birth to him

again from her womb. Depictions of this act are commonly found on the ceilings of temples as well as in the royal tombs in the Valley of the Kings, where they are accompanied on the walls by the nightly journey of the sun through the underworld. The two versions of the path of the sun were not regarded as contradictory. Nut's body was also interpreted as the course of the stars, which are shown as decorations on her dress, and it is thought likely that she also personified one particular constellation, probably located near the celestial equator.

As the renewer of the sun each day, she was clearly regarded as a suitable funerary deity, and several of the utterances in the PYRAMID TEXTS speak of her 'enfolding the body of the king'. Another utterance asks: 'O my mother,

Nut, spread yourself over me, so that I may be placed among the imperishable stars and never die', and a version of this prayer was inscribed on one of the golden shrines of Tutankhamun (1336–1327 BC). Such imagery gave rise to her identification with the lid of the COFFIN, and texts during the Old Kingdom (2686–2181 BC) refer to the chest of the sarcophagus as *mwt* ('mother'). From the New Kingdom (1550–1069 BC) onwards, she was regularly depicted on the underside of the lid of many coffins and sarcophagi, arching her body over that of the deceased. The dead person was thus both back inside the body of the mother, ready for rebirth, and re-enacting the journey of the sun-god between heaven and earth.

Nut has also been identified as the inspiration behind the so-called 'swimming-girl' cosmetic spoons, which date to the New Kingdom and usually portray a nude woman swimming, often holding a goose in outstretched arms. These artefacts are now regarded as rebuses of the divine pair Nut and Geb, whose roles in the funerary equipment may therefore have been more complex and ritualistic than previously thought.

J. BERGMAN, 'Nut – Himmelsgöttin – Baumgöttin – Lebensgeberin', *Humanitas religiosa: Festschrift für H. Biezais* (Stockholm, 1979), 53–69.

E. HORNUNG, *Der ägyptische Mythos von der Himmelskuh: eine Ätiologie des Unvollkommenen* (Freiburg, 1982).

A. KOZLOFF and B. BRYAN, *Egypt's dazzling sun: Amenhotep III and his world* (Bloomington and Cleveland, 1992), 331–48.

D. MEEKS and C. FAVARD-MEEKS, *La vie quotidienne des dieux égyptiens* (Paris, 1993), 166–72, 238–9.

obelisk (Egyptian *tekhen*)

Tapering, needle-like stone monument, the tip of which was carved in the form of a pyramidion (Egyptian *benbenet*). The shapes of both obelisks and pyramidia were derived ultimately from the ancient BENBEN stone in the temple of the sun-god at HELIOPOLIS. This stone was believed to be that on which the rays of the rising sun first fell, and was sacred at least as early as the 1st Dynasty (3100–2890 BC). The Egyptian word for obelisk (*tekhen*) may be related to the word *weben* meaning 'to shine', further emphasizing the connection with the cult of the sun.

The role of the obelisk as a solar symbol was often re-emphasized by carved figures of baboons at the base, since wild baboons were evidently known to greet the rising sun with great chattering and excitement. The pyramidion at the apex of each obelisk was usually gilded in order to reflect the sun's rays.

The masonry obelisk in the 5th-Dynasty sun temple of NYUSERRA (2445–2421 BC) at ABU GURAB would originally have been one of the largest obelisks, although its broad, squat proportions would have been more reminiscent of the *benben* stone than the elegant monolithic obelisks of later periods. The use of obelisks was at first fairly limited, spreading gradually from Heliopolis. As early as the Old Kingdom, small obelisks were sometimes erected outside private tombs, although it is with temples that they are most often associated. The use of such small obelisks in front of tombs continued in the New Kingdom (1550–1069 BC), and a pair of obelisks are represented in the tomb of the 18th-Dynasty vizier REKHMIRA (TT100). They also formed part of the decoration of SHABTI-boxes of the Third Intermediate Period (1069–747 BC), and from the Late Period (747–332 BC) onwards their importance in funerary architecture led to the creation of obelisk-shaped amulets.

In the New Kingdom large monolithic obelisks were often erected in pairs in front of temple pylons. Sadly, no such pairs remain *in situ* today, the last two having been separated when Muhammed Ali presented one of the LUXOR obelisks to the French government in 1819, leaving only one in front of the temple, while the other now stands in the Place de la Concorde in Paris.

An unfinished granite obelisk, probably dating to the New Kingdom, is still lying in the northern quarries at ASWAN. With a length of 41.75 m and a weight of 1168 tons, it would have been the largest monolithic obelisk ever cut if it had not developed a fatal flaw during the initial quarrying. Experiments by Reginald Engelbach showed that it took an hour to remove 5 mm of stone from a strip 0.5 m wide across the obelisk, using basalt pounders. The moving and raising of obelisks was a major feat of organization in itself, presenting difficulties even to those who have attempted it in the twentieth century. Nevertheless, many obelisks were obviously successfully cut in ancient times, and the quarrying and transport of two enormous granite obelisks for Hatshepsut (1473–1458 BC) is recorded in her temple at DEIR EL-BAHRI, while the monuments themselves are still located in the temple of Amun at KARNAK.

The obelisk rapidly became popular with other cultures outside Egypt. It was copied by the Canaanites (see BYBLOS), and the ASSYRIAN ruler Ashurbanipal (669–627 BC) is said to have removed two bronze-clad examples from THEBES after his invasion of 669 BC. In later times, many obelisks were removed by the Ptolemies and the Romans, with the result that Rome now has the greatest number of obelisks

Red granite obelisk of Hatshepsut. 18th Dynasty, c.1473–1458 BC, from Qasr Ibrim, Nubia. H. 1.83 m. (EA1834)

anywhere in the world, including the tallest, the so-called Lateran Obelisk. In modern times obelisks have been re-erected in many major cities throughout the world, for example London, Paris and New York.

R. ENGELBACH, *The Aswan obelisk* (Cairo, 1922).

C. KUENTZ, *Obélisques* (Cairo, 1932). [Part of the catalogue of the Egyptian Museum, Cairo.]

B. DIBNER, *Moving the obelisks* (Cambridge, MA, 1970).

E. IVERSEN, *Obelisks in exile* (Copenhagen, 1972).

L. HABACHI, *The obelisks of Egypt* (London, 1978).

R. HAYWARD, *Cleopatra's needles* (Buxton, 1978).

offering formula

The *hetep-di-nesw* ('a gift which the king gives') or 'offering formula' was a prayer asking for offerings to be brought to the deceased. It first appears as the principal inscription on the FALSE DOOR stelae of the Old Kingdom (2686–2181 BC), which formed the focus of food offerings in early private tombs, but it continued to be used on funerary stelae (and later also on COFFINS), throughout the Pharaonic and Greco-Roman periods. On stelae the formula is often accompanied by a depiction of the deceased sitting in front of an OFFERING TABLE heaped with food, and on coffins of the Middle Kingdom (2055–1650 BC) it was often written on the exterior (see illustration), while a number of different offerings were depicted in neat rows on the interior.

Typically the first line of the offering formula asks for the king to make gifts to the gods OSIRIS or ANUBIS; the rest of the inscription then usually consists of a list of the various quantities of items of food and drink that the *ka* of the deceased requires. The inscription sometimes also asks visitors to the tomb to recite the formula so that the necessary offerings would appear. It is clear from the nature of the formula that the sustenance of the *ka* of the deceased was not simply the responsibility of the surviving relatives – it was necessary for the king to intercede with the gods on his or her behalf. This illustrates the essential role played by the king as divine intermediary at the heart of each individual's funerary cult, establishing the crucial link between the fate of the individual and the festivals of Osiris. It also reflects the common practice of dividing up temple offerings and redistributing them among the funerary cults of individuals.

A. H. GARDINER, *Egyptian grammar*, 3rd ed. (Oxford, 1957), 170–3

R. B. PARKINSON, *Voices from ancient Egypt* (London, 1991), 136–42.

Detail of the offering formula (hetep-di-nesw), *a prayer asking the king to provide offerings, on the exterior of the outer coffin of the physician Seni. Middle Kingdom, c.2000 BC, painted wood, H. 15 cm. (EA30841)*

offering table

One of the most important elements of the Egyptian private tomb throughout the Pharaonic and Greco-Roman periods. It was usually placed in an accessible location such as the chapel, so that offerings could actually be brought to it by the funerary priests or relatives of the deceased.

The hieroglyph representing the ancient Egyptian word *hetep* (the most literal meaning of which is 'offering') consists of a depiction of a woven mat surmounted by a loaf of bread, doubtless reflecting the most basic method of presenting an offering. This simple visual image not only served as a metaphor for the act of offering itself but also came to be the characteristic shape of the physical surface on which offerings were placed from the beginning of the Pharaonic period onwards. The upper surfaces of offering tables were often carved with the loaves, trussed ducks and vessels required by the cult, so that the stone-carved images could serve as magical substitutes for the real food offerings, usually with the additional back-up of the hieroglyphic OFFERING FORMULA and lists of produce. Often there were cups, grooves or channels cut into the surface so that such liquids as water, beer or wine could be poured on to the table.

The so-called 'soul houses' placed beside the mouths of the shaft-burials of comparatively poor individuals of the First Intermediate Period and Middle Kingdom (2181–1650 BC) were essentially an elaborate form of offering table. Flinders Petrie, who excavated large numbers of them at the site of Rifeh, was able to trace the evolution of soul houses from simple pottery trays (imitating stone offering tables) to later more elaborate examples consisting of models of houses, the forecourts of which were strewn with food offerings. In this way the soul house neatly and economically combined the concept of the burial place as the symbolic home of the deceased

Kneeling statue of Rameses II holding an offering table on a hes-vase. 19th Dynasty, c.1250 BC, limestone, from Abydos, H. 98 cm. (EA96)

with the expression of a desire for food offerings to sustain the KA. See also ALTAR.

C. KUENTZ, 'Bassins et tables d'offrandes', *BIFAO* 81 (1981), suppl., 243–82.

H. ALTENMÜLLER, 'Opfer', *Lexikon der Ägyptologie* IV, ed. W. Helck, E. Otto and W. Westendorf (Wiesbaden, 1982), 579–84.

J. BOURRIAU, *Pharaohs and mortals: Egyptian art in the Middle Kingdom* (Cambridge, 1988), 101–3.

Ogdoad (Egyptian *khmun*)

The Hermopolitan Ogdoad were a group of eight deities whom the priests at HERMOPOLIS MAGNA, the principal cult-place of THOTH, identified as the primeval actors in a CREATION myth. During the Pharaonic period Hermopolis even derived its name (Khmun) from the ancient Egyptian word for 'eight', and this ancient toponym has survived in the modern place-name of el-Ashmunein.

The Ogdoad comprised four frog-gods and four snake-goddesses, each frog being paired with one of the snakes. The four pairs symbolized different aspects of the chaos before the creation. Their names were NUN and Naunet (water), AMUN and Amaunet (hiddenness), HEH and Hauhet (infinity), and Kek and Kauket (darkness). It was thought that these deities brought into being the original PRIMEVAL MOUND on which, according to one myth, the egg of the sun-god was placed.

E. HORNUNG, *Idea into image*, trans. E. Bredeck (New York, 1992), 41–2.

oil

Important material in both funerary ritual and daily life during the Pharaonic period. Oil and fat served as the bases for many of the Egyptians' unguents and scents (there were no true – distilled – perfumes). Various aromatic herbs and spices were added to the oil in order to imbue it with certain aromas. At a more prosaic level, oil was the fuel used in lamps, which served as lighting in houses as well as illuminating tombs and mines. It seems that salt was added to the oil to reduce the amount of soot produced when it was burnt. The identification of the ancient names for oils with the actual plants from which the oil was produced has proved to be extremely difficult, and many early attempts seem to have been erroneous.

Jars of oils or fats, possibly once scented, were included in the burial equipment from Predynastic times onwards. One group of scented oils of particular importance is known today as the 'seven sacred oils', although the Egyptians referred to them only as 'the oils'. These formed an integral part of religious ritual and were used for anointing the deceased in the OPENING OF THE MOUTH CEREMONY. They

were also included in daily temple ritual. Some of the seven sacred oils are known from 1st-Dynasty wooden and ivory labels, but the group appears not to have been used collectively until the Old Kingdom (2686–2181 BC), when they were represented as part of the OFFERING FORMULA on the walls or FALSE DOOR stelae of tombs.

The earliest known actual set of the seven sacred oils is from the tomb of Hetepheres, but small stone tablets with depressions for these oils were sometimes placed in burials throughout the Old Kingdom. Like the other known sets of jars from Middle Kingdom (2055–1650 BC) burials, Hetepheres' set contained eight jars, but the identity of the contents in the eighth jar was never consistent. Based on tomb and temple reliefs, it would seem that the group had been further extended to nine or ten oils during the New Kingdom (1550–1069 BC).

They were given the following names, usually listed in this order: *seti-heb* (odour of festivals), *hekenw* (oil of praising), *sefet, nehenem, twawt* (these three untranslatable), *hatet net 'sh* (first-quality oil of conifer?), *hatet net tjehenw* (first-quality oil of Libya).

A. LUCAS, *Ancient Egyptian materials and industries*, 4th ed. (London, 1962), 327–37.

M. SERPICO and R. WHITE, 'Oil, fat and wax', *Ancient Egyptian materials and technology*, ed. P. T. Nicholson and I. Shaw (Cambridge, 2000), 390–429.

Old Kingdom (2686–2181 BC)

Chronological phase consisting of the 3rd to 6th Dynasties, during which most of the royal PYRAMID complexes and private MASTABA tombs of the Memphite necropolis were built (see MEMPHIS and SAQQARA). The first significant ruler of the 3rd Dynasty was DJOSER Netjerikhet (2667–2648 BC), whose Step Pyramid still dominates the skyline of northern Saqqara. Near the southwest corner of Djoser's enclosure is the unfinished step pyramid of his successor SEKHEMKHET.

The 4th Dynasty began with the reign of SNEFERU, who is associated with no fewer than three pyramids (one at MEIDUM, which may have belonged to his 3rd-Dynasty predecessor, Huni, and two at DAHSHUR). Of the next five rulers, three (KHUFU, KHAFRA and MENKAURA) built their pyramids at GIZA, while the burial places of DJEDEFRA and SHEPSESKAF were located at ABU ROASH and SAQQARA respectively. A sixth unknown 4th-Dynasty ruler seems to have had a pyramid complex at ZAWIYET EL-ARYAN. The 4th Dynasty not only represented a distinct peak in terms of the resources devoted to pyramid building but it was also the apogee of the cult of the sun-god, with the adoption of the royal title *sa Ra* ('son of the sun-god').

The 5th-Dynasty rulers (Userkaf, Sahura, Neferirkara, Shepseskara, Raneferef Nyuserra, Menkauhor, Djedkara-Isesi and UNAS) were buried either at ABUSIR or Saqqara, and several of the earlier rulers of this dynasty also built sun-temples, in which the royal cult seems to have been assimilated with the worship of the sun (see ABU GURAB and HELIOPOLIS). Although the architectural and artistic achievements of the 4th and 5th Dynasties are undoubtedly impressive, the intellectual and social developments are poorly known, since few documents have survived.

The pyramids and tombs of the 6th-Dynasty rulers and their court were all constructed at Saqqara. The increased number of surviving texts from this period (particularly the PYRAMID TEXTS and Abusir papyri) has ensured that the religion, society and economy of the late Old Kingdom are better documented than in earlier periods. A number of 6th-Dynasty 'funerary autobiographies' (see LITERATURE) have also enabled aspects of the political history of the period to be tentatively reconstructed, including the launching of campaigns and trading missions to NUBIA and western Asia. It is uncertain as to whether events and political situations were typical of the Old Kingdom as a whole or only of the 6th Dynasty, because of the patchiness of the textual record.

The Old Kingdom effectively came to an end with the death of PEPY II, who was perhaps succeeded by a female ruler named Nitiqret. Some scholars, however, have argued that the 7th and 8th Dynasties continued to rule from Memphis and that the political structure during this period remained relatively intact despite a rapid succession of kings with extremely brief reigns (see FIRST INTERMEDIATE PERIOD). A variety of factors seem to have brought about the fall of the Old Kingdom; suggestions include climatic deterioration, consisting of lower annual rainfall and/or lower Nile INUNDATIONS; a possible increase in power of the provincial rulers, whose offices became hereditary; and a decline in the size and quality of royal funerary monuments which may have been a result or symptom of a decrease in royal wealth and authority (perhaps partly due to the granting of too many tax exemptions).

H. GOEDICKE, *Königliche Dokumente aus dem Alten Reich* (Wiesbaden, 1967).

I. E. S. EDWARDS, C. J. GADD and N. G. L. HAMMOND (ed.), *Cambridge ancient history 1/2: Early history of the Middle East*, 3rd ed. (Cambridge, 1971), 145–207.

E. MARTIN-PARDEY, *Untersuchungen zur ägyptischen Provinzialverwaltung bis zum Ende des Alten Reiches* (Hildesheim, 1976).

P. POSENER-KRIÉGER, *Les archives du temple funéraire de Neferirkarê-Kakaï (les papyrus d'Abousir)*: *traduction et commentaire*, 2 vols (Cairo, 1976).

N. KANAWATI, *The Egyptian administration in the Old Kingdom: evidence on its economic decline* (Warminster, 1977).

B. J. KEMP, 'Old Kingdom, Middle Kingdom and Second Intermediate Period', *Ancient Egypt: a social history*, B. G. Trigger et al. (Cambridge, 1983), 71–182.

J. MALEK, *In the shadow of the pyramids: Egypt during the Old Kingdom* (London and Oklahoma, 1986).

G. HART, *Pharaohs and pyramids* (London, 1991).

N. GRIMAL, *A history of ancient Egypt* (Oxford, 1992), 63–101.

J. VERCOUTTER, 'Le fin de l'Ancien Empire: un nouvel examen', *Atti di VI Congresso di Egittologia* II (Turin, 1993), 557–62.

Omari, el-

Type-site of the el-Omari phase of the Lower Egyptian PREDYNASTIC PERIOD, consisting of several Predynastic settlements and cemeteries clustered around the Wadi Hof, between modern Cairo and Helwan. The two main settlements (el-Omari A and B) have provided radiocarbon dates that suggest they were roughly contemporary with the Amratian and Gerzean phases of the Upper Egyptian Predynastic. The pottery is predominantly red or black, bearing very little decoration. The cemeteries were mingled with the settlement areas, as at Merimda, but each body was laid on the left side with its skull facing to the south, as in Upper Egyptian Predynastic cemeteries. A third area of settlement (el-Omari C) appears to have still been occupied in the Early Dynastic period.

F. DEBONO, 'La civilization prédynastique d'El Omari (nord d'Hélouan)', *BIE* 37 (1956), 329–39.

M. A. HOFFMAN, *Egypt after the pharaohs* (New York, 1979), 191–9.

K. A. BARD, 'The Egyptian Predynastic: a review of the evidence', *Journal of Field Archaeology* 21 (1994), 265–88.

onomasticon

Type of ancient text consisting of lists of various categories of NAMES, from plants and animals to cities or professions. The onomastica were presumably intended to serve both as repositories of knowledge and as training exercises for scribes (see EDUCATION).

A. H. GARDINER, *Ancient Egyptian onomastica* (London, 1947).

M. V. FOX, 'Egyptian onomastica and Biblical wisdom', *Vetus Testamentum* 36 (1986), 302–10.

Cast silver figure of the warrior god Onuris armed with a lance. Third Intermediate Period, H. 4.8 cm. (EA66629)

J. E. OSING, 'Ein späthieratisches Onomaticon aus Tebtunis', *Akten München* 1985 III, ed. S. Schoske (Hamburg, 1989), 183–7.

Onuris (Anhur, Inhert)

God associated with war and hunting, whose name means 'he who brings back the distant one', referring to his principal mythical role in which he returned from Nubia with his consort, the lioness-goddess Mehit. This legend parallels the Heliopolitan myth of the god of the air, SHU, who was also considered to have brought back his consort (the goddess TEFNUT) from Nubia. Onuris' cult is first attested in the Thinite region surrounding ABYDOS in Middle Egypt. By the Late Period (747–332 BC), however, he was closely associated with the Delta site of Schennytos, where a temple was dedicated to Onuris-Shu by NECTANEBO II (360–343 BC). In the Ptolemaic period (332–32 BC) he was identified with the Greek war-god Ares.

He is usually portrayed as a bearded man carrying a spear or rope (with which he pursued Mehit) and wearing a headdress consisting of four long plumes. He held the epithet 'lord of the lance', and his association with the spear and ropes provided an inevitable link with the mythical struggle between HORUS and SETH, in which the hawk-god used the same weapons to entrap and kill his foe, the HIPPOPOTAMUS. Onuris was also portrayed as an avenger defending Egypt on behalf of the sun-god RA. Just as Mehit was identified with another lioness-goddess, SEKHMET, who was the 'EYE OF RA', so (in another parallel with

Shu) Onuris was often given the epithet 'son of Ra'. See also LION

H. JUNKER, *Die Onurislegende* (Berlin, 1917).

J. ENDRODI, 'Statue de bronze d'Onouris et de Mekhit', *Bulletin du Musée Hongrois des Beaux Arts* 55 (1980), 9–16.

opening of the mouth ceremony

Ritual by which the deceased and his or her funerary statuary were brought to life, the 'full version' of which is perhaps an assemblage of different rituals. Most of the surviving evidence derives from the New Kingdom (1550–1069 BC), in the form of vignettes from the BOOK OF THE DEAD and tomb paintings. In the Old Kingdom (2686–2181 BC), a virtually identical ceremony was known as the 'offering ritual' and incorporated into the PYRAMID TEXTS (usually Utterances 20–2 inscribed in the burial chamber). At this date it is likely that the ceremony was regularly carried out on statues of the king in the valley temple of his pyramid complex.

During the New Kingdom the ceremony was codified into seventy-five separate acts, the earliest full copy of which is known from scenes in the tomb of the vizier REKHMIRA (TT100). The ritual was usually carried out by the son and heir of the deceased as a final act of piety. Thus, where royal succession is concerned, it was sometimes a way of legitimizing succession. Such is the case with AY (1327–1323 BC), represented in the robes of a *sem*-priest performing the ceremony on the dead king in the tomb of Tutankhamun (KV62; 1336–1327 BC).

Mummies and statues that underwent this ritual were effectively transformed into vessels for the KA of the deceased. The ritual could be performed in a number of different locations, from the 'house of gold' itself (i.e. the burial chamber) to the workshops of the sculptor or embalmer. New Kingdom papyri frequently depict scenes from the ceremony, showing the coffin standing upright in front of the priest or heir. From the 25th Dynasty (747–656 BC) onwards, an enlarged pedestal base on the coffin may well have assisted in keeping it in this position throughout the ceremony.

The ritual was a very elaborate one involving purification, censing, anointing and incantations, as well as the touching of various parts of the mummy with different objects so that the senses were restored not only to the mouth, so that it might eat and speak, but also to the eyes, ears, nose and other parts of the body. One of the most important objects used in the ritual was the *pesesh-kef*, probably originally a flint knife with a bifurcated blade shaped like a

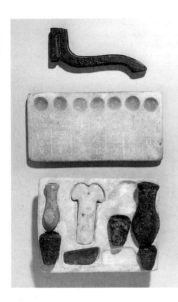

ABOVE *Set of instruments dating from the Old Kingdom which would have been used in the opening of the mouth ceremony. H of limestone table in the centre 8.9 cm. (EA58404)*

fish tail, many fine examples of which have been excavated from Predynastic graves as early as the Naqada I period (*c*.4000–3500 BC), thus probably indicating that a similar ceremony was already being used well before the first evidence for many other aspects of Egyptian funerary ritual. Other implements used are described as *netjeri*-blades and were principally made from meteoric IRON, although occasionally other metals were used. In addition the right leg of a specially slaughtered ox was sometimes extended toward the mummy or statue, perhaps in an attempt to pass on the intrinsic power of the ox.

A. M. BLACKMAN, 'The rite of opening the mouth in ancient Egypt and Babylonia', *JEA* 10 (1924), 47–59.

E. OTTO, *Das ägyptische Mundöffnungsritual* (Wiesbaden, 1960).

R. VAN WALSEM, 'The *pss-kf;* an investigation of an ancient Egyptian funerary instrument', *Oudheidhundige Mededelingen uit het Rijksmuseum van Oudheiden te Leiden* 59 (1978–9), 193–249.

A. R. SCHULMAN, 'The iconographic theme, "opening of the mouth" on stelae', *JARCE* 21 (1984), 169–96.

A. M. ROTH, 'The *pss-kf* and the "opening of the mouth" ceremony: a ritual of birth and rebirth', *JEA* 78 (1992), 113–47.

—, 'Fingers, stars and the "opening of the mouth"', *JEA* 79 (1993), 57–80.

oracles

When important decisions needed to be justified or endorsed, the Egyptians turned to the gods for oracles. When oracles first gained prominence in the early New Kingdom (1550–1069 BC), they were sought even by the pharaoh and the highest government officials, often as a very public means of obtaining divine approval for their actions. In later periods the method was used more regularly to resolve local administrative or legal disputes, although a stelophorous (STELE-bearing) statue of OSORKON II (874–850 BC) at Tanis is inscribed with a prayer to the god Amun in which he asks for an oracle approving his regime.

At a purely local level, as in the workmen's village at DEIR EL-MEDINA, oracles were employed – whether consciously or not – as a mechanism for soothing potential flashpoints of social tension. There must often have been situations in which the *kenbet* (local council) might have been accused of bias or favouritism if they had not been able to call on some form of objective outside guidance (although it is not clear to what extent the oracle could be 'fixed' by the priests).

The consulting of the god for oracles took place when the divine image was being carried through the streets between temples, usually on the occasion of a particular religious FESTIVAL. This provided the ordinary Egyptians with their only real opportunity to approach the god, since his image was usually hidden away in the darkest sanctuary of the temple. When individuals addressed questions to the god (in either spoken or written form) the priests carrying the BARK shrine were able to tilt it one way or another in order to indicate a simple yes or no. At Deir el-Medina the image used for the oracle was usually that of the deified AMENHOTEP I, which was carried through the streets of the village at festival times. The types of questions varied enormously from health problems to disputes over property law. If the verdict given by the oracle of one god was regarded as unsatisfactory, petitioners were evidently able to consult the oracles of one or more other deities.

Part of the Book of the Dead papyrus of Hunefer, illustrating Spell 23, the opening of the mouth ceremony. Priests raise the ritual implements to the mouth of Hunefer's mummy, while behind them a sem-priest in leopard-skin robes holds a censer. Behind the mummy stands a priest wearing an Anubis mask, whilst the wife of the deceased mourns before the coffin. To the right is the funerary chapel with its pyramidal roof and a funerary stele. (EA9901/5)

Copy of a wall-painting from Deir el-Medina showing an image of the deified Amenhotep I being carried in a procession so that his statue could be consulted as an oracle. (COPY BY NINA DE GARIS DAVIES)

From the 21st Dynasty onwards, the 'festival of the oracle' was celebrated in the courtyard between the ninth and tenth pylons at the temple of KARNAK. In the Third Intermediate Period (1069–747 BC) a new form of oracle, known as an 'oracular amuletic decree', was also introduced. This took the form of a small cylindrical amulet worn on a necklace and containing a divine decree said to have been issued in the form of an oracle and effectively protecting the wearer against every conceivable disaster. In the Late Period (747–332 BC) and Ptolemaic period (332–30 BC), a large number of so-called 'dream-texts', written in Greek and DEMOTIC, have been excavated from such sites as the Sacred Animal Necropolis at SAQQARA. These texts suggest that the interpretation of DREAMS had become closely linked with the consulting of oracles. Individuals requiring an answer to a particular problem or dilemma appear to have deliberately slept on sacred ground so that the god would send them dreams serving as somewhat cryptic oracles.

A. L. BLACKMAN, 'Oracles in ancient Egypt I', *JEA* 11 (1925), 249–55.
—, 'Oracles in ancient Egypt II', *JEA* 12 (1926), 176–85.
I. E. S. EDWARDS, *Oracular amuletic decrees of the late New Kingdom* (London, 1960).
G. ROEDER, *Kulte, Orakel und Naturverehrung im alten Ägypten* (Zurich, 1960).
J. ČERNY, 'Egyptian oracles', *A Saite oracle papyrus from Thebes*, ed. R. PARKER (Providence, 1962).
J. D. RAY, *The archive of Hor* (London, 1976), 130–6.
J. M. KRUCHTEN, *Le grand texte oraculaire de Djéhoutymose* (Brussels, 1986).

Orion *see* SAH

Osirid pillar

Square pillar with one of its faces carved into the form of an engaged colossal statue depicting the mummiform figure of the god OSIRIS or the dead king. From the New Kingdom (1550–1069 BC) onwards, porticoes incorporating Osirid pillars were a common feature of royal mortuary temples. Examples are to be found on the upper terrace of the temple of Hatshepsut (1473–1458 BC) at DEIR EL-BAHRI, in the second court of the RAMESSEUM and on the eastern side of the first court of MEDINET HABU at Thebes.

C. LEBLANC, 'Piliers et colosses de type "osirique" dans le contexte des temples de culte royal', *BIFAO* 80 (1980), 69–89.
C. LEBLANC and I. EL-SAYED, *Le Ramesseum* IX/2: *Les piliers osiriaques* (Cairo, 1988).

Osiris

One of the most important deities of ancient Egypt, whose principal association is with death, resurrection and fertility. He is usually depicted as a mummy whose hands project through his wrappings to hold the royal insignia of crook and flail. He wears the distinctive *atef* CROWN, consisting of the tall 'white crown' flanked by two plumes, sometimes shown with the horns of a ram. His flesh was sometimes shown as white, like the mummy wrappings, black to signify the fertile Nile alluvium, or green in allusion to resurrection.

Osiris was one of the earliest Egyptian gods, probably originally regarded simply as a CHTHONIC fertility-god overseeing the growth of crops, and perhaps with some connection to the INUNDATION as a source of fertile alluvium. In later times his connection with the river was still occasionally maintained. As his cult spread through the country, he gradually took on the attributes of those gods on whose cult centres he encroached. It seems likely, for instance, that his insignia were taken from Andjety, a god of Busiris (ancient Djedu) in the Delta. It is likely that the legend of Osiris as the dead form of an earthly ruler was also

Part of the Book of the Dead papyrus of Hunefer, illustrating Spell 125. Osiris is shown seated in judgement under a canopy. Behind him stand Isis and Nephthys, while in front of him are the figures of the four Sons of Horus, standing on a lotus flower. (EA9901/3)

taken over from Andjety's cult. Subsequently, when various sites claimed to be associated with the individual parts of Osiris' dismembered body, Busiris claimed his backbone, the DJED PILLAR, a symbol that had many other connotations and was simply assimilated into the cult of Osiris, perhaps losing its original meaning in the process.

His main southern cult centre was at ABYDOS (ancient Abdjw), which was said to be the burial place of his head. In the New Kingdom (1550–1069 BC), the tomb of the 1st Dynasty ruler DJER (c.3000 BC) was claimed to be his burial place, and the site became a centre of pilgrimage. As well as a chapel for Osiris in the temple of Sety I (1294–1279 BC) there was also the so-called 'Osireion', the masonry of which was evidently intended to resemble a temple of the Old Kingdom (2686–2181 BC), although it was actually the work of Merenptah (1213–1203 BC).

Although his best-known epithet is Wennefer, meaning 'eternally good' or 'eternally incorruptible' (i.e. not suffering the decay of death), he also took on the title 'chief of the westerners', which was the literal meaning of the name of the jackal-god Khentimentiu, the earlier god of the dead at Abydos. Osiris' epithets also included 'he who dwells in HELIOPOLIS', which thus associated him with the cult-centre of the sun-god RA. The Heliopolitan priests attempted to provide a genealogy for Osiris in the form of the ENNEAD, a group of nine deities whose relationships are first described in the PYRAMID TEXTS. Other funerary associations may have evolved as a result of his assimilation with the hawk-headed SOKAR, another underworld god associated with PTAH, patron of the city of Memphis.

The combination of his fertility and funerary aspects naturally transformed Osiris into the quintessential god of resurrection. By at least the 5th Dynasty (2494–2345 BC) the dead king was identified with Osiris, while the living ruler was equated with his son HORUS (see KINGSHIP). With the so-called 'democratization of the afterlife' that took place during the First Intermediate Period (2181–2055 BC) it appears to have become possible for any deceased person to be resurrected in the guise of Osiris (see COFFIN TEXTS). The phrase 'Osiris of X' is frequently used to refer to the deceased, in order to identify him or her with the god.

In order to gain eternal life, it was essential for the mummified body to imitate the appearance of Osiris as closely as possible. The Greek writer HERODOTUS therefore described the most expensive technique of MUMMIFICATION as being 'in the manner of Osiris'. As the judge of the dead, Osiris is shown in judgement scenes illustrating the BOOK OF THE DEAD. Nevertheless, the Egyptians had a somewhat ambivalent attitude toward the underworld (*dwat*) and texts sometimes refer to the negative aspect of Osiris as a malevolent deity. Thus the decreased might also request the protection of Ra, so that they could journey in the light rather than the darkness. It was also perhaps for this reason that the concept of the 'double soul' developed, whereby Osiris was the BA of Ra, and therefore could be thought of as the 'night sun', sometimes equated with the moon. By the same logic, Isis and Nephthys, previously both connected principally with Osiris and Seth, were considered to wait each morning to greet the newborn sun, the resurrection of the god. Between roughly the 18th and 21st Dynasties there was a gradual progression towards the unification of solar and Osirian concepts of resurrection.

As early as the Old Kingdom, many of the main elements of the Osiris myth were in existence, including his death by drowning, and the discovery of his body by Isis. That Seth was his murderer is explicit by the Middle Kingdom (2055–1650 BC), although there is no mention that Osiris was dismembered by him. By the New Kingdom, however, many of the FUNERARY TEXTS connected the deceased much more closely with Osiris, and the descriptions of the fate of the deceased effectively illustrate parts of the story of Osiris. The themes of Osiris' impregnation of Isis and the conception of his son Horus ('avenger of his father') had already developed in Pharaonic times and certain aspects of the myths were illustrated on the walls of the chapel of Sokar in the temple of Sety I at Abydos.

It was at Abydos that the annual FESTIVAL of Osiris took place. This involved the procession of the god in his BARK, known as *neshmet*, preceded by his herald, the jackal-god WEPWAWET. Scenes from Osiris' triumph over enemies were enacted in the course of the journey before the god returned to his sanctuary for purification. The rites connected with the 'mysteries' of Osiris were enacted in the temple, probably celebrating his original function as a fertility god, although little is known of these rituals.

The most coherent, although not necessarily the most accurate, account of the Osiris legend is that compiled by the Greek historian PLUTARCH. Certain of the elements in Plutarch's version can be corroborated from Egyptian sources, while others must remain dubious. He states that Osiris was once an earthly ruler who governed well, and so aroused the jealousy of his evil brother Seth. Seth secretly discovered the measurements of his brother's body and had a magnificent casket made to fit him. He next organized a banquet to which he invited seventy-two accomplices as well as Osiris. During the feast he brought forward the chest and declared that whoever fitted it exactly should have it as a gift. Having stepped into the coffin, Osiris was locked inside and the lid was sealed with molten lead. The coffin was cast into the Nile and then drifted to the city of BYBLOS, where it became entangled in a cedar tree. Although the reference to Byblos is unsupported by Egyptian written accounts, there is a depiction of Osiris in a coffin among the branches of a tree in the temple of Hathor at DENDERA.

Isis eventually rescued the casket and returned it to Egypt, hiding it in the marshes prior to giving a decent burial to her husband. However, while she was engaged in looking for her son Horus (already born in Plutarch's story), Seth is said to have stumbled on the casket and angrily dismembered the body of his brother, scattering the parts throughout Egypt. The account of the number of pieces varies from fourteen to forty-two. Isis then searched for the pieces and buried each at the place where it was found. The phallus, however, had been eaten by the Nile carp (*Lepidotus*), the *Phagrus* and the *Oxyrynchus* FISH, so that an artificial penis had to be manufactured.

In the Egyptian accounts it was at this stage that the dismembered body was reassembled into the form of the first mummy, from which Isis conceived the child Horus. Subsequently Horus was said to have avenged his father's death in a series of contests with his uncle Seth, the so-called Contendings of Horus and Seth. According to these myths, the struggle lasted for eighty years, until Osiris was finally declared ruler of the underworld and his son Horus was confirmed as ruler of the living, leaving Seth to rule the deserts as the god of chaos and evil, the archetypal outsider and the antithesis of Osiris.

E. OTTO, *Osiris und Amun, Kult und Heilige Stätten* (Munich, 1966).

E. CHASSINAT, *Le mystère d'Osiris au mois de Khoiak*, 2 vols (Cairo, 1966–8).

J. G. GRIFFITHS, *Plutarch's De Iside et Osiride* (Swansea, 1970).

—, *The origins of Osiris and his cult* (Leiden, 1980).

M. EATON-KRAUSS, 'The earliest representation of Osiris?', *VA* 3 (1987), 233–6.

A. NIWINSKI, 'The solar-Osirian unity as principle of the theology of the "state of Amun" in Thebes in the 21st Dynasty', *JEOL* 30 (1987–8), 89–106.

M. C. LAVIER, 'Les mystères d'Osiris à Abydos d'après les stèles du Moyen Empire et du Nouvel Empire', *Akten München 1985* III, ed. S. Schoske (Hamburg, 1989), 289–95.

S. QUIRKE, *Ancient Egyptian religion* (London, 1992).

Osiris bed

Item of New Kingdom royal funerary equipment consisting of a wooden frame in the form of the god OSIRIS, which was filled with alluvial silt and sown with seeds of barley. The germination and growth of the grain probably symbolized the act of resurrection and the triumph of Osiris over his adversary SETH. Only seven Osiris beds have been found, including one from the tomb of TUTANKHAMUN (KV62; 1336–1327 BC), which is a virtually life-size figure, measuring 190 cm in height.

It has been suggested that the concept of an Osiris bed (sometimes also described as a 'germinated Osiris figure') may possibly have derived from the observation of pigs tramp-

Osiris bed from the tomb of Tutankhamun. It has been planted with seed corn, the remains of which are clearly visible. 18th Dynasty, c.1330 BC.
L. *190 cm. (CAIRO NO. 288A; REPRODUCED COURTESY OF THE GRIFFITH INSTITUTE)*

pling seed into the ground. Since the pig was associated with the cult of Seth, the sowing of the seeds in the Osiris figure might have symbolized Seth's initial defeat of Osiris, while the eventual sprouting of the barley would, in its turn, have symbolized the rebirth of Osiris. Certainly the overall symbolism of the Osiris bed was concerned not only with resurrection but also with the role of Osiris as a god of fertility and harvest, in which he was closely associated with the grain-god Neper.

There are also a number of ceramic bricks which may be later developments of the Osiris bed; one in the collection of the Metropolitan Museum, New York, measuring 24 cm long and about 10 cm wide, has a hollow figure of Osiris carved into its upper surface, evidently serving as a magical receptacle for soil and grain.

See also CORN MUMMIES.

M. A. LEAHY, 'The "Osiris-bed" reconsidered', *Orientalia* 46 (1977) 424–34.

M. J. RAVEN, 'Corn-mummies', *OMRO* 63 (1982), 7–38.

Osorkon

Libyan name held by five rulers of the 21st to 23rd Dynasties as their 'birth name' or nomen (see ROYAL TITULARY).

Osorkon the elder, Aakheperra Setepenra (984–978 BC), listed in MANETHO's history as Osochor, was the fifth of the 21st-Dynasty rulers. Judging from a pair of inscriptions in the temple of Khons at Karnak, he was the son of a woman called Mehtenweskhet and therefore probably the uncle of the first 22nd-Dynasty ruler, SHESHONQ I (945–924 BC). 'Osorkon the elder' is poorly attested in inscriptions, but it may have been during his six-year reign that the Biblical figure Hadad the Edomite stayed in Egypt, having been initially offered protection by Amenemope (993–984 BC), Osorkon's predecessor.

Osorkon I Sekhemkheperra Setepenra (924–889 BC) was the second ruler of the 22nd Dynasty and successor to Sheshonq I. His reign is much better documented than that of Sheshonq I, and a fine inlaid bronze statuette bearing his cartouches (Brooklyn Museum, New York) was found at TELL EL-YAHUDIYA. The upper part of a statue presented to Elibaal, the ruler of Byblos, has also survived. In the Delta city of Bubastis (TELL BASTA), which was the initial power-base of his father Sheshonq, he constructed a small temple to ATUM and made numerous additions to the principal temple of BASTET. He outlived his son and coregent, Sheshonq II, who was probably also the chief priest of Amun at Thebes,

and was eventually succeeded by a second son, TAKELOT I (889–874 BC).

Osorkon II Usermaatra Setepenamun (874–850 BC) was Takelot I's son and successor and the fifth ruler of the 22nd Dynasty. During the early part of his reign his influence in Upper Egypt was thwarted by the power of the chief priest of Amun at Thebes, Harsiese. However, when Harsiese died, Osorkon II was able to appoint one of his own sons, Nimlot, as the new chief priest, thus regaining control of the Theban region. In the twenty-second year of his reign Osorkon celebrated his SED FESTIVAL, probably at Bubastis, where he constructed a new court and gateway for the occasion. He also constructed additions to the temple of Amun at TANIS (the 22nd-Dynasty capital) and rebuilt an earlier tomb for himself within the temple precincts, eventually sharing it with his son, Hornakht; this tomb was one of those excavated by Pierre Montet in 1939–40.

Osorkon III Usermaatra Setepenamun (777–749 BC) was one of the 23rd-Dynasty pharaohs who ruled from the Theban region, controlling cities such as HERMOPOLIS MAGNA in Middle Egypt, and perhaps Leontopolis (TELL EL-MUQDAM) in the Delta. It was the throne of Leontopolis that Osorkon III inherited from the short-lived Sheshonq IV. He appointed his son Takelot as ruler of Herakleopolis and later also as chief priest at Thebes, thus establishing control over a great deal of Egypt, leaving his contemporary Sheshonq V of Tanis with correspondingly diminished territories.

Osorkon IV Aakheperra Setepenamun (730–715 BC) succeeded Sheshonq V as the last of the 22nd-Dynasty rulers, by which time the geographical area over which he reigned was restricted to the region surrounding Bubastis and Tanis. It was during his reign that the Kushite pharaoh PIY swept northwards to conquer Egypt.

CHICAGO ORIENTAL INSTITUTE, *Reliefs and inscriptions at Karnak* III: *The Bubastite portal* (Chicago, 1954).

R. A. CAMINOS, *The chronicle of Prince Osorkon* (Rome, 1958).

J. YOYOTTE, 'Osorkon, fils de Mehytouskhé, un pharaon oublié', *BSFE* 77–8 (1977), 39–54.

W. BARTA, 'Die Sedfest-Darstellung Osorkons II. im Tempel von Bubastis', *SAK* 6 (1978), 25–42.

K. A. KITCHEN, *The Third Intermediate Period in Egypt* (1100–650 BC), 2nd ed. (Warminster, 1986), 273–4, 287–354, 542–5.

J. YOYOTTE et al., *Tanis, l'or des pharaons* (Paris, 1987).

D. A. ASTON, 'Takeloth II – a king of the "Theban 23rd Dynasty"?', *JEA* 75 (1989), 139–53.

ostracon (Greek *ostrakon*; plural *ostraka*: 'potsherd')

Term used by archaeologists to refer to sherds of pottery or flakes of limestone bearing texts and drawings, commonly consisting of personal jottings, letters, sketches or scribal exercises, but also often inscribed with literary texts, in the HIERATIC, DEMOTIC, COPTIC and Greek scripts (see LITERATURE). The use of ostraca was obviously much cheaper than writing or drawing on PAPYRUS, and many hundreds of these documents have been recovered from excavations.

Thousands of ostraca, including more than fifteen hundred literary excerpts, such as the

Tale of Sinuhe (the largest surviving ostracon, now in the collection of the Ashmolean Museum, Oxford), were excavated at the site of the New Kingdom Theban workmen's village of DEIR EL-MEDINA, providing an invaluable record of the daily lives of the workmen, while also supplying information concerning the nature of Egyptian economy and society at that time. The so-called 'trial sketches', often found on limestone ostraca, are among the liveliest surviving products of Egyptian artists. Many such sketches provide vivid glimpses of Egyptian HUMOUR and satire, which would otherwise be poorly represented in the artistic and literary record.

At urban sites such as EL-AMARNA and QAN-TIR, the vast majority of so-called ostraca belong to the rather different categories of 'jar labels' and 'dockets', which usually simply describe the foodstuffs or liquid contained in the vessel, and, in the case of wine, provide details of the vintage and origins (see ALCO-HOLIC BEVERAGES).

N. DE G. DAVIES, 'Egyptian drawings on limestone flakes', *JEA* 4 (1917), 234–40.

J. ČERNY, *Catalogue des ostraca hiératiques non littéraires de Deir el-Medineh*, 7 vols (Cairo, 1935–70).
J. VANDIER D'ABBADIE, *Catalogue des ostraca figurés de Deir el-Médineh*, 4 vols (Cairo, 1937–46).
J. W. BARNES, *The Ashmolean ostracon of Sinuhe* (Oxford, 1952).
G. POSENER, *Catalogue des ostraca hiératiques littéraires de Deir el Medineh* (Cairo, 1972).
M. A. A. NUR EL-DIN, *The demotic ostraca* (Leiden, 1974).
W. H. PECK, *Egyptian drawings* (London, 1978).
E. BRUNNER-TRAUT, *Egyptian artists' sketches: figured ostraka from the Gayer–Anderson collection in the Fitzwilliam Museum* (Cambridge, 1979).

Limestone chip bearing a sketch of a cockerel, from the Valley of the Kings. 19th Dynasty, c.1200 BC, H. 15.7 cm. (EA68539)

P

paddle dolls *see* SEXUALITY

palace

The close association between the king and his residence reached its logical conclusion in the late New Kingdom (1550–1069 BC), when the term *per-aa* ('great house'), which had previously referred only to the royal palace, was applied instead to the king himself, eventually being transformed into the familiar term 'pharaoh'.

The term *palace* tends to be used rather loosely to refer to any large building in which the king or his immediate family resided, whereas the archaeological and textual evidence suggests that the situation was not quite so straightforward. There were many different types of building associated with the Egyptian royal family, varying primarily in their specific functions and length of use. There were almost ritualistic or symbolic palaces attached to New Kingdom mortuary temples such as the RAMESSEUM and MEDINET HABU (the latter being the best preserved) and there were also huge ceremonial buildings such as the Great Palace at EL-AMARNA and the palace of Sety I at QANTIR, which must have had more to do with the reception of foreign visitors and the enactment of ceremonies than the actual housing of the pharaoh and his family. Relatively few of the surviving 'palaces' have the air of actual residences, but a large villa opposite the Great Palace at el-Amarna was identified by the excavators as the 'king's house'; this seems to have functioned as a set of domestic apartments for the royal family in the very centre of the city. At the more ephemeral end of the scale, a brick platform at Kom el-Abd, in southwestern Thebes, has been interpreted as a royal 'rest-house', perhaps for use during chariot exercises.

Since palaces were constructed primarily of mud-brick and timber they tend not to be as well preserved as stone-built TEMPLES of similar date. On the other hand, they were often less prone to plundering and destruction than the temples, which were frequently deliberately dismantled, even in ancient times, in order to re-use their valuable stone. Although a building from the reign of the Middle Kingdom ruler Amenemhat III at Bubastis (TELL BASTA) has been identified as a palace, most of the surviving Egyptian royal residences date to the New Kingdom, including

those of Amenhotep III (1390–1352 BC) at MALKATA, Akhenaten (1352–1336 BC) at el-Amarna and Merenptah (1213–1203 BC) at Memphis.

Many palaces included a 'window of appearances', consisting of a ceremonial window at which the king appeared in order to undertake such activities as the reception of visitors, the conducting of ceremonies or the dispensing of rewards to his loyal courtiers. In the case of the small palaces associated with the mortuary temples of Rameses II (1279–1213 BC) and III (1184–1153 BC), the window represented a visible threshold between the sacred and profane aspects of the king's rule, a means of passing between palace and temple, the two most important institutions in the central government of Pharaonic Egypt.

The architectural style and decoration of the palaces varied to some extent, although they tended to combine large-scale domestic apartments (sometimes including sets of rooms tentatively identified as the HARIM) with reception halls, courtyards, pools and ceremonial areas in which rituals might have

The throneroom in the palace of Rameses III, beside his mortuary temple at Medinet Habu. The palace was located in the area immediately to the south of the first court of the temple (see entry on Medinet Habu for plan). Although the building was largely constructed of mud-brick, the vestibule, inner hall and throneroom contained stone columns. This is the best preserved throneroom to have survived from Pharaonic Egypt; that of Merenptah at Memphis, for example, is badly damaged. (I. SHAW)

been enacted. A number of surviving fragments of painted plaster and faience tiles suggest that the walls and floors were frequently painted both with the iconography of KINGSHIP (such as depictions of the NINE BOWS and foreign CAPTIVES) and with such pastoral scenes as flocks of birds flying through papyrus marshes.

Probably the most complex surviving groundplan of a New Kingdom palace is that of the Great Palace in the central city at el-Amarna, which was connected by a bridge with the smaller 'king's house' on the other side of the main road. The large courtyards and hypostyle halls of the central palace sug-

gest a building with a very different function to the palaces attached to Ramesside mortuary temples, and it has even been argued that the Great Palace was actually a temple to the Aten. The much later 'palace of Apries' at Memphis, excavated by Flinders Petrie, is equally difficult to interpret and, with its massive casemate mud-brick platform, may have functioned more as a citadel or fortress than a palace.

W. M. F. PETRIE, *The palace of Apries, Memphis II* (London, 1909), 1–13.

E. P. UPHILL, 'The concept of the Egyptian palace as a "ruling machine"', *Man, settlement and urbanism*, ed. P. J. Ucko, R. Tringham and G. W. Dimbleby (London, 1972), 721–34.

R. STADELMANN, 'Tempelpalast und Erscheinungsfenster in der Thebanischen Totentempeln', *MDAIK* 29 (1973), 221–42.

B. J. KEMP, 'The window of appearance at el-Amarna and the basic structure of this city', *JEA* 62 (1976), 81–99.

W. STEVENSON SMITH, *The art and architecture of ancient Egypt* (Harmondsworth, 1981), 279–95, 314–38.

B. J. KEMP, *Ancient Egypt: anatomy of a civilization* (London, 1989), 211–25, 276–81.

Palermo Stone

Broken fragments of a basalt stele dating to the 5th Dynasty (2494–2345 BC) and inscribed on both sides with a set of royal annals stretching back to the quasi-mythical rulers before the beginning of Egyptian history. The principal fragment has been known since 1866 and is currently in the collection of the Palermo Archaeological Museum, Sicily, although there are further pieces in the Egyptian Museum, Cairo, and the Petrie Museum, London.

The slab must originally have been about 2.1 m long and 0.6 m wide, but most of it is now missing, and there is no surviving information about its provenance. The text enumerates the annals of the kings of Lower Egypt, beginning with many thousands of years taken up by mythological rulers, until the time of the god HORUS, who is said to have given the throne to the mortal MENES. Human rulers are then listed up to the 5th Dynasty. The text is divided into a series of horizontal registers divided by vertical lines which curve in at the top, apparently in imitation of the hieroglyph for regnal year (*renpet*), thus indicating the memorable events of individual years in each king's reign. The sorts of events recorded included religious FESTIVALS, military campaigns and the creation of particular royal and divine statues. The name of the ruler was inscribed above the relevant block of compartments.

The Palermo Stone – along with the 'day-books', the annals and KING LISTS inscribed on temple walls, and the papyri held in temple and palace archives (see LIBRARIES and TURIN ROYAL CANON) – was doubtless the kind of document that the historian MANETHO used to compile his list of dynasties.

H. SCHÄFER, *Ein Bruchstück altägyptischer Analen* (Berlin, 1902).

G. DARESSY, 'La pierre de Palerme et la chronologie de l'ancien empire', *BIFAO* 12 (1916), 161–214.

B. J. KEMP, *Ancient Egypt: anatomy of a civilization* (London, 1989), 21–3.

Palestine, Palestinians *see* BIBLICAL
CONNECTIONS; CANAAN; ISRAEL and SYRIA–PALESTINE

palette

Term used to refer to two distinct artefacts: cosmetic and scribal palettes.

Cosmetic/ceremonial palettes, usually of siltstone (greywacke), have been found in the form of grave goods in cemeteries as early as the Badarian period (*c*.5500–4000 BC). They were used to grind pigments such as malachite or galena, from which eye-paint was made.

The earliest examples were simply rectangular in shape, but by the Naqada I period (*c*.4000–3500 BC) they were generally carved into more elaborate geometric forms – including a rhomboid which resembles the symbol of the later fertility-god MIN – or the schematic silhouettes of animals such as hippopotami and turtles (sometimes with inlaid eyes). By this time cosmetic palettes had almost certainly acquired ritualistic or magical connotations. In the Naqada II period (*c*.3500–3100 BC) the

Scribal palette inscribed with the titles of Ahmose I It has depressions for two cakes of pigment and a slot for the reed pens. 18th Dynasty, wood, H 28 cm. (EA12784)

preferred shapes tended to be the forms of fish or birds, rather than animals, and many were shield-shaped, with two birds' heads at the top. By the terminal Predynastic period the range of shapes of the smaller cosmetic palettes had become considerably reduced, but simultaneously a new and more elaborate ceremonial form began to be produced. These palettes (usually oval or shield-shaped) were employed as votive items in temples rather than as grave goods, and a large number were found in the form of a cache in the Early Dynastic temple at HIERAKONPOLIS. They were carved with reliefs depicting the ideology and rituals of the emerging élite, and the quintessential surviving example is the 'Narmer palette' (now in the Egyptian Museum, Cairo; see NARMER for illustration).

Scribal palettes generally consisted of long rectangular pieces of wood or stone (averaging 30 cm long and 6 cm wide), each with a shallow central groove or slot to hold the reed brushes or pens and one or two circular depressions at one end, to hold cakes of pigment. The hieroglyph used as the determinative for the words 'SCRIBE' and 'writing' consisted of a set of scribe's equipment, including a shorter version of the palette.

J. E. QUIBELL, *Archaic objects*, 2 vols (Cairo, 1904–5).

A. EGGEBRECHT et al., *Das alte Ägypten* (Munich, 1984), 347–63.

M. SALEH and H. SOUROUZIAN, *Egyptian Museum, Cairo: official catalogue* (Mainz, 1987), cat. nos 7–8, 233.

A. J. SPENCER, *Early Egypt* (London, 1994), 29–31, 51–8.

pan bedding

Type of construction, usually in mud-brick, consisting of curved courses. It is most often seen in temple enclosure walls from the Late Period (747–332 BC) onwards, which are usually built in sections and with a pronounced BATTER. It has been suggested that this sectional building, along with pan bedding, allowed the walls to move without collapsing as the ground expanded and contracted from the inundation. Others have noted that the wavy effect of the wall tops, resulting from the bedding, can give the impression of water, thus adding to the symbolism of the temple in terms of the PRIMEVAL MOUND surrounded by NUN, the waters of chaos. Good examples of pan bedding can be found in the enclosure-wall of the temple of Hathor at DENDERA and the walls of the town at ELKAB.

A. J. SPENCER, *Brick architecture in ancient Egypt* (Warminster, 1979).

pan-grave culture

Material culture of a group of semi-nomadic Nubian cattle herders who entered Egypt in the late Middle Kingdom (2055–1650 BC) and during the Second Intermediate Period (1650–1550 BC). They are particularly well attested in the Eastern Desert, and their characteristic shallow circular pit-graves, the so-called 'pan graves', are known throughout Upper Egypt as well as Lower Nubia.

The graves preserve the typically Nubian tradition of burying skulls and horns of gazelles, oxen and sheep, sometimes painted. An example from Mostagedda in Upper Egypt depicts what is presumably a chieftain with his weapons. His name is written in hieroglyphs, showing that contact with the Egyptian population was well established. Their POTTERY is of a distinctive handmade tradition, bearing incised decoration. They also used black-topped red ware. These ceramics show links with the C GROUP and KERMA culture as well as with nomads of the Eastern Desert and the Gash Delta near the Red Sea (from which shells must have been taken for some of their distinctive jewellery). Skeletal evidence suggests that they were a robust people, physically different from the C Group and probably also from the Kerma culture. They often appear to have worn distinctive leather kilts. Some have equated them with the MEDJAY who were employed as military mercenaries and as a kind of POLICE force, patrolling specific areas such as the VALLEY OF THE KINGS.

M. BIETAK, *Ausgrabungen in Sayala-Nubien 1961–1965. Denkmäler der C-Gruppe und der Pan-Gräber-Kultur* (Vienna, 1966).

E. STROUHAL and J. JUNGWIRTH, 'Anthropological problems of the Middle Empire and Late Roman Sayala', *Mitteilungen der Anthropologischen Gesellschaft in Wien* 101 (1971), 10–23.

B. J. KEMP, 'Old Kingdom, Middle Kingdom

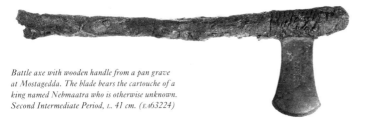

Battle axe with wooden handle from a pan grave at Mostagedda. The blade bears the cartouche of a king named Nebmaatra who is otherwise unknown. Second Intermediate Period, L. 41 cm. (EA63224)

and Second Intermediate Period' *Ancient Egypt: a social history*, B. G. Trigger et al. (Cambridge, 1983), 71–182 (169–71).

J. H. TAYLOR, *Egypt and Nubia* (London, 1991).

papyrus *(Cyperus papyrus)*

The heraldic plant of Lower Egypt. The name for Lower Egypt could be written as several papyrus plants growing out of the sign for 'land'. This was a logical choice since the plant must have grown particularly profusely in the Delta marshes, although it also occurred else-where in Egypt. In modern times it is limited to a few specially planted areas designed to

Papyrus roll from Deir el-Bahri. 21st Dynasty, H. 33 cm. (EA10793)

provide material for the creation of tourist papyri. Growing from the dense Nile mud, it was thought of as the plant that flourished on the PRIMEVAL MOUND of creation and so was chosen for the columns of HYPOSTYLE HALLS, which some scholars have suggested might actually have become flooded during the INUNDATION, adding to the symbolism. Such columns had two types of capital: buds or wide, open umbels. As a symbol of youth or joy (and the hieroglyphic sign meaning 'green'), papyrus was particularly appropriate for presentation to the goddess HATHOR and could serve as a magical sceptre presented to a variety of deities including the cat-goddess BASTET.

The harvested papyrus stems could be used for many purposes, such as the manufacture of ropes (see BASKETRY) and the caulking of boats, although in this use they were gradually replaced, in the post-Pharaonic period, by esparto grass (*Carthago spartaria*). They could also be lashed together to form boats or skiffs for hunting (see SHIPS AND BOATS). Gradually, however, the stems became waterlogged and the boats eventually had to be discarded and replaced.

This ability to absorb water also made the plant suitable for transformation into a paper-like writing material, which is also known as papyrus. Egyptologists have often named individual papyri after the modern owner or finder; thus 'Papyrus Chester Beatty' refers to a document once in the collection of the American-British industrialist and art collector, Sir Alfred Chester Beatty. It is not known when papyrus was first used, although the earliest surviving sheets (uninscribed) were discovered in the 1st-Dynasty tomb of Hemaka at Saqqara (3035).

In the production of papyrus sheets, the triangular stems were cut and their exterior stripped. They were then soaked in water and cut into strips. The length of the page does not usually exceed about one 'short cubit' (*c.*45 cm). The strips would then be beaten with a hammer to break down and flatten the

fibres. Next individual strips would be laid on top of one another at right angles and beaten so that the felted texture of the pith meshed together. Contrary to popular belief, the strips were not woven together. A weight would then be placed on top of the sheet while the strips dried together. The individual squares of papyrus could then be fixed together to make a roll, conventionally consisting of twenty squares, although several rolls might be joined together to make a longer document.

The papyrus was usually unrolled in such a way that the inside, known as the recto, would be written on first. The other side, the verso, was often left blank, and was sometimes the surface used by poorer people who only had access to used papyrus, as in some households in the workmen's village at DEIR EL-MEDINA. Discarded papyri were sometimes used for the production of CARTONNAGE, and valuable texts have sometimes been recovered as a result of this re-use. The use of papyrus continued through the Greco-Roman period and into the Islamic caliphate, until the introduction of cloth paper from the Far East in the eighth to ninth centuries AD.

J. ČERNY, *Paper and books in ancient Egypt* (London, 1952).

E. G. TURNER, *Greek papyri: an introduction* (Oxford, 1968).

N. LEWIS, *Papyrus in classical antiquity* (Oxford, 1974).

M. L. BIERBRIER, ed., *Papyrus: structure and usage* (London, 1986).

J. J. JANSSEN, 'The price of papyrus', *DE* 9 (1987), 33–5.

R. PARKINSON and S. QUIRKE, *Papyrus* (London, 1995).

Pasebakhaenniut *see* PSUSENNES

pataikos

Minor amuletic deity whose modern name derives from the Greek writer Herodotus' description of a form of Phoenician dwarfish protective image. The Egyptian *pataikos*, consisting of a small human figure (usually with a bald human head or a falcon's head) standing in a pose similar to that of the dwarf-god BES, is identified with 'Ptah the dwarf'. Relatively crude figures probably representing *pataikos* first appear in the late Old Kingdom (2686–2181 BC), but the earliest representations that can genuinely be described as *pataikoi* appear in the New Kingdom (1550–1069 BC). Most of the finest examples date to the Third Intermediate Period (1069–747 BC) and later.

C. A. ANDREWS, *Amulets of ancient Egypt* (London, 1994), 38–9.

Pepy (Pepi)

The 'birth name' (nomen) held by two 6th-Dynasty rulers.

Pepy I Meryra (2321–2287 BC) was the successor to the first 6th-Dynasty ruler, TETI, with only the brief reign of Userkara (either a usurper or a regent) intervening between them; his mother, Queen Iput, probably acted as regent when he first came to the throne. He had an active reign, lasting at least forty years, during which he constructed and decorated various temples at ABYDOS, Bubastis (TELL BASTA), DENDERA, ELEPHANTINE and possibly HIERAKONPOLIS. It was at Hierakonpolis that Frederick Green and James Quibell discovered the earliest examples of copper statuary, consisting of a life-size copper statue of Pepy, and inside it a second smaller copper statue which is usually assumed to represent his son and successor, Merenra. Although few substantial monuments of Pepy I have survived, there are many surviving fragments of inscription incorporating his names and titles, both during and after his lifetime.

A block from the funerary chapel of an official called Weni at Abydos is decorated with a long inscription recounting the part that he played in the events of the reigns of Teti, Pepy I and Merenra, the first three rulers of the 6th Dynasty (2345–2181 BC), including a reference to a possible HARIM conspiracy in the reign of Pepy I. This was clearly thwarted, but it has been suggested that it may, in some obscure way, have been the reason behind the late marriage he made to two women called Ankhenesmerira, both daughters of Khui, an official at Abydos. The enormous influence that Khui must have wielded as a result of these two marriages can be gauged from the fact that these two women gave birth to the next two kings, Merenra and Pepy II respectively, and, in addition, Khui's son Djau became VIZIER during both of their reigns.

There are some grounds for arguing that there was a COREGENCY with Merenra during the last few years of Pepy I's reign, since this would then make it more plausible that Weni could have served under Merenra as well as Teti and Pepy I, given the considerable lengths of the two latter reigns. There is, however, no definite proof of such an early coregency.

Pepy I's pyramid complex in south SAQQARA, although not the first to include PYRAMID TEXTS, was the first in which funerary texts of this type were discovered, when it was excavated by Emile and Heinrich Brugsch in 1880–1. Although his sarcophagus had been destroyed, a metre-deep rectangular pit near the south wall of the burial chamber contained a CANOPIC chest still holding one of the bundles

in which his viscera had been placed, and a few pieces of the stone jar in which it had originally been kept.

Pepy II Neferkara (2278–2184 BC) was a son of Pepy I who came to the throne after the premature death of his half-brother Merenra, who had reigned for about nine years. He himself is thought to have been only about ten years old at the time of his accession, a fact which may possibly be documented by the inscriptions on the walls of the tomb of Harkhuf, a governor of Aswan who was buried at Qubbet el-Hawa (Tomb A8). The texts recount various missions that Harkhuf undertook on behalf of the 6th-Dynasty kings, including a journey into southern Sudan during which he acquired a pygmy. The letter sent to him by the young pharaoh has an air of authenticity and perhaps even historical fact, with the king's expressions of eagerness to see the pygmy and his solicitous pleas that guards be set around him to see that he did not fall out of the boat at night. It is also clear from the texts in Harkhuf's tomb that the Egyptians were continuing to exert a certain amount of economic influence over Lower Nubia.

It is thought possible that the very long reign of Pepy II may have partly contributed to the gradual demise of the Old Kingdom, both by causing the central administration to stagnate and by producing a succession crisis as his appointed heirs perhaps died too early, leaving various rivals in contention for the throne.

Pepy II was buried in a pyramid at south SAQQARA, like his father, but the plan of his funerary complex has been preserved much more clearly. It was excavated in 1926–36 by Gustave Jéquier, who uncovered a number of fragments of relief, including not only the usual processions of subjects bearing offerings but also depictions of the king, in the form of a SPHINX and a griffin, trampling his enemies, and a scene showing the goddess SESHAT compiling a list of captives and spoils of war. Much of the decoration is derivative of that in the complex of Sahura (2487–2475 BC) at ABUSIR, and the scene of the defeated Libyan chieftain and his family in the central transverse corridor seems to have been copied faithfully in every detail (thus calling into question the historicity of many scenes containing named individuals in Egyptian religious or funerary contexts). Like several other pyramid complexes of this period (including Pepy I's), the mortuary temple contained fragments of a number of stone statues of bound CAPTIVES, which may have played a role in the celebration of the king's victories over foreign lands.

G. JÉQUIER, *Le monument funéraire de Pepi II*, 3 vols (Cairo, 1936–41).

E. DRIOTON, 'Notes diverses 2: une corégence de Pepy Ier de Merenre (?)', *ASAE* 44 (1945), 55–6.

L. HABACHI, *Tell Basta* (Cairo, 1947).

J. LECLANT, *Recherches dans la pyramide et au temple haut du pharaon Pépi I à Saqqarah* (Leiden, 1979).

—, 'A la quête des pyramides des reines de Pepi Ier', *BSFE* 113 (1988), 20–31.

N. GRIMAL, *A history of ancient Egypt* (Oxford, 1992), 81–9.

I. E. S. EDWARDS, *The pyramids of Egypt*, 5th ed. (Harmondsworth, 1993), 179–94.

Peribsen (Sekhemib) (*c*.2700 BC)

Ruler of the 2nd Dynasty (2890–2686 BC), whose principal surviving monument is Tomb P in the Umm el-Qa'ab cemetery at ABYDOS. Jar-sealings found in the tomb bear two names: Peribsen and Sekhemib. The name Peribsen, which was also found on the two gneiss stelae associated with the tomb, was written in a SEREKH frame surmounted by a SETH animal and sometimes accompanied by the epithet 'conqueror of foreign lands', while the *serekh* surrounding the name Sekhemib was surmounted by a HORUS falcon. While it was initially suggested that these were two consecutive rulers (just as KHASEKHEMWY and Khasekhem were once thought to refer to two separate individuals), most Egyptologists now consider that the two names were held by the same ruler. According to the latter theory the name Sekhemib would have been held by the king in the first part of his reign, when the cult of Horus was still dominant, whereas the assumption of the name Peribsen is taken to indicate a change in policy whereby the god Seth was elevated to greater prominence in the cult of KINGSHIP. It has even been argued that the apparent struggle between the cults of Horus and Seth is indicative of a resurgence of the conflict between the southern and northern halves of Egypt, which would eventually have been resolved in the reign of Khasekhemwy.

Seal-impressions bearing Peribsen's name were found at Elephantine (see ASWAN) in 1985, confirming that the kingdom extended as far south as the first Nile cataract at this date. It is also perhaps significant that a temple of Seth is known to have existed at Elephantine (although the surviving remains are later than the 2nd Dynasty).

W. M. F. PETRIE, *The royal tombs of the earliest dynasties* I (London, 1901), 11–12, pls LVIII, LXI

P. E. NEWBERRY, 'The Set rebellion of the second dynasty', *Ancient Egypt* (1922), 40–6.

A. GARDINER, *Egypt of the pharaohs* (Oxford, 1961), 416–20.

N. GRIMAL, *A history of ancient Egypt* (Oxford, 1992), 55–6.

peripteral
Architectural term denoting a building surrounded by an external colonnade, such as MAMMISI (although the term is sometimes confused with PERISTYLE).

peristyle
Architectural term used to describe a type of open court surrounded by an internal colonnade, as in the case of the second court of the mortuary temple of Rameses III at MEDINET HABU. See also PERIPTERAL.

Persia, Persians
The Persians, like their neighbours the Medes, were an Indo-Iranian group whose heartland lay in the region of modern Iran during the first millennium BC. The land of 'Parsua', apparently situated next to Urartu and to the south of Lake Urmia, is first mentioned in the annals of the Assyrian king Shalmaneser III (c.858–824 BC). The two principal cities of the Persian heartland in the fifth and sixth centuries BC were Pasargadae and Persepolis (Takht-i Shamshid), the latter comprising a succession of palaces built by Darius I and his successors, each of which incorporated elements derived from Egyptian, Median, Babylonian and Greek architecture. The extent to which the Persians also drew on the artistic resources of the various satrapies is indicated by the discovery of an Egyptian-style statue of Darius I (522–486 BC) at the site of Susa in western Iran.

At its height in c.500 BC the Persian empire extended from Libya to the Indus region and from Babylonia to western Turkey, comprising about twenty 'satrapies', each contributing regular tax and tribute to the Persian king. In the late sixth century BC, when the Achaemenid empire was expanding inexorably, the transformation of Egypt into a new satrapy began to look inevitable, although it was temporarily delayed by the death of Cyrus II in 529 BC. Eventually, however, in the spring of 525 BC, Cambyses (525–522 BC) defeated the armies of PSAMTEK III (526–525 BC) at Pelusium and went on to capture Memphis. The most interesting surviving document from the ensuing first Persian period (or 27th Dynasty, 525–404 BC) is the text inscribed on a statue of Udjahorresnet, an Egyptian priest and doctor who collaborated with the new regime, although there is some evidence that he looked after such local interests as the maintenance of the cult of NEITH at his home-city of Sais.

Scene of grape-picking in the tomb-chapel of Petosiris. This combines a traditional theme with the artistic style and costume of the Greek world. (GRAHAM HARRISON)

Egypt was subject to a second period of Persian domination, which some Egyptologists would describe as the '31st Dynasty', covering the decade between the end of the indigenous 30th Dynasty (343 BC) and the arrival of ALEXANDER THE GREAT in 332 BC. The stele of a priest of HERYSHEF called Somtutefnakht (now in the Naples Museum), which originally stood in the temple of Heryshef at Herakleopolis Magna, was inscribed with an autobiographical inscription generally interpreted as a description of a career stretching from the reign of Nectanebo II to that of Alexander the Great. Like Udjahorresnet, Somtutefnakht seems to have prospered by providing assistance to the new regime. When Alexander defeated the armies of Darius III (336–332 BC) and took Egypt, Somtutefnakht appears to have witnessed the battle from the Persian side.

G. POSENER, *La première domination Perse en Egypte* (Cairo, 1936).

J. YOYOTTE, 'Une statue de Darius découverte à Suse', *Journal Asiatique* (1972), 235–66.

M. LICHTHEIM, *Ancient Egyptian literature* III (Berkeley, 1980), 41–4. [Somtutefnakht]

I. HOFMANN, 'Kambysis in Ägypten', *SAK* 9 (1981), 179–200.

A. B. LLOYD, 'The inscription of Udjahorresnet: a collaborator's testament', *JEA* 68 (1982), 166–80.

N. GRIMAL, *A history of ancient Egypt* (Oxford, 1992), 367–82.

Petosiris (c.300 BC)
High priest of THOTH in the late fourth century BC who is best known for the chapel he built for himself and in honour of his father Seshu and brother Djedthutefankh at TUNA EL-GEBEL, near Hermopolis Magna in Middle Egypt. The tomb chapel is in the form of a small rectangular temple of early Ptolemaic style, in front of which stands a horned 'fire' altar of Greek type, which is also known from KARNAK. The temple is entered through a half-columned portico with composite capitals, like those at EDFU or DENDERA. Most of the texts on the walls of the chapel concern Petosiris and his titles. This chamber then gives access to a sanctuary with four square pillars, the walls of which are decorated with texts concerning his father and brother. Towards the southern end of this sanctuary is the shaft leading to the subterranean burial chambers some 8 m below.

The tomb is best known for its carved and painted decoration which combines traditional Egyptian subjects, such as harvesting, wine pressing and furniture-making, with a distinctly Hellenistic style. For instance, the Egyptian farmers are depicted in Greek clothing and in poses reminiscent of the Classical rather than the Egyptian tradition. The scenes in the porticoed *pronaos* are the most stylistically mixed, while those in the sanctuary tend more to the traditional Egyptian style, although some Greek influence can still be detected.

The inner coffin of Petosiris is made from blackened pine wood inlaid with multi-coloured glass hieroglyphs. Early Ptolemaic period, c.350 BC, from the tomb of Petosiris at Tuna el-Gebel, L. 1.95 m. (CAIRO JE46592)

Although the burials of Petosiris, his wife and one of his sons had been robbed in antiquity, the two wooden coffins and the stone sarcophagus of Petosiris were discovered during Gustave Lefèbvre's excavation of the tomb in 1920. The inner coffin of blackened pine is well preserved, with inlaid eyes and five columns of inscription inlaid in multicoloured GLASS hieroglyphs.

G. LEFÈBVRE, *Petosiris*, 3 vols (Cairo, 1923–4).

E. SUYS, *Vie de Petosiris* (Paris, 1927).

C. PICARD, 'Les influences étrangères au tombeau de Petosiris: Grèce ou Perse?' *BIFAO* 30 (1931), 201–7.

M. LICHTHEIM, *Ancient Egyptian literature* III (Berkeley, 1980), 44–9.

Petrie, William Matthew Flinders

(1853–1942)

Widely recognized as the first scientific excavator in the history of Egyptian archaeology, Petrie was born in Charlton, Kent, the son of William Petrie, a civil engineer and surveyor, and Anne Flinders, daughter of an explorer. In a long and illustrious career, he excavated many of the most important ancient Egyptian sites, from the Predynastic cemeteries at NAQADA to the Early Dynastic royal tombs at ABYDOS and the city at EL-AMARNA. His energetic fieldwork was matched by his excellent publication record, including many books dealing with general topics, such as *Tools and weapons, Ancient weights and measures* and *Egyptian architecture*.

It was typical of his work as a whole that his research began with an innovative metrological analysis encompassing Stonehenge and the GIZA pyramids. Much later in his career he developed the ingenious method of 'sequence dating', whereby the PREDYNASTIC PERIOD was divided into a series of cultural stages that are still broadly recognized by modern archaeologists (see ARMANT). He was able to spend long periods of time excavating in Egypt primarily because of the financial support provided by the writer Amelia Edwards, who was also the founder of the Egypt Exploration Fund (Society) and who endowed a chair in Egyptology for him at University College London.

Petrie's techniques of excavation were vastly superior to those employed by most of his contemporaries. Above all, he was determined to preserve and record as much of the evidence as possible, rather than concentrating purely on the kinds of objects that would command a good price on the art market. Perhaps the only aspect of his work that is regretted by modern scholars is his tendency to synthesize and condense his published results, rather than presenting the detailed field notes in their entirety. Since few of the original records have survived, much of his excavated material is now difficult to re-analyse or reinterpret.

W. M. F. PETRIE, *Inductive metrology* (London, 1877).

—, *The pyramids and temples of Gizeh* (London, 1883).

—, *Tell el-Amarna* (London, 1894).

—, *Diospolis Parva* (London, 1901).

—, *Methods and aims in archaeology* (London, 1904).

Portrait of Flinders Petrie. (PETRIE MUSEUM)

—, *Seventy years in archaeology* (London, 1931).

—, *The making of Egypt* (London, 1939).

M. S. DROWER, *Flinders Petrie: a life in archaeology* (London, 1985).

B. G. TRIGGER, *A history of archaeological thought* (Cambridge, 1989), 200–2.

pharaoh

Term used regularly by modern writers to refer to the Egyptian king (see KINGSHIP). The word is the Greek form of the ancient Egyptian phrase *per-aa* ('great house') which was originally used to refer to the royal PALACE rather than the king. The 'great house' was responsible for the taxation of the lesser 'houses' (*perw*), such as the temple lands and private estates. From the New Kingdom (1550–1069 BC) onwards, the term was often used to refer to the king himself.

H. FRANKFORT, *Kingship and the gods: a study of Near Eastern religion as the integration of society and nature* (Chicago, 1948).

J. D. RAY, 'The pharaohs and their court', *Egypt: ancient culture, modern land*, ed. J. Malek (Sydney, 1993), 68–77.

Philae

The original island site of a temple of the goddess Isis, located about eight kilometres south of Aswan. The surviving elements of the sandstone temple, dating from the 30th Dynasty to the late Roman period (380 BC–AD 300), were transferred to the nearby island of Agilqiyya during the early 1970s in order to save it from the rising waters of Lake Nasser (see ASWAN

HIGH DAM). On the adjacent island of Biga is a 'pure mound', which was regarded as a tomb of OSIRIS, the mythical consort of Isis.

The worship of Isis at Philae can be dated back as early as the reign of the 25th-Dynasty pharaoh Taharqo (690–664 BC), since blocks from his reign have been found at the site, but the earliest visible remains date to the reign of Nectanebo I (380–362 BC). Most of the temple was constructed between the reigns of Ptolemy II Philadelphus (285–246 BC) and Diocletian (AD 284–305). The complex incorporates a temple to the Nubian god AREN-SNUPHIS, built by Ptolemy IV Philopator (221–205 BC) and the Meroitic ruler Arkamani

LEFT *The temple of Isis at Philae, showing the first two pylons and the columns of the* mammisi *between them. The temple was moved from its original site to the island of Agilqiyya in order to preserve it from the waters of Lake Nasser.* (P. T. NICHOLSON)

BELOW *The island of Philae prior to the re-siting of the monuments. Mud-brick structures are omitted.*

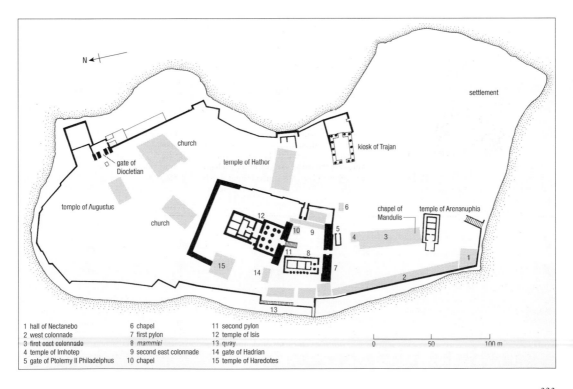

1 hall of Nectanebo	6 chapel	11 second pylon
2 west colonnade	7 first pylon	12 temple of Isis
3 first east colonnade	8 *mammisi*	13 quay
4 temple of Imhotep	9 second east colonnade	14 gate of Hadrian
5 gate of Ptolemy II Philadelphus	10 chapel	15 temple of Haredotes

(*c.*218–200 BC), in a rare instance of Egypto-Nubian architectural collaboration. The cult of Isis on Philae appears to have survived well into the Christian era, and the latest surviving hieroglyphic inscription occurs at the site. It was not until the reign of Justinian (*c.*AD 535) that the temple was finally abandoned.

H. JUNKER, *Der grosse Pylon des Tempels der Isis in Philä* (Vienna, 1958).

H. JUNKER and E. WINTER, *Das Geburtshaus des Tempels der Isis in Philä* (Vienna, 1965).

E. VASSILIKA, *Ptolemaic Philae* (Leuven, 1989).

Phoenicians

West-Semitic-speaking people who occupied the coastal area of the northern Levant (the western half of modern Lebanon) during the first millennium BC. It was in this region that the Phoenician cities of BYBLOS, Sidon and Tyre flourished, having displaced the settlements of earlier CANAANITE people. A number of ancient Egyptian texts (including the Middle Kingdom *Tale of Sinuhe*) use the term *Fenekhw*, apparently with reference to Canaanites living in the region surrounding Byblos, who are presumably to be identified with the Phoenicians. It was perhaps because they were successful sailors and traders, gradually establishing colonies across the Mediterranean region (including the city of Carthage), that their works of art largely consisted of iconography and styles borrowed from Egypt, Mesopotamia and the Aegean. The Phoenicians are also usually said to have been responsible for the invention of the alphabet.

W. WARD (ed.), *The role of the Phoenicians in the interaction of Mediterranean civilizations* (Beirut, 1968).

D. HARDEN, *The Phoenicians* (Harmondsworth, 1971).

D. R. AP THOMAS, 'The Phoenicians', *Peoples of Old Testament times*, ed. D. J. Wiseman (Oxford, 1973), 259–86.

P. M. BIKAU, 'The late Phoenician pottery complex and chronology', *Bulletin of the American Schools of Oriental Research* 229 (1978), 47–56.

Phoenix see BENU-BIRD

Piankhy see PIY

Pigs see ANIMAL HUSBANDRY

Piramesse see QANTIR and TELL EL-DAB'A

Piy (Piye, Piankhy) (747–716 BC)
Kushite ruler of the NAPATAN period who was the first Nubian to conquer Egypt, laying the foundations for the 25th Dynasty (747–656

BC). It is clear that his father, Kashta, had already pushed as far north as ASWAN, where he dedicated a stele to Khnum on Elephantine, and it has even been suggested that he exerted some influence in the Theban region. Piy himself seized control of Upper Egypt within the first decade of his reign, and his sister Amenirdis I was adopted by Shepenwepet I as the next GOD'S WIFE OF AMUN, thus acquiring Theban territories previously controlled by OSORKON III (777–749 BC). In 728 BC, when Tefnakht, the prince of Sais, created an alliance of Delta rulers to counter the growing Nubian threat, Piy swept northwards and defeated the northern coalition, describing his successful campaign on the so-called Victory Stele, which he erected in the temple of Amun at Gebel Barkal (see NAPATA), placing further copies in the principal temples at Karnak and Memphis, although only the original text has survived. Piy's stele borrowed much of its phraseology and style from earlier Egyptian royal 'recitations'. He therefore effectively set the tone of archaism and reverence for the past which was to characterize most of the artistic output of the 25th Dynasty, with the Kushite pharaohs constantly seeking to outdo their Egyptian predecessors in their concern for Egyptian religion and tradition.

In 716 BC Piy died after a reign of over thirty years. He was buried in an Egyptian-style pyramidal tomb at EL-KURRU, accompanied by a number of horses, which were greatly prized by the Nubians of the Napatan period. He was succeeded by his brother SHABAQO (716–702 BC), who reconquered Egypt and took full pharaonic titles, establishing himself as the first full ruler of the 25th Dynasty.

J. H. BREASTED, *Ancient records of Egypt* IV (Chicago, 1906), 796–883.

N. GRIMAL, *La stèle triomphale de Pi('ankh)y au Musée du Caire, JE 8862 et 47086–47089* (Cairo, 1981).

K. A. KITCHEN, *The Third Intermediate Period in Egypt (1100–650 BC)*, 2nd ed. (Warminster, 1986), 363–78.

N. GRIMAL, *A history of ancient Egypt* (Oxford, 1992), 335–43.

Plutarch (*c.*AD 46–126)

Greek writer of the Roman period who spent most of his life in his home town of Chaeronea, although he also visited Athens, Italy and Egypt. He is important to Egyptologists principally for his *De Iside et Osiride*, an account of the myth of HORUS and SETH, but there is debate as to how accurate this is. It is possible that much of what he recorded was based on a late version of the story.

J. G. GRIFFITHS, *Plutarch's De Iside et Osiride* (Swansea, 1970).

D. A. RUSSELL, 'Plutarch', *The Oxford Classical dictionary*, ed. N. G. L. Hammond and H. H. Scullard (Oxford, 1970), 848–50.

police

For most of the Pharaonic period there is evidence of a variety of officials whose roles roughly approximated to certain aspects of a modern police force. They can be divided into two basic categories: those performing a quasi-military role of guarding and patrolling and those enforcing justice and inflicting punishment.

Groups of men called *nww* are described as patrolling the desert with trained dogs in order to guard against BEDOUIN incursions, while the *meniw tjesenw* are credited with the protection of quarrying and mining expeditions in the Middle Kingdom (2055–1650 BC). By the New Kingdom (1550–1069 BC), these tasks seem to have been undertaken increasingly by groups of MEDJAY mercenary soldiers, who also guarded temples, palaces and cemeteries. A more specialized title (*s'sha*) was held by the officials who kept order in palace HARIMS.

The tasks of arresting individuals for such crimes as non-payment of tax (see TAXATION) and the subsequent inflicting of bastinado as punishment were both assigned to the holders of the title *sa-per* in the Old Kingdom (2686–2181 BC), although these same officials are later also mentioned as the guards accompanying Middle Kingdom desert expeditions. The continued use of this title in terms of the maintenance of law and order, however, is indicated by the Ptolemaic inscriptions at KOMOMBO, which elevate the term to a more universal role, describing the crocodile-god Sobek as a *sa-per* smiting rebels.

J. YOYOTTE, 'Un corps de police de l'Egypte pharaonique', *RdE* 9 (1952), 139–51.

J. ČERNY, *A community of workmen at Thebes in the Ramesside period* (Cairo, 1973), 261–84.

G. ANDREU, 'Sobek comparé à un policier', *Livre du Centenaire*, ed. J. Vercoutter (Cairo, 1980), 3–7.

—, 'Polizei', *Lexikon der Ägyptologie* IV, ed. W. Helck, E. Otto and W. Westendorf (Wiesbaden, 1982).

pornography see EROTICA and SEXUALITY

pottery

From the Predynastic period (*c.*5500–3100 BC) onwards pottery was one of the most important of Egyptian artefacts, and is certainly the one which survives most readily in the archae-

ulogical record. Because its broken fragments, or sherds, are almost indestructible, massive quantities of pottery have been preserved at sites throughout Egypt. However, it is only in relatively recent times that Egyptologists have come to value the importance of pottery in the Dynastic period,

LEFT *Badarian pot with blackened rim. Despite their early date and simple technology pots such as these are amongst the finest ever produced in Egypt. Fifth millennium BC, from el-Badari, H. 22.8 cm. (EA59691)*

BELOW *A fine blue-painted biconical jar from el-Amarna. Most ancient Egyptian pottery of the Pharaonic period was undecorated, the blue-painted ware being exceptional in this respect. 18th Dynasty, c.1350 BC, H. 70 cm. (EA56841)*

having previously placed greater reliance on inscriptional sources.

Egyptian pottery can be divided into two broad groups according to the generalized type of clay used. The first is 'Nile silt ware', those pots made from the alluvial deposits of the Nile valley, and which fire to a red-brown colour. This group makes up the great bulk of Egyptian pottery, and is most commonly used for the coarse, utilitarian wares, although it may be decorated as in the case of the 'blue painted' pottery during the New Kingdom (1550–1069 BC). The second group is the 'marl clay' vessels. These are made from calcareous clays which have a limited occurrence in Egypt, the best-known source being around Qena in Upper Egypt. Marl clays tend to be the products of more specialized industries and are usually employed for the better-quality wares. Often their surfaces are deliberately compacted, using a pebble or similar smooth object, before they are fired in the kiln. This process, known as burnishing, leaves them with a shiny surface, which is not a glaze, although it is sometimes mistakenly referred to as such. In fact, the application of a glaze to pottery (as opposed to FAIENCE, which is a non-clay ceramic) does not appear until Roman times.

These two basic pottery fabrics have been subdivided according to the materials added to them, known as filler or temper, as well as natural impurities in the clay. These subdivisions are devised by each archaeological expedition, but are usually related to an internationally recognized system for the classification of Egyptian pottery known as the Vienna System. This has the benefit of allowing archaeologists working all over Egypt to understand one another's pottery descriptions.

Predynastic pottery is often of extremely high quality. From the Badarian period come handmade vessels (i.e. those made without the use of the potter's wheel), burnished to a lustrous finish and fired so that they have a black top section with the rest left red. This is a considerable technical achievement, and demanded great skill on the part of the potter, particularly as it is likely that these vessels were open-fired (using a kind of bonfire) or produced in only the most rudimentary of kilns. Badarian vessels are among the most beautiful pottery ever made in Egypt. Free-form painted decoration is known from Naqada I times (c.4000–3500 BC), with animals, patterns, boats and human figures all being portrayed. This kind of representational art on pottery dies out in the Dynastic period.

The pottery of the Old Kingdom (2686–

2181 BC) was formed by hand and with the aid of a turntable, although by the late Old Kingdom the true potter's wheel, which uses centrifugal force to 'throw' pottery, had developed. This latter device requires finer clay preparation, which in turn necessitates greater control during firing. The chimney-like updraught kiln (with the fire placed beneath the pots and separated from them by a gridded floor) was probably developed in the Dynastic period, perhaps around the time that the wheel came into general use. The first wheels were hand-turned and relied on a smooth bearing to develop centrifugal force. They were very simple, comprising one stone set into another, and highly polished to form the bearing. The more familiar 'kick wheel', with its foot-operated fly-wheel, was probably introduced in Persian or Ptolemaic times (i.e. after c.500 BC).

The wheel allowed vessels to be made more quickly, in a simple form of mass production, but certain types of vessel continued to be handmade, alongside these thrown types. Bread-moulds, the formers for loaves of bread, particularly for offering use, continued to be shaped around a core known as a *patrix*.

Pottery was used for many of those purposes for which we would now use plastics, and alongside BASKETRY provided the main form of container. The differing combination of pottery fabric, technology and form allow archaeologists to use pottery as a chronological indicator, particularly significant on sites where there is no other clear dating evidence. It was the observation of this fact that first allowed Flinders PETRIE to develop his 'sequence dates' for the PREDYNASTIC PERIOD, building up a floating chronology, which, with the advent of radiocarbon dating, has been transformed into a system of absolute dates.

Regional variation and trade can also be traced through pottery, since a familiarity with Egyptian clays allows imported wares to be identified relatively simply, particularly with the use of such scientific techniques as ceramic petrology (thin sectioning) and neutron activation analysis. Recent developments in archaeological science also facilitate the study of the contents of pottery, thus providing information on the use of particular vessels. In addition, the study of the technological development of pottery, and its relationship to other crafts, is of value in itself.

The study of ancient Egyptian pottery is a rapidly developing area of recent EGYPTOLOGY, and one which has considerable potential to modify many of the existing views of Egyptian society and economy, providing information

on aspects of Egyptian culture that have previously been undocumented.

W. M. F. PETRIE, *Diospolis Parva* (London, 1901).

J. D. BOURRIAU, *Umm el-Qa'ab: pottery from the Nile valley before the Arab conquest* (Cambridge, 1981).

B. J. KEMP and R. MERRILLEES, *Minoan pottery from second millennium Egypt* (Mainz, 1981).

P. RICE, *Pottery analysis: a source book* (Chicago, 1987).

J. D. BOURRIAU and P. T. NICHOLSON, 'Marl clay pottery fabrics of the New Kingdom from Memphis, Saqqara and Amarna', *JEA* 78 (1992), 29–91.

D. ARNOLD and J. D. BOURRIAU (ed.), *An introduction to ancient Egyptian pottery* (Mainz, 1993).

Predynastic period (c.5500–3100 BC)

The late Neolithic period in Egypt, generally described as the 'Predynastic', began in the sixth millennium BC. The evidence from Upper Egypt differs significantly from the Lower Egyptian data; not only is each of the two regions apparently characterized by very different sequences of material culture, but the excavated sites in Upper Egypt are mainly cemeteries while those excavated in Lower Egypt primarily consist of settlement remains. This situation makes direct comparisons between the prehistoric cultures of northern and southern regions of Egypt extremely difficult. Excavations from the 1970s onwards have sought to redress the balance by obtaining more settlement data from the south and vice versa. In addition, the provision of radiocarbon dates on material from both Upper and

Lower Egyptian sites has gradually facilitated the construction of a tentative absolute chronology for the whole geographical and chronological range of the Predynastic.

A framework of relative dates for the mid- to late Predynastic period in Upper Egypt, i.e. the Amratian and Gerzean periods (see NAQADA), was first established by Flinders Petrie in the early 1900s (see also CHRONOLOGY; HIWSEMAINA REGION and POTTERY). When Gertrude Caton-Thompson excavated at Hammamia in the EL-BADARI region in the 1920s, she found stratigraphic confirmation of Petrie's dating system and considerable evidence of the earliest Upper Egyptian phase, the Badarian period (c.5500–4000 BC). Petrie's 'sequence dates' SD1–SD30, which he had allocated only in a preliminary fashion, were duly assigned to the various phases of the Badarian. Radiocarbon and thermoluminescence dates from the el-Badari region suggest that the period stretched back at least as early as 5500 BC.

Cemeteries of the Amratian phase (also known as Naqada I; c.4000–3500 BC) have survived at a number of sites in Upper Egypt, from Deir Tasa in the north to the Lower Nubian site of Khor Bahan. A rectangular Amratian house has been excavated at HIERAKONPOLIS and small areas of late Gerzean settlement were excavated at ABYDOS and el-Badari. In addition, a possible Gerzean religious structure has been uncovered at

Predynastic burial in which the body has been naturally desiccated by the hot, dry, desert sand. Naqada II period, c.3200 BC, L. (unflexed) 1.63 m. (EA32751)

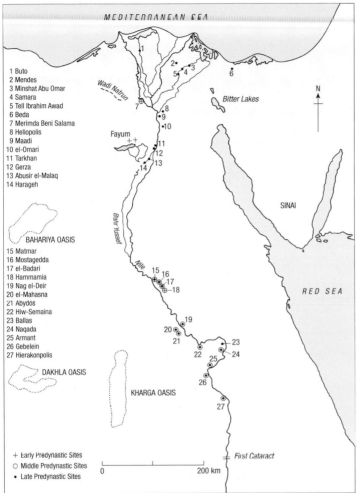

1 Buto
2 Mendes
3 Minshat Abu Omar
4 Samara
5 Tell Ibrahim Awad
6 Beda
7 Merimda Beni Salama
8 Heliopolis
9 Maadi
10 el-Omari
11 Tarkhan
12 Gerza
13 Abusir el-Malaq
14 Harageh

BAHARIYA OASIS

15 Matmar
16 Mostagedda
17 el-Badari
18 Hammamia
19 Nag el-Deir
20 el-Mahasna
21 Abydos
22 Hiw-Semaina
23 Ballas
24 Naqada
25 Armant
26 Gebelein
27 Hierakonpolis

DAKHLA OASIS

+ Early Predynastic Sites
○ Middle Predynastic Sites
• Late Predynastic Sites

First Cataract

0   200 km

MEDITERRANEAN SEA

Wadi Natrun

Bitter Lakes

N

Fayum

SINAI

Bahr Yussef

Nile

RED SEA

KHARGA OASIS

LEFT *Sites associated with Predynastic civilization.*

BELOW *Ivory figurine, with inlaid eyes of lapis lazuli. Fifth millennium BC, H. 11 cm. (EA32141)*

Delta region itself, both sites showing evidence of cultural influences from Gerzean Upper Egypt. The current view of the late Predynastic period in Egypt as a whole is that the inhabitants of Lower Egypt gradually assimilated various aspects of Upper Egyptian material culture in the late fourth millennium BC (this 'transitional' phase being particularly attested at Tell el-Fara'in) and that the Delta was eventually subsumed politically into a unified state dominated by Upper Egypt in about 3100 BC.

The 2500-year period of the Predynastic was once widely considered to have been culturally distinct from the Pharaonic age that succeeded it. Many authorities have argued that the apparently abrupt change at the end of the Predynastic – from the characteristic skeletons and artefacts of the early Gerzean people to those of the Early Dynastic élite buried at Naqada, Hierakonpolis and Abydos – was evidence of a sudden invasion from western Asia. Such 'diffusion theories' for the origins of the Egyptian state have come to seem less plausible, and most scholars now agree

Hierakonpolis. The transition from the Gerzean period to the EARLY DYNASTIC PERIOD was considered by Petrie to have been a separate cultural phase (the 'Semainean'), corresponding to SD65 onwards, but this final phase of the Predynastic is now described by some archaeologists as the 'Protodynastic'.

The earliest Lower Egyptian Neolithic remains are the 'Fayum A' encampments, dating back to c.5000 BC, which were effectively the first agricultural settlements in Egypt. The next stage in the Predynastic sequence is represented by three periods of occupation at

MERIMDA BENI SALAMA, the latest phase of which seems to have been contemporary with the settlements and cemeteries of EL-OMARI, south of Cairo. The next phase of the Lower Egyptian Predynastic is represented at the site of MAADI, which seems to have flourished in the early to mid fourth millennium BC. Most of the available information for the Lower Egyptian Predynastic derives from sites at the southern periphery of the region, but excavations during the 1980s at MINSHAT ABU OMAR and TELL EL-FARA'IN (Buto) have begun to provide crucial new evidence in the heart of the

that there was a steady and relatively unbroken progression in the Upper Egyptian material culture from the Badarian to the Early Dynastic: the archaeological case for social continuity is currently far more convincing than that for sudden invasion or migration.

See also AGRICULTURE; ARMANT and ELKAB.

H. J. KANTOR, 'The final phase of predynastic culture: Gerzean or Semainean?', *JNES* 3 (1944), 110–36.

M. A. HOFFMAN, *Egypt before the pharaohs* (New York, 1979).

B. G. TRIGGER, 'The rise of Egyptian civilization', *Ancient Egypt: a social history*, ed. B. G. Trigger et al. (Cambridge, 1983), 1–70.

F. HASSAN, 'The Predynastic of Egypt', *Journal of World Prehistory* 2 (1988), 135–85.

E. C. M. VAN DEN BRINK (ed.), *The Nile Delta in transition: 4th–3rd millennium BC* (Tel Aviv, 1992).

B. MIDANT-REYNES, *Préhistoire de l'Egypte* (Paris, 1992).

W. WETTERSTROM, 'Foraging and farming in Egypt: the transition from hunting and gathering to horticulture in the Egyptian Nile valley', *The archaeology of Africa: food, metals and towns*, ed. T. Shaw, B. Andah and P. Sinclair (London, 1993), 165–226.

K. A. BARD, 'The Egyptian Predynastic: a review of the evidence', *Journal of Field Archaeology* 21 (1994), 265–88.

prenomen (throne name) *see* ROYAL
TITULARY

priests

The Egyptian priest should not be viewed in the same way as a modern religious leader, such as a clergyman, *mullah* or rabbi. The term 'priest' is simply a modern translation for a number of religious offices connected with the Egyptian TEMPLE. The Egyptian priest, literally described as a 'servant of god' (*hem netjer*), was not necessarily well versed in religious doctrine (see EDUCATION), and, particularly in the Old and Middle Kingdoms, he did not necessarily work full-time for the temple. The common modern translation of *hem netjer* as 'prophet' has led to a certain amount of misunderstanding regarding the role of this official. He was employed at the temple to look after the cult statue of the deity. Like mortals, the god or goddess was thought to have daily needs for food and clothing.

Most priests would not have come into contact with the cult image, and, in theory, only the pharaoh, the high priest of every cult, had the privilege of attending the god. In practice, however, his authority was delegated to the chief priest, who was supported by lesser priests who would have attended to offerings

A sem *priest in leopard-skin robe. In his left hand he holds a censer. Detail from the Book of the Dead papyrus of Ani. 19th Dynasty, c.1250 BC. (EA10470, SHEET 5)*

and minor parts of the temple ritual. The 'second prophet' attended to much of the economic organization of the temple, while lower ranks, known as *wab* priests ('purifiers') attended to numerous other duties. There was also a female version of the *hem netjer* title (*hemet netjer*) and many élite women of the Old and Middle Kingdoms served as priestesses of the goddess HATHOR.

The chief priest, or 'first prophet', could wield significant power, and this position allowed him great influence in what would now be regarded as secular matters. During the 18th Dynasty (1550–1295 BC) the priesthood of the god AMUN became extremely powerful, and it is possible that they may have been temporarily suppressed in the reign of AKHENATEN (1352–1336 BC). In the 21st Dynasty (1069–945 BC), a succession of Libyan generals took control of the Theban region, using the title High Priest of Amun to legitimate their power.

There were also groups of priests with specialist knowledge, including 'hour priests' whom Serge Sauneron interprets as astronomers; he suggests that these men would have determined the time at which FESTIVALS took place. This was an important duty, since the Egyptian CALENDAR was rarely in step with the seasons. Astrologers sometimes determined 'lucky and unlucky' days, and books of these predictions have survived (see ASTRONOMY AND ASTROLOGY). The HOUSE OF LIFE had its own priestly officials, who attended to the teaching of writing and copied out texts, while it was the 'lector priests' (*hery heb*) who would recite the words of the god. Various CULT SINGERS AND TEMPLE MUSICIANS were needed to accompany the rituals, and women of noble birth, who sometimes held titles such as 'chantress of Amun', were occasionally depicted in this role, sometimes holding a SISTRUM. In the cult of Amun the god was also considered to have an earthly wife, the GOD'S WIFE OF AMUN, which also became an important political title, although the title is not attested before the 18th Dynasty.

During the New Kingdom, administrators, in association with the 'second prophet', oversaw the provisioning of the temple from estates and endowments. They ensured that the requisite numbers of offerings were brought in each day, and that the labourers went about their tasks properly. Only the essence of the offerings was thought to be consumed by the god, but the physical substance was consumed by the priests through a process now known as 'reversion of offerings'. Various foods were prohibited by particular temples so that the priests' diet was certainly atypical, but such food TABOOS are common in many religions.

The Greek historian Herodotus states that Egyptian priests were required to wash twice during the day and a further twice during the night, as well as being entirely clean shaven and without body hair. He also says that they were obliged to be circumcised and, since there was no prohibition on marriage, to abstain from sexual intercourse during their period of office. He claims that they were prohibited from the wearing of wool or leather, in favour of fine linen, and that their sandals had to be made from PAPYRUS.

Particular ranks of officials also wore special garments, such as the leopard skin worn by *sem* priests. In addition, there were regulations and prohibitions connected with particular cults. However, although these rules were strict, they applied to individual priests only during three months of the year. This was because the priests were divided into four groups of identical composition. These are now known by the Greek word *phyles*, although the Egyptians called them *saw* ('watches'). Each *phyle* served for only one month before returning to their usual professions for a further three months. Such offices could be very lucrative, in that the priests were granted a fixed portion of temple revenue while in the service of the temple.

Since religious knowledge was not a prerequisite, it is not surprising to find that priests often simply inherited their posts from their fathers, although appointments were also generally endorsed by the king. In certain circumstances, priestly offices could even be purchased, a method that became common under Roman rule. It should be remembered too that in many of the small provincial temples the priests might often have been less important, and the full hierarchy may not have been represented. Despite the apparently prosaic methods of entering the priesthood, there was a definite code of ETHICS, including proscriptions against discussing temple rites or practising fraud. The extent to which such codes were actually obeyed is unknown, although cases of malpractice are recorded.

H. KEES, *Das Priestertum in ägyptischen Staat vom neuen Reich bis zur Spätzeit*, 2 vols (Leiden and Cologne, 1953–8).

—, *Die Höhenpriester von Amun von Karnak von Herihor bis zum Ende der Äthiopienzeit* (Leiden, 1964).

S. SAUNERON, *The priests of ancient Egypt* (New York, 1969).

E. BRESCIANI, 'Tempelpersonal I (AR)', *Lexikon der Ägyptologie* VI, ed. W. Helck, E. Otto and W. Westendorf (Wiesbaden, 1986), 387–401.

A. M. ROTH, *Egyptian phyles in the Old Kingdom* (Chicago, 1991).

S. QUIRKE and A. J. SPENCER, *The British Museum book of ancient Egypt* (London, 1992), 74–8.

E. STROUHAL, *Life in ancient Egypt* (Cambridge, 1992), 223–34.

primeval mound

The hill that emerged from the primeval waters of NUN was an important element in Egyptian religious thought and imagery. The potency of the image of fertile ground emerging from water must have owed a great deal to the cycle of the annual INUNDATION of the Nile, whereby fresh agricultural land regularly appeared out of the flood waters.

The primeval mound was the principal symbol of the act of creation and the Memphite god TATJENEN (whose name means 'raising of the land') was a personification of the hill itself. The sun-god ATUM is sometimes described in the PYRAMID TEXTS as 'hill', and correspond-

ingly the Heliopolitan BENBEN STONE, which was closely asociated with Atum's cult, appears to have been a physical manifestation of the mound. The shape of the pyramids themselves may have derived, like the *benben*, from the primeval mound. The power of the SCARAB as a metaphor for the rebirth of the sun-god was due partly to the observed fact that beetles emerged from dung-hills.

The concept of the original hill of virgin land was maintained in the practice of building the sanctuaries of TEMPLES over low mounds of pure sand. Similarly tombs and cenotaphs, such as the Osireion at ABYDOS, often incorporated a symbolic 'island' at their centres.

A. DE BUCK, *De Egyptische Voorstellingen betreffende den Oerheuvel* (Leiden, 1922).

H. R. HALL, 'Review of De Buck, *De Egyptische* ...(1922)', *JEA* 10 (1924), 185–7.

A. A. SALEH, 'The so-called "primeval hill" and other related elevations in ancient Egyptian mythology', *MDAIK* 25 (1969), 110–20.

H. A. SCHLÖGL, *Der Gott Tatenen* (Freiburg, 1980).

K. MARTIN, 'Urhügel', *Lexikon der Ägyptologie* VI, ed. W. Helck, E. Otto and W. Westendorf (Wiesbaden, 1986), 873 5.

Psammetichus *see* PSAMTEK

Psamtek (Psammetichus)

'Birth name' given to three kings of the 26th (or SAITE) Dynasty (664–525 BC).

Psamtek I Wahibra (664–610 BC) and his father NEKAU I of SAIS (672–664 BC) were both carried off to Nineveh by the ASSYRIANS, following their involvement in a plot led by the Kushite ruler TAHARQO (690–664 BC). While in exile they were supposedly indoctrinated into Assyrian ways (Psamtek being given the name Nabu-shezibanni), before being returned to Egypt as vassals of Ashurbanipal.

At this time power was concentrated in the Delta, and the Assyrians placed Memphis and Sais under Nekau I and Athribis (TELL ATRIB) under Psamtek I. In 664 BC, however, Nekau died and Psamtek I took over his rule, becoming the first true ruler of the new 26th Dynasty. With the help of Carian and GREEK mercenaries, he effectively took control of the whole of the Delta. The increased numbers of foreigners in Egypt led to measures to control them, and archaeological evidence suggests that the site of NAUKRATIS, among others, may have been set up during his reign. Upper Egypt was still in Kushite hands, perhaps under TANUTAMANI (664–656 BC), son of Taharqo. However, by his ninth regnal year Psamtek I was recognized as ruler of both Upper and Lower Egypt.

To cement his rule over Thebes, he obliged the GOD'S WIFE OF AMUN Shepenwepet II and her appointed successor, Amenirdis II, to adopt his daughter Nitiqret (Nitocris) as their ultimate successor. Psamtek then gradually replaced Theban officials, as each died, putting his own protégés in their places and thus tightening his grip on Upper Egypt. Well established as he now was, he ceased any pretence to be an Assyrian vassal.

The 26th Dynasty was to be characterized by renewed nationalism; Psamtek's artists therefore carefully studied and copied the art of the Old Kingdom. There was also a renewed respect for old-established religious practices, including the worship of SACRED ANIMALS, whose cults grew dramatically, eventually becoming a significant part of the economy. Psamtek was succeeded by his son, Nekau II (610–595 BC).

Psamtek II Neferibra (595–589 BC), son and successor to Nekau II, is well known because of the numerous surviving monuments bearing his name. He is also known to have launched an expedition against the Kushites, which penetrated deep into NUBIA. Like his predecessors, he relied heavily on foreign mercenary troops, and at ABU SIMBEL there are graffiti left by his Carian, Greek and Phoenician soldiers. Among his generals was AHMOSE II (570–526 BC), who was eventually to supplant his son APRIES in the succession to the throne.

Psamtek III Ankhkaenra (526–525 BC), the son of Ahmose II, was the last king of the 26th Dynasty. His rule lasted for only some six months, following which he was executed by the Persian ruler Cambyses (525–522 BC) who invaded Egypt in 525 BC.

J. YOYOTTE, 'Le martelage des noms royaux éthiopiens par Psammétique II', *RdE* 8 (1951), 215–39.

F. K. KIENITZ, *Die politische Geschichte Ägyptens* VII (Berlin, 1953).

R. A. CAMINOS, 'The Nitocris adoption stela', *JEA* 50 (1964), 71–101.

E. CRUZ-URIBE, 'On the existence of Psammetichus', *Serapis* 5 (1980), 35–9.

Psusennes (Pasebakhaenniut)

'Birth name' taken by two kings of the 21st Dynasty, who ruled from Tanis in the Delta at the start of the Third Intermediate Period.

Psusennes I Aakheperra Setepenamun (1039–991 BC), successor of Smendes (1069–1043 BC), the founder of the 21st Dynasty, was perhaps the most important ruler of the dynasty. His tomb was discovered at Tanis by Pierre Montet in 1940. The richness of the funerary items (see TANIS) has been described as second only to those from the tomb of TUTANKHAMUN, although the timing of the find led to their being overshadowed by Howard Carter's earlier discovery. It is likely that Psusennes concentrated most of his activities at Tanis, where he built an enclosure wall for the temple complex. During his reign Upper Egypt was under the control of the Libyan generals ruling from Thebes (see NEW KINGDOM). However, there does not seem to have been great rivalry between the Theban and Tanite rulers; Psusennes I himself was probably the son of the Theban High Priest Pinudjem I and, in addition, one of his daughters was married to a Theban priest.

Psusennes II Titkheperura Setepenra (959–945 BC), the last king of the 21st Dynasty, may have been the son of the Theban High Priest Pinudjem II (990–969 BC). He might therefore have reunited the rule of Upper and Lower Egypt when he acceded to the Tanite throne on the death of Siamun (978–959 BC). After Psusennes' death, however, the crown passed into the hands of the Libyan rulers of the 22nd Dynasty, and it has been suggested that the Tanite ruling family may by then have been comparatively poverty-stricken. The 22nd-Dynasty pharaoh OSORKON I (924–889 BC) subsequently seems to have attempted to gain support for his claim by marrying Psusennes' daughter, Maatkara, who gave birth to SHESHONQ II (c.890 BC), thus establishing a blood link between the two dynasties.

P. MONTET, *La nécropole royale de Tanis* I: *Les constructions et le tombeau de Psoussennes à Tanis* (Paris, 1951).

K. A. KITCHEN, *The Third Intermediate Period in Egypt (1100–650 BC)*, (Warminster, 1986), 283–6.

A. DODSON, 'Psusennes II', *RdE* 38 (1987), 49–54.

Ptah

Creator-god of MEMPHIS who was usually portrayed as a mummy, with his hands protruding from the wrappings, holding a staff that combines the DJED pillar, ANKH sign and WAS sceptre. His head was shaven and covered by a tight-fitting skull-cap leaving his ears exposed. From the Middle Kingdom (2055–1650 BC) onwards, he was represented with a straight beard. The basic iconography of his images remained virtually unchanged throughout the Pharaonic period. In Hellenistic times he was identified with the Greek god Hephaistos.

Ptah himself was part of a TRIAD at Memphis, along with his consort (the lioness-goddess SEKHMET) and the lotus-god

Rameses III before the triad of Memphis (from left to right): Nefertem, Sekhmet and Ptah. 20th Dynasty, c.1150 BC, third illustration from the Great Harris Papyrus, H. 42.5 cm. (EA9999/43)

NEFERTEM, whose relationship with Ptah is unclear. IMHOTEP, the deified architect of the Saqqara Step Pyramid, came to be regarded as a son of Ptah, although he was not considered to be a member of the Memphite triad.

Ptah's original cultic association seems to have been with craftsmen, and the High Priest of Ptah held the title *wer kherep hemw* ('supreme leader of craftsmen'). This connection with the production of artefacts probably contributed to the elevation of his cult into that of a universal creator-god. He was thought to have brought the world into existence by the thoughts emanating from his HEART and the words emerging from his tongue. Although he was clearly already regarded as a creator as early as the Old Kingdom (2686–2181 BC), the references to him in the PYRAMID TEXTS are minimal. It has been suggested that this virtual omission from the royal funerary cult may have resulted from the reluctance of the Old Kingdom priesthood of RA at HELIOPOLIS to allow a Memphite deity to rival the sun-god. Ptah was, however, credited with having devised the OPENING OF THE MOUTH CEREMONY, and it was perhaps in a similar spirit of theological rivalry that the priests of Ptah themselves devised a CREATION myth (the Memphite Theology) in which Ptah gave birth to Ra and his ENNEAD.

During the Old Kingdom the cult of Ptah

gradually impinged on that of another Memphite deity, the hawk-god SOKAR, resulting in the emergence of a funerary deity known as Ptah-Sokar (see also PATAIKOS). By the Late Period (747–332 BC) this combined deity had also taken on the attributes of OSIRIS, the god of the dead, resulting in the appearance of Ptah-Sokar-Osiris. Wooden images of Ptah-Sokar-Osiris were regularly included among the funerary equipment of private individuals during the Late Period, usually taking the form of a standing mummiform human-headed figure on a hollow wooden pedestal, sometimes with miniature falcons on the base. An earlier version of this type of funerary figure, first attested in the 19th Dynasty (1295–1186 BC), simply consisted of a mummiform image of Osiris standing on a pedestal (sometimes with a BOOK OF THE DEAD papyrus secreted inside).

The temples of Ptah at Memphis were gradually expanded during the Pharaonic period, and further important cult centres were established at Karnak and the Nubian sites of ABU SIMBEL and Gerf Husein. It has been suggested that the name of one of his Memphite shrines, Hwt-ka-Ptah, may have been corrupted by the Greeks into the word Aiguptos, from which the modern name 'Egypt' derives.

M. STOLK, *Ptah* (Berlin, 1911).

M. SANDMAN HOLMBERG, *The god Ptah* (Lund, 1946).

H. A. SCHLÖGL, *Der Gott Tatenen* (Freiburg, 1980), 110–17.

H. te Velde, 'Ptah', *Lexikon der Ägyptologie* IV, ed. W. Helck, E. Otto and W. Westendorf (Wiesbaden, 1982), 1177–80.

C. Maystre, *Les grands prêtres de Ptah de Memphis* (Freiburg, 1992).

Ptolemaic period *see* PTOLEMY

Ptolemy

Name held by a succession of fifteen Hellenistic rulers of Egypt from 305 to 30 BC.

Limestone relief showing Ptolemy I offering flowers to one of the manifestations of Hathor. Ptolemaic period, c.300 BC, from Kom Abu Billo, H. 33 cm. (EA649)

In this dictionary the 'Ptolemaic period' is taken to include the brief preceding 'Macedonian' phase (332–305 BC), encompassing the reigns of ALEXANDER THE GREAT (332–323 BC), his half-brother Philip Arrhidaeus (323–317 BC) and his son Alexander IV (317–310 BC).

The policy pursued by Alexander the Great, in which he portrayed himself as an Egyptian ruler and effectively grafted the new administration on to the existing political and religious structure, appears to have been followed by his Ptolemaic successors with varying degrees of enthusiasm and success. Many Egyptian temples, including those at DENDERA, EDFU, ESNA and KOM OMBO, were either rebuilt, repaired or newly founded. Such Pharaonic administrative and religious centres as Thebes, Memphis and Tanis were replaced by ALEXANDRIA, a new capital city on the shores of the Mediterranean, the very position of which indicated the Ptolemies' realignment of Egypt towards the Mediterranean region rather than Africa or western Asia.

Ptolemy I Soter I (305–285 BC), founder of the Ptolemaic line, rose to the throne of Egypt after the death of Alexander IV, having administered Egypt as a general (then known as Ptolemy of Lagos), since the death of Alexander the Great. Ptolemy I devised the cult of SERAPIS from the existing cult of Osiris–Apis, hoping

perhaps to use it as a unifying political force, but in practice it was the cult of the goddess ISIS that grew and spread from Egypt.

The Macedonians and other Greeks were already familiar to the Egyptians long before the arrival of Alexander, since the Egyptian army in the Late Period (747–332 BC) had invariably included large numbers of GREEKS as mercenaries. Ptolemaic rule, however, did not remain popular, and there were revolts in the Theban area in 208–186 BC and 88–86 BC. As Ptolemaic rule weakened, so the Ptolemies relied ever more heavily on Rome, and eventually the actions of CLEOPATRA VII (51–30 BC), the daughter of Ptolemy XII (80–51 BC) and sister-wife of Ptolemy XIII (51–47 BC), provided a pretext for the Roman conquest of Egypt under Octavian, the future Emperor Augustus (30 BC–AD 14).

D. J. Crawford, *Kerkeosiris, an Egyptian village in the Ptolemaic period* (Cambridge, 1971).

H. Maehler and V. M. Strocka (eds), *Das ptolemäische Aegypten* (Mainz, 1978).

A. K. Bowman, *Egypt after the pharaohs* (London, 1986).

N. Lewis, *Greeks in Ptolemaic Egypt* (Oxford, 1986).

W. M. Ellis, *Ptolemy of Egypt* (London, 1994).

Punt (Pwenet)

Name used by the ancient Egyptians to describe a region of east Africa to which trading missions were sent from at least the 5th Dynasty (2494–2345 BC) onwards. There is still some debate regarding the precise location of Punt. Although it was once identified with the region of modern Somalia, a strong argument has now been made for its location in southern Sudan or the Eritrean region of Ethiopia, where the flora and fauna correspond best with those depicted in Egyptian reliefs.

Punt (the 'land of the god') was the source of many exotic products, such as GOLD, aromatic resins, African blackwood, ebony, ivory, SLAVES and wild animals, including monkeys and the sacred CYNOCEPHALUS baboons. The Egyptians also appear to have brought pygmies from Punt (see DWARFS AND PYGMIES), judging from the funerary inscription of Harkhuf, an expedition leader of the reign of PEPY II (2278–2184 BC).

Some trading missions evidently travelled overland to Punt, but the more common route was by sea, usually departing from the ports of Quseir or Mersa Gawasis on the west coast of the Red Sea. As a distant and distinctly non-Egyptian land, Punt gradually acquired an air of fantasy, like that of Eldorado or Atlantis. For this reason it sometimes features in narrative tales such as the *Tale of the Shipwrecked Sailor* in the Middle Kingdom (2055–1650 BC), and is also mentioned in various love poems in the New Kingdom (1550–1069 BC; see EROTICA).

The best-documented trading expedition to Punt was that of the reign of Hatshepsut

Limestone relief blocks from the temple of Hatshepsut at Deir el-Bahri. Parehu, ruler of Punt, walks in front of his obese wife Ati, whose condition is considered by some scholars to be the result of Dercum's disease. Behind them come men carrying gifts for Hatshepsut's expedition. 18th Dynasty, 1473–1458 BC, max. H. of block 49.3 cm. (CAIRO JE14276 AND JE89661)

(1473–1458 BC), scenes from which are depicted on the second terrace of her funerary temple at DEIR EL-BAHRI. These reliefs show the process of trading, which may have taken the particular form of barter known to anthropologists as 'silent trade', by which the two parties in the transaction do not negotiate verbally but set out exchange-goods until both are satisfied that the respective amounts are sufficient. Only then does actual exchange take place. The scenes also include depictions of conical reed-built huts built on poles above the ground and entered via ladders. The surrounding vegetation includes palms and 'myrrh trees', some already in the process of being hacked apart in order to extract the myrrh.

Whereas the ruler of Punt was distinguished from the Egyptians primarily by his beard and unusual costume, his wife was evidently much more memorable. She is depicted as an obese woman, and the saddled donkey that carried her is singled out for particular attention, not only because of the queen's great weight but also because it was still relatively unusual for the Egyptians to ride either donkeys or horses at this time. The scenes also show myrrh trees being loaded on to the ships so that the Egyptians could produce their own aromatics from them. Trees such as these might eventually have been replanted in the temple at Deir el-Bahri, judging from the surviving traces of tree-pits.

A stele in the mortuary temple of Amenhotep III (1390–1352 BC) records a speech delivered by the god Amun, in which the king is informed: 'Turning my face to sunrise I created a wonder for you, I made the lands of Punt come here to you, with all the fragrant flowers of their lands, to beg your peace and breathe the air you give.'

W. STEVENSON SMITH, 'The land of Punt', *JARCE* I (1962), 59–60.

R. HERZOG, *Pount* (Glückstadt, 1968).

D. M. DIXON, 'The transplantation of Punt incense trees in Egypt', *JEA* 55 (1969), 55–65.

K. A. KITCHEN, 'Punt and how to get there', *Orientalia* 40 (1971), 184–207.

M. LICHTHEIM, *Ancient Egyptian literature* II (London, 1976), 46–7.

R. FATTOVICH, 'The problem of Punt in the light of recent fieldwork in the eastern Sudan', *Akten München 1985* IV, ed. S. Schoske (Hamburg, 1991), 257–72.

K. A. KITCHEN, 'The Land of Punt', *The archaeology of Africa*, ed. T. Shaw et al. (London, 1993), 587–608.

purification *see* PRIESTS; SACRED LAKE; TABOO and WATER

First pylon of the temple of Isis at Philae. The reliefs on the outer faces of the pylon's towers are typical, showing the king (Ptolemy XII Neos Dionysos) striking foreign captives with a mace. The scenes would originally have been painted. (I. SHAW)

pylon (Greek: 'gate')
Massive ceremonial gateway (Egyptian *bekhenet*) consisting of two tapering towers linked by a bridge of masonry and surmounted by a cornice. Rituals relating to the sun-god were evidently carried out on top of the gateway. The pylon was used in temples from at least the Middle Kingdom to the Roman period (c.2055 BC–AD 395). It has been tentatively suggested that the earliest known pylons may have been constructed in the pyramid complex and sun temple of the 5th-Dynasty ruler Nyuserra (2445–2421 BC) at ABUSIR and ABU GURAB, but the oldest intact examples are those in Theban royal mortuary temples of the New Kingdom (1550–1069 BC), such as MEDINET HABU and the RAMESSEUM.

The pylon was usually filled with rubble (often consisting of blocks plundered from earlier temples, as in the case of TALATAT BLOCKS), but many also contained internal stairs and rooms, the purpose of which is uncertain. Ancient depictions of pylons show that the deep vertical recesses visible along the façades of surviving examples were intended to hold flagstaffs; above each groove was a small window through which the flag could be attached. Such flags would have had particular significance in the context of the temple, in that the Egyptian word for 'god' (*netjer*) took the form of a symbol usually interpreted as a fluttering pennant.

Pylons were frequently decorated with reliefs enhanced with bright paint and inlays, in which the scenes tended to emphasize the theme of royal power, since the outer pylon would have been the most visible part of the temple for the great mass of the population who were forbidden to pass beyond the first courtyard. The most common motif on the pylon was that of the king smiting foreign enemies or offering captives to a god.

Many temples had only one pylon, but the more important religious complexes consisted of long successions of pylons and courtyards, each added or embellished by different rulers; the temple of Amun at KARNAK, for instance, has ten pylons. In the unusual temples dedicated to the Aten in the city at EL-AMARNA, the pylons appear to have been somewhat different, consisting of pairs of separate towers without any bridging masonry between them.

It is likely that the pylon represented the two mountains of the HORIZON (*akhet*) between which the sun rose, thus contributing to the TEMPLE's role as a symbol of the cosmos and the act of creation. The towers were each identified with the goddesses ISIS and NEPHTHYS.

F. W. VON BISSING et al., *Das Re-Heiligtum des Königs Ne-Woser-Re* I (Leipzig, 1905), 8–10, 19–24.

L. BORCHARDT, *Das Grabdenkmal des Königs Ne-user-Re'* (Leipzig, 1907), 97.

T. DOMBARDT, 'Der zweitürige Tempelpylon altägyptischer Baukunst und seine religiöse Symbolik', *Egyptian Religion* I (1933), 87–98.

P. A. SPENCER, *The Egyptian temple: a lexicographical study* (London, 1984), 193–4.

pyramid

Funerary monument, built usually of stone masonry and consisting of four triangular sides meeting in a point. It served as the focal point – or at least the most visible component – of Egyptian royal funerary complexes from the 3rd Dynasty (2686–2613 BC) to the Second Intermediate Period (1650–1550 BC). Throughout the rest of the Pharaonic period private tombs occasionally incorporated small-scale mud-brick or stone 'pyramidia'. The modern term derives from the Greek word *pyramis* ('wheat cake'), presumably because cakes of this type were pyramidal in shape; the ancient Egyptian word, however, was *mer*.

In purely architectural terms, pyramids can be divided into two broad types: 'step pyramids' and 'true pyramids'. The first step pyramids appear to have developed initially out of the rectangular royal and private MASTABA tombs of the Early Dynastic period (3100–2686 BC), but by the early 4th Dynasty the first smooth-sided true pyramid had been constructed at DAHSHUR. Over the next thousand years the pyramid gradually acquired a wide range of symbolic meanings.

The full-scale 'pyramid complex' consisted of a true pyramid with its mortuary and valley temples, a causeway between the two latter, and usually a number of smaller 'subsidiary pyramids'; this had evolved by the beginning of the 4th Dynasty. However, the origins of the pyramid complex can be discerned in the royal tombs and 'funerary enclosures' at Early Dynastic ABYDOS and the Old Kingdom Step Pyramid complex at SAQQARA.

Chronology and development: The first step pyramid was built by the architect IMHOTEP for the 3rd-Dynasty ruler Netjerikhet DJOSER (2667–2648 BC) at SAQQARA. From the reign of Djoser onwards the pyramid complex was established as the royal funerary monument and burial-place. Djoser's pyramid seems to have initially taken the form of a huge mastaba, built in stone rather than mud-brick, but it was gradually extended and elaborated until it became a pyramidal superstructure consisting of six separate steps and reaching a height of 60 m, making it clearly visible from the capital city of Memphis. A passage from the north side led to the subterranean royal burial chamber, and eleven subsidiary chambers for members of the family. A series of ancillary chambers and corridors were decorated with elaborate blue FAIENCE tiles and relief sculpture showing the king performing rites at his royal jubilee (SED FESTIVAL).

In Djoser's complex the recessed, 'palace-façade' style of the superstructures of Saqqara mastaba tombs of the Early Dynastic period

was used to decorate the great enclosure wall surrounding the pyramid and its ancillary buildings. It is thus thought likely that Djoser's monument was a combination of a royal tomb and a 'funerary enclosure' (or *Talbezirk*), such as those of the 1st- and 2nd-Dynasty rulers at Abydos (e.g. the Shunet el-Zebib complex of KHASEKHEMWY).

To the east of Djoser's pyramid was an open area surrounded by rows of solid 'dummy' buildings apparently intended to replicate various provincial shrines. This part of the complex was almost certainly connected with the celebration of the *sed* festival, although it is not clear whether the ritual itself would have been enacted there during the king's lifetime. A mortuary temple, now badly ruined, stood on the north side of the pyramid, and a large rectangular structure known as the 'south mastaba' lay at the south end of the enclosure (perhaps serving as a cenotaph balancing the main pyramid and thus symbolizing the DUALITY of the Egyptian kingship). The complex as a whole seems to have been simultaneously a permanent monumental equivalent of the *sed* festival and the celebration of the royal funerary cult. As later pyramids became more concerned with the king's solar connections, the importance of the *sed* festival as an element of the funerary complex appears to have diminished correspondingly.

The remains of the unfinished step-pyramid complex of SEKHEMKHET (2648–2640 BC) are situated a short distance to the southwest of Djoser's complex. A few other surviving traces of enclosure walls at the western side of the Saqqara necropolis, including the so-called Great Enclosure (currently being investigated by a team from the Royal Museum of Scotland), suggest that further 3rd-Dynasty rulers probably began to erect similar monuments. It is also worth pointing out that the use of steps in pyramid-building never truly died out, in that many true pyramids continued to consist of a stepped structure, which was simply transformed by the application of a smooth outer casing. The late 3rd-Dynasty or early 4th-Dynasty pyramid at MEIDUM, for example, was originally conceived as a step pyramid; in this instance, however, the smooth outer casing eventually collapsed, and the original stepped core of the superstructure was revealed.

The two pyramids of SNEFERU (2613–2589 BC) at DAHSHUR were probably the first royal funerary monuments to be conceived as true pyramids from the outset. The southernmost of these is known as the 'bent pyramid' (or 'rhomboidal pyramid'), owing to the

marked change of angle part-way up its profile, from 54° 27' in the lower part to 43° 22' in the upper. However, the 'northern pyramid' (or 'red pyramid') was successfully completed with a constant angle of 43° 22'. From this time onwards the practice of giving names to pyramids is regularly attested; thus the north pyramid was known as 'Sneferu appears in glory' and the bent pyramid as 'Sneferu of the south appears in glory'.

However, it was Sneferu's son KHUFU (2589–2566 BC) whose name came to be most intimately linked with pyramid construction, since his funerary monument was the Great Pyramid at GIZA, the largest surviving pyramid. It stands alongside two other smaller pyramid complexes belonging to two of his successors, KHAFRA (2558–2532 BC) and MENKAURA (2532–2503 BC) (although the unfinished pyramid complex of his immediate successor, Djedefra (2566–2558 BC), was located further to the north at ABU ROASH).

As far as the overall development of the pyramid complex was concerned, the basic components were already present in the Giza monuments, which were first scientifically studied by Flinders Petrie in 1880–2. Each pyramid was entered by a passage from the north, and on its east side was a mortuary temple, usually interpreted as the royal equivalent of the MASTABA funerary chapel. A walled (later roofed) causeway led down from the mortuary temple to the valley temple, which was associated with the royal funeral rites and statue cults. All of the Giza pyramids, as well as most other surviving pyramids, were accompanied by 'subsidiary pyramids' of varying size and number, located within the main pyramid enclosure; some of these are described as 'queen's pyramids', since they were probably built for the king's wives, while others may have served a similar purpose to the 'south mastaba' in Djoser's complex.

The internal arrangements of the Great Pyramid were atypical in that there were three burial chambers – one subterranean and the other two built into the core of the superstructure – whereas most other pyramids had only one subterranean burial chamber hewn out of the bedrock below the superstructure. Small shafts, usually known as 'air shafts', lead from the uppermost chamber of the Great Pyramid to the outside of the pyramid, while similar ones lead from the so-called 'queen's chamber' several metres below. The investigation of one of these vents in 1993 revealed the presence of a blockage midway along the passage, which may be a door to a fourth chamber or perhaps simply closes off the shaft.

It has long been suggested that the 'air shafts' in the Great Pyramid actually served some astronomical function, since they are evidently carefully aligned with various stars, including the constellation of Orion (the Egyptian god SAH), which might have been the intended destination of the king's BA, when he ascended to take his place among the circumpolar stars. A certain amount of astronomical observation was clearly used in the process of pyramid-building, particularly in terms of the precise alignment with the cardinal points, but there seems to be little foundation for the suggestion that the layout of the three pyramids at Giza was intended to symbolize the shape of the belt of Orion.

The pyramids of ABUSIR, which date to the 5th Dynasty (2494–2345 BC), are regarded as the peak of development of the standard pyramid complex, although both their architectural quality and their size are less impressive than those of the Giza pyramids. It has been suggested that the more modest scale of the Abusir pyramids might have partially resulted from the diversion of resources into the sun temples that began to be erected in the 5th Dynasty (see ABU GURAB). The layout of the complexes differs only in the sense that they show less variability, and a subsidiary pyramid began to be regularly placed in the southeast corner of the enclosure.

The last 5th-Dynasty ruler, UNAS (2375–2345 BC), seems to have been the first to inscribe the PYRAMID TEXTS on the internal walls of his pyramid at Saqqara. This practice was then taken up by the rulers of the 6th Dynasty (2345–2181 BC) and their queens, providing Egyptologists with a set of almost eight hundred early religious 'utterances' that have provided a useful body of evidence with regard to the symbolism and purpose of pyramid complexes.

The standard of workmanship of pyramids appears to have declined along with the political and economic structure of the Old Kingdom, and the pyramid complex all but disappeared in the First Intermediate Period (2181–2055 BC). However, the form began to be used again in the Middle Kingdom, when the state had been reunified. The unusual funerary complex of the 11th-Dynasty ruler MENTUHOTEP II (2055–2004 BC) at DEIR EL-BAHRI may have incorporated a pyramidal superstructure (although opinions differ on this point), but the full pyramid complex was reintroduced with the complexes of AMENEMHAT I and SENUSRET I at EL-LISHT. Later 12th- and 13th-Dynasty pharaohs built pyramids at Dahshur, HAWARA, Saqqara, Mazghuna and EL-LAHUN. These pyramids made extensive use of mud-brick, using stone only for cross walls which were then infilled with rubble or mud-brick, although the whole edifice was given a casing of fine limestone so that externally it would have appeared as well built as those of the Old Kingdom. However, the subsequent removal of these outer casings has reduced them to a more severely weathered state than their stone-built predecessors.

No pyramids have survived from the 14th to 16th Dynasties (1750–1650 BC), although there were a few small mud-brick 17th-Dynasty pyramids at western Thebes, and the 17th-Dynasty ruler AHMOSE I (1550–1525 BC) is known to have constructed a cenotaph at Abydos in the form of a mud-brick pyramid. Thereafter, the 'pyramidion' became a comparatively minor element in the pyramid-shaped superstructures of private funerary chapels, as in the case of the cemetery of the New Kingdom workmen at DEIR EL-MEDINA. Many hundreds of years after the construction of the last Egyptian pyramid complex, the pyramid form was revived – albeit on a smaller scale and with much steeper sides – in the

The pyramids of Khufu, Khafra and Menkaura at Giza, with the subsidiary pyramids of Menkaura in the foreground. 4th Dynasty c. 2589–2503 BC. (GRAHAM HARRISON)

funerary monuments of the Napatan and Meroitic kings of Nubia (see MEROE NAPATA and NURI).

Methods of construction: There has been considerable speculation concerning the means used to construct the pyramids. No textual records outlining such methods have survived, although presumably this omission is a result of the accident of preservation (or perhaps even a proscription on the description of such a sacred task); the suggestion is occasionally made that no records were kept because pyramid construction was regarded as a comparatively prosaic activity not worthy of record, but this is surely unlikely, given the vast resources and amounts of labour involved in such projects.

The careful survey work begun by PETRIE, and extended in recent times by Mark Lehner, has shown that the Giza site was carefully levelled, probably by cutting a series of trenches as a grid and flooding them with water, then reducing the surrounding stone 'islands' to the desired level. The cardinal points would subsequently have been determined astronomically (see ASTRONOMY AND ASTROLOGY). Much of the required stone was obtained from sources immediately adjacent to the complexes themselves, with only the fine limestone for the outer casing being brought from Tura across the river. When granite was needed, for such purposes as the lining of burial chambers or, in the case of Menkaura, part of the casing, it was brought up the Nile from Aswan (and indeed reliefs in the causeway of Unas show granite columns being conveyed by boat from the quarries to the temple). The final stage of transporting the stone would probably not have been as difficult as it now appears, since the flood waters of the annual INUNDATION would have allowed the boats to bring the stone close to the pyramid itself. Since the flood also produced a slack period in the agricultural year, the king was able to employ large bodies of seasonally available labour.

The methods by which the stone blocks were raised into position remains a contentious issue. A variety of techniques have been suggested, from the use of simple cranes (based on the SHADUF style of irrigation) to elaborate systems of levers and rockers, which would certainly have been used in positioning the blocks. What seems certain, from the archaeological evidence, is that ramps were used. These would have grown longer and higher as the pyramid became larger, and would no doubt have been major feats of engineering in themselves. There are only surviving traces of long, straight ramps, but it has been suggested that the terraced nature of the

pyramid core would have often made it more convenient to use a series of much smaller ramps built along the sides of the pyramid from step to step; the remains of these would no doubt have been lost when the outer casing was applied.

The casing would have been smoothed from top to bottom while the scaffolding or ramps were gradually cleared away. Once the debris had been cleared away the mortuary and subsidiary pyramids would no doubt have been completed. It is also possible that the causeways from pyramid to valley temple originally served as construction ramps from quay to building site, and the valley temple would have been built beside a quay connected with the Nile by canal.

Symbolism and purpose: There is general agreement that the fundamental purpose of the pyramid was to serve as a highly visible superstructure for royal burials (with the exception of seven late 3rd-Dynasty non-sepulchral step pyramids, perhaps erected as symbols of royal power at provincial capitals; see NOMES). There is, however, still a great deal of debate concerning the symbolism of its shape and design. It has been suggested that it represented the PRIMEVAL MOUND of creation, on which the sun-god was thought to have been born, and which was probably first symbolized by the Heliopolitan BENBEN STONE.

Since the pyramidion at the top of each pyramid was often gilded and was closely connected with the sun, it has been proposed that the building was intended to symbolize the sloping rays of the sun. However, it has also been suggested that, particularly in the case of the step pyramids, there may have been an association with the idea of ascending to the heavens on a stairway, since it was believed, from at least the Old Kingdom onwards, that the deceased were able to rise up to the night sky, becoming transformed into 'imperishable stars'. There is also a great deal of symbolism in the various locations of such features of the pyramid complex as the entrance to the pyramid, the mortuary and valley temples, the subsidiary pyramids, as well as more detailed features, such as the position of the sarcophagus and the orientation of the internal corridor and chambers.

The Greek historian HERODOTUS (*c.*484–420 BC) gave an account of the pyramids, but Pliny (AD 23–79) seems to have been the first ancient writer to suggest that they might have contained treasure. After the Arab conquest (AD 641), such stories of buried riches led to numerous attempts to open the pyramids, although the contents of the burial chambers were always found to have been long since

plundered. Various myths concerning the origins and significance of pyramids persisted among European travellers, including the ingenious theory that they had functioned as the granaries of the Biblical Joseph. In modern times, much stranger theories continue to be concocted concerning the nature of pyramids, and the pragmatic accounts of generations of archaeologists have done little to dispel the popular belief that they are embodiments of some lost mystic knowledge and/or the key to the understanding of the universe.

W. M. F. PETRIE, *The pyramids and temples of Gizeh* (London, 1883).

D. ARNOLD, *Building in Egypt: pharaonic stone masonry* (Oxford, 1991).

G. HART, *Pharaohs and pyramids* (London, 1991).

J.-P. LAUER, *Les pyramides de Sakkara*, 6th ed. (Cairo, 1991).

I. E. S. EDWARDS, *The pyramids of Egypt*, 5th ed. (Harmondsworth, 1993).

C. SCARRE, 'The meaning of death: funerary beliefs and the prehistorian', *The ancient mind: elements of cognitive archaeology*, ed. C. Renfrew and E. B. W. Zubrow (Cambridge, 1994), 75–82.

R. STADELMANN, 'Die sogenannten Luftkanäle der Cheopspyramide Modellkorridore für den Aufstieg des Königs zum Himmel', *MDAIK* 50 (1994), 53–6.

Pyramid Texts

The earliest Egyptian funerary texts, comprising some eight hundred spells or 'utterances' written in columns on the walls of the corridors and burial chambers of nine pyramids of the late Old Kingdom (2375–2181 BC) and First Intermediate Period (2181–2055 BC). In modern texts and translations of the Pyramid Texts the individual utterances are conventionally numbered in a sequence relating to their usual position in the pyramid, progressing from the burial chamber outwards, although it has been suggested that the opposite order (from the entrance to the burial chamber) may in fact be a more logical sequence. Siegfried Schott, for instance, has argued that the texts make up a ritualistic description of the funereal progress of the king's dead body from its arrival in the valley temple to its deposition in the burial chamber.

Although the earliest surviving Pyramid Texts are inscribed in the 5th-Dynasty pyramid of UNAS (2375–2345 BC) at Saqqara, the examples in the pyramid of PEPY I, a short distance to the south, were the first to be discovered. They were inscribed in the pyramids of six kings altogether (all buried at Saqqara between the 6th and 8th Dynasties), as well as in the three pyramids of Pepy II's queens. No single pyramid contains the whole collection of spells, the maximum number being 675 utterances in the pyramid of Pepy II (2278–2184 BC).

The constant references to the cult of the sun-god in the texts suggest that they were probably composed by the priests of HELIOPOLIS. There appear to have been several basic categories of utterance, including what might be described as 'magical' spells aiming to prevent harm to the deceased; these often use archaic language perhaps indicating the Predynastic origins of the ideas. Indeed, sometimes these magical utterances seem to be referring to aspects of the funerary cult that were no longer current at the time that the pyramids were built, as in the case of Utterances 273–4 (the 'Cannibal Hymn'), which appear only in the pyramids of Unas and TETI (see HUMAN SACRIFICE). Another type of utterance seems to consist of the texts of various rituals which would have been performed at the royal funeral, with the deceased addressed as OSIRIS. This type of spell, which includes texts dealing both with offerings and with the resurrection, was inscribed in the burial chamber itself, no doubt the most sacred part of the pyramid. The OPENING OF THE MOUTH CEREMONY is first recorded in these ritual texts, along with the early offering ritual. Another category of spell, generally inscribed on the walls of the ante-chamber and corridor, seems to have been intended to be uttered by the tomb owner personally.

H. RICKE, *Bemerkungen zur ägyptischen Baukunst des Alten Reichs* (Zurich and Cairo, 1944–50).

S. SCHOTT, *Bemerkungen zum ägyptischen Pyramidenkult* (Cairo, 1950).

R. O. FAULKNER, *The ancient Egyptian pyramid texts* (Oxford, 1969).

J. P. ALLEN, 'The Pyramid Texts of Queens Ipwt and Wdbt-m. (j)', *JARCE* 23 (1986), 1–25.

W. BARTA, 'Die Pyramidentexte auf den Privatsärgen des Mittleren Reiches', *ZÄS* 113 (1986), 1–8.

J. OSING, 'Zur Disposition der Pyramidentexte des Unas', *MDAIK*, 42 (1986), 131–44.

Q

Qa'a (Ka'a) (*c.*2890 BC)

Last ruler of the 1st Dynasty (3100–2890 BC), who was probably buried in Tomb Q at ABYDOS, excavated first by Emile Amélineau and later by Flinders PETRIE at the turn of the century. The tomb was re-excavated by Gunther Dreyer and Werner Kaiser in 1991–2. Two typical royal funerary stelae bearing the king's name were found on the east side of the tomb. The recent excavations show that the tomb was built in stages, with the thick walls of the central burial chamber eventually being hollowed out to create extra magazines. The discovery of seal impressions and other artefacts bearing the name of Hetepsekhemwy, the first ruler of the 2nd Dynasty (2890–2686 BC), suggests that there may have been no real break between the 1st and 2nd Dynasties.

Four tombs at Saqqara have been dated to Qa'a's reign, including the large MASTABA tombs 3500 and 3505. The latter incorporates a set of rooms on the north side of the superstructure, where the lower parts of two wooden statues were found. It has been suggested that this maze of rooms may have served as an offering chapel which would perhaps have been an antecedent of the mortuary temple in pyramid complexes. The stelae of two of Qa'a's officials, Merka and Sabef, bear more complex inscriptions than those of earlier reigns, suggesting an increasingly sophisticated use of the hieroglyphic script.

W. M. F. PETRIE, *The royal tombs of the first dynasty* I (London, 1900).

W. B. EMERY, *Great tombs of the first dynasty* III (London, 1958).

W. B. EMERY, *Archaic Egypt* (London, 1961), 86–91.

A. J. SPENCER, *Early Egypt* (London, 1993), 83–4.

Qadesh (goddess) *see* QEDESHET

Qadesh, Battle of (*c.*1274 BC)

Military clash between RAMESES II (1279–1213 BC) and the HITTITE king Muwatallis, which was the first major conflict in the ancient world to be described in detail. There are thirteen surviving Egyptian accounts of the battle, recorded both on papyri and on the walls of many of Rameses II's temples in Egypt and Nubia. These thirteen versions are also written in three different literary forms: poem, bulletin and captioned reliefs.

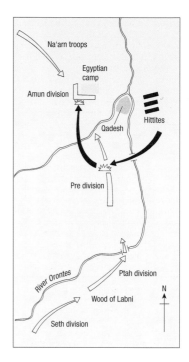

The Battle of Qadesh.

In the summer of the fourth year of his reign (*c.*1275 BC), Rameses II launched a military campaign into the Levant. He succeeded in consolidating Egyptian control of the provinces of Canaan and Upi and recaptured Amurru without coming into direct conflict with the Hittites, Egypt's principal rivals in the region. Because Rameses then forced the prince of Amurru to sign a vassal treaty with Egypt, the Hittite king Muwatallis is said to have sworn to regain the Syrian territories. For his part Rameses was now keen to capitalize on his successes by pushing forward into the area of central Syria and the city of Qadesh in the spring of 1274 BC.

In his second campaign, Rameses sent a division of élite troops (the Na'arn) northwards along the Phoenician coast, while the main army, divided into four divisions (named Amun, Pre, Ptah and Seth), marched through Canaan and Upi to approach Qadesh from the south. Meanwhile, Muwatallis had assembled an army said to have been more than double the size of the Egyptian forces.

While Rameses and his army were passing through the wood of Labni, a few miles to the south of Qadesh, two captured BEDOUIN convinced them that the Hittites were still a considerable distance away, in the area of Aleppo. By the time it was realized that the Hittites were in fact camped nearby, just across the Orontes, Rameses had already set up camp near Qadesh and his three other divisions were still some way behind. Before anything could be done to remedy this situation the Hittite chariots launched their attack, taking the Pre division by surprise and sending them fleeing north towards Rameses and the Egyptian camp.

Although Rameses is said to have rallied the combined troops of Amun and Pre in an attempt to rescue the situation, it is clear that the Egyptians might have been routed at this stage if it had not been for the timely arrival of the Na'arn troops. The Egyptians were then able to regroup and push back the Hittite chariotry, thus allowing the Ptah and Seth divisions finally to catch up with the rest. The following morning the battle resumed but eventually they reached a state of stalemate. In the subsequent exchange of envoys Rameses (unlike his father SETY I) refused to make a treaty and returned to Egypt with the control of Amurru still unresolved. Moreover, as soon as he had retreated, the Hittites gained control of both Amurru and Upi, thus pushing back the Egyptian frontier to the borders of Canaan.

Despite Rameses II's euphemistic accounts of the battle, he was finally obliged to make a treaty with a new Hittite king, Hattusilis III, in 1259 BC, in order that Egypt and the Hittites could form a united front in the face of the growing threat of the ASSYRIAN empire of Shalmaneser I.

J. H. BREASTED, *The Battle of Kadesh, a study in the earliest known military strategy* (Chicago, 1903).

H. GOEDICKE, 'Considerations on the Battle of Kadesh', *JEA* 52 (1966), 71–80.

K. KITCHEN, *Pharaoh triumphant* (Warminster, 1982), 53–62.

H. GOEDICKE (ed.), *Perspectives on the Battle of Kadesh* (Baltimore, 1985).

B. OCKINGA, 'On the interpretation of the Kadesh record', *CdE* 62/123–4 (1987), 38–48.

Qantir (anc. Piramesse)

Site of the ancient Egyptian harbour-town of Piramesse, located in the eastern Delta near modern el-Khatana. Piramesse was founded by Sety I (1294–1279 BC) and transformed into a new royal residence and seat of government by his successor Rameses II (1279–1213 BC). A mud-brick PALACE dating to the earliest phase of the town was discovered in 1929, and exca-

Two polychrome faience tiles showing an aquatic scene, from a palace of Rameses II at Qantir. L. 59.7 cm.
(METROPOLITAN MUSEUM, NEW YORK, ROGERS FUND AND EDWARD S. HARKNESS GIFT, 35.1.104)

vations in the 1980s have revealed military barrack-rooms and workshops, also dating to the Ramesside period. By the end of the New Kingdom (c.1069 BC) the city had diminished in importance and a great deal of its stonework was transferred to the temples at TANIS in the 21st Dynasty and Bubastis (TELL BASTA) in the 22nd Dynasty.

W. C. HAYES, *Glazed tiles from a palace of Ramesses II* at Kantir (New York, 1937).

E. UPHILL, *The temples of Per Ramesses* (Warminster, 1984).

M. BIETAK, *Avaris and Piramesse*, 2nd ed. (Oxford, 1986).

E. PUSCH, 'Bericht über die sechste Hauptkampagne in Qantir' Piramesse-Nord herbst 1988', *GM* 112 (1989), 67–90.

—, 'Ausländisches Kulturgut in Qantir-Piramesse', *Akten München 1985*, ed. S. Schoske (Hamburg, 1989), 249–56.

Qasr Ibrim (anc. Pedeme, Primis)

Site of a Lower Nubian multi-period fortified settlement, now located on a headland in Lake Nasser about 240 km south of Aswan, which has been excavated by the Egypt Exploration Society every two years since 1961. The earliest activity at Qasr Ibrim dates to the late New Kingdom (c. 1000 BC), and the site was occupied throughout successive periods until the early nineteenth century AD, when the garrison was still manned by Ottoman soldiers from Bosnia.

The principal surviving building is a Nubian cathedral dating to the eighth century AD. Remains from earlier periods include four rock-shrines dating to the New Kingdom (c.1550–1069 BC) and a number of temples dating from the 25th Dynasty (747–656 BC) to the late MEROITIC period (c.AD 100–350). To the north and south of the main town-site there are a number of cemeteries, mainly dat-

ing to the Meroitic, BALLANA, Christian and Islamic phases of the site's history.

W. B. EMERY and L. P. KIRWAN, *The excavations and survey between Wadi es-Sebua and Adindan 1919–31* (Cairo, 1935), 268–77.

R. A. CAMINOS, *The shrines and rock inscriptions of Ibrim* (London, 1968).

W. Y. ADAMS, 'Qasr Ibrim: an archaeological conspectus', *Nubian Studies: proceedings of the symposium for Nubian studies, 1978*, ed. J. Plumley (Warminster, 1982), 25–33.

A. J. MILLS, *The cemeteries of Qasr Ibrim* (London, 1982).

M. HINDS and V. MÉNAGE, *Qasr Ibrim in the Ottoman period* (London, 1991).

M. HORTON, 'Africa in Egypt: new evidence from Qasr Ibrim', *Egypt and Africa*, ed. W. V. Davies (London, 1991), 264–77.

Qebehsenuef see SONS OF HORUS

Qedeshet (Qadesh, Qudshu)

SYRIAN goddess, generally portrayed as a naked woman (viewed frontally), holding flowers and snakes, and standing on the back of a lion. Her cult began to be celebrated in Egypt at least as early as the 18th Dynasty (1550–1295 BC).

Limestone relief fragment depicting the Asiatic goddess Qedeshet. She holds a lotus in one hand and snakes in the other. 19th Dynasty, c.1250 BC, H. 25.5 cm. (EA60308)

Such was her assimilation into Egyptian religion that she was considered to be a member of a TRIAD along with the fertility god MIN and the Asiatic deity RESHEF. She was also linked both with the Egyptian goddess HATHOR and with ANAT and ASTARTE, two other Asiatic goddesses whose cults had filtered into Egypt.

J. LEIBOVITCH, 'Une imitation d'époque gréco-romaine d'une stèle de la déesse Qadech', *ASAE* 41 (1941), 77–86.

I. E. S. EDWARDS, 'A relief of Qudshu-Astarte-Anath in the Winchester College collection', *JNES* 14 (1955), 49–51.

R. STADELMANN, *Syrisch-palästinische Gottheiten in Ägypten* (Leiden, 1967), 110–23.

C. CLAMER, 'A gold plaque from Tell Lachish', *Journal of the Tel Aviv University Institute of Archaeology* 7 (1980), 152–62.

Qudshu *see* QEDESHET

queens

Term usually applied to various female relatives of the pharaoh, although considerable caution is necessary in using the word in an ancient Egyptian context, since there is no Egyptian term precisely corresponding to it. Instead, the Egyptian texts tend to highlight a number of important women who are defined by their kinship with the king.

There are three main types of 'queen': the 'great royal wife' (*hemet nesw weret*), the 'king's mother' (*mwt nesw*) and the 'king's wives' (*hemwt nesw*). The great royal wife appears to have been second only to the king in terms of the political and religious hierarchy, and she is often represented alongside him on monuments. Very occasionally, as in the case of NEFERTITI, she was also represented alone. It was usually one of the sons of the great royal wife who was heir to the throne.

For many years scholars believed that succession to the throne was purely via the female line; it was thus suggested that each king, irrespective of whether he was the son of the previous ruler, had to marry a sister or half-sister in order to legitimize his claim to the throne. This so-called 'heiress theory' would have meant that one of the daughters of the previous king would always have become a great royal wife in the subsequent reign. However, it has been pointed out that there are several clear instances where kings married women who were not their sisters, as with the marriage of Amenhotep III (1390–1352 BC) to TIY, the daughter of a chariotry officer, therefore the theory is no longer accepted. It has been suggested that the popularity of the 'heiress theory' may have been due partly to the attempts of earlier scholars to explain the

Bronze statuette of a queen, late New Kingdom, H. 22 cm. (EA54388)

Egyptians' apparent acceptance of the royal practice of incest (see MARRIAGE).

The 'mother of the king' was an important member of the royal family, and, like the great wife (and sometimes also the royal daughter), she was often depicted alongside the king on his monuments. For example, Queen Tiy still enjoyed considerable prominence in the reign of her son AKHENATEN (1352–1336 BC).

The third category of queen, the 'king's wives', were simply the other women to whom he was married, most of whom would have resided in the HARIM. From the New Kingdom (1550–1069 BC) onwards these wives would often have included foreign women married as part of a diplomatic arrangement. It seems to have been common for foreign rulers to be asked to send their daughters to Egypt, where they would have effectively been treated either as tribute or as hostages, guaranteeing the preservation of good relations between the two rulers. The relationship thus established was perhaps more of a link between two ruling families than between two states, since a newly

acceded foreign ruler was often asked to provide a new daughter, even though the daughter of his predecessor was no doubt still living and married to the Egyptian king.

Because the conventions of Egyptian art and literature focus largely on the king and his exploits, little information has survived concerning even the most famous queens, such as Tiy, Nefertiti and NEFERTARI, the wife of Rameses II (1279–1213 BC). There are also comparatively few surviving personal details concerning HATSHEPSUT (1473–1458 BC), who was both a queen and a king, in that she ruled initially as a regent and then assumed the full attributes of kingship for many years. Most of her monuments were damaged and altered by her stepson and successor, Thutmose III (1479–1425 BC) who, late in his reign, appears to have reacted against the idea of a female king, which might have been regarded as an abnormality, a contravention of the Egyptian conception of MAAT (truth and harmony).

It is clear, therefore, that – however powerful queens may have been and however much influence they might have wielded over the kings' decisions – they remain shadowy figures, effectively masked by the powerful iconography of the king, which suggests that it was the place of the king's wife or mother to be the epitome of feminine grace while her husband typified the essence of masculine power.

B. J. KEMP, 'The harim-palace at Medinet el-Ghurab', *ZÄS* 105 (1978), 122–33.

A. R. SCHULMAN, 'Diplomatic marriage in the Egyptian New Kingdom', *JNES* 38 (1979), 177–93.

G. ROBINS, 'A critical examination of the theory that the right to the throne of ancient Egypt passed through the female line in the 18th Dynasty', *GM* 62 (1983) 67–77.

L. TROY, *Patterns of queenship in ancient Egyptian myth and history* (Uppsala, 1986).

G. ROBINS, *Women in ancient Egypt* (London, 1993), 21–55.

R

Ra (Re)

Heliopolitan sun-god whose cult is first attested in the name of the 2nd-Dynasty ruler Raneb (*c*.2865 BC). The cult of the sun was celebrated particularly at HELIOPOLIS (ancient Iunu), now largely covered by the northern suburbs of Cairo. Numerous aspects of the material culture and religion of the Old Kingdom were influenced by the cult of Ra, but it was not until the 4th Dynasty (2613–2494 BC), when the royal title *sa Ra* ('son of Ra') was introduced by Djedefra (2566–2558 BC), that the worship of the sun-god reached its peak. In the 5th Dynasty several sun temples incorporating large masonry OBELISKS (see ABU GURAB and BENBEN) were constructed, apparently all modelled on the earliest temple of Ra at Heliopolis, although no trace of this has survived in the archaeological record.

The sun-god was usually represented as a hawk-headed human figure wearing a sun-disc headdress, but in the underworld, through which he sailed in the SOLAR BARK, he was portrayed as ram-headed. Ra exerted such a strong influence on the rest of the Egyptian pantheon that virtually all of the most significant deities were eventually subsumed into the universalist sun-cult by a process of SYNCRETISM; thus AMUN became Amun-Ra, MONTU became Montu-Ra and HORUS became Ra-Horakhty. In his manifestation as creator-god, the sun-god himself took the name of Atum-Ra, combining with another Heliopolitan sun-god, ATUM, whose name means 'perfection' (see CREATION and ENNEAD). The *Litany of Ra*, a text of the New Kingdom (1550–1069 BC) inscribed on the walls of some of the royal tombs in the VALLEY OF THE KINGS (the earliest example being in that of Thutmose III, KV 34), is essentially a celebration of Ra's identification with OSIRIS, the god of the underworld.

It was during the reign of AKHENATEN (1352–1336 BC) that the concept of the sun-god as a universal deity (into whom all other deities could be absorbed) seems to have come closest to a monotheistic position. The worship of the ATEN (literally the 'disc'), represented almost diagrammatically in the form of a sun-disc from which arms stretched down offering life and power to the royal family, was substituted for the cults of anthropomorphic figures such as Ra-Horakhty or Amun-Ra, and

Sheet from a papyrus depicting the priestess Henttowy prostrating herself in adoration before the sun, which emerges from the desert horizon and contains the eye of Horus, thus spelling out the rebus of the god Ra-Horakhty. 21st Dynasty, H. 20 cm. (EA10018, SHEET 1)

Akhenaten's *Hymn to the Aten* appears to describe a deity whose power permeates all aspects of life, thus effectively superseding the traditional Egyptian 'pantheon'.

A. PIANKOFF, *The litany of Re* (New York, 1964).

J. ASSMANN, *Der König als Sonnenpriester* (Glückstadt, 1970).

D. B. REDFORD, 'The sun-disc in Akhenaten's program: its worship and antecedents I', *JARCE* 13 (1976), 47–61.

S. QUIRKE, *Ancient Egyptian religion* (London, 1992), 21–51.

J. ASSMANN, *Egyptian solar religion in the New Kingdom: Re, Amun and the crisis of polytheism*, trans. A. Alcock (London, 1995).

race

The apparently simple question of the racial origins or characteristic racial type of the Egyptians is both difficult to answer and in some measure irrelevant. We know that their LANGUAGE belonged to the group known as Afro-Asiatic or Hamito-Semitic, which simply means that they shared some common traits with the languages of parts of Africa and the Near East. Languages of this group can be spoken by people of vastly different racial type, just as Spanish may be spoken by Spaniards and South American Indians.

Examination of human remains from the Predynastic period shows a mixture of racial types, including negroid, Mediterranean and European, and by the time that Pharaonic civilization had fully emerged it was no longer meaningful to look for a particular Egyptian racial type, since they were clearly already, to some extent at least, a mixed population. It is in the context of the Protodynastic period (*c*.3100–2900 BC) that the issue of race has

often been most hotly debated, with a number of scholars, including W. B. Emery, claiming that the Predynastic Egyptians were effectively conquered by a new race from the east. Although the skeletal evidence for this theory is still considered to be indicative of some kind of physical or racial change, it is now thought that there was a slower period of transition which probably involved the indigenous Egyptian population gradually being infiltrated by a different physical type from Syria–Palestine, via the Delta region (see PREDYNASTIC PERIOD).

A more fruitful avenue is to inquire how the Egyptians saw themselves. The answer to this is partly defined in the negative, in that they clearly did not consider themselves to be either African or Asiatic; that much is obvious from their art and literature (see CAPTIVES). As 'Egyptians', they were automatically different from all their neighbours, even when certain Egyptian individuals may have appeared 'foreign' in their racial characteristics, as in the case of the New Kingdom military official MAIHERPRI, who held an important post and yet was clearly of negroid origins. Clearly, despite the highly developed iconography of foreigners, it was nevertheless possible for many different racial types to consider themselves

The enemies of Egypt were usually portrayed as captives, in this case an Asiatic and a Nubian are symbolically bound to the staff of Tutankhamun and so always in the royal grip. (CAIRO NO 50UU, REPRODUCED COURTESY OF THE GRIFFITH INSTITUTE)

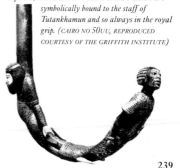

Egyptian. Perhaps the clearest example of this is the case of the skeletal remains from the 'tomb of two brothers' at Rifeh, dating to the Middle Kingdom (2055–1650 BC), where the physical appearance of one of the men was negroid, while that of his brother was more European.

It has recently been argued by certain scholars, notably Martin Bernal, the author of *Black Athena*, that the Egyptians were essentially a 'black African' culture, and that ancient Egypt should therefore be regarded as a pinnacle of negroid achievement, the artistic and cultural influence of which instigated the earliest achievements of the Classical civilizations in the Mediterranean. Although valuable in drawing attention to African contributions to western culture, Bernal's hypothesis might be accused of missing the essential point, in that 'civilizations' cannot necessarily be defined in purely racial terms. While the population at large may consist predominantly of one or another racial group, its 'culture' and the archaeological record of its characteristics are often the product of the interaction of many racial groups.

D. E. DERRY, 'The dynastic race in Egypt', *JEA* 42 (1956), 80–5.

A. C. BERRY, R. J. BERRY and P. J. UCKO, 'Genetical change in ancient Egypt', *Man* n.s. 2 (1967), 551–68.

A. C. BERRY and R. J. BERRY, 'Origins and relations of the ancient Egyptians', *Population biology of the ancient Egyptians*, ed. D. R. Brothwell and B. A. Chiarelli (New York, 1973), 200–8.

B. G. TRIGGER, 'Nubian, Negro, Black, Nilotic?', *Africa in antiquity: the arts of ancient Nubia and the Sudan* I, ed. S. Hochfield and E. Riefstahl (Brooklyn, 1978), 26–35.

M. BERNAL, *Black Athena: the Afro-Asiatic roots of classical civilization*, 2 vols (London, 1987–91).

F. J. YURCO, 'Were the ancient Egyptians black or white?', *BAR* 15/5 (1989), 24–9, 58.

Radjedef (Djedefra) *see* ABU ROASH and KHAFRA

Ra-Horakhty *see* HORUS and RA

ram
Like the BULL, the ram (Egyptian *ba*) was venerated by the Egyptians for its fertility, and although sheep were regarded as unclean, and thus unsuitable food for purified persons, the ram was worshipped from early times. The earliest ram-gods seem to have been based on the *Ovis longipes palaeoaegyptiaca* species, which has long wavy horns and a heavy build; this was the form in which KHNUM and

Banebdjedet (see MENDES) were represented. A second species, *Ovis aries platyra aegyptiaca*, appeared somewhat later in Egypt, perhaps around the 12th Dynasty (1985–1795 BC); this ram had a lighter build, fat tail and curved horns, the form often attributed to the god Amun.

Khnum, the local deity of Esna and Elephantine, was the most prominent of the ram deities, worshipped as the creator of humankind. From the New Kingdom onwards, the cult of the god AMUN absorbed that of Khnum, and Amun himself was commonly represented in ram form, although with the curving horns of the *platyra* species. The Delta town of Mendes was a cult centre for the ram-god Banebdjedet, who held the epithet 'lord of Djedet' and was regarded as the BA of the god OSIRIS. The Greek historian HERODOTUS, who visited Egypt around 450 BC, noted the sacrifice of goats at Mendes, in contrast to the use of sheep elsewhere in Egypt, although his reliability on this point is questionable. At Herakleopolis Magna the ram was worshipped under the name HERYSHEF. At many of these cult centres rams were regularly mummified and buried in catacombs at various cult centres (see SACRED ANIMALS).

L. STÖRK, 'Schaf', *Lexikon der Ägyptologie* V, ed. W. Helck, E. Otto and W. Westendorf (Wiesbaden, 1984), 522–3.

P. BEHRENS, 'Widder', *Lexikon der Ägyptologie* VI ed. W. Helck, E. Otto and W. Westendorf (Wiesbaden, 1986), 1243–5.

R. WILKINSON, *Reading Egyptian art* (London, 1992), 60–1.

Rameses
'Birth name' used in the ROYAL TITULARY of eleven rulers in the 19th and 20th Dynasties. This phase of the New Kingdom is therefore often described as the 'Ramesside' period.

Rameses I Menpehtyra (1295–1294 BC) was a military officer from the eastern Delta who rose to the rank of VIZIER under HOREMHEB and founded the 19th Dynasty (1295–1186 BC). His adoption as heir by Horemheb is recorded in the form of an inscription added to the granite interior coffin (Egyptian Museum, Cairo) which was apparently made for him while he was still vizier. He was married to a woman called Satra, whose father was also a soldier, and she bore him a son, the future SETY I. Although his reign lasted barely two years he managed to build temples at ABYDOS and BUHEN and completed the construction of the second PYLON at KARNAK, as well as almost completing his tomb in the VALLEY OF THE KINGS (KV16), which was decorated with scenes from the *Book of Gates* like those in the

Upper part of a granite figure of Rameses II wearing the double crown and holding the crook and flail, symbols of royalty. 19th Dynasty, c.1250 BC, H. 1.43 m. (EA67)

tomb of Horemheb. The style of the surviving funerary equipment, such as the wooden 'guardian statues' now in the British Museum, is said to be influenced by the art of much earlier rulers at the beginning of the 18th Dynasty.

Rameses II Usermaatra Setepenra (1279–1213 BC) was the third ruler of the 19th Dynasty. A vast number of temples, monuments and statuary were created (or usurped from earlier rulers) during his extremely long reign, including the construction of several Nubian rock-cut temples at ABU SIMBEL, AMARA West, BEIT EL-WALI, Derr and Gerf Husein. He was also an active builder in Egypt itself, where his projects included numerous temples at MEMPHIS, the court and pylon of LUXOR temple, the RAMESSEUM at western Thebes (his mortuary temple), another temple at Abydos, the completion of his father's temple nearby, and the decoration of the great HYPOSTYLE HALL at Karnak (as well as other additions to the complex).

The major event of his reign, celebrated repeatedly on the walls of his major temples, was the confrontation with the HITTITES known as the BATTLE OF QADESH, which – if not the great victory he would clearly have liked – ensured that the Hittite empire was kept at bay and Egyptian interests in the Levant were more or less protected. Eventually he signed a treaty with the Hittites, and the archive of CUNEIFORM tablets at Boghazköy contains a large number of LETTERS sent by Rameses to the Hittite king and his wife. Surviving stelae also record Rameses' further consolidation of relations with Hatti through his marriages to two Hittite princesses in the thirty-third and forty-fourth years of his reign (see QUEENS).

His principal wife was NEFERTARI, to whom the smaller temple at Abu Simbel was dedicated, and when she died his daughter Meritamun was elevated to this position. In the eastern Delta, where his family origins lay, he established a new capital called Piramesse (see QANTIR and TELL EL-DAB'A) at a site near modern el-Khatana where Sety I had previously built a palace. This was to be the capital city for the rest of the Ramesside period, although the royal cemetery was still in the VALLEY OF THE KINGS at Thebes. Rameses' own tomb was KV7 but his mummy was one of those found in the DEIR EL-BAHRI mummy cache.

During the first part of Rameses' lifetime the heir to the throne had been Amunherkhepeshef, one of his sons by Nefertari, but it was Khaemwaset, the son of another wife called Isetnofret, who was heir for most of the latter half of his reign. Despite a vigorous career as chief priest of Ptah at Memphis, Khaemwaset died in the fifty-fifth year of Rameses' reign, about a decade earlier than his father, and when Rameses finally died it was his thirteenth son, MERENPTAH, who succeeded him on the throne. Even Merenptah seems to have been middle-aged by the time that he came to power; he was the first of several short-lived rulers who had perhaps already passed their peak as a result of Rameses' unusually long reign.

Rameses III Usermaatra Meryamun (1184–1153 BC) was the second king of the 20th Dynasty (1186–1069 BC). He appears to have consciously set out to emulate his illustrious predecessor Rameses II, not only in his titles and military campaigns but also in the architectural style of his temple-building. He was

the son of the short-lived ruler Sethnakhte (1186–1184 BC) by his wife Tiye-merenese. He himself married a woman called Ese but, in common with most New Kingdom rulers, he also had many minor wives, by whom he bore numerous children.

Defensive foreign policy occupied much of the early part of his reign. His first conflict, in the fifth year of his reign, was with the LIBYANS and their allies, whom he defeated and brought back to Egypt as slaves. Three years later the great coalition of displaced and migrant peoples from the north, known as the SEA PEOPLES, who had been repulsed by Merenptah in the late thirteenth century BC, advanced into Syria, apparently with the aim of settling. The Sea Peoples, as their name indicates, were backed up by naval forces, including Sherden troops, who were noted seafarers. Although presumably not used to fighting maritime battles, the Egyptian navy managed to destroy the Sea Peoples' fleet, while simultaneously defeating the troops in Syria on land. Apart from another campaign against the Libyans in his eleventh year, the remaining two decades of Rameses III's reign were peaceful.

These campaigns, along with several others that may well be fanciful copies based on scenes from the RAMESSEUM, were recorded in some of the reliefs on the walls of Rameses III's mortuary temple at MEDINET HABU. Details of his life can also be gleaned from the Great Harris Papyrus, the longest known papyrus roll (now in the British Museum), a list of temple endowments compiled by Rameses IV (1153–1147 BC) at the time of his father's death, which concludes with a description of the dead king's achievements. The way in which he died may be indicated by the accounts of a trial of participants in a 'harim conspiracy', preserved in several documents, the most important of which are the Lee and Rollin Papyri and the Turin Judicial Papyrus. It appears that a secondary queen wished to place her son on the throne in place of the king, whom she sought to murder with the assistance of other women of the *harim*. It is not clear whether the plot succeeded, but the king's body, originally buried in KV11, was preserved in the DEIR EL-BAHRI cache and shows no signs of a violent death.

There were, however, other problems in Rameses III's reign, which seem to have resulted from poor communication between the king and his officials. A STRIKE by the workmen of DEIR EL-MEDINA occurred in the twenty-ninth year of his reign as a consequence of the irregular and delayed delivery of rations.

He was succeeded by one of his sons, Rameses IV, who was the first of a series of increasingly weak rulers. Eventually, in the reign of Rameses XI (1099–1069 BC) at the end of the 20th Dynasty, the control of Thebes fell into the hands of Libyan generals bearing the title High Priest of Amun, and by the late 22nd Dynasty much of the kingdom dissolved into independent princedoms.

W. ERICHSEN, *Papyrus Harris* (Brussels, 1933).

A. DE BUCK, 'The judicial papyrus of Turin', *JEA* 23 (1937), 152–67.

A. GARDINER, *Ramesside administrative documents* (Oxford, 1948).

W. F. EDGERTON, 'The strikes in Ramses III's twenty-ninth year', *JNES* 10 (1951) 137–45.

K. KITCHEN, *Pharaoh triumphant: the life and times of Ramesses II* (Warminster, 1982).

D. POLZ, 'Die Särge des (Pa-)Ramessu', *MDAIK* 42 (1986), 145–66.

E. HORNUNG, *Zwei Ramessidische Königsgräber: Ramses IV und Ramses VII* (Mainz, 1990).

F. FÈVRE, *Le dernier pharaon: Ramses III ou le crépuscule d'une civilization* (Paris, 1992).

K. A. KITCHEN, *Ramesside inscriptions*, 7 vols (Oxford, 1993–)

Ramesseum

Mortuary temple of Rameses II (1279–1213 BC), located on the west bank of the Nile at western THEBES, opposite modern Luxor. It was misleadingly described by DIODORUS as the 'tomb of Ozymandias', which in turn inspired Shelley's verse. The principal building, in which the funerary cult of the king was celebrated, was a typical stone-built New Kingdom temple, consisting of two successive courtyards (each entered through a pylon), a HYPOSTYLE HALL with surrounding annexes, leading to a room for the sacred BARK (a ritual boat containing a cult image) and the sanctuary. The complex includes the remains of a royal PALACE and large numbers of mud-brick granaries and storerooms. Both pylons are decorated with scenes from the Battle of QADESH.

The reliefs and architecture, as at other funerary complexes such as the mortuary temple of RAMESES III at MEDINET HABU (the plan of which was closely modelled on that of the Ramesseum), constitute an important body of evidence concerning the beliefs and rituals relating to the royal funerary cult, while the surrounding granaries indicate the importance of the New Kingdom temples with regard to the overall economy of Egypt. Evidence concerning the existence of a scribal training school at the Ramesseum has survived in the form of a large pile of ostraca (see EDUCATION and HOUSE OF LIFE).

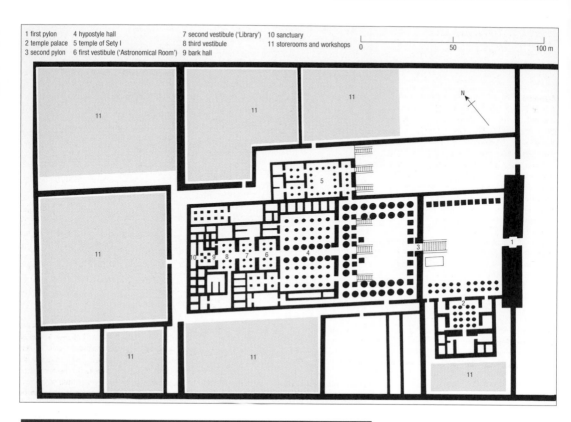

1 first pylon	4 hypostyle hall	7 second vestibule ('Library')	10 sanctuary
2 temple palace	5 temple of Sety I	8 third vestibule	11 storerooms and workshops
3 second pylon	6 first vestibule ('Astronomical Room')	9 bark hall	

ABOVE *Plan of the Ramesseum.*

LEFT *Four of the Osirid pillars of the second court of the Ramesseum, built by Rameses II at Thebes. The building later served as a model for the mortuary temple of Rameses III at Medinet Habu.* (*P. T. NICHOLSON*)

Beneath the floor of the mortuary temple a shaft tomb of a priest of the late Middle Kingdom (*c.*1700 BC) was excavated by James Quibell in the late nineteenth century. The burial chamber contained a box of papyri and a range of religious and magical artefacts (see LIBRARIES, MAGIC and MASKS).

As far as the later history of the site is concerned, a number of papyri of the Third Intermediate Period (including fragments of ONOMASTICA) have been discovered, in addition to the remains of an élite cemetery of roughly the same date.

J. E. QUIBELL, *The Ramesseum* (London, 1898).
B. PORTER and R. L. B. MOSS, *Topographical bibliography* II, 2nd ed. (Oxford, 1972), 432–43.

W. HELCK, *Die Ritualdarstellungen des Ramesseums* I (Wiesbaden, 1972).

R. STADELMANN, 'Ramesseum', *Lexikon der Ägyptologie* V, ed. W. Helck, E. Otto and W. Westendorf (Wiesbaden, 1984), 91–8.

Ramose

Vizier under Amenhotep III (1390–1352 BC) and Akhenaten (1352–1336 BC), whose Theban tomb at Sheikh Abd el-Qurna (TT55) is of particular importance because it includes reliefs executed in both the distinctive 'AMARNA style' of Akhenaten and the more traditional style of his father. The southern wall depicts the funerary processions of Ramose, while the west side preserves one of the earliest depictions of Akhenaten worshipping the ATEN. Like many Theban private tombs, it remained unfinished, and the fate of its owner, as with many of those who held office before Akhenaten's move to el-Amarna, is unknown. The tomb was once known as 'Stuart's Tomb', since it was cleared by H. W. Villiers Stuart in 1879, although it had been known to Egyptologists since 1860.

A. E. P. WEIGALL, *A guide to the antiquities of Upper Egypt* (London, 1910), 160–5.

N. DE G. DAVIES, *The tomb of the vizier Ramose* (London, 1941).

B. PORTER and R. L. B. Moss, *Topographical bibliography* I (Oxford, 1960), 105–11.

red crown *see* CROWNS AND ROYAL REGALIA

Reisner, George Andrew (1867–1942)

American Egyptologist who set new standards in Egyptian archaeology with his meticulous excavation methods, which were then comparable only with those of the British archaeologist Flinders PETRIE. Born in Indianapolis of German parents, he at first studied law at Harvard, but in 1893–6 he acquired a travelling fellowship enabling him to study Semitic languages at Berlin University, eventually gravitating towards Egyptology. Just as Petrie was supported for much of his career by the novelist Amelia Edwards, so Reisner's long-term excavations at GIZA, NAG EL-DEIR, KERMA and DEIR EL-BALLAS relied largely on the financial assistance of the philanthropist Phoebe Apperson. At the Nubian sites of NURI, EL-KURRU and Gebel Barkal (NAPATA) he discovered the pyramidal tombs of seventy-three Nubian rulers, including the 25th-Dynasty pharaohs (747–656 BC). His attention to detail, which involved the earliest Egyptological use of section drawings as well as plans, resulted in lengthy reports (several of which were unfortunately still unpublished at his death) describing such monuments as the valley temple of MENKAURA and

The carving in the tomb of the vizier Ramose at Thebes is amongst the finest of its time. Here two male guests are depicted at a funerary feast. 18th Dynasty, c.1390–1336 BC. (GRAHAM HARRISON)

the shaft-tomb of Queen HETEPHERES I at Giza. The latter was his most famous discovery, since it still contained much of the queen's funerary equipment, although the body itself seems to have been buried elsewhere. Reisner contributed several volumes to the catalogue of antiquities in the collection of the Egyptian Museum at Cairo. After a period of twenty-eight years as Professor of Egyptology at Harvard, he died at Giza in 1942.

G. A. REISNER, *Amulets* (Cairo, 1907).

G. A. REISNER and A. MACE, *The Early Dynastic cemeteries of Naga-ed-Dêr*, 2 vols (Boston, 1908–9).

G. A. REISNER, *Models of ships and boats* (Cairo, 1913).

—, *Excavations at Kerma*, 2 vols (Cambridge, MA, 1923).

G. A. REISNER and W. STEVENSON SMITH, *A history of the Giza necropolis*, 2 vols (Cambridge, MA, 1942–55).

J. A. WILSON, *Signs and wonders upon pharaoh* (Chicago, 1964), 145–58.

M. LEHNER, *The pyramid tomb of Hetep-heres and the satellite pyramid of Khufu* (Mainz, 1985).

Rekhmira

Vizier under Thutmose III (1479–1425 BC) and Amenhotep II (1427–1400 BC), whose tomb (TT100) at Sheikh Abd el-Qurna is unique among the private tombs in the Theban necropolis. Texts on its walls describe the installation of the VIZIER, a post of great importance particularly at a time of imperial expansion. A further set of texts describe the duties of the vizier, and the moral code within which his administration was intended to operate (see ETHICS). It is stated that 'there was nothing of which he [the vizier] was ignorant in heaven, in earth, or in any quarter of the underworld'.

The painted decoration includes numerous scenes relating to agriculture and craftwork, many of which provide information concerning such activities as jewellery-making and the activities in sculptors' studios, which have served to supplement archaeological and experimental data. One of the walls is decorated with scenes from the presentation of foreign tribute by Nubians, Syrians, Cretans and representatives of various other neighbouring countries. These scenes include valuable information on TRADE and tribute, indicating the kinds of raw materials and artefacts that were acquired from particular geographical areas, which has also proved useful in dating surviving imported goods.

Funerary scenes are also represented in the tomb, including the OPENING OF THE MOUTH CEREMONY being performed on Rekhmira's mummy, following the funeral procession to

243

the tomb. The tomb chapel has no burial shaft below it, and it has been suggested that Rekhmira was buried in a shaft tomb in the Valley of the Kings, although the location of this burial-place remains unknown.

K. SETHE, *Die Einsetzung des Veziers unter der 18. Dynastie. Inschrift im Grabe des Rekh-mi-re zu Schech Abd el Gurna* (Leipzig, 1909).

A. E. P. WEIGALL, *A guide to the antiquities of Upper Egypt* (London, 1910), 115–17.

N. DE G. DAVIES, *The tomb of Rekh-mi-re at Thebes* (New York, 1943).

B. PORTER and R. L. B. MOSS, *Topographical bibliography* 1/1 (Oxford, 1960), 206–14.

rekhyt bird

Egyptian term for the lapwing (*Vanellus vanellus*), a species of plover with a distinctive crested head. It was often used as a symbol for subject peoples, probably because, with its wings pinioned behind its back, thus preventing it from flying, it roughly resembled the hieroglyph for a bound CAPTIVE.

The symbol is first attested in the upper register of relief decoration on the late

Section of relief on a column in the temple of Kom Ombo, showing a rekhyt *bird (lapwing), representing the king's subjects in an attitude of worship. (I. SHAW)*

Predynastic 'Scorpion macehead' (*c.*3100 BC); a row of lapwings are shown hanging by their necks from ropes attached to the STANDARDS representing Upper Egyptian NOMES (provinces). In this context the *rekhyt* appears to be representing the conquered peoples of northern Egypt during the crucial period when the country was transformed into a single unified state. In the 3rd Dynasty (2686–2613 BC), however, another row of lapwings were depicted in the familiar pinioned form, alongside the NINE BOWS (symbolizing Egypt's enemies), crushed under the feet of a stone statue of DJOSER from his Step Pyramid at Saqqara. From that point onwards there was a continual ambiguity in the symbolic mean-

ing of the birds (to modern eyes at least) since they could, in different contexts, be taken to refer either to the enemies of Egypt or to the loyal subjects of the pharaoh.

The *rekhyt* bird icon, sometimes taking the form of winged and crested human figure, was used regularly in the decoration of Egyptian palaces and temples throughout the Pharaonic and Greco-Roman periods. The bird was usually depicted with a pair of human arms upraised in the traditional gesture of worship and in many cases it was perched on a *neb* hieroglyph (meaning 'all') with an accompanying star-shaped *dwa* hieroglyph ('to adore'), thus forming a rebus signifying 'all subject peoples adore [the pharaoh]'.

P. F. HOULIHAN, *The birds of ancient Egypt* (Warminster, 1986), 93–5.

A. NIBBI, *Lapwings and Libyans in ancient Egypt* (Oxford, 1986).

—, 'The rhj.t people as permanent foreigners in ancient Egypt', *DE* 9 (1987), 79–96.

C. VANDERSLEYEN, 'The rekhyt and the Delta', *The archaeology, geography and history of the Delta*, ed. A. Nibbi (Oxford, 1989), 301–4.

religion

Ancient Egyptian 'state religion' was concerned with the maintenance of the divine order; this entailed ensuring that life was conducted in accordance with MAAT, and preventing the encroachment of chaos. In such a system it was necessary for religion to permeate every aspect of life, so that it was embedded in society and politics, rather than being a separate category. The Egyptian view of the universe was capable of incorporating a whole series of apparently contradictory CREATION myths. This holistic view also led to the treatment of prayer, MAGIC and SCIENCE as realistic and comparable alternatives; as a result it made good sense to combine what might now be described as medical treatment with a certain amount of ritual and the recitation of prayers (see MEDICINE), each component of the overall treatment having the same aim: to suppress evil and maintain the harmony of the universe.

The TEMPLES and their attendant PRIESTS therefore served as a perpetual means of stabilizing the universe. Each day they attended to the needs of the god (who was thought to be manifested in the cult image), made offerings to him, and thus kept the forces of chaos at bay. A distinction is sometimes made between, on the one hand, the important state gods (e.g. HORUS or ISIS) and local deities (e.g. Banebdjedet at MENDES) and, on the other hand, the 'popular' or 'household' deities such as BES and TAWERET.

In actual practice the only major difference seems to have been the lack of major cult-places dedicated to the latter (and even Taweret effectively had a cult-place at KARNAK, in the form of the temple dedicated to her predecessor Opet).

A more useful distinction can be made between the tendency of the state religion to focus on the concerns of the state and the kingship, whereas surviving ostraca, stelae and votive offerings show that the individual Egyptians regarded religion primarily as a method of averting disaster or harm on a more personal level. Since childbirth was a particularly dangerous time in the lives of ordinary people, it is not surprising that the most popular household gods were credited with particular protective powers in this regard, while the processes of procreation and birth were both areas in which magic, prayer and medicine were inextricably entwined.

Neglect of the gods, or blasphemy against them, could lead to punishment. Various stelae from DEIR EL-MEDINA, for instance, describe how an offence against the cobra-goddess MERETSEGER led to blindness or other complaints, and how, after penitence, the deity had cured the wrongdoer. Although concerned with maintaining Maat, Egyptian religion generally was not overtly directed towards the personal morality that was implicit in upholding Maat. However, the WISDOM LITERATURE provides some insight into the Egyptians' views on morality, and some of the same concepts are reflected in the FUNERARY TEXTS of the New Kingdom.

Egyptian FUNERARY BELIEFS were also directed towards the continuance of the established order. The dead person attempted to ensure that through MUMMIFICATION, and the provision of the established offerings and funerary goods, the KA would receive nourishment and the BA find the body. The deceased would avoid the perils of the underworld and travel safely in the BARK of the sun-god RA. See also ATEN; DEIFICATION; NAOS and SHRINE.

S. SAUNERON, *The priests of ancient Egypt* (London, 1960).

S. MORENZ, *Egyptian religion* (London, 1973).

E. LIPIŃSKI (ed.), *State and temple economy in the ancient near east*, 2 vols (Leuven, 1979).

E. HORNUNG, *Conceptions of god in ancient Egypt: the one and the many* (London, 1983).

J. ASSMANN, *Ägypten: Theologie und Frömmigkeit einer frühen Hochkultur* (Stuttgart, 1984).

J. P. ALLEN et al., *Religion and philosophy in ancient Egypt* (New Haven, 1989).

S. QUIRKE, *Ancient Egyptian religion* (London, 1992).

Renenutet (Greek *Thermouthis*)

Cobra-goddess, protector of the king, and goddess of fertility who was represented as a cobra or a woman with a cobra head, sometimes nursing a child. Her name may be translated as 'the nourishing snake'. In the Old Kingdom (2686–2181 BC) she was regarded as an important guardian of the king, who united with WADJYT as a fire-breathing cobra to protect him in the afterlife. She was also the

Stele showing Setau, the Viceroy of Kush during the reign of Rameses II, pouring a libation before the goddess Renenutet, who is depicted in the form of a serpent. 19th Dynasty, c.1300 BC, limestone, from Buhen, H. 50 cm. (EA1055)

protectress of the linen garment worn by the king, which was thought to instil fear into his enemies in the afterlife. By extension, she was sometimes connected with the provision of mummy bandages.

As the 'lady of fertile fields' and 'lady of granaries' she was responsible for securing and protecting the harvest. Her cult enjoyed particular popularity at the city of Dja (MEDINET MAADI) in the FAYUM REGION where a FESTIVAL was annually celebrated for her, and where she was linked with the gods SOBEK and HORUS (this triad being known by the Greeks as Hermouthis, Sekonopis and Ankhoes). In this role as a corn goddess she was associated with OSIRIS in his youthful form of Neper (Nepri). Her part in the Osiris myth is extended by a mention in the BOOK OF THE DEAD in which she is said to be the mother of Horus from a union with ATUM. This led to her being identified with the goddess ISIS, who was herself regarded as a divine mother.

J. BROEKHUIS, *De godin Renenwetet* (Assen, 1971).

'reserve head'

Type of funerary sculpture, consisting of a limestone human head, usually with excised (or unsculpted) ears and enigmatic lines carved around the neck and down the back of the cranium. About thirty examples are known, all deriving from private mastaba tombs in the Memphite necropolis (principally at GIZA) dating to the Old Kingdom, primarily from the reigns of KHUFU and KHAFRA (2589–2532 BC). They were placed in the burial chamber close to the corpse, whereas other Old Kingdom statues were usually placed in the chapel or the SERDAB.

The English term 'reserve head' refers to the theory that the sculpted head was intended to act as a substitute for the real head of the deceased in the afterlife. The facial features, although idealized, are thought to have been intended to be more 'realistic' than was usually the case with Egyptian statuary, although this view has been contested by Roland Tefnin. According to Tefnin, the heads had a more complex religious function, simultaneously serving both as a means by which the spirit could identify its own body and as a symbol of the ritual decapitation and mutilation of the deceased, thus protecting the living from the ill will of the dead.

E. NAVILLE, *Les têtes de pierre déposées dans les tombeaux égyptiens* (Geneva, 1909).
C. L. VANDERSLEYEN, 'Ersatzkopf', *Lexikon der Ägyptologie* II, ed. W. Helck, E. Otto and W. Westendorf (Wiesbaden, 1977), 11–14.
N. B. MILLET, 'The reserve heads of the Old Kingdom', *Essays in honor of Dows Dunham*, ed. W. K. Simpson and W. M. Davis (Boston, 1981), 129–31.

Limestone 'reserve head' from Giza. Old Kingdom, late 4th Dynasty, c.2550 BC. H. 27 cm. (METROPOLITAN MUSEUM, NEW YORK, ROGERS FUND 48.156)

R. TEFNIN, 'Les têtes magiques de Gizeh' *BSFE* 120 (March 1991), 25–37.

Reshef (Reshep, Reshpu)

Amorite war-god whose cult is strongly attested in Egypt during the 18th Dynasty (1550–1295 BC), no doubt as a result of the influences emerging from the Egyptian 'imperial'

Late Period statue of the war-god Reshef holding a spear and a shield and wearing the white crown with a gazelle's head on the front. It is the only surviving stone statue of Reshef. Late Period, provenance unknown, H. 29 cm. (METROPOLITAN MUSEUM, NEW YORK, GIFT OF JOSEPH W. DREXEL, 1889, 89.2.215)

presence in the Levant. In the same way as the Asiatic goddesses QEDESHET, ANAT and ASTARTE, he became thoroughly absorbed into Egyptian religion and was usually represented as a bearded figure wearing an Upper Egyptian white CROWN with a GAZELLE's head at the front (in place of the sacred cobra or *uraeus* of WADJYT) and a ribbon hanging down at the rear. Sometimes he was portrayed in the act of wielding a mace or spear, like the Egyptian war-god MONTU, with whom he developed considerable affinities. Although there are many bronze statuettes of the god, and he is depicted on a number of stelae from sites such as Memphis and Qantir (often being portrayed alongside other Asiatic deities), only one stone statue has survived (Metropolitan Museum of Art, New York). It should be noted that these images are rarely named, therefore they could, in theory, represent other Asiatic gods.

B. GRDSELOFF, *Les débuts du culte de Rechef en Egypte* (Cairo, 1942).

W. K. SIMPSON, 'An Egyptian statuette of a Phoenician god', *BMMA* x/6 (1952), 182–7.

H. DE MEULENAERE, *De cultus van Resjef in Egypte* (Leuven, 1955).

W. J. FULCO, *The Canaanite god Resep* (New Haven, 1976).

A. R. SCHULMAN, 'Reshep at Zagazig: a new document', *Studien zu Sprache und Religion Ägyptens: Festschrift W. Westendorf* (Göttingen, 1984), 855–63.

Romans

The Romans' earliest involvement in the affairs of Egypt dates to the period when Pompey became engaged in the financial affairs of the Ptolemaic court, ultimately becoming the guardian of CLEOPATRA VII (51–30 BC) on the death of her father PTOLEMY XII (80–51 BC). When Pompey was defeated by Caesar at Pharsalia in 48 BC he fled to Egypt, but was assassinated there. Caesar then entered Egypt and reinstated Cleopatra (who had been briefly deposed in 48 BC) as CO-REGENT with her second brother, Ptolemy XIV (47–44 BC), who became her husband. However, in 47 BC Cleopatra gave birth to a son, Ptolemy Caesarion, whom she claimed to have been fathered by Caesar. Her visit to Rome, in 46 BC, attracted a great deal of attention, as did her political manoeuvres on her return to Egypt, involving the assassination of her brother and the installation of Caesarion on the throne. Having been summoned by the Romans to meet with Mark Antony at Tarsus, she soon afterwards bore him twins.

In 34 BC, Mark Antony divided various parts of the eastern Roman empire between Cleopatra (now his wife) and her children, while informing Rome that he was simply installing client rulers. However, Octavian (later Augustus) organized a propaganda campaign against Antony, and in 32 BC Rome declared war on Cleopatra. The following year Octavian defeated Mark Antony at the naval battle of Actium. Both Mark Antony and

Bronze statue of Horus dressed in Roman armour. Roman period, provenance unknown, H. 47 cm. (EA36062)

Cleopatra committed suicide, and Octavian had Caesarion killed, thus effectively bringing an end to the Ptolemaic Dynasty.

Octavian Augustus appointed himself pharaoh on 30 August 30 BC, thenceforth treating Egypt as an imperial estate, rather than a Roman province. This special status was retained under subsequent emperors. Greek remained the official language, and ALEXANDRIA the dominant city. The country underwent a sparse military occupation, although outposts are known throughout the country as far as QASR IBRIM in Nubia. Augustus ruled from 30 BC to AD 14, during which time he appears to have done little to endear himself to the native Egyptian élite, not least through his contempt for traditional religion and his refusal to visit the sacred APIS bull at Memphis.

Superficially, Roman rule was a continuation of the Ptolemaic period, except that no ruling family was resident in Egypt. This had important consequences, in that it may have removed any incentive for Egypt to create wealth, given that it was effectively being exploited at a distance, as a source of food for Rome. Improvements in irrigation that had been introduced by the Ptolemies were exploited to the full by the Roman administration, and the produce was gathered up in tax

by governors who could be held personally liable for any shortfalls.

The official adoption of Egyptian practices, such as the completion of Ptolemaic temples (e.g. DENDERA, KOM OMBO and PHILAE) in Egyptian style, and the depiction of the emperors in Egyptian garb did little to distract attention from the harsh conditions under which the poor laboured. There were various revolts, including an uprising of Jews in AD 115–17. The emperor Hadrian (AD 117–38) looked more favourably on Egypt, and travelled widely in the country. He even incorporated a SERAPEUM into his villa at Tivoli, along with statues of Egyptian gods. The influence of Egyptian religion on Rome became very great at this period. However, conditions in Egypt probably improved little as a result of the imperial visit, which seems to have resulted only in the founding of new settlements such as Antinoopolis in Middle Egypt.

During the reign of Marcus Aurelius (AD 161–80), Egypt was stricken by a plague, which can only have added to the gradual depopulation of the country, while a rival bid for power made by Avidius Cassius in AD 175 did nothing to help the situation. Conditions improved slightly under Septimius Severus (AD 193–211) who reorganized the local ADMINISTRATION and carried out various building works, notably the repair of the COLOSSI OF MEMNON at Thebes. This conciliatory phase was short lived, and in AD 215 Caracalla (AD 198–217) banned Egyptians from Alexandria, ordering the killing of all the youth of the city because of a slander made by the inhabitants.

The reign of Diocletian (AD 284–305) was infamous for its persecution of Christians (known as Copts in Egypt) and Egypt was not spared, perhaps even suffering more grievously through the influence of Sossianus Hierocles, a fanatical persecutor. This was an attempt to enforce traditional Roman religion, but it was not to be effective. Not only did Christianity survive, but Egyptian cults, notably that of ISIS, were already established within the Roman empire.

Although the FAYUM REGION, heavily settled by Greeks, continued to be favoured by Roman visitors (who needed special permission to visit the country), it too gradually underwent depopulation, evident by the fourth century AD. In AD 384 Theodosius (AD 379–95) issued an edict commanding the closing of all pagan temples, and ordering the adherence of the entire populace to Christianity. However, some areas resisted, and PHILAE remained an outpost of traditional religion for a considerable time. The Egyptian Christians continued to set up churches and monasteries in some of the ancient temples, and to establish settlements (see COPTIC PERIOD).

J. G. MILNE, *A history of Egypt under Roman rule* (London, 1924).

H. I. BELL, *Egypt from Alexander the Great to the Arab conquest* (London, 1956).

P. A. BRUNT, 'The administrators of Roman Egypt', *Journal of Roman Studies* 65 (1975), 124–47.

N. LEWIS, *Life in Egypt under Roman rule* (London, 1983).

A. K. BOWMAN, *Egypt after the Pharaohs* (London, 1986).

D. PEACOCK, *Rome in the desert: a symbol of power* (Southampton, 1992).

Rosellini, (Niccolo Francesco) Ippolito

(1800–43)

Italian Egyptologist, born and educated in Pisa, who accompanied Jean-François CHAM-POLLION on the Franco-Tuscan expedition to Egypt in 1828–9. Although his career was relatively short, his ten-volume description of the major monuments of Egypt, published between 1832 and 1844, was one of the most influential Egyptological publications of the mid-nineteenth century, rivalling the principal publications of his contemporaries, Karl Richard LEPSIUS and Sir John Gardner WILKINSON.

I. ROSELLINI, *I monumenti dell'Egitto e della Nubia, disegnati dalla spedizione scientifico-letteraria Toscana in Egitto*, 3 pts, 10 vols (Pisa, 1832–44).

G. GABRIELI, *Ippolito Rosellini e il suo giornale della spedizione letteraria Toscano in Egitto negli anni 1828–29* (Rome, 1925).

E. BRECCIA (ed.), *Scritti dedicati alla memoria di Ippolito Rosellini ne primo centenario della morte* (Florence, 1945).

G. BOTTI (ed.), *Studi in memoria di Rosellini nel primo centenario della morte*, 2 vols (Pisa, 1949–55).

Rosetta Stone

Black granitic stele discovered in 1799 at the village of el-Rashid (Rosetta) in the western Delta of Egypt. The Rosetta Stone (now in the British Museum) is inscribed with a decree issued at Memphis and dated to 27 March 196 BC, the anniversary of the coronation of PTOLEMY V Epiphanes. The main significance of the text lies not in its content, a record of benefits conferred on Egypt by Ptolemy V, but in the fact that it is written in three scripts: HIERO-GLYPHICS, DEMOTIC and Greek. It should be noted, however, that the text is an important source for the re-establishment of Ptolemaic (Alexandrian) rule over Egypt after the secession of a great deal of the country at the end of the reign of Ptolemy IV, ten years earlier.

The Rosetta Stone, inscribed in hieroglyphics (top), demotic (centre) and Greek (bottom), provided a key to the decipherment of the hieroglyphic script. Although found at el-Rashid (Rosetta) and recording a decree issued in Memphis, it may originally have been erected in Sais. Ptolemaic period, 196 BC, granitic stone, H. 1.14 m. (EA24)

Early Egyptologists such as Silvestre de Saçy, Johann David Åkerblad and Thomas Young recognized the potential of the Rosetta Stone in terms of the decipherment of Egyptian hieroglyphs. Young deciphered the demotic text, but it was Jean-François Champollion who made the final breakthrough, announcing in his famous *Lettre à M. Dacier* in 1822 that the Rosetta Stone had not only enabled him to decipher the names of Ptolemy and Cleopatra, as Young had, but also provided him with the means to understand the basis of the phonetic and ideogrammatic system employed in hieroglyphic texts.

C. A. ANDREWS, *The Rosetta Stone* (London, 1982).

S. QUIRKE and C. A. ANDREWS, *The Rosetta Stone: a facsimile drawing* (London, 1988).

Royal Canon of Turin *see* TURIN ROYAL CANON

royal ka *see* KA

royal titulary

The classic sequence of names and titles held by each of the pharaohs consisted of five names (the so-called 'fivefold titulary'), which was not established in its entirety until the Middle Kingdom (2055–1650 BC). The five epithets to some extent encapsulate Egyptian views on KINGSHIP, in the sense that three of them stress his role as a god, while the other two emphasize

the perceived division of Egypt into two lands, both under the control of the pharaoh.

The 'birth name' (also known as the nomen), such as AMENEMHAT or RAMESES, was introduced by the epithet 'son of RA'. It was usually the last name in the sequence in inscriptions giving the king's name and titles, but it was the only one to be given to the pharaoh as soon as he was born. The other four names (Horus; He of the two ladies; (Horus of) Gold; and He of the SEDGE and BEE) were given to the ruler at the time of his installation on the throne, and their components may sometimes convey something of the ideology or intentions of the king in question.

In the late fourth millennium BC the earliest kings' names are attested. These simple 'Horus names', painted on pottery vessels and carved on fragmentary ivory and wooden labels, typically consisted of a falcon perched on a SEREKH frame containing the name of the king in question. By the end of the 1st Dynasty (3100–2890 BC), all elements of the full titulary, apart from the 'son of Ra' (*sa Ra*) name had appeared, although often they made their initial appearance as isolated symbols and epithets rather than as full-blown names. For

Fragment of ivory from the tomb of King Den at Abydos. The king's 'Horus name' appears in a serekh surmounted by the falcon-god Horus. 1st Dynasty, c.2950 BC, H. 6 cm. (EA35552)

instance, the 'He of the sedge and bee' title (*nesw-bit*) was first used in the reign of DEN (*c.*2950 BC), but it was ANEDJIB (*c.*2925 BC) who was the first to have both the title 'he of the sedge and bee' and also a second name (Merpabia) linked with it.

Two further crucial developments in the royal titulary took place during the 4th Dynasty: Huni (2637–2613 BC) introduced the use of the CARTOUCHE to frame his 'He of the sedge and bee' name, and Djedefra (2566–2558 BC) was the first to use the 'son of Ra' title. By the 11th Dynasty (2055–1985 BC) the two names by which the king was most regularly known were the two 'cartouche names': 'he of the sedge and bee' (the throne name) and 'son of Ra' (the birth name). The religious implication of this change was that the king was no longer first and foremost a manifestation of Horus; instead he was seen primarily in terms of his rule over the two lands and his relationship with the sun-god.

The importance of the royal titulary in terms of legitimizing and enshrining each king's right to the throne is indicated both by the apparent care taken in choosing names and by the lengths to which many foreign rulers of Egypt went to acquire authentic titulary. In the reign of the Persian ruler Cambyses I (525–522 BC), for example, an Egyptian priest called Udjahorresnet was employed to create a suitable throne name for him (see PERSIA).

H. GAUTHIER, *Le livre des rois d'Egypte*, 3 vols (Cairo, 1907–17).

P. KAPLONY, 'Königstitulatur', *Lexikon der Ägyptologie* III, ed. W. Helck, E. Otto and W. Westendorf (Wiesbaden, 1980), 641–59.

N. GRIMAL, *Les termes de la propagande royale égyptienne* (Paris, 1986).

S. QUIRKE, *Who were the pharaohs?* (London, 1990).

S

sa

Hieroglyphic sign meaning 'protection', which may have originally represented the rolled-up reed mat that would have sheltered herdsmen; it might also have served as a type of papyrus 'life-vest' for boatmen. It is clear that the sign soon acquired the more general meaning of 'protection', and, like the ANKH sign, it was used either as an amulet in its own right or as a symbol held by the deities BES and TAWERET. In the Middle Kingdom

Amulet in the form of the sa *hieroglyph made in electrum wire. Middle Kingdom, c.2055–1650 BC, H. 4 cm. (EA65332)*

(2055–1650 BC) the *sa* shape was used as a single, repeated element in jewellery and on magic wands, while in the New Kingdom (1550–1069 BC) it usually occurred in combination with other signs such as the ANKH, DJED or TYET (Isis knot). Virtually all of the surviving amulets in the form of the *sa* sign date to the Middle Kingdom.

R. H. WILKINSON, *Reading Egyptian art* (London, 1992), 196–7.

C. ANDREWS, *Amulets of ancient Egypt* (London, 1994), 43.

sacred animals

The Egyptians held a number of animals to be sacred as the living manifestations of various gods (see BA). The belief may have come from Predynastic times, when animals were revered for particular qualities, such as the bull for its strength and the lion for its aggression. Some of the NOME gods may have had their origins in such totemistic beliefs.

In some cases, after *c.*700 BC, a whole species of animal, bird or fish was revered, as with the IBIS (sacred to the god THOTH) or the falcon (sacred to HORUS and OSIRIS), while in

other cases individual animals might represent the god, as with the CYNOCEPHALUS baboon of Thoth, or more especially the APIS bull at Saqqara (see SERAPEUM). In the latter case only one Apis bull existed at any one time, and this animal was selected and reared with great care because of its distinctive markings.

The sacred animal cults were overseen by their own priesthoods, who cared for the animals and ultimately arranged for their mummification and burial. In the case of an Apis, BUCHIS or MNEVIS bull, the burial would be very elaborate, involving funerary equipment and ceremonies similar to those surrounding a royal funeral. The hawks and the ibises, on the other hand, were donated in their thousands as votive offerings, therefore many of the mummies were placed in wooden boxes or sealed pottery jars. Pilgrims would pay for the embalming and burial of one of these birds as an act of piety. The jars containing mummified birds or animals were buried in underground galleries such as the extensive complexes at SAQQARA or TUNA EL-GEBEL, while the Apis and Buchis bulls, as well as their mothers, were each allocated splendid hypogea (subterranean tomb chambers) with individual granite sarcophagi. At Saqqara the sacred baboons were found buried in wooden shrines set in stone niches in their own gallery. These cults grew in importance from the late New Kingdom onwards, reaching a peak in the Late Period (747–332 BC), when they may have formed an important part of the economy. The Sacred Animal Necropolis at north Saqqara was excavated by the Egypt Exploration Society during the 1960s, and two more recent expeditions at the site, during the 1990s, have concentrated firstly on the analysis of the chronological development of the galleries, and secondly on the use of the mummified remains to study the genetic history of primates.

As well as the numerous galleries of sacred animals at Saqqara, there were important centres for the cult of sacred rams at MENDES, HERAKLEOPOLIS MAGNA, ESNA and ELEPHANTINE, sacred cats at TELL BASTA and BENI HASAN, Mnevis bulls at HELIOPOLIS (and possibly EL-AMARNA), Buchis bulls at ARMANT, the sacred cow of Hathor at DENDERA, and sacred crocodiles at KOM OMBO, MEDINET EL-FAYUM (Crocodilopolis) and el-Maabda.

J. D. RAY, 'The world of North Saqqara', *WA* 10/2 (1978), 149–57.

G. T. MARTIN, *The sacred animal necropolis at North Saqqara* (London, 1981).

Amulets of six sacred animals. TOP LEFT TO RIGHT *Ram in turquoise faience, Third Intermediate Period. Ibis in turquoise and dark blue, representing Thoth; the bill is supported by the feather of Maat, Late Period, L. 4.5 cm. Apis bull in turquoise faience, Saite period, L. 2.9 cm.* BOTTOM LEFT TO RIGHT *Cow, probably representing Hathor, in bronze, Late Period. Lion in pale green faience, representing Nefertem, Saite period. Jackal, probably representing Wepwawet, Third Intermediate Period. (EA11896, 36451, 61622, 11600, 64617, 36448)*

D. KESSLER, *Die Heiligen Tiere und der König* I (Wiesbaden, 1989).

R. PERIZONIUS et al., 'Monkey mummies and north Saqqara', *Egyptian Archaeology* 3 (1993), 31–3.

P. T. NICHOLSON, 'Archaeology beneath Saqqara', *Egyptian Archaeology* 4 (1994), 7–8.

sacred lake

Artificial expanse of water located within the precincts of many Egyptian temples from the Old Kingdom to the Roman period (2686 BC– AD 395). The most common type is that of the Temple of Amun at KARNAK: a rectangular, stone-lined reservoir filled by ground water and entered via several stairways, which the Egyptians described as a *she netjeri* ('divine pool'). The sacred lake fulfilled a number of different cultic purposes, serving as a setting for the sailing of BARKS containing images of the gods, the home of such aquatic sacred animals as geese or crocodiles, and a source of pure water for the daily ritual ablutions and libations of the temple. As well as the conventional rectangular lake found at such sites as

The sacred lake in the precincts of the temple of Hathor at Dendera. (I. SHAW)

ARMANT, MEDINET HABU, DENDERA and TANIS, there were several other forms, such as the horseshoe-shaped pool (known as an *isherw-water*) that enclosed the main buildings in the sacred precinct of Mut at Karnak. There were also circular reservoirs completely surrounding the main cult-place of the Osireion at ABY-DOS and encircling the shrines of the Maru-Aten at EL-AMARNA.

H. BONNET, *Reallexikon der ägyptischen Religionsgeschichte* (Berlin, 1952), 694–5.

P. MONTET, *Le lac sacré de Tanis* (Paris, 1966).

B. GESSLER-LÖHR, *Die heiligen Seen in ägyptischer Tempel* (Hildesheim, 1983).

saff tomb

Type of rock-cut tomb constructed primarily in the el-Tarif area of western Thebes for the local rulers of the Theban 11th Dynasty (INTEF I–III; 2125–2055 BC). The term *saff* (Arabic: 'row') refers to the rows of rock-cut pillars which stood around three sides of a large trapezoidal sunk forecourt, forming the distinctive frontage of each of the tomb chapels. Private *saff* tombs have also been excavated at ARMANT and DENDERA.

D. ARNOLD, *Gräber des Alten und Mittleren Reiches in El-Tarif* (Mainz, 1976).

Saft el-Hinna *see* SOPED

Sah (Orion)

Personification of the principal southern constellation that was later known as Orion. The god was described as the 'glorious soul of OSIRIS' and formed a divine triad along with the dog star SOPDET (Sothis) and his son SOPED, who was the god of the eastern border.

P. CASANOVA, 'De quelques légendes astronomiques arabes considérées dans leurs rapports avec la mythologie égyptienne', *BIFAO* 2 (1902), 1–39 (17–24).

K. PREISENDANZ, *Papyri Graecae magicae: Die griechischen Zauberpapyri* (Stuttgart, 1973), 26–33.

H. BEHRENS, 'Orion', *Lexikon der Ägyptologie* IV, ed. W. Helck, E. Otto and W. Westendorf (Wiesbaden, 1982), 609–11.

Sais (Sa el-Hagar)

Town in the western Delta, the remains of which are mostly covered by the modern village, and date principally to the eighth to sixth centuries BC. Its patron goddess was NEITH, whose cult is attested at least as early as the 1st Dynasty (3100–2890 BC), suggesting that Sais itself must have been occupied from the late Predynastic period onwards. It was the provincial capital of the fifth nome of Lower Egypt and the seat of the rulers of the 24th and 26th Dynasties (727–715 and 664–525 BC). There appear to be no surviving remains earlier than the late New Kingdom (c.1100 BC). The remains of the *tell* have been largely destroyed by *sebakhin* (farmers removing mud-brick deposits for use as fertilizer), leaving only a few relief blocks *in situ*, and the site has not yet been scientifically excavated. See also SAITE PERIOD.

B. PORTER and R. MOSS, *Topographical bibliography* IV (Oxford, 1934), 46–9.

L. HABACHI, 'Sais and its monuments', *ASAE* 42 (1942), 369–416.

R. EL-SAYED, *Documents relatifs à Saïs et ses divinités* (Cairo, 1975).

—, *La déesse Neith de Saïs* (Cairo, 1982).

Saite period

Term applied to the 26th Dynasty (664–525 BC), when Egypt was ruled from the city of SAIS in the Delta. The overall character of the period stems from the fact that the first Saite ruler, PSAMTEK I (664–610 BC), had shaken off ASSYRIAN and Kushite rule, thus ushering in a new era of Egyptian nationalism. This cultural change was expressed primarily by the sculpture and painting of the period, which were often consciously modelled on earlier work, particularly that of the Old and Middle Kingdoms (2686–1650 BC), a process that had already begun in the late Third Intermediate Period and especially in the 25th Dynasty (747–656 BC), when Kushite kings sought to legitimize their rule by using established Egyptian artistic styles.

The enormous care with which Saite artists copied ancient works of art is indicated by the fact that they appear to have overlaid some of the panels in the Step Pyramid at SAQQARA with grid lines in order to reproduce the reliefs, even creating a new entrance into the pyramid in order to gain access to the subterranean chambers. It is interesting to note, however, that the copies did not necessarily reproduce the originals in precise detail. Instead, there were often artistic innovations, as in the case of the reliefs in the tomb of MENTUEMHAT (TT34; c.700–650 BC) which, although apparently drawing on scenes from the nearby 18th-Dynasty tomb of MENNA (TT69; c.1400 BC), nevertheless added new details. Such observations have led to suggestions that the Saite period should be regarded as a time of vigorous renaissance rather than slavish archaizing.

Similarly, traditional religious practices were reinforced but often simultaneously reshaped; thus the SACRED ANIMAL cults grew in importance, and their upkeep became an increasingly important element of the Egyptian economy. The cult-centre of the goddess NEITH at Sais was expanded and embellished, while new temples were constructed at MEMPHIS (still the administrative centre) as well as at Thebes and other major cities throughout Egypt. During this period the Theban region was effectively controlled by the GOD'S WIFE OF AMUN. In another indication that the Saite period was a time of progress as well as revival, the DEMOTIC script, first attested in c.700 BC, gained wide acceptance under the 26th-Dynasty rulers.

The Egyptian army came increasingly to depend upon GREEK mercenaries, and as early as 630 BC a settlement for Greek traders was founded at NAUKRATIS in the Delta. The town was later reorganized under AHMOSE II (570–526 BC), who was traditionally credited with its foundation. This economic connection with the Greeks inevitably led to Egypt's closer involvement in the affairs of the Mediterranean, and a change in outlook. From this time onwards, many Greeks travelled to Egypt, including HERODOTUS, who described Egypt in the period immediately following the Saite dynasty. See also LATE PERIOD.

J. D. COONEY, 'Three early Saite tomb reliefs', *JNES* 9 (1950), 193–203.

H. KEES, 'Zur Innenpolitik der Säitendynastie', *Nachrichten der Geschichte und Wissenschaft, Göttingen Phil.-Hist. Klasse* I (1963), 96–106.

A. B. LLOYD, 'The Late Period, 664–323 BC', *Ancient Egypt: a social history*, B. G. Trigger et al. (Cambridge, 1983), 279–348.

P. DER MANUELIAN, *Living in the past* (London, 1994).

Saqqara

Site of the principal necropolis of the ancient city of MEMPHIS, situated some 17 km from the GIZA suburb of Cairo, which was in use from the 1st Dynasty (3100–2890 BC) to the Christian period (AD 395–540). The entire length of the site is about six kilometres, with a maximum width of about 1.5 km. It has been suggested that the name of the site may be derived from that of the god SOKAR, although Arab chroniclers state, more plausibly, that it derives from the name of an Arab tribe once resident in the area.

The importance of the Saqqara necropolis is indicated by the very crowded nature of the burials, with some having been re-used many times and most having been extensively plundered throughout antiquity. Beneath the ground, Saqqara is honeycombed with inter-

The Step Pyramid of Djoser at Saqqara is surrounded by a complex of ritual buildings and courts, including these 'dummy chapels' in the sed festival court, reconstructed by J.-P. Lauer. (P. T. NICHOLSON)

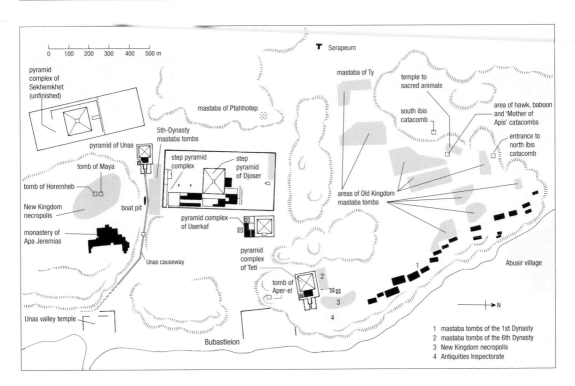

Plan of north Saqqara.

cut tombs, galleries and robber shafts, not always visible on the desert surface.

The 1st-Dynasty ruler NARMER is the earliest king whose name is known from Saqqara; his actual burial was almost certainly in Tomb B17–18 of the Umm el-Qa'ab cemetery at ABYDOS, but a stone bowl bearing his name was discovered in one of the extensive storerooms beneath the Step Pyramid of DJOSER (2667–2648 BC). It is not impossible that there was originally also a monument of the reign of Narmer at Saqqara, since slightly later 1st-Dynasty MASTABA tombs are well attested at the site, forming a distinct group along the northeastern edge of the plateau.

It is thought likely that the original site of the White Walls (one of the names for ancient Memphis) was probably near the modern village of Abusir, which is situated at the northeastern edge of the plateau, close to the 1st- and 2nd-Dynasty tombs. The development of an extensive cemetery of mastaba tombs along the plateau edge during the first two dynasties might have gradually produced a situation when the population at Memphis would have found it difficult to distinguish any particular tomb among the great mass on the edge of the

plateau; it has therefore been suggested that this may be partly why the architect IMHOTEP devised such an innovative structure as Djoser's funerary monument in the early 3rd Dynasty (see PYRAMIDS). This was the first time that stone architecture had been used on such a large scale in Egypt. It therefore still followed closely the earlier building styles connected with mud-brick and organic materials: thus the 'palace-façade' style of decoration continued to be used, and wooden columns were transformed into stone.

Mastaba tombs were constructed at Saqqara for the Memphite élite during the Old Kingdom (2686–2181 BC), many of them focusing closely on the pyramids of the kings, which date from the 3rd-Dynasty complex of Djoser to the 13th-Dynasty monument of Khendjer (c.1748 BC). The 5th-Dynasty pyramid of Unas (2375–2345 BC) was the first to be inscribed with the PYRAMID TEXTS, while the pyramid complex of the 6th-Dynasty ruler Pepy II (2278–2184 BC) was effectively the last major funerary monument of the Old Kingdom at Saqqara. The remains of the small mud-brick pyramid of the 8th-Dynasty ruler Ibi aptly symbolize the decline in the

political and economic system from the Old Kingdom to the First Intermediate Period (2181–2055 BC).

In the Middle Kingdom (2055–1650 BC) and Second Intermediate Period (1650–1550 BC) the area around DAHSHUR and EL-LISHT, as well as the sites of EL-LAHUN, HAWARA and THEBES, became the main centres of royal funerary activity. Although Thebes was probably the religious capital of the New Kingdom, Memphis retained a great deal of its administrative importance and, as for most of Egyptian history, it was the real seat of government. Many important officials of the New Kingdom resided in the city, and although their rulers chose to be buried in the VALLEY OF THE KINGS at Thebes, many nobles constructed elaborate temple-style tomb chapels for themselves at Saqqara, usually surrounded by the smaller tombs of their servants and family.

Some of these New Kingdom tombs were recorded by Karl Richard LEPSIUS during his expedition of 1842–5, but their precise locations were subsequently difficult to ascertain

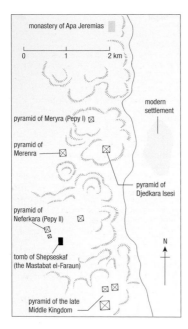

monastery of Apa Jeremias

0   1   2 km

pyramid of Meryra (Pepy I)

modern
settlement

pyramid of
Merenra

pyramid of
Djedkara Isesi

pyramid of
Neferkara (Pepy II)

N

tomb of Shepseskaf
(the Mastabat el-Faraun)

pyramid of the late
Middle Kingdom

RIGHT *Carved relief from the mastaba-chapel of Ptahhotep at Saqqara, showing a herdsman leading forward a group of prize cattle. 5th Dynasty, c.2380 BC. (GRAHAM HARRISON)*

LEFT *Plan of south Saqqara.*

from maps. Since 1975, the joint expedition of the Egypt Exploration Society and Leiden Museum has rediscovered some of these tombs, in a part of the necropolis to the south of the causeway of the pyramid of Unas, where the finest surviving tombs date to the period between the time of TUTANKHAMUN (1336–1327 BC) in the late 18th Dynasty and Rameses II (1279–1213 BC) in the early 19th. The rediscoveries have included the tomb of Maya, the treasury official of Tutankhamun, and that of his colleague, the generalissimo HOREMHEB (1323– 1295 BC), who later became king and was buried in a royal tomb (KV 57) in the Valley of the Kings at Thebes. In the cliffs towards the Early Dynastic remains at the northern end of the Saqqara plateau, a French expedition led by Alain Zivie has also discovered the tomb of Aperia (or Aper-el), who was northern vizier during the reigns of AKHENATEN (1352–1336 BC) and Tutankhamun, thus probably indicating that Memphite officials continued to govern from Memphis even when a new capital had briefly been established at EL-AMARNA.

There was also New Kingdom activity in northwestern Saqqara, in the form of the hypogea (tomb chamber) of the sacred APIS bull, which began to be buried in the underground galleries of the SERAPEUM from at

least the time of Amenhotep III (1390–1352 BC) until the Roman period. By the Late Period (747–332 BC) onwards, large numbers of SACRED ANIMALS were being buried in huge quantities in the vast underground catacombs at the north end of the site; these mummified animals and birds included cows identified as the 'Mothers of Apis', as well as CYNOCEPHALUS baboons, hawks and IBISES. The area was probably chosen for a sacred animal necropolis because of its traditional connection with Imhotep, who had become identified with THOTH, a god particularly associated with baboons and ibises. The texts suggest that rams sacred to the god Banebdjedet (see MENDES), as well as the calves of the Apis bull, may also have been buried in this area, although the actual galleries have not yet been located. Further to the east, there were burials of dogs or jackals connected with the Anubeion (see ANUBIS), and of cats connected with the Bubasteion (see BASTET). So many cats were buried in this part of Saqqara that their mummified remains were deposited in many of the earlier private funerary monuments, including the nearby tomb of Aper-el.

Private tombs of post-New Kingdom date 26th and 27th Dynasties are also located near the pyramid of Unas. Many of the artists decorating tombs of the 26th Dynasty (or SAITE PERIOD) deliberately copied a great deal of the earlier funerary art at Saqqara. Tombs of the 30th Dynasty (380–343 BC) and Greco-Roman period (332 BC–AD 395) are clustered mainly on the northern side of the Step Pyramid, and towards the Serapeum.

Since many of the tombs at Saqqara were constructed from unusually small stone blocks (particularly during the New Kingdom), they could easily be dismantled to provide a ready source of building stone for later building operations. Much of the monastery of Apa Jeremias, to the south of the Unas causeway, for instance, was constructed from such reused blocks. During the time of the monastery, a small Coptic settlement was established to the southeast, close to the valley temple of Unas.

W. B. EMERY, *Great tombs of the first dynasty*, 3 vols (Cairo and London, 1949–58).

J. D. RAY, 'The world of North Saqqara', *WA*, 10 (2) (1978) 149–57.

G. T. MARTIN, 'The New Kingdom necropolis at Saqqara', *Acts of the First International Congress of Egyptology*, ed. W. F. Reinecke (Berlin, 1979), 457–63.

—, *The sacred animal necropolis at north Saqqara* (London, 1981).

J. MALEK, 'Saqqara, Nekropolen NR', *Lexikon der Ägyptologie* V, ed. W. Helck, E. Otto and W. Westendorf (Wiesbaden, 1984), 410–12.

G. T. MARTIN, *The hidden tombs of Memphis* (London, 1991).

J. VAN DIJK, *The New Kingdom necropolis of Memphis: historical and iconographical studies* (Groningen, 1993).

Sarapis *see* SERAPIS

sarcophagus *see* COFFINS AND SARCOPHAGI

Satet (Satis)

Goddess associated with the island of Elephantine near ASWAN and guardian of the southern frontiers of Egypt. She was usually depicted as a woman wearing the white CROWN of Upper Egypt, with ANTELOPE horns on either side of it. From the New Kingdom onwards, she was regarded as the wife of the creator god KHNUM. She was also considered to be the mother of ANUKET the huntress. The principal cult centre of Satet at Elephantine (on the site of an earlier Predynastic shrine) was excavated by a German expedition during the 1980s and 1990s.

Although she was most commonly worshipped in the region of Aswan, her name has also been found inscribed on jars excavated from the subterranean galleries of the Step Pyramid of Djoser at SAQQARA, and she is mentioned in the PYRAMID TEXTS as a goddess specifically concerned with purifying the deceased. Her temple at Elephantine is situated at the point at which the first waters of the annual Nile INUNDATION would be heard before the flood itself became visible. This geographical situation would perhaps have emphasized the aspects of her role relating to fertility. In her function as protectress of the southern border she was considered to repel Egypt's enemies with her arrows.

G. ROEDER, 'Sothis und Satis', *ZÄS* 45 (1908), 22–30.

D. VALBELLE, *Satis et Anoukis* (Mainz, 1981).

G. DREYER, *Der Tempel der Satet: die Funde der Frühzeit und des Alten Reiches* (Mainz, 1986).

Satis *see* SATET

scarab

Common type of amulet, seal or ring-bezel found in Egypt, Nubia and Syria–Palestine from the 6th Dynasty until the Ptolemaic period (*c.*2345–30 BC). The earliest were purely amuletic and uninscribed; it was only during the Middle Kingdom (2055–1650 BC) that they were used as seals. The scarab seal is so called because it was made in the shape of the sacred scarab beetle (*Scarabaeus sacer*), which was personified by KHEPRI, a sun-god associated with resurrection. The flat underside of the scarab, carved in stone or moulded in faience or glass, was usually decorated with designs or inscriptions, sometimes incorporating a royal name. Scarabs, however, have proved to be an unreliable means of dating archaeological contexts, since the royal name is often that of a long-dead ruler; Menkheperra, the prenomen of Thutmose III (1479–1425 BC), being a particularly common example.

During the reign of AMENHOTEP III (1390–1352 BC), a series of unusually large

Glazed steatite commemorative scarab of Amenhotep III describing a lion hunt undertaken by the king. 18th Dynasty, c.1360 BC, H. 8.5 cm. (EA29438)

scarabs were produced to celebrate certain events or aspects of Amenhotep's reign, from the hunting of bulls and lions to the listing of the titles of Queen TIY. There were also a number of funerary types of scarab, such as the large 'winged scarab' (virtually always made of blue faience and incorporated into the bead nets covering mummies), and the 'HEART scarab' (usually inscribed with Chapter 30b of the BOOK OF THE DEAD), which was included in burials from at least the 13th Dynasty (1795–1650 BC) onwards.

The term *scaraboid* is used to describe a seal or amulet which has the same ovoid shape as a scarab but may have its back carved in the form of some creature other than the scarab beetle. This appears to have developed out of the practice of carving two-dimensional animal forms on the flat underside of the scarab, which is known as early as the First Intermediate Period (2181–2055 BC).

P. E. NEWBERRY, *Ancient Egyptian scarabs: an introduction to Egyptian seals and signet rings* (London, 1906; repr. Chicago, 1979).

C. BLANKENBERG-VAN DELDEN, *The large commemorative scarabs of Amenhotep III* (Leiden, 1969).

E. HORNUNG and E. STAEHELIN, *Skarabäen und andere Siegelamulette aus Basler Sammlungen* (Mainz, 1976).

M. MALAISE, *Les scarabées de coeur dans l'Egypte ancienne* (Brussels, 1978).

B. JAEGER, *Essai de classification des scarabées Menkheperré* (Göttingen, 1982).

G. T. MARTIN, *Scarabs, cylinders and other ancient Egyptian seals* (Warminster, 1985).

C. ANDREWS, *Amulets of ancient Egypt* (London, 1994), 50–9.

science

The need to solve particular problems, such as the moving of large weights of stone, or the calculation of the height or angles of PYRAMIDS, was usually the inspiration for particular developments in Egyptian 'science', which does not seem to have existed as a word or concept in its own right. Research appears not to have been undertaken for its own sake, and no attempt was made to derive general laws, such as mathematical theorems, from practical solutions. In a society in which religion played a major role it is unsurprising to find that pure research was not conducted. Any phenomenon could be explained by reference to the actions of the gods, and such science as there was may be seen as practical measures, such as the prediction of the Nile INUNDATION (see NILOMETERS) and the construction of temples and funerary complexes.

Nevertheless, the Egyptians were clearly capable of keeping accurate scientific records, when necessary, and such surviving documents as the Edwin Smith Medical Papyrus (New York Historical Society) even suggest that they sometimes conducted what amount to scientific experiments. Similarly, the attention to astronomy in the development of the CALENDAR shows careful observation, although they do not seem to have sought reasons for the discrepancy between the seasons and their calendar, a phenomenon which was due to the need for an additional quarter-day each year.

There are undoubtedly still aspects of ancient Egyptian technology that remain poorly understood (such as the precise methods by which many of the monuments were constructed), but there is no reason to believe that the Egyptians had any special hidden knowledge that has since been lost.

See also ASTRONOMY AND ASTROLOGY; MAGIC; MATHEMATICS and MEDICINE.

O. NEUGEBAUER, *The exact sciences in antiquity*, 2nd ed. (Providence, 1957).

R. J. GILLINGS, *Mathematics in the time of the pharaohs* (New York, 1982).

W. WESTENDORF, 'Wissenschaft', *Lexikon der Ägyptologie* VI, ed. W. Helck, E. Otto and W. Westendorf (Wiesbaden, 1986), 1278–9.

M. CLAGETT, *Ancient Egyptian science*, 2 vols (Philadelphia, 1989).

scorpion

Arachnid which, like the SERPENT, became the object of cults and spells from the earliest times in Egypt, doubtless principally because of the fear of its sting. Two main species of scorpion are found in Egypt: the paler, more poisonous *Buthridae* and the darker, relatively harmless *Scorpionidae*. The scorpion ideogram, one of the earliest known hieroglyphic signs, was depicted on wooden and ivory labels found in the late Predynastic/Early Dynastic royal cemetery at ABYDOS and also among the cache of cult equipment in the Early Dynastic temple at HIERAKONPOLIS. A Protodynastic ruler called SCORPION was portrayed on the 'Scorpion macehead' from Hierakonpolis.

The goddess SERKET was the principal divine personification of the scorpion (although Isis was also said to have been protected from her enemies by seven scorpions), and was usually depicted with a scorpion perched on her head. Another, less well-known deity, the god Shed (also described as 'the saviour'), was linked with the scorpion and considered to afford protection against its sting; two stelae dedicated to Shed were found

Line-drawing of the relief scene on the Scorpion macehead from Hierakonpolis, showing King Scorpion wearing the white crown and conducting a ritual, c.3100 BC. (DRAWN BY RICHARD PARKINSON AFTER MARIAN COX)

in a chapel associated with the workmen's village at EL-AMARNA. Images of scorpions are also depicted on *cippi*, a type of stele used to ward off scorpion stings and snake bites from the Late Period onwards (see HORUS). See also TA-BITJET.

H. KANTER, 'Giftschlangen und Skorpione Nordafrikas', *Die Sahara und ihre Randgebiet* I, ed. H. SCHIFFERS (Munich, 1971).

E. HORNUNG and E. STAEHELIN, *Skarabäen und andere Siegelamulette aus Basler Sammlungen* (Mainz, 1976), 131–3.

J.-C. GOYON, 'Hededyt: Isis-scorpion et Isis au scorpion: en marge du papyrus de Brooklyn 47.218.50', *BIFAO* 78 (1978), 439–58.

P. BEHRENS, 'Skorpion', *Lexikon der Ägyptologie* v, ed. W. Helck, E. Otto and W. Westendorf (Wiesbaden, 1984), 987–9.

F. KÁNEL, '*La nèpe et le scorpion': un monographie sur la déesse Serket* (Paris, 1984).

Scorpion (*c.*3150 BC)

Name held by two Protodynastic rulers, one of whom was perhaps buried in Tomb U-j of the Umm el-Qaʿab cemetery at ABYDOS.

A fragmentary pear-shaped limestone macehead (Ashmolean Museum, Oxford), bearing a depiction of a man wearing the white CROWN of Upper Egypt and identified as King Scorpion, was excavated from the 'main deposit' in the temple precinct at HIERAKONPOLIS in 1896–8. The stratigraphic context of the 'Scorpion macehead' was poorly recorded by the excavators, James Quibell and Frederick Green, but the style of its decoration almost certainly dates it to the late Predynastic period when the early Egyptian state was first appearing (*c.*3150 BC). Like the NARMER palette and macehead, it is decorated with a raised relief depiction of an early pharaoh

engaged in ritualistic activities. On the Scorpion macehead this royal figure, identified by scorpion and rosette ideograms, wears the white crown of Upper Egypt and is apparently excavating a ceremonial irrigation canal with the help of attendants.

Tomb U-j at Abydos was excavated by a team of German archaeologists in 1988, revealing a twelve-chambered subterranean tomb, originally roofed with wood, matting and mud-brick. Although it had been plundered in antiquity, one chamber still contained over four hundred vessels imported from southern Palestine, and the excavation of the burial chamber revealed fragments of a wooden shrine and an ivory model *heka*-sceptre (see CROWNS), suggesting that the tomb's owner was a ruler. Throughout the site there were large quantities of fragments of pottery dating to the late Predynastic (NAQADA) period, many of which bore ink inscriptions consisting of the scorpion hieroglyph; it is considered unlikely, however, that this Scorpion was the same ruler as the figure represented on the Scorpion macehead.

J. E. QUIBELL and F. W. GREEN, *Hierakonpolis*, 2 vols (London, 1900–2).

A. J. ARKELL, 'Was King Scorpion Menes?', *Antiquity* 46 (1963), 221–2.

E. J. BAUMGARTEL, 'Scorpion and rosette and the fragment of the large Hierakonpolis macehead', *ZÄS* 92 (1966), 9–14.

M. A. HOFFMAN, *Egypt before the pharaohs* (London, 1980), 312–17.

G. DREYER, 'Umm el-Qaab: Nachuntersuchungen im frühzeitlichen Königsfriedhof 5./6. Vorbericht', *MDAIK* 49 (1993), 23–62.

scribe

Term used to translate the Egyptian word *sesh*, which was applied not only to clerks or copyists but to the class of bureaucratic official around whom the entire Egyptian political, economic and religious system revolved (see ADMINISTRATION). Throughout the Pharaonic period it is likely that only a small percentage of the population was literate, and the scribal élite tended to pass on their profession from father to son, thus enabling power to be retained by the same family groups over long periods. The prestige attributed to the scribal profession is indicated by the popularity of the 'scribe statue', portraying members of the élite

in typical cross-legged scribal pose, even if they had never served as professional scribes.

Many of the HIERATIC texts used in the EDUCATION of scribes, in preference to the slower and more ceremonial HIEROGLYPHS, consisted of descriptions of the comfort and prestige enjoyed by scribes, in contrast to the rigours of manual labour (see WISDOM LITERATURE and LITERATURE). Much of the work and training of scribes is thought to have taken place in an institution known as the HOUSE OF LIFE.

The hieroglyphic signs used for the terms 'scribe' and 'writing' were both essentially depictions of the scribal equipment, consisting of a stone or wooden PALETTE containing two cakes of ink (usually red and black), a leather bag or pot holding water, and a set of reed brushes. During the Pharaonic period, the brushes were made from the stem of *Junctus maritimus*, but from the Ptolemaic period (332–30 BC) onwards reed pens cut from the stems of *Phragmites aegyptiaca* were more frequently used. The surfaces on which scribes wrote varied from simple OSTRACA (chips of stone and potsherds) to more expensive manufactured materials such as PAPYRUS, leather sheets and thinly plastered wooden boards.

R. J. WILLIAMS, 'Scribal training in ancient Egypt', *JAOS* 92 (1972), 214–21.

J. R. BAINES, 'Literacy and ancient Egyptian society', *Man* 18 (1983), 572–99.

RIGHT Quartzite statue of the chamberlain Pesshuper, who is holding a papyrus roll in his left hand in the attitude of a scribe. 25th or 26th Dynasty, provenance unknown, H. 53 cm. (EA1514)

Sea Peoples

Loose confederation of peoples of the eastern Mediterranean, who attempted to settle in Syria–Palestine and Egypt between the thirteenth and twelfth centuries BC. The names and characteristics of the individual peoples, some of whom probably originated from the Aegean and Asia Minor, are known from reliefs at MEDINET HABU and KARNAK as well as from the text of the Great Harris Papyrus (now in the British Museum), a historical text at the end of a list of temple endowments from

Detail of the head of a Sherden soldier from the reliefs depicting the battle of Qadesh on the outer wall of the temple of Rameses II at Abydos. (I. SHAW)

the reign of RAMESES III (1184–1153 BC). It is clear from these sources that the Sea Peoples were not bands of plunderers but part of a great migration of displaced peoples. When they moved overland, the warriors were generally accompanied by their wives and families carrying their possessions in ox-drawn carts; there was a clear intention to settle in the areas through which they passed.

Their first attack on Egypt took place in the fifth regnal year of the 19th-Dynasty ruler MERENPTAH (1213–1203 BC). The LIBYANS, allied with these migrant peoples, named as the Ekwesh, Lukka, Meshwesh, Shekelesh, Sherden and Teresh, launched an attack on the Delta. Merenptah gained a victory, killing more than six thousand of them and routing the rest. He then recorded his victory on one of the walls of the temple of Amun at Karnak and on the so-called ISRAEL Stele in his funerary temple.

In the eighth regnal year of Rameses III, the Sea Peoples returned. They had perhaps already brought about the destruction of the HITTITE empire, and are probably to be held responsible for the sacking of the client city of Ugarit on the Syrian coast as well as cities

such as Alalakh in northern Syria. This time the list included the Denen, Peleset, Shekelesh, Sherden, Tjeker, Teresh and Weshwesh, and the attack came by both land and sea. Rameses III's troops in Palestine defeated the land-based attack, while the Egyptian navy destroyed the enemy fleet on the Delta coast. Like Merenptah, Rameses III recorded his victory in stone, on the outer walls of his mortuary temple at Medinet Habu, while the compiler of the Great Harris Papyrus included them in a broader account of the campaigns of his reign.

Study of the 'tribal' names recorded by the Egyptians and Hittites has shown that some groups, notably the Denen, Lukka and the Sherden, were already active by the reign of Akhenaten (1352–1336 BC), while the Lukka and Sherden were also recorded, along with the Peleset, serving as mercenaries in the army of Rameses II (1279–1213 BC) at the BATTLE OF QADESH.

Attempts have been made to link the various groups of Sea Peoples with particular homelands, or at least with the places in which they eventually settled. The Ekwesh have been identified with the Homeric Achaean Greeks, the Peleset with the Biblical Philistines (who gave their name to Palestine), and, more contentiously, the Sherden with Sardinia.

G. A. WAINWRIGHT, 'Some Sea-Peoples and others in the Hittite archives', *JEA* 25 (2) (1939), 148–53.

G. A. WAINWRIGHT, 'Some Sea Peoples', *JEA* 47 (1961), 71–90.

R. STADELMANN, 'Die Abwehr der Seevölker unter Ramses III', *Saeculum* 19 (1968), 156–71.

W. HELCK, *Die Beziehungen Ägyptens und Vorderasiens zur Agäis bis ins 7.Jh. v. Chr.* (Darmstadt, 1979).

N. K. SANDARS, *Sea Peoples* (London, 1985).

Sebek *see* SOBEK

Second Intermediate Period

(1650–1550 BC)

As the MIDDLE KINGDOM (2055–1650 BC) went into decline, groups of Asiatics appear to have migrated into the Delta and established settlements (see HYKSOS). The Second Intermediate Period began with the establishment of the 15th Dynasty at Avaris (TELL EL-DAB'A) in the Delta. The 15th-Dynasty rulers were largely contemporary with the line of minor Hyksos rulers who comprise the 16th Dynasty. The precise dates of these two dynasties, and more particularly their rulers, are uncertain, as are those of the 17th Dynasty, the last of the period. The 17th Dynasty ruled from Thebes, effectively

acting as the 'native' Egyptian government, as opposed to the foreign northern rulers.

Having established their capital at Avaris, the political influence of the Hyksos appears to have gradually spread, with the development of centres such as TELL EL-YAHUDIYA and TELL EL-MASKHUTA, and the probable seizure of the important Egyptian city of MEMPHIS. The discovery of a small number of objects inscribed with the names of Hyksos kings at sites such as Knossos, Baghdad and Boghazköy (as well as the remains of Minoan frescos at 15th-Dynasty Avaris) suggests that the new rulers maintained trading links with the Near East and the Aegean. Seals at the Nubian site of KERMA bear the name Sheshi, apparently a corrupted form of Salitis, the earliest known Hyksos king. The presence of these seals probably indicates that there was an alliance between the Hyksos and the kingdom of Kerma, which would have helped them to counter the opposition of the 17th Dynasty in Upper Egypt. The last rulers of the 17th Dynasty, SEQENENRA TAA II and KAMOSE, campaigned openly against the Hyksos, and AHMOSE I, the first ruler of the 18th Dynasty, was eventually able to drive them from power, thus establishing the NEW KINGDOM.

J. VON BECKERATH, *Untersuchungen zur politischen Geschichte der zweiten Zwischenzeit in Ägypten* (Glückstadt and New York, 1965).

J. VAN SETERS, *The Hyksos, a new investigation* (New Haven, 1966).

B. J. KEMP, 'Old Kingdom, Middle Kingdom and Second Intermediate Period', *Ancient Egypt: a social history*, ed. B. G. Trigger et al. (Cambridge, 1983), 71–182.

D. B. REDFORD, *Egypt, Canaan and Israel in ancient times* (Princeton, 1992), 98–129.

Sedeinga

Religious site in Upper Nubia, consisting of the ruins of a temple of Amenhotep III (1390–1352 BC), located only a few kilometres to the north of the temple of SOLEB. The Sedeinga temple was probably dedicated to the cult of Amenhotep III's wife, Queen TIY, and the modern toponym appears to be a considerably distorted version of the ancient name of the temple (*hwt-Tiy*). Certain significant parts of the temple have survived, such as columns with HATHOR-headed capitals and a fragment of relief bearing a representation of Tiy in the form of a SPHINX, which was perhaps also intended to suggest a leonine form of the 'eye of HORUS'. The temple was restored and elaborated during the reign of the 25th Dynasty pharaoh TAHARQO (690–664 BC).

M. SCHIFF GIORGINI, 'Première campagne des

fouilles à Sedeinga 1963–4', *Kush* 13 (1965), 112–30.

J. LECLANT, 'Taharqa à Sedeinga', *Festschrift W. Westendorf* (Göttingen, 1984), 1113–20.

sed festival (Egyptian *heb-sed*: 'royal jubilee')

Ritual of renewal and regeneration, which was intended to be celebrated by the king only after a reign of thirty years had elapsed. In practice the surviving inscriptions and monuments associated with this festival seem to show that many kings whose entire reigns were much shorter than thirty years have left evidence of the celebration of their *sed* festivals. There are two possible interpretations of this situation: first, that many kings actually celebrated the *sed* festivals well before the requisite thirty years had elapsed, or, second, that they ordered the depiction of the ritual in anticipation of the actual event happening later in the reign.

The *sed* festival (which derives its name from a jackal-god called Sed, closely related to WEPWAWET of Asyut), is inextricably linked with the Egyptian perception of KINGSHIP, being documented from a very early stage in Egyptian history. The two essential elements of the ceremony (the paying of homage to the enthroned king and the ritual of territorial claim) are depicted on an ebony label from the tomb of King DEN at Abydos (now in the British Museum, see illustration above). The right-hand corner of the label shows the king, at first, seated inside one of the special festival pavilions, wearing the double CROWN, and, later, running between two sets of three cairns or boundary markers (probably symbolizing the BORDERS of Egypt). The two scenes are framed by the king's name in a SEREKH frame on the left and the hieroglyphic sign for a regnal year on the right.

The first royal mortuary complexes were concerned with the king's enactment of the *sed* festival. The eastern side of the Step-Pyramid complex of Djoser at SAQQARA incorporates the earliest surviving architectural setting for the festival, in the form of a courtyard surrounded by 'dummy' chapels, each representing the shrines of the local gods in different provinces. At the southern end of the court is the base of a double pavilion which would have held two thrones like the one shown on the ebony label of Den. It is presumed that the king would have sat on each throne dressed in the Upper and Lower Egyptian regalia respectively, thus symbolizing his dominion over the 'two lands' of Egypt.

In the adjoining court to the south of the pyramid traces were found of boundary markers like those between which the king was

LEFT *Block of relief from the Red Chapel of Hatshepsut at Karnak, showing the queen taking part in one of the rituals of her* sed *festival, with the boundary-markers visible behind her. 18th Dynasty, c.1473–1458 BC. (I. SHAW)*

BELOW *Oil-jar label bearing a scene depicting the* sed *festival of King Den. In the upper right-hand corner the king is shown running between two markers probably representing the borders of Egypt. 1st Dynasty, c.2900 BC, ebony, H. 5.5 cm. (EA32650)*

required to run. A relief from the subterranean chambers of the pyramid shows Djoser himself running between two sets of cairns; this dynamic image of the running pharaoh (often holding strange implements) continued to be depicted in *sed*-festival reliefs throughout the Pharaonic period, as in the case of one of the blocks from the red chapel of Hatshepsut (1473–1458 BC) at KARNAK temple.

From the 4th Dynasty onwards the importance of the *sed* festival in the royal mortuary complex was to some extent eclipsed by reliefs associated with the cult of the dead king, but there were still large numbers of buildings constructed and decorated in connection with the royal jubilee, not least the mortuary temple of Amenhotep III (1390–1352 BC) at Thebes, the Aten temple of AKHENATEN in east Karnak and the *sed*-festival court of OSORKON II (874–850 BC) at Bubastis (TELL BASTA).

Although there is enormous continuity in the depictions of *sed* festivals from Den to Osorkon, it seems from the descriptions of the three *sed* festivals celebrated by Amenhotep III that the liturgy and symbolism of the ceremony could sometimes be adapted to suit the occasion or the place. The huge lake excavated to the east of the palace of Amenhotep III at MALKATA appears to have functioned as the setting for a reinvented *sed* festival, in which the king and the divine statuary were carried along on barges, in imitation of the voyage of the solar BARK through the netherworld.

H. KEES, 'Die weisse Kapelle Sesostris' I. in Karnak und das Sedfest', *MDAIK* 16 (1958), 194–213.

E. UPHILL, 'The Egyptian sed-festival rites', *JNES* 24 (1965), 365–83.

E. HORNUNG and E. STAEHLIN, *Studien zum Sedfest* (Geneva, 1974).

W. J. MURNANE, 'The sed festival: a problem in historical method', *MDAIK* 37 (1981), 369–76.

sedge

Term used to refer to the plant, the hieroglyph for which formed part of the ROYAL TITULARY as early as the 1st Dynasty (3100–2890 BC), when one of the titles of the king of Upper Egypt was 'he who belongs to the sedge' (apparently referring to the eternal, divine aspect of the kingship). From the unification of Egypt (*c.*3100 BC) onwards, the sedge and the bee became part of the titulary of the King of Upper and Lower Egypt: *nesw-bit* ('he of the sedge and the bee').

S. QUIRKE, *Who were the pharaohs?* (London, 1990), 11, 23.

Sekhemib *see* PERIBSEN

Sekhemkhet (2648–2640 BC)

One of the principal rulers of the 3rd Dynasty, whose reign probably lasted for only about eight years. It has been suggested that he may be the same ruler as Djoserti (or Djoserteti) whom the TURIN ROYAL CANON, a king list preserved on a papyrus dating to the reign of Rameses II (1279–1213 BC), lists as the successor of DJOSER Netjerikhet (2667–2648 BC). It was Sekhemkhet who sent one of the earliest expeditions to the TURQUOISE mines at Wadi Maghara in the Sinai, where three rock-carved depictions of the king (still *in situ*) show him in the act of smiting an Asiatic prisoner.

His unfinished step-pyramid complex lies close to the southwest corner of the Step Pyramid of his predecessor, Djoser, at SAQQARA; it was excavated by Zakaria Goneim during the period 1951–9 and by Jean-Philippe Lauer in 1963–76. Sekhemkhet's name was found inscribed on the clay stoppers of jars from the pyramid. The burial chamber contained a closed travertine sarcophagus with a wreath placed on top, which was nevertheless found to be completely empty, suggesting that either the burial chamber or the sarcophagus may have been duplicates, perhaps serving some ritual purpose or designed to fool tomb-robbers. In the so-called 'south mastaba' at the south end of the enclosure (similar to that in Djoser's complex), the excavations revealed a wooden coffin of 3rd Dynasty type, which was found to contain the skeleton of an eighteen-month-old child of unknown identity.

M. Z. GONEIM, *The buried pyramid* (London, 1956).

—, *Horus Sekhem-khet: the unfinished step pyramid at Saqqara* I (Cairo, 1957).

J.-P. LAUER, 'Recherche et découverte du tombeau sud de l'Horus Sekhem-khet à Saqqarah', *BIE* 48–9 (1969), 121–31.

I. E. S. EDWARDS, *The pyramids of Egypt*, 5th ed. (Harmondsworth, 1993), 58–65.

sekhem sceptre

Symbol of power which was sometimes shown in the hand of the king from the Early Dynastic period (3100–2686 BC) onwards, but which also served as a badge of office for the highest officials, who are commonly shown holding it in funerary reliefs. When the king held a *sekhem* sceptre in his right hand he would usually hold a MACE or censer in the left, whereas officials generally held only a staff in the left hand if the *sekhem* was in the right.

The term *sekhem* meant 'power' or 'might' and was associated with a number of deities (as well as being incorporated into such royal names as SEKHEMKHET). Thus the name of the lioness-goddess SEKHMET means 'she who is powerful', while the god OSIRIS was sometimes described as 'great *sekhem* who dwells in the THINITE nome'. The term was also associated with ANUBIS, another god of Abydos, who, as god of the underworld and Khentimentiu ('chief of the westerners'), had a particular association with the royal cemetery and the supposed burial place of Osiris at Abydos. The *sekhem* sceptre was sometimes depicted behind the reclining figure of Anubis.

Stele of Sarenenutet, steward of the double granary, showing him seated and holding a sekhem *sceptre. 12th Dynasty, c.1950 BC, limestone, from Abydos, H. 52 cm. (EA585)*

Occasionally the sceptre was shown with two eyes or a face carved into it.

The sceptre also played a role in the mortuary cult, in that it was often held by individuals making offerings. It appears that the sceptre was waved over the items being offered to the KA of the deceased. A gilded *sekhem* sceptre was found in the tomb of Tutankhamun (1336–1327 BC; KV 62), and on its back were carved five registers showing a slaughtered bull, which may possibly have signified the number of times that the sceptre was waved during the offering ritual.

R. H. WILKINSON, *Reading Egyptian art* (London, 1992), 182–3.

Sekhmet (Sakhmet)

Lioness-goddess whose name simply meant 'she who is powerful'. She personified the aggressive aspects of female deities and acted as the consort of PTAH and probably the mother of NEFERTEM in the Memphite TRIAD. She was usually portrayed as a woman with a lioness's head but, as the daughter of the sun-god RA, she was also closely linked with the royal *uraeus* in her role as the fire-breathing 'EYE OF RA' (see also WADJYT). The PYRAMID TEXTS twice mention that the king was conceived by Sekhmet.

Because of the rise to power of the Theban rulers of the New Kingdom (1550–1069 BC),

the Theban triad (AMUN, MUT and KHONS) became correspondingly more important and began to 'absorb' the attributes of other deities. This meant that Sekhmet was increasingly represented as an aggressive manifestation of the goddess Mut, and large numbers of statues of the lioness-goddess were therefore erected by AMENHOTEP III (1390–1352 BC) both in the temple of Mut at KARNAK and in his mortuary temple in western THEBES.

J. YOYOTTE, 'Une monumentale litanie de granit: les Sekhmet d'Aménophis III et la conjuration permanente de la déesse dangereuse', *BSFE* 87–8 (1980), 46–75.

P. GERMOND, *Sekhmet et la protection du monde* (Geneva, 1981).

Two statues of the goddess Sekhmet from Thebes. 18th Dynasty, c.1400 BC, H. 2.18 m, 2.28 m. (EA62, 80)

Selkis *see* SERKET

Semainean *see* PREDYNASTIC PERIOD

Semerkhet (*c.*2900 BC)

Penultimate ruler of the 1st Dynasty, who succeeded ANEDJIB on the throne and was probably buried in Tomb U at Abydos. His name is not listed on the Saqqara Tablet (a Ramesside KING LIST) and, in contrast to the other 1st-Dynasty rulers, no MASTABA tombs of his reign have yet been discovered at Saqqara; it has therefore been suggested that he usurped Anedjib's jubilee vessels in order to bolster somewhat shaky claims to the throne. On the other hand, his *nesw-bit* name ('he of the sedge and bee', see ROYAL TITULARY), Semenptah, is probably that rendered by MANETHO as Semempses, and he is also mentioned on the PALERMO STONE (a 5th-Dynasty king list). It is also perhaps significant, in terms of his legitimacy, that his tomb at Abydos is larger and more elaborate than that of Anedjib.

W. M. F. PETRIE, *The royal tombs of the first dynasty* I (London, 1900).

W. B. EMERY, *Archaic Egypt* (London, 1961), 84–6.

A. J. SPENCER, *Early Egypt* (London, 1993), 83–4.

Semna

Fortified town established in the reign of Senusret I (1965–1920 BC) on the west bank of the Nile at the southern end of a series of FORTRESSES founded during the 12th Dynasty (1985–1795 BC) in the second-cataract area of Lower Nubia. The Semna gorge, at the southern edge of ancient Egypt, was the narrowest part of the Nile valley. It was here, at this strategic location, that the 12th-Dynasty pharaohs built a cluster of four mud-brick fortresses: Semna, Kumma, Semna South and Uronarti (all covered by the waters of Lake Nasser since the completion of the ASWAN HIGH DAM in 1971). The rectangular Kumma fortress, the L-shaped Semna fortress (on the opposite bank) and the much smaller square fortress of Semna South were each investigated by the American archaeologist George REISNER in 1924 and 1928. Semna and Kumma also included the remains of temples, houses and cemeteries dating to the New Kingdom (1550–1069 BC), which would have been roughly contemporary with such Lower Nubian towns as AMARA West and SESEBI-SUDLA, when the second cataract region had become part of an Egyptian 'empire', rather than simply a frontier zone.

G. A. REISNER, 'Excavations in Egypt and Ethiopia', *BMFA* 22 (1925), 18–28.

D. DUNHAM and J. M. A. JANSSEN, *Second cataract forts* I: *Semna, Kumma* (Boston, 1960), 5–112.

B. J. KEMP, *Ancient Egypt: anatomy of a civilization* (London, 1989), 174–6.

Senenmut (*fl. c.*1470 BC)

Chief steward in the reign of HATSHEPSUT (1473–1458 BC), who appears to have been born at ARMANT of relatively humble parents (Ramose and Hatnefer). He entered royal ser-

Seated statue of Senenmut nursing Princess Neferura, to whom he was tutor, within his cloak. 18th Dynasty, c.1470 BC, black granite, from Karnak (?), H. 71 cm. (EA174)

vice in the reign of Thutmose II (1492–1479 BC), and under Hatshepsut he became the most influential member of the court. His numerous titles included the role of steward of Amun and tutor to Hatshepsut's only daughter, Neferura. There is no evidence that Senenmut ever married, and he is usually depicted only with his parents or with Neferura. This has led some scholars to speculate that he was the lover of Hatshepsut, although evidence for this theory is distinctly flimsy.

His responsibilities included the overseeing of royal building works at Thebes, a duty mentioned on one of his many surviving statues. It was probably as a result of his influence in construction projects that he had himself portrayed in the temple at DEIR EL-BAHRI, although his figures stand behind shrine doors, where they were not readily visible. He is also credited with organizing the transport and erection of the two great OBELISKS of Hatshepsut in the temple of Amun at KARNAK.

He built two tombs for himself; the first (TT71) is high on the hillside at Sheikh Abd el-

Qurna and still preserves a rock-cut BLOCK STATUE portraying him in his role as royal tutor, with Neferura seated on his lap. This is one of six surviving block statues of Senenmut and Neferura, although the rest are freestanding. About 150 OSTRACA were found in his tomb, including sketch-plans of the tomb itself and various literary texts. He later began a second grander tomb (TT353) to the east of the first court of the temple of Hatshepsut at DEIR EL-BAHRI, which is sometimes described as the 'secret tomb'. Its walls are decorated with scenes from the BOOK OF THE DEAD and its roof is the earliest known 'astronomical ceiling' (see ASTRONOMY AND ASTROLOGY). The tomb was never completed, and, like the images of Senenmut at Deir el-Bahri and elsewhere, it was defaced in antiquity. This defacement was probably caused by some kind of fall from grace, since there is no further record of Senenmut from late in the reign of Hatshepsut. Neferura is not attested after Hatshepsut's eleventh regnal year, and it has been suggested that Senenmut then sought to ally himself with Thutmose III (1479–1425 BC) with whom Hatshepsut was supposedly co-regent. Peter Dorman has suggested that Senenmut may well have outlived Hatshepsut and continued as an unrecorded official during the sole reign of Thutmose III.

W. C. HAYES, *Ostraka and name stones from the tomb of Sen-Mut (no. 71) at Thebes* (New York, 1942).

B. PORTER and R. L. B. MOSS, *Topographical bibliography* 1/1 (Oxford, 1960), 139–42, 417–18.

P. DORMAN, *The monuments of Senenmut: problems in historical methodology* (London, 1988).

—, *The tombs of Senenmut* (New York, 1991).

Senusret (Senwosret, Senusert, Sesostris)

'Birth name' taken by three kings of the 12th Dynasty (1985–1795 BC).

Senusret I Kheperkara (1965–1920 BC) was the second ruler of the 12th Dynasty, who succeeded to the throne after the assassination of his father AMENEMHAT I (1985–1955 BC), with whom he had ruled as coregent for up to a decade. The unusual circumstances of his accession form the background to the *Tale of Sinuhe* and the *Instruction of Amenemhat I*. He continued the policy of expansion in Lower Nubia and established a garrison at the fortress of BUHEN. As far as relations with Syria-Palestine were concerned, the policy was very different, concentrating on maintaining commercial and diplomatic links rather than achieving territorial gains. He protected the Delta region and the oases of the Western Desert from Libyan invasion by means of a series of military expeditions.

He had already begun a programme of temple construction during his coregency with his father, extending and embellishing most of the major temples, including those at KARNAK and HELIOPOLIS. His pyramid complex at EL-LISHT, near the new 12th-Dynasty capital, Itjtawy, was located to the south of that of Amenemhat I; the burial chambers of both these monuments are currently inaccessible. Two painted wooden figures, one wearing the white crown and the other the red crown, were excavated from the neighbouring MASTABA tomb of the priest Imhotep; these may possibly be portraits of Senusret I but have also been interpreted as dating to the 13th Dynasty (1795–1650 BC).

Senusret II Khakheperra (1880–1874 BC), the fourth ruler of the 12th Dynasty, succeeded Amenemhat II (1922–1878 BC) after a coregency. He constructed his funerary complex at EL-LAHUN, placing the entrance to the pyramid not on the north side, as in most other pyramids, but a short distance to the south, perhaps because the practice of aligning the monument with the circumpolar stars was considered less important than the security of the tomb. Stronger connections with the cult of Osiris may be indicated by the presence of a row of trees around the base of the pyramid as well as the first instances of balls of mud containing grain (see OSIRIS BED). The burial chamber, excavated by Flinders PETRIE in 1887–8, contained an empty red granite sarcophagus. In the vicinity of the valley temple Petrie also excavated the settlement of Kahun, which was originally built in order to house the community associated with the pyramid and the royal funerary cult.

During his reign, the tomb of Khnumhotep at BENI HASAN (BH3) records the arrival of a BEDOUIN trading party apparently bringing supplies of galena for use in cosmetics. This incident is indicative of the fact that Senusret's foreign policy was characterized by an expansion in commerce with western Asia and Nubia. He also inaugurated an ambitious irrigation system in the FAYUM REGION, which enabled large areas of new agricultural land to be brought under cultivation.

Senusret III Khakaura (1874–1855 BC) succeeded Senusret II, and was to be instrumental in re-shaping Egypt's internal and foreign affairs. His domestic policy centred on the re-organization of the administrative system. Since the Old Kingdom (2686–2181 BC), the major threat to royal power had probably come from the nomarchs, the provincial governors (see NOMES); a shift in the funerary patterns of the élite (a decline in provincial tombs) may

ern NUBIA. These three ministries (*waret*) were each headed by an official and an assistant.

In the preceding two reigns, there had been little military activity, and Nubian tribes had perhaps gradually moved northwards, toward the second cataract. Senusret III took military action against these tribes in his eighth, tenth and sixteenth regnal years, thus enabling the frontier to be established at SEMNA, south of the second cataract. This border was further secured by a series of eight FORTRESSES between Semna and BUHEN, further to the north, although it is not clear how many of these were built, and how many extended, by Senusret III. Communication between Elephantine and the fortresses was facilitated by the enlargement of a canal built by Pepy I (2321–2287 BC) near the island of Sehel, south of Aswan. So great was his hold on Nubia that

LEFT *Black granite statue of Senusret III, from Deir el-Bahri. 12th Dynasty, c.1860 BC, H. 1.22 m. (EA686)*

BELOW *The reconstructed White Chapel of Senusret I, which was found in fragments inside the 3rd pylon of Amenhotep III at Karnak. The exterior is decorated with lists of the Egyptian nomes (provinces). (P. T. NICHOLSON)*

indicate that Senusret III reduced their authority drastically by removing many of their established privileges. The means by which this was achieved is unclear, but henceforth it was the king's VIZIERS who oversaw all branches of administration. There were three viziers. one for the north, another for the south and a third for Elephantine (see ASWAN) and north-

by the New Kingdom the deified Senusret was worshipped in northern Nubia.

The king seems to have personally led a campaign into Palestine, and to have taken the town of Sekmem, probably to be equated with Shechem in the Mount Ephraim region, This is the only recorded campaign in western Asia during his reign, although useful insights concerning attitudes towards foreign enemies are provided by the EXECRATION TEXTS, many of which have been excavated at the Nubian fortress of Mirgissa. The names of Sekmem, Ashkelon, Byblos and Jerusalem are mentioned in these texts, as well as many of the Nubian peoples, including the Kushites and the MEDJAY.

Senusret constructed a temple to Montu, god of war, at the Upper Egyptian site of MEDAMUD, and chose DAHSHUR, at the southern end of the Memphite necropolis, as the site of his pyramid complex. The pyramid itself, however, has suffered from the overzealous investigations of Richard Vyse and John Perring, causing damage to its already weathered profile. In 1894–5 Jacques de Morgan undertook a more careful investigation, discovering a wealth of JEWELLERY in the tombs of women of the royal family in the vicinity. The site has recently been re-examined by Dieter Arnold on behalf of the Metropolitan Museum of Art, New York. Although the superstructure of the pyramid is in poor condition the subterranean chambers of the king are spectacular; the corridors are lined in fine white limestone, with a granite burial chamber and sarcophagus. However, there is no evidence that Senusret III was ever buried here. In 1994 the jewellery and sarcophagus of Nefret, the queen of Senusret III, were discovered.

After his death his feats were conflated with those of Senusret I and II, and by Classical times he was probably also confused with Rameses II (1279–1213 BC). He thus eventually became regarded as 'high Senusret', the archetypal Egyptian ruler.

K. LANGE, *Sesostris* (Munich, 1954).

P. LACAU and H. CHEVRIER, *Une chapelle de Sésostris ter à Karnak*, 2 vols (Paris, 1956–69).

G. POSENER, *Littérature et politique dans l'Egypte de la XII dynastie* (Paris, 1956).

H. GOEDICKE, 'Remarks on the hymns to Sesostris III', *JARCE* 7 (1968), 23–6.

W. K. SIMPSON, 'Sesostris II and Sesostris III', *Lexikon der Ägyptologie* v, ed. W. Helck, E. Otto and W. Westendorf (Wiesbaden, 1984), 899–906.

D. WILDUNG, *Sesostris und Amenemhet: Ägypten in Mittleren Reich* (Freiburg, 1984).

Senwosret *see* SENUSRET

Seqenenra Taa II (*c.*1560 BC)
Theban ruler of the 17th Dynasty, who began the series of campaigns against the HYKSOS rulers in the Delta, which were eventually to culminate in the liberation of Egypt by his son AHMOSE I (1550–1525 BC), the first ruler of the 18th Dynasty. The Ramesside tale of the *Quarrel of Apophis and Seqenenra*

(Papyrus Sallier I) consists of part of an eccentric account of Seqenenra's struggles with the Hyksos ruler Aauserra APEPI. Although his tomb has not been located, it probably lies somewhere in the Dra Abu el-Naga region of western Thebes, and fortunately his body was one of those preserved (along with Ahmose I's) in the DEIR EL-BAHRI mummy cache discovered in 1881. His head and neck had clearly been badly wounded, suggesting that he died in battle. A forensic examination of the body in the early 1970s succeeded in obtaining a good match between the gashes and the typical dimensions of a Palestinian axe-head of the correct date, confirming the suspicion that he died in a battle against the Hyksos, although more recent analysis of the skeleton has suggested that some of the wounds had been inflicted at a later date and that he may therefore have survived the first onslaught.

B. GUNN and A. H. GARDINER, 'New renderings of Egyptian texts II: The expulsion of the Hyksos', *JEA* 5 (1918), 36–56.

H. WINLOCK, 'The tombs of the kings of the seventeenth dynasty at Thebes', *JEA* 10 (1924), 217–77.

M. BIETAK and E. STROUHAL, 'Die Todesumstände des Pharaohs Sequenenre (17. Dynastie)', *Annalen des Naturhistorischen Museum, Wien* 78 (1974), 29–52.

C. VANDERSLEYEN, 'Un seul roi Taa sous la 17e dynastie', *GM* 63 (1983), 67–70.

Serabit el-Khadim *see* TURQUOISE

Serapeum
Term usually applied to buildings associated with the cult of the APIS bull or that of the later syncretic god SERAPIS. The Memphite Serapeum at SAQQARA, the burial-place of the Apis bull, consists of a series of catacombs to the northwest of the Step Pyramid of Djoser. From the 30th Dynasty onwards, funerary processions would have approached the Serapeum via a *dromos* (sacred way) running from the city of Memphis to the Saqqara plateau.

The Saqqara Serapeum was excavated in 1851 by Auguste Mariette, who was led to the site through his discovery of traces of some of the sphinxes lining the *dromos*, which are faithfully described by the Greek writer STRABO (*c.*63 BC–AD 21). The catacombs date back at least as early as the 18th Dynasty (1550–1295 BC) and continued in use until the Ptolemaic period (332–30 BC); they contain many massive granite sarcophagi weighing up to 80 tons, although all but one had been robbed of their burials. Mariette also found the

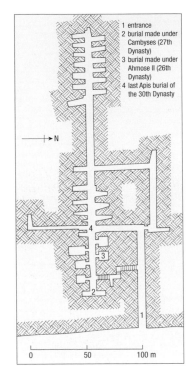

1 entrance
2 burial made under Cambyses (27th Dynasty)
3 burial made under Ahmose II (26th Dynasty)
4 last Apis burial of the 30th Dynasty

→N

0   50   100 m

Plan of the Serapeum at Saqqara.

burial of Prince Khaemwaset, a son of RAMESES II (1279–1213 BC), who had been responsible for constructing some of these vaults.

The Serapeum serving as the cult centre of Serapis was located at ALEXANDRIA, close to Pompey's pillar, but it was sacked by Christians when Theodosius (AD 379–95) issued an edict in AD 391, ordering it to be razed to the ground, and only the subterranean section has survived. Some of the underground chambers served for jackal burials associated with the temple of ANUBIS, while other parts were shelved to hold the temple LIBRARY. With the spread of the cult of Serapis, other such cult-centres were constructed, including the Greek holy site of Delos, which was founded by an Egyptian priest in the third century BC.

A. MARIETTE, *Le Sérapéum de Memphis*, ed. G. Maspero (Paris, 1882).

E. OTTO, *Beiträge zur Geschichte des Stierkulte in Ägypten* (Berlin, 1938).

J. VERCOUTTER, *Textes biographiques du Sérapéum de Memphis* (Paris, 1962).

M. MALININE, G. POSENER and J. VERCOUTTER, *Catalogue des stèles du Sérapéum de Memphis* I, 2 vols (Paris, 1968).

P. M. FRASER, *Ptolemaic Alexandria* I (Oxford, 1972), 246–76.

The underground catacomb known as the Serapeum was the burial place of the Apis bulls. Near the entrance, niches which once contained votive stelae can be seen, along with the lid of one of the massive bull sarcophagi. (P. T. NICHOLSON)

Serapis (Sarapis)

Composite god resulting from the fusion of the Egyptian god Osorapis (himself combining the gods OSIRIS and APIS) with attributes of a number of Hellenistic gods, notably Zeus, Helios, Hades, Asklepios and Dionysos. From the latter, Osorapis took solar, funerary, healing and fertility aspects, although in fact he already encompassed some of these. The fertility aspect of the god is emphasized by his protection of the corn supply, denoted by a corn measure (see MODIUS) on his head.

Serapis is first attested in the reign of PTOLEMY I Soter (305–285 BC) and was considered to be representative of the essence of Egyptian religion, while at the same time blending it with Greek theology. Unlike the Apis bull, the main cult-centre of Serapis was not at Memphis or Saqqara but at the Alexandrian SERAPEUM, which functioned as an important centre of learning. His consort was ISIS, whose cult was also popular among the Romans, and the pair came to embody the natural forces of male and female fertility. In Alexandrian iconography they were sometimes represented on door jambs as a pair of

human-headed serpents, the bearded one representing Serapis. His cult was adopted by the Romans, and spread very widely through the empire. One text mentions a temple of Serapis in Britain, and indeed a sculpted head of the god was found at the Walbrook Mithraeum in London. The Romans thus appear to have kept alive the very Egyptian animal deities that they are initially said to have despised.

L. VIDMAN, *Isis und Sarapis bei den Griechen und Römern* (Berlin, 1970).

P. M. FRASER, *Ptolemaic Alexandria* I (Oxford, 1972), 246–76.

J. E. STAMBAUGH, *Sarapis under the early Ptolemies* (Leiden, 1972).

W. HORNBOSTEL, *Sarapis* (Leiden, 1973).

G. J. F. KATER-SIBBES, *Preliminary catalogue of Sarapis monuments* (Leiden, 1973).

serdab (Arabic: 'cellar'; Egyptian *per-twt*: 'statue-house')

Room in MASTABA tombs of the Old Kingdom (2686–2181 BC), where statues of the KA of the deceased were usually placed. There were often eye-holes (known as the 'eyes of the ka-house') or a narrow slit in the wall of the chamber, both enabling the *ka* to leave the chamber and allowing offerings to pass through to the statues from the tomb chapel. The earliest *serdabs* in private mastaba tombs date to the 4th Dynasty (2613–2494 BC).

A. M. BLACKMAN, 'The ka-house and the serdab', *JEA* 3 (1916), 250–4.

G. A. REISNER, *The development of the Egyptian tomb down to the accession of Cheops* (Cambridge, MA, 1936), 267–9.

A. J. SPENCER, *Death in ancient Egypt* (Harmondsworth, 1982), 60–1.

serekh

Hieroglyphic symbol comprising the recessed panelling described in modern times as 'palace-façade' decoration, which is believed to have been modelled on the design of the earliest royal residences. The palace-façade design is imitated in mud-brick on the mastaba tombs of the Early Dynastic period (3100–2686 BC) and Old Kingdom (2686–2181 BC), on FALSE DOOR stelae, COFFINS, sarcophagi and numerous other funerary and ceremonial contexts throughout Egyptian history.

The term is usually employed to refer to a rectangular frame surmounted by the HORUS falcon, within which the king's 'Horus name' was written (see ROYAL TITULARY). This frame seems to have effectively symbolized the domain of Horus, the royal residence. Occasionally the royal name in its *serekh* surmounted by Horus was combined with a sculpture as in the statue

Granite stele bearing the serekh of Raneb from Mitrahina (Memphis). 2nd Dynasty, c.2850 BC, H 99 cm. (METROPOLITAN MUSEUM, NEW YORK, JOSEPH PULITZER BEQUEST 1960, 60,144)

of the 6th-Dynasty ruler Pepy I (2321–2287 BC; Brooklyn Museum, New York), where it forms the back of his throne. Such iconography is typical of the close relationship between Egyptian ART and writing. More spectacular examples are the monumental falcon panels which formed part of a palace-façade wall for the enclosure of the pyramid complex of Senusret I (1965–1920 BC) at EL-LISHT.

For a brief period, in the 2nd Dynasty (2890–2686 BC), SETH replaced Horus as the god surmounting the *serekh* (see PERIBSEN and KHASEKHEMWY), thus transforming it into a 'Seth name', but the change was short lived. The Horus name continued to be written in a *serekh* even after the introduction of the CARTOUCHE for the 'birth' and 'throne' names.

W. KAISER, 'Einige Bemerkungen zur ägyptischen Frühzeit III. die Reicheinigung', *ZÄS* 91 (1964), 86–125.

R. H. WILKINSON, 'The Horus name and the form and significance of the serekh in the royal Egyptian titulary', *JSSEA* 15 (1985), 98–104.

W. BARTHA, 'Der Palasthorustitel und seine Vorläufer in der Frühzeit', *GM* 117–18 (1990), 55–8.

S. QUIRKE, *Who were the pharaohs?* (London, 1990), 19–23.

A. O'BRIEN, 'The Serekh as an aspect of the iconography of early kingship', *JARCE* 33 (1996), 123–38.

serpent, snake

As in most cultures, the snake was regarded by the Egyptians as a source of evil and danger; it was the principal form of the god APOPHIS, who threatened the sun-god during his voyage through the netherworld (see FUNERARY TEXTS). In the same way that the scorpion-deities SERKET and Shed were worshipped and propitiated in order to avert the danger posed by their physical manifestations, so prayers and offerings were made to the serpent-goddesses RENENUTET and MERETSEGER, so that snake-bites could be avoided or cured. There was also a snake-god called Nehebkaw, first attested in the PYRAMID TEXTS of the late 5th and 6th Dynasty (c.2375–2181 BC). It was not until the Third Intermediate Period (1069–747 BC) that the first amulets of Nehebkaw were made, usually representing him as a man with a snake's head and tail.

The most highly regarded serpent-deity was the cobra-goddess WADJYT, who was the patroness of Lower Egypt and, along with the vulture-goddess NEKHBET, a symbol of the king's rule over the two lands of Egypt. The *uraeus* (cobra), traditionally poised at the forehead of the pharaoh as a potent symbol of his KINGSHIP, was given the epithet *weret hekaw*, 'great of magic', and there were strong associations between serpents and the practice of magic. A 13th-Dynasty bronze serpent (now in the Fitzwilliam Museum, Cambridge), found entangled in a mass of hair in 'Tomb 5' under the RAMESSEUM at Thebes, has been interpreted as a magician's 'wand' like those held by a statuette representing a lioness-headed (or lioness-masked) female magician, which was found in the same context and is now in the Manchester Museum (see MAGIC). A type of stele called a *cippus*, used during the Late Period (747–332 BC) as a means of warding off such dangers as snakes, scorpions and disease, usually depicts Harpocrates (see HORUS) holding snakes and other desert creatures in either hand.

Serpents were also regarded as primeval, chthonic creatures intimately linked with the process of creation, therefore the four goddesses of the Hermopolitan OGDOAD were sometimes described as having snakes' heads, and Kematef, the cosmogonic aspect of the god AMUN, took the form of a serpent. There was also the ouroboros, the serpent whose body coiled around the universe, eventually allowing it to bite its own tail, which served as a metaphor for the relationship between being and non-being. This serpent, the earliest surviving depiction of which is on the small golden shrine of TUTANKHAMUN (1336–1327 BC), represented the powers of resurrection and

Serket (Selket, Selkis)

Scorpion-goddess usually depicted as a woman with a rearing SCORPION on her head, although, like many Egyptian goddesses, she could also be represented as a lioness or serpent. Her name appears to be an abbreviation of the phrase *serket hetyt* ('the one who causes the throat to breathe'), presumably in an attempt to neutralize the threat posed by scorpions. The cult of Serket is attested as early as the 1st Dynasty (3100–2890 BC), on the inscribed funerary stele of Merka from Tomb 3505 at Saqqara, and she also appears in the PYRAMID TEXTS as the 'mistress of the beautiful house'. This latter epithet relates to her role in the embalming process, and she was regarded as the protector of the hawk-headed CANOPIC-JAR deity Qebehsenuef (see SONS OF HORUS). Along with three other goddesses, Isis,

Gilded and painted wooden figures of three of the four goddesses who protected the golden shrine of Tutankhamun, including (from left to right) Neith, Isis and Serket, whose head is surmounted by a scorpion. 18th Dynasty, c.1336–1327 BC, H. 90 cm. (CAIRO JE60686, REPRODUCED COURTESY OF THE GRIFFITH INSTITUTE)

Nephthys and Neith, she was charged with guarding the royal coffin and canopic chest. Although she often features in spells to cure or avoid venomous bites (and was probably the patroness of magicians dealing with such bites), she is rarely invoked in spells relating to scorpion stings.

F. KANEL, *'La nèpe et le scorpion': un monographie sur la déesse Serket* (Paris, 1984).

—, *Les prêtres-ouab de Sekhmet et les conjurateurs de Serket* (Paris, 1984).

Stele of Paneb, a foreman of the tomb-workers at Deir el-Medina, showing Paneb worshipping the goddess Meretseger in the form of a serpent. 19th Dynasty, c.1195 BC, H. 19.3 cm. (EA272)

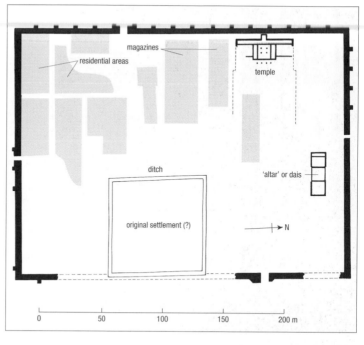

ABOVE *Plan of Sesebi.*

renewal, and it was thought that the regeneration of the sun-god was re-enacted every night within its body. While the ouroboros conveyed a sense of endless spatial length encompassing the universe, another snake called the *metwi* ('double cord') served as a manifestation of the infinity of time, and a depiction from the *Book of Gates* in the tomb of Sety I (1294–1279 BC) shows the undulating coils of a vast snake accompanied by the hieroglyphs signifying 'lifespan'.

J. BOURRIAU, *Pharaohs and mortals: Egyptian art in the Middle Kingdom* (Cambridge, 1988), 111–13.
S. JOHNSON, *The cobra goddess of ancient Egypt* (London, 1990).
E. HORNUNG, *Idea into image*, trans. E. Bredeck (New York, 1992), 49–51, 63–4.

Sesebi-Sudla

Walled settlement situated in the Upper Nubian Abri-Delgo reach, between the second and third cataracts, which was founded by the 18th-Dynasty pharaoh Akhenaten (1352–1336 BC). The roughly contemporaneous Nubian towns at BUHEN and MIRGISSA, dating to the New Kingdom (1550–1069 BC), were essentially extensions of garrisons established in the Middle Kingdom (2055–1650 BC), but Sesebi-Sudla was a newly established town and very much a product of the New Kingdom Egyptian policy of colonization of Nubia. It covered an area of more than five hectares and the population has been estimated at about 1000–1500.

RIGHT *Faience vessel decorated with blue lotuses found at Sesebi. New Kingdom, H 14.5 cm. (EA64041)*

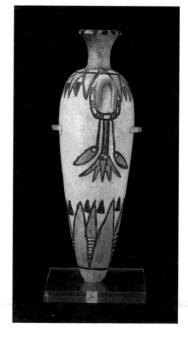

The principal areas excavated by Aylward Blackman and H. W. Fairman in 1936–8 were the northwestern and southwestern corners of the site. The remains in the northwestern corner of the town were dominated by a large tripartite temple dedicated to the Theban triad (AMUN, MUT and KHONS), which must therefore have been founded in the early years of Akhenaten's reign, before his full-scale adoption of the cult of the ATEN. The southwestern area comprised a dense block of houses arranged along a regular grid of streets. The examination of the central eastern area of the town has also revealed traces of a small enclosure surrounded by a ditch, which may be the remains of an earlier settlement established in advance of the main town.

Since the date of the town's foundation was within a few years of the establishment of a new Egyptian capital city at EL-AMARNA, comparisons between the two sites are potentially revealing. The few élite houses at Sesebi-Sudla, unlike the villas in the main city at el-

Amarna, were not set in extensive private gardens, and many of the smaller houses, like those in the Theban workmen's village at DEIR EL-MEDINA, were regularly furnished with cellars. The colony as a whole showed signs of 'careful, regular and economic planning', making it more similar to the peripheral workmen's village at el-Amarna than the main city. These fundamental differences suggest that the town of Sesebi-Sudla was probably a specialized, state-run community rather than simply a cross-section of Egyptian society transplanted into Upper Nubia.

A. L. BLACKMAN, 'Preliminary report on the excavations at Sesesbi, Northern Province, Anglo-Egyptian Sudan, 1936–7', *JEA* 23 (1937), 145–51.

H. W. FAIRMAN, 'Preliminary report on the excavations at Sesebi (Sudla) and 'Amarah West, Anglo-Egyptian Sudan, 1937–8', *JEA* 24 (1938), 151–6.

R. MORKOT, 'The excavations at Sesebi (Sudla) 1936–38', *Beiträge zur Sudanforschung* 3 (1988), 159–64.

Seshat

Goddess of writing and measurement, usually represented as a woman clad in a long panther-skin dress and wearing a headdress consisting of a band surmounted by a seven-pointed star and a bow. From at least the 2nd Dynasty (2890–2686 BC) onwards she was recorded as assisting the pharaoh in the foundation ritual of 'stretching the cord' (see ASTRONOMY AND ASTROLOGY), although the goddess Sefkhet-Abwy ('she who has laid aside the [two] horns') sometimes replaced her in this role. Temple reliefs of the Old and Middle Kingdoms (2686–1650 BC) show her in the act of recording the quantities of foreign captives and booty in the aftermath of military campaigns, but in the New Kingdom (1550–1069 BC) she became much more associated with the SED FESTIVAL (the royal jubilee ritual); she is therefore often depicted with the notched palm rib that traditionally represented the passing of time, and, like her male equivalent THOTH, she was sometimes shown writing the names of the king on the leaves of the persea tree (see TREES).

R. ENGELBACH, 'A foundation scene of the second dynasty', *JEA* 20 (1934), 183–4.

G. A. WAINWRIGHT, 'Seshat and the pharaoh', *JEA* 26 (1940), 30–40.

H. BONNET, *Reallexikon der Ägyptischen Religionsgeschichte* (Berlin, 1952), 699–701.

W. HELCK, 'Seschat', *Lexikon der Ägyptologie* v, ed. W. Helck, E. Otto and W. Westendorf (Wiesbaden, 1984), 884–8.

Sesostris see SENUSRET

Seth (Set, Setekh, Suty, Sutekh)

God of chaos and confusion, who was generally depicted with a human body but with the head of a mysterious animal, often described as 'Typhonian' (because of his later identification with the Greek god Typhon). With its long nose and squared ears, the 'Seth animal' has sometimes been compared with an anteater, but was probably a completely mythical beast. The full animal form of the god was depicted with an erect forked tail and a canine

Limestone stele of Aapehty, a royal craftsman, showing him adoring the god Seth. The craftsman's name is a play on the phrase aa-pehty *meaning 'great of strength', one of the epithets of Seth who, in Ramesside times, became a patron of Egypt along with Amun, Ra and Ptah. 19th Dynasty, c.1200 BC, from Thebes, H. 21.2 cm. (EA35360)*

body, but he was also occasionally represented in the guise of other abhorred animals, such as the hippopotamus, pig and donkey. The earliest known representation of Seth takes the form of a carved ivory artefact (perhaps a comb) from Tomb H29 at el-Mahasna, dating to the NAQADA I period (c.4000–3500 BC), while the distinctive figure of the Seth-animal is also portrayed on the macehead of the Proto-dynastic ruler SCORPION (c.3150 BC).

According to surviving religious texts, Seth was the son of the sky-goddess NUT, the brother of OSIRIS, ISIS and NEPHTHYS (the latter being also his wife), and was said to have been

born in the region of NAQADA. Since the deserts and foreign lands were equated with enmity in the Egyptian world view, Seth became patron of such countries, and was also sometimes associated with the foreign goddesses ANAT and ASTARTE.

According to legend, Seth was supposed to have murdered his brother Osiris and then to have engaged in a long and violent contest with his nephew HORUS, who sought to avenge the death of his father. In this contest, Seth put out the eye of Horus, while the latter castrated Seth, part of whose violent nature probably derived from his sexual potency. It has been suggested, in this context, that the struggle between the two gods may have served as a metaphor for the role of male SEXUALITY in the cult of the Egyptian king. In the various contests, Seth took on many forms, including those of a black boar and HIPPOPOTAMUS, and it is common to see Horus spearing him in one of these animal guises, as in the ambulatory of the temple of Horus at EDFU. Eventually the gods were called upon to judge which of the two should be the earthly ruler. Despite his great evil, Seth was favoured by RA on account of his seniority. However, it was eventually decreed that Horus should be the ruler of the living (hence his identification with the king) while Osiris would govern the underworld (hence his identification with the dead king). As god of chaos and confusion, Seth lay outside the ordered universe, thus serving as a necessary complement to the divine order, since everything within the Egyptian system needed an opposing force in order to maintain the necessary balance (see DUALITY).

Despite his failure to gain the throne Seth was said to have remained a 'companion of Ra', dwelling with him and causing storms and bad weather. He is also supposed to have journeyed with the sun-god in his BARK through the twelve hours of the night. In this context his violent nature was put to good use, defending Ra from the coils of the serpent APOPHIS, whom he speared from the bow of the boat. Since the deceased king also journeyed with Ra, he too enjoyed the protection of Seth. Similarly Seth might be called upon to provide good weather by withholding the chaotic aspect of his character that would usually have instigated his storms.

Despite his unsavoury reputation, Seth was nevertheless the object of veneration; his cult had been centred at Naqada since the Predynastic period, as well as in the north-eastern Delta. The 2nd-Dynasty ruler Peribsen chose to write his principal name in a SEREKH surmounted by an image of Seth rather than Horus, in a radical change from traditional iconography, while his successor, KHASEKHEMWY, placed images of both gods above his name. Thereafter, however, the *serekh* remained uniquely associated with Horus.

In the Second Intermediate Period (1650–1550 BC) Seth was worshipped by the HYKSOS at Avaris (TELL EL-DAB'A), perhaps because he was a thunder-god, like the Levantine deity, Baal. He was also venerated by the rulers of the 19th and 20th Dynasties (1295–1069 BC), some of whom took his name, as in the case of Sety I (1294–1279 BC) and Sethnakhte (1186–1184 BC). The rulers of this period occasionally made reference to the strength of Seth when describing their own deeds in battle.

From the late Third Intermediate Period (*c*.800 BC) onwards, there appears to have been a change in the way that Seth was viewed. Whereas previously he had been regarded simply as an ambivalent force, avoided for most purposes but invoked for others, he began instead to be seen as evil and undesirable, to the extent that some of his statues were recarved with the attributes of the god Amun, and his defeat by Horus was widely celebrated.

H. TE VELDE, *Seth, god of confusion* (Leiden, 1967).

C. ONASCH, 'Der ägyptische und der biblische Seth', *Archiv für Papyrusforschung* 27 (1980), 99–119.

S. QUIRKE, *Ancient Egyptian religion* (London, 1992), 61–70.

Sety

'Birth name' forming part of the ROYAL TITULARY of two pharaohs of the 19th Dynasty (1295–1186 BC).

Sety I Menmaatra (1294–1279 BC) was the second ruler of the 19th Dynasty, the son of RAMESES I and the father of Rameses II. His COREGENCY with his father appears to have lasted virtually from the beginning of the dynasty, perhaps in a conscious effort to avoid the problems of succession that had contributed to the decline of the 18th-Dynasty royal family. The concern with historical continuity is evident in his temple at ABYDOS, where the cult of the royal ancestors was celebrated with a relief showing his son reading a papyrus inscribed with the names of sixty-seven predecessors stretching back to the semi-mythical MENES (see KING LISTS).

His reign seems to have been successful on virtually all levels, with military campaigns in the Levant and wars with the LIBYANS and HITTITES effectively securing the country's sphere of influence in north Africa and the Near East. In terms of architecture, the reliefs

Watercolour by Henry Salt of a scene in the tomb of Sety I at Thebes, painted c.1818.

in his temple at Abydos and the paintings in his tomb in the VALLEY OF THE KINGS (KV17) were among the most elegant of the New Kingdom. His mummy was among the group which survived the tomb-robbery of the Third Intermediate Period (1069–747 BC) through reburial in the 'DEIR EL-BAHRI cache'.

Sety II Userkheperura Setepenra (1200–1194 BC) was the designated heir of MERENPTAH (1213–1203 BC), but it seems likely that he was initially prevented from reigning by the emergence of a rival claimant called Amenmessu, son of a relatively unknown daughter of Rameses II. About five years after the death of Merenptah, Sety finally became king, and there is surviving evidence of work which he commissioned at Karnak and the Ramesseum. His tomb in the Valley of the Kings (KV15) was never completed but the standard of the reliefs on the walls was high. His mummy was among those re-interred in the tomb of AMENHOTEP II in the 21st Dynasty (1069–945 BC).

H. CHEVRIER, *Le temple reposoir de Séti II* (Cairo, 1940).

A. R. DAVID, *A guide to religious ritual at Abydos* (Warminster, 1981).

E. HORNUNG, *The tomb of Seti I* (Zurich and Munich, 1991).

K. A. KITCHEN, *Ramesside inscriptions*, 7 vols (Oxford, 1993).

sexuality

Until comparatively recently it was often implied that the ancient Egyptian attitudes to sexuality were somewhat naïve or coy. It is

now recognized, however, that the Egyptians' view of sexual behaviour was relatively uninhibited and straightforward; like most societies, they applied their code of ETHICS to certain aspects of sexuality, in that adultery was not condoned and sexual intercourse in sacred places was prohibited, but their general attitude was distinctly pragmatic and unprudish.

Sexuality and fertility were clearly of great significance in many of their religious beliefs. The ithyphallic god MIN was a popular symbol of fertility, to whom cos lettuces were offered, allegedly because the white sap of the lettuce was identified with semen. The Egyptians were aware that semen (*mw*) was the male contribution to conception, although they also believed that the semen emerged from a man's bones and thus provided the child with its skeleton, while women were thought to supply the baby's soft tissues. As far as contraception was concerned, some of the surviving 'medical papyri' prescribe recipes for potions to avoid pregnancy.

From at least the Badarian period onwards, figurines of women, made from clay, wood, ivory or stone, were included among funerary equipment. These were often highly stylized and generally emphasized one or more of the sexual characteristics. The interpretation of the various different types of 'fertility figurines' has proved extremely difficult. Two areas of confusion have persisted until recent times: on the one hand, some figures were described by their excavators as 'dolls' and therefore incorrectly viewed as TOYS; on the other hand, even when their sexual significance was recognized by scholars, they were often automatically assumed to have been intended for the posthumous sexual gratification of the deceased (despite the fact that they have been found in the tombs of women as well as men).

It is now believed by most Egyptologists that the function of such female figurines within the tomb was to reinforce or symbolize the sexual aspects of regeneration and rebirth. There are a number of specialized types such as the wooden 'paddle dolls', so called because of their shape, which have been found mainly in 11th-Dynasty Theban tombs. Another very common Middle Kingdom type, often misleadingly described as 'concubines of the dead', consisted of clay or faience female figures, often truncated at the knees, which were found in both tombs and houses.

Medical papyri make it clear that physicians were familiar with the male sexual organs but less so with the female genitalia. The hieroglyphic sign showing female genitalia was often used for the word 'woman', while the erect penis was sometimes used to denote 'male' or 'husband'. The two hieroglyphs were occasionally even superimposed to express sexual intercourse. The art in temples and tombs frequently depicts or alludes to the sexual act. In the temple of Hathor at DENDERA, for example, ISIS, in the form of a kite, is shown poised on the phallus of the mummified OSIRIS as part of the Osiris myth. Similarly, the coffin of the deceased might be identified with the sky-goddess NUT, as though the deceased had returned to her body to await rebirth.

Homosexuality was not unknown, and tended to be described somewhat disapprovingly, as in the attempted rape of the god HORUS by his enemy SETH. The Greek historian Herodotus made reference to the practice of bestiality in Egypt, but his reliability in this matter is uncertain, and he may even have been confusing mythological references and ritual acts with actual sexual preferences.

P. J. UCKO, *Anthropomorphic figurines of Predynastic Egypt and Neolithic Crete* (London, 1968).

H. BRUNNER, 'Fruchtbarkeit', *Lexikon der Ägyptologie* II, ed. W. Helck, E. Otto and W. Westendorf (Wiesbaden, 1977), 336–44.

L. MANNICHE, *Sexual life in ancient Egypt* (London, 1987).

Shabaqo (Shabaka) (716–702 BC)

Second ruler of the Egyptian 25th Dynasty (747–656 BC). He rose to power over the kingdom of NAPATA after the death of his brother PIY (747–716 BC), who had already conquered Egypt but apparently failed to consolidate his military success. Shabaqo soon re-established control over Lower Egypt, defeating his main

rival, the 24th-Dynasty Saite king Bakenrenef (Bocchoris; 720–715 BC) and replacing him with a Kushite governor. Throughout his reign he made many additions to Egyptian temples, such as those at MEMPHIS, ABYDOS and Esna, while at KARNAK he erected a 'treasury'. The 'archaism' that characterized the art and architecture of the 25th and 26th Dynasties was already apparent in the reign of Shabaqo, particularly in the case of the 'Shabaqo Stone' (now in the British Museum), an account of the creation of the universe by the god Ptah which was inscribed on a slab of basalt and claimed to be copied from an old worm-eaten document.

Shabaqo appointed his son, Horemakhet, to the post of High Priest of Amun at Thebes, although the real power in the Theban region still lay in the hands of Shabaqo's sister, Amenirdis I, the GOD'S WIFE OF AMUN, who constructed a mortuary chapel and tomb for herself within the precincts of MEDINET HABU. When Shabaqo died, he was buried in a pyramidal tomb at the Napatan royal necropolis of EL-KURRU and was succeeded by Piy's son Shabitqo.

K. A. KITCHEN, *The Third Intermediate Period in Egypt (1100–650 BC)*, 2nd ed. (Warminster, 1986), 378–83.

shabti (Egyptian *ushabti, shawabti*)

Funerary figurine, usually mummiform in appearance, which developed during the Middle Kingdom out of the funerary statuettes and models provided in the tombs of the Old Kingdom. The etymology of the word *shabti* is unknown, as is the variant *shawabti*, but by the Late Period (747–332 BC) the term *ushabti*, meaning 'answerer', was in general use.

The purpose of the statuettes was to spare their owner from menial corvée labour in the afterlife, which would be required for the deceased to produce his or her food. The figures stood in for both the deceased (in whose name they would answer the call to work) and the servants of the deceased. Some *shabtis* are uninscribed but most are decorated with Chapter 6 of the BOOK OF THE DEAD, which is therefore known as the '*shabti* chapter'. Several forms of this text have been identified by Hans Schneider, but its basic purpose was to enable the *shabtis* to accomplish their tasks: 'O *shabti*, if [name of deceased] be summoned to do any work which has to be done in the realm of the dead – to make arable the fields, to irrigate the land or to convey sand from east to west; "Here am I", you shall say, "I shall do it".'

Early New Kingdom *shabtis* were sometimes

Shabtis *of the princess Henutmehyt and the box in which they were contained. The box shows her adoring the jackal-headed Duamutef and the human-headed Imsety, two of the four Sons of Horus. 19th Dynasty, c.1290 BC, wood, from Thebes,* H *of box 34 cm.* (EA41549)

accompanied by model hoes and baskets and from the Third Intermediate Period (1069–747 BC) onwards some 'overseer figures' were provided with a whip, while later examples have such details moulded or carved as part of the statuette. New Kingdom *shabtis* were also occasionally shown in ordinary dress rather than in the guise of a mummy. Initially the deceased was provided with only one *shabti*, but by the New Kingdom the numbers had increased significantly so that there might be 365 figures, one for every day of the year, accompanied by thirty-six 'overseers', giving a total of 401, although as many as seven hundred are said to have been found in the tomb of Sety I (1294–1279 BC). The increasing number of *shabtis* led to the manufacture of special containers now known as *shabti*-boxes.

The quality of *shabtis* and their material varies widely, although wood, clay, wax, stone, bronze, FAIENCE and even GLASS are known. Faience is the material most commonly associated with *shabtis*, particularly in the fine examples of the 26th to 30th Dynasties (664–343 BC). The poorest quality *shabtis* were barely recognizable as such, and some – especially of the 17th Dynasty

(1650–1550 BC) – were little more than wooden pegs. The use of *shabtis* died out during the Ptolemaic period (332–30 BC).

W. M. F. PETRIE, *Shabtis* (Warminster, 1974)

H. D. SCHNEIDER, *Shabtis*, 3 vols (Leiden, 1977).

H. M. STEWART, *Egyptian shabtis* (Princes Risborough, 1995).

shadow, shade (Egyptian *shwt*)

The shadow was regarded by the Egyptians as an essential element of every human being; as with the AKH, BA, KA and NAME, it was considered necessary to protect it from harm. Funerary texts describe the shadow as an entity imbued with power and capable of moving at great speed, but the Egyptian word for shadow (*shwt*) also had the connotations of 'shade' and 'protection', consequently the pharaoh is generally portrayed under the shade of a feather- or palm-fan (the same hieroglyphic sign being used for both fan and sunshade). The painted scenes decorating the royal tombs in the Valley of the Kings take account of the sun's shadow as it passes through the netherworld, and it was felt that power was transferred to those over whom the solar shadow fell. In the city at EL-AMARNA there was a special type of shrine dedicated to the god ATEN, known as a *shwt-Ra* ('sun-shade').

B. GEORGE, *Zu den altägyptischen Vorstellungen vom Schatten als Seele* (Bonn, 1970).

E. HORNUNG, *Idea into image*, trans. E. Bredeck (New York, 1992), 178–9.

shaduf

Irrigation tool consisting of a long wooden pole with a receptacle at one end and a counterbalancing weight at the other, by means of which water could be transferred out of a river or canal. It is first depicted on an AKKADIAN cylinder seal of the late third millennium BC but it was probably not introduced into Egypt until the 18th Dynasty (1550–1295 BC) and the earliest surviving depictions are on the walls of the tomb chapels of Neferhotep and Merira II at the time of Akhenaten (1352–1336 BC). It was eventually superseded, first by the Archimedes screw (Arabic *tanbur*) in the fifth century BC and, second, by the waterwheel (Arabic *saqiya*) in the early Ptolemaic period, although small *shadufs* are still occasionally used, even in modern Egypt, to water garden plots.

K. W. BUTZER, 'Shaduf', *Lexikon der Ägyptologie* V, ed. W. Helck, E. Otto and W. Westendorf (Wiesbaden, 1984), 520–1.

E. STROUHAL, *Life in ancient Egypt* (Cambridge, 1992), 97.

Shay

God who served as a symbol of allotted life-span or destiny, and was therefore occasionally portrayed in vignettes of the weighing of the heart of the deceased (the Egyptian last judgement). In the Ptolemaic period he became closely identified with the Greek serpent-god of fortune-telling, Agathodaimon.

J. QUAEGEBEUR, *Le dieu égyptien Shaï dans la religion et l'onomastique* (Louvain, 1975).

sheep *see* ANIMAL HUSBANDRY and RAM

Sheikh el-Beled (Arabic: 'headman of the village')

Popular name for the wooden statue of a chief lector-priest called Ka-aper, whose tomb, mastaba C8, was excavated by the French archaeologist Auguste Mariette at north Saqqara, near the pyramid complex of the

The life-like statue of the chief lector priest Ka-aper is better known as the 'Sheikh el-Beled', apparently because he reminded Mariette's workmen of their village headman. The original cane and sceptre held in his hands were missing and the cane he now holds is modern; the legs have also been partly restored. 4th Dynasty, c.2490 BC, sycamore wood with copper and rock crystal eyes, from Saqqara, mastaba C8, H 1.12 m. (CAIRO CG34)

5th-Dynasty pharaoh Userkaf (2494–2487 BC). The life-size standing figure (Egyptian Museum, Cairo), carved from sycamore wood, is widely regarded as one of the masterpieces of Old Kingdom private sculpture. Ka-aper is portrayed as a thick-set, middle-aged figure clad in a straight skirt and holding a staff in his left hand and a SEKHEM SCEPTRE in his right (both traditional symbols of authority). His eyes are made of rock-crystal rimmed with copper and furnished with pupils in the form of drilled holes filled with black pigment.

The dates of mastaba C8 and the statue have been a matter of some debate, but most scholars place Ka-aper and his tomb in the late 4th Dynasty (c.2500 BC). The Sheikh el-Beled is comparable with other 4th-Dynasty realistic sculptures, such as the bust of Ankhhaf in Boston; it was found in association with a large granite stele and part of a wooden figure of a woman thought to represent Ka-aper's wife (Cairo). Another wooden statue of a man (Cairo), although of inferior quality, is considered to be a representation of Ka-aper at a younger age and probably derives from the same mastaba.

J. VANDIER, *Manuel d'archéologie égyptienne* III (Paris, 1958), 90–1, 104–5, 125–8.

C. VANDERSLEYEN, 'La date du Cheikh el-Beled (Caire CG 34)', *JEA* 69 (1983), 61–5.

M. SALEH and H. SOUROUZIAN, *The Egyptian Museum, Cairo: official catalogue* (Mainz, 1987), no. 40.

shen

Hieroglyphic symbol depicting a circle or ring of rope folded and knotted at the bottom; since the circle effectively had no end, it came to denote infinity. When the *shen* sign was depicted encircling the sun, it appears to have symbolized the eternity of the universe. This property of encirclement was extended to denote protection as well as eternity, making the sign doubly potent. Consequently it is frequently found as a decorative element in designs, and is particularly associated with HORUS the falcon or NEKHBET the vulture who hold the sign in their claws above the king, offering him eternal protection. Similarly it appears as an amuletic element in jewellery from the Middle Kingdom (2055–1650 BC) onwards. The shape is well suited to finger rings, but also occurs in pendants, earrings and pectorals. Richard Wilkinson suggests that the upcurved wings of some jewellery in the form of birds deliberately imitate the shape of the *shen* that they hold in their claws.

On sarcophagi the sign commonly appears in the hands of the goddesses who kneel on the

Double-sided amulet in pale green faience in the form of the shen *sign symbolizing infinity, eternity and protection. Saite period, H 3.7 cm. (EA58025)*

nebw sign ('gold'), at the ends of royal sarcophagi of the New Kingdom such as that of Amenhotep II (1427–1400 BC). The shape of the sign is imitated by the ouroboros, the snake which bites its own tail, and that the two are related is shown by the sarcophagus lid of Merenptah (1213–1203 BC), which is carved in the shape of a CARTOUCHE (the elongated form of the *shen* sign in which royal names were written) surrounded by an elongated ouroboros.

R. H. WILKINSON, *Reading Egyptian art* (London, 1992).

Sheshonq (Shoshenq, Sheshonk, Shishak)

Libyan name held by five kings of the 22nd and 23rd Dynasties (945–715 BC and 818–715 BC respectively) as their 'birth name' or nomen (see ROYAL TITULARY).

Sheshonq I Hedjkheperra Setepenra (945–924 BC), a nephew of OSORKON the elder, was a descendant of the LIBYAN 'great chiefs of the Meshwesh'. He rose to power through his role as general and adviser to PSUSENNES II (959–945 BC), whom he eventually succeeded, thus inaugurating the period of Libyan domination. He succeeded in restoring Egyptian political influence over Palestine, an act commemorated on the 'Bubastite portal', which was the gateway leading into the first court of the temple of Amun at KARNAK. His reliefs on an exterior wall of this court at Karnak depict his victory over the two Jewish kingdoms of ISRAEL and Judah (see BIBLICAL CONNECTIONS). The presentation of a statue of himself to King Abibaal of BYBLOS probably also indicated the full resumption of economic links with the Levant.

Sheshonq II Heqakheperra Setepenra (c.890 BC) was the designated heir of OSORKON I (924–889 BC), but died before him, having ruled only in a COREGENCY with his father

rather than as a pharaoh in his own right. In 1939 Pierre Montet discovered his silver coffin in the vestibule of the tomb of Psusennes I (1039–991 BC) at TANIS, and the age of the mummified body which it contained is estimated to have been about fifty years at death. He is probably the same person as Sheshonq Meryamun, who is recorded as chief priest of Amun at Thebes at roughly the same time; a quartzite statue of Hapy the god of the inundation, now in the collection of the British Museum, was dedicated by Sheshonq Meryamun, whose figure is carved in relief at Hapy's side (see HAPY for illustration).

Sheshonq III Usermaatra Setepenra/amun (825–773 BC) was the successor to Takelot II (850–825 BC), having apparently usurped the throne from the heir, prince Osorkon. It was around the eighth year of his reign that he was somewhat eclipsed by Pedubastis I (818–793 BC), ruler of Leontopolis (TELL EL-MUQDAM), who also declared himself king, thus creating the 23rd Dynasty, whose rulers were contemporaneous with the last four rulers of the Tanite 22nd Dynasty. This left Sheshonq III with his territories restricted to parts of the eastern and central Delta, while it was Pedubastis whose reign was apparently endorsed by the influential priests of Amun at Thebes.

Sheshonq IV Usermaatra Meryamun (c.780 BC) had a brief reign (six years at most) as the 23rd-Dynasty successor to the throne of Pedubastis I at Leontopolis.

Sheshonq V Aakheperra (767–730 BC), the penultimate 22nd-Dynasty ruler, reigned for nearly forty years and is relatively well attested, particularly at Tanis, where he constructed a small temple dedicated to the triad of Amun and, in the thirtieth year of his reign, a chapel relating to his SED FESTIVAL.

K. A. KITCHEN, *The Third Intermediate Period in Egypt (1100–650 BC)*, 2nd ed. (Warminster, 1986), 287–354, 575–6.

J. YOYOTTE et al., *Tanis, l'or des pharaons* (Paris, 1987).

D. A. ASTON, 'Takeloth II – a king of the "Theban 23rd Dynasty"?', *JEA* 75 (1989), 139–53.

N. GRIMAL, *A history of ancient Egypt* (Oxford, 1992), 319–30.

shesmet girdle

Belt or girdle from which an apron of beads was suspended, forming part of the symbolic attire of Early Dynastic and Old Kingdom rulers such as Djoser (2667–2648 BC), which perhaps evolved from Predynastic beaded girdles. The belt was also worn by certain deities, and there was a goddess Shesmetet, attested from the Early Dynastic period

(3100–2686 BC) onwards, who personified the girdle. By at least the 5th Dynasty Shesmetet was represented with the head of a lioness and considered as a form of the goddess BASTET.

It is possible that the *shesmet* itself eventually developed into other forms of belt, such as those found in male burials from the Old Kingdom onwards, which were later extended to women by the Middle Kingdom (2055–1650 BC). The tomb of Senebtisy, a woman of the 12th-Dynasty royal family buried at EL-LISHT, contained numerous items of jewellery, including a *shesmet* girdle. The cultic significance of the girdle is perhaps also indicated by the fact that the epithets of the god SOPED included the phrase 'lord of the *shesmet*'.

P. E. NEWBERRY, 'ŠSmit', *Studies presented to Francis Llewellyn Griffith* (London, 1932), 316–23.

E. STAEHELIN, 'Schesemet-Gürtel', *Lexikon der Ägyptologie* v, ed. W. Helck, E. Otto and W. Westendorf (Wiesbaden, 1984), 586–7.

ships and boats

The importance of water transport, both as a practical means of communication and as a recurring religious metaphor, arose inevitably from the existence of the river Nile and its tributaries as the principal artery of communication in ancient Egypt. The prevailing wind in the Nile valley came from the north, so that sails could be used to propel boats travelling south, while those heading north, against the wind, relied on oars and the current. For this reason, the hieroglyph for 'travelling north', even in the case of overland travel, consisted of a boat with its sails down, while that for 'travelling south' shows a boat with billowing sails. Boats were already being used as early as the Gerzean period (c.3500–3100 BC).

A great deal of information has survived concerning Egyptian ships and boats, principally in the form of depictions on the walls of tombs, funerary models and textual references. There have also been a number of finds of actual boats, ranging from the reconstructed SOLAR BARK of Khufu (2589–2566 BC) to the fragments of boat timber preserved through their reuse for such purposes as the construction of slipways.

Travel by boat was so ingrained in the Egyptian psyche that it was considered natural to depict the sun-god RA travelling through the sky or the netherworld in his bark. However, when sailing outside the Nile valley, on the Mediterranean or Red Sea, the ships seem to have stayed close to the shore. Unlike the Greeks, the Egyptians were evidently not enthusiastic seafarers.

Probably the earliest and simplest boats were PAPYRUS skiffs, made of bundles of reeds lashed together. These would have been used for fishing and HUNTING game in the marshes, for crossing the river and for travelling short distances, and this type probably remained in use throughout Pharaonic history. Even from Predynastic times there is evidence for larger vessels, though perhaps still of reed construction. Painted pottery of the Naqada period shows elaborate, many-oared, ships with numerous sailors. The prows and sterns of such vessels are usually upturned; they would normally have been provided with at least one large steering oar, and sometimes also a sail and cabin.

The boats and ships of the Old Kingdom (2686–2181 BC) were usually made of WOOD

the boats carrying the great granite papyrus columns for his valley temple.

The typical craft of the Middle Kingdom (2055–1650 BC) were similar in design, although, from the late Old Kingdom onwards, the steering oar was operated as a rudder by means of ropes. The mast was collapsible and rested on a stand when not in use, while the cabin was usually located at the stern. Many models of these boats have survived in tombs, where they played an important role in the funerary cult, symbolizing the journey of the deceased to ABYDOS. There are also surviving fragments of timber from actual vessels reused for slipways and ramps in the pyramid complexes at EL-LISHT.

In the New Kingdom (1550–1069 BC) vessels seem to have become more specialized;

Boats of the Late Period (747–332 BC) seem to have remained roughly similar, but the stern was generally higher. With increasing Greek influence from the SAITE PERIOD onwards, however, sea-going vessels began to be modelled on those used by the Greeks and Phoenicians, and by the time of the sea battle of Actium, between CLEOPATRA VII (51–30 BC) and the Roman consul Octavian (later Emperor Augustus), the Egyptian ships appear to have been similar in design to those of the Romans.

G. A. REISNER, *Models of ships and boats* (Cairo, 1913).

P. LIPKE, *The royal ships of Cheops* (Oxford, 1984).

M. BIETAK, 'Zur Marine des Alten Reiches', *Pyramid studies and other essays presented to I. E. S. Edwards*, ed. J. Baines et al. (London, 1988), 35–40.

D. A. JONES, *A glossary of ancient Egyptian nautical titles and terms* (London, 1988).

R. H. WILKINSON, *Reading Egyptian art* (London, 1992), 152–7.

S. VINSON, *Egyptian boats and ships* (Princes Risborough, 1994).

D. A. JONES, *Boats* (London, 1995).

Model boats frequently accompanied burials of the Middle Kingdom and symbolized the pilgrimage to Abydos. 12th Dynasty, c.1900 BC., provenance unknown, H. of hull 10.2 cm, L. 66.7 cm. (EA9524)

obtained either locally or from Syria-Palestine. They had a characteristically curving hull and were usually provided with several steering oars, a mast and a long narrow sail. Oars would also have been used for propulsion when there was insufficient breeze to fill the sails. The best-known surviving Old Kingdom boat is that found beside the pyramid of Khufu at GIZA, which was made of large planks of wood 'sewn' together with ropes. Rather less elaborate vessels would have been used to transport stone from the quarries to the construction sites of pyramid complexes. The reliefs decorating the causeway of the pyramid complex of Unas (2375–2345 BC) included depictions of

there were usually cabins on both the stern and the prow in addition to a main cabin in the centre of the boat. The helmsman operated double steering oars by a system of ropes and levers as before, and the width of the sail was greater than its height. The Egyptian navy of this period was put to the test when it repulsed the invasion of the SEA PEOPLES, according to the reliefs of Rameses III (1184–1153 BC) at MEDINET HABU. As in the Old Kingdom, huge masses of stone were also moved by barge, including OBELISKS for the temple of Hatshepsut (1473–1458 BC) at DEIR EL-BAHRI. The same queen also sent a seaborne expedition to PUNT. A late 20th-Dynasty literary (or possibly quasi-historical) text, *The Report of Wenamun*, outlines a seajourney by an official to obtain timber from BYBLOS; this expedition was initially unsuccessful due to Egypt's poor political fortunes at the time (see HERIHOR).

shrine

Term which is to some extent synonymous with NAOS, in that it is often used to refer either to the innermost element of a temple (where the cult image or BARK of the deity was placed) or to the elaborate boxes containing funerary statuary (such as those in the tomb of TUTANKHAMUN (KV62)). The Egyptian term *per* is used to refer to the pavilion-style shrines of Upper and Lower Egypt.

The traditional Upper Egyptian shrine (*per-wer* or *kar*) has a shape identical to that of the golden shrine of Tutankhamun, consisting of a square box topped by a CAVETTO CORNICE and a roof or lid sloping down from the front. Although the hieroglyphic image was initially used simply to designate the chapel of the goddess NEKHBET at ELKAB, it came to symbolize the whole geographical region of Upper Egypt itself. The Lower Egyptian shrine (*per-nu* or *perneser*) was a dome-roofed box with high posts on either side, which became the model for various other objects such as sarcophagi (see COFFINS AND SARCOPHAGI) and SHABTI-boxes. The original shrine was located at Buto (TELL EL-FARRA'IN), the city of the cobra-goddess WADJYT, but it too came to represent the region as a whole.

The English term 'shrine', however, is often used to describe various small freestanding buildings which in themselves were miniature temples or chapels, such as the 'BARK-shrines', which were placed along processional ways as temporary resting places for the divine bark as it was carried between one temple complex and another. The gardens of the larger houses

Granite shrine from Philae, carved during the reign of Ptolemy VIII Euergetes II (170–116 BC) and bearing texts including a dedication to the goddess Isis, the principal deity of Philae. H. 2.51 m. (EA1134)

at EL-AMARNA often contained unusual shrines in the form of small decorated PYLONS or stelae, which were dedicated to the royal family of AKHENATEN (1352–1336 BC).

M. EATON-KRAUSS and E. GRAEFE, *The small golden shrine from the tomb of Tutankhamun* (Oxford, 1985).

Shu

God of the air and sunlight, whose name probably means 'he who rises up'. He was usually depicted as a man wearing a headdress in the form of a plume (which was the hieroglyph denoting his name). Apart from references in the PYRAMID TEXTS and COFFIN TEXTS, his cult is not attested until the New Kingdom, when his comparative prominence is probably a reflection of his association with the force of life, which was an increasingly important element of Egyptian religion in the New Kingdom.

While Shu symbolized dry air, his sister-

wife, TEFNUT, was goddess of moisture or corrosive air; they were the first two gods created by ATUM according to the CREATION myth of Heliopolis, in which they were said to have come into being from the semen of Atum or from the mucus of his sneeze. Their children were GEB the earth-god and NUT the sky-goddess, and it was Shu's role to support the outstretched figure of Nut, thus effectively separating the sky from the earth.

He was not a solar deity (indeed he was often linked with the lunar deities KHONS and THOTH), but his role in providing sunlight led to an obvious connection with the sun-god RA, and it was believed that he brought the sun to life each morning. Similarly, in the underworld, it was thought that he protected the sun from the snake-god APOPHIS, although at the same time he was portrayed at the head of a group of the torturers threatening the deceased. During the reign of Akhenaten (1352–1336 BC) the cult of Shu escaped proscription because of his solar associations, and he was considered to dwell in the sun-disc (see ATEN). With a typical Egyptian sense of DUALITY, his wife, Tefnut, was linked with the moon. His connections with the sun, with resurrection and with separating heaven and earth are exemplified in a headrest of Tutankhamun (1336–1327 BC) in which Shu, flanked by two lions, supports the head of the sleeper, so that the composition as a whole forms the HORIZON hieroglyph, thus perhaps allowing the head of the king to be identified with the sun poised on the horizon.

P. DERCHAIN, 'Le nom de Chou et sa fonction', *RdE* 27 (1975), 110–16.

H. VAN DE WALLE, 'Survivantes mythologiques dans les coiffures royal de l'époque atonienne', *CdE* 55/109 (1980), 23–6.

Grey-green faience amulet of Shu, god of air and sunlight, supporting a sun-disc. Saite period, c.664–525 BC, H. 3 cm. (EA60439)

H. TE VELDE, 'Schu', *Lexikon der Ägyptologie* v, ed. W. Helck, E. Otto and W. Westendorf (Wiesbaden, 1984), 735–7.

S. QUIRKE, *Ancient Egyptian religion* (London, 1992), 25–31.

sidelock of youth

Egyptian children, particularly boys, are usually portrayed with their heads shaved, apart from a single plaited 'sidelock', which features in the hieroglyph for 'child' (*khered*) and was considered to be the archetypal symbol of youth. Four actual examples of sidelocks were found in 6th-Dynasty graves at Mostagedda by Guy Brunton. The childlike versions of

Fragment from the tomb of Anherkhau, showing a child with the sidelock of youth. 20th Dynasty, c.1160 BC, from Deir el-Medina. (EA1329)

such gods as HORUS and KHONS were regularly portrayed with a sidelock, as were royal offspring, including the 'Amarna princesses', the daughters of AKHENATEN (1352–1336 BC). The *sem* priest, who usually performed the final rites of resurrection on the mummy of the deceased, often wore a sidelock, presumably in imitation of Horus, who would have performed the same filial rites on the body of his father OSIRIS.

silver

Although the Egyptians could obtain GOLD and electrum (the natural alloy of silver and gold) from the mountains of the Eastern Desert and Nubia, silver was comparatively rare, and may even have been unknown in early times, since the Egyptian language lacks a word for it. They described it only as the 'white metal', and seem to have regarded it as a variety of gold.

When silver was first introduced into the Egyptian economy, its value seems to have been higher than that of gold, judging from

Cult image of the god Amun from his temple at Karnak. New Kingdom, c.1300 BC, silver and gold, H. 23 cm. (EA60006)

the fact that silver items were listed before those of gold in descriptions of valuables during the Old Kingdom (2686–2181 BC). The value of the earliest silver imports is indicated by the thinness of the bracelets of the 4th-Dynasty queen HETEPHERES I (c. 2600 BC), in marked contrast to the extravagance of her goldwork. A silver treasure excavated at the site of TOD comprised vessels probably made in Crete, or perhaps somewhere in Asia but under Cretan influence. This cache dates to the reign of Amenemhat II (1922–1878 BC), in the 12th Dynasty, and is roughly contemporaneous with finds of fine silver JEWELLERY at el-Lahun and Dahshur.

By the Middle Kingdom (2055–1650 BC), however, silver may have been regarded as less valuable, presumably as a result of increased availability; according to the Rhind Mathematical Papyrus (written in the Second Intermediate Period but perhaps originally composed in the 12th Dynasty), silver had acquired a value approximately half that of gold. It was imported into Egypt from western

Asia and the Mediterranean, and became readily available only from the New Kingdom (1550–1069 BC) onwards. A study by Jaroslav Černy, based on New Kingdom ostraca recording sales and other transactions, suggests that metal prices remained relatively constant between the 12th and the 19th Dynasties (c.1985–1186 BC), with silver maintaining half the value of gold, and copper about one-hundredth the value of silver.

Despite (or perhaps even because of) the increased quantity of silver available in the New Kingdom, the tomb of Tutankhamun (1336–1327 BC; KV62) contained relatively little silverwork. The rulers of the 21st and 22nd Dynasties, who were buried at TANIS, made greater use of silver in their burials. Sheshonq II (c. 890 BC) had a solid silver coffin with gilded details in the form of the hawk-god SOKAR. Silver was regarded as the material from which the bones of the gods were fashioned, while their flesh was considered to be made from gold.

F. BISSON DE LA ROQUE, 'Le trésor de Tod', *CdE* 12 (1937), 20–6.

J. ČERNY, 'Prices and wages in Egypt in the Ramesside period', *Cahiers d'Histoire Mondiale* I (1954), 903–21.

A. LUCAS, *Ancient Egyptian materials and industries*, 4th ed. (London, 1962), 245–9.

N. H. GALE and Z. A. STOS-GALE, 'Ancient Egyptian silver', *JEA* 67 (1981), 103–15.

Z. A. STOS-GALE and N. H. GALE, 'Sources of galena and silver in Predynastic Egypt', *Actes du XXe Symposium international d'archéometrie, Paris 26–29 mars 1980* III [*Revue d'Archéométrie*, Supplément 1981] (Paris, 1981), 285–96.

Sinai

Peninsula situated between Egypt and the Levant at the northern end of the Red Sea and to the east of the Suez canal, which has tradi-

Relief fragment of King Sanakht from the turquoise mines at Wadi Maghara, central Sinai. 3rd Dynasty, c.2680 BC, sandstone, H. 33 cm. (EA691)

tionally been settled by BEDOUIN. The people of the Nile valley and southern Palestine periodically exploited its mineral resources (primarily consisting of TURQUOISE and COPPER), and created settlements, shrines and rock-carvings at sites such as Serabit el-Khadim, Wadi Maghara, Wadi Arabah and Timna. A major archaeological survey of the Sinai was undertaken by Flinders PETRIE in 1904–5, and in the 1990s many sites were investigated in northwestern Sinai in advance of the construction of a new canal.

Texts written in an unusual script known as Proto-Sinaitic have been found at a number of places in the Sinai, including Serabit el-Khadim, as well as at sites in Palestine. The script consists of at least twenty-three signs, about half of which appear to derive from Egyptian hieroglyphs, and the texts probably date from the late Middle Kingdom (c.1800–1650 BC) or Second Intermediate Period (1650–1550 BC), but it has still not been properly deciphered. It is possible that Proto-Sinaitic represents a crucial early stage in the development of the alphabet.

W. M. F. PETRIE and C. T. CURRELLY, *Researches in Sinai* (London, 1906).

W. F. ALBRIGHT, *The proto-Sinitic inscriptions and their decipherment* (Cambridge, MA, and London, 1966).

B. ROTHENBERG et al., *Sinai: pharaohs, miners, pilgrims and soldiers* (New York, 1979).

W. V. DAVIES, *Egyptian hieroglyphs* (London, 1987), 57–60.

Sinuhe, Tale of *see* LITERATURE

Sirius *see* SOPDET

sistrum (Egyptian *seshesht*; Greek *seistron*) Musical rattling instrument played primarily by women, except when the pharaoh was making offerings to the goddess HATHOR. Although most surviving Greco-Roman examples are made mainly of bronze, many ritual or funerary examples, which would often have been non-functional, were made from other materials such as wood, stone or faience.

Priestesses, princesses and royal wives were often represented shaking the instrument while participating in rituals or ceremonial activities. There were two basic types of sistrum, hooped and NAOS-shaped, both of which were closely associated with the cult of Hathor, whose head was often depicted on the handle. An early travertine sistrum inscribed with the names of the 6th-Dynasty ruler TETI (2345–2323 BC) takes the form of a papyrus topped by a *naos*, which is itself surmounted by a falcon and cobra, thus forming a rebus of

Detail of a Book of the Dead papyrus bearing the figure of the priestess Anhai shaking a sistrum and holding a length of vine. 20th Dynasty, c.1100 BC. (EA10472, SHEET 7)

the name of Hathor (i.e. *hwt Hor*). The *naos*-style sistrum thus dates back at least as early as the Old Kingdom (2686–2181 BC), but it was the hooped style which became most common by the Greco-Roman period (332 BC–AD 395).

N. DE G. DAVIES, 'An alabaster sistrum dedicated to King Teta', *JEA* 6 (1920), 69–72.

F. DAUMAS, 'Les objects sacrés de la déesse Hathor à Dendara', *RdE* 22 (1970), 63–78.

C. ZIEGLER, *Catalogue des instruments de musique égyptiens* (Paris, 1979), 31–40.

Siwa Oasis (anc. Sekhet-imit; Ammonium)

Natural depression in the Libyan Desert about 560 km west of Cairo, where the earliest remains date to the 26th Dynasty (664–525 BC). The site includes the cemetery of Gebel el-Mawta, dating from the 26th Dynasty to the Roman period, and two temples dedicated to the god AMUN, dating to the reigns of Ahmose II (570–526 BC) and Nectanebo II (360–343 BC) respectively. In 332 BC the famous oracle of Amun at Siwa is said to have been visited by ALEXANDER THE GREAT, where he was officially recognized as the god's son

and therefore the legitimate pharaoh. In the Middle Ages, the caravan route from northwest Africa passed through the Siwa Oasis.

A. FAKHRY, *The oases of Egypt* I: *Siwa Oasis* (Cairo, 1973).

K. P. KUHLMANN, *Das Ammoneion: Archäologie, Geschichte und Kultpraxis des Orakels von Siwa* (Mainz, 1988).

slaves

Attempts to analyse the use of slaves in ancient Egyptian society have often been thwarted by problems of definition and translation, as well as by the emotive connotations of a term that invariably conjures up anachronistic visions either of ancient Rome or of the nineteenth-century plantations of the New World.

Most of the population of Pharaonic Egypt were tied to the land or followed strictly hereditary professions; these men or women were often included among the possessions of kings, high-ranking officials or TEMPLE estates. They might, however, be better described as 'serfs' (*semedet* or *meret*), although even this translation is perhaps too closely connected with images of feudal society in medieval Europe, especially in view of the fact that Egyptian farmers were 'tied to the land' not legally but by tradition and economic circumstances. *Semedet* and *meret* were allowed to own property but appear to have enjoyed very limited freedom by modern western standards.

True slavery, in the Classical sense of the word, seems to have been rare in Egypt before the Ptolemaic period (332–30 BC). Most Egyptian slaves (*hemw* or *bakw*) would have been Asiatic prisoners of war (*khenetw*, or, more commonly, *sekerw ankhw*), although it is clear from records of the Late Period (747–332 BC) that Egyptians too could be slaves, and indeed that they were sometimes obliged to sell themselves into slavery, presumably in order to gain food and shelter or to pay debts. The Jewish mercenaries at Elephantine (ASWAN), for instance, are said to have had Egyptian slaves during the Late Period. It appears that slaves were generally well treated, and some at least seem to have owned property. Both male and female owners of slaves had the right to free them, and it was possible for slaves to marry free-born women and even to own land.

The popular assertion that the PYRAMIDS were built by slave labour finds little support in the surviving textual records of the Old Kingdom (2686–2181 BC), since the work on royal funerary monuments was mostly conducted through corvée labour. Quarrying and mining, however, were sometimes carried out by convicts or foreign prisoners of war. It was

not until the Middle Kingdom and the New Kingdom that prisoners of war became numerous enough to play any perceptible role in Egyptian society. The records of the workmen's village at DEIR EL-MEDINA show that slaves were employed on a communal basis, particularly to help with the grinding of grain for bread-making, and some workmen in the community even owned personal slaves. One 19th-Dynasty worker, Ken, buried in tomb TT4 at Deir el-Medina, appears to have had about twelve slaves, thus illustrating that the ownership of slaves was by no means the exclusive preserve of the élite.

A. EL-M. BAKIR, *Slavery in pharaonic Egypt* (Cairo, 1952).

S. P. VLEEMING, 'The sale of a slave in the time of pharaoh Py', *OMRO* 61 (1980), 1–17.

E. S. BOGOSLOVSKIY, 'On the system of the ancient Egyptian society of the epoch of the New Kingdom', *Altorient Forschungen* 8 (1981), 5–21.

E. CRUZ-URIBE, 'Slavery in Egypt during the Saite and Persian periods', *Revue International des Droits de l'Antiquité* 29 (1982), 47–71.

Smenkhkara *see* AKHENATEN

snake *see* SERPENT

Sneferu (Snofru) (2613–2589 BC)

First pharaoh of the 4th Dynasty, who was deified by the Middle Kingdom and celebrated in later literature as a benevolent and good-humoured ruler. He was the son of his predecessor Huni by Meresankh I (probably a concubine rather than one of the principal wives) and father of KHUFU, the builder of the Great Pyramid at Giza. According to the PALERMO STONE, he sent military expeditions against the Nubians and Libyans as well as quarrying expeditions to the TURQUOISE mines in the Sinai. His 'Horus name' was Nebmaat, but his ROYAL TITULARY was the first to have his other name (i.e. Sneferu) enclosed within an oval ring or CARTOUCHE. It was by this 'cartouche name' that he and subsequent kings were known.

The time of Sneferu is also crucial in terms of the development of the royal pyramid complex, since the three funerary monuments constructed during his reign (one at MEIDUM and two at DAHSHUR) represented the first attempts at true pyramids, moving away from the step-pyramid complexes of the 3rd Dynasty. The North Pyramid (or 'Red Pyramid') at Dahshur is thought to have been the actual burial-place of Sneferu.

A. FAKHRY, *The monuments of Sneferu at Dahshur*, 2 vols (Cairo, 1959–61).

R. STADELMANN, 'Snofru und die pyramiden von

Meidum und Dahschur', *MDAIK* 36 (1980), 437–9.

E. GRAEFE, 'Die gute Reputation des Königs "Snofru"', *Studies in Egyptology presented to Miriam Lichtheim*, ed. S. Isarelit-Groll (Jerusalem, 1990), 257–63.

I. E. S. EDWARDS, *The pyramids of Egypt*, 5th ed. (Harmondsworth, 1993), 70–96.

Snofru *see* SNEFERU

Sobek (Sebek, Suchos)

Crocodile-god who was portrayed either as a CROCODILE (often perched on a shrine or altar) or as a man with a crocodile's head, often wearing a headdress consisting of the horned sun-disc and upright feathers. His two main cult-centres were at the Upper Egyptian site of KOM OMBO, where he shared a temple with HORUS, and at MEDINET EL-FAYUM in the centre of the Fayum region, where the town of Shedyet, later known as Crocodilopolis, once stood. There were, however, numerous other shrines and temples dedicated to Sobek throughout the Nile valley, such as GEBEL EL-SILSILA and GEBELEIN. The temples of crocodile-gods were usually provided with a pool containing sacred crocodiles.

During the 12th and 13th Dynasties the cult of Sobek was given particular prominence, as the names of such rulers as SOBEKHOTEP and SOBEKNEFERU indicate. From

Section of relief in the mammisi at Kom Ombo, showing Ptolemy IX making offerings to a seated figure of the crocodile-god Sobek, c.116–107 BC. (I. SHAW)

the Middle Kingdom onwards, like many other deities, he gradually became assimilated into the cult of the pre-eminent 'state' god AMUN, and in the form Sobek-Ra was worshipped as another omnipotent manifestation of the sun-god. By the Ptolemaic period his association with the sun-god was sufficiently close that he was identified with the Greek god Helios.

C. DOLZANI, *Il dio Sobk* (Rome, 1961).

L. KÁKOSY, 'Krokodilskulte', *Lexikon der Ägyptologie* III, ed. W. Helck, E. Otto and W. Westendorf (Wiesbaden, 1980), 801–11.

Sobekhotep

'Birth name' held by eight rulers of the 13th Dynasty (1795–c.1650 BC), most of whom had very short reigns. The few surviving monuments from the reign of *Sobekhotep II Amenemhat* (c.1750 BC) include relief blocks from MEDAMUD and DEIR EL-BAHRI. *Sobekhotep III Sekhemrasewadjtawy* (c.1745 BC), the son of a Theban prince called Mentuhotep, is credited with the construction of a colonnade and a number of gateways in the temple of Montu at Medamud. A pair of important papyri relating to ADMINISTRATION during the Pharaonic period (one of which lists a month's income and expenditure incurred by the royal court during a period of residence at Thebes) have also survived from his reign. The period encompassed by the reigns of *Sobekhotep IV Khaneferra* (c.1730–1720 BC) and his two brothers, Neferhotep I and Sihathor, was the most stable phase in the 13th Dynasty. There are a number of surviving colossal statues of Sobekhotep IV, as well as several relief

fragments from temples embellished during his reign.

J. VON BECKERATH, *Untersuchungen zur politischen Geschichte der zweiten Zwischenzeit* (Glückstadt and New York, 1964).

D. FRANKE, 'Zur Chronologie in des Mittleren Reiches II', *Orientalia* 57 (1988), 245–74.

S. QUIRKE, 'Royal power in the 13th Dynasty', *Middle Kingdom Studies*, ed. S. Quirke (New Malden, 1991), 123–39.

Sobekneferu (1799–1795 BC)

Last ruler of the 12th Dynasty, whose name means 'beauty of Sobek'. The sister (and perhaps also the wife) of AMENEMHAT IV (1808–1799 BC), she became the first definitely attested female pharaoh, although Queen Nitiqret (c.2180 BC) may have come to power in similar circumstances at the end of the 6th Dynasty. The reign of Sobekneferu appears to have lasted only about three years, but she is credited with completing the construction of the mortuary temple of Amenemhat III (1855–1808 BC) at HAWARA, the so-called 'labyrinth'. The location of her own tomb has not yet been definitely ascertained; it has been suggested that she may have been buried in the uninscribed northern pyramid complex at Mazghuna, immediately to the north of the complex ascribed to Amenemhat IV, but both identifications have been questioned on architectural grounds.

W. M. F. PETRIE, G. A. WAINWRIGHT and E. MACKAY, *The Labyrinth, Gerzeh and Mazguneh* (London, 1912).

I. E. S. EDWARDS, *The pyramids of Egypt*, 5th ed. (Harmondsworth, 1993), 227.

Sokar

God of the Memphite necropolis, who was usually shown as a human figure, often mummiform in appearance, with the head of a hawk. He was also sometimes portrayed as a low mound of earth surmounted by a boat containing the hawk's head – an image that was connected with the title 'he who is upon his sand' in the *Amduat* (see FUNERARY TEXTS). The most spectacular surviving image of the hawk-headed Sokar is the silver coffin of SHESHONQ II (c.890 BC) from TANIS.

The origins of the god, and indeed the very etymology of his name, are obscure; he seems originally to have been a god of the Memphite region, possibly a patron of craftsmen, although he was also venerated as an earth or fertility god. By the Old Kingdom (2686–2181 BC) he was identified with the god of the dead, OSIRIS, who, according to legend, was slain by the evil god SETH at ABYDOS, thus extending the domain of Sokar into

A wooden Ptah-Sokar-Osiris figure standing on a sarcophagus on which are seated four hawks with sun-discs. The bases of such figures, or the figures themselves, were often hollowed out to contain funerary papyri. 26th Dynasty, 664–525 BC, H. 90 cm. (EA9737)

Upper Egypt. This association is doubtless the origin of his funerary role, and it is in this context that he is described in the PYRAMID TEXTS as the creator of 'royal bones' and in the BOOK OF THE DEAD as the maker of foot-basins from silver, which was the material of which divine bones were believed to have been composed.

Sokar was also linked with the god PTAH (at an earlier date than the connections with Osiris), no doubt because both deities shared associations with MEMPHIS and craftsmen, and consequently SEKHMET, the lioness wife of Ptah, came to be regarded as Sokar's consort. In the Old Kingdom, the combined cult of Ptah-Sokar became more elaborate, and by the Middle Kingdom (2055–1650 BC) it had expanded further into Ptah-Sokar-Osiris. From the New Kingdom (1550–1069 BC) onwards, the FESTIVAL of Sokar was lavishly celebrated, particularly in the necropolis of western Thebes, where it is portrayed in some of the reliefs decorating the walls of the second court of the mortuary temple of Rameses III at MEDINET HABU.

It was in the syncretic form of Ptah-Sokar-Orisis that Sokar was most often represented, particularly from the Late Period (747–332 BC) onwards, when many tombs were equipped with wooden statuettes depicting Ptah-Sokar-Orisis as an anthropomorphic mummiform figure, with or without a hawk's head, combined with curled ram horns, sun-disc, plumes and *atef* CROWN. The Ptah-Sokar-Orisis figure was usually shown standing on a miniature sarcophagus base, sometimes surmounted by figures of Sokar-hawks. It was sometimes hollow, in which case it would often have originally contained a copy of a Book of the Dead papyrus or a CORN MUMMY; alternatively, a small piece of the Book of the Dead was occasionally placed in the sarcophagus base. The distinctive amuletic figure of PATAIKOS almost certainly derived from the Ptah-Sokar-Osiris figure.

G. A. GABALLA and K. KITCHEN, 'The festival of Sokar', *Orientalia* 38 (1969), 1–76.

M. J. RAVEN, 'Papyrus-sheaths and Ptah-Sokar-Osiris statues', *OMRO* 59–60 (1978–9), 251–96.

E. BRESCIANI, 'Sokar', *Lexikon der Ägyptologie* V, ed. W. Helck, E. Otto and W. Westendorf (Wiesbaden, 1984), 1055–74.

solar bark (solar boat)

Just as the images of gods were carried between temples or shrines in ceremonial BARKS, so the sun-god and the deceased pharaoh were considered to travel through the netherworld in a 'solar bark'. There were two different types of solar bark, that of the day (*mandet*), and that of the night (*mesektet*). It is possible that the well-known solar barks discovered in the pyramid complex of Khufu at GIZA (one of which has been reconstructed and displayed *in situ*) were intended to serve as a means of conveying the pharaoh through the netherworld.

G. FOUCART, 'Un temple flottant: le vaisseau d'or d'Amon-Ra', *Fondation Eugène Piot: Monuments et mémoires publiés par l'Academie des Inscriptions et Belles Lettres* 25 (1921–2), 143–69.

O. FIRCHOW, 'Königsschiff und Sonnenbark', *WZKM* 54 (1957), 34–42.

K. A. KITCHEN, 'Barke', *Lexikon der Ägyptologie* I, ed. W. Helck, E. Otto and W. Westendorf (Wiesbaden, 1975), 619–25.

P. LIPKE, *The royal ships of Cheops* (Oxford, 1984).

R. H. WILKINSON, *Reading Egyptian art* (London, 1992), 152–3.

Soleb

Site in the third cataract region of Upper Nubia, which was excavated by a team from the University of Pisa between 1957 and 1977. It consists primarily of a sandstone temple built by Amenhotep III (1390–1352 BC), the remains of a town which became the capital of Kush in the late 18th Dynasty, and cemeteries dating mainly to the New Kingdom (1550–1069 BC) and the Meroitic period (300 BC–AD 350).

The temple of Amenhotep III was dedicated both to AMUN-RA of Karnak and to Nebmaatra, lord of Nubia (a deified version of Amenhotep III himself). Nebmaatra was portrayed as an anthropomorphic moon-god wearing the ram's horns of Amun, in effect a local version of KHONS, the son of Amun-Ra and MUT. The temple formed the setting both for the celebration of a SED FESTIVAL and for the ritual of 'illuminating the dais', whereby Nebmaatra was invoked to ensure the regular appearance of the full moon by healing the eye of HORUS. Several myths describe the 'eye' as having fled to Nubia, where it was frequently said to have taken on the appearance of a lioness. It is therefore possible that a pair of red granite lions inscribed with the name of Amenhotep III and originally installed at the temple (and later moved to Gebel Barkal) may have represented the lioness-goddess of the full moon, Tefnut-Mehit. These statues – the 'Prudhoe

The ruins of the temple at Soleb, built by Amenhotep III. From a 19th-century drawing by George Alexander Hoskins. (REPRODUCED COURTESY OF THE GRIFFITH INSTITUTE)

Lions' – are now in the British Museum (see illustration under LION).

M. SCHIFF GIORGINI, *Soleb*, 2 vols (Florence, 1965–71).

Somtutefnakht *see* PERSIA, PERSIANS

Sons of Horus

Four deities (Duamutef, Qebehsenuef, Imsety and Hapy) who were responsible for protecting the internal organs of the deceased (see CANOPIC JARS). Each of the four gods was associated with a particular canopic vessel and its contents, while the gods themselves were said to be protected by particular goddesses. The four are first mentioned in the Old Kingdom (2686–2181 BC), when the PYRAMID TEXTS describe them as the 'friends of the king', assisting him in his ascension to the heavens. Their connection with the god HORUS also dates to this period. In the Middle Kingdom (2055–1650 BC) their association with particular goddesses and specific internal organs was not well defined, but their roles had become clearer by the New Kingdom (1550–1069 BC), by which time they had also become members of the group known as the 'seven blessed ones', who were considered to guard the coffin of the god OSIRIS (father of Horus) in the northern sky.

From the late 18th Dynasty onwards the stoppers of the canopic jars were fashioned in the forms of the heads of each of the four gods (i.e. a jackal, a cynocephalus baboon, a hawk and a man). Drawings and paintings of the four sons consisted of human figures (sometimes mummiform) each with their characteristic head. Their forms and functions are summarized below:

Name of deity	Jar contents	Head	Cardinal point
Imsety	liver	human	south
Hapy	lungs	ape	north
Duamutef	stomach	jackal	east
Qebehsenuef	intestines	falcon	west

Faience figures of the four Sons of Horus. They are (from left to right) Imsety, Duamutef, Qebehsenuef and Hapy. Such canopic figures might be placed within mummy wrappings. Late New Kingdom, H. of Imsety 14.6 cm. (EA26230)

When portrayed on coffins, from the Middle Kingdom onwards, the depictions of Hapy and Qebehsenuef were placed on the west side at the head and foot respectively, while those of Imsety and Duamutef were located in the corresponding positions on the east side. The north (head) end of the coffin was usually protected by NEPHTHYS, while the south (foot) was associated with ISIS.

W. C. HAYES, *The scepter of Egypt* (New York, 1953), 320–1.

A. J. SPENCER, *Death in ancient Egypt* (Harmondsworth, 1982), 157–9.

A. DODSON, *The canopic equipment of the kings of Egypt* (London, 1994).

Sopdet (Sothis)

The goddess Sopdet, known as Sothis in the Greco-Roman period (332 BC–AD 395), was the personification of the 'dog star', which the Greeks called Seirios (Sirius). She was usually represented as a woman with a star poised on her head, although the earliest depiction, on an ivory tablet of the 1st-Dynasty king DJER (c.3000 BC) from Abydos, appears to show her as a seated cow with a plant between her horns. It has been pointed out that, since the plant is symbolic of the year, the Egyptians may have already been correlating the rising of the dog star with the beginning of the solar year, even in the early third millennium BC.

Along with her husband SAH (Orion) and her son SOPED, Sopdet was part of a triad which paralleled that of OSIRIS, ISIS and HORUS. She was therefore described in the PYRAMID TEXTS as having united with Osiris to give birth to the morning star.

J. VANDIER, *Manuel d'archéologie égyptienne* I (Paris, 1952), 842–3.

L. KÁKOSY, 'Die Mannweibliche Natur des Sirius in Ägypten', *Studia Aegyptiaca* 2 (Budapest, 1976), 41–6.

G. CLERC, 'Isi-Sothis dans le monde romain', *Hommages à Maarten J. Vermaseren* (Leiden, 1978), 247–81.

C. DESROCHE-NOBLECOURT, 'Isis Sothis – le chien, la vigne – et la tradition millénaire', *Livre du Centenaire, IFAO 1880–1980* (Cairo, 1980), 15–24.

Soped (Sopdu)

Hawk-god and personification of the eastern frontier of Egypt, whose primary cult-centre was in the twentieth Lower Egyptian nome at the city of Per-Soped (modern Saft el-Hinna), although there are also inscriptions attesting his worship at Serabit el-Khadim in the Sinai peninsula (see TURQUOISE). He was represented either as a crouching falcon or as a bearded man wearing a SHESMET GIRDLE and a head-dress of two falcon feathers, often carrying a WAS SCEPTRE, a battle-axe and an ANKH sign. The PYRAMID TEXTS associate him with the teeth of the deceased pharaoh, but they also describe him as a star who was born from the union of the king (as OSIRIS) and the dog star SOPDET (as Isis). He therefore became associated with the more important hawk-god HORUS (producing the syncretic form Har-Soped), and the triad of Sopdet, SAH and Soped thus paralleled the divine family of ISIS, Osiris and Horus.

I. W. SCHUMACHER, *Der Gott Sopdu, der Herr der Fremdländer* (Freiburg, 1988).

Sothic cycle

In terms of the Egyptian CALENDAR, the dog star Sirius, whose Egyptian name was Sothis (SOPDET) was the most important of the stars or constellations known as decans (see ASTRONOMY AND ASTROLOGY), and the 'Sothic rising' coincided with the beginning of the solar year only once every 1460 years. This astronomical event (known as a heliacal rising) took place in AD 139, during the reign of the Roman emperor Antoninus Pius, and was commemorated by the issue of a special coin at Alexandria. There would have been earlier heliacal risings in 1321–1317 BC and 2781–2777 BC, and the period that elapsed between each such rising is known as a Sothic cycle. The Egyptian textual records of Sothic risings (surviving from the reigns of Senusret III, Amenhotep I and Thutmose III) form the basis of the conventional CHRONOLOGY of Egypt, which, in turn, influenced that of the whole Mediterranean region.

Bronze statuette of the goddess Sopdet. Late Period, after c.600 BC, H. 19 cm. (EA11143)

R. A. PARKER, 'Sothic dates and calendar "adjustment"', *RdE* 9 (1952), 101–8.

J. ČERNY, 'Note on the supposed beginning of a Sothic period under Sethos I', *JEA* 47 (1961), 150–2.

M. F. INGHAM, 'The length of the Sothic cycle', *JEA* 55 (1969), 36–40.

R. KRAUSS, *Sothis- und Monddaten: Studien zur astronomischen und technischen Chronologie* (Hildesheim, 1985).

Sothis *see* SOPDET

soul house *see* OFFERING TABLE

speos (Greek: 'cave')

Term used in Egyptian archaeology to refer to a small rock-cut temple. Egyptologists in the nineteenth century tended to apply the term to comparatively large temples, such as the rock-cut shrines of Rameses II (1279–1213 BC) at ABU SIMBEL, but its use has since become much more restricted.

Speos Artemidos

Rock-cut temple dedicated to the lioness-goddess Pakhet (or Pasht), located about three kilometres east of the Middle Kingdom rock-cut tombs of BENI HASAN, in Middle Egypt.

The temple, locally known as Istabl 'Antar (the 'stable' of Antar, a pre-Islamic hero) was built by Hatshepsut (1473–1458 BC) and Thutmose III (1479–1425 BC). Pakhet ('she who scratches') is known from the COFFIN TEXTS as a night-huntress, which was presumably the reason why the Greeks later identified her with their own Artemis. There is no evidence for any cult of Pakhet in the area of Beni Hasan before the New Kingdom (1550–1069 BC).

The temple consists of a vestibule, supported by eight HATHOR-headed columns, connected by a short corridor with an inner chamber where the cult image would once have stood, although only the niche now survives. An inscription on the architrave above the vestibule describes the ravages of the HYKSOS rulers, and the work of Hatshepsut in restoring the damage they caused. It is usually assumed that this text simply uses the Hyksos as convenient personifications of disorder, since their expulsion had taken place more than seventy-five years earlier, under the reign of her great-grandfather, AHMOSE I (1550–1525 BC). Ironically, the queen's own name was later hacked out when Sety I (1294–1279 BC) inserted his own cartouches instead. The temple is surrounded by the much-plundered burials of sacred CATS, most of which date to the Late Period (747–332 BC).

A. FAKHRY, 'A new speos from the reign of Hatshepsut and Tuthmosis III at Beni-Hasan', *ASAE* 39 (1939), 709–23.

A. H. GARDINER, 'Davies's copy of the great Speos Artemidos inscription', *JEA* 32 (1946), 43–56.

S. BICKEL and J.-L. CHAPPAZ, 'Missions épigraphiques du fonds de l'Egyptologie de Genève au Speos Artemidos', *BSEG* 12 (1988), 9–24.

J. MALEK, *The cat in ancient Egypt* (London, 1993), 97, 126–8.

sphinx

Mythical beast usually portrayed with the body of a lion and the head of a man, often wearing the royal *nemes* headcloth, as in the case of the Great Sphinx at Giza. Statues of sphinxes were also sometimes given the heads of rams (criosphinxes) or hawks (hierakosphinxes). In one unusual case from the mortuary temple of Amenhotep III (1390–1352 BC) a sphinx was given the tail of a crocodile, evidently in imitation of a beast associated with one of the Egyptian constellations. Women are rarely represented in the guise of a sphinx, and even Queen HATSHEPSUT (1473–1458 BC) assumed the form in her masculine role as king rather than as a woman.

The Great Sphinx at Giza probably represents the 4th-Dynasty ruler, Khafra. Although much of the body is carved from a knoll of rock, substantial stone cladding has been added at intervals since Pharaonic times both in response to erosion and as a means of improving areas of poor quality rock. Further conservation work has recently been undertaken. (P. T. NICHOLSON)

Although the ancient Greek term sphinx meant 'strangler', it has been suggested that the origin of the word may have been the Egyptian phrase shesep ankh ('living image'), which was an epithet occasionally applied to sphinxes. The Egyptian sphinx, associated with both the king and the sun-god, was clearly very different from the malevolent female sphinx that features in Greek myths such as the tales of Oedipus and Perseus. Even when Egyptian sphinxes are depicted in the act of trampling on foreign enemies, as in a depiction on a shield from the tomb of TUTANKHAMUN (KV62), the slaughter was clearly regarded simply as one of the archetypal aspects of the kingship. This theme was popular in jewellery, as in the case of the 12th-Dynasty pectoral of Mereret from DAHSHUR, which bears a scene of two falcon-headed sphinxes crushing the enemies of the pharaoh.

The head of a statue of Djedefra (2566–2558 BC), discovered in his pyramid complex at ABU ROASH, is thought to be the earliest

surviving fragment of a sphinx (now in the Louvre). The same site also yielded a small limestone sphinx statuette. However, the Great Sphinx at GIZA, located beside the causeway of the pyramid of KHAFRA (2558–2532 BC), remains the best-known example. Measuring 73 m long and a maximum of 20 m in height, it was carved from a knoll of rock left behind after quarrying. The face probably represents Khafra himself, although it has been argued that it may represent his predecessor Djedefra. On many occasions it has been all but buried by sand and recleared, the most famous instance being recorded on the 'Dream Stele' erected directly in front of the Sphinx by Thutmose IV (1400–1390 BC), describing the promise made to him in a dream that if he cleared the sand he would become king.

A detailed study of the Great Sphinx was undertaken by the American archaeologist Mark Lehner during the 1980s, leading to the suggestion that a standing figure of a king was added between the paws of the Sphinx in the New Kingdom. As early as the 18th Dynasty (1550–1295 BC) the Sphinx was already subject to reconstruction work in the form of limestone cladding, and there has been growing concern with regard to the gradual deterioration of the monument, which has lost its nose, uraeus and divine beard (fragments of the two latter features being in the collections of the

British Museum and the Egyptian Museum, Cairo). More recently erosion and rising ground water have become a problem, and the site is currently the subject of environmental monitoring.

An incomplete 4th-Dynasty temple, apparently made from the same stone as the sphinx itself, was built immediately in front of the monument. It was probably intended for the worship of the three forms of the sun: KHEPRI in the morning, RA at midday, and ATUM in the evening. In the New Kingdom, the Sphinx was identified with Horemakhet ('Horus in the horizon'), and a new temple dedicated to Horemakhet was constructed to the north of the earlier building, which would by then have been completely immersed in sand. This New Kingdom temple was also dedicated to the cult of Hauron, a Canaanite desert-god who may have become identified with the Great Sphinx partly because it was buried in the desert.

From at least as early as the New Kingdom, avenues of sphinxes lined the processional ways (dromoi) leading to many temples, including those of KARNAK and LUXOR. The main entrance to the temple of Amun at Karnak is flanked by rows of criosphinxes, while the pylon of the Luxor temple was approached through avenues of human-headed sphinxes bearing the cartouche of the 30th-Dynasty ruler Nectanebo I (380–362 BC).

E. Chassinat, 'A propos d'une tête en grès rouge du roi Didoufri', *Fondation Eugène Piot: Monuments et mémoires publiés par l'Academie des Inscriptions et Belles Lettres* 25 (1921–2), 53–75.

S. Hassan, *The Sphinx: its history in light of recent excavations* (Cairo, 1949).

C. De Wit, *Le rôle et le sens du lion dans l'Egypte ancienne* (Leiden, 1951).

A. Dessenne, *Le sphinx: étude iconographique* (Paris, 1957).

H. Demisch, *Die Sphinx* (Stuttgart, 1977).

M. Lehner, 'Reconstructing the Sphinx', *CAJ* 2/1 (1992), 3–26.

I. E. S. Edwards, *The pyramids of Egypt*, 5th ed. (Harmondsworth, 1993), 121–4.

standards

Wooden standards, comprising poles surmounted by cult images, were used from the Predynastic period onwards as a means of displaying fetishes or representations of deities symbolizing the different towns and NOMES (provinces) of Egypt. There are depictions of standards on many of the ceremonial PALETTES, maceheads and labels of the late Predynastic and Early Dynastic periods (c.3200–2890 BC). The Bull Palette (now in the

Early Dynastic ivory label showing King Den smiting an Asiatic; on the right-hand side is a standard surmounted by the figure of a jackal. 1st Dynasty, c.2950 BC, from Abydos, H. 4.5 cm. (EA55586)

Louvre) shows a rope clutched by hands on the end of several standards each of which evidently personified regions controlled by an early Egyptian ruler. The SCORPION macehead (Ashmolean Museum, Oxford) inventively used a row of standards as gibbets from which to hang the subject-peoples in the form of REKHYT BIRDS. More conventionally, the NARMER palette (Egyptian Museum, Cairo) shows the king wearing the 'red crown' and preceded by a group of four standard-bearers as he inspects enemy dead.

The term 'standard-bearer' was a military rank designating the commander of a unit of about two hundred men, and the title was held by numerous individuals throughout the Pharaonic period. Whereas the NOME standards usually appear to have been three-dimensional images at the top of the poles, military standards are often represented as rectangular wooden stelae bearing painted figures of gods or occasionally aggressive scenes such as the pair of wrestlers on a Nubian soldiers' standard depicted in the Theban tomb of Tjanuny (TT74, c.1400 BC).

Priests are regularly portrayed in the act of carrying standards bearing either stelae or figurines of deities, as in the case of the wooden statue of a priest called Penbuy holding two standards, each surmounted by divine statuettes (now in the Museo Egizio, Turin). A pair of ebony statuettes of AMENHOTEP III and TIY (Römer-Pelizaeus Museum, Hildesheim) and a faience figurine of Ptah (University of Pennsylvania, Philadelphia) are thought to have derived from temple standards of this type. See also illustration under ART.

C. C. Seligman and M. Murray, 'Note upon an early Egyptian standard', *Man* ii (1911), 165–71.

R. O. Faulkner, 'Egyptian military standards', *JEA* 27 (1941), 12–18.

C. Chadefaud, *Les statues porte-enseignes de l'Egypte ancienne* (Paris, 1982).

S. Curto, 'Standarten', *Lexikon der Agyptologie* v, ed. W. Helck, E. Otto and W. Westendorf (Wiesbaden, 1984), 1255–6.

stars *see* ASTRONOMY AND ASTROLOGY; CALENDAR; SAH; SOPDET and SOTHIC CYCLE

stele

Slab of stone or wood bearing inscriptions, reliefs or paintings, usually of a funerary, votive, commemorative or liminal nature, although these four categories often overlap. The earliest funerary stelae were excavated from the cemetery of 1st- and 2nd-Dynasty kings at ABYDOS The royal stelae at Abydos consisted of pairs of large stone-carved slabs bearing the name of the king written in a SEREKH frame, while the private stelae from the tombs of their courtiers at Abydos and SAQQARA were smaller and less carefully carved.

By the 3rd Dynasty a new type of funerary stele, the FALSE DOOR, had emerged out of a combination of early slab stelae and the inscribed niches into which they were set. This was to be the focal point of the private offering cult for much of the Pharaonic period, providing a symbolic door between the world of the living and the afterlife, through

LEFT Granite stele of Peribsen from tomb P at Abydos. 2nd Dynasty, c.2700 BC, H. 1.13 m. (EA35597)

BELOW Ptah, the patron of craftsmen, receives offerings and adoration from the royal craftsman Penbuy. Painted limestone stele of Penbuy from Deir el-Medina, 19th Dynasty, c.1250 BC, H. 38 cm. (EA1466)

which the KA of the deceased could pass back and forth to partake of the offerings in the chapel. In the early Middle Kingdom a new round-topped type of funerary stele began to be used, particularly in votive contexts such as the offering chapels at Abydos.

Votive stelae, usually placed in temples, were principally rectangular, round-topped slabs decorated with either painted relief decoration or painting over a thin layer of plaster. Large numbers of votive stelae were erected at particularly sacred sites such as Abydos and the Saqqara SERAPEUM, although they are less prominent in the archaeological record than funerary stelae. Most stelae were decorated with scenes of an individual bearing offerings to a deity or simply in the act of worshipping the god or goddess whose assistance was sought, but a special form, known as an 'ear stele', was also decorated with sets of ears, apparently so that the prayer recorded on the stele was heard by a particular aspect of the deity in question: 'he/she who listens to prayers'. These stelae constitute part of the evidence for the growth in 'personal piety' in the New Kingdom, whereby individuals attempted to make their own approaches to deities, rather than relying on PRIESTS to intercede on their behalf.

Commemorative stelae were a form of votive stelae erected in temples by the pharaohs or their courtiers in order to describe royal exploits on behalf of the gods. This category includes the 'KAMOSE Stelae' describing the conquest of the HYKSOS, the 'ISRAEL Stele'

Quartzite stelophorous (stele-bearing) statue of Amenwahsu The stele is inscribed with a prayer to the sun-god and a figure of the god Ra-Horakhty in his bark. 18th Dynasty, c.1450 BC, H. 56 cm. (EA480)

enumerating MERENPTAH'S campaigns against Libyans, Sea Peoples and Asiatics, the 'Victory Stele' of the Kushite ruler PIY, recounting his glorious crusade through Egypt, supposedly re-conquering it on behalf of the god Amun, and the 'Restoration Stele' of TUTANKHAMUN, describing the religious reforms introduced in the immediate aftermath of the Amarna period. A more specialized group of commem-

orative stelae were the rock-cut and freestanding inscriptions carved at sites such as GEBEL EL-SILSILA and HATNUB in order to mark the achievements of quarrying and mining expeditions (see STONE AND QUARRYING AND TURQUOISE).

Liminal stelae were set up to mark the edges of territory, the simplest version being the stones that marked the edges of fields. On a more sophisticated level were the unique 'boundary stelae' at the edges of the city of Akhetaten at EL-AMARNA, and such far-flung monuments as the SEMNA and KURGUS stelae, marking the southernmost BORDERS of Egypt in the 12th and 18th Dynasties respectively.

Stelophorous statues, consisting of human figures holding or offering stelae, were produced from the 18th Dynasty onwards. Such stelae were usually inscribed with hymns to the sun-god.

W. M. F. PETRIE, *The royal tombs of the earliest dynasties* II (London, 1901), pls XXVI–XXXI.

P. LACAU, *Stèles du Nouvel Empire* (Cairo, 1909).

J. VANDIER, *Manuel d'archéologie égyptienne* II/I (Paris, 1954).

L. HABACHI, *The second Kamose stele* (Glückstadt, 1972).

S. WIEBACH, *Die ägyptische Scheintür* (Hamburg, 1981).

W. J. MURNANE and C. VAN SICLEN III, *The boundary stelae of Akhenaten* (London, 1993).

stelophorous statue *see* STELE

stone and quarrying

Whereas many ancient peoples were obliged to trade with other cultures in order to obtain the mineral resources they needed, the Egyptians were well provided with a diverse range of types of stone in the deserts on either side of the Nile valley. Their exploitation of stone is first attested in the form of small chert quarries of the Palaeolithic period, dating to c.35000 BC. In the Predynastic period (c.5500–3100 BC), relatively small pieces of such favoured stones as siltstone, basalt, breccia, limestone, sandstone and granodiorite were being quarried for the production of cosmetic PALETTES, MACES and vessels. The carving of stone vessels, often from very hard stones, for funerary use virtually reached the level of mass production in the Early Dynastic period (3100–2686 BC).

By the mid-third millennium BC there were hundreds of quarries scattered across the western and eastern deserts and the SINAI peninsula and southern Palestine, often in extremely remote areas, since the use of stone was an essential component of the Pharaonic economy, particularly once the reign of DJOSER

and the construction of his Step Pyramid at SAQQARA had ushered in a new era of monumental stone masonry on an unprecedented scale.

The amount of quarrying that took place in each reign of the Pharaonic period (3100–332 BC) can be employed as a kind of measure of political centralization and stability. There are

Unfinished statuette of a woman or goddess, with the surface still showing the marks of the sculptor's chisel. Late Period, c.600 BC, basalt, H. 32 cm. (EA55251)

even some Egyptian rulers who would barely be known if it were not for the remote rock-cut inscriptions commemorating their quarrying expeditions, as in the case of the 11th-Dynasty pharaoh Mentuhotep IV (1992–1985 BC), who sent expeditions to Wadi el-Hudi for amethysts and to the Wadi Hammamat for siltstone (greywacke).

Egyptian kings would often supply their loyal courtiers with the stone they needed for their funerary equipment, and this arrangement seems to have been an important element in the political and personal links between the pharaoh and his officials. The tomb of an official called Weni at Abydos describes the quarrying expeditions that he organized for the king and mentions the royal gift of a fine limestone sarcophagus from the Tura quarries.

Although the scale of many expeditions would have effectively made them royal monopolies, archaeological evidence from the HATNUB travertine ('Egyptian alabaster') quarries, the Umm el-Sawwan gypsum quarries and the Gebel el-Zeit galena (lead sulphide) mines suggests that there was intermittent private exploitation of certain raw materials throughout the Pharaonic period, perhaps following in the footsteps of the major expeditions.

K.-J. SEYFRIED, *Beiträge zu den Expeditionen des Mittleren Reiches in die Ost-Wüste* (Hildesheim, 1981).

J. A. HARRELL, 'An inventory of ancient Egyptian quarries', *NARCE* 146 (1989), 1–7.

D. ARNOLD, *Building in Egypt: pharaonic stone masonry* (New York and Oxford, 1991).

D. and R. KLEMM, *Steine und Steinbrüche im alten Ägypten* (Berlin, 1993).

I. SHAW, 'Pharaonic quarrying and mining: settlement and procurement in Egypt's marginal regions', *Antiquity* 68 (1994), 108–19.

B. G. ASTON, J. HARRELL and I. SHAW, 'Stone', *Ancient Egyptian materials and technology*, ed. P. T. Nicholson and I. Shaw (Cambridge 2000).

Strabo (*c.*63 BC–*c.*AD 21)

Greek historian and geographer, who was born in Pontus but spent several years at Alexandria, which he describes in some detail in the eighth book of his *Geography*. As in HERODOTUS' *Histories*, much of Strabo's information concerns Lower Egypt, but he also discusses the Theban monuments, including the tourist attractions of his day such as the COLOSSI OF MEMNON and the New Kingdom rock-tombs. He also travelled as far south as the first cataract near Aswan in *c.*25 BC, recording the presence of the NILOMETER at Elephantine. Although not generally as informative as the work of Herodotus, Strabo's *Geography* is nevertheless a valuable record of Egypt in the first century BC.

STRABO, *The geography*, trans. H. L. Jones (London, 1932).

strikes

The only evidence for the very modern concept of the 'strike' or withdrawal of labour occurs in some of the surviving documents from the DEIR EL-MEDINA community of royal tomb-workers. The records of the scribe Amennakhte show that the government supplies for the village were repeatedly delayed over a period of six months in the twenty-ninth year of the reign of RAMESES III (1184–1153 BC). The workers therefore eventually went on strike and staged protests in front of the mortuary temples of Thutmose III, Sety I and Rameses II, on the Theban west bank. Despite attempts by the central administration to remedy the situation, further strikes took place later in the year and later documents seem to show that the rest of the Ramesside period was dogged by poor relations between the village and the government. It is possible that the Deir el-Medina strikes are part of the evidence for a steady decline in the political and economic stability of Egypt as it slid gradually towards the fragmentation of

the country in the Third Intermediate Period (1069–747 BC).

W. EDGERTON, 'The strikes in Ramesses III's twenty-ninth year', *JNES* 10 (1951), 137–45.

C. J. EYRE, 'A "strike" text from the Theban necropolis', *Orbis Aegyptiorum Speculum, Glimpses of ancient Egypt: studies in honour of H. W. Fairman*, ed. J. Ruffle, G. A. Gaballa and K. Kitchen (Warminster, 1979), 80–91.

Suchos *see* SOBEK

Sumer, Sumerian

Early Mesopotamian ethnic and linguistic group comprising a series of autonomous city-states, which emerged in about 3400 BC. It was probably the first 'civilization' in the world, perhaps appearing as a result of the stimulation of the organizational demands of irrigation agriculture. Among the principal Sumerian cities were Ur, Eridu, Lagash and Uruk, some of whose rulers are known from king lists compiled in the second millennium BC. Sumerian, the spoken language of the people of Sumer, is unrelated to any other known linguistic group; it was recorded in the CUNEIFORM script, archaic versions of which already appear to be in the Sumerian language in the later fourth millennium BC (i.e. the Uruk and Jemdet Nasr periods). The presence of Sumerian cylinder seals at late Predynastic sites in Egypt has raised the possibility that early cuneiform may have inspired the development of HIEROGLYPHS in Egypt, but there is still considerable debate concerning the connections, if any, between these two ancient scripts. Around 2300 BC Sumer was incorporated into the AKKADIAN empire.

S. N. KRAMER, *The Sumerians* (Chicago, 1963).

H. CRAWFORD, *Sumer and the Sumerians* (Cambridge, 1991).

sun *see* ATEN; ATUM; RA and SHADOW

symplegma (Greek: 'intertwined')

Greek term used to describe a type of sculptural group depicting a group of intertwined figures engaged in sexual intercourse, usually executed in painted terracotta. Votive sculptures of this type were sometimes deposited in shrines and temples, especially in the Ptolemaic period (332–30 BC). The largest surviving *symplegma*, now in the collection of the Brooklyn Museum, New York, is a terracotta Ptolemaic sculpture portraying a nude woman receiving the sexual attentions of four male figures (each wearing the distinctive SIDELOCK of a *sem*-priest), while two attendants hold a representation of a bound oryx. In this instance it has been suggested that orgiastic

scenes were probably associated with the procreative powers of the god OSIRIS, while the bound oryx perhaps symbolized the containment of evil.

R. S. BIANCHI et al., *Cleopatra's Egypt: age of the Ptolemies* (Mainz, 1988), no. 130.

—, 'Symplegma', *Ancient Egyptian art in the Brooklyn Museum*, ed. R. A. Fazzini et al. (New York and London, 1989), no. 82.

syncretism

The process of syncretism, by which two or more deities were fused into the object of a single cult, was a fundamental aspect of the development of Egyptian RELIGION. Erik Hornung has made an eloquent study of the ways in which the attributes and associations of 'local' and 'national' deities were rearranged and combined by the Egyptians in a form of visual and iconographic theology. Thus the recurring concept of a single underlying 'universal' deity was considered to be manifest in a huge variety of Egyptian gods and goddesses. The syncretizing of one god with another, such as the transformation of AMUN and RA into Amun-Ra, and the fusion of PTAH, SOKAR and OSIRIS into the consummate funerary image of Ptah-Sokar-Osiris, was a natural consequence of this flexibility in Egyptian theology. The same process could also be used to assimilate Asiatic, Nubian, Greek or Roman deities into the Egyptian pantheon, as in the case of the Meroitic god Shu-ARENSNUPHIS, the Asiatic goddess ANAT-Hathor, and the Greco-Roman god SERAPIS (Zeus, Helios and Osorapis).

H. BONNET, 'Zum Verständnis des Synkretismus', *ZÄS* 75 (1939), 40–52.

—, 'Synkretismus', *Reallexikon der ägyptischen Religionsgeschichte*, ed. H. Bonnet (Berlin, 1952), 237–47.

J. G. GRIFFITHS, 'Motivation in early Egyptian syncretism', *Studies in Egyptian religion dedicated to Professor Jan Zandee*, ed. M. H. van Voss et al. (Leiden, 1982), 43–55.

E. HORNUNG, *Conceptions of God in ancient Egypt: the one and the many* (London, 1983), 91–9.

Syria–Palestine

Geographical area in western Asia, comprising the southern and northern sections of the Levant, bordered by the SINAI peninsula to the southwest, the Mediterranean to the west, Anatolia to the north, and the Arabian desert and Mesopotamia to the south and east. See BYBLOS; CANAAN; ISRAEL; MEGIDDO and QADESH.

T

Ta-bitjet

Scorpion-goddess closely associated with the bleeding caused by loss of virginity. She is described as the consort of the hawk-god HORUS in certain magical spells intended to avert the consequences of poisonous bites.

taboo (Polynesian *tabu*)

Originally a term applied to the various mechanisms by which Polynesian social divisions were created and maintained. In Egyptology, as in the study of many other ancient civilizations, the term is commonly used in a slightly different sense, to describe the various phenomena that posed a threat to the structure of the universe. Taboos were in effect the means by which the social and metaphysical framework was preserved and reinforced.

The Egyptians believed that taboos were instilled by the creator in particular objects, people and actions, and it was felt that only the creator-god himself, or sometimes the king (functioning as a demiurge), could alter this situation. The word used by the Egyptians to refer to the concept of taboo seems to have been *bwt*, according to Pierre Montet's analysis of cult-topographical lists of the Late Period (747–332 BC). Unless some parts of the universe were declared *bwt* it was considered to be impossible to recreate the primordial state of the universe at the moment of creation, since the act of cosmogony was effectively concerned with the creation and maintenance of the very boundaries from which taboos were derived. One type of taboo affected access to such ceremonial and ritualistic structures as temples, tombs and palaces, in the sense that individuals were prohibited unless they adhered to certain rules of purity, such as abstinence from sexual activity. Other forms of taboo were concerned with the avoidance of such activities as the consumption of certain foodstuffs, including pigs, FISH and honey, or walking upside down (an action somehow connected with faeces). Since the epagomenal days at the end of each year (see CALENDAR) were taboo, it was considered essential for the names of each of the days to be memorized.

Taboos could affect physical entities ranging from bodily orifices to national borders, but they could also apply to events such as copulation or birth. It is important to note,

however, that the most important factor was often the geographical or cultural context rather than the event or act itself. Taboos could often be purely local, affecting only the inhabitants of a region dominated by a particular deity.

In the Victory Stele of the Kushite ruler PIY (747–716 BC) the description of the surrender of the Delta princes involves reference to two taboos regarding CIRCUMCISION and the consumption of fish: 'They were forbidden to enter the palace because they had not been circumcised and they were eaters of fish, which is an abomination to the palace, but King Nimlot was able to enter the palace because he was clean and did not eat fish.'

P. MONTET, 'Le fruit défendu', *Kêmi* II (1950), 85–116.

J. ZANDEE, *Death as an enemy* (Leiden, 1960).

P. J. FRANDSEN, 'Tabu', *Lexikon der Ägyptologie* VI, ed. W. Helck, E. Otto and W. Westendorf (Wiesbaden, 1986), 135–42.

—, 'Bwt – divine kingship and grammar', *Akten München 1985* III, ed. S. Schoske (Hamburg, 1989), 151–8.

Taharqo (Taharka, Taharqa) (690–664 BC)

Third pharaoh of the NAPATAN 25th Dynasty, who inherited the throne of Egypt and Nubia at the age of about thirty-two, on the death of his nephew (or possibly cousin), Shabitqo (702–690 BC). During the first half of his twenty-six-year reign he was able to undertake a considerable amount of construction, particularly in the temple complexes of KARNAK, KAWA, MEDINET HABU and Sanam. He also had his daughter, Amenirdis II, adopted as GOD'S WIFE OF AMUN at Thebes, partly no doubt in order to ensure that MENTUEMHAT, the power-

ful 'fourth prophet of Amun', did not exert too much independent control over the Theban region.

He recorded the early years of his reign on a series of stelae in his temple at KAWA, the first of which dated to the sixth year of his reign. In the seventeenth year (*c*.674 BC) he defeated the invading armies of the ASSYRIAN king Esarhaddon, but three years later Esarhaddon returned and succeeded in driving him out of Memphis, apparently capturing his son and brother in the process. Although Esarhaddon died in 669 BC, his successor Ashurbanipal wasted no time in reconquering Egypt, this time pushing down much further south to Thebes, forcing Taharqo to retreat in exile to the Kushite heartland around Napata.

Once the Assyrian armies had withdrawn, the rulers of the princedoms of Lower Egypt plotted with Taharqo to restore him to power. The Assyrians, however, were alerted to the potential rebellion and promptly killed most of the Delta princes, leaving only the favoured Saite prince NEKAU I (672–664 BC) and his son PSAMTEK I (664–610 BC) as the Assyrian-backed joint rulers of Lower Egypt. Shortly afterwards, Taharqo died in Napata, leaving the throne to his nephew TANUTAMANI (664–656 BC); he was buried in a pyramidal tomb at the royal cemetery of NURI.

M. F. LAMING MACADAM, *The temples of Kawa*, 2 vols (Oxford, 1949–55).

K. MYSLIEWIEC, 'Das Königsporträt des Taharka in Napata', *MDAIK* 39 (1983), 151–7.

W. Y. ADAMS, *Nubia: corridor to Africa* (London and Princeton, 1984), 246–93.

J. LECLANT, 'Taharqa', *Lexikon der Ägyptologie* VI, ed. W. Helck, E. Otto and W. Westendorf (Wiesbaden, 1985), 156–84.

K. A. KITCHEN, *The Third Intermediate Period in Egypt (1100–650 BC)*, 2nd ed. (Warminster, 1986), 387–93.

talatat blocks

Small sandstone relief blocks dating to the Amarna period (*c*.1352–1336 BC), the name for which probably derives from the Arabic word meaning 'three hand-breadths', describing their dimensions (although it has also

Granite sphinx of Taharqo from Temple T at Kawa, Nubia. 25th Dynasty, 690–664 BC, L. 74.7 cm. (EA1770)

been suggested that the word may have stemmed from the Italian for 'cut masonry', *tagliata*). Their distinctive shape derives from the rapid construction techniques employed by AKHENATEN (1352–1336 BC) in commissioning the temples of the Aten at EL-AMARNA and KARNAK, which necessitated the provision of large quantities of smaller, more roughly carved blocks compared with the temples constructed during the rest of the New Kingdom. When the 'heretical' Amarna-period temples were comprehensively dismantled in the reign of HOREMHEB and the early Ramesside period, the *talatat* blocks were preserved through their re-use as rubble in the construction of new temples; Horemheb, for instance, used them to fill the Ninth and Tenth PYLONS in the temple of Amun at Karnak. The largest numbers of *talatat* blocks have been found in the temples of Karnak, LUXOR and HERMOPOLIS MAGNA, although smaller numbers have also been found at several other sites, including Medamud, Asyut and Abydos. The tens of thousands of blocks now form vast and complex jigsaw puzzles, the partial solution of which has already assisted archaeologists in their attempts to reconstruct the plan and appearance of the various Amarna-period temples at el-Amarna and Karnak.

D. B. REDFORD, *Akhenaten, the heretic king* (Princeton, 1984), 65–71.

C. ALDRED, *Akhenaten, king of Egypt* (London, 1988), 69–87.

Talmis *see* KALABSHA

Tanis (anc. Djanet; San el-Hagar)

Most important archaeological site in the northeastern Delta, and capital of the nineteenth Lower Egyptian nome in the Late Period (747–332 BC). The principal excavations at Tanis were carried out in 1860–80 by Auguste MARIETTE, in 1883–86 by Flinders PETRIE and in 1921–51 by Pierre Montet, and the site is still being studied by French archaeologists.

Although many blocks and fragments of reliefs and statuary from the Old and Middle Kingdoms as well as the reign of Rameses II (1279–1213 BC) have been discovered at the site, all of this earlier material appears to have been re-used. Montet believed that the Ramesside sculpture identified the site as Piramesse, the new capital established by Sety I (1294–1279 BC) and Rameses II, but this theory has been invalidated by work at TELL EL-DAB'A and QANTIR (the latter being the actual site of Piramesse). The earliest recorded building at Tanis dates to the reign of

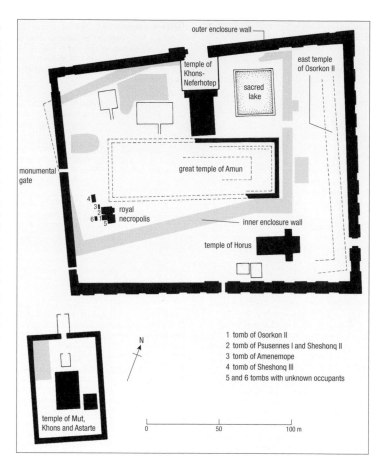

Plan of Tanis.

PSUSENNES I (1039–991 BC) of the 21st Dynasty, who was responsible for constructing the huge mud-brick enclosure wall (430 m × 370 m) surrounding the temple of Amun. Later rulers of the 21st and early 22nd Dynasty added to the temple complex, while NECTANEBO I (380–362 BC) of the 30th Dynasty also built there, removing stone from the temple buildings of SHESHONQ V (767–730 BC) and PSAMTEK I (664–610 BC) for use in the construction of the SACRED LAKE. On the southwestern side of the site, beyond the temple enclosure, is a smaller temple dedicated to MUT and KHONS, where the Asiatic goddess ASTARTE was also worshipped. This building was reconstructed during the reign of Ptolemy IV (221–205 BC).

Montet's discovery, in 1939, of the royal tombs of the 21st and 22nd Dynasties was overshadowed by the outbreak of the Second World War; therefore the finds are less widely known than would otherwise have been the case. Six tombs were discovered: all were subterranean and constructed of a combination of mud-bricks and re-used stone blocks, many of them inscribed. The occupants of two of the tombs are unknown, but the remaining four belonged to Psusennes I, Amenemope (993–984 BC), Osorkon II (874–850 BC) and Sheshonq III (825–773 BC). However, two further royal burials had been placed in these tombs: the tomb of Psusennes I contained the hawk-headed silver coffin of Sheshonq II (c.890 BC) as well as the coffin and sarcophagus of Amenemope, while that of Osorkon II held the sarcophagus of Takelot II (850–825 BC).

The goldwork and other equipment from the Tanis necropolis are the most important source of knowledge concerning royal funerary goods of the Third Intermediate Period (1069–747 BC).

W. M. F. PETRIE, *Tanis*, 2 vols (London, 1885–7).

P. MONTET, *Les nouvelles fouilles de Tanis* (Paris, 1933).

—, *La nécropole royale de Tanis*, 3 vols (Paris, 1947–60).

—, *Le lac sacré de Tanis* (Paris, 1966).

K. A. KITCHEN, *The Third Intermediate Period in Egypt (1100–650 BC)*, 2nd ed. (Warminster, 1986).

G. GOYON, *La découverte des trésors de Tanis* (Paris, 1987).

J. YOYOTTE et al., *Tanis, l'or des pharaons* (Paris, 1987).

—, *Gold of the pharaohs* (Edinburgh, 1988).

Tanutamani (Tantamani, Tanwetamani) (664–656 BC)

Last of the 25th-Dynasty pharaohs, who defeated and killed the ASSYRIAN-backed Saite ruler NEKAU I (672–664 BC) in 664 BC, and was then recognized as king by the Delta princes. He left a stele in the temple at Gebel Barkal which described how, in a dream, the throne of Egypt had been offered to him by goddesses. This method of legitimizing and strengthening his claim to the throne drew not only on the text of the Victory Stele of the NAPATAN ruler PIY (747–716 BC) but also harked back to the 18th-Dynasty Dream Stele of THUTMOSE IV (1400–1390 BC).

Tanutamani's reign over the whole kingdom of Egypt and Nubia lasted for little more than a year. In 663 BC he was overthrown in the same way as his uncle (or cousin) TAHARQO, by the Assyrian king Ashurbanipal, whose armies plundered the temple treasures of Thebes. Despite maintaining control over the Napatan territories in Nubia, Tanutamani was unable to regain control of Egypt itself, where the Assyrians established Nekau's son, PSAMTEK I (664–610 BC), as a vassal ruler. In the Theban region, however, the dates continued to be written in terms of the years of Tanutamani's reign until at least 657 BC, although a local priest, MENTUEMHAT, appears to have wielded the genuine political power. In 656 BC Tanutamani died and was interred in a typical Napatan pyramidal tomb (accompanied by horse burials) in the royal cemetery at EL-KURRU.

K. A. KITCHEN, *The Third Intermediate Period in Egypt (1100–650 BC)*, 2nd ed. (Warminster, 1986), 393–400.

A. A. GASM EL-SEED, 'La tombe de Tanoutamon à El Kurru (Ku.16)', *RdE* 36 (1985), 67–72.

Tatjenen (Tatenen: 'risen land')

Primeval god who is mentioned on the SHABAQO Stone (see OGDOAD and PTAH) in connection with the emergence of the PRIMEVAL MOUND at the moment of creation, as his name suggests. His cult was initially attested at Memphis and became closely associated with the various myths of CREATION; he was effectively the Memphite equivalent of the BENBEN STONE at Heliopolis, although he was also symbolic both of Egypt itself and of the fertile land rising annually from the waters of the inundation. Often portrayed as a bearded man wearing a crown consisting of ram's horns, a sun-disc and two plumes, he was an 'earth god' or chthonic deity, like AKER and GEB, guarding the passage of the SOLAR BARK through the netherworld. In the *Litany of Ra*, however, he is listed as the personification of the phallus of the dead king.

E. A. E. REYMOND, 'The children of Tanen', *ZÄS* 92 (1966), 116–28.

H. A. SCHLÖGL, *Der Gott Tatenen* (Freiburg, 1980).

tattoos *see* COSMETICS

Taweret (Taurt, Thoeris)

Household deity in the form of a female hippopotamus, who was particularly associated with the protection of women in childbirth. She was usually portrayed with the arms and legs of a lion and the back and tail of a crocodile (or even a complete crocodile perched on her back), while her pendulous breasts and full belly clearly conveyed the idea of pregnancy. Her headdress comprised a low MODIUS surmounted by two plumes, sometimes with horns and a disc, and she often held a large SA amulet ('protection') and sometimes an ANKH symbol ('life'). As a result of Mediterranean trade, her image was absorbed into the iconography of the Minoan civilization on the island of Crete, where she was eventually transformed into the somewhat different 'Genius' figure.

The hippopotamus-goddess is attested as early as the Old Kingdom, when she took three principal names: Opet or Ipy ('harim' or 'favoured place'), Taweret ('the great goddess') and Reret ('the sow'). Although there is a temple of Opet at KARNAK, dating to the Late Period and Ptolemaic period, it was the cult of

Figure of the household deity Taweret resting on a sa *sign. She was especially associated with the protection of women in childbirth and is one of the most commonly represented amuletic deities. New Kingdom, rock crystal, H. 9.5 cm. (EA24395)*

Taweret that gained particular importance over time. Like the dwarf-god BES, she appears to have had no cult temples of her own, although a few statues have survived, and she was sometimes portrayed in temple reliefs. The Egyptian system of constellations connected the hippopotamus with the northern sky, and it was in this role as Nebetakhet ('mistress of the horizon') that Taweret was depicted on the ceiling of the tomb of Sety I (1294–1279 BC) in the Valley of the Kings (KV15).

Essentially a benevolent figure, Taweret was widely represented on amulets from the Old Kingdom (2686–2181 BC) onwards, including large numbers excavated from houses at EL-AMARNA (*c.*1340 BC). Because of her protective powers during childbirth, the image of the hippopotamus-goddess was considered a suitable motif for the decoration of beds and headrests. Faience vases in the shape of the goddess, provided with a small pouring hole at the nipple, were sometimes used to

serve milk, presumably in an attempt to instil extra potency into the liquid.

The male hippopotamus was essentially regarded as a destructive animal and therefore closely associated with the evil god SETH. It was presumably with this connection in mind that the Roman historian Plutarch described Taweret as the 'concubine' of Seth, who had changed her ways to become one of the 'followers' of HORUS.

S. QUIRKE, *Ancient Egyptian religion* (London, 1992), 107.

G. ROBINS, *Women in ancient Egypt* (London, 1993), 85–7.

C. ANDREWS, *Amulets of ancient Egypt* (London, 1994) 40–1.

taxation

From at least the Old Kingdom (2686–2181 BC) onwards, the government of Egypt revolved mainly around the collection of taxes by the central and provincial administrators. It is important, however, to try to distinguish between tax and rent and between regular and *ad hoc* taxes. The PALERMO STONE and other surviving documents suggest that there were biennial censuses of agricultural produce so that the 'treasury' could assess the amount of tax to be paid by individuals (although even these censuses may have actually taken place at irregular intervals). Because of the non-monetary economy that operated for almost

Detail of a fragment of wall-painting from the tomb-chapel of Nebamun, showing cattle being paraded in front of a scribe (at the extreme left of the upper register) so that a tax assessment can be made. 18th Dynasty, c.1400 BC, painted plaster from Thebes. H. 58.5 cm. (EA37976)

the whole of the Pharaonic period, taxes were paid in kind. The surviving scenes of daily life in private tombs show that scribes were sent out to measure the precise areas of land under cultivation and to calculate meticulously the numbers of livestock from geese to cattle.

The seriousness with which this system was enforced is indicated by such evidence as the scene depicted in the 6th-Dynasty MASTABA tomb of the vizier Khentika at Saqqara (*c*.2300 BC), showing five men in the process of being punished for corruption in the collection of taxes. A painting in the tomb chapel of Menna, dating to the reign of Thutmose IV (1400–1390 BC), shows a stock scene of the assessment of produce and collection of taxes by SCRIBES, and the subsequent beating of a farmer who has not paid his tax, while Papyrus Lansing, a well-known 20th-Dynasty text (now in the British Museum), describes the severe penalties suffered by a defaulting farmer and his family, despite their failed harvest. The tomb of an 18th-Dynasty vizier called REKHMIRA (*c*.1425 BC) is decorated with a portrayal of the reception of taxes on behalf of the king, including detailed descriptions of specific amounts of such products as cakes, barley, honey, reed mats, gold ingots and linen. It is interesting to note that the scribes themselves usually seem to have been exempt from taxation, although it has been pointed out that the tax was generally levied on agricultural produce, which the non-farming scribes would rarely have owned in the first place. 'Exemption decrees' could be issued to individuals and institutions; these are our chief source of knowledge of taxation.

A. H. GARDINER, 'A protest against unjustified tax demands', *RdE* 6 (1951), 115–24.

B. J. KEMP, *Ancient Egypt: anatomy of a civilization* (London, 1989), 234–8.

Tefnut

Goddess associated with moisture or damp, corrosive air. She and her brother-husband SHU were the first gods created by ATUM, according to the doctrine of Heliopolis (see CREATION). Because she was considered to have been created by a process of ejaculation and spitting, a pair of lips could be used to denote her name. The children of Shu and Tefnut were GEB and NUT.

In the same way that the myths and attributes of Atum gradually merged with those of RA, so Tefnut and Shu became 'EYES OF RA'; in these roles, Tefnut took the head of a lioness, and Shu that of a lion. Both were worshipped in these forms at Leontopolis (TELL EL-MUQDAM) in the Delta. Tefnut was also identified with the *uraeus* (see WADJYT), thus establishing an association with the KINGSHIP, and it was in this connection that she appeared in the PYRAMID TEXTS in the form of a serpent rearing from a sceptre.

W. SPIEGELBERG, *Der ägyptische Mythus von Sonnenauge* (Leiden, 1917).

S. WEST, 'The Greek version of the legend of Tefnut', *JEA* 55 (1969), 161–83.

S. QUIRKE, *Ancient Egyptian religion* (London, 1992), 25–31.

tekenu

Enigmatic figure which played an uncertain role in private funerary rites. Scenes on the walls of tombs of the early New Kingdom, such as that of Reneni at ELKAB (EK7), dating to the reign of Amenhotep I (1525–1504 BC), portray the *tekenu* as a man wrapped in a skin or bag, usually taking the form of a human-headed sack-like bundle placed on a sledge and drawn along by cattle as part of the funeral ceremonies. Since it was carried alongside the coffin and canopic equipment, it has been suggested that the sack may have simply contained the parts of the body that could neither be mummified nor placed in CANOPIC JARS but were nevertheless essential to the full resurrection of the deceased. It would perhaps also have served as an image of the body itself.

The *tekenu* has also been interpreted as a symbolic survival of the practice of funerary HUMAN SACRIFICE or even as a symbol of the contracted form of corpses of the Predynastic period, although there is little evidence to substantiate either of these views.

J. GWYN GRIFFITHS, 'The tekenu, the Nubians and the Butic burial', *Kush* 6 (1958), 106–20.

E. HORNUNG, *Idea into image*, trans. E. Bredeck (New York, 1992), 169–70.

Scene from the tomb of Reneni at Elkab (EK7) showing funerary rites, including the opening of the mouth (middle register), and procession. In the upper register the tekenu *can be seen being pulled along on a sledge in front of men carrying a chest. 18th Dynasty, c.1520 BC. (P. T. NICHOLSON)*

Tell

All site names beginning with 'Tell' are alphabetized under the second part of the name, e.g. Yahudiya, Tell el-.

tell (Arabic: 'mound')

Term usually employed to describe an artificial mound consisting of superimposed settlement remains. Although many Egyptian toponyms incorporate the word it is more accurately applied to sites elsewhere in the Near East – the site of 'TELL EL-AMARNA', for instance, derives from local tribal names rather than topography.

temenos

Ancient Greek term used to describe the sacred precinct surrounding the cult place of a deity. In Egyptian religious architecture it is usually loosely applied to the area within the enclosure wall of a temple. The religious complex at KARNAK consisted of three distinct *temenoi*: the precincts relating to the temples of AMUN, MUT and MONTU respectively.

temple

Building or complex of buildings regarded by the ancient Egyptians as the 'house' of a deity (or deities). The most essential component of

the Egyptian temple was the innermost cult-chamber or SHRINE, where the image of the deity was kept. The activities of the temple revolved around the worship and celebration of the deity's cult via the image in the shrine, and the building itself was not a meeting-place for worshippers but an architectural setting for the celebration of the cult.

The modern conception of the Egyptian temple is biased by two principal factors of archaeological preservation. First, very few pre-New-Kingdom temples have survived, primarily because Egyptian temples were repeatedly rebuilt in the same sacred area, therefore the earliest structural phases were often obliterated, buried and recycled in constructing the later versions of the temple.

Second, most Lower Egyptian religious complexes, such as the temple of Ptah at MEMPHIS and the sun temple at HELIOPOLIS (Iwnw), have been heavily pillaged over the centuries, therefore comparatively little of their plan and decoration has been preserved. The result of these two archaeological distortions is that the modern view of the Egyptian temple is based almost entirely on Upper Egyptian temples dating from the New Kingdom (1550–1069 BC) onwards. The most elaborate surviving example of the Upper Egyptian temple is the precinct of Amun at KARNAK, while the best-preserved such building is the temple of Horus at EDFU, dating to the Ptolemaic period (332–30 BC).

The typical post-Middle Kingdom Upper Egyptian temple appears to have consisted of a series of processional ways through which the king and his priests could gradually approach the cult image in its NAOS. The same conduits also provided the backdrop for religious FESTIVALS, which usually consisted of the transportation of the cult image, carried in a BARK, from one temple to another. Within the confines of the temple, these processional ways passed through open courtyards, HYPOSTYLE HALLS and massive ceremonial gateways known as PYLONS. The decoration of the external walls of the temple tended to concentrate on the motif of the king's conquest over enemies and wild beasts, symbolizing the protection of the god's cult. The painted reliefs on the internal walls usually depicted aspects of the performance of rituals, showing the king engaged in the presentation of offerings to the various deities associated with the temple, and thus performing his role of intermediary between the human and the divine.

The temple was also considered to be an architectural metaphor both for the universe

Reconstruction drawing of the temple of Khons at Karnak, built during the 20th Dynasty, c.1100 BC. (DRAWN BY CHRISTINE BARRATT)

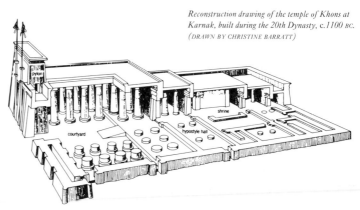

and for the process of CREATION itself. The floor gradually rose, passing through forests of plant-form columns and roofed by images of the constellations or the body of the sky-goddess NUT, allowing the priests to ascend gradually from the outermost edge of the universe towards the sanctuary, which was a symbol of the inner core of creation, the PRIMEVAL MOUND on which the creator-god first brought the world into being.

Apart from serving as universal metaphors and eternal backdrops for the celebration of cult and ritual, the temples also served as important parts of the Egyptian economic infrastructure. Each was founded not merely as a hollow building but as an important institution employing large workforces and endowed with such reliable sources of income as agricultural land and gold mines. The main temple was therefore invariably surrounded by ancillary buildings such as granaries and slaughter-houses, in which the daily offerings were stored and processed, usually eventually being re-distributed to feed the temple staff themselves. The administration of the temple, which in modern terms might be divided into ritualistic and economic activities, is documented both in the temple reliefs and in certain surviving archives of papyri, particularly those that have been excavated from the Old Kingdom mortuary temples of Neferirkara (2475–2455 BC) and Raneferef (2448–2445 BC) at ABUSIR.

H. W. FAIRMAN, 'Worship and festivals in an Egyptian temple', *Bulletin of the John Rylands Library, Manchester* 37 (1954), 165–203.

A. R. DAVID, *A guide to religious ritual at Abydos* (Warminster, 1981).

P. SPENCER, *The Egyptian temple: a lexicographical study* (London, 1984).

B. J. KEMP, *Ancient Egypt: anatomy of a civilization* (London, 1989), 91–105.

D. O'CONNOR, 'The status of early Egyptian temples: an alternative theory', *The followers of Horus*, ed. R. Friedman and B. Adams (Oxford, 1992), 83–98.

Teti (2345–2323 BC)

First ruler of the 6th Dynasty (2345–2181 BC) whose reign probably does not represent any sharp break with the preceding reign of UNAS, in that he married Iput, one of Unas' daughters, although it seems likely that his father came from outside the 5th-Dynasty royal family. Teti was the first of many rulers to take the Horus name Sehetep-tawy ('pacifier of the two lands') in his ROYAL TITULARY, possibly suggesting a desire on his part to remedy problems in the administration, which had become less stable by the end of the 5th

Dynasty, as a result of the increasing power of nomarchs (provincial governors). The evidence of his more concrete attempts to adjust the balance of power includes firstly a stele at Abydos exempting temples from TAXATION and secondly the marriage of his eldest daughter to the vizier MERERUKA, who was later to be chief priest of his funerary cult.

The historian MANETHO claims that Teti was eventually assassinated by his bodyguards, and although there is no other evidence for this, it seems likely that PEPY I, his true heir and eventual successor, was initially usurped by Userkara. Little is known about the latter who reigned for only a year and may have been a descendant of a 5th-Dynasty pharaoh.

Teti's pyramid complex, excavated by James Quibell in 1907–8, is situated in north Saqqara, accompanied by the MASTABA tombs of several of his officials, including that of Mereruka. In a revival of a 4th-Dynasty tradition, the complex included pyramids for two queens (Iput and Kawit). The internal passage of the pyramid was only the second to be inscribed with PYRAMID TEXTS, and the burial chamber contained a grey basalt sarcophagus, the body and funerary equipment having been plundered in ancient times. A plaster death-mask (now in the Egyptian Museum, Cairo) was found in his mortuary temple, but it is uncertain whether it was taken from the body of Teti himself.

C. M. FIRTH and B. GUNN, *The Teti pyramid cemeteries*, 2 vols (Cairo, 1926).

J.-P. LAUER and J. LECLANT, *Le temple haut du complexe funéraire du roi Téti* (Cairo, 1972).

N. GRIMAL, *A history of ancient Egypt* (Oxford, 1992), 80–1.

I. E. S. EDWARDS, *The pyramids of Egypt*, 5th ed. (Harmondsworth, 1993), 179–80.

Tetisheri (c.1590–1540 BC)

Wife of the 17th-Dynasty Theban ruler Senakhtenra Taa I and mother of SEQENENRA TAA II, who appears to have been of non-royal origin. She survived until the early 18th Dynasty and, like her descendants AHHOTEP I and AHMOSE NEFERTARI, appears to have been an unusually influential woman. Her grandson, AHMOSE I, established cenotaphs and funerary estates for both himself and Tetisheri at ABYDOS, where she was granted a posthumous cult as the most important female ancestor of the 18th-Dynasty rulers. Despite her importance, only one statue has survived, the lower portion of a limestone statuette, the present location of which is now unknown. The collection of the British Museum includes a seated statuette purporting to represent Tetisheri, but this has been identified as a forgery.

M. H. GAUTHIER, *Livre des rois d'Egypte* II, 159–60.

—, 'Monuments et fragments appartenant à l'Institut Français d'Archéologie Orientale du Caire', *BIFAO* 12 (1916), 125–44 (128–9).

W. V. DAVIES, *A royal statue reattributed* (London, 1981).

Thebes (anc. Waset)

Principal city of Upper Egypt and capital of the fourth Upper Egyptian nome. The archaeological remains of the city and temples of Thebes surround the modern city of Luxor on the east bank of the Nile, while the west bank is the site of the mortuary temples and tombs of kings and high officials from the Middle Kingdom to the end of the Pharaonic period (c.2055–332 BC). Because of its long and important history, Thebes has been a centre of archaeological research since at least the time of the Napoleonic expedition (1798–1802; see EGYPTOLOGY).

The ancient Egyptians knew the town as Waset, symbolized by the WAS SCEPTRE, but the Greeks called it Thebes, after their own city of the same name in Boeotia. Unlike other major cities of the Pharaonic period, such as MEMPHIS, HELIOPOLIS or ABYDOS, its origins were comparatively recent; it probably emerged as a small provincial town during the Old

Gilded wooden rishi *coffin of King Nubkheperra Intef from his tomb at Dra Abu el-Naga. The necropolises of Thebes are a major source of knowledge on funerary practices. 17th-Dynasty, c.1650 BC, H. 1.93 m. (EA6652)*

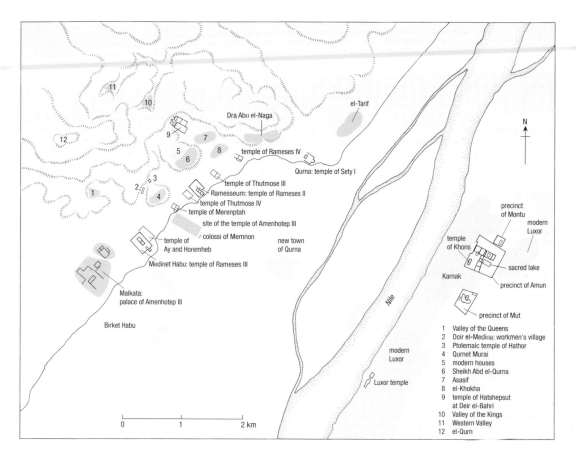

Plan of Thebes.

1 Valley of the Queens
2 Deir el-Medina: workmen's village
3 Ptolemaic temple of Hathor
4 Qurnet Murai
5 modern houses
6 Sheikh Abd el-Qurna
7 Asasif
8 el-Khokha
9 temple of Hatshepsut
   at Deir el-Bahri
10 Valley of the Kings
11 Western Valley
12 el-Qurn

Kingdom (2686–2181 BC), but eventually assumed a more prominent role in the First Intermediate Period (2181–2055 BC), as the principal rival to the 'Herakleopolitan' dynasty of Lower Egypt (see HERAKLEOPOLIS MAGNA and MENTUHOTEP II).

The 9th and 10th Dynasties of Lower Egypt ruled from the traditional administrative centre, Memphis, but the roughly contemporary 11th-Dynasty rulers of Upper Egypt came from ARMANT and therefore established Thebes as their seat of power. At the end of the First Intermediate Period the Theban rulers emerged victorious, ousting the Herakleopolitans and gaining control of the whole of Egypt. The Middle Kingdom pharaohs then ruled from the newly founded city of Itjtawy ('taking possession of the two lands'), situated near the new necropolis of EL-LISHT, although they clearly still regarded Thebes as their sacred city. The rulers of the 12th Dynasty (1985–1795 BC; see AMENEMHAT and SENUSRET) established Thebes as the capital of Upper Egypt, and henceforth AMUN, the local god of Thebes, became increasingly prominent. In the 11th Dynasty royal burials were already being made on the west bank, notably at el-Tarif in the north but also at DEIR EL-BAHRI, where Mentuhotep II (2055–2004 BC) built his funerary complex. By the New Kingdom (1550–1069 BC) the Theban west bank was developing into a great necropolis that would eventually rival the Memphite necropolis of SAQQARA in importance.

At the end of the Second Intermediate Period (1650–1550 BC) it was once again a local Theban dynasty that rose to power, expelling the HYKSOS from Egypt and reunifying the country. Burials of the 17th Dynasty are concentrated around Dra Abu el-Naga between el-Tarif and Deir el-Bahri. The 114 known rock-tombs at Dra Abu el-Naga include those of officials from the early New Kingdom to the Late Period (c.1550–500 BC), as well as the pyramidal royal burials of the 17th-Dynasty rulers and their families (c.1650–1550 BC). The area has been extensively plundered and many of the tombs have now been badly damaged or lost.

The New Kingdom was the most important period in Theban history, and it was during this period that successive rulers began to enlarge and elaborate the temple complex of KARNAK, the *ipet-isut*, 'most favoured of places', founded in the 12th Dynasty and dedicated to the divine triad of Amun, MUT and KHONS, as well as MONTU (another local god). In the reign of AMENHOTEP III

(1390–1352 BC) the LUXOR temple (the *ipet-resyt*, 'private chambers to the south') was founded, a short distance to the south of Karnak.

On the west bank the VALLEY OF THE KINGS became the burial place of the New Kingdom rulers from at least as early as the reign of THUTMOSE I (1504–1492 BC), while many of the highest officials of each of the reigns were buried nearby on the hill slopes of Dra Abu el-Naga, Deir el-Bahri, el-Khoka, Asasif, Sheikh Abd el-Qurna and Qurnet Murai. A long row of mortuary temples also stood on the west bank, usually with communities of officials, priests and servants housed in the vicinity (see MEDINET HABU and RAMESSEUM). At DEIR EL-MEDINA was the walled settlement and cemetery of the workmen responsible for constructing the royal tombs. A number of royal palaces were also constructed on the west bank, ranging from the comparatively small buildings attached to the mortuary temples to the sprawling complex of buildings from the reign of Amenhotep III at MALKATA.

Even in the Ramesside period (1295–1069 BC), when the royal palace and the central administration were transferred to the Delta (see QANTIR and TELL EL-DAB'A), Thebes retained a great deal of its religious and political significance, and the bodies of rulers were still brought to western Thebes for burial in the Valley of the Kings. The kings of the 21st and 22nd Dynasties (1069–747 BC) governed from various cities in the Delta, but they lacked the strength to control the whole country, and at this time Libyan generals, from HERIHOR onwards, controlled Upper Egypt from their power-base at Thebes. It was only in the Late Period (747–332 BC) that the importance of the city finally seems to have dwindled in favour of Memphis, TANIS, SAIS and BUBASTIS.

B. PORTER and R. L. B. MOSS, *Topographical bibliography* I–II (Oxford, 1964–72).

E. RIEFSTAHL, *Thebes in the time of Amunhotep III* (Norman, OK, 1964).

J. BAINES and J. MALEK, *Atlas of ancient Egypt* (Oxford, 1980), 84–105.

L. MANNICHE, *City of the dead: Thebes in Egypt* (London, 1987).

Thinis, Thinite period

The remains of the ancient town of Thinis, capital of the Thinite region, have never been located, although it has been suggested that they may have been situated in the vicinity of the modern village of Girga, several kilometres to the north of the Predynastic and Early Dynastic cemeteries of ABYDOS.

The Thinite region appears to have been the most important of the small states that were competing for control of Upper and Lower Egypt, at the end of the Predynastic period. The first two Egyptian dynasties, covering a period of over four hundred years (*c*.3100–2686 BC), were described by the Egyptian historian Manetho as the 'Thinite period', in recognition of the fact that Early Dynastic Thinis enjoyed a short period of pre-eminence, when it was the seat of power of the first rulers of a united Egypt. It is unclear, however, precisely when the centre of power transferred northwards to MEMPHIS, thus diminishing the political role of Thinis and leaving Abydos as a site of purely ceremonial and ritualistic importance (see ABYDOS and SAQQARA for discussion of the possible roles of the Thinite and Memphite necropolises).

Third Intermediate Period (1069–747 BC)

Chronological phase following the NEW KINGDOM. Smendes (1069–1043 BC) succeeded RAMESES XI (1099–1069 BC) as first king of the 21st Dynasty (1069–945 BC), but his was only one line of succession in this period of divided government. Smendes ruled from TANIS, while the High Priests of Amun at Thebes, under Pinudjem I, continued to rule an area stretching from as far north as EL-HIBA (south of the Fayum) to ASWAN in the south. The two lines intermarried, and the Thebans recognized the official Tanite dating system, but maintained Upper Egypt as a separate state.

The Delta-based 22nd Dynasty (945–715 BC) began with the reign of the Libyan ruler SHESHONQ I (945–924 BC). His accession coincided with the decline in power of the Theban High Priests, so that he was able to install his son at Thebes, lending some degree of unity to the two lands. Later in the Dynasty, however, the Thebans appear to have objected to the establishment of Osorkon, son of Takelot II (850–825 BC), as High Priest of Amun, and embarked on a civil war with the northern rulers. The establishment of rival dynasties followed, with the result that 22nd to 24th Dynasties were all ruling simultaneously in different parts of the country.

Osorkon III (777–749 BC) established his daughter Shepenwepet as GOD'S WIFE OF AMUN in Thebes. The importance of this post as, at the very least, a symbol of the political control of Thebes, meant that it was subsequently filled by a series of adoptions imposed by the dominant ruler of the time. It was perhaps by this means that the Kushite 25th Dynasty demonstrated that it had secured religious as well as political authority in the region. Despite having gained the Theban region,

however, the 25th Dynasty was still thwarted for a while by the 24th Dynasty (727–715 BC) ruling from the town of SAIS in the Delta. The Napatan ruler PIY (747–716 BC) campaigned as far north as Memphis until he was satisfied that he had secured control of the Nile valley, then he withdrew to NAPATA. His campaigns, however, were inconclusive, necessitating further military activity by his successor, SHABAQO (716–702 BC) at the beginning of the LATE PERIOD (747–332 BC).

M. BIERBRIER, *The late New Kingdom in Egypt (c.1300–664 BC): a genealogical and chronological investigation* (Warminster, 1975).

D. O'CONNOR, 'New Kingdom and Third Intermediate Period, 1552–664 BC', *Ancient Egypt: a social history*, ed. B. G. Trigger et al. (Cambridge, 1983), 183–278.

K. KITCHEN, *The Third Intermediate Period in Egypt*, 2nd ed. (Warminster, 1986).

R. FAZZINI, *Egypt: Dynasty XXII–XXV* (Leiden, 1988).

K. JANSEN-WINKELN, 'Das Ende des Neuen Reiches', *ZÄS* 119 (1992), 22–37.

—, 'Der Beginn der Libyschen Herrschaft in Ägypten', *BN* 71 (1994), 78–97.

Thoeris *see* TAWERET

Thoth (Djehuty)

God of writing and knowledge, who was depicted in the form of two animals: the baboon (*Papio cynocephalus*; see CYNOCEPHALUS) and the sacred IBIS (*Threskiorn aethiopicus*), both of which are elegantly portrayed on the exterior of the unusual early Ptolemaic tomb-chapel of a priest of Thoth called PETOSIRIS. In his baboon form Thoth was closely associated with the baboon-god, Hedj-wer ('the great white one') of the Early Dynastic period (3100–2686 BC). By the end of the Old Kingdom (2686–2181 BC) he was most frequently portrayed as an ibis-headed man, usually holding a scribal palette and pen or a notched palm-leaf, engaged in some act of recording or calculation. Utterance 359 of the PYRAMID TEXTS describes how the gods gained access to the netherworld by travelling 'on the wing of Thoth' across to the other side of the 'winding waterway'.

He was worshipped, along with his little-known consort, Nehmetaway, at the ancient city of Khmun (HERMOPOLIS MAGNA) in Middle Egypt, although there was also a temple of Thoth at DAKHLA OASIS and at Tell Baqliva in the Delta. There are few surviving remains of the temple at Khmun, but two colossal baboon statues erected by Amenophis III (1390–1352 BC) still dominate one area of the site (see illustration under HERMOPOLIS MAGNA).

Squatting figure of the god Thoth in the form of a baboon, inscribed with the cartouches of Amenhotep III. 18th Dynasty, c.1390 BC, quartzite, H. 67 cm. (EA38)

Thoth was closely associated with the moon (the second 'EYE OF RA') and was regularly shown with a headdress consisting of a disc and crescent symbolizing the lunar phases. It is possible that the long curved beak of the ibis was identified both with the crescent moon and with the reed pen. An association with the passing of time is reflected in those depictions that show him recording the king's names on the leaves of the persea tree. In vignettes of the 'judgement of the dead', regularly included in Book of the Dead papyri in the New Kingdom (1550–1069 BC), Thoth was often shown both in his anthropomorphic, ibis-headed manifestation, recording the results of the weighing of the heart of the deceased, and, less frequently, as a baboon. Sometimes, in addition, he is shown as a baboon perched on top of the scales. It was probably because of his role as guardian of the deceased in the netherworld, and as an intermediary between the various deities, that he became associated with the Greek god Hermes in the Ptolemaic period (332–30 BC), hence the renaming of the city of Khmun as Hermopolis Magna.

C. BOYLAN, *Thoth, the Hermes of Egypt* (Oxford, 1922).

C. J. BLEEKER, *Hathor and Thot* (Leiden, 1973).

A. P. ZIVIE, *Hermopolis et le nome de l'ibis: recherches sur la province du dieu Thot en Basse Egypte* (Cairo, 1975).

M. T. DERCHAIN-URTEL, *Thot: rites égyptiens 3* (Brussels, 1981).

—, 'Thot à Akhmim', *Hommages à F. Daumas*, ed. A. Guillamont (Montpellier, 1986), 173–80.

J. QUAEGEBEUR, 'Thot-Hermès, le dieu le plus grand!', *Hommages à F. Daumas* (Montpellier, 1986), 525–44.

V. WESSETSKY, 'Tier, Bild, Gott: über die Affen des Thot', *Akten München 1985 III*, ed. S. Schoske (Hamburg, 1989), 425–30.

throne name (prenomen) *see* ROYAL TITULARY

Thutmose (Tuthmosis)

Birth name, meaning 'Thoth is born', held by four 18th-Dynasty pharaohs.

Thutmose I Aakheperkara (1504–1492 BC) was the successor of AMENHOTEP I and the third ruler of the 18th Dynasty. Although his reign was comparatively short, his achievements in terms of foreign policy were significant. The inscriptions at Tombos, in the area of the third Nile cataract, and Kurgus, south of the fourth cataract, indicate that he had consolidated and expanded Egyptian control over Nubia. Another stele (known only from later records) erected on the far side of the river Euphrates and commemorating a successful military incursion into the territory of MITANNI, suggests that he was the first of the New Kingdom pharaohs to gain control of a substantial area of the Levant. The main motivation for Egyptian expansion into Nubia and western Asia lay in the desire to secure trade routes for such raw materials as OILS, timber, COPPER, SILVER and SLAVES, all of which were more difficult to obtain within Egypt itself.

Thutmose I is considered to have been buried in KV38, the earliest tomb in the VALLEY OF THE KINGS at Thebes, but his body was probably among those reinterred in the cache of royal mummies at DEIR EL-BAHRI. Although a sarcophagus bearing his name was discovered in KV38, a second one was also found in the tomb of his daughter HATSHEPSUT (KV20).

Thutmose II Aakheperenra (1492–1479 BC) was the son of Thutmose I by a lesser wife called Mutnofret. In the first year of his reign he erected a victory stele at Aswan, describing the crushing of a revolt in Nubia, thus signaling that he was continuing his father's aggressive foreign policy. A virtually undecorated

tomb in the Valley of the Kings (KV42) containing an uninscribed sarcophagus, was once thought to be his burial place but this is now considered unlikely. His mortuary temple in western Thebes was excavated by French archaeologists in 1926.

Thutmose III Menkheperra (1479–1425 BC) was the son of Thutmose II and a minor wife called Aset. When Thutmose II died, his wife and half-sister Hatshepsut acted as regent for the first few years of the reign of Thutmose III. By year seven of his reign she herself had assumed the full titulary of a pharaoh, thus

Head from a green schist statue probably representing Thutmose III or Hatshepsut. 18th Dynasty, c.1450 BC. H. 45.7 cm. (EA986)

delaying the full accession of her nephew for more than twenty years. He finally came to the throne in his own right in about 1458 BC, presumably on the death of Hatshepsut. It was probably not until relatively late in his reign that he began systematically to remove Hatshepsut's name from her monuments, replacing it with his own.

In his foreign policy he emulated the exploits of Thutmose I, re-establishing

Egyptian suzerainty over Syria–Palestine with the BATTLE OF MEGIDDO in the first year after Hatshepsut's death, thus neutralizing the military threat posed by the Prince of Qadesh and his Mitannian allies. This battle and his subsequent Levantine campaigns were recorded in the Hall of the Annals in the temple of Amun at KARNAK. As well as expanding the cult-centre of Amun, he also built temples at Deir el-Bahri and MEDINET HABU as well as numerous sites in Nubia and the Delta. At ARMANT and SPEOS ARTEMIDOS he completed his stepmother's constructions.

His tomb in the Valley of the Kings (KV34) is decorated with scenes from the *Amduat* ('that which is in the underworld') and his mortuary temple on the Theban west bank has survived, although in poor condition. His mummy was one of those discovered in the Deir el-Bahri cache.

Thutmose IV Menkheperura (1400–1390 BC) was the son of Amenhotep II, the father of Amenhotep III and the grandfather of AKHEN-ATEN. The so-called Dream Stele at Giza describes how he was offered the throne of Egypt in return for removing the sand from the Great Sphinx. Since he does not seem to have been the actual heir to the throne, it is possible that this inscription formed part of the legitimizing of his accession. In terms of foreign policy his reign marked a period of rec-onciliation with Mitanni, including a 'diplo-matic marriage' to the daughter of Artatama I, the Mitannian ruler. He also left a stele at the island of Konosso, near Aswan, commem-orating an expedition to quell rebellion in Nubia. Both his Theban funerary temple and his tomb (KV43 in the Valley of the Kings) have survived, and his mummy was among those recovered from the tomb of Amenhotep II in 1898.

H. E. WINLOCK, 'Notes on the reburial of Tuthmosis I', *JEA* 15 (1929), 56–68.

W. F. EDGERTON, *The Thutmosid succession* (Chicago, 1933).

D. B. REDFORD, *History and chronology of the Eighteenth Dynasty of Egypt: seven studies* (Toronto, 1967).

A. TULHOFF, *Thutmosis III* (Munich, 1984).

B. M. BRYAN, *The reign of Thutmose IV* (Baltimore and London, 1991).

N. GRIMAL, *A history of ancient Egypt* (Oxford, 1992), 207–21.

Thutmose (Djehutymose, Tuthmosis) (*c.*1340 BC)

One of the principal sculptors of the reign of AKHENATEN (1352–1336 BC), whose titles describe him as 'king's favourite and master of works, the sculptor Thutmose'. His house

and workshop, buildings P.47.1–3 in the south suburb of EL-AMARNA, were discovered by Ludwig Borchardt in December 1912. Most of the identifications of occupants of houses at Amarna have been made on the basis of inscribed door lintels or jambs, but Thutmose's house was ascribed to him through the excavation of a fragment of an ivory horse-blinker from a domestic rubbish pit. A storeroom of Thutmose's atelier (P.47.2: room 19) was found to contain numerous artist's 'trial pieces', as well as many unfinished statues and heads, including those of the king, queen and princesses. There were also a number of plaster heads probably representing various members of the Amarna-period royal family, which were initially interpreted as death-masks but are now usually assumed to have been the 'master images' from which sculptures in stone may have been copied. The most spectacular find was the brightly painted limestone bust of NEFERTITI, the principal wife of Akhenaten (now in the collection of the Ägyptisches Museum, Berlin).

L. BORCHARDT, *Porträts der Königin Nofret-ete* (Leipzig, 1923).

L. BORCHARDT and H. RICKE, *Die Wohnhäuser in Tell el-Amarna* (Berlin, 1980), 96–7.

R. KRAUSS, 'Der Bildhauer Thutmose in Amarna', *Jahrbuch der Preussischer Kulturbesitz* 20 (1983), 119–32.

C. ALDRED, *Akhenaten King of Egypt* (London, 1988), 59.

time see CALENDAR; CHRONOLOGY; CLEPSYDRA and HISTORY AND HISTORIOGRAPHY

titulary see ROYAL TITULARY

Tiy (Tiye) (*c.*1410–1340 BC)

Principal wife of the late 18th-Dynasty ruler AMENHOTEP III (1390–1352 BC). Her father was a chariot officer (see YUYA AND TUYU) and her brother, Anen, rose to the position of Second Prophet of AMUN. She seems to have exerted considerable influence both on her husband and on her son AKHENATEN (1352–1336 BC).

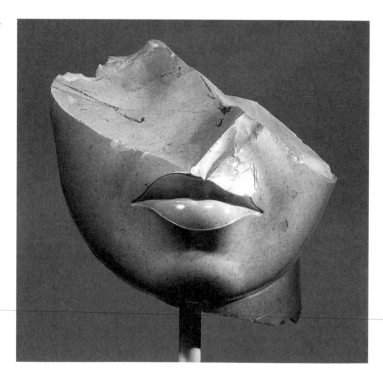

The lips of Queen Tiy. 18th Dynasty, c.1380 BC, yellow jasper, H. 12.6 cm. (METROPOLITAN MUSEUM, NEW YORK, EDWARD S. HARKNESS GIFT. 1926, 26.7.1396)

After the death of Amenhotep III, for instance, the correspondence from Tushratta, the ruler of MITANNI, was addressed directly to Tiy. She was regularly being portrayed alongside her husband in sculptures, and her titles were listed on one of a series of commemorative SCARABS issued by the king.

On the accession to the throne of her son, Akhenaten, the centre of power transferred from Thebes to a new capital city at EL-AMARNA. A relief in the rock-cut tomb of Huya at el-Amarna shows that Tiy visited

C. ALDRED, *Akhenaten, King of Egypt* (London, 1988), 146–52, 219–21.
G. ROBINS, *Women in ancient Egypt* (London, 1993), 21–55.

tjet *see* TYET

Tod (anc. Djerty, Tuphium)
Site on the east bank of the Nile, south of ARMANT, which dates from at least the Old Kingdom until the Islamic period. A mud-brick chapel was constructed there as early as the 5th Dynasty (2494–2345 BC), but the site gained in importance in the Middle Kingdom (2055–1650 BC), when temple construction for the local god MONTU was undertaken by MENTUHOTEP II (2055–2004 BC), Mentuhotep III (2004–1992 BC) and SENUSRET I (1965–1920 BC). Although these structures are now almost entirely destroyed, a number of impressive fragments of relief have survived, including part of a wall decorated on both sides with depictions of the goddess Tjanenent and the god Montu, dating to the reign of Mentuhotep III (now in the Louvre).

In February 1936 the French archaeologist François Bisson de la Roque discovered the so-called 'Tod treasure' underneath the Middle Kingdom temple. The treasure comprised SILVER vessels (which may have been made in Crete, or perhaps somewhere in Cretan-influenced western Asia), a silver lion, lapis lazuli cylinder seals from Mesopotamia, and gold ingots. These were found in four bronze chests bearing the cartouche of Amenemhat II (1922–1878 BC) of the 12th Dynasty. Not only was this discovery one of the richest finds of silver in Egypt, but the evidence it provides

Green steatite head of Tiy from the temple of Hathor at the turquoise-mining site of Serabit el-Khadim, Sinai. 18th Dynasty, c.1370 BC, H. 7.2 cm. (CAIRO JE38257)

Akhenaten at the new city in the twelfth year of his reign, and she may even have had her own residence there. She was perhaps buried with her son in the royal tomb at Amarna, but this is by no means certain. It is likely, at any rate, that her body was eventually taken to Thebes. Some of her funerary equipment was found in tomb KV55 in the VALLEY OF THE KINGS, although the body associated with these objects is believed to be that of Smenkhkara, the short-lived coregent of Akhenaten. A body of a royal woman discovered among the cache of royal mummies in the tomb of Amenhotep II (KV35) is thought to be that of Tiy, although this identification has not been universally accepted. A lock of her hair was also found in a miniature coffin in the tomb of TUTANKHAMUN (KV62).
A. ROWE, 'Inscriptions on the model coffin containing the lock of hair of Queen Tiy', *ASAE* 40 (1941), 627

The Tod treasure, discovered by François Bisson de la Roque in the temple of Montu in 1936, is one of the largest finds of silver from ancient Egypt. 12th Dynasty, c.1900 BC, L. of box 45 cm. (LOUVRE E15128–15318, PHOTOGRAPH: JEAN-LUC BOVOT)

concerning contacts with Greece and the Near East during the Middle Kingdom is a valuable indication of trade contacts at the time.

From the New Kingdom have survived the remains of a BARK shrine erected by Thutmose III (1479–1425 BC) for Montu, the decoration of which includes restoration work undertaken by other kings of the 18th, 19th and 20th Dynasties. Many of the blocks of Thutmose III's temple were later re-used in the construction of the Deir Anba Ibshay church to the east of the site. In front of the site of the temple of Senusret I, Ptolemy VIII (170–116 BC) built a new temple and sacred lake, and a KIOSK was added in the Roman period.
F. BISSON DE LA ROQUE, 'Le trésor de Tod', *CdE* 12 (1937), 20–6.
J. VANDIER, 'A propos d'un dépôt de provenance asiatique trouvé à Tod', *Syria* 18 (1937), 174–82.
F. BISSON DE LA ROQUE, G. CONTENEAU and F. CHAPOUTHIER, *Le trésor de Tôd* (Cairo, 1953).
C. DESROCHES-NOBLECOURT and J. VERCOUTTER, *Un siècle de fouilles françaises en Egypte 1880–1980* (Paris, 1981), 137–63.

tombs
In the strictest sense of the word the ancient Egyptian tomb underwent very little development over the course of the six millennia from the beginning of the Predynastic period to the end of the Roman period (c.5500 BC–AD 395). In essence the tomb itself was almost always subterranean, usually comprising a simple pit,

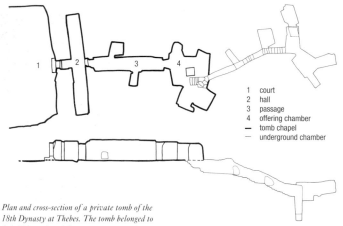

1 court
2 hall
3 passage
4 offering chamber
— tomb chapel
— underground chamber

Plan and cross-section of a private tomb of the 18th Dynasty at Thebes. The tomb belonged to Sobekhotep whose life at court is recorded in scenes in his tomb-chapel, which was located above ground. In the 19th Dynasty, tomb chapels were decorated with funerary texts. The subterranean parts of the tomb were largely undecorated and were blocked except for burials. (DRAWN BY CHRISTINE BARRATT)

a rock-cut room or a chamber of mud-brick or stone, within which the body was placed, usually accompanied by funerary equipment of various kinds. The pit style of burial was particularly persistent, being used not only by most of the Predynastic population but also by poorer people throughout Egyptian history.

The full study of the development of the Egyptian tomb is therefore principally concerned with the evolution of the superstructure, which was invariably the architectural form of the 'offering chapel' rather than the burial chamber itself. Since the purpose of the funerary monument was to ensure the continued survival of the deceased, the attention of the funerary architects and artists naturally focused not so much on the body itself but on the chapel, which was the interface between the dead and the living, and the means by which the KA ('spiritual essence') and the BA ('potency') of the individual could communicate with the world outside. Although there were obvious differences in scale and elaboration between the PYRAMID complexes of the Old Kingdom and the simplest MASTABA tombs of some of the more lowly officials of the time, all of these buildings were essentially performing the same function, providing a vehicle for the making of offerings to the deceased. From the SERDABS containing statuary of the deceased to the STELAE bearing inscriptions naming and describing the individual, and listing the required offerings for

the cult, the basic components of the funerary chapel and mortuary temple were very similar.

There were certain subtle architectural and artistic means by which royal tombs could be distinguished from those of their courtiers, and equally there were ways in which the design and iconography of the tomb could be used to indicate the prerogatives and privileges held by certain members of the non-royal élite and not by others. However, some of the major differences in the outward appearance of tombs were the result of simple geological and geographical variations, such as the availability of good

quality building stone (as at GIZA and SAQQARA) or the suitability of the desert cliffs for the excavation and decoration of rock-cut chambers (as at ASYUT, BENI HASAN and MEIR). Factors such as these would have determined whether private funerary chapels were rock-cut or built. In addition, the chronological changes in architectural style within particular necropolises, such as SAQQARA or THEBES, were generally the result of dynastic or religious change, as well as an increasing reaction to the threat of tomb-robbery. Indeed, the problem of security seems to have been one of the main factors that led to the move away from the highly visible pyramid complexes of the Old and Middle Kingdom to the hidden corridors of the VALLEY OF THE KINGS at Thebes in the New Kingdom.

See also FALSE DOOR; FUNERARY BELIEFS; MUMMIFICATION; VALLEY OF THE QUEENS.

G. A. REISNER, *The development of the Egyptian tomb down to the accession of Cheops* (Cambridge, MA, 1936).

A. J. SPENCER, *Death in ancient Egypt* (Harmondsworth, 1982).

W. KAISER, 'Zu Entwicklung und Vorformen der frühzeitlichen Gräber mit reich gegliedert Oberbaufassade', *Mélanges Gamal Eddin Mokhtar* (Cairo, 1985), 25–38.

N. CHERPION, *Mastabas et hypogées d'Ancien Empire: le problème de la datation* (Brussels, 1989).

E. HORNUNG, *The Valley of the Kings: horizon of eternity* (New York, 1990).

I. E. S. EDWARDS, *The pyramids of Egypt*, 5th ed. (Harmondsworth, 1993).

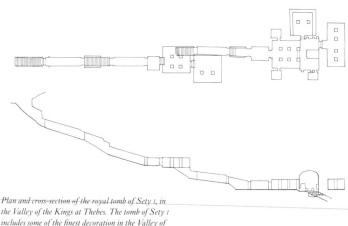

Plan and cross-section of the royal tomb of Sety I, in the Valley of the Kings at Thebes. The tomb of Sety I includes some of the finest decoration in the Valley of the Kings, and was the first to be well known in Britain, through the efforts of its discoverer, Giovanni Belzoni. (DRAWN BY CHRISTINE BARRATT)

towns

Although Egypt was once described as a 'civilization without cities', the archaeological evidence to the contrary has been steadily growing over the last hundred years, as more settlement sites have been surveyed and excavated. By the 1970s, with the inauguration of new programmes of research at such sites as EL-AMARNA, ELEPHANTINE and TELL EL-DAB'A, 'settlement archaeology' can be said to have arrived as a subdiscipline within Egyptology. These long-term excavations have played a crucial role in demonstrating the ways in which the development of Egyptian towns was influenced both by geographical location and by the particular political and social conditions in which they were founded. It has been suggested, for instance, that the orthogonal grid-plan of most surviving Old and Middle Kingdom settlements indicates a high degree of state control and bureaucracy, as in the case of Kahun (see EL-LAHUN).

The phenomenon of urban life in Egypt is currently best studied in terms of its New Kingdom phase, when the expansion of the Egyptian empire was reflected in the cosmo-

ABOVE *Schematic models of two Egyptian houses. Third Intermediate Period, limestone, H. 21 cm and 14 cm. (EA2462, 27526)*

Cross-section of a typical house in the workmen's village at Deir el-Medina. Similar houses are known from the workmen's village at Amarna. 20th Dynasty, c.1150 BC.

politan nature of its major cities. The site of el-Amarna, on the east bank of the Nile in Middle Egypt, midway between the modern towns of Minya and Asyut, is the location of the only virtually complete city to have survived from ancient Egypt. Small patches of settlement have survived from the contemporary cities of Memphis and Thebes, which, in their time, would have been considerably larger, but el-Amarna is the only Egyptian site at which a relatively complete and representative range of official and residential buildings have been excavated. There are at least ten other substantial excavated town-sites dating principally to the New Kingdom (c. 1550–1069 BC): DEIR EL-BALLAS, BUHEN, SESEBI, SOLEB, AMARA West, DEIR EL-MEDINA, MALKATA, GUROB, MEMPHIS (Kom el-Rabia)

and Piramesse (QANTIR and TELL EL-DAB'A). A few smaller areas of New Kingdom settlement have also been excavated at other sites, such as ABYDOS, MEDINET HABU, KARNAK and HERMOPOLIS MAGNA (el-Ashmunein). Substantial Late Period settlements have been excavated at TANIS, NAUKRATIS and Hermopolis Magna.

The textual and archaeological evidence suggest that, although there were evidently cities in the New Kingdom with a strong agricultural economic *raison d'être* (such as the nome capitals, Ninsu and Hardai, which are known from textual references rather than excavation), many New Kingdom towns were focused on religious or administrative buildings. As David O'Connor has pointed out, 'the definition of Egypt as "civilization without cities" can only be accepted if "city" is understood in a most narrow and specialized sense; a more broadly defined type (or types) of urbanism was certainly characteristic of historic Egypt'.

B. J. KEMP, 'The early development of towns in Egypt', *Antiquity* 51 (1977), 185–200.
M. BIETAK, 'Urban archaeology and the "town problem" in ancient Egypt', *Egyptology and the social sciences*, ed. K. Weeks (Cairo, 1979), 95–144.
E. UPHILL, *Egyptian towns and cities* (Princes Risborough, 1988).
B. J. KEMP, *Ancient Egypt: anatomy of a civilization* (London, 1989).

toys

The identification of 'toys' or playthings in the archaeological record is fraught with problems. The Egyptians' frequent use of models, statuettes and figurines, both in religious cults and in the practice of MAGIC, means that many ritual artefacts can appear disconcertingly similar to dolls or puppets to the modern eye. A number of unfired (or lightly fired) clay figures of humans and animals have survived in urban contexts, particularly from the town of Kahun (see EL-LAHUN), dating to the Middle Kingdom (2055–1650 BC), and may therefore be toys.

The balls of string or rag and the wooden tops excavated at settlement sites, and sometimes also in private tombs, are almost certainly playthings. A few relatively elaborate toys have survived, including human figures, rattles and models of animals (one example, in the collection of the British Museum, being a crocodile with a moving jaw). As with some of the clay figures from Kahun, it is possible that some of these dolls had ritual functions. It is also possible that the two purposes may sometimes have been combined, in that some 'dolls' may have been intended both as girls' toys and as the amuletic means to fertility in later life.

T. KENDALL, 'Games', *Egypt's golden age*, ed. E. Brovarski, S. K. Doll and R. E. Freed (Boston, 1982), 263–72.

M. STEAD, *Egyptian life* (London, 1986), 63.

Selection of toys: model feline figure with articulated jaw, inlaid eyes and bronze teeth, probably dating to the New Kingdom; painted linen and reed ball, Roman period; faience spinning top from the Fayum, Roman period. (EA15671, 46709, 34920)

trade

Ancient Egypt did not have a monetary economy until the end of the Late Period (747–332 BC), and indeed the Egyptians of the Pharaonic period had no word or concept corresponding to the modern category of 'economy'. The economic aspects of their lives were embedded in the social system as a whole, and trading primarily took a form akin to bartering. The system, however, was very sophisticated, and, at least as early as the New Kingdom (1550–1069 BC), it was related to a definite scale of value based on weights of metal (see MEASUREMENT). Copper was the main standard for small transactions, and silver and gold were used for those of higher value. Fragments of the metals themselves were sometimes used in transactions, but not in such a precise way as to constitute coinage.

Most of the evidence for trade among ordi-

nary Egyptians of the New Kingdom comes from the workmen's community at DEIR EL-MEDINA. It seems that each given commodity had a value that could be expressed in terms of numbers of copper *deben*. Many transactions therefore seem to have taken the form of a calculation of the value of the two sets of goods that were being exchanged, in order to ascertain that each was worth the same amount of *deben*. Some Egyptologists consider that these prices were fairly stable and resulted from traditional usage, whereas others have argued that the prices were fixed much more fluidly through the supply and demand of the market. Whether ancient economies should be subject to 'formalist' (market-oriented) or 'substantivist' (non-market) analysis is a matter of some controversy in anthropology, particularly where ancient states are concerned, and in Egypt a case can be made for either. Barry Kemp has been able to show that the process of exchange was an accepted part of social relations, and so helps to bring the two schools of thought closer together.

Records of bartering transactions necessarily show the exchange of a number of items of relatively low value in order to buy something of a higher value. Clearly this system would work only in a community in which people were prepared to be flexible about what they took in exchange, otherwise an enormous chain of smaller exchanges would have been necessary in order to obtain goods purely for the purpose of a transaction, and the whole system would have become impractical. The vendor usually seems to have tried to ensure that some of the goods obtained in exchange could, if necessary, be bartered again in the future. Many of the surviving records of transactions at Deir el-Medina list a bed (valued at 20–25 *deben*) among the items traded; it is unlikely that households would actually have wished to receive and store numerous beds, therefore it is usually assumed that the bed was included in the record of the transaction simply as surety, to facilitate the exchange. In this way, Egyptian economic activity can be seen to be the material expression of social relations. The economist Karl Polanyi and the anthropologist Marshall Sahlins have shown that in many societies commodities may have one price for those within the community and another for outsiders; it is possible that such a system operated in Pharaonic Egypt.

Foreign trade probably also operated mainly through barter. The expedition to the African country of PUNT, which is recorded in the mortuary temple of Hatshepsut (1473–1458 BC) at Deir el-Bahri, seems to depict the oper-

ation of 'silent trade', whereby each of the parties gradually laid out more or fewer items until both felt satisfied with their return on the deal. This system is particularly likely to have been used when dealing with relatively unsophisticated foreigners, who would have had no knowledge of the prices of objects or goods within Egypt.

Trade with developed states in the Mediterranean and the Near East seems to have taken a different form. Here goods of high value were regularly exchanged by way of diplomatic gifts. The AMARNA LETTERS contain lists of goods sent by foreign rulers to Egypt, and requests by them for gifts such as gold statues. The luxury goods acquired in this way could often be given to loyal courtiers as rewards, serving as marks of status conferred by the king.

Many tomb-paintings in the New Kingdom depict the arrival of trade goods, but they often portray them as if they were gifts given as tribute. In practice traders from Crete, and elsewhere in the Greek world, visited Egypt to exchange goods, and were no doubt themselves visited by Egyptian traders (or at least traders bearing Egyptian goods such as those found on the Bronze Age shipwrecks at Cape Gelidonya and Ulu Burun). Egyptian traders themselves are not well attested, although the term *shwty* apears to be used to refer to merchants. There are also references to the sending of royal trading missions throughout the Pharaonic period; these were usually organized by officials serving as 'expedition leaders', from Harkhuf, who travelled to Africa in the time of Pepy II (2278–2184 BC), to the semi-fictional character Wenamun, who was supposed to have been sent to the Syrian port of BYBLOS in the time of HERIHOR (*c.*1070 BC).

When the word *shwty* was used to identify traders in the New Kingdom, they were always state employees. Nevertheless, there seems to have been a level of trade that was intermediate between the international commerce of the highest courtly officials and the local bartering of the workmen. This is demonstrated by numerous finds of Mycenaean pottery at sites such as EL-AMARNA, where its occurrence outside purely royal contexts perhaps indicates that it arrived through Mycenaean merchants or Egyptian middlemen. At any rate, there may well have been unofficial exchanges between Egyptians and members of the retinues of visiting foreign potentates, just as the anthropologist Bronislaw Malinowski recorded among the peoples of the Pacific.

In the Late Period (747–332 BC) foreign trade was dominated by GREEKS, and Egyptian rulers controlled them by confining them to trading cities such as NAUKRATIS. During the 29th Dynasty the first coinage was introduced into Egypt, which was to lead to a full monetary economy in the Ptolemaic period, thus effectively beginning the process of integrating the Nile valley into the early monetary economy of the Mediterranean world.

B. MALINOWSKI, *Argonauts of the Western Pacific* (London, 1922).

K. POLANYI, 'The economy as instituted process', *Trade and market in the early empires*, ed. K. Polanyi, C. Arensberg and H. Pearson (Glencoe, IL, 1957).

D. M. DIXON, 'The transplantation of Punt incense trees in Egypt', *JEA* 55 (1969), 55–65.

M. SAHLINS, *Stone age economics* (London, 1974).

J. J. JANSSEN, *Commodity prices from the Ramessid period* (Leiden, 1975).

M. G. RASCHKE, 'Papyrological evidence for Ptolemaic and Roman trade with India', *Proceedings of the XIV International Congress of Papyrologists* (London, 1975), 241–6.

S. ALLAM, 'Wie der Altägypter in der Zeit des Neuen Reiches kaufte und verkaufte', *Das Altertum* 27 (1981), 233–40.

J. PADRO, 'Le role de l'Egypte dans les relations commerciales d'Orient et d'Occident au premier millénaire', *ASAE* 71 (1987), 213–22.

B. J. KEMP, *Ancient Egypt: anatomy of a civilization* (London, 1989), 232–60.

trees

Among the more common species of tree in Egypt were the acacia, tamarisk, date palm, dom palm and sycamore. Perhaps because of the comparative rarity of trees, many of them developed associations both with specific deities and with the afterlife. The goddess HATHOR, for instance, was sometimes described as 'lady of the sycamore', and this tree was also linked with other goddesses, including ISIS and NUT. Chapter 109 of the Book of the Dead describes two 'sycamores of turquoise' growing at the point on the eastern horizon where the sun-god rises each morning. It was the sycamore tree that was often depicted in funerary decoration as a semi-anthropomorphic figure, often with arms and hands offering food or sacred water to the deceased. Perhaps the most unusual version of the sacred sycamore is in the burial chamber of Thutmose III (1479–1425 BC), where the tree goddess – probably in this instance Isis – is shown suckling the king with a breast emerging from the branches.

The *ished* tree was connected with the sun-god and, like the sycamore, had connections with the horizon. Reliefs sometimes depict THOTH and SESHAT, the two deities associated with writing, inscribing the leaves of either the *ished* or persea tree (*Mimusops laurifolia*) with the ROYAL TITULARY and the number of years in

Shabti-*box bearing painted decoration depicting the priestess Henutmehyt receiving water from a tree-goddess. 19th Dynasty, c.1290 BC, wood, from Thebes, H. of box 34 cm. (EA41549)*

the pharaoh's reign. The link between trees and the duration of kings' reigns was reiterated in the use of a date-palm branch as the hieroglyph signifying year (*renpet*), which is often shown in association with the god of eternity, HEH. When covered in notches indicating the passing of time, the palm branch formed an important element of scenes depicting the SED FESTIVAL.

There are only a few surviving depictions of the felling of trees, the earliest of which is probably the relief in the 4th-Dynasty tomb of Personet at Giza, showing one man in the act of chopping at a trunk, while others hack off the branches. According to the PALERMO STONE (a 5th-Dynasty king list) the 4th-Dynasty ruler Sneferu (2613–2589 BC) was already importing large quantities of coniferous timber from BYBLOS. Live species were sometimes also brought back from trading missions, according to the painted scenes of the expedition to the African kingdom of PUNT, in the temple of Hatshepsut (1473–1458 BC) at Deir el-Bahri, which show Egyptians carrying off small trees in ceramic pots, as well as trimming branches from ebony logs in preparation for their transportation back to Egypt.

M. L. BUHL, 'The goddesses of the Egyptian tree cult', *JNES* 6 (1947), 80–97.

I. WALLERT, *Die Palmen in alten Ägypten: eine Untersuchung ihrer praktischen, symbolischen und religiösen Bedeutung* (Berlin, 1962).

R. MOFTAH, 'Die uralte Sykomore und andere Erscheinungen der Hathor', *ZÄS* 92 (1965), 40–7.

I. GAMER-WALLERT, 'Baum, heiliger', *Lexikon der Ägyptologie* I, ed. W. Helck, E. Otto and W. Westendorf (Wiesbaden, 1975), 655–60.

E. HERMSEN, *Lebensbaumsymbolik im alten Ägypten: eine Untersuchung* (Cologne, 1981)

N. BAUM, *Arbres et arbustes de l'Egypte ancienne* (Louvain, 1988).

R. H. WILKINSON, *Reading Egyptian art* (London, 1992), 116–19.

triad

Term used to describe a group of three gods, usually consisting of a divine family of father, mother and child worshipped at particular cult centres. The triad was often a convenient means of linking together three formerly independent gods of an area, and seems to have been primarily a theological development of the New Kingdom. The process of forming a triad provided a frame of reference for each of the deities, placing them into a detailed mythological context. Among the most important triads were AMUN, MUT and KHONS at Thebes, PTAH, SEKHMET and NEFERTEM at

The tomb chapel of Ptolemais at Tuna el-Gebel is one of a number of Graeco-Roman tomb chapels at the site, located close to the sacred animal catacombs. (P. T. NICHOLSON)

Memphis, the Behdetite HORUS (see WINGED DISC), HATHOR and Harsomtus (Horus the child) at Edfu, and KHNUM, SATET and ANUKET (daughter or second consort) at Elephantine. The best-known triad is that of OSIRIS, Isis and Horus, but this grouping was not associated with any specific cult-centre, Osiris being worshipped at Abydos, ISIS at Philae and Horus at Edfu.

The term is also occasionally used to refer to a 'group statue' consisting of three figures, as in the case of the statues from the 4th-Dynasty valley temple of MENKAURA (2532–2503 BC) at Giza. These five 'triads' (now in the collections of the Egyptian Museum, Cairo and the Museum of Fine Arts, Boston) each show the king in the company of the goddess Hathor and a female personification of one of the nomes (provinces) of Egypt in which Hathor was particularly venerated. In private statuary, such a sculptural triad would usually consist of a man and two of his dependants, as in the case of the painted limestone statue of the 5th-Dynasty official Meresankh and two of his daughters (now in the Egyptian Museum, Cairo). Triads, however, are far less common than DYADS (pair-statues).

E. HORNUNG, *Conceptions of god in ancient Egypt: the one and the many*, trans. J. Baines (London, 1983).

Tuna el-Gebel

Site of the necropolis of HERMOPOLIS MAGNA, including a complex of catacombs for the burial of SACRED ANIMALS and an associated temple of THOTH, located on the west bank of the Nile, near the modern town of Mallawi in Middle Egypt. The temple, now much damaged, is connected with the subterranean galleries, which date from at least as early as the 19th Dynasty until Ptolemaic times (c.1295–100 BC). Close to the animal catacombs is a boundary stele of AKHENATEN, labelled Stele A by Flinders Petrie, marking the incorporation of this agricultural territory within the bounds of his new capital on the east bank, at EL-AMARNA (see also STELE).

One catacomb at Tuna el-Gebel is devoted primarily to the ritual storage of mummified votive IBISES, although many of the sealed pottery jars also contain falcons and other birds. Mummified baboons, the other creatures sacred to Thoth, were also buried in the galleries, in some cases accompanied by the bodies of the priests who had tended them in life. A variety of other animals, including crocodiles, are also represented in smaller numbers. The galleries, and other parts of the site, were partly excavated by Egyptian Egyptologist Sami Gabra in the inter-war period, and have been excavated during the 1980s and 1990s by a team of German archaeologists under the direction of Dieter Kessler.

There are also surviving remains of the buildings constructed to accommodate the numerous ancient pilgrims visiting the site. A site of such importance also attracted private burials, including about sixty brick-built funerary houses and nine limestone tomb chapels, many of Ptolemaic and Roman date. The names of some of the owners of these 'funerary houses' and tomb chapels are known, including Isadora (c.AD 150), a woman who is said to have drowned in the Nile and subsequently became the object of a popular cult. The tomb chapel of a chief priest of Thoth called PETOSIRIS (c.300 BC) is the most important private tomb at the site, principally because its decoration consists of an unusual combination of Egyptian and Hellenistic styles.

S. GABRA, E. DRIOTON, P. PERDRIZET and W. G. WADDELL, *Rapport sur les fouilles d'Hermopolis Ouest* (Cairo, 1941).

S. GABRA, *Chez les derniers adorateurs du Trimégiste: la nécropole d'Hermopolis-Touna el-Gebel* (Cairo, 1971).

J. BOESSNECK, A. VON DEN DRIESCH and D. KESSLER, *Tuna I: Die Tiergalerien* (Hildesheim, 1987).

D. KESSLER, *Die heiligen Tiere und der König* (Wiesbaden, 1989).

Turin Royal Canon

Papyrus dating to the reign of Rameses II (1279–1213 BC), inscribed in HIERATIC with a list of the names of Egyptian rulers (originally numbering about three hundred), evidently copied from a more complete original. When it was first acquired by the traveller Bernardino Drovetti in the early nineteenth century, it

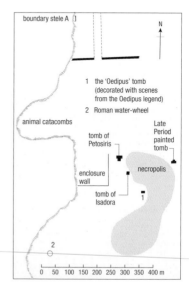

Plan of Tuna el-Gebel.

seems to have been largely intact, but by the time it had become part of the collection of the Museo Egizio, Turin, its condition had deteriorated. The diligent work of such Egyptologists as Jean-François CHAMPOLLION and Gustavus Seyffarth ensured that the many fragments were placed in the correct order, but many lacunae still remain.

The list included the HYKSOS rulers (often left out of other KING LISTS), although they were not given CARTOUCHES, and a hieroglyphic sign was added to indicate that they were foreigners. Apart from the names of each of the rulers, the list also cited the precise duration of each reign, and occasionally provided a summary of the numbers of years that had elapsed since the time of the semimythical ruler MENES. There was also an attempt to go back beyond the reigns of known kings and to assign regnal lengths to the series of unnamed spirits and gods who had ruled before the appearance of the human pharaohs. It was presumably this type of document that provided MANETHO with the basis for the history that he compiled in the early third century BC, which has supplied the sequence of DYNASTIES still used by Egyptologists.

E. MEYER, *Aegyptische Chronologie* (Berlin, 1904), 105–14.

G. FARINA, *Il papiro dei re restaurato* (Rome, 1938).

A. H. GARDINER, *The Royal Canon of Turin* (Oxford, 1959).

J. MALEK, 'The original version of the Royal Canon of Turin', *JEA* 68 (1982), 93–106.

turquoise

Mined by the Egyptians from the late Predynastic period onwards, turquoise is an opaque blue-green or pale sky-blue mineral (hydrated phosphate of copper and aluminium), which forms as veins and nodules in the fissures of sandstone and trachyte. The greener variety was highly prized by the ancient Egyptians, who preferred it to the more porous blue variety, which tends to fade when exposed to the air. Turquoise (probably corresponding to the Egyptian term *mefkat*) was used in jewellery as early as the Gerzean period, and one of the most exquisite early examples of its use is a bracelet consisting of thirteen gold and fourteen turquoise SEREKH-plaques, each crowned by a falcon, excavated from the 1st-Dynasty tomb of DJER (*c*.3000 BC) at Abydos.

The Sinai peninsula was the major Egyptian source of turquoise and copper throughout the Pharaonic period. The mines at Wadi Maghara, 225 km southeast of Cairo, were particularly exploited during the Old and

Middle Kingdoms (2686–1650 BC), and there are impressive rock-carvings (usually depicting the king in the act of smiting foreign captives), dating back to the reign of the 3rd-Dynasty ruler SEKHEMKHET (2648–2640 BC). Petrie examined the site in 1904–5 and found an Old Kingdom hill-top miners' settlement consisting of about 125 stone-built structures. His excavations also revealed numerous artefacts, including evidence of copper-smelting *in situ*.

Another set of mines, at Serabit el-Khadim, about 18 km to the north of Wadi Maghara, were also accompanied by rock-carved stelae, as well as an unusual associated temple complex dating to the Middle and New Kingdoms (*c*.2055–1069 BC). In the temple precincts and the surrounding area, numerous rock-cut and freestanding stelae were dedicated by mining expeditions to the goddess HATHOR in her aspect of *nebet mefkat* ('lady of turquoise') and the god SOPED 'guardian of the desert ways'.

R. WEILL, *Receuil des inscriptions égyptiennes du Sinai* (Paris, 1904).

W. M. F. PETRIE and C. T. CURRELLY, *Researches in Sinai* (London, 1906).

A. H. GARDINER, T. E. PEET and J. CERNY, *Inscriptions of Sinai*, 2 vols, 2nd ed. (London, 1952–5).

R. GIVEON, 'Le temple d'Hathor à Serabit el-Khadem', *Archéologia* 44 (1972), 64–9.

M. CHARTIER-RAYMOND, 'Notes sur Maghara (Sinai)', *CRIPEL* 10 (1988), 13–22.

Tutankhamun (1336–1327 BC)

Ruler of the late 18th Dynasty who was, ironically, one of the most poorly known of the pharaohs until Howard CARTER's discovery of his tomb in the VALLEY OF THE KINGS (KV62) in 1922. Although the tomb had been partially robbed and resealed in ancient times, most of the funerary equipment, including the coffins and sarcophagi, were found in excellent condition, and it was certainly the best-preserved of any of the royal tombs (although the contents of the 21st- and 22nd-Dynasty royal burials at TANIS, excavated by Pierre Montet in 1939, were in similarly good condition). The tomb is also architecturally different from other pharaohs' tombs in the Valley of the Kings, in that it consists of only four very small rooms rather than the long corridor-style tomb that is typical of the 18th to 20th Dynasties. It is possible that a more conventional tomb near that of AMENHOTEP III (KV23) may have originally been intended for him but this was usurped by his successor, the ageing courtier AY, who probably acted as regent and wielded the real power during his reign.

Tutankhamun was born during the Amarna

The body of Tutankhamun, which disintegrated when it was unwrapped in November 1923 and had to be re-assembled on a tray. 18th Dynasty, c.1336–1327 BC, H. 1.63 m. (REPRODUCED COURTESY OF THE GRIFFITH INSTITUTE.)

period, probably at el-Amarna itself, where he was at first known as Tutankhaten ('living image of the Aten'), but later changed his name, presumably in order to distance himself from the Atenist heresies of the reigns of AKHENATEN and Smenkhkara. His wife, Ankhesenpaaten, who was one of the daughters of Akhenaten, similarly changed her name to Ankhesenamun, although a throne found in his tomb portrays them together underneath the rays of the Aten, since this item was presumably created in the late Amarna period. In his decoration of the colonnade in the temple at LUXOR constructed by Amenhotep III, he describes the latter as his 'father'. This raises the question of whether he may in fact have been Akhenaten's brother, although it is usually assumed that the term is to be translated more generally as 'ancestor', and that the supposed link with Amenhotep III was simply a convenient way of dissociating himself from his two heretical predecessors.

When he reached the throne, at the age of perhaps only eight years old, he moved the royal court back up to Memphis. It was therefore at SAQQARA that the tombs of a number of his high officials were located (rather than at Thebes, as in the earlier 18th Dynasty), including those of the general HOREMHEB, the chancellor Maya and the vizier Aper-el, all three of which were excavated during the 1970s and 1980s. Although his 'restoration stele' (enumerating a number of reforms designed to undo the excesses of the Amarna period) was erected at Karnak, it was actually

issued from Memphis. The Theban tomb of his VICEROY OF KUSH, Huy, is decorated with painted scenes showing Tutankhamun's reception of tribute from the Nubian prince of Miam (ANIBA).

H. CARTER, *The tomb of Tutankhamun*, 3 vols (London, 1923–33).
C. DESROCHES-NOBLECOURT, *Tutankhamen, life and death of a pharaoh* (London, 1963).
THE GRIFFITH INSTITUTE, *Tut'ankhamun's tomb series*, 10 vols (Oxford, 1963–90).
R. KRAUSS, *Das Ende der Amarnazeit: Beiträge zur Geschichte und Chronologie des Neuen Reiches*, 2nd ed. (Hildesheim, 1981).
M. EATON-KRAUSS, 'Tutankhamun at Karnak', *MDAIK* 44 (1988), 1–11.
C. N. REEVES, *The complete Tutankhamun* (London, 1990).
G. T. MARTIN, *The hidden tombs of Memphis: new discoveries from the time of Tutankhamun and Ramesses the Great* (London, 1991).

'Two Ladies' see NEKHBET and WADJYT

Ty (Ti) (*c.* 2500 BC)
Important 5th-Dynasty official who was overseer of the pyramid complexes and sun temples of the 5th-Dynasty rulers Neferirkara (2475–2455 BC) and Nyuserra (2445–2441 BC) at ABUSIR, as well as the sun temples of Sahura (2487–2475 BC) and Raneferef (2448–2445 BC). His career, which roughly coincided with the reign of Nyuserra, is documented in the painted reliefs decorating the interior of one of the finest MASTABA tombs at SAQQARA (no. 60).

Head of a black granite statue of Hapy with the facial features of Tutankhamun. It is inscribed with the names of Horemheb who usurped many monuments of Tutankhamun.
H. 1.68 m. (EA75)

His wife, Neferhetpes, was a prophetess of the goddesses Neith and Hathor, and is frequently portrayed at his side.

The funerary chapel, which would originally have formed the superstructure of the tomb, was discovered and cleared by Auguste MARIETTE in the late nineteenth century, but its exterior walls are now partly buried in the desert. Its porticoed doorway – probably similar to the entrances of the houses of the élite during the Old Kingdom (2686–2181 BC) – led to a columned hall beneath which a passageway led down to the actual burial. The walls of this hall were decorated with agricultural scenes emphasizing the wealth and official duties of Ty. A corridor in the southwest corner led past the FALSE-DOOR stele of Neferhetpes (and the accompanying offering scenes) into a chamber on the west side which is decorated with scenes showing the bringing and preparing of offerings, including an interesting depiction of a potters' workshop (see POTTERY). Further southwards along the corridor was a larger hall, the roof of which was supported by two pillars, while the walls were decorated with further agricultural scenes, as well as dancers, temple craftsmen and boatbuilders, some of these workers apparently being 'inspected' by Ty in his official capacity. There were also typical scenes of the deceased engaged in hippopotamus HUNTING and fowling in the marshes.

The SERDAB (statue chamber) was placed on the south side of the large hall, and a plaster cast of the statue of Ty is currently visible through three spy-holes in the wall (the original having been transferred to the Cairo Museum).

A. MARIETTE, *Les mastabas de l'Ancien Empire* (Paris, 1882–9).
G. STEINDORFF, *Das Grab des Ti* (Leipzig, 1913).
L. EPRON and F. DAUMAS, *Le tombeau de Ti* (Cairo, 1939).

tyet (Egyptian *tjet*: 'knot of Isis')
The so-called *tyet* 'knot' or 'girdle' was already a sacred symbol during the Old Kingdom (2686–2181 BC), and was commonly depicted alongside the ANKH and the DJED PILLAR. By the New Kingdom (1550–1069 BC) it was described as the 'knot of Isis', perhaps partly in order to parallel the association between the *djed* pillar and the god OSIRIS, consort of the goddess ISIS. It was during this period that *tyet* amulets became comparatively common; the loop of the knot was sometimes replaced by a head of the cowgoddess HATHOR, thus emphasizing the links between Isis and Hathor.

The *tyet* resembles an *ankh* sign with its

U

V

Protective tyet *amulet in red jasper, New Kingdom, H. 6.6 cm. (EA20639)*

horizontal bar turned down at either side, and Spell 156 of the Book of the Dead states that it should be made of red jasper, which would have been symbolic of the 'blood of Isis'. Some *tyet* amulets were carved from carnelian, while others were manufactured in red faience or glass.

W. WESTENDORF, 'Beiträge aus und zu den Medizinischen Texten', *ZÄS* 92 (1966), 128–54 (144–54).

—, 'Isisknoten', *Lexikon der Ägyptologie* II, ed. W. Helck, E. Otto and W. Westendorf (Wiesbaden, 1980), 204.

Udimu *see* DEN

Udjahorresnet *see* ART and PERSIA

udjat see HORUS

Unas (Wenis) (2375–2345 BC)
Final ruler of the 5th Dynasty (2494–2345 BC), whose reign is poorly documented in many respects, despite the comparatively good preservation of his funerary complex at the southwest corner of the Step Pyramid complex of Djoser (2667–2648 BC) in north SAQQARA. His funerary causeway (linking the mortuary temple and the valley temple) includes a number of reliefs apparently depicting events during his reign, such as the transportation by barge of granite COLUMNS from the quarries at Aswan to the mortuary temple, and a scene of emaciated figures that has been interpreted as a portrayal of a FAMINE, perhaps heralding the economic and political decline of the late Old Kingdom. Another scene shows Asiatic traders apparently arriving in Egypt by boat, which probably indicates continued economic contacts with BYBLOS.

Although Unas' pyramid is the smallest of those built during the Old Kingdom (2686–2181 BC), it is particularly significant because it was the earliest to have its internal walls inscribed with the various spells making up the PYRAMID TEXTS.

E. DRIOTON, 'Une représentation de la famine sur un bas-relief égyptien de la Ve Dynastie', *BIE* 25 (1942–3), 45–54.

S. HASSAN, 'The causeway of Wnis at Sakkara', *ZÄS* 80 (1955), 136–44.

A. LABROUSSE, J.-P. LAUER and J. LECLANT, *Le temple haut du complex funéraire du roi Ounas* (Cairo, 1977).

I. E. S. EDWARDS, *The pyramids of Egypt*, 5th ed. (Harmondsworth, 1993), 173–6.

uraeus see COBRA and WADJYT

Uto *see* WADJYT

Valley of the Kings (Biban el-Muluk)
New Kingdom royal necropolis located on the west bank of the Nile, about 5 km to the west of modern Luxor, which actually consists of two separate valleys. The eastern valley is the main royal cemetery of the 18th to 20th Dynasties, while the so-called Western Valley (or Cemetery of the Monkeys/Apes) contains only four tombs: those of AMENHOTEP III (1390–1352 BC; KV22) and AY (1327–1323 BC; KV23), and two others which are uninscribed (KV24–5). There are sixty-two tombs in the cemetery as a whole: the earliest is perhaps KV38, at the far end of the main valley, which has been identified as that of THUTMOSE I (1504–1492 BC) and the latest is KV4, belonging to Rameses XI (1099–1069 BC). It has been suggested that KV39 may be the tomb of Thutmose I's predecessor, Amenhotep I, but most scholars still believe that his tomb was at Dra Abu el-Naga (see THEBES).

One of the major features of the royal tombs at the Valley of the Kings was their separation from the mortuary temples, which, for the first time since the Early Dynastic period, were built some distance away, in a long line at the edge of the desert. Each of the tombs was therefore a long series of rock-cut corridors and chambers, sloping downwards into the cliffs. The earlier tombs (from Thutmose I to Amenophis III) consisted of a bent-axis corridor leading down to a burial chamber which was at first oval (or CARTOUCHE-shaped) and later square. The wall-decoration in these 18th-Dynasty tombs consisted of scenes from the *Amduat* (see FUNERARY TEXTS) executed in a simplified linear style, apparently imitating painted papyrus, with the background colour changing from one tomb to another.

The most famous tomb in the valley, that of TUTANKHAMUN (1336–1327 BC; KV62), is also ironically probably the most unusual. It is a small tomb, almost certainly intended for a private individual, leaving Tutankhamun's original tomb (KV23) to be usurped by his successor, AY. More importantly, however, the discovery of much of Tutankhamun's funerary equipment still intact and unplundered has given a good indication of the riches that were robbed from the other tombs over the centuries. When discovered, most tombs contained only remnants of funerary

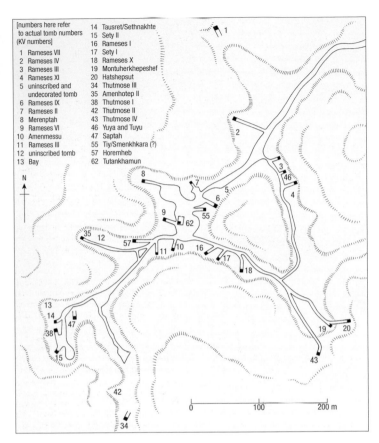

[numbers here refer
to actual tomb numbers
(KV numbers]

1 Rameses VII	14 Tausret/Sethnakhte
2 Rameses IV	15 Sety II
3 Rameses III	16 Rameses I
4 Rameses XI	17 Sety I
5 uninscribed and	18 Rameses X
undecorated tomb	19 Montuherkhepeshef
6 Rameses IX	20 Hatshepsut
7 Rameses II	34 Thutmose III
8 Merenptah	35 Amenhotep II
9 Rameses VI	38 Thutmose I
10 Amenmessu	42 Thutmose II
11 Rameses III	43 Thutmose IV
12 uninscribed tomb	46 Yuya and Tuyu
13 Bay	47 Saptah
	55 Tiy/Smenkhkara (?)
	57 Horemheb
	62 Tutankhamun

N

0   100   200 m

Plan of the Valley of the Kings.

equipment, including sarcophagi, CANOPIC equipment and pieces of wooden furniture and statuary.

The tomb of HOREMHEB (KV57) was the first to consist simply of one straight corridor, like that of AKHENATEN at EL-AMARNA, and also the first to be decorated with scenes from the *Book of Gates*. The tomb of SETY I (KV17), which is arguably the finest in the valley, was discovered by Giovanni BELZONI in October 1817. It was the first to be decorated with the *Litany of Ra*, in which the cult of the sun-god RA was combined with that of the dead king as OSIRIS. As far as the ceilings of the tombs were concerned, those from Thutmose I to Rameses III (1184–1153) were decorated with astronomical scenes depicting constellations and listing their names (see ASTRONOMY AND ASTROLOGY). From the reign

of Rameses IV onwards, scenes from the *Books of the Heavens* were painted on the ceiling of the burial chamber.

As far as the bodies of the New Kingdom pharaohs were concerned, some were moved in the 21st Dynasty, forming a cache in the tomb of Inhapy at DEIR EL-BAHRI, where they were discovered in 1871 by the Abd el-Rassul family. The majority of the others were discovered in the tomb of Amenhotep II (KV35), which was excavated by Victor Loret in March 1898.

See Appendix 2 for a list of owners of royal tombs.

J. ROMER, *Valley of the Kings* (London, 1981).

E. HORNUNG, *Valley of the Kings* (New York, 1990).

C. N. REEVES, *Valley of the Kings: the decline of a royal necropolis* (London, 1990).

C. N. REEVES (ed.), *After Tutankhamun* (London, 1991).

Valley of the Queens (Biban el-Harim)

Cemetery of the royal wives and sons of some of the New Kingdom pharaohs, located on the west bank at Thebes, about a kilometre to the northwest of Medinet Habu. Although the site includes the tombs of some members of the late 17th and early 18th Dynasty royal family, most of the 18th-Dynasty rulers' wives were buried in the same tombs as their husbands in the VALLEY OF THE KINGS. However, many of the 19th- and 20th-Dynasty royal wives and their offspring were buried in their own rock-cut tombs in the Valley of the Queens. There are about seventy-five tombs at the site, usually consisting of a small antechamber followed by a narrow corridor leading to the burial chamber, and virtually all of them were excavated by Ernesto Schiaparelli in 1903–5. The earliest inscribed tomb is QV38, belonging to Satra, the wife of RAMESES I (1295–1294 BC), but the best-known and undoubtedly the finest is QV66, the tomb of NEFERTARI, the principal wife of Rameses II (1279–1213 BC), although the deterioration of much of its painted decoration has necessitated a great deal of expensive (and, to some extent, successful) restoration work since the 1970s. Some of the tombs of the princes include beautifully preserved painted decoration, as in the case of QV55 and QV44, belonging to Amenherkhepeshef and Khaemwaset II, two sons of Rameses III.

See Appendix 2 for a list of owners of royal tombs.

E. SCHIAPARELLI, *Esplorazione della 'Valle delle Regine'* (Turin, 1923).

G. THAUSING and H. GOEDICKE, *Nofretari: eine Dokumentation der Wandgemälde ihres Grab* (Graz, 1971).

M. A. CORZO (ed.), *Wall paintings of the tomb of Nefertari: scientific studies for their conservation* (Cairo and Malibu, 1987).

Viceroy of Kush (King's son of Kush)

Administrative post established in the New Kingdom, under either KAMOSE (*c.*1555–1550 BC) or AHMOSE I (1550–1525 BC) and ending with the close of the 20th Dynasty (1186–1069 BC). This high official governed the whole of Nubia, then known as Wawat and Kush, each of which was administered by a 'deputy' (*idenw*). This seems to have been somewhat different to the situation in Syria–Palestine, where Egyptian governors worked alongside local potentates during the New Kingdom. Under Amenhotep III (1390–1352 BC) the powers of the Viceroy were extended so that he controlled the gold mining areas in the deep south of Nubia.

The Theban tomb of Amenhotep (known

Cast of scenes from the walls of the temple of Beit el-Wali, Nubia, showing the Viceroy, Amenope, being rewarded with gold collars by Rameses II, while exotic animals and products of Africa are brought into the king's presence, 19th Dynasty, c.1250 BC.

as Huy; TT40), who was Viceroy, or 'King's son of Kush', in the reigns of Akhenaten (1352–1336 BC) and Tutankhamun (1336–1327 BC), depicts his investiture, and his close relationship with the king. The collection and distribution of tribute and taxes appears to have been his main role, along with the organization of the gold mining regions. The title was a civil one, the army being under the control of the 'battalion-commander of Kush', although, in case of emergency, viceregal authority took precedence. Many of the viceroys were drawn from the ranks of the royal stables or chariotry, presumably because they were felt to have the necessary experience of desert campaigns through their military service, and were loyal to the king who promoted them so highly.

Late in the 20th Dynasty Rameses XI (1099–1069 BC) requested the Viceroy of Kush, Panehsy, to command troops in Upper Egypt in order to strengthen his reign. Many of the troops brought by Panehsy were Nubians, and there was well founded fear of usurpation and foreign invasion, on top of which he seems to have destroyed the town of Hardai in Upper Egypt, and appears as an enemy in Papyrus Mayer A. Panehsy was eventually buried at Aniba in Nubia.

G. A. REISNER, 'The viceroys of Kush', *JEA* 6 (1920), 28–55, 73–88.

N. DE G. DAVIES and A. H. GARDINER, *The tomb of Huy, viceroy of Nubia* (London, 1926).

T. SÄVE-SÖDERBERGH, *Ägypten und Nubien* (Lund, 1941), 177–84.

D. O'CONNOR, 'New Kingdom and Third Intermediate Period, 1552–664 BC', *Ancient Egypt: a social history*, B. G. Trigger et al. (Cambridge, 1983), 262–3.

W. Y. ADAMS, *Nubia: corridor to Africa*, 2nd ed. (London and Princeton, 1984), 229–32, 242–3.

vizier (Egyptian *tjaty*)

Term usually employed to refer to the holders of the Egyptian title *tjaty*, whose position in the ancient Egyptian ADMINISTRATION is generally considered to have been roughly comparable with that of the vizier (or chief minister) in the Ottoman empire. The office of *tjaty* is first attested in the 2nd Dynasty (2890–2686 BC), later than the title of 'chancellor of Lower Egypt' held by such men as Hemaka at Saqqara. It is possible, however, that the role of the *tjaty* may eventually be traced back to the beginning of the Pharaonic period and the emergence of the king's own titles.

It was in the 4th Dynasty (2613–2494 BC) that the vizier attained his full range of powers, serving as the king's representative in most areas of government (apart from the royal military and religious duties) and usually bearing a string of further titles such as 'chief of all of the king's works' and 'royal chancellor of Lower Egypt'. All of the 4th-Dynasty viziers were also kings' sons, but from the 5th Dynasty (2494–2345 BC) onwards this practice seems to have stopped. In the Middle Kingdom there is evidence for a 'bureau of the vizier' (*kha n tjaty*) at various places (including Thebes) but the post was not split into northern and southern offices until the 18th Dynasty.

During the Second Intermediate Period (1650–1550 BC), which was characterized by a long and rapid succession of short-lived rulers, it appears to have been the viziers who provided the essential stability that prevented the administrative system from breaking up completely. Ankhu, for instance, served under two different kings and is attested, unlike other viziers of the time, on papyri and the stele of another official. This probably had the effect of bolstering the influence of the vizier in the long term, so that even when the stability of the kingship was restored in the New Kingdom (1550–1069 BC) viziers such as RAMOSE and REKHMIRA continued to play a significant role in the government. In addition, it appears that the position had once more become hereditary, as in the 4th Dynasty, when the title was passed on from one king's son to another.

Rekhmira's tomb chapel in western Thebes presents a particularly revealing snapshot of the state of the vizierial office in the reign of Thutmose III (1479–1425 BC), since the texts inscribed on its walls (which are duplicated in three other 18th-Dynasty viziers' tombs) disclose details of the installation and responsibilities of the vizier, while the paintings of the reception of foreign tribute and the armies of craftsmen working at his command indicate his key position in the administration.

From the 18th Dynasty (1550–1295 BC) onwards the title was divided into two viziers, one dealing with Upper Egypt and the other with Lower Egypt. This had happened twice before, in the reigns of Pepy II (2278–2184 BC) and Senusret I (1965–1920 BC), but from the 18th Dynasty onwards the division became a permanent fixture, perhaps partly as a result of the polarization of the two Theban and Delta-based sets of dynasties during the Second Intermediate Period. More is known about the southern vizier during the 18th Dynasty, primarily because most of the archaeological and prosopographical evidence for this period derives from the Theban region rather than from the north. Even in the 19th and 20th Dynasties (1295–1069 BC), when the founding of the new capital of Piramesse (see QANTIR

Flexible collar in the form of a vulture from the tomb of Tutankhamun. Both the vulture and the counterpoise are inlaid with dark blue, red and green glass. 18th Dynasty, c.1336–1327 BC. (CAIRO JE61876, REPRODUCED COURTESY OF THE GRIFFITH INSTITUTE)

and TELL EL-DAB'A) moved the centre of government northwards, the southern vizier continued to wield power at least equal to that of his northern counterpart.

By the Late Period (747–332 BC) the vizier had become a far less influential figure, and it has been pointed out that Papyrus Rylands IX, which documents the fortunes of a family of priests between the reigns of Psamtek I and Darius I (c.664–486 BC), does not mention the vizier, despite numerous references to the central administration. On the other hand, some of the finest monuments of the Late Period belonged to viziers.

W. C. HAYES, *A papyrus of the late Middle Kingdom in the Brooklyn Museum* (New York, 1955).
T. G. H. JAMES, *Pharaoh's people: scenes from life in imperial Egypt* (Oxford, 1984), 51–72.
N. STRUDWICK, *The administration of Egypt in the Old Kingdom* (London, 1985), 300–35.
G. P. F. VAN DEN BOORN, *The duties of the vizier: civil administration in the early New Kingdom* (London, 1988).

vulture

Manifestation of the goddesses NEKHBET and MUT, depicted in a variety of forms, from the typically outstretched wings of the vultures painted on the ceilings of many temples to the crouched attitude of the Nekhbet-vulture, which was regularly depicted in the motifs associated with KINGSHIP. Of several different species of vulture found in ancient Egypt it was the 'griffon vulture' (*Gyps fulvus*) that was most frequently represented, whereas the hieroglyph with the phonetic value 'a' was the so-called Egyptian vulture (*Neophron percnopterus*).

One of the earliest representations of Nekhbet as the griffon vulture, on a 2nd-Dynasty stone vase of KHASEKHEMWY (c.2686 BC) from Hierakonpolis, incorporates a SHEN-sign (representing encirclement and therefore also infinity and protection) underneath her left talon. Many later representations show both vultures and falcons grasping *shen*-signs in their talons, often when they are poised protectively behind or above the king.

See also CROWNS AND ROYAL REGALIA.
P. F. HOULIHAN, *The birds of ancient Egypt* (Cairo, 1988), 39–43.
R. H. WILKINSON, *Reading Egyptian art* (London, 1992), 84–5, 192–3.

W

Wadi Hammamat *see* MAPS AND PLANS and STONE AND QUARRYING

Wadi Maghara *see* TURQUOISE

Wadi Tumilat *see* TELL EL-MASKHUTA

Wadj Wer *see* GREAT GREEN

Wadjyt (Edjo, Uto, Wadjet)
Cobra-goddess whose name means 'the green one' or 'she of the papyrus'. Her cult was particularly associated with the Lower Egyptian town of Buto (TELL EL-FARA'IN), which dates back to the Predynastic period. Usually portrayed as a rearing cobra, she was thus inextricably linked with the *uraeus*, the archetypal serpent-image of kingship, which protruded just above the forehead in most royal crowns and headdresses. It has been suggested that the original meaning of the Greek word *uraeus* may have been 'she who rears up'.

Wadjyt and the vulture goddess NEKHBET

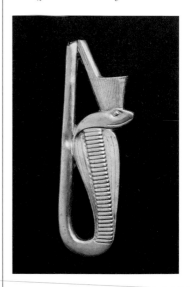

Uraeus wearing the red crown, which was probably originally part of a statue or item of furniture. Late Period (?), after 600 BC, gold sheet, H. 15 cm. (EA16518)

RIGHT *Bronze seated figure of Wadjyt as a lioness-headed goddess, which originally contained a mummified animal, possibly an ichneumon. Late Period, provenance unknown, H. 32.5 cm. (EA24785)*

were described as the *nebty* ('two ladies'), who served as tutelary deities of Lower and Upper Egypt respectively, symbolizing the essential DUALITY of the Egyptian world. Together they presided over one of the elements of the ROYAL TITULARY, the 'two ladies' name, which is attested as early as the 1st Dynasty.

Wadjyt was also sometimes portrayed in leonine form, since she and the *uraeus* were often identified with the lioness-goddess known as the 'EYE OF RA'. In the Late Period (747–332 BC) bronze statuettes of the lioness form of the goddess were used as coffins for ICHNEUMONS.

B. V. BOTHMER, 'Statues of W'd.t as ichneumon coffins', *JNES* 8 (1949), 121–3.

J. VANDIER, 'Ouadjet et Horus léontocéphale de Bouto', *Fondation Eugène Piot: Monuments et mémoires publiés par l'Academie des Inscriptions et Belles Lettres* 55 (1967), 7–75.

T. G. H. JAMES, 'A wooden figure of Wadjet with two painted representations of Amasis', *JEA* 68 (1982), 156–65.

H.-W. FISCHER-ELFERT, 'Uto', *Lexikon der Ägyptologie* VI, ed. W. Helck, E. Otto and W. Westendorf (Wiesbaden, 1986), 906–11.

S. JOHNSON, *The cobra goddess of ancient Egypt* (London, 1990).

warfare

From the primordial conflict of the gods HORUS and SETH to the well-documented battles of the New Kingdom (1550–1069 BC) at MEGIDDO and QADESH, warfare was a recurrent element in Egyptian mythology and history. Although the Egyptians may be customarily regarded as a comparatively peaceful nation, particularly in comparison with the peoples of western Asia, such as the ASSYRIANS and the PERSIANS, there was a large military and bureaucratic infrastructure devoted to the expansion and maintenance of their imperial ambitions in NUBIA and SYRIA–PALESTINE.

The range of sources for the study of Egyptian warfare is far from complete and certain historical periods are poorly known. For instance, little has survived concerning the organization of the Egyptian army until the beginning of the second millennium BC, while the primary sources for international diplomacy (the AMARNA LETTERS) are restricted to only a few decades in the fourteenth century BC. Overall, however, the atmosphere of Egyptian army life has been well preserved in the surviving art and texts, from paintings of new recruits being given military-style haircuts to the enthusiastically pedantic military despatches from the Nubian front.

The very fact that the Egyptians retained their national autonomy for almost three millennia is evidence enough of their military abilities. The Middle Kingdom FORTRESSES in Nubia, and the numerous indications of political intervention in the Levant, indicate that a vigorous policy of expansionism and imperialism was pursued by Egypt for many hundreds of years. This policy was a fundamental part of the Egyptian world-view whereby the pharaoh's domains were considered to have originally comprised the whole of creation. Any act of warfare perpetrated by Egypt – whether a punitive raid on a Nubian village or a major expedition into Syria–Palestine – was therefore considered to be a legitimate restoration of the natural order of things (see BORDERS, FRONTIERS AND LIMITS).

See also BEDOUIN; CANAAN; CAPTIVES; CHARIOT; HITTITES; LIBYANS; NINE BOWS; SHIPS AND BOATS; STANDARDS.

Y. YADIN, *The art of warfare in Biblical lands in the light of archaeological discovery* (London, 1963).

I. SHAW, *Egyptian warfare and weapons* (Aylesbury, 1991).

Two joining fragments of a ceremonial palette (the so-called 'Battlefield Palette') with relief decoration showing, on the side here illustrated, a scene of captives and slain victims of battle, the latter in the process of being devoured by vultures and a lion. The other side shows two long-necked gazelles browsing on a date palm. Late Predynastic to 1st Dynasty, c.3100 BC, grey siltstone, H. 32.8 cm. (EA20791)

E. STROUHAL, *Life in ancient Egypt* (Cambridge, 1992), 201–14.

I. SHAW, 'Battle in ancient Egypt: the triumph of Horus or the cutting edge of the temple economy?', *Battle in Antiquity*, ed. A. B. Lloyd (London, 1996).

was sceptre

Sceptre consisting of a straight shaft with its handle in the form of the head of a canine animal, and its base ending in two prongs. This unusual appearance may derive from an early totemic or fetish animal, which would probably have been associated with prosperity and well-being, given that the sceptre acquired these connotations in the Pharaonic period. Its primary function in funerary contexts was to ensure the continued welfare of the deceased. Until the Middle Kingdom (2055–1650 BC) the sceptre was sometimes represented in wood alongside the mummified body. In later times, rows of *was* sceptres were incorporated into the decorative friezes on the coffin or the walls of the tomb. It has also been suggested that the sceptre may have been used as a gnomon (the upright section of a sundial), perhaps representing the divine measurement of time. When adorned with a streamer and feather, it became the emblem of the Theban nome (province) of Waset.

K. MARTIN, 'Was-Zepter', *Lexikon der Ägyptologie* VI, ed. W. Helck, E. Otto and W. Westendorf (Wiesbaden, 1986), 1152–4.

R. H. WILKINSON, *Reading Egyptian art* (London, 1992), 180–1.

C. ANDREWS, *Amulets of ancient Egypt* (London, 1994), 80.

water

In Egyptian CREATION myths, the primeval waters of NUN were a formless mass of fecundity from which the universe was born. This fundamental role in the process of cosmogony itself must have contributed to the Egyptian sense that pure water was a sacred substance (see SACRED LAKE), and the role of the Nile INUNDATION (personified as HAPY) in the annual agricultural cycle must have automatically imbued water with an aura of fertility and power. There was also a belief in the ability of water to acquire magical and healing powers when it was poured over statues or other sacred objects, such as *cippi* (see HORUS).

RIGHT *Fragment of a wall-painting from the tomb-chapel of Nebamun, showing a garden pool surrounded by fruit trees; the water is indicated by repeated wavy lines, as in the hieroglyphs for water. 18th Dynasty, c.1400 BC, painted plaster, H. 64 cm. (EA37983)*

See also AGRICULTURE; INUNDATION; CLEPSYDRA; GREAT GREEN; NILE; NILOMETER.

R. A. WILD, *Water in the cultic worship of Isis and Sarapis* (Leiden, 1981).

C. VANDERSLEYEN, 'L'Egypte pharaonique et ses symboles: l'eau, les colonnes lotiformes et papyriformes', *Le symbolisme dans le culte des grandes religions* (Louvain, 1985), 117–23.

R. H. WILKINSON, *Reading Egyptian art* (London, 1992), 136–7.

water clock *see* CLEPSYDRA

wedjat *see* HORUS

Weighing of the Heart *see* HEART

Wenamun, Report of *see* HERIHOR and LITERATURE

Wenis *see* UNAS

Wepwawet ('opener of the ways')

Jackal-god who was already portrayed on the NARMER palette at the end of the fourth millennium BC. His cult was particularly connected with ASYUT in the Pharaonic and Greco-Roman periods, with the result that the city was renamed Lykopolis ('wolf city') in the Ptolemaic period (332–30 BC). At Abydos

his cult was celebrated in connection with that of OSIRIS. He was usually depicted either as a figure of a jackal or other wild canid (often standing on a nome STANDARD) or as a jackal-headed man.

ABOVE *Limestone stele from Abydos, carved in sunk relief with a depiction of King Wepwawetemsaf in the presence of the jackal-headed god Wepwawet, who is holding a* was*-sceptre and an ankh sign. 13th Dynasty, c.1650 BC, H. 27.4 cm. (EA969)*

His iconographic and mythical connections related mainly to the various interpretations of his name. In a political context he could be the god who opened up the way for the king's foreign conquests, while in the PYRAMID TEXTS he performed the OPENING OF THE MOUTH CEREMONY on the king and led the deceased through the netherworld, a task with which he was also later credited in the funerary papyri of private individuals. Wepwawet was closely linked with another canine deity, Sed, who was also depicted as a canid perched on a standard; Sed's name has been preserved primarily in the ancient term for the royal jubilee or SED FESTIVAL.

J. SPIEGEL, *Die Götter von Abydos* (Wiesbaden, 1973), 179–80.

E. GRAEFE, 'Upuaut', *Lexikon der Ägyptologie* VI, ed. W. Helck, E. Otto and W. Westendorf (Wiesbaden, 1986), 862–4.

white crown *see* CROWNS AND ROYAL REGALIA

Wilkinson, (Sir) John Gardner

(1797–1875)
Early nineteenth-century Egyptologist who was the first British scholar to make a serious study of Egyptian antiquities. The son of the Reverend John Wilkinson and Mary Anne Gardner, he was born in Hardendale, Westmorland. While he was still a young boy, both of his parents died and the Reverend Dr Yates was appointed as his guardian. He was educated at Harrow School and Exeter

Portrait of Sir John Gardner Wilkinson in Oriental dress, by Henry Wyndham Phillips. (REPRODUCED COURTESY OF THE GRIFFITH INSTITUTE)

College, Oxford, but in 1820, as a result of poor health, he travelled to Italy. There he met Sir William Gell, a Classical archaeologist, who persuaded him to undertake a career in Egyptological research.

In 1821 the twenty-four-year-old Gardner Wilkinson arrived in Egypt. Based in Cairo, he was to spend the next twelve years travelling through Egypt and Nubia. Along with other intrepid scholars of the same period, such as James Burton, Robert Hay and the Fourth Duke of Northumberland, he rediscovered numerous ancient sites and undertook some of the earliest surveys and scientific excavations at such sites as KARNAK, the VALLEY OF THE KINGS and the ancient Nubian capital of Gebel Barkal (see NAPATA). He was the first archaeologist to produce a detailed plan of the ancient capital city of Akhenaten at el-Amarna, and his map of the Theban temples and tombs was undoubtedly the first comprehensive survey of the region. The records of his excavations and epigraphy at THEBES are still an invaluable source of information for modern Egyptologists. He also conducted the first excavations at the Greco-Roman settlement of Berenice, on the Red Sea coast, which had been discovered by GIOVANNI BELZONI.

When he returned to Britain in 1833, his copious notes and drawings and his diverse collection of antiquities provided the basis for his most famous book, *The manners and customs of the ancient Egyptians*, which was to earn him a knighthood in 1839. He undertook two further seasons of study in Egypt, in 1842 and 1848–9, and in 1849–50 he studied the TURIN ROYAL CANON, publishing a detailed facsimile of this important KING LIST.

J. G. WILKINSON, *Topography of Thebes and general view of Egypt* (London, 1835).

—, *The fragments of the hieratic papyrus at Turin, containing the names of Egyptian kings, with the hieratic inscription at the back*, 2 vols (London, 1851).

—, *The manners and customs of the ancient Egyptians*, 3 vols (London, 1837; rev. 1878).

J THOMPSON, *Sir Gardner Wilkinson and his circle* (Austin, 1992).

window of appearance *see* PALACES and MEDINET HABU

wine *see* ALCOHOLIC BEVERAGES

winged disc (Egyptian *'py wer*: 'the great flyer')
The image of the solar disc with the wings of a hawk was originally the symbol of the god HORUS of Behdet (or the 'Behdetite Horus') in the eastern Delta. An ivory comb dating to the

reign of the 1st-Dynasty ruler DJET (*c*.2980 BC) already shows a pair of wings attached to the SOLAR BARK as it passes through the sky, and an inscribed block from the mortuary temple of the 5th-Dynasty ruler Sahura (2487–2475 BC) includes a winged disc above his names and titles, with the phrase 'Horus of Behdet' written beside it.

Since Horus was associated with the king, the winged disc also came to have both royal and protective significance, as well as representing the heavens through which the sun moved. Alan Gardiner argued that the disc represented the 'actual person' of the king, syncretized with the sun-god. It was presumably because of these royal associations, as well as the connections between the Behdetite Horus and the Lower Egyptian cobra-goddess WADJYT at Buto, that *uraei* (sacred cobras) were added on either side of the disc during the Old Kingdom (2686–2181 BC). By the New Kingdom (1550–1069 BC) it was a symbol of protection to be found on temple ceilings and above PYLONS and other ceremonial portals.

R. EGELBACH, 'An alleged winged sun-disk of the First Dynasty', *ZÄS* 65 (1930), 115–16.

M. WERBROUCK, 'A propos du disque ailé', *CdE* 16/32 (1941), 165–71.

A. H. GARDINER, 'Horus the Behdetite', *JEA* 30 (1944), 23–61 [46–52].

D. WILDUNG, 'Flügelsonne', *Lexikon der Ägyptologie* II, ed. W. Helck, E. Otto and W. Westendorf (Wiesbaden, 1977), 277–9.

wisdom literature

Genre of didactic texts that is arguably the most characteristic form of Egyptian literature. There are two basic types of wisdom literature: the *sebayt* or 'instruction' (see EDUCATION and ETHICS) and the reflective or pessimistic 'discourse.'

The earliest surviving *sebayt* (a series of maxims on the 'way of living truly') is the text said to have been composed by the 4th-Dynasty sage Hardjedef (*c*.2550 BC), while another such document was attributed to Ptahhotep, a vizier of the 5th-Dynasty ruler Djedkara-Isesi. It is likely that few of these instructions were written by their purported authors, and many, including that of Hardjedef, were almost certainly composed much later than they claim.

The instructions retained their popularity throughout the Pharaonic period, two of them being attributed to kings. The first of these was the *Instruction for King Merikara*, set in the First Intermediate Period (2181–2055 BC), and the second was the *Instruction of Amenemhat I*, set at the beginning of the 12th Dynasty (*c*.1950 BC). The instructions of Any and Amenemipet son of Kanakht, composed during the New Kingdom (1550–1069 BC), are similar in some respects to such Biblical wisdom texts as Proverbs (see BIBLICAL CONNECTIONS). The two most important surviving instructions from the Greco-Roman period are the *Sayings of Ankhsheshonqy* (now in the British Museum) and the maxims recorded on Papyrus Insinger (Rijksmuseum, Leiden), which were both written in the DEMOTIC script, consisting of much shorter aphorisms compared with the *sebayt* of the Pharaonic period. As well as the narrative form of instruction, there is also some evidence for the existence of less elaborately structured collections of maxims, as in the case of Papyrus Ramesseum II.

The second type of wisdom text, the pessimistic discourse, tended to focus on the description of order and disorder, as opposed to the prescription of a set of ethics. These include such works of the Middle Kingdom (2055–1650 BC) as the *Admonitions of Ipuwer*, the *Discourse of Neferty*, the *Dialogue of a Man with his Ba*, the *Dialogue of the Head and the Belly* (now in the Museo Egizio, Turin), the *Discourse of Khakheperraseneb* and the *Discourse of Sasobek*, the two latter (now in the British Museum) being preserved only on an 18th-Dynasty writing board and a 13th-Dynasty papyrus respectively.

M. LICHTHEIM, *Ancient Egyptian literature* I (Berkeley, 1975), 58–80.

W. BARTA, 'Die Erste Zwischenzeit im Spiegel der pessimistischen Literatur', *JEOL* 24 (1975–6), 50–61.

L. FOTI, 'The history in the Prophecies of Noferti: relationship between the Egyptian wisdom and prophecy literatures', *Studia Aegyptiaca* 2 (1976), 3–18.

M. V. FOX, 'Two decades of research in Egyptian wisdom literature', *ZÄS* (1980), 120–35.

B. OCKINGA, 'The burden of Kha 'kheperre 'sonbu', *JEA* 69 (1983), 88–95.

R. B. PARKINSON, *Voices from ancient Egypt: an anthology of Middle Kingdom writings* (London, 1991), 48–54, 60–76.

—, 'Teachings, discourses and tales from the Middle Kingdom', *Middle Kingdom Studies*, ed. S. Quirke (New Malden, 1991), 91–122.

women

The role of women in ancient Egyptian society and economy has been seriously studied only in recent years. The previous neglect of the subject was partly a question of academic bias, in that Egyptologists – consisting mostly of male scholars until modern times – were apparently uninterested in examining the evidence for female activities and roles. On the other hand, there are also problems in terms of the bias of the surviving evidence itself, which largely consists of élite male funerary assemblages, male-dominated religious monuments and ancient texts which were written primarily by men.

The true roles played by women, therefore, invariably have to be carefully extracted from the records left by their husbands, fathers, brothers and sons. Although a small number of surviving documents, including a few ostraca from the Ramesside village at DEIR EL-MEDINA, are said to have been written by women, there is no surviving ancient Egyptian text that can yet be definitely ascribed to a woman. Even when women (such as SOBEKNEFERU and HATSHEPSUT) attained the highest office in ancient Egypt, the KINGSHIP, they were effectively portrayed as men, since the pharaoh was regarded as intrinsically male.

There are, however, many other ways in which the study of ancient Egyptian women has been fruitfully pursued. The excavations of cemeteries have provided a vast amount of data concerning the bioanthropology of both male and female illiterate members of society (perhaps 99 per cent of the population). In addition, the recent excavations at settlement sites such as EL-AMARNA, MEMPHIS and TELL EL-DAB'A have begun to provide insights into such subjects as diet, work practices, patterns of residence and levels of education and hygiene, all of which can be used to shed light on the activities of women.

The study of RELIGION and MYTHOLOGY often provides evidence concerning ancient Egyptian attitudes to women and femininity. The goddess ISIS, for instance, was regarded as the ideal wife and mother, while HATHOR was the epitome of female SEXUALITY and fertility. Many of the goddesses, however, could also present the more negative, destructive aspects of womanhood, in the form of the EYE OF RA, the daughter of the sun-god sent to persecute the human race.

Although women are frequently depicted in Egyptian art, there seems little doubt that their status was generally lower than that of men at all levels of society. The political structure of ancient Egypt was clearly dominated by the male scribal élite, and women were given very few overt opportunities to participate in the ADMINISTRATION or public ceremonies. On the other hand, women such as NEFERTITI and TIY, who were the wives and mothers of pharaohs (see QUEENS), must have been both rich and powerful by virtue of their social rank, regardless of their rights as women; in other words, the differences between peasant women and royal women must have been far greater than the differences between Egyptian men and women as a whole.

Although women were not usually part of the political or administrative hierarchy, they were able to participate in certain spheres of life outside the home: at various periods they were able to be bakers, weavers, musicians, dancers, priestesses (until the 18th Dynasty), gardeners and farmers. They were also able to engage in business deals, inherit property, own and rent land and participate in legal cases; in other words, their legal and economic rights and freedoms were often similar to those of men. On the other hand, there is no evidence for girls of 'scribal' class being educated as their male equivalents were; and there were clearly various ethical distinctions made between the activities of men and women. Married men, for instance, were allowed to sleep with unmarried women, whereas women's infidelity was considered morally wrong (perhaps as a practical means of being sure of the paternity of children).

On a more visible level, as in most cultures, Egyptian women were distinguished from their male counterparts by such aspects of their appearance as CLOTHING and HAIR. Egyptian artistic conventions not only idealized the bodily proportions of men and women but also usually dictated skin colour; thus men were shown with reddish-brown tanned skin while women were given a paler, yellowish-brown complexion. This difference is thought to have originated from the greater proportion of time that women spent indoors, protected from the sun (a theory perhaps corroborated by the paler skin of some important officials of the Old Kingdom (2686–2181 BC), whose high status no doubt exempted them from outdoor work).

The status and perceptions of women were by no means static aspects of Egyptian society; clearly there was a reasonable amount of change during the period of almost three millennia from the Early Dynastic period to the end of the Pharaonic period. There is evidence, for instance, to indicate that there were more women involved in temple rituals in the Old Kingdom than in later periods; that they held more administrative titles in the Old Kingdom than in later periods; and that they were once able to participate in business transactions in the late New Kingdom.

There is no obvious sense of progress or 'emancipation' in these changes, or at least no sense that the overall lot of women was being improved over the centuries; the impression is much more that ancient Egyptian women's roles and appearances in the world outside the domestic cycle were simply adapted in response to overall changes in society. The *Instruction of Ptahhotep*, probably originally composed in the early Middle Kingdom, thus appears to summarize a view of women that remained relatively intact throughout the Dynastic period: 'If you are excellent, you shall establish your household, and love your wife according to her standard: fill her belly, clothe her back; perfume is a prescription for her limbs. Make her happy as long as you live! She is a field, good for her lord. You shall not pass judgement on her. Remove her from power, suppress her; her eye when she sees (anything) is her stormwind. This is how to make her endure in your house: you shall restrain her.'

See also CHILDREN; DIVINE ADORATRICE; EROT-ICA; GOD'S WIFE OF AMUN; HARIM; MARRIAGE; MEDICINE.

A. THEODORIDÈS, 'Frau', *Lexikon der Ägyptologie* II, ed. W. Helck, E. Otto and W. Westendorf (Wiesbaden, 1977), 280–95.

C. J. EYRE, 'Crime and adultery in ancient Egypt', *JEA* 70 (1984), 92–105.

L. TROY, *Patterns of queenship in ancient Egyptian myth and history* (Uppsala, 1986).

B. LESKO (ed.), *Women's earliest records from ancient Egypt and Western Asia* (Atlanta, 1989).

G. ROBINS, *Women in ancient Egypt* (London, 1993).

J. TYLDESLEY, *Daughters of Isis: women of ancient Egypt* (London, 1994).

wood, timber

Despite the fertility of the Nile valley, timber was clearly always a precious commodity in ancient Egypt. Although many TREES (such as the date palm, dom palm and fig) were grown principally for their fruit, they were also good sources of wood, which was principally used for building or the construction of furniture. Its use as a fuel must have been very limited, dried dung usually being burnt in domestic fires.

The date palm (*Phoenix dactylifera*) and dom palm (*Hyphaene thebaica*) were both carved into planks, while the date palm was also regularly employed, with relatively little preparation, for the production of COLUMNS or roof joists. The tamarisk (*Tamarix aphylla*) and the sycamore fig (*Ficus sycomorus*) were both widely used for the making of COFFINS as well as for carving into statuary. Ash (*Fraxinus excelsior*) was sometimes used for weapons, particularly those requiring flexibility, such as the bow found in the tomb of Tutankhamun (1336–1327 BC; KV62). Acacia wood (*Acacia sp.*) was often used for boat building (see SHIPS AND BOATS) and other large-scale construc-tions. However, the finest timber used by the

Egyptians was imported cedar wood from the Lebanon (*Cedrus libani*), which was much prized for sea-going boats as well as for the best COFFINS. The Aleppo pine (*Pinus halepen-sis*) was also imported for similar purposes, while juniper (*Juniperus sp.*) was also used in architecture and as a veneer. Finally, ebony (*Diospyrus sp.*) was imported from the lands of tropical Africa, including PUNT, and used prin-cipally for furniture and veneering.

The ancient Egyptian methods of stone-working were probably partly derived from skills that were first perfected by wood-workers, and many of the tools used by stone-masons are derived from those of carpenters and joiners. As well as developing veneering techniques, the Egyptians also produced a

Wooden funerary statue of Rameses II, from his tomb in the Valley of the Kings (KV2). 19th Dynasty, c.1250 BC. (EA882)

form of plywood, fragments of which, perhaps deriving from a coffin, were found in the Step Pyramid of the 3rd-Dynasty ruler Djoser (2667–2648 BC) at SAQQARA. The Egyptians' inventive use (and re-use) of timber empha-sizes its high value, a point which is further illustrated by Egyptian carpenters' skilful use of joints, producing well-crafted rectangular coffins from small, irregular fragments of tim-ber planking. Wooden objects could be deco-rated by painting, gilding or veneering, as well as with inlays of ivory, GLASS or gem-stones.

A. LUCAS, *Ancient Egyptian materials and industries*, 4th ed. (London, 1964), 429–56.

V. TÄCKHOLM, *Students' flora of Egypt* (Cairo, 1974).

H. VEDEL, *Trees and shrubs of the Mediterranean* (Harmondsworth, 1978).

G. KILLEN, *Egyptian woodworking and furniture* (Princes Risborough, 1994).

X

X Group *see* BALLANA AND QUSTUL

Yahudiya, Tell el- (anc. Naytahut,
Leontopolis)
Town-site in the eastern Delta, dating from at
least as early as the Middle Kingdom until the
Roman period (*c.*2000 BC–AD 200), which was
first excavated by Edouard Naville and
Flinders PETRIE. The main feature of the site is
a rectangular enclosure (about 515 m × 490 m)
surrounded by huge earthworks, the function
of which is not clear; it is usually dated to the
late Middle Kingdom, and may perhaps relate
to the HYKSOS occupation of the Delta. Among
the other remains at Tell el-Yahudiya are a

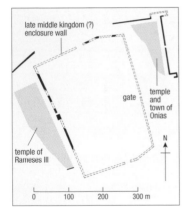

Plan of Tell el-Yahudiya.

temple built by Rameses III (1184–1153 BC)
and a small settlement established by Onias, an
exiled Jewish priest, which flourished between
the early second century BC and the late first
century AD.

The pottery dating to the Hyksos period
and the Middle Kingdom at Tell el-Yahudiya is
particularly characterized by a type of juglet
named after the site, which has been found as
far afield as Cyprus, Syria–Palestine and the
Nubian town-sites of Buhen and Aniba.
These juglets were made in a distinctive black-
fired material described as 'Tell el-Yahudiya
ware', which was often decorated with
incised zigzag designs filled with white pigment. The wide geographical distribution of
the ware has been the subject of considerable
research, including the identification of

*One of several polychrome faience tiles,
here depicting a captive Libyan, one of the
traditional enemies of Egypt, from a Ramesside
palace at Tell el-Yahudiya. He wears a sidelock
and a penis sheath, both characteristic of his
homeland. 20th Dynasty, c.1170 BC, H. 30.5 cm.
(EA12337)*

centres of production in Egypt and the Levant.
H. E. NAVILLE, *The Mound of the Jew and the city
of Onias* (London, 1890).
W. M. F. PETRIE, *Hyksos and Israelite cities*
(London, 1906).
S. ADAM, 'Recent discoveries in the eastern
Delta', *ASAE* 55 (1958), 301–24.
R. S. MERRILLEES, 'El-Lisht and Tell el-Yahudiya
ware in the Archaeological Museum of the
American University of Beirut', *Levant* 10
(1978), 75–98.
M. K. KAPLAN, *The origin and distribution of Tell
el-Yahudijah-ware* (Gothenburg, 1980).
M. BIETAK and C. MLINAR, *Tell el-Dab'a* V
(Cairo, 1987).

Yam *see* KERMA

Young, Thomas (1773–1829)
Egyptologist and polymath, who pursued a
brilliant career as both a scientist and a linguist. By the age of fourteen he was already
able to read twelve languages (including
Hebrew, Latin, Greek, Arabic, Persian, French

and Italian). Although he qualified as a physician and made important discoveries in the
field of physics (including the formulation of
the undulatory theory of light), he retained a
strong interest in linguistics. While practising
as a physician in London in the early nineteenth century, he began to take an interest in
the decipherment of Egyptian HIEROGLYPHS,
and he published a study of the ROSETTA STONE
in 1815. Three other scholars, Johann David
Åkerblad, Antoine Silvestre de Saçy and Jean-
François CHAMPOLLION, were also examining
copies of the trilingual Rosetta inscription at
roughly the same time, although it was the latter who was to achieve the first great breakthrough. Young, on the other hand, was the
first modern scholar to translate the DEMOTIC
script, in a posthumous paper which was published as an appendix to Henry Tattam's
Coptic grammar in 1831.
T. YOUNG, *Remarks on Egyptian papyri and on the
inscription of Rosetta* (London, 1815).
—, *Egypt*, supplement to the 4th and 5th
editions of the *Encyclopaedia Britannica*
(London, 1819).
H. TATTAM and T. YOUNG, *A compendious
grammar of the Egyptian language as contained in
the Coptic and Sahidic dialects… with an appendix
consisting of the rudiments of an Egyptian
dictionary in the ancient enchorial character;
containing all the words of which the sense has been
ascertained* (London, 1831).
J. D. RAY, 'Thomas Young et le monde de
Champollion', *BSFE* 119 (October 1990), 25–34.

Yuya and Tuyu (Yuia and Thuiu) (*c.*1400 BC)
The parents of Queen TIY, the wife of AMEN-
HOTEP III (1390–1352 BC), whose well-
preserved tomb (KV46) was excavated in the
VALLEY OF THE KINGS in 1905. Yuya held the
unusual title of 'god's father', and 'master of
the horse' and Tuyu, who was also mentioned
on some of the commemorative SCARABS of
Amenhotep III, was the 'chief lady of the HARIM
of Amun'.

The inscriptions indicate that Yuya came
from AKHMIM in Upper Egypt, but various
aspects of the evidence, including his unusual
name and tall stature, have suggested to some
scholars that he was not a native Egyptian. The
next holder of the title 'divine father' was AY
(1327–1323 BC), who also came from Akhmim
and was eventually to succeed TUTANKHAMUN
(1336–1327 BC) as pharaoh. It has therefore been
argued that Ay was the son of Yuya and Tuyu and
hence the brother of Tiy, but until genetic work
is carried on the mummies of the 18th-Dynasty
family this theory cannot be proved.

The political rise of Yuya and Tuyu, including the granting of the rare privilege of a tomb

in the royal necropolis, was no doubt a direct consequence of the marriage of their daughter to the king. Their tomb was discovered by James Edward Quibell while carrying out excavations on behalf of Theodore Davis. Until the discovery of the tomb of Tutankhamun (KV62) the contents of their tomb (now in the Egyptian Museum, Cairo) comprised the most complete set of funerary equipment found in the royal valley, including a canopic box, a *shabti*-box, a model coffin, a statuette from a MAGIC BRICK, a chair inscribed with the name of Queen Tiy, a kohl tube, jewel box and vase of Amenhotep III, and several beds and chairs. The mummies of the couple are among the finest to have survived. Although the tomb had been entered in antiquity, few objects had been removed, indeed a golden CHARIOT yoke was one of the first objects to be found. Tragically, Davis' decision to have the tomb cleared in a matter of days, in the absence of Quibell, meant that virtually no record was made of the positions of the contents, which has greatly diminished the value of the find to archaeology.

T. M. DAVIS, G. MASPERO, P. E. NEWBERRY and H. CARTER, *The tomb of Iouiya and Touiyou* (London, 1907).

J. E. QUIBELL, *The tomb of Yuaa and Thuiu* (Cairo, 1908).

B. PORTER and R. L. B. MOSS, *Topographical bibliography* I/2 (Oxford, 1964), 562–4.

Mummy mask of Tuyu, mother of Queen Tiy. Made from gilded cartonnage with details inlaid in gemstones and glass. Part of the linen gauze still adheres to the mask. 18th Dynasty, c.1390–1352 BC, from the tomb of Yuya and Tuyu (KV46), H. 40 cm. (CAIRO JE95251/CG51009)

Z

Zawiyet el-Aryan

Site of two unfinished PYRAMIDS, a number of MASTABA tombs of the Old Kingdom (2686–2181 BC) and a cemetery of the New Kingdom (1550–1069 BC), situated on the west bank of the Nile, between GIZA and ABUSIR. The earlier of the two pyramids is known as the 'Layer Pyramid' or 'el-Medowwara', and was possibly constructed for the 3rd-Dynasty ruler Khaba (2640–2637 BC). The 84-metre-square superstructure is almost identical to that of the unfinished step pyramid of Sekhemkhet (2648–2640 BC) at SAQQARA, both consisting of slanting layers of masonry, and both being originally planned as six- or seven-stepped pyramids. The subterranean section was entered via a vertical burial shaft descending from the north face of the pyramid. At the base of the shaft were three corridors, one leading southwards to the burial chamber (beneath the centre of the pyramid) and two others leading to east and west, each with sixteen side-chambers that were presumably intended for the deposition of funerary goods. The pyramid was excavated first by Alexandre Barsanti and later by George REISNER, who also cleared some of the associated MASTABA tombs. It was Reisner who located fragments bearing the name of Khaba, as well as a pottery fragment with the name of NARMER, leading him to suggest that the monument should be dated to the 2nd Dynasty. However, the subsequent excavation of the pyramid of Sekhemkhet indicated that a 3rd-Dynasty date was the most likely.

The second pyramid at Zawiyet el Aryan probably dates to the 4th Dynasty (2613–2494 BC) and was also excavated by Barsanti. Its main feature is a long sloping trench, at the bottom of which an unusual oval granite sarcophagus was discovered. Fragments of a similar type of sarcophagus were found by Flinders PETRIE in the pyramid complex of Djedefra (2566–2558 BC) at ABU ROASH, leading to the suggestion that the Zawiyet el-Aryan monument was constructed by the same ruler, although more recently it has been suggested that it may have belonged to an unknown ruler between the reigns of Djedefra and Khafra.

B. PORTER and R. L. B. MOSS, *Topographical bibliography* III/1 (Oxford, 1974), 312–14.

D. DUNHAM, *Zawiyet el-Aryan: the cemeteries adjacent to the Layer Pyramid* (Boston, 1978).

I. E. S. EDWARDS, *The pyramids of Egypt*, 5th ed. (Harmondsworth, 1993), 64–6, 146–7.

—, 'Chephren's place among the kings of the 4th Dynasty', *The unbroken reed: studies in honour of A. F. Shore*, ed. C. Eyre et al. (London, 1994), 97–105.

Zoser *see* DJOSER

CHRONOLOGY

All dates before 690 BC are approximate.

Predynastic	5500–3100 BC
Badarian period	5500–4000
Amratian (Naqada I) period	4000–3500
Gerzean (Naqada II) period	3500–3100
Early Dynastic Period	3100–2686
1ST DYNASTY	3100–2890
Narmer	c.3100
Aha	c.3100
Djer	c.3000
Djet	c.2980
Den	c.2950
[Queen Merneith	c.2950]
Anedjib	c.2925
Semerkhet	c.2900
Qa'a	c.2890
2ND DYNASTY	2890–2686
Hetepsekhemwy	c.2890
Raneb	c.2865
Nynetjer	
Weneg	
Sened	
Peribsen	c.2700
Khasekhemwy	c.2686
Old Kingdom	2686–2181
3RD DYNASTY	2686–2613
Sanakht (=Nebka?)	2686–2667
Djoser (Netjerikhet)	2667–2648
Sekhemkhet	2648–2640
Khaba	2640–2637
Huni	2637–2613
4TH DYNASTY	2613–2494
Sneferu	2613–2589
Khufu (Cheops)	2589–2566
Djedefra (Radjedef)	2566–2558
Khafra (Chephren)	2558–2532
Menkaura (Mycerinus)	2532–2503
Shepseskaf	2503–2498

5TH DYNASTY	2494–2345
Userkaf	2494–2487
Sahura	2487–2475
Neferirkara	2475–2455
Shepseskara	2455–2448
Raneferef	2448–2445
Nyuserra	2445–2421
Menkauhor	2421–2414
Djedkara	2414–2375
Unas	2375–2345
6TH DYNASTY	2345–2181
Teti	2345–2323
Userkara	2323–2321
Pepy I (Meryra)	2321–2287
Merenra	2287–2278
Pepy II (Neferkara)	2278–2184
Nitiqret	2184–2181
First Intermediate Period	2181–2055
7TH AND 8TH DYNASTIES	2181–2125
Numerous ephemeral kings	
9TH AND 10TH DYNASTIES (HERAKLEOPOLITAN)	2160–2025
Khety (Meryibra)	
Khety (Wahkara)	
Merykara	
Ity	
11TH DYNASTY (THEBES ONLY)	2125–2055
[Mentuhotep I ('Tepy-aa')]	
Intef I (Sehertawy)	2125–2112
Intef II (Wahankh)	2112–2063
Intef III (Nakhtnebtepnefer)	2063–2055
Middle Kingdom	2055–1650
11TH DYNASTY (ALL EGYPT)	2055–1985
Mentuhotep II (Nebhepetra)	2055–2004
Mentuhotep III (Sankhkara)	2004–1992
Mentuhotep IV (Nebtawyra)	1992–1985

12TH DYNASTY*	1985–1795
Amenemhat I (Sehetepibra)	1985–1955
Senusret I (Kheperkara)	1965–1920
Amenemhat II (Nubkaura)	1922–1878
Senusret II (Khakheperra)	1880–1874
Senusret III (Khakaura)	1874–1855
Amenemhat III (Nimaatra)	1855–1808
Amenemhat IV (Maakherura)	1808–1799
Queen Sobekneferu (Sobekkara)	1799–1795
13TH DYNASTY	1795– after 1650
Some seventy rulers, of which the five more frequently attested are listed below	
Hor (Awibra)	
Khendjer (Userkara)	
Sobekhotep III (Sekhemrasewadjtawy)	
Neferhotep I (Khasekhemra)	
Sobekhotep IV (Khaneferra)	c.1725
14TH DYNASTY	1750–1650
Minor rulers probably contemporary with the 13th Dynasty	
Second Intermediate Period	1650–1550
15TH DYNASTY (HYKSOS)	1650–1550
Salitis	
Khyan (Seuserenra)	c.1600
Apepi (Aauserra)	c.1555
Khamudi	
16TH DYNASTY	1650–1550
Minor Hyksos rulers contemporary with the 15th Dynasty	
17TH DYNASTY	1650–1550
Several rulers based in Thebes, of which the four most prominent examples are listed below	
Intef (Nubkheperra)	
Taa I (Senakhtenra)	
Taa II (Seqenenra)	c.1560
Kamose (Wadjkheperra)	1555–1550

New Kingdom	1550–1069
18TH DYNASTY	1550–1295
Ahmose (Nebpehtyra)	1550–1525
Amenhotep I (Djeserkara)	1525–1504
Thutmose I (Aakheperkara)	1504–1492
Thutmose II (Aakheperenra)	1492–1479
Thutmose III (Menkheperra)	1479–1425
Hatshepsut (Maatkara)	1473–1458
Amenhotep II (Aakheperura)	1427–1400
Thutmose IV (Menkheperura)	1400–1390
Amenhotep III (Nebmaatra)	1390–1352
Amenhotep IV / Akhenaten (Neferkheperurawaenra)	1352–1336
Nefernefruaten (Smenkhkara)	1338–1336
Tutankhamun (Nebkheperura)	1336–1327
Ay (Kheperkheperura)	1327–1323
Horemheb (Djeserkheperura)	1323–1295
19TH DYNASTY	1295–1186
Rameses I (Menpehtyra)	1295–1294
Sety I (Menmaatra)	1294–1279
Rameses II (Usermaatra Setepenra)	1279–1213
Merenptah (Baenra)	1213–1203
Amenmessu (Menmira)	1203–1200
Sety II (Userkheperura Setepenra)	1200–1194
Saptah (Akhenra Setepenra)	1194–1188
Tausret (Sitrameritamun)	1188–1186
20TH DYNASTY	1186–1069
Sethnakhte (Userkhaura Meryamun)	1186–1184
Rameses III (Usermaatra Meryamun)	1184–1153
Rameses IV (Hekamaatra Setepenamun)	1153–1147
Rameses V (Usermaatra Sekheperenra)	1147–1143
Rameses VI (Nebmaatra Meryamun)	1143–1136
Rameses VII (Usermaatra Setepenra Meryamun)	1136–1129
Rameses VIII (Usermaatra Akhenamun)	1129–1126

Rameses IX (Neferkara Setepenra)	1126–1108
Rameses X (Khepermaatra Setepenra)	1108–1099
Rameses XI (Menmaatra Setepenptah)	1099–1069
Third Intermediate Period	1069–747
21ST DYNASTY (TANITE)	1069–945
Smendes (Hedjkheperra Setepenra)	1069–1043
Amenemnisu (Neferkara)	1043–1039
Psusennes I [Pasebakhaenniut] (Aakheperra Setepenamun)	1039–991
Amenemope (Usermaatra Setepenamun)	993–984
Osorkon the elder (Aakheperra Setepenra)	984–978
Siamun (Netjerkheperra Setepenamun)	978–959
Psusennes II [Pasebakhaenniut] (Titkheperura Setepenra)	959–945
22TH DYNASTY (BUBASTITE / LIBYAN)	945–715
Sheshonq I (Hedjkheperra Setepenra)	945–924
Osorkon I (Sekhemkheperra)	924–889
Sheshonq II (Hekakheperra Setepenra)	c.890**
Takelot I	889–874
Osorkon II (Usermaatra Setepenamun)	874–850
Takelot II (Hedjkheperra Setepenra / amun)	850–825
Sheshonq III (Usermaatra)	825–773
Pimay (Usermaatra)	773–767
Sheshonq V (Aakheperra)	767–730
Osorkon IV (Aakheperra Setepenamun)	730–715
23RD DYNASTY (TANITE / LIBYAN)	818–715
Several contemporary lines of rulers at Herakleopolis Magna, Hermopolis Magna, Leontopolis and Tanis, only three of whom are listed below	
Pedubastis I (Usermaatra)	818–793

Sheshonq IV	c.780
Osorkon III (Usermaatra Setepenamun)	777–749
24TH DYNASTY	727–715
Bakenrenef (Bocchoris)	727–715
Late Period	747–332
25TH DYNASTY (KUSHITE)	747–656
Piy (Piankhy)	747–716
Shabaqo (Neferkara)	716–702
Shabitqo (Djedkaura)	702–690
Taharqo (Khunefertemra)	690–664
Tanutamani (Bakara)	664–656
26TH DYNASTY (SAITE)	664–525
[Nekau I	672–664]
Psamtek I (Wahibra)	664–610
Nekau II (Wehemibra)	610–595
Psamtek II (Neferibra)	595–589
Apries (Haaibra)	589–570
Ahmose II (Khnemibra)	570–526
Psamtek III (Ankhkaenra)	526–525
27TH DYNASTY (FIRST PERSIAN PERIOD)	525–404
Cambyses	525–522
Darius I	522–486
Xerxes I	486–465
Artaxerxes I	465–424
Darius II	424–405
Artaxerxes II	405–359
28TH DYNASTY	404–399
Amyrtaios	404–399
29TH DYNASTY	399–380
Nepherites I	399–393
Hakor (Khnemmaatra)	393–380
Nepherites II	c.380
30TH DYNASTY	380–343
Nectanebo I (Kheperkara)	380–362
Teos (Irmaatenra)	362–360
Nectanebo II (Senedjemibra Setepenanhur)	360–343

SECOND PERSIAN PERIOD	343–332
Artaxerxes III Ochus	343–338
Arses	338–336
Darius III Codoman	336–332

Ptolemaic Period	332–30
MACEDONIAN DYNASTY	332–305
Alexander the Great	332–323
Philip Arrhidaeus	323–317
Alexander IV***	317–310
PTOLEMAIC DYNASTY	
Ptolemy I Soter I	305–285
Ptolemy II Philadelphus	285–246
Ptolemy III Euergetes I	246–221
Ptolemy IV Philopator	221–205
Ptolemy V Epiphanes	205–180
Ptolemy VI Philometor	180–145
Ptolemy VII Neos Philopator	145
Ptolemy VIII Euergetes II	170–116
Ptolemy IX Soter II	116–107
Ptolemy X Alexander I	107–88
Ptolemy IX Soter II (restored)	88–80
Ptolemy XI Alexander II	80
Ptolemy XII Neos Dionysos (Auletes)	80–51
Cleopatra VII Philopator	51–30
Ptolemy XIII	51–47
Ptolemy XIV	47–44
Ptolemy XV Caesarion	44–30

Roman Period	30 BC–AD 395
Augustus	30 BC–AD 14
Tiberius	AD 14–37
Gaius (Caligula)	37–41
Claudius	41–54
Nero	54–68
Galba	68–69
Otho	69
Vespasian	69–79
Titus	79–81
Domitian	81–96
Nerva	96–98
Trajan	98–117
Hadrian	117–138
Antoninus Pius	138–161
Marcus Aurelius	161–180
Lucius Verus	161–169
Commodus	180–192
Septimius Severus	193–211
Caracalla	198–217
Geta	209–212
Macrinus	217–218
Didumenianus	218
Elagabalus	217–222
Severus Alexander	222–235
Gordian III	238–242
Philip	244–249
Decius	249–251
Gallus and Volusianus	251–253
Valerian	253–260

Gallienus	253–268
Macrianus and Quietus	260–261
Aurelian	270–275
Probus	276–282
Diocletian	284–305
Maximian	286–305
Galerius	293–311
Constantine I	306–337
Maxentius	306–312
Maximinus Daia	307–324
Licinius	308–324
Constantine II	337–340
Constans	337–350
Constantius II	337–361
Magnetius	350–353
Julian the Apostate	361–363
Jovian	363–364
Valentinian I	364–375
Valens	364–378
Gratian	375–383
Theodosius the Great	379–395
Valentinian II	383–392
Eugenius	392–394
Division of the Roman Empire	395

*   there are some overlaps between the reigns of 12th-Dynasty kings, when there appear to have been 'coregencies' during which father and son would have ruled simultaneously

**   died after having served only one year of a coregency with his father, Osorkon I

*** only titular ruler 310–305 BC

APPENDIX I
List of Egyptologists mentioned in the text

J. D. Åkerblad	1763–1819
Emile Amélineau	1850–1915
Alexandre Barsanti	1858–1917
Giovanni Belzoni	1778–1823
Georges Aaron Bénédite	1857–1926
Frederick von Bissing	1873–1956
Fernand Bisson de la Roque	1885–1958
Aylward Manley Blackman	1883–1956
Ludwig Borchardt	1863–1938
James Henry Breasted	1865–1935
Emile Brugsch	1842–1930
Heinrich Ferdinand Karl Brugsch	1827–1894
Guy Brunton	1878–1948
Bernard Bruyère	1879–1971
E. A. Wallis Budge	1857–1934
Jean-Louis Burckhardt	1784–1817
James Burton	1788–1862
Howard Carter	1874–1939
Gertrude Caton-Thompson	1888–1985
Jaroslav Černy	1898–1970
Jean-François Champollion	1790–1832
Jacques-Joseph Champollion-Figeac	1778–1867
Dorothy Charlesworth	1927–1981
Emile Chassinat	1868–1948
J. D. Cooney	1905–1982
C. T. Currelly	1876–1957
Bon Joseph Dacier	1742–1833
Theodore Davis	1837–1915
James Dixon	1891–1915
Bernardino Drovetti	1776–1852
Amelia Edwards	1831–1892
Walter Bryan Emery	1903–1971
Reginald Engelbach	1888–1946
H. W. Fairman	1907–1982
Ahmed Fakhry	1905–1973
Clarence Stanley Fisher	1876–1941
Sami Gabra	1892–1973
Alan H. Gardiner	1879–1963
Ernest Arthur Gardner	1862–1939
John Garstang	1876–1956
Robert Grenville Gayer-Anderson	1881–1945
Zakaria Goneim	1911–1959
Frederick William Green	1869–1949
F. Llewellyn Griffith	1862–1934
William Hayes	1903–1963
D. J. Hogarth	1862–1927
Gustave Jéquier	1868–1946
Athanasius Kircher	1602–1680
Gustave Lefèbvre	1879–1957
Karl Richard Lepsius	1810–1884
W. L. S. Loat	1871–1932
Victor Loret	1859–1946
Albert Lythgoe	1868–1934
Auguste Mariette	1821–1881
Gaston Maspero	1846–1916
Robert Mond	1867–1938
Pierre Montet	1885–1966
Jacques de Morgan	1857–1924
Oliver Humphrys Myers	1903–1966
Edouard Naville	1844–1926
Percy E. Newberry	1869–1949
Frederick Ludwig Norden	1708–1742
T. Eric Peet	1882–1934
Lord Algernon Percy (fourth Duke of Northumberland)	1792–1865
John Shae Perring	1813–1869
W. M. Flinders Petrie	1853–1942
Richard Pococke	1704–1765
James Edward Quibell	1867–1935

George Reisner	1867–1942
Gunther Roeder	1881–1966
(Niccolo Francesco) Ippolito Rosellini	1800–1843
Olivier Charles de Rougé	1811–1872
Henry Salt	1780–1827
A. H. Sayce	1845–1933
Heinrich Schäfer	1868–1957
Ernesto Schiaparelli	1856–1928
Siegfried Schott	1897–1971
Veronica Seton-Williams	1910–1992
Gustavus Seyffarth	1796–1885
Claude Sicard	1677–1726
Grafton Elliot Smith	1871–1937
Henry Windsor Villiers Stuart	1827–1895
Henry Tattam	1789–1868
Richard Howard Vyse	1784–1853
John Gardner Wilkinson	1797–1875
Leonard Woolley	1880–1960
Thomas Young	1773–1829

APPENDIX 2
Alphabetical list of owners of tombs in Western Thebes

VALLEY OF THE KINGS

Name	Dynasty	KV Number
Amenemopet	18	48
(vizier in reign of Amenhotep II)		
Amenhotep II	18	35
Amenhotep III	18	22
Amenmessu	19	10
Ay	18	23
Bay	19	13
(chancellor in reign of Saptah)		
'Golden tomb'	19?	56
Hatshepsut	18	20
Horemheb	18	57
Maiherpri	18	36
(standard-bearer in reign of Hatshepsut)		
Merenptah	19	8
Montuherkhepeshef	20	19
(son of Rameses IX)		
Rameses I	19	16
Rameses II	19	7
Rameses II (sons)	19	5
Rameses III	20	3, 11
Rameses IV	20	2
Rameses VI	20	9
Rameses VII	20	1
Rameses X	20	18
Rameses IX	20	6
Rameses XI	20	4
Saptah	19	47
Sety I	19	17
Sety II	19	15
Tausret	20	14
Thutmose I	18	38
Thutmose II	18	42
Thutmose III	18	34
Thutmose IV	18	43
Tiy/Smenkhkara	18	55
Tutankhamun	18	62
Userhat (official)	18	45
Yuya and Tuyu	18	46
(parents of Queen Tiy)		
unknown		12, 21, 24–33, 37, 39–41, 44, 49–54, 58–61

VALLEY OF THE QUEENS

Name	Dynasty	QV Number
Ahmose	17	47
(daughter of Seqenenra Taa II)		
Amunherkhepeshef	20	55
(son of Rameses III)		
Bentanta	19	71
(daughter of Rameses II)		
Imhotep	?	46
(vizier)		
Isis II	20	51
(mother of Rameses VI)		
Khaemwaset II	20	44
(son of Rameses III)		
Meritamun	19	68
(daughter of Rameses II)		
Nebiri	18	30
Nebtawy	19	60
(daughter of Rameses II)		
Nefertari	19	66
(wife of Rameses II)		
Paraherwenemef	20	42
(son of Rameses III)		
Rameses	20	53
(son of Rameses II)		
Satra	19	38
(wife of Rameses I)		
Sethherkhepeshef	20	43
(son of Rameses III)		
Tanedjem	20?	33
Tentopet	20?	74
(wife of Rameses IV?)		
Titi, wife of a Rameses	20	52
unknown queen	?	31
unknown queen	?	40
unknown queen	?	75
unknown princess	?	36
unknown princess	?	73
unknown	?	1–29, 32, 34–5, 37, 39, 41, 45, 48–50, 54, 56–9, 61–5, 67, 69–70, 72, 76–79

PRIVATE TOMBS IN WESTERN THEBES

Name	Dynasty	TT Number*
Abau	19/20	351
Ahmose (Humay)	18	224
Ahmose	18	121
Ahmose	18	241
Ahmose Meritamun	18	358
(daughter of Thutmose III and wife of Amenhotep II)		
Akhamenerau	25	404
Amenarnefru	18	199
Amenemhat (Surer)	18	48
Amenemhat	18	53
Amenemhat	18	82
Amenemhat	18	97
Amenemhat	18	122
Amenemhat	18	123
Amenemhat	19	163
Amenemhat	18	182
Amenemhat	18	340, 354
Amenemhat	18	A1
Amenemhat	18	c2
Amenemheb	19/20	25
Amenemheb	19/20	44
Amenemheb (Mahu)	18	85
Amenemheb	19/20	278
Amenemheb	19	364
Amenemheb	18/19	A8
Amenemib	19/20	A15
Amenemonet	20	58

* Numbers A1–D3 are tombs which were explored
in the past but have now been lost.

Names in brackets are alternative names
of the tomb owner.

List of bibliographical abbreviations

ASAE Annales du Service des Antiquités de l'Egypte
BACE Bulletin of the Australian Centre for Egyptology
BAR Biblical Archaeology Review
BES Bulletin of the Egyptological Seminar
BiOr Bibliotheca Orientalia
BIE Bulletin de l'Institut de l'Egypte
BIFAO Bulletin de l'Institut Français d'Archéologie Orientale
BMFA Bulletin of the Museum of Fine Arts, Boston
BMMA Bulletin of the Metropolitan Museum of Art, New York
BN Biblische Notizen
BSEG Bulletin de la Société d'Egyptologie de Genève
BSFE Bulletin de la Société Française d'Egyptologie
CAJ Cambridge Archaeological Journal
CdE Chronique d'Egypte
CRIPEL Cahiers de Recherche de l'Institut de Papyrologie et Egyptologie de Lille
DE Discussions in Egyptology
ET Etudes et Travaux
GM Göttinger Miszellen
JAOS Journal of the American Oriental Society
JARCE Journal of the American Research Center in Egypt
JEA Journal of Egyptian Archaeology

JEOL Jaarbericht van het Vooraziatisch–Egyptisch Genootschap 'Ex Oriente Lux'
JMA Journal of Mediterranean Archaeology
JNES Journal of Near Eastern Studies
JSSEA Journal of the Society for the Study of Egyptian Antiquities
LAAA Liverpool Annals of Archaeology and Anthropology
MIDAIK Mitteilungen des Deutschen Archäologischen Instituts, Abteilung Kairo
MIO Mitteilungen des Instituts für Orientforschung
NARCE Newsletter of the American Research Center in Egypt
OLZ Orientalistische Literaturzeitung
OMRO Oudheidkundige Mededelingen uit het Rijksmuseum van Oudheden te Leiden
Orientalia Orientalia Lovaniensa Periodica
PSBA Proceedings of the Society of Biblical Archaeology
RdE Revue d'Egyptologie
SAK Studien zur Altägyptischen Kultur
VA Varia Aegyptiaca
WA World Archaeology
WZKM Wiener Zeitschrift für die Kunde des Morgenlandes
ZÄS Zeitschrift für Ägyptische Sprache und Altertumskunde

Note on the illustrations

Each illustration is credited in its accompanying caption. Wherever possible object numbers are included. The following abbreviations have been used to refer to those institutions which kindly supplied photographs:

Cairo	The Egyptian Museum, Cairo
CM	The Department of Coins and Medals at the British Museum
DAI, Cairo	Deutsches Archäologisches Institut in Cairo
EA	The Department of Ancient Egypt and Sudan at the British Museum
Griffith Institute	The Griffith Institute at the Ashmolean Museum, Oxford
Metropolitan Museum	The Metropolitan Museum of Art, New York
Petrie Museum	The Petrie Museum of Egyptian Archaeology, University College London
WA	The Department of the Ancient Near East at the British Museum